TERRORIST EVENTS WORLDWIDE 2019-2020

EDWARD MICKOLUS

WW

WANDERING
WOODS
PUBLISHERS

Terrorist Events Worldwide 2019-2020

By Edward Mickolus

First Edition 2021

ISBN: 978-1-949173-13-0

Published in the United States by
Wandering Woods Publishers

Book Design, Cover and Typesetting by
Cynthia J. Kwitchoff (CJKCREATIVE.COM)

DISCLAIMER

OTHER BOOKS BY EDWARD MICKOLUS

Terrorism Worldwide 2021 (forthcoming)

Terrorism Worldwide 2019-2020

Terrorism Worldwide, 2018

Terrorism Worldwide, 2017

Terrorism Worldwide, 2016

Terrorism 2013-2015: A Worldwide Chronology

Terrorism 2008-2012: A Worldwide Chronology

Terrorism, 2005-2007

with Susan L. Simmons Terrorism, 2002-2004: A Chronology, 3 volumes

with Susan L. Simmons Terrorism, 1996-2001: A Chronology of Events and a Selectively Annotated Bibliography, 2 volumes

with Susan L. Simmons Terrorism, 1992-1995: A Chronology of Events and a Selectively Annotated Bibliography

Terrorism, 1988-1991: A Chronology of Events and a Selectively Annotated Bibliography

with Todd Sandler and Jean Murdock International Terrorism in the 1980s: A Chronology, Volume 2: 1984-1987

with Todd Sandler and Jean Murdock International Terrorism in the 1980s: A Chronology, Volume 1: 1980-1983

with Peter Flemming Terrorism, 1980-1987: A Selectively Annotated Bibliography

International Terrorism: Attributes of Terrorist Events, 1968-1977, ITERATE 2 Data Codebook

with Susan L. Simmons The 50 Worst Terrorist Attacks

with Susan L. Simmons The Terrorist List: North America

with Susan L. Simmons The Terrorist List: South America

with Susan L. Simmons The Terrorist List: Eastern Europe

with Susan L. Simmons The Terrorist List: Western Europe

with Susan L. Simmons The Terrorist List: Asia, Pacific, and Sub-Saharan Africa

The Terrorist List: The Middle East, 2 volumes

The Literature of Terrorism: A Selectively Annotated Bibliography

Transnational Terrorism: A Chronology of Events, 1968-1979

ITERATE: International Terrorism: Attributes of Terrorist Events, Data Codebook

Combatting International Terrorism: A Quantitative Analysis

Spycraft for Thriller Writers: How to Write Spy Novels, TV Shows and Movies Accurately and Not Be Laughed at by Real-Life Spies

Stories from Langley: A Glimpse Inside the CIA

More Stories From Langley: Another Glimpse Inside the CIA

Briefing for the Boardroom and the Situation Room

The Counterintelligence Chronology: Spying by and Against the United States from the 1700s through 2014

TABLE OF CONTENTS

INTRODUCTION

This is the 19th in a series of chronologies of international and domestic terrorist attacks and global, regional, and individual government and private responses.

The year 2020 was sufficiently different from preceding years in this series that it merits separate treatment in the Introduction and has a separate chronology.

This book uses the same **definition** of terrorism as found in its predecessors, allowing comparability across decades. Terrorism is the use or threat of use of violence by any individual or group for political purposes. The perpetrators may be functioning for or in opposition to established governmental authority. A key component of international terrorism is that its ramifications transcend national boundaries, and, in so doing, create an extended atmosphere of fear and anxiety. The effects of terrorism reach national and worldwide cultures as well as the lives of the people directly hurt by the terrorist acts. Violence becomes terrorism when the intention is to influence the attitudes and behavior of a target group beyond the immediate victims. Violence becomes terrorism when its location, the victims, or the mechanics of its resolution result in consequences and implications beyond the act or threat itself.

The book includes a **region-by-region** (and within each, a country-by-country) look at terrorist **incidents**—including a separate section updating events that occurred prior to 2019—and a **bibliography**. The Incidents section is based solely on publicly available sources, in-cluding the *Associated Press, Agence France-Presse, UPI, NPR, al-Jazeera, Reuters, CNN, Newsweek, NBC News, ABC News, CBS News, Fox News, New York Times, Washington Post, Miami Herald, Wall Street Journal, BBC, Sky News, Air Force Times, Navy Times, Marine Corps Times, Stars and Stripes, Long War Journal, U.S. News and World Report, Washington Examiner, USA Today, Times of London, Washington Post 202, The Guardian, Daily Telegraph, Radio Free Europe, Fars, Anadolu, IRNA, Florida Times Union*, overseas national and local media, and a host of United Nations, government agency, and non-governmental organization press releases and press conferences and research service reports. If not otherwise specified in the text, the *Associated Press* was the principal source of an incident's details.

This section is not intended to be analytical, but rather comprehensive in scope. As such, the section also includes descriptions of non-international attacks that provide the security and political context in which international attacks take place. In some cases, the international terrorists mimic the tactics of their stay-at-home cohorts. Often, these are the same terrorists working on their home soil against domestic, rather than foreign, targets. Domestic attacks often serve as proving grounds for techniques later adopted for international use. I have therefore included material on major technological, philosophical, or security advances, such as: the use of letter bombs; food tampering; major assassinations; attempts to develop, acquire, smuggle, or use precursors for an actual chemical, biological, radiological, or nuclear weapon; key domestic and international legislation and new security procedures; key arrests and trials of major figures; and incidents involving mass casualties. Non-international entries do not receive an eight-digit code (described below).

The section also provides follow-up material to incidents first reported prior to January 1, 2019. For example, updates include information about the outcome of trials for terrorist acts occurring prior to 2019 and "where are they now" information about terrorists and their victims. The update is identified by the original incident date, and includes enough prefatory material to give some context and to identify the original incident in the earlier volumes.

The international terrorist incidents and airline hijackings are identified by an eight-digit code. The first six digits identify the date on which the incident became known as a terrorist attack to someone other than the terrorists themselves (e.g., the date the letter bomb finally arrived at the recipient's office, even though terrorists had mailed it weeks earlier; or the date on which investigators determined that an anomalous situation was terrorist in nature). The final two digits ratchet the number of attacks that took place on that date. In instances in which either the day of the month or the month itself is unknown, "99" is used in that field.

The information cutoff date for this volume is December 31, 2020.

The Bibliography section includes references drawn from the same public sources that provide the incidents, literature searches, and contributions sent by readers of previous volumes. It does not purport to be comprehensive. The citations are grouped into topic areas that were chosen to make the bibliography more accessible, and includes print and web-based material. The Bibliography gives citations on key events and may be referenced for more detail on specific attacks described in the Incidents section.

DEVELOPMENTS IN 2019

ACTIVITIES OF KEY TERRORIST GROUPS

Fragmentary reported suggested that **al-Qaeda** may have experienced a loss of the services of two key leaders, one to illness, a second to death.

- In the summer, **Ayman al-Zawahiri**, titular albeit marginalized successor to Osama Bin Laden, was reported to have suffered an otherwise unspecified major heart difficulty. While he had not been that effective as a leader, limiting his activities to occasional propaganda pronouncements and clashing with other members of the jihadi movement, his further sidelining due to medical issues would further erode al-Qaeda's leadership contingent.

- A follow-up report that **Hamza Bin Laden**, Osama's son who had apparently been groomed for eventual takeover of the group, had been killed in an airstrike within the past two years, further was at least a symbolic loss for the group. While the 20-something was nowhere near ready to take the mantle of leadership, his death nonetheless took another household name off the group's roster.

- Observers speculated that the successor would probably come from a cadre believed to be under a loose form of house arrest in Iran, such as Saif al-Adel, already wanted for the August 1998 bombing of the U.S. Embassy in Kenya.

Despite these reverses at the top, all was not bad news for al-Qaeda's worldwide network of affiliates.

- The most active al-Qaeda affiliate was AQ in the Arabian Peninsula, which used Yemen, where the civil war showed no signs of abating, as its base of operations. The previously active al-Qaeda in the Islamic Maghreb was comparatively quiet, as was the Boko Haram affiliate in Nigeria's neighborhood. Al-Shabaab in the region around Somalia remained splintered between ISIS and AQ affiliates.

- A U.N. report in early 2019 noted that AQ Syria affiliate Hayat Tahrir al-Sham, with 20,000 fighters in Idlib Province, "remains the largest terrorist group in the country", and was in competition with another AQ affiliate, Hurras al-Deen, which was "steadily growing and attracting fighters disillusioned with HTS".

Despite its large membership, al-Qaeda has not engaged in—or at least claimed responsibility for—attacks outside of the home turf of its affiliates since January 2015. The affiliates have been happy keeping their eye on the ball, in this case, conducting localized anti-regime insurgencies which at the time can involve foreign, including U.S., interests. Focus on "the near enemy" has meant that operations against "the far enemy"—the U.S. and its (shrinking number of) allies—have taken a back seat.

However, an insider attack in Pensacola, Florida, underscored the continuing ability of the message of late al-Qaeda propagandists to radicalize. While green-on-blue insider attacks by Afghans inspired by the Taliban are near-commonplace, two attacks in December, one by an individual apparently motivated by personal considerations in Pearl Harbor, and one by a Saudi pilot on training at the naval base in Pensacola, Florida, showed that the insider problem exists in the U.S. homeland as well. The Saudi attack brought to the fore concerns that the foreign military training program could have security loopholes that needed addressing. Others suggested that pre-program vetting was fine, but radicalization can occur after an individual gets a clean bill of health to travel to the U.S. Surprisingly, tweets attributed to the attacker used not the language of ISIS, but of al-Qaeda founder Osama bin Laden and radical AQ cleric Anwar al-Aulaqi.

Key developments for ISIS

- The collapse of the Islamic State's self-declared caliphate in Iraq and Syria was completed in 2019, although ISIS was able to conduct hit-and-run attacks and suicide bombings in the area. Its days of governance of a wide swathe of the region gone, the group moved on to a new iteration, one of loosely-connected affiliates and individuals inspired by its calls to action. Its leader, Abu Bakr al-Baghdadi, committed suicide at the end of October during an American Special Operations raid. Kurdish militias conducted mopping-up operations, seizing thousands of ISIS alumni while Western governments squabbled over their duties to accept for extradition the fighters and repatriate family members, including children born on ISIS soil with little tie to Western metropoles. By December, some 30,000 former ISIS fighters were imprisoned in Iraq and Syria and tens of thousands of their children were in refugee camps. Syria's al-Hol camp alone hosted 70,000 ISIS women, including foreign-born expats, and children.

- ISIS's spread to neighboring countries was particularly effective in Afghanistan, where ISIS-Khorasan conducted numerous attacks and threatened to derail progress on the Taliban's talks with Washington regarding potential American withdrawal. Taliban refusal to involve the Kabul government in the talks presaged an expansion of Taliban violence against the government once American protectors leave.

- The ISIS main propaganda organs, particularly its *Aamaq* news service, appeared intact and continued pumping materials, including claims for specific attacks, to its subscribers.

- The Pentagon's Inspector General warned that ISIS, with the drawdown of a U.S. presence in the area, was rebuilding its cadres in Iraq and Syria and keeping up its operational tempo with assassinations, suicide attacks, abductions, and arson of crops. The IG added that "the drawdown could cause U.S.-backed forces in Syria to look for 'alternate partnerships and resources' to replace the reduced U.S. support". These warnings were echoed during testimony to the U.S. House Armed Services Committee by U.S. Central Command chief General Joseph Votel, who noted that ISIS was quietly blending into holding camps, biding its time. The withdrawal from the Turkish-Syrian border area of U.S. troops in October 2019 gave hope to

ISIS of a return to the area, and perhaps a return to the caliphate, at least initially in a small footprint.

Terrorists getting substantially more attention than in earlier years claimed no affiliation to specific groups, but rather were motivated by alt-right anti-immigrant, racist, **white nationalistic ideologies** articulated by a host of fringe groups all the way up to world leaders. Several individuals around the world, including in the United States and New Zealand, conducted mass murders using automatic weapons. One individual killed 22 people in 30 seconds, getting off 41 rounds before being shot to death by police who responded within seconds.

FATES OF KEY TERRORISTS

Government and international organizations expanded their lists of designated international terrorist groups and individual supporters. The most eye-catching was the designation by the U.S. in April of the Iranian Revolutionary Guard Corps as a terrorist group. The expected Iranian retort was, of course, "you're the real terrorists", or words to that effect, regarding U.S. Central Command. Expansion of the terrorist group designation beyond its historic use against individuals and non-state actors to a government organization was innovative, and while it placed another block to negotiation between the governments, it might provide a new, untested legal/economic/diplomatic tool for anti-terrorist forces.

Individuals whom earlier volumes in the series suggested that terrorism-hunters concentrate on remained at large, including

- **Samantha Louise Lewthwaite**, believed to be an al-Shabaab strategist.

- **Abubakar Shekau**, Boko Haram leader.

- **Ayman Mohammed Rabie al-Zawahiri**.

- **Returning jihadis** from ISIS territory. Hundreds of terrorism tourists proved a difficult task for surveillance teams.

- **Lone wolves**. Many popped up throughout the rest of the world. Security forces stopped many, but not all, before they could attack.

An alumnus of the list, **Abu Bakr al-Baghdadi**, true name Ibrahim Awwad Ibrahim al-Badri, ISIS caliph, for whose capture the U.S. offered a $25 million reward, died in October at his own hand.

SENIOR TERRORISTS KILLED IN 2019

This list includes those killed by coalition and Russian forces, including by airstrikes, and by rival terrorist groups, plus those who died of natural causes. The list is comparatively small compared to litanies for recent years.

Al-Qaeda
- Jamel Ahmed Mohammed Ali al-Badawi, variant Jamal al-Badawi, who was involved in the October 12, 2000 attack on the *U.S.S. Cole* in Yemen

- Hamza bin Laden, son of Osama bin Laden believed to be prepping to become leader of al-Qaeda if Ayman al-Zawahiri ever stepped down

- Asim Omar, head of operations in South Asia

Ansar Ghawzat-ul-Hind, an al-Qaeda-linked Kashmiri jihadi group
- Hamid Lelhari, operations chief

Afghan Taliban
- Mullah Sayed Azim, Taliban shadow governor for Anar Dara district in Farah Province

- Mawlavi Nooruddin, Taliban shadow governor for Samangan Province

ISIS
- Abu Bakr al-Baghdadi, nee Ibrahim Awwad Ibrahim al-Badri, caliph of ISIS

- Abu Hassan al-Muhajir, ISIS spokesman and key aide to al-Baghdadi

Islamic State in Pakistan
- Mohammad Islam, believed to be the mastermind behind a November 2018 attack in Klaya that killed 35 Shi'ites

Palestinian Islamic Jihad
- Baha Abu al-Ata, north command PIJ leader living in the Gaza Strip, who was believed to be behind a spate of rocket attacks on Israel

OTHER TERRORISTS KILLED IN 2019

Al-Qaeda
- Adeel Hafeez and Usman Haroon, who were involved in the August 13, 2011 kidnapping of American Warren Weinstein and the 2013 kidnapping of former Pakistani Prime Minister Yusuf Raza Gilani's son, Ali Haider
- Raihan, courier between Asim Omar, AQ chief of operations for South Asia, and Ayman al-Zawahiri

Abu Sayyaf
- Talha Jumsah, a local commander behind suicide attacks who was in contact with ISIS
- Sibih Pish, a commander in Sulu Province, Philippines

Al-Shabaab
- Yahya Haji Fiile, alias Abu Zakariye, a pro-ISIS commander in Bu'ale, Somalia, who had defected from al-Shabaab

Ansarul Islam in Burkina Faso
- Abdoul Hadi, a local commander who helped the group establish a presence in the area

Revolutionary Armed Forces of Colombia (FARC) breakaway dissidents
- Gildardo Cucho, a unit leader

ISIS
- Hayat Boumedienne, a Frenchwoman suspected as an accomplice in a 2015 attack in Paris
- Fabien Clain, a French-born ISIS member who was on European most-wanted lists, and his brother, Jean-Michel Clain
- Muhammad Saifuddin, alias Abu Walid, an Indonesian who appeared in ISIS videos executing foreigners, including Japanese journalist Kenji Goto

Kashmiri rebels
- Zeenatul Islam, a commander in the Shopian area

Jaish-e-Mohammad
- Munna Bihari, a local commander of the Pakistani group, killed in India

Lashkar-e-Taiba
- Asif Maqbool Bhat

Afghan Taliban
- Noman, a commander believed responsible for an attack in January 2019 that may have killed up to 126 security officers

TERRORISTS WHO DIED OF NATURAL CAUSES

- Varuzhan Karapetian, a Syrian of Armenian descent, who headed the French branch of the Armenian Secret Army for the Liberation of Armenia and carried out a fatal 1983 bombing attack on Orly Airport in Paris. He apparently sustained a heart attack.

KEY TERRORISTS CAPTURED/ SURRENDERED IN 2019

Italian Armed Proletarians for Communism
- Cesare Battisti, who was on the run for 37 years, avoiding a life sentence for killing four people

REGIONAL DEVELOPMENTS

On three continents in the space of six weeks in March-April, places of worship—churches, mosques, and a synagogue—were subjected to mass casualty attacks.

The deadliest attack outside a war zone occurred in heretofore peaceful New Zealand, where a lone rightwing anti-immigration gunman killed 50 people and injured another 48, murdering more people in one day than an average year in the country. The attack raised the issue of the threat posed by the radical right, and spurred New Zealand to impose further restrictions on firearms.

In **Africa**, al-Shabaab's mid-January attack on a Nairobi hotel complex established that despite U.S. airstrikes on its facilities in Somalia, the group could still conduct complex cross-border operations against countries contributing to the African Union coalition. Its siphoning tens of millions of dollars per year via protection rackets and other methods of shaking down legitimate businesses ensured that it had enough money to finance its hundreds of attacks per year, bankroll its own courts, pay its roughly 10,000 adherents, and even staff road toll booths.

Other prominent jihadi organizations in West Africa, principally Boko Haram and its splinters in Nigeria and its neighbors and al-Qaeda and IS affiliates, continued their operations. Clashes between English- and French-speakers plagued Senegal. Rebels in the Congo harried hospitals attempting to deal with a growing Ebola problem.

In **Asia**, Sri Lanka, quiet for a decade after more than 30 years of Tamil Tigers violence, was the scene of eight simultaneous bombings against Christian churches and five-star hotels in April that killed more than 200 and injured 450. Kashmiri rebels, benefiting from a sympathetic local population, conducted numerous attacks against Indian governmental authority. The Indian government exacerbated the problem by nullifying the special status of Kashmir, further sparking local dissatisfaction and helping rebel recruitment efforts. Indonesian authorities were faced with Papuan independence fighters and jihadis allied with ISIS, but managed some victories against remnants of an al-Qaeda-linked group. Pakistani Taliban gunmen continued their attacks, mainly assassinations and bombings. While Abu Sayyaf had fewer operatives, it maintained its pace of operations against Philippine and regional targets.

In **Latin America**, the peace agreement between the government and the Revolutionary Armed Forces of Colombia showed signs of fraying, with a group of key rebel negotiators announcing their withdrawal from the pact and return to armed conflict. The government took immediate steps to quash their action.

Europe was faced with attacks by individuals—born locally as well as emigres—inspired by ISIS. Many jihadis who went to territory previously held by ISIS now longed to return to their European homelands, but faced stiff resistance by local populations. Germany cracked down on a growing neo-Nazi white supremacist alt-right movement.

The **Middle East and South Asia** saw the end of ISIS as we know it, with a complete shriv-

eling of its territory and declaration of the end of the caliphate on March 23, 2019. Questions remained as to the location of thousands of local and foreign hostages, such as John Cantlie, who was forced to serve as their propaganda tour guide.

The shrinking of ISIS territory and al-Baghdadi's death led to considerations about what next. Lack of ISIS-held turf would force its leaders to hide out either in ungoverned territory or in areas at least titularly under the governance of semi-supportive regimes. ISIS faces several options. It could:

- Name a successor and morph into its next iteration. Identifying that successor will pose difficulties for the group. No one has yet developed the operational, organizational, or ideological sweep that comes close to that of al-Baghdadi. No obvious successor comes to mind, although a few in his inner circle are likely to jockey for position. ISIS was quick to announce a successor with Quraysh tribe ties, although his precise identity was not specified.

  o Al-Baghdadi does not appear to have been in close daily operational control of the group's activities, suggesting that while the group has taken a blow in terms of inspirational and ideological leadership, it can still plan and conduct operations thanks to its decentralized approach to attacks. His loss might inspire some affiliates to engage in revenge operations throughout the world with the added effect of heightening their recognition amongst the global jihadi movement.

  o Would-be successors, however, will need to battle others within ISIS as well as ISIS rivals who will jump at the chance to recruit ISIS members feeling adrift or previously disillusioned with the harsh treatment of those who lived in the caliphate.

  o With the withdrawal of American forces, the thousands of ISIS fighters imprisoned in Iraq and Syria, and tens of thousands of its supporters detained in camps, could suddenly be in play if Kurdish forces are unable to ensure their continued detention.

○ A successor could give ISIS a new direction, and perhaps a new name, to indicate a fresh start, new thinking, and a new vision for the worldwide jihadi movement. Such a leader could also develop a modus vivendi at minimum with al-Qaeda, perhaps leading to a merger should al-Zawahiri retire, die, be captured, or be forcibly removed.

○ Perhaps a key part of becoming al-Baghdadi's successor will be an ability to get one's hands on the tens of millions of dollars analysts believed the group squirrelled away while it controlled oil fields and local graft.

• Merge with al-Qaeda. The option would entail possibly insurmountable roadblocks for the group, with limited communication opportunities between the groups and still-festering rivalries and feuds which often broke out into pitched battles in Syria, according to the ODNI's Worldwide Threat Briefing of 2019. It would be difficult for ISIS leaders to swallow a litany of "told you so's" by al-Zawahiri and his cohorts. Moreover, the operational ideology of al-Qaeda's operations wing—go after the far enemy—would pose problems for ISIS's views on establishing local caliphates first.

• Allow the ISIS affiliates even greater autonomy, with a named figurehead with little daily control over the groups. The affiliates in, say, Nigeria, the Philippines, Somalia, India, and Europe, inter alia, are unlikely to be affected because they operated independently of the central leadership headquartered in caliphate turf. Fissures could well result if a successor lacks Baghdadi's charisma and organizational skills, much the way al-Qaeda had fractured under the less-than-ideal leadership of bin Laden successor Ayman al-Zawahiri.

• End operations, and let its membership slink back to their home countries.

The demise of ISIS as a territory holder led to questions about the endgame: what to do with the women who left their homelands to join ISIS, marry fighters, and have their babies. Many governments turned their backs on their former citizens, arguing that supporting beheadings of their nationals was beyond the pale. Others questioned their claims of nationality. Still others were willing to consider whether the children were citizens even if their parents had cut ties to the homeland. Yet other governments worried about inadvertently making people stateless.

Houthi rebels in Yemen ushered in the new year with an attack on a military parade by its Qasef-2 drone, killing six people among 8,000 participating. The Houthis had stepped up their drone technology from simple kits to what was believed to be adaptations of Iranian military weapons, often sending drones across the Saudi border.

In Afghanistan, the Taliban conducted near-daily attacks on police outposts, military checkpoints, schools, government facilities, media outlets, and many other targets while engaged in negotiations with the United States over American withdrawal from its longest war. American military leaders cautioned that a no-deal-Brexit-like crash out of Afghanistan would likely lead to extensive bloodletting against Afghan security forces poorly prepared to go it alone against the Taliban and its ISIS-K rivals. That said, at least the Afghan Taliban is likely to stay in its area of operations and maintain its links to the original al-Qaeda leadership, perhaps with a tentative return by AQ back to Afghan turf.

In the **United States**, ISIS lurked in the background while rightwing loners conducted mass shootings in various public fora. Terrorism-watchers also worried about Iranian sleeper cells, including those trained by Hizballah and Shi'a radicals as well as members of the Iranian Revolutionary Guards Corps' Quds Force, awaiting a further uptick in U.S.-Iranian tensions that could become the spark for their activation. This likelihood increased with the January 2, 2020 U.S. airstrike on Baghdad Airport that killed General Qassem Soleimani, head of the Quds Force, along with Kataeb Hizballah leader Abu Mahdi al-Muhandis.

WHAT'S NEXT?

INNOVATIONS IN TERRORIST METHODS

Terrorists by and large continued with simple operations, although some engaged in by large insurgent groups were often described as "complex", usually referring to a suicide vehicle bomber taking out a security gate, guard house, or other perimeter defense, followed by a second group of terrorists storming into a facility. Terrorists have not upped the ante on innovative tactics for the simple reason that they do not have to. There are precious few effective defenses against suicidal terrorists willing to storm defended facilities, or who are willing to blend in with individuals at a softer target. Gun attacks and knifings by lone individuals are similarly easy to conduct and hard to detect and prevent. Until targets are able to devise more effective defense measures, terrorists will not feel under pressure to change their tactics. However, when environments have changed—such as when aerial hijackings were effectively shut down by closed cockpit doors—terrorists historically have shifted, rather than thrown in the towel.

When such shifts are called for, the likeliest, and cheapest, new techniques could include use of armed drones, computer hacking, and dazzling pilots with standoff laser attacks by ground-based terrorists. All of these techniques have been seen in some form around the world by various entities, although as far as we can tell, they have been little-used by organized terrorist groups.

Higher-tech operations continued to be rarities. While it is difficult to attribute cyber attacks, most of these incidents appeared to be conducted by nation-states or computer science criminals rather than terrorists. Terrorists rarely claim credit for cyber attacks, even the groups that otherwise opportunistically take credit for events not involving them. The proliferation of nations willing to hack elections, either via propagandabots or via direct attacks on sites, could provide a model for terrorists interested in damaging governmental authority.

The 2018 volume looked at what would be needed for a next-generation terrorist leader. Few groups have designated formal handovers, although the Taliban is a world leader in formulating quick succession plans when local commanders are removed from the battlefield. Al-Qaeda, earlier losing several operations chiefs to airstrikes, has not recently had such urgent succession requirements, but al-Zawahiri's medical difficulties may necessitate a terrorist-in-waiting plan. The late Hamza bin Laden had a toe-in-the-water attempt to establish propaganda credentials, but remained a callow youth on the actual battlefield before his demise. Before the apparent confirmation of his death, al-Qaeda continued issuing Hamza's catalog of previously unreleased recordings, hoping to establish the persona of a new, youthful jihadi leader. Not even al-Zawahiri, despite his occasional audio releases, has established himself as a charismatic presence who can easily rally the troops nor an innovator in attack methodologies. ISIS has lost numerous senior commanders, and it is unclear who would replace al-Baghdadi as the movement's figurehead and rallying crier. AQ and ISIS has so far not named operations chiefs capable of conducting complex, mass casualty attacks away from their home soil. Moreover, none of the terrorist bench appear to have a resume of orchestrating eyecatching operations in any locale.

This trend could shift with the withdrawal of U.S. and coalition forces from Afghanistan, Syria, Iraq, and other battle zones. AQ and ISIS forces could re-establish themselves on uncontested turf, according themselves safe havens and training camps. During its cautious negotiations over the status of U.S. forces, the Taliban has never backtracked on its willingness to host like-minded groups (read al-Qaeda). Continuous chaos in Libya also presents operational opportunities for these groups.

RESPONSES

A spate of lone gunman attacks, including several by individuals emboldened by alt-right language on the Internet, led observers to note limitations in domestic U.S. law. As of August 2019, when several attacks killed dozens, prosecutors lacked domestic terrorism legislation similar to international terrorism laws, requiring them to use a patchwork of other laws, including hate crime legislation, weapons laws, and other approaches, to charge individuals who would otherwise be deemed terrorists in courtrooms. Lack of a formal list of designated domestic terrorist groups, such as white supremacist organizations and incel (involuntarily celebate) groups, further limited statutory prosecutorial discretion. Surveillance of individuals not apparently affiliated with designated terrorist groups is limited. The formal international terrorism lists maintained by the Departments of State and the Treasury included 68 groups, none of which included white supremacists.

A growing problem is the dilemma of what to do with those returning to the West and other regions from their ISIS adventures in the shriveled caliphate. The *New York Times* reported that ISIS recruited more than 40,000 foreign fighters and their families from 80+ countries; 5,000 of them came from European countries. While many died, some 40% were unaccounted for. Kurdish militias in Syria in August 2019 held some 13,000 foreign ISIS followers in pop-up prisons, noting that they were ill-prepared to keep the ISIS alumni imprisoned and monitored over the medium term. Such conditions allowed fertile recruiting opportunities at the camps for a second generation of ISIS.

Repatriation plans were iffy at best.

- At one end of the spectrum is Kazakhstan's Rehabilitation Center of Good Intentions, which provides ISIS brides with art therapy, daycare, and psychologists. A similar art therapy program is offered in Syria. Other programs offer short incarceration terms (sometimes a month of rehabilitation training) before they are sprung into society.

- On the other end of the spectrum are Western governments who ignored President Trump's calls to receive their wayward citizens.

Many question whether the ISIS brides, never mind the foreign fighters, often showing little remorse, can be reassimilated into the societies they foreswore for a culture of on-street beheadings. The former citizens of the caliphate return to their initial home countries with military skills developed in training camps and on the battlefield, and with their original motivations still simmering. Jailing them often gives them the opportunity to radicalize their cellmates. Many of the first wave of prisoners were expected to be released in 2020.

In 2019, the Taliban attacked military targets—including military camps and police checkpoints—and other symbols of government authority, including government offices. Even if it eased up after withdrawal of foreign forces in a U.S. peace deal—an unlikely longterm ceasefire—its rival ISIS-K has developed a taste for civilian blood, bombing voter registration centers, mosques, wedding halls, hospitals, Shi'ite cultural centers, and markets, inter alia, that kill dozens at a time. ISIS-K and the Taliban have also engaged in pitched battles against each other. ISIS-K will feel no compunction in stepping up such operations, not being part of any peace deal involving the Taliban.

DEVELOPMENTS IN 2020

Fates of Key Terrorists

Government and international organizations expanded their lists of designated international terrorist groups and individual supporters.

SENIOR TERRORISTS KILLED IN 2020

This list includes those killed by coalition and Russian forces, including by airstrikes, and by rival terrorist groups, plus those who died of natural causes. The list is comparatively small compared to litanies for recent years. Rumors continued of the death by natural causes of al-Qaeda leader Ayman al-Zawahiri, but as of this writing, remained unconfirmed wishful thinking.

Al-Qaeda
- Abdullah Ahmed Abdullah, alias Abu Mohammed al-Masri, deputy to al-Zawahiri, believed to be the mastermind behind the al-Qaeda bombings of the U.S. Embassies in Tanzania and Kenya on August 7, 1998.

Al-Qaeda in the Arabian Peninsula (AQAP)
- Qassim al-Rimi, AQAP leader

Al-Qaeda in the Islamic Maghreb (AQIM)
- Abdelmalek Droukdel, AQIM's leader

Al-Qaeda in the Indian Subcontinent (AQIS)
- Abu Muhsin al-Masri, deputy commander of AQIS

West Papua Liberation Army (military wing of the Free Papua Organization of Indonesia)
- Hengky Wanmang, a senior commander

Al-Shabaab
- Muse Moalim, who had run al-Shabaab's Amniyat intelligence service

Colombian National Liberation Army (ELN)
- Andres Vanegas, alias Commander Uriel, one of the group's senior commanders

Iranian Revolutionary Guards Qods Force
- Qassem Soleimani, intelligence chief and head of the Qods Force, designated by U.S. administration as a global terrorist

Group to Support Islam and Muslims (GSIM) in Mali
- Ba Ag Moussa, the group's military commander

Houthis in Yemen
- Mohamed Abdel Karim al-Hamran, special forces commander

Kataeb Hizballah
- Jamal Jaafar Ibrahimi, alias Abu Mahdi al-Muhandis, who was in a Kuwait prison for years for bombing the U.S. Embassy in Kuwait. He died in a U.S. airstrike on January 2, 2020 on Baghdad Airport that also killed Iranian General Qassem Soleimani, head of the Revolutionary Guards Quds Force.

Hizbul Mujahedeen, Kashmir's largest rebel group
- Riyaz Naikoo, chief of operations
- Junaid Ashraf Sehrai, an HM commander

OTHER TERRORISTS KILLED IN 2020

Al-Qaeda in the Indian Subcontinent
- Mohammad Hanif, a Pakistani bombmaker who trained Taliban terrorists

Hizballah
- Ali Mohammed Younes, a Hizballah commander in Lebanon

Islamic State affiliate in Egypt
- Abdel-Qader Sweilam, an Egyptian IS leader

Afghan Taliban
- Mullah Nangyalay, commander of a Taliban splinter group in Herat Province

KEY TERRORISTS CAPTURED/ SURRENDERED IN 2020

Abu Sayyaf
- Anduljihad Susukan, a commander who was linked to beheadings of hostages, including two Canadians and a Malaysian

ISIS
- Shifa al-Nima, alias Abu Abdul-Bari, senior mufti in issuing fatwas, the 300-pounder advocated enslavement, rape, torture and ethnic cleansing
- Mahmut Ozden, senior ISIS emir in Turkey

ISIS-K
- Abdullah Orakzai, alias Aslam Farooqi, head of ISIS-K

Jemaah Islamiyah
- Aris Sumarsono, alias Zulkarnaen, believed to be the military leader of the al-Qaeda-linked Jemaah Islamiyah

Muslim Brotherhood (Egypt)
- Mahmoud Ezzat, acting chief

South Asia Islamic State (Afghanistan)
- Abu Ali, intelligence chief
- Abu Omar Khorasani, alias Zia-ul-Haq, chief for South Asia
- Saheeb, head of public relations

REGIONAL DEVELOPMENTS

In **Africa**, local groups began 2020 with several multi-casualty operations.

Date	Country/ Group	# Deaths	# Injuries
Jan. 6	Nigeria ISWAP	30	35
Jan. 9	Niger Islamic State	89	
Jan. 18	Somalia al-Shabaab	2	20
Jan. 20	Chad Boko Haram	9	2
Jan. 21	Burkina Faso Boko Haram	36	

Equally worrisome is that terrorists conducted attacks in nine African countries in the first month of the year, more than in the Middle East and Europe combined. March saw a continuation of this spike in multi-casualty attacks in Africa. Despite the start of the coronavirus era in Africa, the March casualty tally was worse:

Date	Country/ Group	# Deaths	# Injuries
March 1	Nigeria "bandits"	50	
March 9	Burkina Faso "defense groups"	43	
March 19	Mali suspected al-Qaeda	29	
March 20	Nigeria Boko Haram	50	
March 23	Chad Boko Haram	92	

Another 81 people were killed in Nigeria in early June.

Attacks continued unabated in the second half of the year, particularly in Congo, Somalia, Burkina Faso, Niger, and Mali, with jihadis also making serious inroads in Mozambique. The high body counts also continued with one especially noteworthy one at the end of November, when suspected Boko Haram (or perhaps Islamic State West Africa Province) terrorists killed 110 villagers near their rice farms in Nigeria.

A promising development for security forces in the region was the death of Abdelmalek Droukdel, head of al-Qaeda in the Islamic Maghreb (AQIM). The organization continued its campaign of attacks without him.

In **Asia**, Pakistan, India, and the Philippines continued to be plagued by internal insurgencies that often included terrorist attacks.

In **Latin America**, decommissioned and disarmed erstwhile members of the Revolutionary Armed Forces of Colombia (FARC) found themselves sitting ducks for vengeful attacks.

In **Europe**, the withdrawal of the United Kingdom from the European Union (Brexit) threatened economic upheaval but also stirred sectarian rifts on the emerald isle. Poverty left many young men open to radicalization, a term previously limited to Islamic fundamentalist recruiting efforts, but now also referring to potential growth of next-generation Protestant and Catholic paramilitaries. The call for a post-Brexit united Ireland under the European Union threatened a campaign of violence from the New IRA. Polls cited by the *New York Times* showed Protestant majorities supporting Brexit, whereas 85% of Catholics wanted to remain in the EU. Pro-independence groups in Scotland also saw Brexit as their opportunity to press for their turf to remain in the EU.

In the final quarter of 2020, as Covid lockdown fatigue set in and people doffed masks and vigilance, terrorists also came out of quarantine, conducting knifings in France and a mass shooting in Vienna, Austria. Radical jihadis were stirred by the trial regarding the attack on *Charlie Hebdo*, with the magazine further roiling the waters by publishing another skein of cartoons denigrating the Prophet Muhammad and Islam in general.

Europe also saw arrests for and the beginning of trials regarding major attacks that occurred years, sometimes decades, earlier. These developments underscored the determination of authorities to provide justice, no matter how long it may take, for society and the victims.

The **Middle East and South Asia** began the year with the death by U.S. drone strike of the head of the Iranian Revolutionary Guard's Qods Force, General Qassem Soleimani, credited with killing hundreds of foreigners during a several-decade career as a state sponsor of terrorism via his control of Iranian proxies. Some observers suggested that his removal from the field overshadowed the deaths of al-Qaeda founder Osama bin Laden and ISIS caliph Abu Bakr al-Baghdadi.

Soleimani had led Shi'a efforts against the Sunni ISIS in the region, and his passing may have facilitated ISIS's attempts to reconstitute itself. His death also gave Shi'a and Sunni wannabe terrorists yet another excuse for attacking American interests in the area and abroad, although his name was rarely cited in terrorist confessor videos.

Late February saw the signing of a peace agreement between the Taliban and the U.S. administration, which would entail the withdrawal of all U.S. troops from the battlefield in return for the Taliban agreeing to not support terrorists on its soil. Ongoing strife with ISIS-K would make that promise easy to uphold, but continuing contacts with al-Qaeda led many pundits to question the long-term likelihood of the Taliban adhering to the terms of the agreement. Attacks by ISIS-K, the Taliban, and unknown individuals were logged in seven provinces (Badghis, Baglan, Faryab, Ghazni, Herat, Kandahar, and Kunduz) in early 2020, compared to 21 provinces in the last half of 2019.

The Trump Administration's handling of the negotiations with the Taliban came under close scrutiny in late June when the *New York Times* and scores of other media outlets disclosed that intelligence briefings indicated that Russian military intelligence officers offered bounties to Taliban gunmen to kill American troops. Some intelligence reporting suggested that the program began in 2018, and may have been directly responsible for the killings of American Marines in April 2019. Questions of what-did-he-know, when-did-he-know-it, why-didn't-he-do-anything swirled around the President, who denied having received contemporaneous briefing of the intelligence reports. Later reports of Iranian bounties received less press coverage.

Outgoing President Trump's withdrawal of troops from Afghanistan stoked worries of an increase in terrorist violence.

In the **United States,** attacks, including Molotov cocktails, knifings and shooting of police, were conducted on the margins of the massive nationwide protests against institutional racism and the killing of black men by individual police officers. Despite the Administration's efforts to pin protest-related violence on antifa instigators, nearly all of the attacks chronicled herein were by white supremacists, rightist militias, and other right-leaning individuals. Of special note was a plot by Bugaloo right-wingers to kidnap Michigan Governor Gretchen Whitmer (D) and Virginia Governor Ralph Northam (D) for their assertive response to the COVID-19 crisis. The FBI continued its excellent record of wrapping up plot before attacks could take place.

Effects of the Coronavirus

The coronavirus dominated the world's headlines and attention spans, necessitating new whole-of-world responses to an existential threat. Even terrorists were taken aback by its deadliness.

- ISIS told its adherents, via its newsletter, to stand down on travel home and/or to likely operational areas.

- In a more altruistic response, Colombia's National Liberation Army (ELN) declared a unilateral one-month ceasefire to begin on April 1.

- Later that month, ELN guerrillas in Bolívar Department warned that it would be "forced to kill people in order to preserve lives" because residents had not "respected the orders to prevent COVID-19".[1] Human Rights Watch logged eight murders between March and June by Latin American armed groups of civilians who apparently did not abide by the gunmen's COVID rules.[2]

---

[1] Ciara Nugent "Why Armed Groups in Latin America Are Enforcing COVID-19 Lockdowns" *Time Magazine,* July 22, 2020, https://www.msn.com/en-us/news/world/why-armed-groups-in-latin-america-are-enforcing-covid-19-lockdowns/ar-BB1745J8; Megan Janetsky and Anthony Faiola "Colombian Guerrillas Are Using Coronavirus Curfews To Expand Their Control. Violators Have Been Killed" *Washington Post,* July 26, 2020.

[2] "Colombia: Armed Groups' Brutal Covid-19 Measures: Killings, Threats, and Social Control" Human Rights Watch, July 15, 2020 https://www.hrw.org/news/2020/07/15/colombia-armed-groups-brutal-covid-19-measures

- HRW reported that FARC splinters enforcing COVID-19 lockdowns included the Oliver Sinisterra Front and the United Guerrillas of the Pacific, in Nariño State; the Jaime Martínez mobile column and the Dagoberto Ramos mobile column, in Cauca State; the 10th Front, in Arauca State; the 7th and the 1st fronts in Guaviare State; and the Carolina Ramírez Front, in Putumayo State. HRW reported that the right-wing Gaitanist Self-Defense Forces of Colombia (AGC) was involved in similar actions.

- Carlos Ruiz Massieu, U.N. envoy for Colombia, said that 22 former FARC combatants were making face masks at a textile cooperative to respond to the coronavirus pandemic; eight other former FARC fighters' cooperatives were doing similar work.

- In Lebanon, Hizballah mobilized 24,500 members and volunteers for a campaign against the coronavirus pandemic, sending paramedics and volunteers via trucks and on foot to spray disinfectants on shops and buildings and care for virus patients. Many had blamed the organization for inadvertently bringing the virus into the country. Hizballah leader Sayyed Hassan Nasrallah countered by giving regularly televised speeches on COVID-19 responses, observing, "We should feel that we are in a battle and we should fight this battle." Hizballah's Islamic Health Society plans to open testing centers.

- The Communist Party of the Philippines called on its New People's Army to halt fighting rebel groups until April 15.

- In early April, the Taliban announced its willingness to declare a cease-fire in areas it controlled if they were hit by a coronavirus outbreak. Taliban spokesman Zabihullah Mujahed said, "If, God forbid, the outbreak happens in an area where we control the situation then we will stop fighting in that area." It also said it would guarantee the security of health and aid workers traveling to their areas offering assistance to prevent the spread of COVID-19. It was unclear how many cases would trigger a cease-fire. Meanwhile, the group enforced quarantines of everyone who returned from Iran, a regional hotspot, and distributed gloves, soap and masks. The Taliban warned, however, that it would exact revenge "upon the cold-hearted enemy" if Taliban prisoners lost their lives to the virus while in government jails.

- Hayat Tahrir al-Sham, which dominates Syria's Idlib Province, restricted gatherings and issued medical information to the public.

At least one prominent extremist may have succumbed to the virus. In early June, *Foreign Policy* reported that senior Taliban military official Moulawi Muhammad Ali Jan Ahmed said that Afghan Taliban supreme leader Mullah Haibatullah Akhunzada had contracted COVID-19 and might have died during treatment.[3]

A survey of 100 counterterrorist practitioners by the Daniel K. Inouye Asia-Pacific Center for Security Studies noted that terrorists and security services had been forced to adapt to the pandemic, and that terrorists had gained relatively little in the short term.[4] In the long term, however, as governments divert more resources to propping up the economy and away from security programs, terrorists could prey upon youths who find themselves unemployed, broke, and fed up with government incompetence in meeting their economic, societal, and public health needs.

Ever alert for opportunities to sew discomfort, propaganda wings of terrorist groups offered messages tying their brand of radicalism to the Covid-19 crisis:

- U.N. Secretary-General Antonio Guterres warned that extremists had stepped up their social media campaigns, aiming at young people who were spending more time online during lockdowns. Estonia's U.N. Ambassa-

---

[3] Lynne O'Donnell and Marwais Khan "Leader of Afghan Taliban Said To Be Gravely Ill with Coronavirus" *Foreign Policy,* June 1, 2020.

[4] Daniel Mullins "Assessing the Impact of the COVID-19 Pandemic on Terrorism and Counter-Terrorism: Practitioner Insights" vol. 21, *APCSS Perspectives,* August 2020, 9 pp., https://apcss.org/nexus_articles/assessing-the-impact-of-the-covid-19-pandemic-on-terrorism-and-counter-terrorism-practitioner-insights/?fbclid=IwAR0awqpVErX5GppIB3t-3o1fmsvim2H-pz2maO-IZO7Fcq8yyNv1keMGr1PI

dor Sven Jürgenson added that worsening poverty "will lead to increased educational gaps, serious damage to the prospects for a better future and can potentially lay seeds of radicalization among young people, constituting a threat to peace and security"[5]. That said, on April 30, the U.N. announced that Guterres's March 23 call for a cease-fire was positively received by 16 armed groups from Yemen, Myanmar, Ukraine, Philippines, Colombia, Angola, Libya, Senegal, Sudan, Syria, Indonesia and Nagorno-Karabakh.[6]

- Al-Shabaab warned that the coronavirus was spread "by the crusader forces who have invaded the country and the disbelieving countries that support them". The group upped the ante in June by opening in Jilib a COVID-19 isolation and care facility, which featured a 24/7 hotline. The Jilib building had earlier housed UNICEF.[7]

- Al-Qaeda and ISIS saw the virus as punishment for non-Muslims and called on followers to repent and take care of themselves. It saw COVID-19 as a consequence of "our own sins and our distance from the divine methodology".[8] Al-Qaeda said that non-Muslims should use their quarantine time to learn about Islam.

- The mid-March edition of ISIS's *al-Naba* newsletter called for followers to show no mercy and launch attacks during the crisis. An audiotape in late May complained about the closure of a shrine in Mecca to combat the coronavirus, hinting that Muslims are immune.

- ISIS adherents crowed about ongoing COVID-19 deaths and violence related to

demonstrations in the U.S. in early June. An ISIS follower posted the hashtag "#AmericaBurning" in a discussion on *Telegram*, and another posted "You are waking up this morning to news of the destruction of America, the dismantling of its States, and civil war." Another ISIS website posted, "Destruction, fragmentation. America is burning," and an ISIS supporter posted photos in the same *Telegram* forum of the riots, adding "O Allah, burn them like they burned the lands of the Muslims."[9]

- Houthi rebels claimed Saudi Arabia had airdropped masks infected with coronavirus.[10]

- Boko Haram assessed that coronavirus was a punishment for those who disobey Islam and advocated piety as a solution.[11]

- An Indonesian ISIS supporter deemed coronavirus retribution for al-Baghdadi's death and called for attacks on the UN.[12]

- Filipino ISIS adherents threatened Muslims who followed government directives on COVID-19.[13] Social media accounts with possible ties to ISIS-East Asia threatened attacks if mosques were not reopened. The accounts said that the Philippine government was incompetent. Manila had diverted counterterrorism resources to the COVID-19 response.[14]

[5] Edith M. Lederer "UN Chief: Extremists Using COVID-19 To Recruit Online Youths" *Associated Press*, April 27, 2020.
[6] Edith M. Lederer "UN Chief: 16 Armed Groups Have Responded to Cease-Fire Appeal" *Associated Press*, April 30, 2020.
[7] Abdi Guled "Extremist Group al-Shabaab Sets Up COVID-19 Center in Somalia" *Associated Press* June 12, 2020. https://www.washingtonpost.com/world/africa/extremist-group-al-shabab-sets-up-covid-19-center-in-somalia/2020/06/12/9e288142-ac9b-11ea-a43b-be9f6494a87d_story.html
[8] Joseph Hincks "With the World Busy Fighting COVID-19, Could ISIS Mount a Resurgence?" *Time*, April 29, 2020.

[9] Brian Glyn Williams, Professor of Islamic History, University of Massachusetts Dartmouth "Islamic State Calls for Followers to Spread Coronavirus, Exploit Pandemic and Protests" MSN.com's The Conversation June 23, 2020. https://www.goskagit.com/opinion/conversation/islamic-state-militants-incite-attacks-gloat-at-us-protests-and-pandemic-deaths/article_c3d663e2-4fe1-543b-b04e-4fd7d9793f8c.html
[10] Kevin Sieff, Susannah George and Kareem Fahim "Now Joining the Fight Against Coronavirus: The World's Armed Rebels, Drug Cartels, and Gangs" *Washington Post*, April 14, 2020.
[11] Joseph Hincks "With the World Busy Fighting COVID-19, Could ISIS Mount a Resurgence?" *Time*, April 29, 2020.
[12] Ibid.
[13] Ibid.
[14] "COVID-19 Is an 'Ally' for ISIS in the Philippines, DoD Report Finds" *Military Times*, August 14, 2020. https://www.militarytimes.com/news/your-military/2020/08/13/covid-19-is-an-ally-for-isis-in-the-philippines-dod-report-finds/?utm_source=Sailthru&utm_medium=email&utm_campaign=EBB%2008.14.20&utm_term=Editorial%20-%20Early%20Bird%20Brief

- White supremacists and neo-Nazis cited an "obligation" of infected members to spread the virus to law enforcement and minority communities. Other right-wing extremists posted "What to Do if You Get Corona 19", suggesting that one "visit your local mosque, visit your local synagogue, spend the day on public transport, spend time in your local diverse neighborhood".[15] Their calls continued into July.[16]

ISIS soon got back on its feet in Iraq, however, quintupling its operations by conducting a spate of bombings, ambushes of police and military officers, and complex attacks as authorities were stretched thin trying to police the coronavirus lockdown while also protecting against terrorist attacks.[17] A UN monitoring team reported in late July 2020 that ISIS "exploited security gaps caused by the pandemic and by political turbulence in Iraq to relaunch a sustained rural insurgency, as well as sporadic operations in Baghdad and other large cities".[18] The Pentagon's Inspector General's report to Congress noted that ISIS had taken advantage of restrictions placed on security forces due to COVID-19.[19] ISIS had similarly kept up operations in Syria.

Terrorist trials were conducted using social distancing measures that would otherwise have raised due process concerns. Gokmen Tanis, 38, a Dutch man of Turkish descent accused of shooting in and around a tram in Utrecht on March 18, 2019, killing four people and wounding three others, was not permitted in court during the announcing of his sentencing due to coronavirus concerns.

Prisoners in Guantanamo Bay feared the disease's spread after a Navy sailor tested positive. Prisoners in jails throughout the world shared the same fears, some resorting to rioting. Others were given compassionate release. A Gitmo defense attorney warned of the likely propaganda exploitation by al-Qaeda-affiliated terrorists if an aging, ill detainee dies of Covid-19 while incarcerated.[20]

Unexpected secondary effects of the COVID-19 crisis included difficulties of ISIS victims in returning to their home countries. Yazidi women who were kidnapped found closed borders and restrictions on movement in Iraq and Syria hampered their repatriations.[21]

In addition to affecting soldiers' readiness and mobility, government restrictions on movements as part of coronavirus responses impaired the ability of local self-defense volunteers to patrol against terrorists.[22]

Colombia's cash-strapped government was forced to divert money to coronavirus response that had earlier been earmarked for implementing the peace agreement with former rebels, putting the retired fighters in harm's way from vengeful foes. Erstwhile rebels worried that quarantines made them sitting ducks for assas-

---

[15] Lydia Khalil "COVID-19 and America's Counter-Terrorism Response" *War on the Rocks*, May 1, 2020. https://warontherocks.com/2020/05/covid-19-and-americas-counter-terrorism-response/?utm_source=Sailthru&utm_medium=email&utm_campaign=EBB%2005.01.20&utm_term=Editorial%20-%20Early%20Bird%20Brief

[16] Amy Woodyatt "Neo-Nazis Encouraging Followers To 'Deliberately Infect' Jews and Muslims with Coronavirus" CNN July 9, 2020, https://www.msn.com/en-us/news/world/neo-nazis-encouraging-followers-to-deliberately-infect-jews-and-muslims-with-coronavirus/ar-BB16xb1A

17 Qassim Abdul-Zahra, Bassem Mroue and Samya Kullab "IS Extremists Step Up as Iraq, Syria, Grapple with Virus" *Associated Press*, May 3, 2020.

[18] Paul Cruickshank "ISIS Exploiting Coronavirus Security Gaps To Relaunch Insurgency, UN Report Warns" CNN July 23, 2020. https://www.cnn.com/2020/07/23/politics/isis-coronavirus-un-terrorism-report/index.html

[19] Richard Sisk "ISIS Took Advantage of COVID-19 Restrictions To Ramp Up Attack in Iraq, Report Finds" military.com August 5, 2020. https://www.military.com/daily-news/2020/08/05/isis-took-advantage-of-covid-19-restrictions-ramp-attack-iraq-report-finds.html?utm_source=Sailthru&utm_medium=email&utm_campaign=DEF%20EBB%208.6.20&utm_term=Editorial%20-%20Early%20Bird%20Brief

[20] Aaron Shepard "What Happens When the Coronavirus Hits Guantanamo Bay?" *Pittsburgh Post-Gazette*, July 1, 2020. https://www.post-gazette.com/opinion/Op-Ed/2020/06/30/Aaron-Shepard-coronavirus-Guantanamo-Bay-Nazir-Bin-Lep/stories/202006300013?utm_source=Sailthru&utm_medium=email&utm_campaign=EBB%2007.01.20&utm_term=Editorial%20-%20Early%20Bird%20Brief

[21] "After IS Captivity, Virus Blocks One Yazidi's Homecoming" *Agence France-Presse*, May 6, 2020. https://www.msn.com/en-us/news/world/after-is-captivity-virus-blocks-one-yazidis-homecoming/ar-BB13Gkog

[22] Sam Mednick "Burkina Faso's Volunteer Fighters Are No Match for Jihadists" *Washington Post* July 9, 2020 https://www.washingtonpost.com/world/africa/burkina-fasos-volunteer-fighters-are-no-match-for-jihadists/2020/07/09/715ca7f2-c1b2-11ea-8908-68a2b9eae9e0_story.html

sins who could more easily track them down.[23]

The buildup of the virus's curve focused media attention away from terrorist attacks and toward almost exclusive reporting on the pandemic's effects. The concomitant drop in ITERATE numbers for 2020 may reflect a drop in reporting, rather than in actual attacks.

A terrorist-like attack on coronavirus responders occurred on March 31, when a train engineer tried to crash his train into the hospital ship *USNS Mercy*, which was treating non-COVID-19 patients at the Port of Los Angeles so that hospitals could focus on COVID-19 cases. Pundits suggested that terrorists around the world might similarly attempt to hamper medical assistance missions, as they had done with attacks on polio and Ebola workers, out of baseless anti-government conspiracy theories.

In Burkina Faso, jihadis blocked food, water and medicine trucks while trying to annex territory in the north and east.[24]

Conspiracy theorists also filled in some of the violence vacuum left by more commonly-recognized terrorist groups. Conspiracists linked the building of 5G mobile communications cell towers with the advent of Covid-19, and despite the assurances of the scientific community that there is no causal link, began torching cellular radio towers. During the first three weeks of April, the UK logged 50 fires against cell towers and other equipment, while police arrested three perpetrators. An attack in Birmingham denied voice and data traffic to a field hospital treating coronavirus patients, denying the victims' families the ability to chat with their dying loved ones. Another 16 towers were hit in the Netherlands. Other attacks occurred in Ireland, Cyprus, and Belgium.[25]

Frustrations with ongoing state-government-imposed restrictions in response to Covid-19 led to increasingly disturbing actions by protestors, who showed up to state capitols with automatic weapons. The FBI and ATF caught an individual in Loveland, Colorado, who had stockpiled four pipe bombs and had called for protestors to bring assault rifles to the state capital for a rally on May 1.

If there's an illegal buck to be made, criminal organizations will find a way to make it. Police organizations reported an uptick in scams, theft of personal protective equipment, ransomware attacks on hospitals, other cybercrime, and counterfeiting during the crisis.[26] Hacking was especially popular amongst those targeting hospitals, health care bodies, pharmaceutical companies, academics, medical research organizations and local government; some appeared to have been sponsored by governments.[27] Computer-sophisticated terrorists could be taking notes on which techniques were most effective.

Similar funding campaigns were used by terrorists. In August, the U.S. Department of Justice seized $2 million in 300 cryptocurrency accounts held by ISIS, al-Qaeda, and Hamas's al-Qassam Brigades. On of the scams entailed ISIS creating a site in February in which it offered personal protective equipment to shield against coronavirus.[28] The U.S. Department of Justice shut down another ISIS-affiliated site, FaceMaskCenter.com, in August that offered to sell FDA-approved N95 respirator masks and other PPE. The site even accepted credit cards.[29]

---

[23] Christine Armario "Bullets, Virus: Fears Multiply for Colombia's Ex-Rebels" *Associated Press*, April 30, 2020.

[24] Henry Wilkins and Danielle Paquette "Terror in the Countryside, Coronavirus in the City: In Burkina Faso, There's No Safe Haven" *Washington Post*, April 15, 2020

[25] Kelvin Chan, Beatrice Depuy and Arijeta Lajka "Conspiracy Theorists Burn 5G Towers Claiming Link to Virus" *Associated Press*, published in *Florida Times-Union*, April 22, 2020, p. A4.

[26] Samuel Petrequin "Criminals Quick to Exploit COVID-19 Crisis in Europe" *Associated Press*, April 30, 2020.

[27] Zachary Cohen "State-Backed Hackers Behind Wave of Cyberattacks Targeting Coronavirus Response, US and UK Warn" CNN May 6, 2020. https://www.cnn.com/en-us/news/us/state-backed-hackers-behind-wave-of-cyber-attacks-targeting-coronavirus-response-us-and-uk-warn/ar-BB13DFtP

[28] David Shortell "Justice Department Seizes Millions in Cryptocurrency From Terror Groups" CNN, August 13, 2020, https://www.cnn.com/2020/08/13/politics/justice-department-cryptocurrency-terror-groups/index.html

[29] David Choi "Fake N95 Face Masks Were Being Sold on This ISIS-linked Website—and It Shows How Terror Groups Are Using COVID-19 as a Propaganda Tool" *Business Insider* August 29, 2020. https://www.msn.com/en-us/news/world/fake-n95-face-masks-were-being-sold-on-this-isis-linked-website-%e2%80%94-and-it-shows-how-terror-groups-are-using-covid-19-as-a-propaganda-tool/ar-BB18uTgD

What's Next?

Innovations in Terrorist Methods

The most noteworthy attack breakthrough was employed not by terrorists, but by a spree killer in April who dressed in a Royal Canadian Mounted Police uniform and drove a decommissioned RCMP cruiser that still had the service's distinctive markings. After targeted shootings, he then drove the vehicle, stopping random drivers who pulled over after seeing a police vehicle behind them, then shooting them. His killing spree included 16 crime scenes, highlighted by several torchings of buildings. The double technique of police disguise and rolling attacks could be mimicked by future terrorists. Counterfeit vehicles, usually ambulances and captured armed forces vehicles, have earlier been used by terrorists overseas, but strictly as a way to gain access, not halt potential victims.

Vehicles being used to kill and maim victims without explosives—esesentially used by non-suicide bombers with an exit strategy—have been seen in Europe, Israel and the U.S., the latter site a favorite of right-wing individuals targeting street protests.

In late July, hundreds of individuals in various U.S. states reported receiving unsolicited deliveries of unknown plant seeds. While most authorities attributed the mass mailing to likely scam artists looking to steal identities for fake product reviews on social media sites, terrorists could adapt the technique to offshore attacks. The seed packages, labeled "jewelry" and using (according the Chinese Foreign Ministry fake) return addresses from the Chinese postal services apparently sailed through postal service scanners designed to detect biological weapons such as anthrax. Use of the seeds, perhaps bolstered by an online misinformation campaign attributing positive aspects of the seeds (e.g., that they have protective properties against Covid-19; that they are a superior food plant, etc.) could wreak havoc for minimal cost and no loss of lives for the terrorists.

Responses

Affecting nearly every human endeavor worldwide, the coronavirus also affected antiterrorist efforts. On June 25, Afghan security forces in Nangarhar, Ghazni, Logar, and Kunduz Provinces were reporting that suspected infection rates in their units were hitting between 60 and 90 percent.[30] Minimal testing capabilities meant that troops were isolated for two weeks out of an abundance of caution, siphoning forces away from security duties. Senior commanders had died from COVID-19 complications, including the chief of police in Kunduz, a district-level police chief in Balkh Province and a mid-level police officer in Kabul. While authorities assumed that the virus was also affecting ISIS-K and Taliban fighters, terrorist attacks continued unabated.

Iraqi antiterrorist efforts were similarly hampered by lockdowns called to halt the spread of the coronavirus.[31]

Patient tracking down of major terrorists and foot soldiers, sometimes taking decades, has managed to take many household (well, my household) names off the streets and into jails or the grave. Since the late 1970s, when this chronology series began, the following individuals have had their careers ended through death by natural causes, their own hand, rival assassinations, government raids, or the death penalty, retirement, or incarceration. A surprising number of them lived into their golden years. Among the major names are:

- **Yasser Arafat**, born Mohammed Yasser Abdel Rahman Abdel Raouf Arafat al-Qudwa al-Husseini, alias Abu Ammar, Chairman of the Palestine Liberation Organization,

[30] Susannah George, Aziz Tassal, and Sharif Hassan "Coronavirus Sweeps Through Aghanistan's Security Forces" *Washington Post*, June 25, 2020, https://www.washingtonpost.com/world/asia_pacific/afghanistan-coronavirus-security-forces-military/2020/06/24/0063c828-b4e2-11ea-9a1d-d3db1cbe07ce_story.html

[31] Brian Glyn Williams, Professor of Islamic History, University of Massachusetts Dartmouth "Islamic State Calls for Followers to Spread Coronavirus, Exploit Pandemic and Protests" MSN.com's *The Conversation* June 23, 2020. https://www.goskagit.com/opinion/conversation/islamic-state-militants-incite-attacks-gloat-at-us-protests-and-pandemic-deaths/article_c3d663e2-4fe1-543b-b04e-4fd7d9793f8c.html

founding member of Fatah, first president of the Palestinian National Authority, died at age 75 in France after winning the Nobel Peace Prize.

- **Shoko Asahara**, born born Chizuo Matsumoto, founder of the doomsday cult Aum Shin Rikyo, was executed for murder in Japan at age 63.

- **Anwar Nasser al-Aulaqi**, imam and key ideological supporter of jihadi operations, was killed by a Hellfire missile in Yemen at age 40.

- **Berndt Andreas Baader**, a leader of the West German Red Army Faction, commonly known as the Baader-Meinhof Group, committed suicide in prison in West Germany at age 34.

- **Abu Bakr al-Baghdadi**, born Ibrahim Awad Ibrahim Ali al-Badri al-Samarrai, founder and Caliph of the Islamic State of Iraq and the Levant, died in a raid on October 26, 2019 at age 48 in Syria.

- **Carlos the Jackal**, born Illich Ramirez Sanchez, age 71, a Venezuelan Marxist affiliated with the Popular Front for the Liberation of Palestine; currently serving a life sentence in France.

- **Manuel Rubén Abimael Guzmán Reynoso**, alias Chairman Gonzalo, age 86, founder of Peru's Sendero Luminoso (Maoist Shining Path); currently serving a life sentence in Peru.

- **George Habash**, alias al-Hakim, founder of the Popular Front for the Liberation of Palestine, died at age 81 of a heart attack while battling cancer in Jordan.

- **Wadi Haddad**, alias Abu Hani, founder of the Popular Front for the Liberation of Palestine-External Operations, died at age 51 in East Germany.

- **Nayef Hawatmeh**, alias Abu an-Nuf, age 82, founder of the Marxist Democratic front for the Liberation of Palestine, resides in Syria. He remains active in left-wing Palestinian politics.

- **Theodore John Kaczynski**, alias The Unabomber, age 78, an anarchist lone wolf who is serving a life sentence in the U.S.

- **Leila Khaled**, age 76, a serial hijacker for the Popular Front for the Liberation of Palestine, served a prison term and now lives in Israel. She remains active in Palestinian politics.

- **Osama bin Mohammed bin Awad bin Laden**, founder of al-Qaeda, died in a raid in Pakistan on May 2, 2011 at age 54.

- **Ulrike Marie Meinhof**, a leader of the West German Red Army Faction, commonly known as the Baader-Meinhof Group, committed suicide in prison in West Germany at age 41.

- **Khalid Sheikh Mohammed**, age 56, Pakistani terrorist commonly viewed as the principal architect of, inter alia, the 9/11 attack, is awaiting trial at the Guantanamo Bay detention facility on terrorism charges.

- **Abu Nidal**, born Sabri Khalil al-Banna, founder of Fatah-Revolutionary Council, commonly known as the Abu Nidal Organization, died at age 65 on August 16, 2002 in Baghdad, Iraq.

- **Qasim al-Rimi**, emir of Al-Qaeda in the Arabic Peninsula, was killed in Yemen at age 41.

- **Fusako Shigenobu**, age 75, founder of the Japanese Red Army, is serving time in prison in Japan.

- **Ramzi Yousef**, age 52, Pakistani terrorist involved in numerous high profile jihadi attacks, including the 1993 World Trade Center bombing, is serving a life term in the U.S.

- **Abu Musab al-Zarqawi**, born Ahmad Fadeel al-Nazal al-Khalayleh, Jordanian leader of al-Qaeda in Iraq, died in an airstrike in Iraq at age 39.

We can add to this list two of the most notorious state sponsors of terrorism:

- Colonel **Muammar Muhammad Abu Minyar al-Qadhafi** of Libya, killed at age 69 while attempting to flee a mob

- **Saddam Hussein Abd al-Majid al-Tikriti**, ousted President of Iraq, executed at age 69 by Iraqi authorities

Governments continue to work on adding to this tally by ending the careers of al-Qaeda titular leader Ayman al-Zawahiri, age 69, and Boko Haram leader Abubakar Shekau, age 47, who remained at large as of this writing.

Courts, police and prosecutors followed up in pursuing sometimes decades-in-the-making justice in several longstanding cases at the end of 2020, including:

- **Early October**: A French court sentenced ISIS follower Farid Ikken, who charged a police officer outside the Notre Dame cathedral in Paris with a hammer on June 6, 2017, to 28 years in jail.

- **October 1**: Authorities at Frankfurt Airport arrested Kim A., a German woman, on her return from Syria on allegations she had joined ISIS. She was charged with membership in a terrorist organization and other crimes.

- **October 2**: The Hamburg State Court sentenced Omaima A., widow of German-born rapper Denis Cuspert, alias Deso Dogg, who joined ISIS in Syria and was killed in an airstrike in 2018, to three years and six months in prison for membership in a terrorist organization, failing to properly care for her children, weapons violations, and aiding and abetting the enslavement of a Yazidi girl.

- **October 6**: The U.S. Department of Justice petitioned the U.S. Supreme Court to review the case of Boston Marathon bomber Dzhokhar Tsarnaev, whose death sentence was tossed out by the 1ˢᵗ U.S. Circuit Court of Appeals on July 31, 2020 due to concerns over the jury selection process.

- **October 6**: U.S. District Judge Leonie Brinkema in Alexandria, Virginia denied the request for compassionate release of Ardit Ferizi, a computer hacker who gave ISIS personal data of more than 1,300 U.S. government and military personnel, and ruled that the Kosovo native should remain in federal prison in Lewisburg, Pennsylvania, to serve his 20-year sentence.

- **October 7**: The U.S. Department of Justice charged Alexanda Kotey and El Shafee Elsheikh, two of the British-accented ISIS "Beatles", in Alexandria, Virginia federal court with hostage-taking resulting in death, conspiracy to murder U.S. citizens outside the United States, conspiracy to provide material support to a foreign terrorist organization, and related conspiracy charges for involvement in the torture and beheading of American journalists James Foley and Steven Sotloff and relief workers Peter Kassig and Kayla Mueller. The duo were also suspected of involvement in the killing of two Britons, Alan Henning and David Haines, and several other hostages, including two Japanese nationals.

- **October 7:** Pakistan's government ordered the continued detention for at least another three months of British-born Pakistani Ahmed Omar Saeed Sheikh, who had been on death row for the January 23, 2002 beheading of U.S. journalist Daniel Pearl.

- **October 7:** Kenyan Chief Justice/Magistrate Francis Andayi found guilty Mohamed Ahmed Abdi and Hassan Hussein Mustafa for conspiring with and aiding the four al-Shabaab gunmen who attacked Nairobi's Westgate Mall on September 21, 2013, killing 67 people. The duo were sentenced to 18 years.

- **October 7:** The trial began of Russian citizen Vadim Krasikov, alias Vadim S., for shooting to death Georgia national and former Chechen commander Tornike K. in Kleiner Tiergarten park in Berlin on August 23, 2019.

- **October 7:** At the end of a five-year trial that featured 453 hearings, more than 200 witnesses, and 60 lawyers, Greek Presiding Judge Maria Lepenioti ruled that neo-Nazi party Golden Dawn founder and leader Nikos Michaloliakos and seven other senior members were guilty of running a criminal organization. The judge later sentenced Michaloliakos and seven other former lawmakers to 13 years in prison.

- **October 8**: The Rotterdam District Court convicted six male jihadis for plotting to fire AK-47 assault rifles and set off a car bomb at a September 2018 festival and sentenced them to 10-17 years.

- **October 8**: Pakistani counter-terrorism police arrested two people in Muzaffargarh district in Punjab Province on charges of collecting funds for radical cleric Hafiz Saeed's outlawed Jamaat-ud-Dawa and Falah-e-Insaniat charities, suspected of being fronts for Lashkar-e-Taiba. Saeed is wanted by the U.S. for his role in the 2008 Mumbai attacks.

- **October 10**: Philippine police and troops arrested suspected Indonesian suicide bomber wannabe Rezky Fantasya Rullie with two Filipino women, who were suspected to be the wives of Abu Sayyaf terrorists, in a house in Jolo in Sulu Province where they found an explosive vest and bomb components.

- **October 12**: British Justice Mark Warbury sentenced sheep farmer Nigel Wright to 14 years in prison for plotting to use baby food laced with metal shards to blackmail Tesco, one of Britain's biggest supermarket chains.

- **October 13**: The U.S. Attorney's office for the Eastern District of Virginia sought the extradition to the U.S. of five American citizens—Waqar Hussain Khan, Ahmed Minni, Ramy Zamzam, Aman Yemer, and Umar Farooq—who had fled the country to Pakistan in 2009 to fight for the al-Qaeda-linked Lashkar-e-Taiba and Jaish-e-Mohammed terrorist groups.

- **October 16**: Self-described skinhead and white supremacist Richard Holzer, of Pueblo, Colorado, pleaded guilty in federal court to federal hate crime and explosives charges. He planned to bomb Colorado's second-oldest synagogue and poison members of the synagogue as part of a "racial holy war" before his arrest in November 2019.

- **October 19**: The back-to-back terrorism trials in Paris began of Josu Urrutikoetxea, 69, alias Josu Ternera, the last known head of the separatist Basque Nation and Liberty (ETA). He was charged with "criminal association with a view to preparing a terrorist act" for alleged attack plots in the 2000s and 2010s. When the French trials end, France has agreed to extradite him to Spain for crimes against humanity, multiple killings and belonging to a terrorist organization.

- **October 20**: India's National Investigation Agency filed charges at an NIA special court at Mohali in Punjab against ten people, including the slain senior Hizbul commander Riyaz Naikoo and Punjab-based drug traffickers, in the Hizbul Mujahideen (HM) narco-terror case.

- **October 23**: Enrique Marquez, who purchased guns for Syed Rizwan Farook in 2011 and 2012 before Farook and his wife, Tashfeen Malik, conducted a terrorist attack on December 2, 2015 on the Inland Regional Center in San Bernardino, California that killed 14 people and wounded 22, was sentenced to 20 years in prison.

- **October 26**: Prominent Holocaust denier Horst Mahler, 84, was freed from a Brandenburg, Germany prison. Authorities issued a new arrest warrant for the erstwhile far-left terrorist turned neo-Nazi. He was jailed in 2009 after being sentenced to ten years for repeated incitement to racial hatred and for Holocaust denial. In the 1960s and early 1970s, he was an attorney representing prominent leftists in West Germany and later founded the Red Army Faction with Andreas Baader, Gundrun Ensslin, Ulrike Meinhof and others. He participated in some of the group's criminal activities, including bank robberies and kidnappings.

- **October 27**: The trial in Mali began against three jihadis accused of killing more than two dozen people in attacks targeting foreigners in 2015. In March 2015, gunmen fired at Bamako's La Terrasse nightclub and threw a grenade inside, killing a Frenchman, a Belgian, and three Malians. In November 2015, gunmen took guests and staff hostage at the 190-room Radisson Blu Hotel, killing 20 people, including 14 foreigners.

- **October 28:** Federal authorities charged Haji Najibullah, an Afghan man, for the November 2008 kidnapping of former *New York Times* journalist David Rohde, Afghan journalist Tahir Ludin, and their Afghan driver Asadullah Mangal.

- **November 3:** The trial in a Dutch courtroom began of Oleg Putalov, who was one of four people charged in the July 17, 2014 shoot-down of Malaysia Airlines Flight 17, a B-777, over Grabovo, Ukraine. Prosecutors said that a Russian-made Buk missile launched from territory controlled by pro-Russian rebels hit the jet, killing all 298 passengers and crew on board en route from Amsterdam to Kuala Lumpur. Also accused were two other Russians—Igor Girkin and Sergey Dubinskiy—and Ukrainian Leonid Kharchenko.

- **November 5:** A Paris criminal court sentenced Sidi Ahmed Ghlam, an Algerian man, to life in prison for killing fitness instructor Aurélie Chatelain and trying to bomb a church near in the Paris suburb of Villejuif in a failed April 2015 attack plotted by ISIS in Syria.

- **November 5:** Authorities in Ciudad Juarez arrested Alfredo L. in connection with the November 4, 2019 murder of nine Mormon American-Mexican citizens—including three women and six children—in an attack on their three-vehicle convoy on a remote dirt road in Bavispe in Sonora State.

- **November 9:** U.S. District Court Judge Philip P. Simon sentenced Samantha Elhassani, alias Samantha Sally, formerly of Elkart, Indiana, to 78 months in prison for aiding ISIS terrorists by smuggling more than $30,000 in cash and gold in multiple trips from the U.S. to Hong Kong between November 2014 and April 2015 to help fund their actions in Syria.

- **November 10:** The trial began in Spain's National Court in San Fernando de Henares near Madrid of three men accused of helping members of an ISIS cell that conducted two attacks in Barcelona and the nearby seaside town of Cambrils that killed 16 people and wounded 140 on August 17-18, 2017. A driver had crashed a van into pedestrians on Barcelona's Las Ramblas boulevard, killing 14. Five accomplices of the driver rammed into pedestrians in Cambrils and stabbed to death a woman.

- **November 11:** Libyan refugee Khairi Saadallah pleaded guilty at a pre-trial hearing in London's Old Bailey court to three murders and three attempted murders after stabbing six people in Forbury Gardens in Reading during the evening of June 20, 2020.

- **November 16:** An Amsterdam appeals court upheld the conviction for attempted murder with a terrorist motive of Afghan asylum-seeker Jawed S., 21, who stabbed two American tourists, seriously injuring them, at Amsterdam's main railway station on August 31, 2018.

- **November 18:** West Midlands Police and counterterrorism officers from the Police Service of Northern Ireland detained a 65-year-old man at his Belfast home under the Terrorism Act for the November 21, 1974 bombings of the Mulberry Bush and Tavern in the Town pubs in Birmingham that killed 21 and injured 182. The bombings were blamed on the Provisional Irish Republican Army (PIRA), which never claimed responsibility.

- **November 25:** The trial in Antwerp began of four people, among them two Iranians including an Iranian diplomat believed to be the mastermind, accused of plotting to bomb a rally of 25,000 Iranian Mujahedeen-e-Khalq (MEK) opposition supporters in Villepinte, a Paris suburb, on June 30, 2018.

- **November 25:** U.S. federal prosecutors charged Maria Bell of Hopatcong, New Jersey, with concealing multiple efforts to transfer money to jihadis connected to the Nusra Front, a former al-Qaeda affiliate based in Syria's Idlib Province.

- **November 27:** Norway announced that it would extradite to France Walid Abdulrahman Abu Zayed, in his 60s, who is suspected of taking part in an attack that killed six people and wounded 20 others in the Jo Goldenberg restaurant in the Marias quarter of Paris in August 1982. Arrest warrants had been issued in 2015 against three former members of the Abu Nidal Organization for the attack.

• **December 7:** Pre-trial hearings began at the former NATO headquarters, now called Justitia, in Belgium regarding the March 22, 2016 ISIS suicide bombings that killed 32 and injured hundreds at the Brussels subway and airport.

• **December 10:** Indonesian counterterrorism police raided at a house in East Lampung district on Sumatra island and arrested biologist Aris Sumarsono, alias Zulkarnaen, believed to be the military leader of the al-Qaeda-linked Jemaah Islamiyah network who had been at large since 2003. Zulkarnaen was suspected of involvement in making bombs used in several attacks, including the 2002 Bali bombings that killed 202 people, mostly foreign tourists, and a 2003 attack on the J.W. Marriott Hotel in Jakarta that killed 12.

• **December 11:** The special tribunal set up to prosecute those responsible for the February 14, 2005 assassination of former Lebanese Prime Minister Rafiq al-Hariri sentenced Hizballah member Salim Jamil Ayyash to five life sentences.

• **December 14:** The U.S. formally blamed Iran for the presumed death of retired FBI agent Robert Alan Levinson, who had disappeared on March 9, 2007 from a hotel on Iran's Kish Island. The administration announced sanctions, including blocking their assets in the U.S., against Mohammad Baseri and Ahmad Khazai, two Iranian intelligence officers believed responsible for his abduction.

• **December 16:** A French court convicted all 14 defendants in the trial of those linked to the January 7-9, 2015 Paris attacks on *Charlie Hebdo* and a kosher supermarket.

• **December 16:** The Kyoto District Public Prosecutors Office formally filed charges of murder, attempted murder, arson and two other counts against Shinji Aoba for a deadly fire at the Kyoto Animation's No. 1 anime studio on July 18, 2019, that killed 36 and wounded more than 30 in Japan.

• **December 16:** Federal prosecutors indicted Barry Croft, Daniel Harris, Ty Garbin, Kaleb Franks, Adam Fox and Brandon Caserta on a federal kidnapping conspiracy charge in an alleged plot to kidnap Michigan Governor Gretchen Whitmer in October 2020. Michigan had charged another eight people; seven of them are associated with the Wolverine Watchmen group.

• **December 18:** A Paris court sentenced Moroccan national Ayoub el-Khazzani to life in prison for attempted murder with intent to commit terrorism in his attack moments after the Thalys train crossed into France from Belgium on August 21, 2015.

• **December 18:** The trial in Canada of Alek Minassian, charged with ten counts of first-degree murder and 16 counts of attempted murder for killing ten people in an April 23, 2018 van attack in North York, a Toronto suburb, was due to end.

• **December 21:** U.S. brought charges against Abu Agila Mohammad Mas'ud, a suspect in the Pan Am 103 bombing over Lockerbie, Scotland, on December 21, 1988 that killed 270 people.

• **December 21:** The Naumburg Higher Regional Court convicted right-wing extremist Stephan Balliet of 13 charges, including murder, attempted murder, and incitement, and sentenced him to life in prison for his Yom Kippur attack on a synagogue in Halle, Germany on October 9, 2019 when he killed two people.

Not all courts kept accused terrorists locked up. On December 24, Pakistan's Sindh High Court ordered the immediate release of four men accused of orchestrating the January 25, 2002 kidnapping and later beheading of American journalist Daniel Pearl. Acting U.S. Attorney

General Jeffrey Rosen said that the U.S. was willing to prosecute Ahmed Omar Saeed Sheikh if Pakistan's appeals were not upheld.

ADDITIONAL RESEARCH SOURCES

For those who prefer to run textual searches for specific groups, individuals, or incidents, a computer version of the 1960-2020 ITERATE (International Terrorism: Attributes of Terrorist Events) textual chronology is available from Vinyard Software, Inc., 502 Wandering Woods Way, Ponte Vedra, Florida 32081-0621, or e-mail via vinyardsoftware@hotmail.com The data set comes in a WordPerfect and Word textual version and looks remarkably like the volumes in this series of hardcopy chronologies. A numeric version offers circa 150 numeric variables describing the international attacks from 1968-2020. The data sets can be purchased by specific year of interest. See www.vinyardsoftware.com for further details.

Vinyard also offers the Data on Terrorist Suspects (DOTS) project, a detailed biographical index of every terrorist suspect named in the previous volumes of this chronology.

Comments about this volume's utility and suggestions for improvements for its likely successors are welcome and can be sent via vinyardsoftware@hotmail.com. Please send your terrorism publication citations to Vinyard to ensure inclusion in the next edition of the bibliography.

ACKNOWLEDGEMENTS

Once again, there are many individuals who have contributed to this research effort. Of particular note is Cynthia Kwitchoff, who has a well-earned reputation for quality and for being exceptionally easy to work with; ace coder Dr. Peter Flemming; and my family.

2019 CHRONOLOGY

WORLDWIDE

January 24, 2019: The *Voice of America* reported that Jane's Terrorism and Insurgency Center's annual Global Attack Index indicated a one-third decrease in global terrorist attacks in 2018, while fatalities dropped to a decade low. ISIS attacks in 2018 dropped 75 percent. Jane's recorded 15,321 attacks in 2018, with 13,483 nonmilitant fatalities.

UNITED NATIONS

March 28, 2019: The U.N. Security Council voted 15-0 in favor of a French-drafted resolution strengthening global efforts to combat terrorist financing. It called on the U.N.'s 193 member states to ensure that all measures they take to combat terrorism and its financing comply with international humanitarian, human rights and refugee law.

May 7, 2019: The U.N. Office of Counter-Terrorism instituted the Countering Terrorist Travel Program to help countries detect and disrupt travel by foreigners who have fought for extremist groups such as ISIS and al-Qaeda. The "go-Travel" software system will collect, process and share passenger information with national and international authorities.

August 3, 2019: A UN Security Council Counter-Terrorism Committee report warned that ISIS leaders were "adapting, consolidating and creating conditions for an eventual resurgence" in Syria and Iraq. It also suggested that ISIS could launch international terrorist attacks designed to "exacerbate existing dissent and unrest" in Europe before the end of 2019. The group was looking to "reinvest in the capacity to direct and facilitate complex international attacks". It had already surveilled potential targets and positioned explosives, according to the *New York Times*.

AFRICA

BENIN

May 1, 2019: *AP* reported on May 5 that observers feared that jihadis had kidnapped French tourists Laurent Lassimouillas and Patrick Picque after the duo failed to return from a game drive in the Pendjari National Park wildlife reserve near the border with Burkina Faso on May 1. They were last seen with their African male driver. Interior Minister Sacca Lafia said that on May 3, the body of the driver, who had been shot to death, was found in the park.

On the evening of May 9, two decorated French soldiers, petty officers Cédric de Pierrepont and Alain Bertoncello, died in a rescue operation in Burkina Faso that freed four people from the U.S., France, and South Korea who were kidnapped in Benin. Two hostages were the French citizens, another was an American woman. The French government did not identify the kidnappers. Four kidnappers died in the pre-dawn military operation. Officials said the hostages and their captors were crossing Burkina Faso en route to Mali.

On May 14, French President Emmanuel Macron hosted a national tribute for the Barkhane special forces soldiers at Les Invalides in Paris. Crowds lined the Alexander III Bridge in central Paris for the funeral cortege. 1905010.

BURKINA FASO

January 4, 2019: Government spokesman Remis Dandjinou said intercommunal clashes that began on December 31, 2018 had killed 46 people. On that date, the Yirgou village chief and seven other people were killed by suspected extremists in the north central region. Reprisals followed against local Fulani Muslims.

January 16, 2019: *BBC, Reuters,* and *AP* reported that jihadis were suspected of the nighttime kidnapping of Kirk Woodman, a Canadian whose body was found the next day. He was grabbed during a raid on a gold mining site in Tiabongou, about 12 miles from Mansila in Yagha Province in the north near the Niger border. His bullet-riddled body was found 62 miles from where he worked for Progress Mineral Mining Company. *Linked-In* indicated that Woodman was vice-president of exploration for Vancouver-based Progress Minerals. 19011601

January 27, 2019: Minister of Security Ousseni Compaore said a dozen gunmen attacked civilians at a Sunday market in Sikire in Soum Province in the Sahel region, killing ten people and injuring two.

January 28, 2019: The director of the local national television, Bouma Nebie, reported that in the morning, gunmen raided a base of anti-terrorist forces in Nassoumbou in Soum Province, burning tents and equipment and killing four people.

February 2019: Jihadis killed a Catholic priest in Bittou.

February 4, 2019: Gunmen attacked Kain village in Yatenga Province in the morning, killing 14 people. Army commander General Moise Minougou said the armed forces had responded and killed 146 jihadists in three counterterror operations in Bahn in the north region and Bomboro in the Boucle du Mouhoun region in the northwest near the border with Mali. There were light injuries and no deaths among security forces.

February 5, 2019: Army Commander General Moise Minoungou said that during the night, armed forces killed 21 jihadis who attacked a military base in Oursi.

February 6, 2019: Army General Moise Minoungou said jihadis killed five gendarmes and wounded three in retaliation for counterterror operations that killed 146 of their fighters.

February 19-20, 2019: Defense and security forces claimed to have killed 29 extremists in Kompienbiga, Kabonga and a touristic hunting area, seizing weapons, ammunition and other materials.

April 26, 2019: *AFP* and *AP* reported that jihadis shot to death five teachers and a municipal worker in Maitaougou in Koulpelogo Province.

April 28, 2019: *AP* and *AFP* reported that at 1 p.m., jihadis on motorbikes attacked a Protestant church after Sunday services in Silgadji, near the Mali border and Djibo, capital of Soum Province. They demanded that everyone convert to Islam. They shot to death five men wearing crosses and a pastor. Two other people were missing.

May 12, 2019: The *Washington Post, AP* and *BBC* reported that gunmen killed six people, including a priest and five worshippers, at a Catholic church in Dablo during morning Mass and then torched the church, nearby shops, a medical clinic, and all places serving alcohol. Jihadis were suspected.

May 13, 2019: *CNN* on May 15 reported that gunmen attacked a Catholic religious procession, killing four adults and burning a statue of the Virgin Mary in the remote village of Zimtenga, in the Kongoussi area of the country's northwest, according to Paul Ouédraogo, president of the Episcopal Conference of Burkina Faso and Niger.

August 2019: Jihadi gunmen attacked Catholic and Protestant churches in Tialboanga, killing three worshippers.

August 20, 2019: Jihadi gunmen killed 24 soldiers in an attack on the Koutougou barracks in Soum Province near the border with Mali. Several soldiers were wounded and five were missing.

October 11, 2019: Gunmen attacked the grand mosque in Salmossi, killing 16 people and wounding two others during evening prayers. No one claimed credit.

October 18, 2019: Four soldiers and a policeman were killed during two nighttime attacks in the north.

October 20-21, 2019: North Central Regional Councilor Adama Sawadogo said gunmen attacked Zoura in Bam Province in the night and into the next morning, killing nine civilians. A separate weekend attack on a funeral in Boulga in Sanmatenga Province killed four people. A third attack in Loroum Province killed six. Jihadis were suspected.

October 25-26, 2019: Suspected jihadis killed 19 people in attacks in northern Burkina Faso over the weekend. *Radio Omega* said that gunmen attacked Pobe Mengao in the Sahel region, killing 16 people, stealing motorcycles and other vehicles and burning shops. The *Burkina Faso News Agency* reported that three people, including a teacher, were killed in Rounga in Lorum Province on October 25 and 26.

November 6, 2019: *AP* and *AFP* reported that gunmen attacked a convoy near the Montreal-based Semafo Boungou mine in Tapoa Province, killing 37 people and wounding 60 others. The attack involved five buses of employees who were being accompanied by a military escort. *AFP* reported that a security source said "a military vehicle that was escorting the convoy hit an explosive device… Two buses carrying workers were then fired upon." Canadian foreign ministry spokeswoman Sylvain Leclerc said there were no reports of any Canadian citizens among the casualties. No one claimed credit; jihadis were suspected. Semafo operates two gold mines in the country. 19110602

November 15-16, 2019: The army announced that 32 jihadis and one soldier were killed over the weekend in the country's north and several women used as sex slaves were freed. When a military patrol in Yorsala was ambushed on November 15, two dozen terrorists died in hours of fighting. The next day, the army killed eight jihadis and confiscated weapons.

November 29, 2019: Soldiers killed extremist leader Abdoul Hadi, who helped Ansarul Islam establish a presence in the area, and five supporters in Nahouri Province. The army seized a large cache of weapons.

December 1, 2019: Gunmen attacked a Protestant church service in Hantoukoura, killing 14 people and wounding several others. The terrorists fled on motorcycles. No one claimed credit, but jihadis were suspected.

December 2-3, 2019: Soldiers killed 20 terrorists and wounded another 20 gunmen after jihadis conducted simultaneous overnight attacks on military positions. Troops seized dozens of motorcycles and other material following attacks on the military detachment in Toeni in Sourou Province and another in Bahn in Loroum Province. General Moise Minougou said three soldiers were killed and seven others were wounded.

December 24, 2019: President Roch Marc Christian Kabore said terrorists attacked Arbinda in Sahel region, killing 35 civilians, most of them women. A gun battle with security forces that lasted several hours killed 80 jihadis and seven members of the security forces. No one claimed credit.

CAMEROON

February 13, 2019: *AFP* reported that 187 Cameroonians who had joined Boko Haram had returned home and surrendered to authorities in the towns of Kolofata and Meme in Mayo-Sava district in Cameroon's Far North Province. Many of them walked home from Nigeria.

February 16, 2019: *NPR* reported that gunmen in the English-speaking region of the country kidnapped 170 schoolchildren and some of their teachers. The hostages were freed the next day.

June 28, 2019: In the afternoon, gunmen kidnapped John Fru Ndi, leader of Cameroon's main opposition Social Democratic Front party, from his residence in the Ntarikon neighborhood in the English-speaking town of Bamenda. Nkedze Emilia, a senator of the party, said "They were heavily armed with weapons. When they got to his house, his guards resisted and one of them was shot on the leg. But our leader was forced into a car and taken to an unknown destination." Fru Ndi "has not been in good health for quite some time now and we are afraid." Fru Ndi was kidnapped by members of Cameroon's separatist movement in April as he was leading a delegation to a legislator from his party, but was later released. He refused to pay a ransom.

August 20, 2019: A military tribunal sentenced to life in prison Julius Ayuk Tabe, the head of the Anglophone secessionist movement, and nine others, after finding them guilty of charges including secession, terrorism and hostility against the state. The tribunal ordered them to pay millions of dollars to the state and civil claimants. The defense counsel boycotted the trial, claiming bias. Defense lawyer Edwin Fongo vowed to appeal. The ten were arrested in Nigeria and extradited to Cameroon in January 2018 along with 46 others alleged to support the campaign for a separatist Ambazonia English-speaking state in Cameroon's North West and South West regions.

CENTRAL AFRICAN REPUBLIC

January 25, 2019: During the night, Union for Peace gunmen fired on a funeral ceremony in Ippy, killing 18 civilians and wounding 23.

April 4, 2019: On April 9, Doctors Without Borders said one of its health workers, assistant nurse Gaulbert Mokafe, had been killed by an armed group between Batangafo and Bouca while traveling by motorcycle to visit family.

May 22, 2019: French-Spanish nun Sister Ines Nieves Sancho, 77, was found decapitated in Nola near Berberati near the border with Cameroon. She taught poor schoolgirls. 19052201

May 23, 2019: The 3R militia attacked several villages in the area of Ouham Pende prefecture, killing more than 50 people near the border with Chad.

CONGO

February 24, 2019: During the night, gunmen attacked an Ebola treatment center run by Doctors Without Borders in Katwa, killing a caretaker and injuring another. The patients, four confirmed with Ebola and six suspected cases, were transferred to other centers for continued treatment. Medecins Sans Frontieres said the attackers threw stones at the facility and then burned down parts of the treatment center and destroyed wards and equipment. The caretaker brother of a patient died while reportedly trying to escape.

February 27, 2019: Butembo Mayor Sylvain Kanyamanda said raiders burned tents and other equipment at an Ebola treatment center run by Doctors Without Borders. Four Ebola patients were missing. The Health Ministry reported that 32 of the 38 people being treated for suspected cases of Ebola fled during the attack, while eight of the 12 patients with confirmed cases remained in bed.

March 9, 2019: In the early morning, gunmen attacked an Ebola treatment center in Butembo, killing a police officer. One attacker was wounded.

March 15, 2019: *NPR* reported that an attack on a transition center for Ebola patients killed one person and injured one.

April 18, 2019: The *Long War Journal* reported that the Islamic State Central African Province announced its establishment, saying IS fighters killed three Congolese soldiers and wounded five others in an attack in eastern Beni near Congo's border with Uganda. *Aamaq* reported that "[Members of] The Congolese Army were killed and wounded in an attack in the village of Kamango near the borders of the Congo and Uganda." The attack was blamed on the Allied

Democratic Forces (ADF). The Congo Research Group reported that the ADF rebranded itself as "Madinat al Tawhid wal Muwahedeen," or the City of Monotheism and Monotheists (MTM). 19041801

Earlier in the week, the U.S. Department of the Treasury designated an ally of ISIS financier Waleed Ahmaed Zein, an East African-based Islamic State financier, Halima Adnan Ali.

April 19, 2019: Gunmen broke into a conference room at an Ebola treatment center in the clinic of the Catholic University of Graben in Butembo, forced people to the floor, stole their belongings, accused them of perpetuating false rumors about Ebola, and shot in the abdomen a Cameroonian epidemiologist with the World Health Organization, killing him.

Reuters reported on August 8, 2019 that three Congolese doctors were arrested for planning the April 2019 attack on a hospital that killed senior WHO epidemiologist and Cameroonian doctor Richard Mouzoko. Senior military prosecutor Lieutenant Colonel Jean-Baptiste Kumbu said militiamen involved in attacking treatment centers had implicated four doctors in planning the raids, including against the Butembo hospital. Three were arrested; the fourth remained at large. Kumbu said 54 people were being held in connection with attacks on Ebola treatment centers. 19041902

April 20, 2019: Butembo deputy mayor Patrick Kambale Tsiko said that overnight, militia members armed with machetes tried to burn down an Ebola treatment center in Katwa district hours after another attack killed a Cameroonian epidemiologist. Military and police guarding the center killed one militia member and arrested five others. The attackers wrongly blamed foreigners for introducing Ebola into the region.

May 8, 2018: Mai-Mai gunmen attacked Butembo during the morning; seven terrorists and a police captain were killed, according to Butembo Mayor Sylvain Kanyamanda. He said, "Before this attack on Wednesday, leaflets of Mai-Mai militia were circulating to tell the teams of foreign doctors to leave the region as soon as possible before the worst happens." World Health

Organization emergencies chief Michael Ryan said that there had been 119 attacks recorded since January including 42 directed at health facilities.

May 12, 2019: Butembo Mayor Sylvain Kanyamanda said that during the night, gunmen attacked an Ebola treatment center in Katwa. The nursing staff fled. Two patients and a terrorist died.

June 3, 2019: Allied Democratic Forces rebels were blamed for an attack near Beni, wracked by the Ebola virus, that killed 13 civilians. Beni interim Mayor Modeste Bakwanamaha said two Congolese soldiers were killed. Spokesman Zachee Mathima said one attacker was killed and a teenage girl was kidnapped.

June 18, 2019: Jean Bamanisa, governor of Ituri Province, announced that two weeks of intercommunal violence between the Lendu and Hema communities killed 161 people in several villages. Authorities blamed militia fighters from the Lendu community linked to Mathieu Ngudjolo, who was acquitted of war crimes at the International Criminal Court in 2012.

July 8, 2019: Presiding Judge Robert Fremr announced that the International Criminal Court at The Hague convicted Congolese militia commander Bosco Ntaganda, alias The Terminator, of 18 counts of crimes against humanity and war crimes including murder, rape and sexual slavery for his role in atrocities in the ethnic conflict in a mineral-rich region of the Democratic Republic of the Congo in 2002-2003. He faced a life sentence. Ntanganda was the deputy chief of staff and commander of operations for the Patriotic Forces for the Liberation of Congo rebel group. The ICC in 2012 convicted the force's leader, Thomas Lubanga, of using child soldiers and sentenced him to 14 years. Some 102 witnesses testified at Ntaganda's trial, including a woman who survived having her throat slit by Ntaganda's forces. Judge Fremr said Ntaganda had shot to death an elderly Catholic priest.

July 22, 2019: The administrator for Beni territory, Kasereka Kibwana Donat, said that rebels killed 12 people in an area of eastern Congo where an Ebola virus outbreak had persisted for nearly a year. Nine people died in Oicha and three in Eringeti in overnight attacks.

July 29, 2019: Army spokesman for South Kivu Province Captain Dieudonne Kasereka said that during the previous week, gunmen kidnapped a South African, a Zimbabwean and two Congolese working for the Canadian gold mining company Banro in Maniema Province. Mai Mai rebels were suspected. Three people were arrested on suspicion of involvement. As of the first day of the incident, no ransom was demanded. 19072902

September 18, 2019: Army spokesman General Richard Kasonga said during the night, the army killed General Sylvestre Mudacumura, commander of the Rwandan Hutu militia group FDLR, in Rutshuru territory in North Kivu Province. An International Criminal Court arrest warrant was issued in 2012 on counts of war crimes in North Kivu and South Kivu Provinces. He had been under U.N. sanctions since 2005 for involvement in arms trafficking.

November 2, 2019: *ABC News* reported that terrorists killed Papy Mahamba Mumbere, who worked at a radio station in Ituri Province, and had been serving as a community health worker in Lwemba. His wife was critically injured. Authorities arrested two suspects. He had tried to spread awareness about Ebola.

November 7, 2019: The International Criminal Court passed its highest ever sentence, sentencing Congolese warlord Bosco Ntaganda, alias "The Terminator", to prison for 30 years for murder, rape and sexual slavery. He was found guilty in July 2019 of 18 counts of war crimes and crimes against humanity for his role as a military commander in atrocities during a bloody ethnic conflict in a mineral-rich region of Congo in 2002-2003. Presiding Judge Robert Fremr issued sentences ranging from eight years to 30 years for individual crimes and an overarching sentence of 30 years, the court's maximum sentence. Judges may impose a life sentence. Ntaganda was the deputy chief of staff and commander of operations for the Patriotic Forces for the Liberation of Congo. In 2012, the ICC convicted its leader, Thomas Lubanga, of using child soldiers. He is serving a 14-year prison sentence.

November 19-20, 2019: Army spokesman Mak Hazukay Mongba said Allied Democratic Forces rebels conducted an overnight attack in Beni, killing eight people and kidnapping a dozen others.

November 24-25, 2019: Civil society leader Kizito Bin Hangi said rebels attacked Beni, killing eight people and kidnapping nine overnight. Angry residents burned the town hall and protested the United Nations peacekeeping mission, accusing the Congolese army of responding too slowly. Some protesters vowed to continue their demonstrations until the U.N. mission leaves. By November 27, the WHO had evacuated 49 of its staffers there, leaving 71 in place.

November 26, 2019: Authorities killed a protester armed with a petrol bomb who was trying to enter a U.N. compound. 19112602

November 26-27, 2019: In an overnight attack, gunmen killed more than a dozen people in Oicha, 18 miles outside Beni. Beni territory administrator Donat Kibwana blamed the Uganda-based Allied Democratic Forces.

November 27-28, 2019: In a nighttime attack, Mai-Mai rebels attacked Biakato, killing four Ebola response workers, including a member of a vaccination team, two drivers and a police officer, and wounding five other workers, several with Congo's health ministry. Congolese forces killed one attacker and captured two others.

Beni territory administrator Donat Kasereka Kibwana said Allied Democratic Forces rebels attacked an Ebola response coordination office in Mangina.

December 13, 2019: Allied Democratic Forces rebels were blamed for an 8:30 p.m. attack in Beni that killed six people, including a pregnant woman.

ETHIOPIA

September 21, 2019: *Borkena.com* and Fana Broadcasting Corporate reported that the Ethiopian National Intelligence and Security Services (NISS) said that it foiled attacks on hotels, government institutions and popular religious gatherings being planned by ISIS and al-Shabaab, arresting ten people in the Somali region, Oromo region and Addis Ababa. The terrorists planned to set off bombs near large public gatherings and then engage in shootings.

NISS said that al-Shabaab's team, led by Mohammed Abdulahi, alias Yahya Ali Hassan, entered Ethiopia via Djibouti. He picked targets for the attack, but was arrested in Bole area of Addis Ababa. Abdek Mohammed Hussien and Redwan Mohammed, based in Djibouti, along with Sumter Mohammed Iman Yousouf, were captured in a coordinated raid with a Djibouti intelligence unit.

Another group entered Hargessa, Somaliland, from Southern Somalia. They took suicide bomb training, but were captured in coordination with a Somaliland intelligence body. They included Isaq Ali Saden who obtained ID with the alias Ibrahim Ali Aden from Ethiopia Somali region. He opened two accounts with Commercial Bank of Ethiopia from which 2.5 million Ethiopian birr was seized.

NISS added that two other suspects were arrested in the Chercher zone of Ethio-Somali region and Moyale town in the Oromo region. ISIS members entered from the Bosaso area of Somaliland and headed to Addis Ababa. NISS arrested them near the Bole area of Addis Ababa. Another ISIS member was detained in the Awash area of Ethiopia NISS seized communication devices. NISS thanked the assistance of federal and regional security authorities, and intelligence services from Djibouti, Somaliland, Puntland, United States, Italian, France and Spain. NISS said that it shared information with 16 countries from the Middle East, Europe, Africa and Asia regarding persons with links to arrested terrorists in Ethiopia.

November 21, 2019: A man locked himself in a restroom of Ethiopian Airlines flight ET817 from Addis Ababa to Burundi and claimed to have a bomb. Police broke down the door and arrested the man, calling him a "suspected terrorist". The plane was evacuated. No bomb was found. 19112101

GHANA

June 6, 2019: Gunmen kidnapped two Canadians who were attending Kumasi Technical University on an exchange program run by Global Affairs Canada. The Information Ministry announced on June 12 that the duo were rescued that morning in the Ashanti region. 19060601

KENYA

January 15, 2019: At 3:30 p.m., five al-Shabaab gunmen wearing green and firing AK47s attacked the upscale DusitD2 Hotel and office park on Riverside Drive in Nairobi's Westlands neighborhood, taking hostages. The hotel is part of a Thai-owned chain. One bomb targeted three vehicles outside a bank. A suicide bomber in the hotel foyer severely wounded several guests. Gunmen shot at people sitting at the Secret Garden café. The complex's five buildings include the hotel, bars, banks, restaurants, shops, and offices of many multinational companies, including Visa and Shell. Witnesses heard explosions and gunfire and saw corpses, body parts and burning cars. Police and ambulances surrounded the area. Police detonated a car bomb. Witnesses spotted an unexploded grenade in a hallway at the complex. Ministry of Interior and Coordination of National Cabinet Secretary Fred Matiang'i said police evacuated scores of people from Kenya and other countries. Ultimately, 700 civilians were evacuated. A police officer said there was "no time to count the dead". Initial reports said 21 people, including 16 Kenyans, a Briton, an American, and three Africans of indeterminate nationality, and all five terrorists died in the 19-hour siege. One police officer and 20 civilians were killed. Four of the 100 hotel employees on duty were killed; another three were injured. *Citizen TV* aired surveillance footage showing four gunmen.

The dead included:

- American Jason Spindler, 40, one of three brothers from Houston. He had served in a remote area of Peru with the Peace Corps. He graduated from the University of Texas-Austin in 2000 and worked as an investment banker on Wall Street. He pulled people out of the rubble during 9/11, according to his roommate, Kevin Yu. He earned his law degree at NYU and moved abroad to work on social entrepreneurship. He was CEO of a consulting firm headquartered in the complex. He was co-founder and managing director of the San Francisco-based I-DEV International. Nine others in its Nairobi office were safely evacuated.

- Abdalla Dahir, variant Abdalla Sheikh Mohamed Dahir, and Feisal Ahmed, variant Feysal Rashid Haji, two Kenyans of Somali descent, close friends and colleagues at Adam Smith International, an economic-advising company, according to Kenyan lawmaker Fatuma Gedi. They died on the terrace of a restaurant in the complex where the company's Kenya office is located. They worked on the Somalia Stability Fund, which dealt with more than 100 local community initiatives. The firm had lost James Thomas in the 2013 terrorist attack on the Westgate mall in Nairobi. Some 50 Adam Smith staffers and consultants were safely evacuated.

- British citizen Luke Potter, Africa programs director for British charity Gatsby Africa.

- James Oduor, variant James Radido, nicknamed "Odu Cobra", who tweeted during the attack that he was among those "trapped in our buildings". "Gunshots and non-stop explosions." Three minutes later, he wrote "Waaaah. What's happening at 14 Riverside fam? Any news from out there?" Kenyan radio station *Capital FM* said that his account then fell silent. He worked for the East African operation of LG Electronics.

- Revenue manager Bernadette Konjalo, one of four DusitD2 employees who were killed.

- Two officers with Senaca International Security, Ltd.

- Six employees of digital payments company Cellulant, part of a group of 17 Cellulant staff members who tried to flee their offices during the attack but a "barrage of gunfire"

forced some of them to retreat. A January 22 memorial program described the employees as "The Brave Six".

Some 28 people were injured. A RECCE Squad member of the Kenyan special forces was hospitalized. Two commandos suffered leg injuries from grenades thrown by the attackers.

Police identified a Kenyan Defense Forces sergeant as the father of Ali Salim Gichunge, a suspected attacker. Gichunge's mother was arrested and taken to Nairobi for questioning. Violet Kemunto Omwoyo was also named as an attacker in court documents.

On January 16, Kenyan police detained a man and two women following a raid on a house where one of the Nairobi attackers was said to live. Police conducted the raid after neighbors identified a vehicle that had been parked outside the hotel complex. Police announced the arrests of nine more people on January 17. The next day, a Canadian national and five other suspects, identified as Osman Ibrahim, Guleid Abdihakim (the Canadian), Gladys Kaari Justus, Oliver Kanyango Muthee and Joel Nganga Wainaina appeared at a hearing at Milimani law courts in Nairobi. Hussein Mohammed, who was arrested in Mandera County along the border with Somalia, was brought to court separately. Prosecutors suspected the alleged accomplices, including two taxi drivers and an agent for a mobile phone-based money service, of "aiding and abetting" the attackers. The court agreed that five suspects should be held for 30 days while the police conducted their investigation.

Suicide bomber Mahir Khalid Riziki, 25, was born in Mombasa.

Al-Shabaab said on its *Radio Andalus* that it was responding to President Trump's recognition of Jerusalem as Israel's capital, and that the U.S. and Israeli economies would suffer as long as they continued to challenge the rights of Palestinians. Al-Shabaab was following the "guidelines" of al-Qaeda leader Ayman al-Zawahiri.

On January 21, a judge ordered three suspects to be held for 30 days during the investigation; a fourth was to be held for ten days. 19011501

January 20, 2019: Gunmen fired on Chinese construction facilities at Shimbirey near Garissa.

National police chief Joseph Boinnet announced that security forces fought off the attackers. No casualties were reported. 19012001

January 26, 2019: A bomb exploded outside a movie theater in Nairobi, injuring a handcart pusher who received a small piece of luggage from an individual who fled and a newspaper vendor.

January 31, 2019: Interior Minister Fred Matiangi said authorities arrested ten people in a crackdown on extremists at the Dadaab refugee camp, which hosts 200,000 Somali refugees. Among the detainees was a man with two New Zealand passports. On February 8, a court in Garissa freed New Zealander Sulub Warfaa, 36, who told journalists, "Just because I was born in Mogadishu does not mean that I am a terrorist… I did not get tortured. The officers they were just doing their jobs, you know, that's what they were doing… I'm really happy that I am free, you know, and actually finally justice has been served."

April 12, 2019: David Ohito, communications director of the Mandera County government, said suspected jihadis kidnapped two Cuban doctors—Dr. Assel Herera Correa, a general physician, and Dr. Landy Rodriguez, a surgeon—after killing their bodyguard as they headed to work near the Somali border. Governor Ali Roba said the gunmen's vehicle blocked the doctors' vehicle "and opened fire at their bodyguards, killing one instantly". More than 100 Cuban doctors were brought to Kenya in an exchange program that saw around 50 travel to Cuba for specialized training in 2018. The kidnappers may have taken the doctors into Somalia. Al-Shabaab was suspected. Police detained the doctors' driver to help with investigations.

AP reported on October 7, 2020 that during the October 3-4, 2020 weekend, al-Shabaab released the two Cuban doctors it had kidnapped in Kenya and held in Somalia. Cuban foreign ministry official Juan Antonio Fernández Palacios denied the reported release. *AP* reported that Cuba had requested Somali intelligence to negotiate for the doctors' release after obtaining a video a few months ago showing the hostages. 19041201

May 9, 2019: Mombasa court chief magistrate Evans Makori sentenced British suspect Jermaine Grant to four years in prison for possession of bomb making material. Grant had been in prison since his arrest in 2011. He was believed to be part of an al-Shabaab-linked cell that planned multiple attacks over Christmas in 2011. The prosecution had wanted a seven-year sentence. Grant was serving a nine-year sentence for forging immigration documents; the four years will be added to his sentence. Authorities said the cell included Samantha Lewthwaite, widow of Jermaine Lindsay, one of the bombers who killed 52 people on London's transport system on July 7, 2005.

June 15, 2019: Ten police officers died when their vehicle struck a bomb in Wajir County near the Somali border. Thirteen officers were chasing suspected al-Shabaab terrorists who had kidnapped three police reservists in Konton center in Wajir East the previous day. 19061501

October 1, 2019: A police counterterrorism task force foiled an attack, killing three suspects and recovering bomb-making material such as ammonium nitrate, weapons and ammunition including more than 1,600 bullets and military and police uniforms at a house in Likoni on the coast. An internal police circular dated September 23 warned officers to "treat with suspicion" government and United Nations-branded vehicles as intelligence indicated that al-Shabaab was planning attacks on key installations and social places using stolen police vehicles from the north.

October 30, 2019: Police suspected al-Shabaab of raiding the Dadajabula police post in Wajir County near the border with Somalia in an attempt to free two suspects who died in the attack. Two policemen were wounded. North Eastern regional police chief Paul Soi said there had been plans to transfer the suspects. Officers fled heavy gunfire by men speaking Somali.

December 6, 2019: Al-Shabaab claimed credit for stopping a bus in the north near Somalia and killing eight non-Muslim non-local passengers. Most of those killed were police officers returning to their stations in Elwak and Mandera. 19120602

MALI

January 1, 2019: Gunmen dressed as Dozo hunters attacked Kouloghon village in the morning, killing 37 civilians. Fulani Association head Tabital Pulaaku said the victims were from the Fulani ethnic group and included the village chief.

January 10, 2019: On January 19, 2019, *AP* reported that on January 10, French airstrikes in central Mali killed 15 members of an unnamed extremist group that had been preparing an attack on a "symbolic institution" in the Dialoube region.

January 15, 2019: Mohamed Ag Albachar, spokesman for the Azawad Tuareg self-defense group, said that armed men attacked two villages about 25 miles from Menaka near the border with Niger, killing 20 civilians, including elderly people and some security personnel. Jihadis were suspected.

January 20, 2019: In the morning, al-Qaeda-linked jihadis in cars and on motorcycles attacked a United Nations peacekeeping base in Aguelhoc in Kidal region, killing ten peacekeepers from Chad and injuring 25 others. Several of the terrorists were killed. Jama'at Nusrat al-Islam Muslimeen said the attack was in response to Chad renewing diplomatic ties with Israel and that this was the first of many "responses" to Chad's relations with Israel. 19012001

January 25, 2019: Myriam Dessables, spokeswoman for the United Nations mission in Mali, said two Sri Lankan peacekeepers were killed after their convoy struck an explosive device in the morning in the Douentza area of the Mopti region. Several other people were wounded, one critically. 19012501

February 26, 2019: A booby-trapped corpse exploded in Gondogourou in the Mopti region, killing ten men from the Dogon community who were conducting a burial. No one claimed credit. Malian armed forces buried the victims and the body's remains.

March 1, 2019: Nine soldiers serving with the regional G5 Sahel force were killed when they drove over a roadside bomb in Boulkessy in the Mopti region. The G5 Sahel Joint Force is made up of military from Burkina Faso, Chad, Mali, Mauritania and Niger. 19030102

March 12, 2019: Seven Malian U.N. peacekeeping soldiers were killed when their vehicle hit a mine in Mopti region near Dialoube.

March 17, 2019: Gunmen attacked a camp in Dioura in central Mali, killing 23 soldiers. The army blamed Ba Ag Moussa, a former Malian army colonel who deserted in 2012 to join the Tuareg rebellion before joining al-Qaeda.

March 23, 2019: At 5 a.m., a Dogon militia attacked Ogossagou, a village of ethnic Peulhs, killing 115 people, according to Abdoul Aziz Diallo, president of Tabital Pulaaku, who said the victims included the elderly, pregnant women and small children. Another 55 were wounded. A Peulh militia leader said the village chief of Ogossagou and some of his grandchildren were also killed. Dogons claim Peulhs support jihadis linked to terrorist groups in the country's north and beyond. Peulhs accuse Dogons of supporting the Malian army in its effort to stamp out extremism. By March 24, the death toll was 134. Youssouf Toloba, head of the Dogon militia Dan Na Ambassagou, denied involvement. The *New York Times* reported that the victims were Fulani herders and that the village of Welingara was also attacked. An Ogossagou resident said the attack could have been in retaliation for an al-Qaeda affiliate's raid the previous week that killed 23 soldiers.

April 20, 2019: In a morning attack on a U.N. convoy, gunmen killed an Egyptian peacekeeper and wounded four other peacekeepers between Douentza and Boni in the Mopti region. One attacker was killed and eight were detained. 19042001

April 21, 2019: In the morning, motorcycle-rider gunmen attacked a Malian army camp, killing a dozen people in Guire near the border with Mauritania. Al-Qaeda-linked groups were suspected. No one claimed credit.

May 2019: Jihadi gunmen set afire a church in a northern village, killing a priest and five parishioners. The next day they attacked a procession, killing four. Two weeks later, they attacked a Sunday Mass in the same area, killing four people.

May 19, 2019: Interior Security Ministry spokesman Amadou Sangho announced that gunmen on motorcycles killed four civilians, two gendarmes and a customs official in a nighttime attack in Koury, near the border with Burkina Faso. A similar attack in Boura, 34 miles away, led to no deaths. Jihadis were suspected.

June 2019: Jihadi gunman attacked Beni village, shooting to death four men wearing crucifixes.

June 10, 2019: At 3 a.m., gunmen killed 95 people in Sobane, variant Sobame Da, an ethnic Dogon village. Nineteen people were missing. Homes were burned and animals slaughtered. There was no immediate claim of responsibility. Peuhl leaders had threatened to retaliate for an attack by Dogon militia that killed 157 people in March. *AP* reported that the Peuhl were accused of working alongside jihadists from the Islamic State of Greater Sahara. On June 12, the Mopti governor's office lowered the death toll to 35.

June 15, 2019: The *Long War Journal* reported on June 17 that the IS West Africa Province released a short video on June 15 of fighters from Mali and Burkina Faso, featuring Abu Salmah al-Mangawi, renewing their pledge of fealty to the Caliph of the Muslims, mujahid Sheikh Abu-Bakr al-Husseini al-Qurashi al-Baghdadi. They said they would continue to battle the forces of unbelief, which claim to have "eradicated the caliphate".

June 17, 2019: *AFP* reported on June 18 that during the evening, gunmen attacked the Dogon villages of Gangafani and Yoro, near the Burkina Faso border, killing 38 and wounding many. Fulani and Peuhl jihadi militia were suspected. A local official said, "They are terrorists because they killed and then disemboweled some bodies and burned crops."

July 11, 2019: A U.N. Mission in Mali vehicle hit a mine outside Kidal, injuring 10 U.N. peacekeepers, four seriously. 19071101

September 3, 2019: *Reuters* reported that a roadside bomb exploded under a bus carrying 60 passengers traveling in the Mopti region, killing 14 people and wounding 24, seven critically. A person at the scene said his sister and nephew were killed.

September 26, 2019: A military convoy escorting two vehicles full of fertilizer between the communities of Douentza and Sevare hit a land mine. The survivors were ambushed. Seven soldiers were killed. No group claimed responsibility; al-Qaeda-linked groups were suspected.

September 30, 2019: International Criminal Court judges ordered alleged Malian Ansar Dine jihadi leader al-Hassan Ag Abdoul Aziz Ag Mohamed Ag Mahmoud to stand trial on charges of war crimes and crimes against humanity including torture, rape, sexual slavery and deliberately attacking religious buildings and historic monuments in Timbuktu during the group's occupation from April 2012 until January 2013. Defense attorney Melinda Taylor claimed her client was tortured into confessing. Prosecutor Fatou Bensouda argued that al-Hassan was the de facto chief of the Islamic police during Ansar Dine's occupation, noting that he "played an essential and undeniable role in the system of persecution established by the armed groups throughout the period of occupation of Timbuktu".

In 2016, Ansar Dine member Ahmad al-Faqi al-Mahdi was convicted and sentenced to nine years in prison for intentionally directing attacks against nine mausoleums and a mosque door in Timbuktu in 2012.

September 30, 2019: Gunmen from al-Qaeda-linked groups attacked an army base in central Mali, killing 25 people. Another 60 were missing. Terrorists drove into Boulikessi overnight on September 30 to attack a Malian battalion of the regional G5 Sahel Force, according to force commander Niger General Oumarou Namatou Gazama, who blamed "the terrorist group" Ansarul Islam. Mali claimed soldiers killed 15 extremists and destroyed five of their vehicles. A joint Mali-Burkina Faso military force pursued the attackers, who caused "heavy equipment losses and major damage", according to Malian government spokesman Yaya Sangaré. 19093001

October 1, 2019: Gunmen attacked an army camp in Mondoro, killing four people, including two civilians.

AP reported on October 3 that Defense Ministry spokesman General Dahirou Dembele said that the death toll from two attacks in Boulikessi and Mondoro against Malian members of the G5 Sahel regional counterterror force was now 38, with 33 soldiers missing.

October 6, 2019: A UN peacekeeping convoy hit a roadside bomb in Aguelhok, killing a Chadian peacekeeper and seriously wounding three colleagues. 19100601

Gunmen attacked a temporary U.N. operating base in Bandiagara in central Mali, wounding a peacekeeper from Togo. 19100602

November 1, 2019: Jihadis were suspected in an attack in the Menaka area that killed 15 soldiers.

November 2, 2019: At lunchtime, jihadists attacked the Malian military in Indelimane in the Menaka region near the border with Niger, killing 53 soldiers and one civilian, wounding three, and leaving 20 survivors. The Islamic State said, "Soldiers of the caliphate attacked a military base where elements of the apostate Malian army were stationed in the village of Indelimane." The Army tweeted that it was a "terrorist attack".

ISIS claimed credit when an armored vehicle hit a roadside bomb near Menaka, killing French corporal Ronan Pointeau, 24. The French military was escorting a convoy between Gao and Menaka. 19110201

November 7, 2019: *Reuters* reported that the U.S. Treasury Department announced economic sanctions against Amadou Koufa, a Salafist preacher and a leader of Jama'at Nusrat al-Islam wal-Muslimin (JNIM), an al-Qaeda affiliate in the Sahel region. In 2018, French officials had said the militant leader had died in a raid in Mali, but he appeared in a propaganda video in February 2019. The sanctions froze any assets Koufa may have under U.S. control and barred any

persons or entities in the United States from any dealings or transactions with him.

November 11, 2019: The army killed several extremists in a large-scale offensive in parts of the central Mopti region. Soldiers found identity cards of several nationalities.

November 18, 2019: In an overnight attack, jihadis killed 24 soldiers and wounded 29 at Tabankort in Gao region. Seventeen terrorists were killed. Soldiers from Mali and Niger were carrying out a joint operation along their border to track extremists. Nigerien troops detained nearly 100 suspects. On November 21, the Islamic State's West African affiliate said it had killed 30 soldiers and wounded another 30 while acknowledging no deaths among its members. On November 22, Tabankort villagers said the bodies of six more soldiers were found, increasing the total to 30 dead soldiers. Residents in neighboring Infokaritene found seven other bodies and buried them.

November 22, 2019: Malian Intelligence services spokesman Col. Modibo Traore announced the arrests in Bamako of two men, Ousmane Hama Diallo and Harouna Diallo, accused of providing logistical support to the Islamic extremist group Ansarul Islam in Burkina Faso. He said they arrived in Bamako on November 19 from Boulekessi to purchase high-definition cameras, laptops, GPS, radios and binoculars for Ansarul Islam.

December 21, 2019: French President Emmanuel Macron said that French forces killed 33 Islamic extremists in central Mali. Macron added that the Operation Berkhane forces took one prisoner and freed two Malian gendarmes who had been held hostage. The French Defense Ministry announced two days later that on December 21 it had launched its first Reaper drone strike in Mali, killing seven jihadis in the Ouagadou forest, where the Macina Liberation Front is active.

MOZAMBIQUE

May 28, 2019: *AFP* reported that jihadis were suspected of an attack on a Mitsubishi truck carrying passengers and goods on a dirt road in the Macomia coastal district, killing 16 people, including three soldiers guarding the truck, and injuring ten. At least seven attackers threw explosives into the truck and then opened fire.

August 1, 2019: Mozambique's President Filipe Nyusi and Ossufo Momade, leader of RENAMO rebels, signed a peace agreement at Gorongosa National Park, ending decades of hostilities that included a 15-year civil war that killed one million people. RENAMO (the Portuguese acronym for National Resistance of Mozambique) kept an armed base in the area for more than 40 years. Although the group signed a peace accord in 1992 and became an opposition party, it had never disarmed. Under the new agreement, 5,200 fighters were to disarm. Longtime RENAMO leader Afonso Dhlakama died in Gorongosa in 2018. Momade succeeded him. Nyusi declared Gorogosa a peace park of 1,570 square miles.

NIGER

January 3, 2019: The Defense Ministry said land and air raids that began on December 28, 2018 killed more than 280 Boko Haram terrorists near the border with Nigeria.

May 14, 2019: Jihadis armed with explosives ambushed soldiers near Mangaize near Tongo Tongo near the border with Mali, killing 17 soldiers. Another 11 were reported missing. *AP* reported on May 16 that the Islamic State West Africa Province claimed credit for killing the 28 soldiers. IS-WAP also claimed credit for an attack earlier in the week on a prison.

June 8, 2019: During the night, an American military vehicle struck a roadside bomb near a Nigerien military base in Ouallam, causing damage but no injuries. 19060801

October 29-30, 2019: The Defense Ministry announced that Boko Haram was suspected of attacking Bilabrine in the Diffa region near the border with Chad overnight, killing 12 soldiers and injuring eight others. Several Boko Haram terrorists were killed. 19102901

December 9, 2019: In the morning, heavily armed jihadi "terrorists" in a dozen 4x4 vehicles attacked an army post in Agando in western Tahoua region, killing three Nigerien soldiers. Fourteen terrorists died in the gun battle.

December 11, 2019: *AFP* reported that hundreds of jihadis firing shells and mortars ambushed an army camp during the night in Inates in western Tillaberi region, 30 miles from Ouallam, killing 71 soldiers and wounding 122. Others were missing. The Islamic State's West Africa Province claimed credit, observing, "The mujahideen took control over it for a few hours, and captured weapons and ammunition, 16 vehicles, and multiple tanks as spoils." The Defence Ministry said that "a substantial number of terrorists were neutralized" in the three-hour gun battle.

NIGERIA

January 2, 2019: Air Commodore Ibikunle Daramola tweeted that air force helicopter crashed in fighting against Boko Haram at Damasak in northern Borno State. News media added that 53 police were missing after a Boko Haram raid the previous week.

January 28, 2019: Boko Haram gunmen on motorcycles killed 60 people in Rann, near the Cameroon border, during the morning, setting hundreds of houses on fire.

February 15, 2019: The Armed Conflict Location and Event Data Project claimed that more civilians were killed in targeted attacks in Nigeria in 2018 than in either Yemen or Afghanistan. The attacks included those by Boko Haram, the Islamic State's West Africa affiliate, and ethnic militias of herding and farming communities.

February 20, 2019: Herdsmen were suspected in an attack on the Ebete community of Agatu in Benue State that killed 16 people.

February 23, 2019: Terrorists conducted attacks during national voting.

Several explosions were heard in Maiduguri. Authorities initially claimed that it was a show of force to warn off terrorists but later said Boko Haram had "attempted to infiltrate" the Borno State capital by launching artillery fire. State police said "some missiles strayed into vulnerable locations" but there were no casualties and the terrorists retreated. Later, security sources claimed that one soldier was killed and 20 wounded.

At 6:30 a.m., before polls opened, gunmen attacked a military outpost on Geidam, hometown of Yobe State's governor, but were turned back. No casualties were reported.

Witnesses heard gunfire in parts of Port Harcourt.

Days before the originally scheduled voting date, Boko Haram attacked a large convoy carrying Borno's governor. The government said only three people were killed, but witnesses told *Reuters* that 100 may have died and between 100 and 200 were taken captive.

February 24, 2019: The air force claimed it "neutralized" dozens of fighters with the Islamic State West Africa Province in the northeast near Lake Chad as fighters met in Kolloram in Borno State.

March 6, 2019: A vehicle hit a land mine hidden by Boko Haram in Khaddamari outside Maiduguri in Borno State, killing five farmers and wounding dozens. BH had tried to attack the town. The government said the farmers ignored soldiers' warnings not to use the road because they wanted to reach their cucumber farms.

April 19, 2019: Gunmen attacked the Kajuru Castle holiday resort in Kaduna State and shot to death a Nigerian citizen and a British woman, Faye Mooney, who had worked for the aid group Mercy Corps for two years as a communications specialist. Kaduna State police said that the gunmen kidnapped three other people of indeterminate nationalities. Mooney was in a group of 12 tourists who traveled from Lagos. 19041901

April 29, 2019: Boko Haram was suspected of attacking the Kuda-Kaya village in Adamawa State during the night, killing 25 people returning home from a wedding. Rebecca Malgwi lost two brothers-in-law. She said the terrorists moved from house to house.

May 13, 2019: Military spokesman Sagir Musa announced that during the weekend, the army rescued 29 women and 25 children held captive by Boko Haram.

May 25, 2019: Boko Haram was suspected of a morning ambush of a military and civilian convoy that was relocating civilians to a displacement camp in Damboa. Twenty people were killed and others were missing.

June 16, 2019: Usman Kachalla, head of operations at the State Emergency Management Agency (SEMA), said a suicide bomber killed 30 people and hospitalized 40 who were watching a televised nighttime soccer match in Konduga in Borno State. Boko Haram was suspected.

July 18, 2019: Gunmen attacked a convoy of the Action Against Hunger international aid group, killing a driver. A staffer, two drivers and three health workers were missing. The group was heading to the border community of Damasak. Boko Haram was suspected. On July 25, the *Washington Post* reported that on the previous day, kidnappers calling themselves Calipha released a video showing a woman wearing a blue hijab and calling herself Grace saying that she was a Christian and worked for an international aid group. Five Nigerian men sat next to her. She asked Action Against Hunger and the Christian Association of Nigeria for help. 17071801

July 20, 2019: Okasanmi Ajayi, police spokesman in Kwara State, said that four Turkish construction workers were kidnapped during the night by six gunmen who walked in to their drinking spot in Gbale village in the Edu area of Kwara State. 19072001

July 27, 2019: Boko Haram was suspected when gunmen on motorbikes killed 65 and wounded 11 in an attack on villagers leaving a midday funeral in Nganzai in the northeast. Villagers and civilian self-defense forces had fought off Boko Haram a fortnight earlier, killing 11 terrorists. Among the injured as Hassan Ahmadu, 38, hit in the right thigh and shoulders, who lost five family members, including his grandfather, uncle, half-brother and two cousins.

September 25, 2019: *Reuters* reported that ISIS said via *Aamaq* that it ambushed and killed 14 Nigerian soldiers in Borno State.

October 11, 2019: The newly-elected Governor of Borno State, Babagana Zulum, announced support for 10,000 hunters, armed with charmed amulets, who planned an offensive against Boko Haram. The government had discouraged a similar proposal five years earlier. One leader of the hunters, Baba Maigiwa, said more than 5,000 hunters were mobilizing from Nigeria, Burkina Faso, Niger and Chad.

November 27, 2019: The military announced it had freed 983 people, including five women, detained for suspected links to Boko Haram.

December 25, 2019: *AP* and *Reuters* reported that the Islamic State West Africa Province released a video on *Telegram* showing 11 hostages, most of them Christian men, being executed, probably on Christmas Day, as revenge for the killing of ISIS leader Abu Bakr al-Baghdadi and his spokesman Muhajir in Iraq and Syria in October. The video was circulated on December 26. The hostages were believed to have been kidnapped in November. The killers wore beige uniforms and black masks. They shot one and beheaded the rest of the hostages, all of whom were blindfolded. *Reuters* reported that an earlier video claimed that the captives had been taken from Maiduguri and Damaturu.

RWANDA

October 4, 2019: National police spokesman John Bosco Kabera said gunmen attacked a popular tourist area near Volcanoes National Park in Musanze district near the Congo border, killing 14 people and wounding 18 other Rwandans. Police killed 19 terrorists and arrested five.

SOMALIA

January 1, 2019: The government ordered UN envoy Nicholas Haysom to leave the country amid questions over the arrest of former al-Shabaab deputy leader Mukhtar Robow, who had run for a regional presidency. The Foreign Ministry accused Haysom of diplomatic over-reach that violated Somali sovereignty, declaring him "persona non grata". He arrived a few months earlier. Haysom had questioned the legal basis used in the December 2018 arrest by Ethiopian troops and Somali police and whether U.N.-funded regional police in the Southwest were involved.

Al-Shabaab claimed credit for firing seven mortars that landed inside the U.N. compound in Mogadishu, injuring two UN staffers and a contractor. 19010101

January 3, 2019: U.S. Africa Command said an airstrike near Dheerow Sanle in southwestern Somalia killed ten al-Shabaab terrorists.

January 6, 2019: A U.S. airstrike killed six al-Shabaab members near Dheerow Sanle in Lower Shabelle region.

January 7, 2019: U.S. Africa Command announced that two airstrikes killed four al-Shabaab terrorists in the vicinity of Baqdaad after the military's Somali partners "were engaged by al-Shabab militants".

January 14, 2019: The *Long War Journal* and Somali website *Garowe Online* reported that al-Shabaab gunmen recently killed Yahya Haji Fiile, alias Abu Zakariye, a pro-ISIS commander in Bu'ale. The website noted that he split with AS in 2016 after al-Shabaab's Amniyat internal security force in 2015 killed Bashir Abu Numan, one of the first AS commanders to defect to IS.

January 19, 2019: U.S. Africa Command said an airstrike near Jilib in Middle Juba region killed 52 al-Shabaab terrorists after a "large group" mounted an attack on Somali forces. No U.S. casualties were reported. Al-Shabaab said on its *Shahada* news agency that its attack on two Somali army bases killed 41 soldiers at the Bar Sanjuni area near Kismayo. The Ethiopian Defense Ministry said on state television that more than 60 al-Shabaab terrorists were killed and four vehicles carrying explosives were destroyed.

January 23, 2019: U.S. Africa Command announced that two airstrikes against al-Shabaab killed one terrorist. It announced that it would no longer give details on casualties or damage, leaving that up to Somali authorities. The strikes occurred near Jilib in Middle Juba region.

January 29, 2019: Mogadishu Deputy Mayor Mohamed Tulah announced that an explosion at a gas station near the Ministry of Petroleum killed two people and wounded five. Tulah said the car carried explosives that were meant to be set off elsewhere but exploded prematurely.

January 30, 2019: U.S. Africa Command said an airstrike killed 24 al-Shabaab terrorists near an extremist camp near Shebeeley in the central Hiran region.

February 1, 2019: U.S. Africa Command announced an airstrike had killed 13 al-Shabaab members near Gandarshe in Lower Shabelle region.

February 4, 2019: Authorities said al-Shabaab gunmen killed a Maltese man who was working as a construction project manager for the Dubai government-owned P&O Ports port operator in the Puntland region. Three other P&O employees were injured in Bosaso. Al-Shabaab said he worked for a company that "occupies" Somalia's Bosaso Port. 19020401

A car bomb went off near a mall close to local government offices in Mogadishu's Hamarweyne district, killing seven and injuring nine. No one claimed credit. Al-Shabaab was suspected.

February 6, 2019: The *Long War Journal* reported that al-Shabaab's *Shahada News Telegram* channel claimed, "Colonel Abdisalan Sheikh Aden Kurjow, an operations commander of the 12 April Brigade from the government's militias, and Colonel 'Adu and several of their guards were killed and their vehicle was destroyed by an IED planted by Shabaab". Somali media indicated that Kurjow and Abdirahman Jim'ale Muse (referred to as Colonel 'Adu by Shabaab) were killed by an IED near Dhanaane in the Lower Shabelle region south of Mogadishu.

February 6-7, 2019: U.S. Africa Command said targeted airstrikes against suspected extremists killed 15 fighters. The airstrikes occurred near Gandarshe, Lower Shabelle region, on February 6, killing 11, and near Bariire on February 7, killing four.

February 8, 2019: U.S. Africa Command said an air strike killed eight el-Shabaab terrorists near Kobon, near Kismayo.

February 11, 2019: U.S. Africa Command reported that two air strikes against al-Shabaab killed 12 terrorists in Janaale, 40 miles southwest of Mogadishu.

February 23, 2019: Police Captain Mohamed Hussein said al-Shabaab gunmen killed Osman Elmi Boqore, Somalia's oldest legislator estimated to be over 80, in the north of Mogadishu during the night. The terrorists pulled up near his car as he was being driven through Karan district.

February 24, 2019: USAFRICOM said its airstrike killed 35 al-Shabaab terrorists traveling in a rural area about 23 miles (37 kilometers) east of Beledweyne in central Hiran region near the Ethiopian border.

February 25, 2019: The United States military said its airstrike near Shebeeley in the Hiran region against a training camp used as a staging area for attacks killed 20 al-Shabaab terrorists.

February 28, 2019: Al-Shabaab conducted a 24-hour takeover of a hotel in Mogadishu, with 29 people, including two soldiers and all of the attackers, reported killed and 80 wounded. Two car bombs exploded during the night, one near the home of appeals court chief Judge Abshir Omar; security forces fought off gunmen who tried to force their way inside. Eight people were injured in that attack, which tore off part of the roof of Omar's home. Al-Shabaab said the target was the neighboring Maka Almukarramah hotel, which is patronized by government officials.

Four gunmen fired at nearby buildings and businesses along Maka Almukarramah Road, sparking clashes with hotel guards. Dozens of cars caught fire. Authorities freed more than ten people stuck in the hotel. Nurse Sadiya Yusuf at Daru Shifa Hospital said some victims had lost limbs. Doctors at Erdogan Hospital received 55 wounded people, with three dying. Hospital manager Dr. Ismail Yamas said many were in critical condition and 15 had undergone surgeries. U.S. Africa Command said an airstrike in the Hiran region killed 26 al-Shabaab terrorists.

March 7, 2019: A remotely-detonated parked car bomb went off near a security checkpoint near the presidential palace in Mogadishu, killing two people and injuring one. Capt. Mohamed Hussein said it appeared to have been targeting security forces stationed at the checkpoint. Security forces arrested a man suspected to have been the driver.

March 11, 2019: *CNN* reported that U.S. Africa Command said it conducted an airstrike in Somalia after a Somali-led force and its accompanying US military advisers were attacked by al-Shabaab. The airstrike killed eight al-Shabaab fighters.

March 23, 2019: *NPR* and *AP* reported that an al-Shabaab suicide bomber hit the Ministry of Labor and Works building near the headquarters of the country's intelligence agency in Mogadishu. Five gunmen then ran into the building, trapping dozens of hostages and killing five people, including Deputy Minister of Labor and Social Affairs Saqar Ibrahim Abdalla in his ground-floor office. Security forces retook the building and killed the terrorists. The *New York Times* and *Reuters* reported that 15 people were killed.

March 26, 2019: No one claimed credit when a bomb hidden in a private luxury car exploded in Mogadishu's Hodan district, killing the driver and injuring a nearby pedestrian.

March 28, 2019: An al-Shabaab vehicle bomb exploded outside a restaurant in Mogadishu's Waberi district, killing 16 and wounding 17.

March 31, 2019: Al-Shabaab announced on its *Andalus* radio station that it had executed four men accused of spying for the British, Djibouti and Somali intelligence agencies. It said a firing squad killed them in a public square in Kamsuma in the Lower Jubba region.

April 4, 2019: In the evening, a car bomb exploded near the gate of the General Kahiye Police Academy in Mogadishu, injuring six people.

April 14, 2019: *AP* and *Air Force Times* reported that U.S. Africa Command announced that an airstrike on a vehicle near Xiriiro, a village in northern Somalia's semi-independent Puntland State, killed Abdulhakim Dhuqub, deputy leader of the Somali extremists linked to ISIS. Dhuqub ran the group's daily operations, planning attacks and obtaining resources. Puntland Security Minister Abdisamad Mohamed Galan said the airstrike killed other members of the group, which had broken away from al-Shabaab. ISIS-Somalia has roughly 300 members.

May 14, 2019: Police Captain Mohamed Hussein said an al-Shabaab suicide vehicle bomber hit the gate of a district headquarters in Mogadishu, killing three people and injuring three.

May 22, 2019: An al-Shabaab suicide car bomber killed nine people, including former foreign minister Hussein Elabe Fahiye, who was an advisor to the current president, and wounded 13 at a security checkpoint near the presidential palace in Mogadishu. Most of the casualties were soldiers conducting security checks on vehicles on the main road. The group said it targeted vehicles carrying government officials. Witness Madey Ahmed said, "In the past I was wounded in this area, and again today my daughter has been killed in this attack which also destroyed my home. This is terrible."

Stars and Stripes reported on May 24 that U.S. Africa Command said it killed two ISIS-Somalia fighters in the Golis Mountains on May 22.

June 15, 2019: National police chief General Bashir Abdi Mohamed announced that two car bombs in Mogadishu killed eleven people, including at least two women, and wounded 25. Al-Shabaab claimed credit. The first car bomb exploded near a security checkpoint for the presidential palace, killing nine people. *Reuters, AP,* and the *New York Times* reported that the second car bomb killed the driver and his accomplice near a checkpoint on the road to the airport. Al-Shabaab said it was aiming at the first line of security checkpoints for the airport and palace.

July 12, 2019: *Reuters* reported that an al-Shabaab car bomb exploded at the Hotel Asasey in Kismayo where local elders and lawmakers were discussing the August regional election. Abdiasis Abu Musab, al-Shabaab's military operation spokesman, explained, "First we targeted (the hotel) with a suicide car bomb and then armed mujahideen (guerrilla fighters) stormed the hotel. We are still fighting inside the hotel… There are many dead bodies inside the hotel, including a dead white man. We control the hotel now." Ahmed Madobe, the president of Jubbaland regional state which controls Kismayo, said that the 26 dead included three Kenyans, three Tanzanians, two Americans, one Canadian and one Briton, said. The *New York Times* reported that 56 people, including two Chinese, were injured. Mogadishu-based independent radio station *Radio Dalsan* and *AP* reported that Canadian-Somali journalist Hodan Nalayeh, 43, and her husband, Farid Jama Suleiman, fellow journalist Mohamed Sahal Omar, variant Mohamed Omar Sahal, and entrepreneur Mahad Nur were killed. Nalayeh was born in Somalia in 1976, but lived mostly in Canada, including Alberta and Toronto. She founded the international web-based video production company *Integration TV*, aimed at Somali viewers around the world. The *Washington Post* reported that she had 60,000 *YouTube* followers. She was the first Somali woman media owner in the world. She left behind two young sons. After a 14-hour gun battle, troops shot dead all four attackers. 19071201

July 22, 2019: In the morning, al-Shabaab remotely detonated a car bomb near a security checkpoint by Mogadishu's airport, killing 10 and injuring 15, many critically.

July 24, 2019: *AP, AFP* and *al-Jazeera* reported that a female al-Shabaab suicide bomber walked into the office of Mogadishu mayor Abdirahman Omar Osman during a security meeting and set off explosives strapped to her waist, killing seven people, including two district commissioners and three directors, and critically wounding six people, including the mayor, his deputy, and other district commissioners. The attack occurred shortly after UN envoy James Swan made a courtesy call to Osman's office. Al-Shabaab military spokesman Abdiaziz Abu Musab and the government said that the bomber was aiming at the American diplomat. By July 25, Osman remained in a coma. Osman died on August 1 in Qatar, where he had been airlifted for medical treatment. 199072401

July 27, 2019: *Reuters* reported that a U.S. air strike killed an al-Shabaab facilitator in the northern Golis mountain region.

August 14, 2019: Al-Shabaab set off a car bomb, then terrorists attacked an army base in Awdhegle, a farming town, killing four soldiers and a photographer embedded with the army. General Yusuf Rage, commander of the Somali infantry division, said that eight attackers died.

August 20, 2019: U.S. Africa command said an airstrike killed an al-Shabaab terrorist near Qunyo Barrow.

August 30, 2019: The *Washington Post* reported that al-Shabaab was making tens of millions of dollars per year in shaking down legitimate businesses in a protection money racket. In rural Somalia, the group had established courts, road tolls and tax collection and was making inroads into Mogadishu. The group had nearly 10,000 members. AS had conducted more than 850 attacks in 2019, killing 1,600 people, according to the Armed Conflict Location and Event Data Project.

September 30, 2019: Al-Shabaab claimed credit for two attacks on Western forces backing the government. The Somali government said no coalition members were injured or killed.

After a car bomb exploded, dozens of terrorists ran through the gates of Baledogle airfield in the Lower Shabelle region, where the U.S. military stations drones and trains Somali soldiers. Deputy Interior Minister Aden Isak said the "failed attack" killed only al-Shabaab fighters. *NPR* reported that 25 terrorists were killed. Al-Shabaab said that "After breaching the perimeters of the heavily fortified base, the mujahideen [holy warriors] stormed the military complex, engaging the crusaders in an intense firefight." *Military.com* reported that next day that a U.S. service member was wounded. 190930012

The Italian Defense Ministry announced that an Italian military convoy returning to base from a training exercise as part of a European Union training mission in Somalia was hit by an explosion in Mogadishu, destroying a building and damaging an armored personnel carrier. 19093003

Military.com and *Military Times* reported that on October 1, AFRICOM retaliated, killing 10 terrorists and the vehicle used in the base attack with small-arms fire and an airstrike. A second airstrike killed another terrorist near Qunyo Barrow, along the coast southeast of Mogadishu.

October 13, 2019: In the early afternoon, mortar rounds landed inside the U.N. and African Union compounds in Mogadishu, injuring several people. Al-Shabaab was suspected. 19103101

October 25, 2019: A U.S. Africa Command drone hit a vehicle traveling to Golis, killing three senior officers with ISIS affiliation. A Somali official said those killed included a bomb expert who had been sought for nearly a year.

November 19, 2019: A Somali intelligence official announced that a U.S. drone strike on a vehicle outside Kunya Barrow in the Lower Shabelle region killed a senior al-Shabaab officer who had maintained links with foreign terrorist groups with the aim of coordinating future attacks. The U.S. military said the al-Shabaab member had direct ties to al-Qaida.

December 9, 2019: A U.S. Africa Command airstrike on a vehicle outside Sakow, in the Middle Jubba region, killed a senior al-Shabaab terrorist and wounded another.

December 10, 2019: Five al-Shabaab terrorists attacked the presidential palace in Mogadishu. Security forces killed all five after a seven-hour shootout spread from the heavily fortified government complex to the nearby SYL Hotel. Police Captain Mohamed Hussein said that soldiers shot dead three terrorists near the entrance to the presidential residence and then killed two near the hotel parking lot after they took positions by the kitchen area. Authorities rescued 20 people, including government officials, from the hotel. *CNN* reported that three civilians and two soldiers were killed. Eleven people, including two members of the security forces, were injured.

Al-Shabaab claimed credit on its *Andalus* radio station.

December 16, 2019: *Air Force Magazine* reported that a U.S. Africa Command airstrike near Dujuma killed an al-Shabaab member.

December 28, 2019: *NPR* and *CNN* reported that at 8 a.m., an al-Shabaab truck bombing at the Ex-control Afgoye checkpoint at a busy intersection in Mogadishu killed 76 people, including 16 university students and soldiers, and injured more than 70. A taxation office was nearby. Turkey's Foreign Minister Mevlüt Çavuşoğlu said that two Turkish brothers who were engineers for an En-Ez Construction road project died in the attack. The *Washington Post, AP* and the *New York Times* said 79 were killed when a bus carrying university students to their campus was hit. *Reuters* reported that an international organization and a Somali Member of Parliament claimed 90 died, including 17 police officers. Aamin Ambulance service director Abdiqadir Abdulrahman said another 125 were wounded. The *New York Times* cited government authorities who said 149 were wounded. Fatuma Mohamud Ali, a Benadir University student, was wounded in her hands. A Turkish military cargo plane brought 24 doctors to the area, then evacuated at least ten wounded Somalis to Turkey. 19122801

AFP reported that the next day, U.S. Africa Command conducted three airstrikes in two locations in Somalia, killing four al-Shabaab terrorists. Two terrorists died and two vehicles were destroyed in Qunyo Barrow; another two died in Caliyoow Barrow.

SOUTH SUDAN

December 1, 2019: Gunmen attacked the compound of Relief International in Maban, sexually assaulted two staffers and wounded three others. 19120101

UGANDA

April 2, 2019: Four gunmen ambushed a group of foreign tourists and kidnapped U.S. citizen

Kimberley Sue Endicott, variant Endecott, 35, and local driver Jean-Paul Mirenge while on an evening game drive to see gorillas in the Ishasha area of Queen Elizabeth National Park, a protected area near the border with Congo. The kidnappers, using the phone of one of their hostages, demanded a ransom of $500,000. The *Uganda Media Centre* reported that the four other tourists were "left abandoned and unharmed". On April 7, Ugandan police said they had rescued Endicott and her driver from the Democratic Republic of the Congo. Reports conflicted regarding whether a ransom was paid. An official with Wild Frontiers Uganda Safaris said that Endicott was released, "not rescued", after money was paid. Endicott, of Costa Mesa California, owned a small skin care shop. A follow-up *AP* report said she was in her 50s and had a daughter and granddaughter, citing Phoenix resident Rich Endicott, 62, her cousin. *CNN* reported on April 9 that Ugandan police had arrested eight suspects. Ugandan police spokesman Fred Enanga said the arrests occurred with the assistance of a joint task force consisting of the Ugandan security services and representatives from the United States military. 19040201

ASIA

BANGLADESH

February 24, 2019: Bangladesh air force official Mofidur Rahman said a "terrorist" tried to hijack a Biman Bangladesh Airlines Boeing 737-800 flight that took off from Dhaka at 4:35 p.m. bound for Dubai via Chittagong. *Somoy TV* reported that the plane made an emergency landing 40 minutes after takeoff at the Shah Ananta International Airport in Chittagong, Bangladesh after crew reported that the individual was acting suspiciously. The Bangladeshi hijacker asked to speak to his wife and to Bangladeshi Prime Minister Sheikh Hasina. Soon after the hijacker died in a gun battle with military commandos. The hijacker was armed with a pistol. No other injuries were reported; the 143 passengers and seven crew were safely evacuated. Air Vice Marshal M.

Naim Hassan, chairman of the Civil Aviation Authority, said that the suspect could have been "mentally imbalanced". Narayanganj district police chief Mohammed Moniruzzaman identified the hijacker as Mahmud Polash Ahmed, 24, who lived near Dhaka. Late on February 25, civil authorities filed a criminal case, naming Ahmed as the attacker. The complaint said he tried to enter the cockpit 15 minutes after takeoff. Carrying "bombs-like and arms-like" objects, he started shouting. Complainant Debabrata Sarker, a technical assistant at Hazrat Shah Amanat International Airport in Chittagong, said Ahmed exploded "two cracker-like objects" inside the plane. Mufti Mahmud Khan, director of the law and media wing of Bangladesh's Rapid Action Battalion security agency, said that the suspect was listed in its database as Md. Polash Ahmed, who was arrested in 2012 in a kidnapping case. 19022401

March 19, 2019: During the evening, gunmen shot at two cars returning from a polling station at Baghaichhari in Rangamati district with ballot boxes, killing seven people and wounding 15 in southeastern Bangladesh.

May 26, 2019: The Islamic State claimed credit for setting off a bomb targeting a police van in Dhaka's Malibagh area during the night, injuring three people, including a police officer. Police were not sure who was behind it. Dhaka Police Commissioner Asaduzzman Mia said that the bomb had been planted in the van. The government often denies ISIS activity in the country, frequently blaming the domestic Jumatul Mujahedeen Bangladesh.

August 31, 2019: During the night, the Islamic State claimed credit for setting off a crude bomb against a car carrying a Cabinet minister passing through Dhaka's Dhanmondi area, injuring a policeman from his security team and a traffic officer. Local Government and Rural Development Minister Tazul Islam was not hurt. IS posted on an IS-affiliate website that two traffic police officers were severely wounded when a "security detachment from the soldiers of the Caliphate" targeted the two officers.

October 5, 2019: Student activists loyal to Prime Minister Sheikh Hasina were suspected in the murder of Abrar Fahad, a second-year student at a Bangladesh University of Engineering and Technology in Dhaka dormitory after he criticized on *Facebook* a recent water-sharing deal with India. He also questioned another agreement for exporting petroleum gas to India from Bangladesh. Police spokesman Masudur Rahman said police arrested eleven students. An autopsy determined that Fahad died of severe internal bleeding from beatings with blunt objects such as cricket game stumps or sticks. The suspects were tied to the Bangladesh Chhatra League, an influential student body of the ruling party.

CHINA

January 8, 2019: Xicheng district government said that at 11:17 a.m., a man, surnamed Jia, 49, with a hammer injured 20 children, three seriously, inside Beijing No. 1 Affiliated Elementary School of Xuanwu Normal School. Police arrested Jia, who was from northern Heilongjiang Province and employed through a labor service company to perform daily maintenance work at the school. His contract was set to expire in January. Founded in 1908, the school has 2,537 students and 199 teaching personnel.

February 21, 2019: A man with a history of mental illness attacked morning commuters with a knife in Ji'an city, wounding 11 people, including students. Police and onlookers tackled Guo Kaibing, 33.

March 22, 2019: Restaurant owner Cui Lidong, 44, tried to kill his wife and daughter, then crashed his car into pedestrians in Zaoyang city in Hubei Province in northern China, killing six, including a child, before he was shot dead by police. Cui's wife and daughter were among the eight people injured, four of them children.

March 25, 2019: A gunman killed five people in Inner Mongolia's eastern Kailu County before police apprehended him.

March 27, 2019: *CNN* reported on September 28, 2020 that the Jiaozuo Intermediate People's Court in Henan Province sentenced to death Jiaozuo kindergarten teacher Wang Yun, who in 2019 had poisoned 25 children, killing one of them, after an argument with a rival staff member regarding how to handle the students. The Court called her "despicable" and "vicious" for adding nitrite to the breakfast porridge supplied by the school and intended for the other teacher's students. She had earlier been caught trying to poison her husband, surnamed Feng, in February 2017 after an argument, pouring nitrite into his glass and causing minor injuries.

June 7, 2019: Gasoline bombs went off outside Hong Kong police headquarters and a police station, causing no injuries. Authorities arrested a suspect. Police on vehicle patrol saw a man holding an ignited glass bottle at 3:30 a.m. at the intersection where the police headquarters is located. When they slowed down, he threw the bottle toward the building before fleeing in a black car. The bottle landed next to their car. A second gasoline bomb exploded in the afternoon near the Happy Valley police station. The *South China Morning Post* reported that a man in his 20s with a previous arson conviction was later detained after police stopped a black Mercedes. Hong Kong police on June 8 announced the arrests of four men between the ages of 22 and 60.

July 19, 2019: Hong Kong Police arrested a man after finding two kilograms of tri-acetone tri-peroxide (TATP) during a nighttime raid on a commercial building. They also found materials against an extradition bill that had sparked a month of protest. The bill permits authorities to send suspects to mainland China to face trial.

September 2, 2019: At 8 a.m. on the first day of the new semester, a man, 40, surnamed Yu, killed eight students and wounded two students at Chaoyangpo Elementary School in Enshi in Hubei Province. The attacker was arrested. The motive was unclear.

October 13, 2019: Police announced that a homemade bomb was remotely detonated during the night near riot officers who had been clearing away a protestor-built roadblock in Hong Kong's

Kowloon area. Police said it was intended to "kill or to harm". Deputy Commissioner Tang Ping-keung said, "It exploded less than 2 meters away from a police vehicle. We have reason to believe that the bomb was meant to target police officers."

November 3, 2019: Hong Kong Police arrested a 48-year-old knife-wielding man who slashed two people and bit off part of the ear of district councilor Andrew Chiu local during weekend protests, along with two men who attacked him in retaliation. The man struck a couple with a knife outside a mall late in the day after an argument, before biting the politician's ear. An angry crowd jumped the attacker; they included two men aged 23 and 29. Five people were injured, including two who were in critical condition. Before going on a rampage, the man told his victims that Hong Kong belongs to China.

November 6, 2019: Hong Kong Police said an anti-government supporter stabbed Junios Ho, a pro-Beijing lawmaker who was campaigning for local elections. Ho, his assistant and the attacker were hospitalized. A video showed a man giving flowers to Ho before asking permission to take a picture with him. He then pulled a knife from his bag and stabbed Ho in the chest but was quickly overpowered by Ho and several others. The man called Ho "human scum".

November 12, 2019: *AP* and *CNN* reported that in the afternoon, a man climbed over the wall of a kindergarten in Kaiyuan in Yunnan Province and sprayed people with a corrosive chemical (sodium hydroxide, also known as caustic soda) as "revenge on society", hospitalizing 51 children and three teachers. *Xinhua* reported that two were seriously injured. Police arrested a 23-year-old with the family name of Kong. Police said on their *WeChat* social media account, "his parents divorced during his childhood and the lack of family warmth resulted in psychological distortion, plus his work and life was unsatisfactory, which created a pessimistic mentality and thoughts about retaliating against society."

November 17, 2019: A Hong Kong Police media liaison officer was hospitalized after being hit in the leg by an arrow as authorities fired tear gas and water cannons to drive back protesters occupying the Hong Kong Polytechnic University campus and blocking a major road tunnel under the city's harbor. Protestors also used catapults to launch gasoline bombs.

December 9, 2019: Hong Kong Police defused two large radio-controlled homemade bombs packed with nails and designed "to kill and to maim people". Police said the bombs that they found in the evening were "complete, fully functional and ready to be used", to be triggered with mobile phones. They contained 10 kilograms (22 pounds) of high explosives.

December 14, 2019: Hong Kong police arrested three men for testing homemade explosives that they suspect were intended for use during protests.

India

January 12, 2019: *AP* and the *Long War Journal* reported that Indian security forces killed Zeenat-ul-Islam, bomb-maker and chief commander of the Pakistani-connected al-Badr organization in the Jammu and Kashmir region. He was linked to Hizbul Mujahideen. His aide, Shakeel Dar, also died in the nighttime "cordon-and-search" operation in Kulgam district based on tips from residents. Zeenat-ul-Islam was on the Indian Army's list of 22 Most Wanted Terrorists as part of Operation All Out, designated as A++. Moderate political parties, along with Hizbul Mujahideen and Lashkar-e-Taiba, paid tribute to the commander. Thousands of people attended his funeral in his native Sugan village, where gunfire broke out as Indian forces tried to disperse the crowds south of Srinagar in the Shopian area the next day; 16 people were injured. *Hindustan Times* reported that seven civilians were injured.

February 7, 2019: Police officer Mohit Garg said security forces killed ten Maoist Naxalite rebels during a 2 ½ hour attack on their training camp in a forested area in Bijapur district in Chhattisgarh State. Police retrieved 12 rifles and sustained no casualties.

February 10, 2019: Indian forces cordoned off a village in Kashmir's Kulgam area in search of rebels. In an ensuing gun battle, five rebels died.

February 13, 2019: An explosion in a 10th grade classroom in a school in the Kakapora area of Kashmir injured 25 high school students.

February 14, 2019: A car bomb exploded at 3:15 p.m. amidst a convoy of 70 vehicles on a major highway near Srinagar, Kashmir, killing 40 paramilitary police officers. Jaish-e-Mohammed (Army of Mohammed) claimed credit. Journalists ran a confessor video of a man who claimed that he joined JeM a year earlier, observing, "By the time this video reaches you, I will be in heaven."

India conducted airstrikes against an alleged terrorist training camp across the Pakistani border on February 26 in retaliation for the attack. Pakistan reported by downing an Indian air force MiG-21 fighter on the Pakistani-held side of Kashmir on February 27 and capturing the pilot, Wing Commander Abhinandan Varthaman. Pakistani television aired Varthaman in his green flight suit saying he was rescued by two Pakistani military personnel when he ejected and found himself surrounded by angry residents. Some observers said this was a violation of Geneva conventions on the treatment of prisoners. He was accompanied to the border by the International Committee of the Red Cross and returned to India at 9 p.m. on March 1 near the Pakistani border town of Wagah. On March 5, 2019, *AP* reported that Shehryar Afridi, the state minister of the interior, announced the arrests of 44 people from outlawed organizations, including Mufti Abdul Rauf, the brother of Masood Azhar, the leader of Jaish-e-Muhammad, the group responsible for a February 14 terrorist attack in India that killed 40 Indian paramilitary troops. The brother and Hammad Azhar were on a list of suspects submitted by India. *AFP* reported on March 11, 2019 that Indian police said that Mudasir Ahmed Khan, one of the "key conspirators" and top commander with Jaish-e-Mohammad (JeM), died in a shootout with government forces in Tral in Pulwama district on March 10. A second gunman from Pakistan died in the clash.

February 18, 2019: Four soldiers, including an Army major, three gunmen, a police official, and a civilian died in a gun battle as government forces surrounded a village in Pulwama in Kashmir in a search for separatist gunmen believed tied to the February 14 suicide attack. Three army officers, a senior police officer and three other soldiers were wounded.

March 7, 2019: A grenade was thrown and exploded under a bus at the main bus station in Jammu in Kashmir, killing a civilian and wounding 30 others, four critically.

March 21, 2019: Security forces killed five rebels and a hostage, 11, in three clashes in Kashmir. Army spokesman Rajesh Kalia said authorities found the bodies of two insurgents and the boy after a gunfight in Bandipora district. Another hostage was rescued.

Authorities killed two gunmen in Baramulla district and another in southern Shopian area during search operations.

A rebel grenade attack wounded three police officers in the Sopore area.

April 4, 2019: Police officer D.M. Awasthi said that Maoist Naxalite rebels ambushed and killed four Indian paramilitary soldiers and wounded another two who were on a patrol in the forest area of the Kanker district of Chhattisgarh State.

April 9, 2019: Maoist rebels attacked a convoy of India's ruling Bharatiya Janata Party in the Dantewada district of Chhattisgarh State, killing state party lawmaker Bhima Mandavi, his driver and three security personnel in his vehicle with an improvised explosive device. India's paramilitary Central Reserve Police Force added that five soldiers were critically wounded when their escort vehicle was hit by the explosion.

April 30, 2019: The National Investigation Agency arrested Indian man Riyas Aboobacker, 29, who admitted being a follower for a year of Mohammed Zahran, alleged leader of the Easter Sunday bombings in Sri Lanka, who was plotting a suicide attack in India's Kerala State. Three others were brought in for questioning regarding ISIS ties.

May 2019: The National Investigation Agency arrested a man, 29, they said was a follower of Zahran Hashim, mastermind of the Easter Sunday bombings in Sri Lanka, for plotting a suicide bombing in Kerala State.

May 1, 2019: Maharashtra State Minister S. Mungantwar said Maoist rebels set off a land mine under a van carrying police commandos in the forested Gadchiroli area in Maharashtra State in western India, killing 15 officers and their driver.

The *Press Trust of India* said that in the early morning, Maoist rebels burned more than 20 vehicles of a road construction company. They hid in the forest and attacked police commandos searching for them.

May 10, 2019: *Al-Jazeera* and *Reuters* reported that during a battle with rebels, authorities in Shopian, Kashmir killed Ishfaq Ahmad Sofi, a gunman claiming affiliation with ISIS. He had been involved in several rebel groups in Kashmir for more than a decade before pledging allegiance to ISIS. He was suspected of several grenade attacks on security forces in the region.

May 12, 2019: *Al-Jazeera* reported that ISIL (alias ISIS) announced that it had established a "Province" in India. Police in India-administered Kashmir called it "pure propaganda". *Aamaq News Agency* called the new province "Wilayah of Hind", and also claimed the group inflicted casualties on Indian army soldiers in Amshipora in India-administered Kashmir's Shopian district.

May 15, 2019: A grenade attack on a police checkpoint in Gauhati injured ten people. Paresh Baruah, exiled leader of a rebel group that for 40 years has been seeking Assam's independence from India, claimed credit. *AP* reported on May 16 that Gauhati Police Commissioner Deepak Kumar said planning for the attack was carried out in TV soap opera actress Jahnavi Saikia's rented house in Gauhati, the capital of Assam State. Police raiding her house found 99 pounds of explosive material, grenade-making equipment, small arms including pistols, and bullets.

May 21, 2019: Rebels with automatic weapons were suspected in an ambush in Arunachal Pradesh State on Legislative Assembly member Tirong Aboh of the National People's Party and ten relatives and party workers who were traveling to Aboh's constituency along a route used by rebels to reach hideouts in neighboring Myanmar. The attack occurred two days before votes were to be tallied in India's national elections. NPP leader Kumar Waii called Aboh's death "a political killing".

Three political workers in Arunachal Pradesh were killed in recent weeks by suspected rebels.

May 23, 2019: Government forces in Indian-controlled Kashmir killed Zakir Musa, a senior militant commander linked to al-Qaeda, in a gunfight in the Tral area. He had refused to surrender and fired grenades at troops raiding his hideout in a civilian home, which soldiers destroyed using explosives. He joined Hizbul Mujahideen in 2013 after dropping out of his engineering course. In mid-2017, an al-Qaeda-linked propaganda network said he became the head of Ansar Ghawzat-ul-Hind, with less than a dozen others. Musa regularly issued audio messages saying that Kashmir's struggle for self-rule was part of a global jihadi agenda. He was a close aide of Burhan Wani, a charismatic Kashmiri rebel leader who was killed in 2016.

The *Long War Journal* reported on June 7, 2019 that the previous day al-Qaeda's *as-Sahab* propaganda arm posted an audio recording and a written transcript of a eulogy for Zakir Musa, a young jihadist commander of the al-Qaeda-linked Ansar Ghazwat-ul-Hind (AGH), which was established in 2017. AQ's video lauded the group's efforts in Kashmir. The eulogy was recorded by Usama Mahmood, spokesman for al-Qaeda in the Indian Subcontinent (AQIS). Mahmood noted that the "shocking news of the martyrdom of brother Zakir Musa" has "filled the hearts of the Mujahideen here in Afghanistan" with a "grief" that is "equal" to that "of our Kashmiri brothers". Mahmood claimed that despite a "number of obstacles" put in place by "the Hindu army", "more than 40,000 people of Kashmir" attended Musa's funeral. He said Musa joined a "galaxy" of other martyr stars, including Burhan Wani (Musa's fallen comrade), Afzal Guru (who was executed for his role in the December 2001 attack on Indian parliament), Taliban founder Mullah Omar, Osama bin Laden, and Abdul Rashid Ghazi (a cleric who was killed by Pakistani forces at the "Red Mosque" in 2007). Mahmood later cited the sacrifice made by Azfal Guru and named Ghazi Baba, a Jaish-e-Mohammed (JeM) terrorist who was also implicated in the December 2001 assault on the Indian parliament.

AQIS also released a video entitled, "The Soldiers of Ghazwat ul-Hind", featuring a jihadist from Srinagar identified as Faisal Ashfaq Butt, accompanied by two masked men. Butt said that he followed Ghazi Baba's example, conducting jihad against Indian authorities via small-scale operations in Srinagar.

AGH's *al-Hurr Media* released a message "He Kept His Promise." from the group's spokesman, Abu Ubaidah, who said Zakir Musa's replacement would be Abdul Hameed Lelhari (also known as Abbas Musa). His deputy emir is Ghazi Ibrahim.

May 28, 2019: Police officer D.K. Pandey said Maoist rebels set off a bomb buried in a dirt track in Ranchi, wounding eight paramilitary soldiers belonging to a special jungle warfare unit and three police officers who were conducting a search in a forest.

May 29, 2019: Indian troops raided two villages in Shopian and Kulgam in Kashmir based on intelligence that rebels were hiding there. Soldiers set off explosives at three civilian homes with explosives. Hundreds of residents turned on the soldiers, who fired back, killing one person and injuring 100. In Kulgam, residents rescued two rebels from the rubble of a home. Many of the injured were hit by shotgun pellets in the eyes.

June 6, 2019: In the evening, police and soldiers surrounded a village in southern Kashmir's Pulwama area on a tip that terrorists were hiding there. In the ensuing firefight that went into the morning, four terrorists, including two counter-insurgency police officers who had defected to the rebels with their rifles and had not reported to work, were killed.

June 11, 2019: Police came under fire while searching for suspects in Zainapora, Kashmir. The Islamic State claimed "soldiers of the caliphate" were wounded. Police headquarters in Srinagar said that two militants killed in the gun battle were "inspired by IS ideology" and were wanted in connection with "terror crimes".

June 12, 2019: Police raided the home of Mohammed Azarudeen in Tamil Nadu State. He was a *Facebook* friend of the late Zahran Hashim, the suspected mastermind of the Easter Sunday bomb attacks in Sri Lanka. Prosecutors charged Azarudeen with spreading ISIS ideology on social media to recruit young people to participate in a terrorist attack in southern India. The National Investigation Agency, which oversees counterterrorism efforts, said six other raids netted five others for questioning.

Two rebels in a car approached Indian paramilitary soldiers on patrol in Anantnag, Kashmir, and jumped out, firing at them. Five soldiers and a terrorist died. A police officer and two of three injured soldiers were critically injured.

June 13, 2019: The *Washington Post* profiled Hindu ascetic Sadhvi (nun) Pragya Singh Thakur, 49, who said she was involved in the destruction of a medieval mosque in Malegaon, called Nathuram Godse, the murderer of Mohandas Gandhi, a "patriot" and was on trial for conspiring to target Muslims in a 2008 bombing. In May 2019, she was elected with more than 860,000 votes to India's Parliament as part of the ruling BJP party in Bhopal, capital of Madhya Pradesh State. In September 2008, a bomb on a motorbike outside the Malegaon mosque killed six people and injured more than 100. The motorbike was registered in her name. Police accused her of attending a meeting that organized the bombing. She was jailed for eight years before obtaining bail. Her trial began in December 2018; she was represented by attorney J.P. Mishra.

June 17, 2019: During the night, a car bomb hit an armored army vehicle passing through the Pulwama area of Kashmir, killing two Indian soldiers and wounding more than a dozen soldiers and two civilians. No one claimed credit.

Two rebels, Sajad Ahmad Bhat and Tawseef Ahmad Bhat, and a soldier were killed and two other soldiers were wounded in a gunfight in the southern Bijbehara area. The dead terrorists were involved in a February car bombing. The car used in the blast was owned by Sajad, who joined militant ranks few days after the blast. Atul Goel, a senior police officer, said Tawseef was his handler.

Two other Indian soldiers and three rebels died in separate gun battles.

An army officer and a terrorist were killed and two other soldiers were injured in a gunfight in the Anantnag area.

June 27, 2019: Air India flight 191, a B-777 flying 327 passengers from Mumbai to Newark, New Jersey, was diverted to London's Stansted Airport after a security alert. Royal Air Force Typhoon fighter jets escorted the plane. British media reported that there was a bomb threat on board.

June 28, 2019: Police Director-General D.M. Awasthi said Maoist rebels fired at soldiers patrolling on motorbikes, killing three paramilitary soldiers and a young girl riding on a passing bus in Bijapur district in Chhattisgarh State. The *Press Trust of India* reported that the rebels stole an assault rifle, bullets, a bulletproof vest and a wireless set from the dead soldiers.

July 28, 2019: Jammu and Kashmir police chief Dilbagh Singh said that Munna Bihari, a commander of Pakistan's Jaish-e-Mohammad, was killed with a local associate after a nighttime operation in Shopian in the southern part of the Indian-administered part of Kashmir. Bihari was believed behind bomb-making and a series of civilian killings and attacks on the military in the area.

August 2, 2019: Police and soldiers cordoned off a village in Shopian on a tip that terrorists were holed up there. During a gun battle with the rebels, an Indian soldier died.

September 4, 2019: The Home Ministry designated Masood Azhar, chief of Jaish-e-Mohammed, and Hafiz Muhammad Saeed, founder of Lashkar-e-Taiba, as terrorists under the amended Unlawful Activities (Prevention) Amendment Act. The two groups are Pakistan-based. The UN

earlier placed Azhar on a sanctions blacklist, imposing a travel ban, arms embargo, and freeze on his assets.

September 6, 2019: Gunman shot at a fruit trader in northern Sopore in Indian-controlled Kashmir, injuring him and four of his family members.

September 11, 2019: Jammu and Kashmir police chief Dilbagh Singh said that Indian troops killed suspected militant Asif Maqbool Bhat in a shootout in Sopore in northern Indian-controlled Kashmir. Bhat was a member of the Pakistan-backed Lashkar-e-Taiba. Singh said Bhat was involved in a recent shootout in which three members of a fruit trader's family and a girl, 5, were wounded, and an earlier shooting of a migrant laborer from India.

September 28, 2019: Security forces killed three insurgents in a clash in Batote town in Jammu region in Indian-controlled Kashmir and rescued a civilian in whose house five gunmen had holed up. The fate of the other two was unreported. The *Press Trust of India* news agency quoted Lt. Col. Devender Anand as confirming that an Indian soldier was killed.

October 5, 2019: Director General of Police Dilbagh Singh said a grenade went off near the office of a civil administrator in Anantnag in India-administered Kashmir, injuring 10 people, including a police official and a journalist. He blamed militants.

October 14, 2019: Two suspected terrorists shot and killed a truck driver near an apple orchard in Indian-controlled Kashmir where he had picked up fruit boxes. Senior police officer Muneer Ahmed Khan said masked gunmen hijacked the truck from outside the orchard, where the vehicle was loaded with 800 apple boxes. They killed the driver after he had driven them about a half mile from the spot. The gunmen torched the truck and fled from Sindoo Shirmal, a village in southern Kashmir.

October 22, 2019: In a nighttime gun battle, Indian forces killed senior terrorist commander Hamid Lelhari and two associates in a counterinsurgency operation in the Awantipora area of Indian-controlled Kashmir. Police say Lelhari became the operations chief of Ansar Ghawzat-ul-Hind, an affiliate of al-Qaeda, after Indian troops killed Zakir Musa in 2018. In mid-2017, an al-Qaeda-linked propaganda network said Zakir Musa joined its affiliate group after he quit Kashmir's largest rebel group, Hizb-ul-Mujahi-deen.

October 24, 2019: Six gunmen fired at three vehicles laden with apple boxes in Indian-controlled Kashmir, killing an Indian truck driver and his attendant and wounding another driver in an apparent protest of New Delhi's stripping the region of its semi-autonomous status in August. Senior police officer Muneer Ahmed Khan said the victims were from Rajasthan and Haryana states and were about to drive away with the apple consignment from southern Shopian area of Kashmir. The attackers torched the vehicles.

October 29, 2019: Gunmen killed five Indian laborers from West Bengal State who were working in Indian-controlled Kashmir during the night. The attackers were believed to be protesting New Delhi's stripping the disputed region of its semi-autonomous status in early August. Six gunmen broke into two rented rooms where the laborers were staying. Another laborer was hospitalized, and three more were missing.

Gunmen critically injured a laborer near a southern Kulgam district town.

November 4, 2019: *ABC News* reported that a terrorist threw a grenade at a market in Srinagar, Kashmir, killing a street vendor from Uttar Pradesh State and hospitalizing 25. Police blamed insurgents. Two people were critically injured with head trauma and required surgery.

November 26, 2019: A terrorist threw a grenade at a meeting of government and village officials in a government building in Badasgam in Indian-controlled Kashmir, killing an elected village official and a government employee and injuring four others.

An explosion outside a Srinagar restaurant injured three civilians.

Police blamed Kashmiri rebels for the two attacks.

December 4, 2019: State administrator Dinesh Kumar Nag said that an Indian paramilitary soldier fatally shot five of his colleagues and later killed himself in a firing incident in a camp in Narayanpur district in Chhattisgarh State. The soldiers were walking in a group when the shooting started. The soldier killed those who tried to seize the weapon. Five soldiers were killed on the spot and one of the three injured soldiers later died in a hospital.

INDONESIA

January 9, 2019: Papua Province military spokesman Colonel Muhammad Aidi said separatist fighters ambushed soldiers on a logistics mission to Sinak Airport in the mountainous Puncak Jaya district, injuring a soldier in the leg. A Papuan rebel died with the Morning Star flag that serves as a symbol of Papuan independence fighters. The West Papua National Liberation Army was suspected.

January 18, 2019: President Joko Widodo announced that he would release from prison ailing radical cleric Abu Bakar Baaysir, 80, who inspired the Bali bombers from the al-Qaeda-affiliated Jemaah Islamiyah who killed 202 people, and other violent extremists in Indonesia, ending his 15-year sentence that began in 2011. Baaysir was represented by attorney Muhammad Mahendradatta. Another Baaysir lawyer who is also an adviser to Widodo, Yusril Ihza Mahendra, told Indonesian TV that Baaysir accepted conditions and would do nothing except rest and be close to his family. Australian Prime Minister Scott Morrison said he would protest if Baaysir was released early, urging Indonesia to show respect for the victims of the 2002 Bali nightclub bombings that Baaysir inspired. On January 22, Widodo said that Baaysir would not be released unless he renounced radicalism and swore loyalty to the state and the national ideology.

January 28, 2019: In the morning, separatists shot at a light aircraft carrying military personnel and local government officials from Kenyam airport in Nduga district in Papua region, killing a soldier and injuring a second soldier. The chief of Nduga district and two other district chiefs were on the plane, which was transporting supplies to a remote area. The rebels fled into the jungle.

March 7, 2019: Some 50-70 Papuan independence insurgents armed with military-grade weapons, spears and arrows opened fire on 25 soldiers near Yigi village in Nduga district in Papua region mid-day, killing three Indonesian soldiers during a battle that lasted several hours. A Papuan independence fighter also died; the military claimed it killed 7-10 fighters, but found only one body. West Papua National Liberation Army spokesman Sebby Sambom said five soldiers were killed. Both sides claimed to have captured weapons.

March 13, 2019: The wife of Husein, a jihadi who had been arrested by police on March 12, set off a bomb during a siege of their home in Sibologa, North Sumatra, killing herself and her two-year-old child. Police said the man was plotting attacks in Jakarta. Police said that hours earlier, she had thrown a homemade bomb that injured an officer. Police officers reported two explosions and smoke at the house about 1:30 a.m. She had refused calls from her husband, police and local leaders to surrender. Husein was arrested following the March 9 arrest of suspected jihadi Rinto Sugiharto in Lampung regarding plans for attacks on police in Jakarta and Lampung. The men belonged to Jemaah Anshorut Daulah, which is affiliated with ISIS.

March 28, 2019: Egianus Kogoya, a Papuan independence liberation army commander, released video purportedly recorded the previous week in the Nduga area of Papua Province's central highlands in which he vowed to conduct more attacks on a highway development project. The video showed 40 fighters, some with Indonesian military assault rifles and other weapons. Kogoya said, "We cannot step back, we will not hesitate, we would pursue (military and police) until Jakarta gives us independence, our nation must unite to separate from the Republic of Indonesia." The statement said the liberation army recovered three Indonesian-made SS-2 assault rifles during a March 7 attack in Nduga that the military said killed three soldiers and a Papuan.

May 2019: *AP* reported on May 16 that police arrested four suspected militants in Jakarta's suburb of Bekasi and killed a terrorist who tried to set off bomb during a police raid.

May 14, 2019: *AP* reported on May 16 that Indonesian police arrested nine suspected militants following a tipoff about a possible attack during the announcement of presidential election results on May 22. National police spokesman Dedi Prasetyo said that the counterterrorism squad arrested suspected militant instructor Joko Supriono in East Java's Madiun town on May 14; eight others were detained separately in Central Java Province. Seven of the suspects recently returned from Syria. Police said that Supriono was believed to be linked to the ISIS-affiliated Jemaah Anshorut Daulah. The *Washington Post 202* and the *New York Times* reported on May 17 that Indonesian authorities believed they foiled a terrorist attack by using WiFi to set off explosive devices.

May 28, 2019: National police chief Tito Karnavian announced that interrogations of six arrested individuals revealed a plot to assassinate four top Indonesian officials, including two Cabinet ministers, among them security minister Wiranto and his predecessor, maritime minister Luhut Binsar Panjaitan, and the National Intelligence Agency chief Budi Gunawan and the head of the presidential special staff for intelligence and security, Gories Mere, possibly as part of last week's riots around the national election. The head of an opinion polling company was also a target. One suspect was arrested at a hotel in Jakarta after participating in the riots, another was arrested at Jakarta's airport, and others were detained around Jakarta and Bogor. Police confiscated four weapons.

June 29, 2019: National Police spokesman Dedi Prasetyo announced the arrest of Para Wijayanto, a man believed to be the leader of the al-Qaeda-linked Jemaah Islamiyah network who had been at large since 2003. Counterterrorism police arrested him and his wife in Bekasi, a Jakarta suburb. He was suspected of making bombs used in the 2002 Bali bombings that killed 202 people and a 2004 attack on the Australian Embassy in Jakarta that killed nine. Wijayanto was a civil engineer who received military training at a jihadi camp in the southern Philippines in 2000. He was involved in the sectarian conflict in Poso on Indonesia's Sulawesi island. Since 2013, he recruited and trained members of JI's military wing, sending some to Syria to fight with extremist groups. Prasetyo said, "He was appointed as amir (leader) of Jemaah Islamiyah because of his capability and track record as an Islamic fighter." Reformed jjihadi Sofyan Tsauri said Wijayanto became leader of JI in 2007, replacing Zarkasih, who was arrested and sentenced to 15 years in prison. An Indonesian court banned JI in 2008.

September 23, 2019: The nation's counterterrorism squad arrested nine suspected militants, aged between 18 and 28, accusing them of plotting a suicide bomb attack on police. National Police spokesman Dedi Prasetyo said that six people were arrested in Bekasi, two others in northern Jakarta and another in western Jakarta. Prasetyo said they were led by Abu Zee Ghurobah, and were believed linked to ISIS affiliate Jemaah Anshorut Daulah. Prasetyo said authorities defused a powerful bomb from one of the suspects, Muhammad Arshad, when they raided his house in northern Jakarta.

North Jakarta police chief Budhi Herdi Susianto, said police found a goodbye letter written by Arshad, who allegedly planned an imminent suicide bombing at a police station. Police seized a rifle, a gun, two knives, military-style uniforms, jihadi books and bombs.

October 10, 2019: Syahril Alamsyah, alias Abu Rara, stabbed Coordinating Minister for Politics, Law and Security Wiranto, 72, and wounded a local police chief and another person in Banten Province's Menes community in Pandeglang town. President Joko Widodo called Alamsyah a terrorist. Alamsyah was suspected of membership in a jihadi group. He had been under surveillance but did not appear to pose an imminent threat. National police spokesman Brigadier General Dedi Prasetyo said Alamsyah apparently feared that he and his militant wife, Fitri Andriana, would be arrested soon. Armed forces chief in 1998-1999, Wiranto suffered two stab

wounds in the stomach. Wiranto had stepped out of his SUV and was shaking hands with a local police chief when Alamsyah stabbed Wiranto while his wife attacked the police chief. Alamsyah and Andriana were married in a religious ceremony presided by Fazri Pahlawan, alias Abu Zee Ghurobah, suspected leader of Jamaah Ansharut Daulah, a jihadi group aligned with ISIS. Authorities said Pahlawan trained Alamsyah on launching attacks. Authorities arrested Pahlawan in September. Police said Abu Rara would face heavier sanctions for handing a knife to his daughter, 15, to help assault the police. The child declined out of fear.

Bali police spokesman Hengky Widjaja said Indonesia's counterterrorism squad in Bali's Jembrana district arrested two suspected terrorists—a man, AT, and his son, ZAI—accused of plotting to attack Bali police with a bayonet. Police acted on information from interrogations of suspected associates of Jamaah Ansharut Daulah, including Syahril Alamsyah, who wounded the country's security minister hours earlier, and Fazri Pahlawan.

October 16-17, 2019: The Densus 88 anti-terrorism unit arrested 40 suspected terrorists in eight provinces ahead of a weekend presidential inauguration to be attended by Asian leaders and Western envoys. The unit was operating from a tipoff about possible attacks against police and places of worship. Six militants, including a woman, were brought before a news conference at police headquarters. Police confiscated explosive chemicals for bomb-making, knives, jihadi books, ten pipe bombs, computers, cellphones, airsoft guns, and rifles with silencers and sniper scopes. Police spokesman Muhammad Iqbal said the suspects included two radicalized female police officers who were willing to become suicide bombers. Three suspects in West Java's Cirebon district were working on a chemical bomb containing methanol, urea fertilizer and rosary pea seeds, which are the main ingredient of abrin, an extremely toxic poison.

November 13, 2019: Suicide bomber Rabbial Muslim Nasution, 24, a university student, blew himself up at the Medan city police station, wounding four police and two civilians. National Police spokesman Muhammad Iqbal said the terrorist passed through a guard post and into the station's yard, which was crowded with people who were lining up to get various police certificates. He set off his bomb near a parking lot after being confronted by other officers. Police spokesman Dedi Prasetyo said Nasution seemed to be trying to reach a canteen where police and civilians were having coffee or breakfast, but his explosives went off prematurely. Nasution told officers he was at the station to get a background check certificate he needed to apply for a job. Police had twice checked his backpack, which contained books, and had opened his jacket to be checked. On November 18, National Police spokesman Dedi Prasetyo said police in seven provinces had arrested 43 suspected accomplices, including the group's leader, believed to be members of the local ISIS affiliate Jama'ah Anshorut Daulah (JAD). Police seized explosives, guns, knives, arrows and jihadi documents. Prasetyo said the suspects included 20 JAD members who had attended military-style jihadi training in North Sumatra's Mount Sibayak.

On November 16, 2019, North Sumatra police chief Agus Andrianto said members of a police counterterrorism squad shot to death two suspected terrorists who may have had links to a suicide attack at a busy police station in Medan earlier in the week. Three suspected terrorists refused to surrender and shot at police during a raid in North Sumatra Province's Hamparan Perak village. An officer was hospitalized with a gunshot wound to his thigh. The third suspect escaped. Police were tipped off to the suspects after interrogations of detainees arrested after the suicide bomb attack in Medan. Police believed the duo were the Medan attack's bombmakers.

On November 17, four jihadis surrendered to authorities.

December 2, 2019: Two suspected West Papua National Liberation Army rebels were killed in a gun battle in Lanny Jaya District. The WPNLA is the military wing of the Free Papua Movement.

December 3, 2019: Jakarta Police Chief Gatot Eddy Pramono said a smoke grenade exploded near the presidential palace, wounding two sol-diers who were exercising in Jakarta's National Monument Park when they spotted the non-lethal grenade on the ground. It exploded when they tried to pick it up. They were in stable condition at an army hospital with injuries to their hands and thighs.

December 5, 2019: *AP* reported on December 14 that Papua police's deputy chief, Yakobus Marjuki, said the elite counterterrorism squad on December 5 arrested a man, Karwanto, in a raid at a house in Sentani after receiving a tip from intelligence that some members of the extremist group have fled to Papua from other Indonesian islands since 2018. On December 14, Indonesian police, acting on information from his interrogation, arrested seven suspected jihadis in Jayapura, capital of Papua Province. Police seized knives, laptops, explosive materials and a bomb from three houses rented by the suspects. The detainees are suspected members of a local affiliate of the Islamic State group known as Jama'ah Anshorut Daulah (JAD) from Lampung and Medan on Sumatra island.

December 13, 2019: Five members of the East Indonesia Mujahideen were suspected of shooting a police officer to death in eastern Indonesia. National Police spokesman Argo Yuwono said that the gunmen kidnapped villagers and police officers who had just returned from Friday prayers at a small mosque near a police post in Salubanga in Central Sulawesi Province. The hostages fled when the gunmen entered the mosque's yard and fired at the officers and villagers, killing a police officer, and fled to a nearby forested area in Parigi Moutong district. The group is led by Ali Kalora.

December 17, 2019: Military spokesman Colonel Taibur Rahman said two soldiers were killed when rebels fired at troops on patrol in a village in Intan Jaya district in Papua Province.

December 20, 2019: Gunmen shot at a small commercial plane carrying nine passengers as it landed in Puncak district in Papua Province. No casualties were reported. The plane was co-piloted by Purwanto Condro Usodo, an Indonesian who said that he and Australian pilot Michael Cumming landed safely at Beoga airport from the mining town of Timika. Thirty minutes later, gunmen fired on people who were unloading supplies and luggage from the plane. The gunmen fled into the jungle when soldiers returned fire. Observers suspected the West Papua National Liberation Army (TPNPB), the military wing of the Free Papua Movement.

JAPAN

January 1, 2019: *AP, CNN, TV Asahi, Kyodo News* and *NHK TV* reported that a man, Kazuhiro Kusakabe, 21, crashed a minivan into pedestrians at 12.10 a.m., on Takeshita Dori Street where people had gathered for New Year's festivities in downtown Tokyo, injuring nine, one seriously. The attacker exited the vehicle and attacked one of the injured. The injured ranged in age from teens to those in their 50s. A male university student was in critical condition. The driver eluded arrest for around 20 minutes. Police arrested the driver on suspicion of attempted murder. The street, popular among tourists and pop culture and fashion fans that runs by Meiji Shrine in Harajuku, Shibuya ward, had been closed to car traffic for holiday celebrations. The suspect told police that he had conducted a terrorist act to protest the death penalty, telling police he "would not make any excuse" for his actions. Police found a large amount of kerosene in the car and traces of the liquid on his clothes. He said he was retaliating "for the execution of Aum cult members". The Aum Shin Rykyo cult members who were found to be responsible for the March 20 1995 sarin gas attack on a Tokyo subway, were executed in July 2018.

July 18, 2019: The *Washington Post, CNN* and *Reuters* reported that at 10:30 a.m., a man, 41, sprayed flammable liquid throughout Kyoto Animation's (KyoAni) 1st Studio building in Kyoto's Fushimi-ku district, yelled "You die!", and set the four-story (other reports said three-story) building alight, killing 34 people, including 20 women, many of carbon dioxide poisoning, and injuring 36, ten seriously. Several victims collapsed while climbing stairs, trying to reach the roof. Some jumped out of windows, sustaining bone fractures. Studio president Hideaki Hatta told *NHK* it had received several threats. The arsonist

was arrested and treated at a hospital for serious burn injuries. *Kyodo* reported that firefighters in 48 fire engines were dispatched and extinguished the blaze after five hours. The animation studio produces "Free!", the TV manga series "K-On!", "Lucky Star", the anime TV adaptation of "the Melancholy of Haruhi Suzumiya", and "Violet Evergarden" which *Netflix* picked up in 2018, "Clannad", and "Miss Kobayashi's Dragon Maid," inter alia. Its website says the firm also publishes novels, comics and visual books, designs characters and manages a school. A Kyoto prefectural police spokesperson said the man had a backpack containing several knives.

The next day *NHK* said police identified the suspect as Shinji Aoba, 41, who had no connection with Kyoto Animation and was thought to have been living near Tokyo. He told police someone had plagiarized his novel; the media speculated that it was intellectual property used by KyoAni. He sustained burns all over his body. *CNN* reported that police said he had mental health issues. On July 21, Japanese police obtained an arrest warrant for Aoba on arson and murder allegations. *NHK* reported that Aoba had served prison terms for robbing a convenience store in 2012.

A GoFundMe page set up by the Texas-based animation company Sentai Filmworks raised $1.3 million for victims and their families within a day.

AFP reported on May 27, 2020 that Japanese authorities formally arrested Shinki Aoba, 42, on suspicion of murder for the July 18, 2019 arson attack on Kyoto Animation's anime studio that killed 22 women and 14 men and injured dozens. Police had detained Aoba after the fire but did not charge him while he was hospitalized with serious burns. He was unconscious for weeks. No motive was established, although some said he yelled "drop dead". He also faced murder charges for the 34 people who were injured, and with possessing knives on the street without legitimate reasons. Among the dead were Sachie, daughter of Shinichi Tsuda, and Yasuhiro, son of Yasuo Takemoto.

AP reported on December 16, 2020 that the Kyoto District Public Prosecutors Office formally filed charges of murder, attempted murder, arson and two other counts against Shinji Aoba after he had recovered enough from his own severe burns to his face, torso and limbs and was deemed mentally fit to stand trial.

Malaysia

March 2019: On February 5, 2020, Presiding Judge Kadwanto in East Jakarta District Court sentenced ISIS sympathizer Asmar Husin, alias Abu Hamzah, to life in prison for plotting bomb attacks against police and Christians. He was arrested in March 2019 in North Sumatra Province's Sibolga district. His indictment said the interrogation of Rinto Sugiharto uncovered plans for several suicide bombings in Jakarta and Lampung by a ten-member cell Husin led. His wife set off a bomb during a siege of their home, killing herself and their 2-year-old child. Hours earlier, she threw a homemade bomb that injured an officer as police tried to search the house. Separately, the same court sentenced the nine co-conspirators, including Rinto Sugiharto, to prison terms ranging from six to 20 years.

March 5, 2019: National police chief Mohamad Fuzi Harun announced the deportation of six Egyptians and a Tunisian man believed to be linked to the African-based Ansar al-Sharia al-Tunisia terrorist group. Two were detained in 2016 for trying to illegally enter an African country. Harun said they used fake passports to enter Malaysia in October 2018 and were planning to sneak into a third country to launch attacks. Five other Egyptians and two Malaysians were detained in February 2019 for providing food, shelter, air tickets and employment for the two suspected terrorists.

May 13, 2019: Police detained four men planning to assassinate "high-profile targets" and bomb places of worship and entertainment centers during Ramadan. National police chief Abdul Hamid Bador said raids the previous week netted a Malaysian, 34, who was the alleged mastermind, an Indonesian and two ethnic Rohingya Muslims, plus a pistol and six homemade explosives. They were part of an IS-allied cell aimed at avenging a Muslim firefighter who died during riots over the relocation of an Indian temple in

November 2018. Bador said they had planned to attack entertainment outlets and churches, Hindu and Buddhist temples around Kuala Lumpur. The suspects accused the alleged targets of insulting Islam or failing to defend Muslim rights. A Rohingya waiter, 20, was registered with the United Nations High Commission for Refugees and supported the Arakan Rohingya Salvation Army insurgent group. He was planning to attack the Myanmar Embassy in Kuala Lumpur. Police were searching for two other Malaysians and an Indonesian.

May 30, 2019: Authorities arrested three ISIS suspects, one of whom was reported to be en route to Syria through Egypt.

June 18, 2019: Filipino kidnappers in two vessels raided two fishing boats and abducted ten crew members in waters off Borneo island. The attackers boarded the fishing boats, confiscated documents and kidnapped ten crew members before sailing toward Sitangkai Island in the Philippines. A Malaysian official said Abu Sayyaf terrorists were suspected. 19061801

Late September 2019: *AP* reported that three Indonesians were reported kidnapped off Sabah State on northern Borneo island near the sea border with the southern Philippines, where Abu Sayyaf operates. As of October 4, Philippine authorities were trying to verify the reports. *AP* reported on December 22, 2019 that Task Force Sulu of the Philippines' Western Mindanao Command rescued Indonesians Maharudin Lunani and Samion Bin Maniue, two of the three Indonesian hostages, after a gun battle with their Abu Sayyaf captors in the southern jungles. A soldier and a kidnapper were killed in two dawn firefights near Panamao. 19099901

AP reported that Philippine troops killed Abu Sayyaf commander Talha Jumsah near Sulu's mountainous Patikul town. He was a key link between ISIS and local jihadis and helped set up a series of deadly suicide attacks in Sulu Province in 2019.

MALDIVES

December 18, 2019: Mohamed Basheer, a police officer in charge of serious and organized crime, announced a raid on an isolated "quasi community" religious group that led to the arrests of three people suspected of spreading violent extremism and recruiting people to join foreign terrorist groups. The community had deprived women and children of their basic rights, forcing women and children to sever all ties with the outside community, preventing children from attending schools and being vaccinated, and forcing them into child marriages.

MYANMAR

January 4, 2019: The *Myanmar News Agency* said 250 members of the rebel Arakan Army, which seeks autonomy for Rakhine State, conducted morning attacks on three police outposts in Buthidaung and Maungdaw townships in Rakhine State, killing 13 policemen and injuring nine. The group is not affiliated with the Arakan Rohingya Salvation Army (ARSA), a virtually inactive Muslim insurgent group. The attackers seized 40 small weapons, ammunition and a walkie-talkie. Arakan Army sympathizers claimed that 14 government security personnel were captured by the rebels.

March 9, 2019: During the night, sixty Arakan Army rebels attacked a police post in Rakhine State, killing nine policemen who were safeguarding question and answer sheets from the national high school matriculation examination.

April 9, 2019: The *Global New Light of Myanmar* newspaper reported that 200 insurgents claiming to represent the Rakhine minority attacked a security police headquarters in Mrauk-U in Rakhine State during the night, killing three people and kidnapping seven civilians—four women and three children. One officer's family member was killed. Two policemen died and seven were missing. The gunmen retreated after six hours when soldiers arrived. Authorities blamed the Arakan Army rebel group, which is aligned with Rakhine's Buddhist population. The government

declared the Arakan Army a terrorist organization after it killed 13 police officers and wounded nine in attacks on January 4, 2019.

August 15, 2019: The Northern Alliance, a coalition of armed rebels from the Kokang, Rakhine and Ta-ang, or Palaung, claimed credit for attacks in five locations, including at a military academy outside normal combat zones, where a civilian was killed and a soldier wounded. Two attacks hit the Mandalay Region, where the Defense Services Technology Academy is located. The others were in Northern Shan State, where 14 people were killed.

September 25, 2019: *AP* reported on September 27 that Canada, Australia, the UK and the U.S. issued travel advisories regarding possible violent attacks in Naypyitaw, Yangon and Mandalay on September 26, October 16 and October 26. The Canadian and British embassies warned against bombings.

October 13, 2019: *Agence France Presse* reported that Rakhine rebels disguised as a sports team were suspected of kidnapping 31 hostages, mostly off-duty firefighters and construction workers, after storming a Myanmar bus en route to Sittwe. The state-backed *Global New Light of Myanmar* said a man dressed in civilian attire flagged down the bus. Eighteen gunmen in sportswear ran from the forest and ordered the passengers off the bus.

October 26, 2019: The Information Ministry announced that 30 Buddhist rebels captured 58 soldiers, police and civilian officials from a ferry carrying 165 civilians passengers and 50 government personnel from Sittwe, Rakhine's capital, north to Buthidaung. On October 27, the Arakan Army said that an attack by three government helicopters on three boats carrying the captured personnel had sunk two of the boats, killing some of the hostages and rebels. The website of the military commander-in-chief said the helicopters suffered some damage from gunfire and a crewman was lightly wounded, but 14 hostages were rescued.

November 26, 2019: Ko Myo of Charity Without Borders, a nonprofit organization that provides ambulance services, said police in Hsipaw township in northern Shan State took to the hospital an Argentine woman who was injured by a land mine that killed a person initially identified as a Dutch male, 40. The next day, the German Foreign Ministry said a German citizen was killed. 19112601

NEPAL

February 22, 2019: A nighttime explosion outside the Ncell mobile network operator company in Kathmandu killed one person and injured two others. The dead man bled out when both feet were severed by the blast. Police detained six people for questioning. No one claimed responsibility. Ncell is mostly owned by Malaysia-based Axiata Group Berhad.

May 21, 2019: Masked assailants killed nine people in two families in their homes at night in Miklajung, a remote mountain village. Government administrator Murari Wasti said neighbors found the bodies the next morning. A girl, 12, survived with injuries. The two families were related and lived in nearby separate houses.

May 26, 2019: Police official Shyam Lal Gyawali said three explosions (two of them about an hour apart; the other a few hours later) killed three people and wounded eight in three Kathmandu neighborhoods. Police suspected an outlawed communist group that once split from the ruling Maoist Communist party was responsible because its members had been protesting the arrests of their supporters. The first explosion in northern Kathmandu killed two people and injured five, police said. The second bomb in a house in central Kathmandu killed one and injured one. Police believed the men in the house were linked to the outlawed group, having found pamphlets from the group at the second explosion site. The third bomb injured two people believed to be members of the group who were transporting the bomb.

December 14, 2019: After midnight, a bomb exploded in a house in Mahendranagar, killing three people, including the owner, his son and a police officer who responded to the call about the device, and injuring another police officer and the son and daughter of the house owner, a local businessman who ran a medicine store. The owner called police after discovering a suspicious device planted at the entrance gate of his house. The officers were checking the device when it exploded. No one claimed credit.

PAKISTAN

January 1, 2019: Four Pakistani Taliban gunmen, including a suicide bomber, raided a security forces facility in Loralai. In the ensuing gun battle, the terrorists and four security forces were killed. The terrorists failed to enter a main residential area where families of the soldiers and security forces live. They settled for entering another compound near a security checkpoint, where three of the assailants were shot and killed by troops and the suicide bomber detonated his explosives.

January 5, 2019: Police officer Dost Mohammad said a car bomb exploded outside a mosque in the Kali Bari area of Peshawar, hospitalizing three people, including a woman, and damaging several shops. No one claimed credit.

January 6, 2019: Officer Shams Uddin of the Levies Force said a roadside bomb planted in a motorcycle hit the convoy of the force's senior officer Abdul Malik in Pishin district in Baluchistan Province, wounding Malik, his two subordinates, and three civilians.

A remotely-controlled bomb exploded as a Frontier Corps paramilitary vehicle was driving by in Panjgur district in Baluchistan Province, wounding a paramilitary soldier and a civilian.

No one claimed responsibility for the attacks.

January 16, 2019: Security forces raided a terrorist hideout in Hangu, killing three suspects, including Mohammad Islam, mastermind of the November 23, 2018 bombing that killed 35 Shi'ites at a food market in Klaya in Khyber Punktunkhwa Province. A civilian was accidentally killed during the gun battle. The Islamic State (ISIS) had claimed credit for the Klaya attack on "Shi'ite apostates".

January 19, 2019: Senior officer Rai Tahir said counterterrorism officers killed four insurgents, including two women, in a shootout on a highway in Punjab Province. The authorities claimed that terrorists traveling in a car opened fire when police acting on intelligence gleaned from a previous operation stopped them near Sahiwal. No officer was hurt. Three suspects escaped on a motorcycle. Relatives of those killed said they lived in the Kot Lakhpat area in the suburbs of Lahore and identified them as grocery store owner Mohammad Khalil, 42, his wife Nabila, 38, their daughter Areeba, 13, and their friend, Zeeshan Javed, who was driving the car and was on Pakistan's wanted terrorist list. Kalil was survived by his wounded son, Umair, who said that the family was going to attend a wedding. Pakistani authorities arrested 16 counterterrorism officials as hundreds of friends, relatives, and neighbors protested what they deemed an extrajudicial killing of a family. On January 22, provincial minister Raja Bisharat said five police officers were charged with murder after a probe concluded that three people were wrongly killed. Bisharat said four police officers were also charged with mismanaging the raid on the car.

January 29, 2019: Four Pakistani Taliban terrorists armed with guns and grenades attacked a regional police station in Baluchistan Province's Loralai district, killing eight police officers and a civilian and wounding 17 others. Security forces killed two gunmen.

February 4, 2019: Arsonists torched statues and holy books at a Hindu temple in Kumb. No one claimed credit.

February 12, 2019: Gunmen shot at a police vehicle in Dera Ismail Khan, killing four police officers and injuring two. No one claimed credit.

February 16, 2019: Gunmen killed two soldiers in Loralai in Baluchistan Province.

February 17, 2019: Gunmen fired on security forces in Turbat in Baluchistan Province, killing four troops.

February 22, 2019: Police spokeswoman Nabila Ghazanfar said that in a nighttime raid, counterterrorism police arrested two male Baluchistan Liberation Army separatist insurgents attempting to blow up the main gas pipeline in Bahawalpur. Ghazanfar said the duo confessed to similar sabotage of gas pipelines in the adjacent district of Rahim Yar Khan. Police seized 4.5 pounds of explosives, a timing device, detonators and connecting cords.

February 28, 2019: Police said gunmen riding on a motorcycle shot at a car carrying Judge Mohammad Ayub of the Peshawar High Court, critically wounding him and his driver in the Hayatabad neighborhood in Peshawar, capital of Khyber Pakhtunkhwa Province bordering Afghanistan, then fled. No one claimed credit.

March 14, 2019: Police official Jamil Ahmed said a roadside bomb exploded in a market near Panjgur, killing two people, wounding seven, and damaging shops and vehicles. Jihadis and separatists were suspected.

March 17, 2019: Police Officer Abdullah Jamali said a bomb exploded aboard a moving Quetta-bound train in the morning, killing three passengers, including two men and a woman, wounding several others, including women and children, and damaging five cars. Baluch separatists were suspected.

March 20, 2019: The Pakistani Taliban overran a remote security outpost in Ziarat district in Baluchistan Province in the morning, killing six members of the paramilitary forces. Tehreek-e-Taliban Pakistan said it was avenging the deaths of their comrades at the hands of the paramilitary Baluchistan Levies Force.

March 22, 2019: Karachi police chief Ameer Shaikh said four gunmen on two motorcycles fired more than a dozen shots at a convoy carrying prominent religious scholar Maulana Taqi Usmani and his associates in an eastern neighborhood of Karachi, killing the cleric's private guard and an official police escort and seriously wounding his driver. Usmani and his two grandsons who were in the convoy were unhurt. Usmani runs a religious seminary and preached tolerance. No group immediately claimed responsibility.

April 12, 2019: A suicide bomber hit an open-air market near the Shi'ite Hazarganji residential area in Quetta, killing 20 people and wounding 40 others, some critically. Four paramilitary troops who were guarding the fruit and vegetable market were wounded. Senior police chief Abdur Razzaq Cheema said, "It seems people from the (Shi'ite) Hazara community were the target," noting that eight Shi'ites died, along with a paramilitary soldier and seven other people. Sunnis were killed as well, according to Mir Ziaullah Langau, the provincial home minister. ISIS said that it targeted Shi'ites and elements of the Pakistani army.

April 16, 2019: Security forces raided a jihadi hideout in Peshawar, sparking an 18-hour shootout in which a police officer and all five suspected terrorists were killed. The suspects threw grenades, killing the officer. Security forces found explosives in the basement of the house, but no additional suspects. They had been living in the house for the past two weeks, plotting to target government and security forces.

April 18, 2019: Before dawn, dozens of gunmen clad in Pakistani police and paramilitary uniforms ambushed a bus traveling on the Makran coastal highway between Karachi and Gwadar, killing 14 people after examining their ID cards and forcing them out on a remote part of a coastal highway in Baluchistan Province. Hours later, the new Baloch Raji Aajoi Sangar separatist group claimed credit. Local official Jehangir Dashti could not confirm if all the victims were Punjabis. Ten Navy employees were killed, along with three from the Air Force and one from the Coast Guard. The Pakistani Foreign Ministry said the attackers had crossed the border from Iran earlier in the week and told the Iranian government that they were based in Iran's adjacent Baluchistan Province. Pakistan claimed the attackers fled back to Iran. 19041801

April 23, 2019: Gunmen killed a policeman assigned to escort polio workers in Bannu during a three-day nationwide campaign against the disease.

April 24, 2019: Gunmen killed a policeman escorting polio workers in Buner in Khyber Pakhtunkhwa Province.

April 25, 2019: Gunmen on motorcycles shot at female polio vaccination workers in Chaman in Baluchistan Province, killing one and wounding the other. The terrorists fled. On April 27, Pakistani health officials suspended the nationwide anti-polio campaign.

April 27, 2019: A bomb went off near a security checkpoint in North Waziristan, wounding a paramilitary soldier.

A bomb near the Afghan border killed three security personnel.

May 1, 2019: Dozens of gunmen who snuck into the country across the Afghan border fired on troops in North Waziristan. In the shootout, three soldiers were killed and seven were wounded. Scores of militants were killed or wounded, according to the military.

Pakistan's Foreign Ministry announced that the United Nations had added to a sanctions blacklist Masood Azhar, the leader of the outlawed Jaish-e-Mohammad, blamed by India for a February 14, 2019 suicide attack in Kashmir that killed 40 of its soldiers. The designation included a travel ban and freeze on Azhar's assets.

May 6, 2019: Gunmen conducted two attacks within hours of each other on security convoys in North Waziristan district, killing four soldiers and wounding 10 others. The attackers fled toward the Afghan border. No one claimed credit.

May 8, 2019: A suicide bomber attacked security forces guarding a famous Sufi shrine in Lahore, killing five police and five passers-by and wounding 20, some critically. Hundreds of pilgrims were in the area, where a local Sufi saint is buried. Hizbul Ahrar, a Pakistani Taliban splinter group, claimed credit, saying it was targeting police.

May 9, 2019: Gunmen fired on coal miners in Hernai in Baluchistan Province, killing two. The vehicle of paramilitary forces rushing to the scene rolled over a mine, killing three soldiers. No one claimed credit.

May 11, 2019: Three gunmen carrying rifles and grenades attacked the luxury five-star Pearl Continental Hotel in Gwadar in the afternoon in an attempt to take hostages, sparking an hours-long shootout in which naval special forces soldier Abbas Khan, a hotel security guard, three staff members, and all the attackers were killed. Six people, including two soldiers, were wounded. All guests were safely evacuated. After being stopped by a hotel guard, the terrorists ran up a staircase, firing at hotel workers. On the fourth floor, the terrorists deactivated hotel cameras and placed bombs at the entrances to the floor. Commandos opened special entry points onto the floor. The Baluch Liberation Army said its four fighters (later amended by the government to three) were involved and released pictures of the attackers. *NPR* quoted them as saying that they were targeting international investors and Chinese citizens. 19051101

May 15, 2019: A bomb attached to a motorcycle killed four police guarding a mosque in Quetta in Baluchistan Province. The Pakistani Taliban claimed credit.

May 16, 2019: Authorities raided a militant hideout in Mastung in Baluchistan Province, sparking a gun battle that killed nine terrorists and wounded four officers.

May 24, 2019: A remotely-detonated bomb containing 2.5 kilograms of explosives went off during Friday prayers at a mosque in the Pashtoonabad neighborhood of Quetta, capital of Baluchistan Province, killing two people, including the prayer leader, wounding 28 worshippers, breaking windows, and partially destroying the ceiling. It appeared that the prayer leader was the target. Pashtoonabad is a Sunni majority area and the mosque was attended by Sunni Muslims.

May 25, 2019: Police arrested six people for allegedly collecting funds for the banned Jaish-e-Mohammed and Lashkar-e-Jhangvi.

May 26, 2019: Supporters of a local, minority Pashtun group attacked the Khar Kamar security post in the country's northwest near the Afghan border, wounding five soldiers. Three attackers were killed and 10 were wounded. The group was led by lawmakers Ali Wazir and Mohsin Dawar, whose followers wanted to pressure authorities to release terror suspects arrested recently in North Waziristan. It said Wazir and eight others were arrested. Dawar countered that their convoy was attacked by security forces while traveling to a protest in North Waziristan against arresting innocent people. Troops later found five bullet-riddled bodies about a mile away from the Khar Kamar post; it was unclear who the victims were and who killed them. On May 30, authorities arrested Mohsin Dawar in a raid in North Waziristan.

During the night, gunmen attacked the Makki Garh security post in North Waziristan near the Afghan border, killing a soldier and wounding five soldiers.

Authorities arrested three suspected militants in two raids in Punjab Province, foiling possible attacks. In a raid in Dera Ghazi Khan district, authorities arrested a man suspected of links to ISIS and seized grenades and "funds for terrorism financing". In the second raid, authorities arrested two Sunni Lashkar-e-Jhangvi members for planning to target minority Shi'ites.

May 29, 2019: Sarfraz Ahmad, an official at the counter-terrorism department, said authorities arrested six men accused of raising funds for an outlawed Pakistan-based Jaish-e-Mohammed group that claimed responsibility for the suicide bombing that killed 40 Indian troops in Kashmir on February 14, 2019. The six appeared before a judge in Gujranwala who ordered them held for two weeks for questioning.

May 31, 2019: A court sentenced three local Jaish-e-Mohammed leaders to five years in prison after finding them guilty of collecting funds for the outlawed group that claimed responsibility for the suicide bombing that killed 40 Indian troops in Kashmir on February 14, 2019. Three men began serving their sentences.

June 1, 2019: Terrorists with guns and bombs attacked a military vehicle on patrol in the Boya area of North Waziristan district, killing a soldier.

June 6, 2019: Gunmen fired on a paramilitary vehicle patrolling in Hernai in Baluchistan Province, killing two troops before escaping. No one claimed credit.

June 7, 2019: Two bombs went off hours apart, hitting vehicles carrying minority Shi'ite tourists in Ziarat, killing five people and wounding several others. Police officer Noor Ahmed said a bomb went off in a car, killing three Shi'ites from Karachi. A second bomb killed two Shi'ites from Quetta. Both groups were in Ziarat to celebrate the Muslim holiday Eid al-Fitr, which marks the end of Ramadan. No group claimed credit; Sunni extremists were suspected.

A roadside bomb hit a security vehicle in North Waziristan, killing three army officers and an enlisted soldier and wounding four soldiers. The dead included Lt. Col. Karim Baig, Major Moeez Maqsood and Captain Arif Ullah, who were traveling in the area of Kharkamar. Two lawmakers led a mob attack on a military post to get the suspects released, sparking a shootout that wounded five soldiers and killed several assailants.

Local police officer Tariq Mahmood said that a vehicle carrying three suspected militants fell into the Jehlum canal in Punjab Province, killing all of them. Police had asked them to halt but the suspects sped away. Their car fell into the canal when officers were chasing it. Police found explosives and weapons in the car.

June 17, 2019: During the night, gunmen killed Mohammad Bilal Khan, a freelance journalist/activist known for his online criticism of the country's military and politicians, in a wooded area of Islamabad. Police said that someone called Khan to come to the Karachi Company neighborhood, where he and his cousin were attacked with daggers. The cousin was critically injured. Hours earlier, Khan had criticized the newly appointed intelligence director Lt. Gen. Faiz Hameed, who had previously led internal security at Inter-Services Intelligence. The next day, army spokesman Major General Asif Ghafoor condemned "ill-intended propaganda to implicate state agencies" and said that state security forces were not responsible.

June 26, 2019: The Pakistan Taliban attacked a police station in Loralai in Baluchistan Province. The gun battle killed a policeman and all three terrorists and wounded a policeman. District police chief Jawad Tariq said that two suicide bombers detonated their explosive vests while the third was killed by police officers.

June 30, 2019: The provincial Counter-Terrorism Department raided a Pakistani Taliban hideout, triggering a shootout that killed three gunmen in Gujrat. The gunmen had gathered near a key road in Gujrat to plan attacks on security forces. Authorities linked them to the 2007 bomb attack on a Pakistan Air Force bus in which several people were killed.

July 2, 2019: The U.S. Department of State declared the separatist Baluchistan Liberation Army a terrorist group and would seek to deny it resources for planning and carrying out attacks.

July 3, 2019: An explosion killed five soldiers and wounded one near the border with India in Kashmir.

July 5, 2019: Officer Ilyas Khan of the provincial Counter-Terrorism Department announced the arrest of Ali Nawaz, who was funding al-Qaeda terrorists using multiple bank accounts linked with the NGO Human Concern International. Counterterrorism forces in Peshawar raided the NGO offices, arresting regional director Nawaz and three others.

July 11, 2019: Radical Pakistani cleric Maulana Sufi Mohammad, 94, died in Peshawar. He had traveled to Afghanistan to fight international forces after the 2001 U.S.-led invasion. Pakistan arrested the cleric upon his return from Afghanistan in 2009 and sentenced him on multiple charges. He was released in 2018 for health reasons. He was the father-in-law of Mullah Fazlullah, a Pakistani Taliban leader who was killed in a U.S. drone strike in Afghanistan in 2018.

July 17, 2019: Authorities arrested Hafiz Saeed, leader of Lashkar-e-Taiba and accused mastermind of the four days of November 2008 terrorist attacks in Mumbai that killed 160 people. Counterterrorism officials arrested Saeed as he was traveling from Lahore to Gujranwala to post pre-arrest bail in connection with terrorism charges. In 2014, the United States offered $10 million for evidence leading to Saeed's arrest. The arrest came days before Pakistani Prime

Minister Imran Khan's first official visit to the United States to meet with President Trump. Saeed's spokesman, Nadim Awan, said the arrest would be challenged in a higher court. Saeed was charged with financing terrorist organizations and using charitable donations for his own personal enrichment.

July 21, 2019: Gunmen on motorcycles shot at police in a residential area of Dera Ismail Khan, killing two. A female suicide bomber set off 15 pounds of explosives packed with nails and ball bearings outside a hospital as wounded were being brought in from the attack, killing four people and three civilians who were visiting their relatives. Eight police were among the wounded; many were in critical condition. The explosion shut down the damaged emergency room. The Pakistani Taliban attacks killed nine people and wounded 30. Police arrested 16 suspects who belonged to banned organizations. Authorities seized weapons.

July 22, 2019: Provincial home minister Mir Ziaullah Longove said that a bomb exploded in a market in the Quetta suburbs, killing two people and wounding 29, calling it an "act of terrorism" by the "enemies of Pakistan". No one claimed credit.

July 27, 2019: The Pakistani Taliban fired from across the Afghan border at a military patrol near a security post in the Gurbaz area of North Waziristan, killing six soldiers. The Pakistani Taliban claimed credit for an attack in South Waziristan. 19072701

Gunmen killed four members of the paramilitary Frontier Corps on a search operation near Turbat in Baluchistan Province. No one claimed credit.

CNN added that the victims were Captain Aaqib, Havaldar Khalid and Sepoys Hafeezullah, Naveed, Bachal, Babar, Ehsan, Ali Raza, Nadir and Atif Altaf.

July 30, 2019: A roadside bomb hit a security vehicle in Quetta, killing four people and wounding 26. No one claimed credit.

August 16, 2019: A bomb was remotely detonated during Friday prayers inside a mosque in the Quetta suburbs, killing four worshippers, including the prayer leader, Maulvi Ahmadullah, and wounding 20. No one claimed credit. Unconfirmed reports said Ahmadullah was a relative or friend of Taliban leader Maulvi Hibatullah Akhunzada. The Taliban said Akhunzada had earlier lived in Kuchlak.

Gunmen shot to death mosque prayer leader Mohammad Azam in front of a Quetta grocery store. No group claimed credit.

Gunmen killed Mir Amanullah Zehri, a tribal elder and senior politician from a Baluch nationalist party, Zehri's grandson, and his two bodyguards as they were traveling together in a vehicle in Khuzdar district. The district administrator blamed a tribal dispute.

August 17, 2019: In the afternoon, a roadside bomb hit a security forces vehicle patrolling in the Ladha area of South Waziristan, killing two army soldiers. No one claimed credit. The Pakistan Taliban was suspected.

August 18, 2019: The Pakistani Taliban remotely detonated a bomb planted in the vehicle of a pro-government tribal elder, killing him and four others and wounding six who were traveling in the Upper Dir district of Khyber Pakhtunkhwa Province.

August 23, 2019: Al-Qaeda alleged "treacherous Pakistani forces" detained the wife of Ayman al-Zawahiri and two other families of the insurgent group's "martyrs" for nearly a year after capturing them as they left Waziristan during continuous airstrikes, adding, "We ... hold Pakistan's government and its treacherous army and their American masters responsible for their criminal acts."

August 23-24, 2019: Around midnight, eight Pakistani Taliban motorcyclists attacked a security post in the Daraban Kalan area, killing two employees at a nearby gas station and wounding two people in a bus getting gas.

September 4, 2019: Security forces raided a terrorist hideout in the Quetta suburbs, killing the six suspects, including a woman. Five police officers were wounded.

September 5, 2019: Two bombs exploded minutes apart near a police vehicle at a bus terminal in Quetta, killing a passer-by and wounding 10 others. City police chief Abdur Razzaq Cheema said a person was killed and two others were wounded in the first bombing. The second bomb wounded eight people, including policemen and a local TV journalist. No one claimed credit. The bombings came less than a week before Ashoura, the holiest day on the Shi'ite calendar.

September 13, 2019: During the night, gunmen ambushed a security patrol in North Waziristan, killing a soldier. Troops fired back, killing two terrorists.

September 14, 2019: Gunmen killed three Pakistani troops and critically wounded one in an attack on soldiers who were building a fence in the Dir area along the Afghan border.

September 20, 2019: An Army vehicle hit a roadside bomb near the Afghan border, killing two soldiers who were overseeing border fence work in Khyber Pakhtunkhwa Province. The armed forces said the bomb was planted by militants coming from Afghanistan's side of the border. No group claimed credit.

November 10, 2019: Police spokesman Kaleem Qureshi said that in the evening, gunmen ambushed a security force vehicle in Punjab Province, killing two police officers and two intelligence officers en route to raid a militant hideout in the Arbi Tabba area of Rajanpur district. No one immediately claimed credit.

November 12, 2019: A roadside bomb hit a military patrol vehicle in North Waziristan, killing three soldiers and wounding another. No one claimed credit.

November 14, 2019: Police chief Zahur Babar Afridi said gunmen fired on a police vehicle in Peshawar's suburbs, killing senior counter-terrorism officer and deputy superintendent of police Ghani Khan and wounding his driver and a passer-by before escaping. No one claimed credit.

Security officials arrested two suspected male ISIS members in their hideout in Bahawalnagar in Punjab Province and seized bombmaking equipment.

November 15, 2019: Zia Lango, home minister for Baluchistan Province, said that a remote-controlled bomb placed in a motorcycle parked in Kuchlak, a Quetta suburb, hit a Frontier Corps vehicle, killing three paramilitary troops and wounding five overnight. No one claimed responsibility.

December 5, 2019: Soldiers raided a militant hideout near Boya in the North Waziristan district bordering Afghanistan, sparking a shootout that killed two soldiers and two militants.

December 7, 2019: An evening explosion near where a religious congregation in Lahore was gathered to pray near a mosque said to be run by supporters of the banned group Jamaat-ud-Dawa killed one and wounded four, one critically. Officer Zulfiqar Hameed said the blast could have come from a burst air compressor at an air conditioner repair shop nearby.

December 11, 2019: A court in Lahore indicted radical cleric Hafiz Saeed, wanted by Washington for his role in the 2008 Mumbai attacks that killed 166 people, and four of his associates, on terror financing charges. They pleaded not guilty. Saeed founded the outlawed Lashkar-e-Taiba group. His charity organizations, Jamaat-ud-Dawa and Falah-e-Insaniat, are alleged fronts for Lashkar-e-Taiba. Pakistan arrested Saeed in July 2019.

December 18, 2019: Gunmen shot at policemen on foot patrol en route to Lower Dir in Khyber Pakhtunkhwa Province, killing two of them. The police were to escort a team of medics going house-to-house to vaccinate children in an anti-polio drive in the northwest. The terrorists fled. No one claimed credit.

PHILIPPINES

January 27, 2019: *AP* and *CNN* reported that a bomb exploded at 8:15 a.m. before Mass at the Roman Catholic Cathedral of Our Lady of Mount Carmel on Jolo Island in Sulu Province in Mindanao region. A second bomb went off minutes later as soldiers responded to the attack. Some 27 people, including five soldiers, were killed and 111, including 14 Armed Forces of the Philippines soldiers and two Philippine National Police officers, were wounded. On January 21, a referendum involving 2.8 million people in five provinces had passed the Bangsamoro Organic Law peace agreement, although the town of Jolo rejected it. Defense Secretary Delfin Lorenzana blamed Abu Sayyaf commander Hatib Sawadjaan, who he said has pledged allegiance to ISIS. The Islamic State claimed responsibility, saying two suicide bombers wore explosive belts, one detonating at the gate and the other in the parking lot.

AP reported on February 4, 2019 that five suspected Abu Sayyaf members accused of involvement in the bombing surrendered to authorities. Complaints for murder and attempted murder were filed against the five, as well as several other suspected Abu Sayyaf fighters who remained at large. Police Director-General Oscar Albayalde said that before the bombing, the suspects taken into custody had escorted the two Indonesians thought to have carried out the suicide attack around Jolo and to a meeting with Hatib Hajan Sawadjaan, who was accused of plotting and funding the attack. Police claimed the five suspects were led by Kammah Pae, a suspected local militant who denied involvement.

On July 23, 2019, *AP* reported Indonesia's National Police spokesman Dedi Prasetyo said that Indonesian police believed that an Indonesian couple carried out the suicide bombing. He added that a jihadi arrested in East Kalimantan in June had confessed that he'd recruited Rullie Rian Zeke and his wife, Ulfah Handayani Saleh, for the Philippine bombing. Prasetyo said the bombers were part of an Indonesian group linked to ISIS.

January 30, 2019: In the morning, a terrorist threw a grenade into a mosque in Zamboanga where Muslim teachers were sleeping, killing two of them and injuring four. The victims were from Basilan and nearby provinces and planned to teach Islam to children.

February 2, 2019: Regional military spokesman Colonel Gerry Besana said troops battled 150 Abu Sayyaf jihadis for two hours in the jungles off Patikul in Sulu Province. The *New York Times*

reported that five soldiers and three terrorists were killed and five soldiers and 15 gunmen were wounded. Besana said the gunmen were led by Abu Sayyaf commander Hatib Hajan Sawadjaan, who was suspected of plotting the bombing of a cathedral in Jolo on January 27.

February 7, 2019: Interior Secretary Eduardo Ano said that Abu Sayyaf commander Hatib Hajan Sawadjaan could be harboring a foreign Arab would-be suicide bomber in his jungle base.

March 11, 2019: Soldiers battled more than 20 Muslim gunmen near Pagayawan in Lanao del Sur Province. Fighting killed two soldiers and two terrorists.

March 11-12, 2019: Philippine troops, assisted by airstrikes and artillery fire, killed several gunmen linked to the Islamic State. Army Major General Cirilito Sobejana said several key commanders, including Muhamad Ali Abdul Rahiman, alias Muawiya, a long-wanted Singaporean; local commander Esmael Abdulmalik, alias Abu Toraype; and bomb-maker Salahudin Hassan were among the more than 100 gunmen who came under attack at daybreak in the hilly hinterland near Shariff Saydona Mustapha in Maguindanao Province. One soldier was killed and seven others were wounded. The gunmen belonged to the Bangsamoro Islamic Freedom Fighters and the Dawla Islamiya, two small groups aligned with the Islamic State group. Authorities found six bodies of gunmen at the scene. Sobejana suggested that 20 terrorists were killed by the airstrikes and artillery fire.

March 14, 2019: On April 14, 2019, *AP* reported that Philippine Interior Secretary Eduardo Ano announced that U.S. DNA tests confirmed the death of jihadi leader Owaida Marohombsar, variant Benito Marohombsar, alias Abu Dar, who helped lead the May 23, 2017 five-month siege of Marawi and helped the Islamic State group gain a foothold in the region. Abu Dar was one of four terrorists killed in a March 14, 2019 clash that also left four soldiers dead near Tubaran in Lanao del Sur Province. Regional official Zia Adiong that Marohombsar escaped from Marawi with at least 30 million pesos ($566,000) in stolen money. A Philippine police profile indicated that Marohombsar underwent military and explosives training in Afghanistan in 2005 and returned to the south a few years later and established the armed group Khilafa Islamiyyah Mindanao. KIM was implicated in the 2013 bombing of a bar in a shopping mall in Cagayan de Oro that left several people dead and wounded. The *Guardian* reported that Abu Dar was the last surviving member of the Maute Group.

March 28, 2019: *AP* reported on April 1, 2019 that national police chief General Oscar Albayalde announced the March 28 arrest by police, backed by army troops, of two jihadis. Police seized four pistols, two homemade bombs and two ISIS-style black flags from each of the houses of the two detainees in Baggao in Cagayan Province at the northern tip of Luzon island, a northern Philippine province far from the traditional southern territory of jihadis. Altero Bello and Greg Bello belonged to the IS-aligned jihadist Syuful Khilafa Fi Luzon, which was established in 2016. Albayalde said, "In our view, these groups only want to be known and so far they have not carried out any hostilities or atrocities in that region… When we monitor something like this, the police do preventive measures with the military."

April 3, 2019: Regional army commander Major General Cirilito Sobejana said a bomb exploded outside a restaurant in Isulan in Sultan Kudarat Province, injuring 18 people. They suspected the attack was either an extortion attempt or retaliation for battle losses by jihadis in the south. Unidentified people had previously tried to extort money from the restaurant owner, who refused to pay. The attack may also have been carried out by Bangsamoro Freedom Fighters who have been targeted by military offensives.

April 11, 2019: The army's Western Mindanao Command announced that it had killed twelve Abu Sayyaf gunmen in four clashes with 120 jihadis led by Hajan Sawadjaan and Radullan Sahiron near the village of Panglayahan in Patikul in Sulu Province after the terrorists were blamed for the deadly bombing of a Roman Catholic cathedral. Several army scout rangers were wounded.

April 16, 2019: Police in Zamboanga city arrested four wives of Abu Sayyaf commanders who took care of their financial transactions, helped procure guns and bomb parts and arranged the travels of foreign fighters to the country. Authorities seized two grenades, a bag of suspected ammonium nitrate and electrical parts that can be used in making bombs. The women worked under Abu Sayyaf leader Hajan Sawadjaan.

June 28, 2019: Regional military commander Major General Cirilito Sobejana said Abu Sayyaf gunmen were suspected in a noontime attack on the headquarters of an army brigade combat team in Indanan on Jolo island in Sulu Province that killed three soldiers and two civilians and wounded 22 civilians and soldiers. Army spokesman Lt. Col. Ramon Zagala said that an explosion went off at a checkpoint in front of the army camp, where fresh troops had arrived. An earlier report blamed two suicide bombers, saying troops stopped one terrorist, who set off his bomb while the second terrorist ran into the camp, yelled "Allahu akbar" and detonated an explosive near a parking lot. The next day, Interior Secretary Eduardo Ano said intelligence indicated that AS leader Hajan Sawadjaan most likely harbored the two suicide bombers and plotted the attack. The Islamic State said that two of its fighters carried out the attack with explosive belts but overstated the military casualties at about 100. It posted a picture of the two young terrorists before the attack, wearing what appeared to be explosive vests and standing beside a black IS-style flag. On July 2, Sobejana said that the first known Filipino suicide bomber was Norman Lasuca, 23. Lasuca left his family in Sulu's Asturias district five years earlier and joined an AS faction led by Sawadjaan. The second bomber had Caucasian features and was suspected to be the son of a foreign jihadist of Moroccan descent who died in a suicide bombing attack on Basilan island in 2018. Interior Secretary Eduardo Ano suggested that the other suicide attacker could be a Filipino terrorist from Sulu.

July 2019: The *New York Times* reported on March 22, 2020 that authorities in the Philippines arrested Cholo Abdi Abdullah, an al-Shabaab operative from Kenya studying to be a pilot at a local aviation academy. He was accused of conducting research on "aviation threats, aircraft hijacking and falsifying travel documents".

September 8, 2019: A suicide bomber wearing an abbaya attacked a military detachment in Indanan in Sulu Province, damaging the facility's gate but failing to hurt anyone else. Military spokesman Lt. Col. Gerard Monfort said, "A wary soldier yelled at the militant, 'Don't enter, go away, go away' and other soldiers who heard him took cover and assumed combat positions. Then an explosion killed the militant." Regional military chief Lt. Gen. Cirilito Sobejana said "The suicide bomber was ... foreign looking with long hair based on the recovered mutilated head, however, the recovered dismembered hand is similar to that of a man." The Islamic State and Abu Sayyaf were suspected.

September 23, 2019: In the evening, authorities arrested Hassan Akgun, a suspected Swedish militant of Turkish descent, with two local Muslim militant women—Norshiya Camsa and Normhiya Camsa—in Bagumbayan in Sultan Kudarat Province. They were linked to bombings. Troops seized firearms, explosives and an ISIS-style flag. Regional military commander Lt. Gen. Cirilito Sobejana said Akgun was a member of an ISIS-linked organization in Sweden and has been linked to a bombing in August 2018 in Sultan Kudarat's capital town of Isulan. The women were linked to a bombing in Isulan in September 2019 that wounded eight people.

October 4, 2019: During the night, six gunmen armed with pistols kidnapped British businessman Allan Arthur Hyrons, 70, and his Filipino wife, Welma Paglinawan-Hyrons, from a hut at their southern Philippine beach resort within sight of several young men in a nearby bar and dragged them across the beach to two motorboats in Tukuran in Zamboanga del Sur Province. The couple own the resort and two schools. No one initially claimed credit. Abu Sayyaf (Bearers of the Sword) was suspected. The *New York Times* reported that regional police Major Helen Galvez said that a day earlier, two suspects checked into the resort and apparently surveilled the couple. Members of the former Moro Islamic Liberation Front assisted police in the search for the couple. *AP* reported on November 25, 2019 that troops from Armed Forces of the Philippines, Task Force Sulu, following a 10-minute gun battle with IS-affiliated Abu Sayyaf terrorists, freed the hostages from jungle hideouts in the mountainous hinterlands off Parang in Sulu Province. The *New York Times* reported that the kidnappers had abandoned their hostages during the fighting in which five terrorists were killed. The hostages were unhurt. No ransom was paid.

AFP reported on November 26 that the couple told the media that they had been chained and threatened with beheading. She said, "They chained our legs... It was very difficult, but we endured because we believe in God... One of them treated us well, but then he told me he would be the one assigned to cut off my head if the money does not arrive on time... We tried to scream but no one comes because they have the guns." 19100401

November 22, 2019: Joint Task Force Sulu announced that in the morning, troops near the mountain village of Tanum in the jungles off Patikul town in Sulu Province killed "high value" terrorist Talha Jumsah, alias Abu Talha, who was a key link between ISIS and local jihadis and helped orchestrate a series of deadly suicide attacks in the south. The Arabic-speaking member of Abu Sayyaf served as a bomb-making instructor and arranging the transfer of foreign funds and movement of foreign terrorists for the suicide attacks. He and Sawadjaan, who remained at large, were blamed for plotting the January 27 suicide bombing by a suspected Indonesian militant couple at Our Lady of Mount Carmel Cathedral in Sulu's main island of Jolo that killed 23 people, including the bombers, and wounded scores of other churchgoers and soldiers.

November 24, 2019: Troops killed five Abu Sayyaf terrorists, including two commanders, in a clash in Sulu. One of the slain commanders, Sibih Pish, had been blamed for past ransom kidnappings.

November 26, 2019: Army troops and police arrested Maoist guerrilla leader and spokesman Jaime Padilla, alias Ka Diego, and three men guarding him in a room at Manila's Cardinal Santos Medical Center in the upscale residential and shopping Greenhills district. He was being secretly treated for hypertension. President Rodrigo Duterte earlier visited the hospital for medical tests. Padilla is in his 60s and wears a Maoist rebel cap.

December 22, 2019: *AFP* reported that bombs went off during the night, wounding 17 people, including soldiers. A terrorist threw a hand grenade into a military truck in Cotabato on Mindanao island, injuring eight soldiers and four civilians. A bomb exploded in Libungan, wounding five civilians, one seriously. Another bomb went off in Maguindanao. No one claimed credit.

South Korea

July 19, 2019: A South Korean man named Kim, 78, died after setting himself on fire inside his car parked in front of the Japanese Embassy in Seoul. Police said he told an acquaintance that he would set himself on fire due to his hatred of Japan.

Sri Lanka

February 27, 2019: Acting Colombo Magistrate Jayantha Dias Nanayakkara ordered the release of Indian citizen Mersalin Thomas, who was arrested in September 2018 for an alleged plot to kill Sri Lanka's President Maithripala Sirisena after police cleared him of wrongdoing. The court remanded him for violating Sri Lanka's immigration law for overstaying without a valid visa. Police arrested Thomas at the house of Namal Kumara, a police informant and self-described Sri Lankan anti-corruption activist. Kumara said he had a taped conversation with Nalaka de Silva, head of the terrorism investigation department, describing a plan for a hired killer to assassinate Sirisena. Silva was also arrested. Sirisena fired the entire cabinet, including Prime Minister Ranil Wickremesinghe, in October 2018, saying that a Cabinet minister was involved in the plot and blaming Wickremesinghe's government for moving slowly to investigate. Sirisena appointed former president Mahinda Rajapaksato to replace Wickremesinghe.

April 21, 2019: *NPR, AP, CNN,* and the *Washington Post* reported that on Easter Sunday, bombs went off at Christian churches and five-star hotels, killing 359, including 39 foreigners (according to Tourism Minister John Amaratunga; 31 according to the Foreign Ministry) and 39 tourists, and wounding 560, including 28 foreigners who were hospitalized. The government lowered the official death toll to 253 on April 25. Several Americans were injured. Three children were in intensive care. The churches were packed with worshippers. *AP* later reported nine explosions. Sri Lankan Prime Minister Ranil Wickremasinghe told reporters that elements of the government had prior intelligence about jihadi plans for attacks, but did not act on it.

The government initially blamed a local Muslim militant group, National Thowheed Jamaath (National Monotheism Organization), later saying that two terrorist groups had sent seven suicide bombers.

Some 66 people were killed in Colombo; 104 in Negombo; and 28 in Batticaloa.

Islamic State supporters said the attacks avenged strikes on mosques and Muslims.

The explosions occurred at 8:45 a.m. and 9:30 a.m. at three churches in Colombo, Negombo and Batticaloa and three hotels and a banquet hall in Colombo. Targets included

- St. Anthony's Shrine, Kochchikade Church, the largest Roman Catholic congregation in Colombo, was built in the 18th Century Dutch colonial period when priests held services in secret.

- St. Sebastian's Catholic Church in Negombo. The church is in the Gothic style, patterned on the Reims Cathedral in France. It was completed in the 1940s. Some 104 people died there. More than 1,000 were attending Mass, which was being celebrated by assistant priest Sanjeewa Appuhamy.

- Zion Church in Batticaloa, which was founded in the 1970s. A bomber initially targeted St. Mary's Cathedral, but left when he learned Mass was over. He moved on to Zion, carrying a backpack and another bag. He tried to enter the congregation area where 500 people were praying, but was stopped by suspicious priests. He set off his explosives in the courtyard, where some children were eating breakfast, killing 28 people.

- the Shangri-La Hotel in Colombo has 500 guest rooms and suites and 41 serviced apartments. Two suspects had checked into a room at the hotel earlier in the morning and gave a local address to hotel staff. Police visited the address, where other terrorists set off explosives.

- the Cinnamon Grand Colombo Hotel's Taprobane restaurant on the ground floor was the scene of the bombing. The hotel has 483 rooms and 18 suites.

- the Kingsbury Colombo Hotel has 229 rooms

- the New Tropical Inn

- *CNN* reported that a bomb went off at 2:45 p.m. in front of the Dehiwala Zoo in Dehiwala-Mount Lavinia, 20 minutes outside of the capital. The media later clarified that two explosions occurred later on Easter Sunday at a home under a flyover in the Demtagoda area of Colombo, killing three police officers—a sub-inspector and two constables—in a raid as they attempted to interrogate a suspect. Another constable was hospitalized.

- A bomb went off at a banquet hall around 2 p.m.

UNICEF said that 45 children were killed; 27 died and 10 were injured at St. Sebastian's Church; 13 died and 15 were injured in Batticaloa. Twenty children were hospitalized in Colombo. Five foreign children were victims.

The dead included

- Mathew, 8 months old. His nationality was unclear.

The vast majority of the dead were Sri Lankans, most of them Roman Catholics. Among them were

- Dileep Roshan, 37, a carpenter who left behind a wife and daughter.

- An entire family: Berlington Joseph Gomez, 33; his wife, Chandrika Arumugam, 31; and their three sons: Bevon, 9; Clavon, 6; and Avon, 11 months; at St. Anthony's Shrine.

- Ravi Fernando died at St. Anthony's Shrine, according to his wife, Delicia Fernando, 52, who was sitting toward the front of the sanctuary.

- Sister Ramoshini Fernando, a Catholic nun, said that several of her friends and parishioners died in St Anthony's Shrine. Her father sustained shrapnel wounds.

- celebrity chef Shantha Mayadunne and her daughter, according to Sri Lankan news outlet *Hiru News*. The women and their family were eating Easter breakfast at the Shangri-La Hotel. She was the first chef to have a live TC cooking show in Sri Lanka, according to *ABC Australia*. She published two books, taught cooking classes and workshops, and ran the Shantha Mayadunne School of Cooking Art, according to *Gulf News*.

- Sneha Savindi, 12, who died at St. Sebastian's. Her uncle, Duminda, said her body was so mangled by shrapnel that the family could identify her only by a birthmark on her foot.

- Anusha Kumari, 43, lost her husband, daughter, son, sister-in-law and two nieces in Negombo. She was injured with shrapnel in her face, but was able to leave the hospital for the funerals.

- Reverend Niroshan Perera lost 16 relatives and friends. He grew up with Kumari's husband, Dulip Appuhami, and his siblings.

- Kumari's brother-in-law, Jude Prasad Appuhami, said he was not in St. Sebastian's church with his 15 relatives because he had to drive a vehicle carrying a statue of Christ for a parade after Mass. He heard the explosion from the parking lot. One of his sisters-in-law, who survived, shouted for him to help their niece, whom he picked up and rushed to the hospital, only to find that she was dead. Appuhami's wife and a daughter, 10, sitting in an alcove to the left of the altar, had minor injuries. His daughter, Rusiri, 17, who was sitting at the front of the church because she was going to do a reading from Scripture, sustained nerve damage that makes eating painful.

- Prathap Kanagasabai, his wife Anistie Napoleon and two daughters, Andreena, 7, and Abriana, 1, died at St. Anthony's.

- Negombo resident Herman Peiris lost two sisters, Celine and Elizabeth, and two nieces, one of whom was about to get married. His sisters spent most of their time as involved members at St. Sebastian church.

- three Shangri-La employees

Eight British citizens, including

- two U.S.-UK dual nationals, Daniel, 19, and Amelie, 15, children of Matt Linsey, 61, a U.S. investment banker. Matt Linsey was scarred by the shrapnel from the bomb that went off near the elevators on the third floor of the Shangri-La Hotel. Their brother, David, 21, Ethan, 12, and mother stayed at home in London while the trio went on vacation in Colombo. Daniel volunteered to help orphans in Ethiopia.

- lawyer Anita Nicholson, son Alex, 14, and daughter Annabel, 11; the family was on holiday, according to Anita's husband, Ben, an attorney working in Singapore. They died at a table of the restaurant of the Shangri-La Hotel.

- retired Greater Manchester Borough Commander Billy Harrop, 56, and his wife, doctor Sally Bradley, according to the UK Fire Service. The *Manchester Evening News* reported that he had been cited for heroism during the IRA bombing of Manchester in 1996. It was believed he had recently retired to Australia.

- Lorraine Campbell, 55, from Manchester, lived in Dubai, worked in technology, and died in the Cinnamon Grand Hotel.

Four Americans, including:

- Dieter Kowalski, a Madison, Wisconsin native living in Colorado. He worked as a senior leader of the operation technical services group for educational publisher

Pearson and was on a business trip to meet with local engineers. He had arrived at the ground floor restaurant of the Cinnamon Grand Hotel for an Easter breakfast buffet.

- The German Foreign Ministry said that a German-American dual national was killed.

- Kieran Shafritz de Zoysa, a 5th grader, who had been on a year's leave from Washington, D.C.'s private Sidwell Friends School

Ten Indians, including five who had worked on India's recent general election, who were staying at the Shangri-La. Other Indians were injured. Among the dead were

- Lakshmana Gowda Ramesh

- K.M. Lakshminarayan

- K.G. Hanumantharayappa, a Janata Dal Secular party member

- M. Rangappa, a Janata Dal Secular party member

- Narayan Chandrashekhar

- A. Maregowda

- H. Puttaraju

Others:

- three Danish children of Anders Holch Povlsen, billionaire owner of the Bestseller clothing chain. Bestseller is the biggest shareholder in British fashion retailer Asos with a stake of over 26%. He also owns a 10% stake in German online retailer Zalando. Holch Povlsen and his wife, Anne, had four children, according to Danish media. He is worth $5.7 billion and is the 304th richest person in the world, according to *Forbes. CNN Business* reported that Bestseller had 2,700 stores in 70 countries and reported sales of €3.3 billion ($3.7 billion) in financial year 2018. The company has 17,000 employees; brands include Vero Moda and Jack&Jones. He owned a 50% stake in Bestseller Fashion Group China, an independent company with more than 7,000 stores in the country. He was a member of Zalando's supervisory board since 2013. The couple were among the biggest private landowners in Scotland.

- two Chinese cousins. The Chinese Foreign Ministry said that as of April 23, five other Chinese citizens were missing and five were injured, two severely.

- Turkish engineers Serhan Selcuk Narici and Yigit Ali Cavus

- a Spanish man and woman in their 30s from Pontecesures in northwest Spain, according to *Europa Press*

- two Australian members of the same family, Manik Suriaaratchi and her daughter Alexendria, 10, were killed in the St. Sebastian Catholic Church in Negombo and two other Australian women were injured by shrapnel. One suffered a broken leg. Manik's husband, Sudesh Kolonne, told Australian Broadcasting Corporation that he had walked out ahead of his family moments before the explosion. He saw his daughter dead on the floor. The family moved from Melbourne to Sri Lanka in 2014; his wife started a consultancy business. Alexendria studied at an international school in Colombo.

- Kaori Takahashi, a Sri Lankan resident and Japanese citizen who was at the Shangri-La's second floor restaurant eating breakfast with her family, according to *NHK World-Japan*

- a Dutch citizen

- Rui Lucas, a Portuguese man who worked for the sustainable energy company T&T

- a Saudi

- a person from France

- two Swiss nationals, one of whom also had the citizenship of another country, according to the Swiss Foreign Ministry, which added that a third member of the family, who had two non-Swiss citizenships, also was killed.

- Zayan Chowdhury, 8, a family member of several politicians in Bangladesh, including Prime Minister Sheikh Hasina. Zayan was Hasina's cousin's grandson. Zayan died while eating breakfast with his family in the Shangri-La Hotel. British Labour Member of Parliament Tulip Siddiq, Hasina's niece,

tweeted that one of her relatives was killed. One thousand Bangladeshis attended his memorial service.

As of April 23, another 14 foreign nationals were unaccounted for. Seventeen injured foreign nationals were being treated at the Colombo National Hospital and a private hospital in Colombo.

Authorities established a nationwide curfew and blocked *Facebook, Instagram, YouTube, Snapchat, Viber,* and *WhatsApp* to stop false and inflammatory messages. Schools were closed for two days.

Authorities arrested 40 suspects by April 23. On April 22, police arrested two men "behaving suspiciously" at a hotel in Dambulla. *CNN* reported that the U.S. believed that it had identified a key operative in the attacks, and that person had connections to international terrorists, including ISIS.

Defense Minister Ruwan Wijewardene blamed religious extremists. Sri Lankan military spokesman Brigadier General Sumith Atapattu said six suicide bombers were involved.

Police spokesman Ruwan Gunasekara said police found a safe house and conducted a controlled detonation of a van used by the terrorists near St. Anthony's Church in Colombo.

The Air Force defused a fix-foot-long pipe bomb containing 110 pounds of explosives near Colombo's Bandaranaike International Airport at 10:15 p.m.

Rightwing commentators in the UK, Germany, France, and the U.S., including Vice President Mike Pence, claimed that this was further evidence of an attack on Christianity throughout the world.

U.S. President Donald J. Trump inadvertently inflated the number of dead when he initially tweeted, "Heartfelt condolences from the people of the United States to the people of Sri Lanka on the horrible terrorist attacks on churches and hotels that have killed at least 138 million people and badly injured 600 more. We stand ready to help!" He later amended the figure to 138 killed.

Health Minister Rajitha Senaratne said that a foreign network was probably involved. "We do not believe these attacks were carried out by a group of people who were confined to this country. There was an international network without which these attacks could not have succeeded." He said intelligence agencies issued the warnings on April 4. A police warning on April 11 named several members including the group's alleged leader, Mohamed Zaharan. Mujibur Rahman, a member of Sri Lanka's Parliament who was briefed on the report, said it was based on input from Indian intelligence agencies. Strains between the Prime Minister and the President may have contributed to the intelligence not being shared.

A Sri Lankan security official said Thowheed Jamaath was a shell for the Islamic State and was active in Kattankudy, an area in the east. All of the bombers were Sri Lankans. *CNN* reported that a U.S. official said the attacks were inspired by ISIS.

On April 22, investigators found 87 detonators at a private terminal of the Central Bus Stand in Colombo.

The government announced that it would pay compensation of one million Rupees ($5,722) to each victim and $572 to defray funeral expenses. Cabinet spokesperson Rajitha Senaratne said that the government would pay from $570 to $1,718 to the injured. He added, "All damaged churches will be completely repaired by the government. After all as the government we will take the responsibly and we apologized for everyone."

The U.S. Department of State issued a travel advisory for Sri Lanka which read:

"Exercise increased caution in Sri Lanka due to terrorism.

"Terrorist groups continue plotting possible attacks in Sri Lanka. Terrorists may attack with little or no warning, targeting tourist locations, transportation hubs, markets/shopping malls, local government facilities, hotels, clubs, restaurants, places of worship, parks, major sporting and cultural events, educational institutions, airports, and other public areas.

"Read the Safety and Security section on the country information page. If you decide to travel to Sri Lanka:

- Be aware of your surroundings when traveling to tourist locations and crowded public venues.

- Follow the instructions of local authorities.

- Monitor local media for breaking events and adjust your plans based on new information.

- Enroll in the Smart Traveler Enrollment Program (STEP) to receive Alerts and make it easier to locate you in an emergency.

- Follow the Department of State on Facebook and Twitter.

- Review the Crime and Safety Report for Sri Lanka.

- US citizens who travel abroad should always have a contingency plan for emergency situations. Review the Traveler's Checklist."

NPR and *CNN* reported on April 23 that ISIS claimed credit. *Aamaq* said "The attackers who targeted citizens of the (anti-ISIS) coalition state members and Christians in Sri Lanka the day before yesterday were fighters of the Islamic State." ISIS released a photo of the supposed ringleader. *Aamaq* said an attacker clashed with police in Dematagoda.

State Minister of Defense Ruwan Wijewardene told Parliament that two local jihadi groups, National Thowheed Jamath and the Jammiyathul Millathu Ibrahim, were responsible, and were avenging the New Zealand attacks. The local groups might have had outside help from international terrorists. National Thowheed Jamath is a splinter group from the better-known Sri Lanka Thowheed Jamath, which in 2018 was linked to the defacement of Buddhist statues. The *Washington Post* reported that the Thowheed group has links to ISIS.

Sri Lanka state TV *SLRC* showed a video of a man walking around St. Sebastian's church and patting a child on the head before the bomb went off. The man was carrying a large backpack and walking across the church courtyard, then entering via a side door.

The *Washington Post* reported on April 23 that for the previous three years, Mohammed Zahran, alias Zahran Hashmi, apparent leader of the National Thowfeek Jamaath had posted videos calling for non-Muslims to be "eliminated". Warnings of jihadi radicalism extended back to 2007. His name was on an intelligence warning shared among Sri Lankan security forces. Some people were arrested at a large home in Colombo belonging to the family of Zahran, who was believed to have died at the Shangri-La attack.

On April 23, the Sri Lankan Prime Minister warned that other terrorists were "out there". Ranil Wickremesinghe acknowledged the prior warning, and said India's embassy was seen as a possible target. Other reports said politicians were in the terrorists' plans. He said a planned attack at a fourth hotel failed and that the leader of a local group blamed for the assault may have led the attacks and been killed. The warning issued on April 11 named six potential terrorists, including the group's leader. The text included, "Foreign intelligence has informed that Mohammed Cassim Mohamed Zaharan alias Zaharan Hashmi [sic] the leader of the National Thowheeth Jama'ath and his followers are planning suicide attacks in this country... The reports noted that these attacks could target Catholic churches and the Indian High Commission in Colombo." Authorities said Hashmi conducted the Shangri-La bombing.

On April 23, authorities reported three bomb scares, including one at the U.S. Embassy, within 24 hours. Police were searching for five bikes, a cab and a van suspected of carrying more explosives.

The *Long War Journal* reported on April 24 that the ISIS *Aamaq News Agency* released a photo showing the eight terrorists responsible. So far, ISIS had released three confessor statements and a video. The group claimed that 1,000 people were killed or injured, and that Christians, allegedly at war with ISIS, were the target. It provided several kunyas for the terrorists. The third statement showed a photo of the eight bombers standing in front of the ISIS flag. Seven were masked. The unmasked individual apparently was Zahran Hashim. A video showed the eight pledging allegiance to Abu Bakr al-Baghdadi.

The ISIS *al-Naba* newsletter's 174th edition called it "ignorant" to think that the "Islamic State waits for an attack like this on Muslim's mosques to incite its soldiers to kill *mushrikin* [polytheists]." ISIS's "jihad and fight against *mushrikin* is a duty even if they [Christians or polytheists] were weak and can't harm Muslims, as long as they lack faith and covenant... The war

waged by Crusader nations against Muslims did not start when one of their citizens attacked the mosques" in New Zealand. The jihad "is ongoing, hasn't stopped and will not stop", as both New Zealand and Australia are part of "the Crusader military coalition".

President Maithripala Sirisena demanded the resignations of Pujith Jayasundara, the country's police chief, and defense secretary Hemasiri Fernando, who is the top civil servant at the Defense Ministry. The president holds the title of defense minister. Fernando resigned over the failure to prevent the attacks.

By April 24, authorities were beginning to sort out identities of the nine suicide bombers. They included

- Mohammed Cassim Mohamed Zaharan, alias Zaharan Hashmi, leader of the National Thowheeth Jama'ath. He died at the Shangri-La. Authorities said he had issued a warning, and local Muslim leaders had warned of his intemperate jihadist rhetoric for three years. He was believed to be in his 40s. Junior defense minister Ruwan Wijewardene said the attackers had broken away from National Towheed Jamaat and "JMI".

- Inshan Seelavan, described as the "mastermind" who blew himself up at the Shangri-La. Reports differed as to whether he or Zaharan was the leader of the bombers.

- Abdul Lathief Jameel Mohamed, who studied in southeast England in 2006-2007, according to *Sky News*

- a married couple. A woman who was the wife of another bomber, two children and three policemen died in an explosion as authorities closed in on her.

- one terrorist had a law degree

- two brothers Imsath Ahmed Ibrahim and Ilham Ahmed Ibrahim, members of one of the wealthiest Muslim families in Colombo, with connections to the country's business and political elite, according to India's *Firstpost*. The brothers and a woman killed three police officers and herself when she detonated explosives as police closed in on a house in Colombo. Hilmy Ahamed, vice president of the Muslim Council of Sri Lanka, said their father, Mohamed Ibrahim, was a prominent member of the community. He called him "very rich" and added that his sons were "well educated overseas".

- *NPR* and *AP* reported on April 24 that the junior defense minister said that one of the bombers studied in Australia and the UK.

The others had similar demographic profiles, coming from well-off families and were "quite well-educated people". State Minister for Defense Ruwan Wijewardene said that the bombers used two safe houses in Colombo and Negombo.

By April 24, authorities had arrested 60 suspects, including Mohamed Ibrahim, a wealthy spice importer and founder of the Colombo-based Ishana Exports who owned the home in Colombo's Dematagoda neighborhood which police conducted a raid on Easter Sunday. Two of his sons were suicide bombers, and his daughter-in-law set off explosives when police officers came to the house. The next day, the prime minister said Ibrahim was known as "Ibrahim Hajiar", the Sri Lankan term for Muslims who have gone on religious pilgrimages to Mecca.

A senior intelligence official told *CNN* the NTJ was planning a second wave of attacks across the country. The group had, as of April 24, not claimed credit for the Easter Sunday bombings.

The U.S. Embassy announced that it was closed to the public through April 26. The Embassy issued a travel warning to avoid places of worship during the weekend. Archbishop of Colombo Cardinal Malcolm Ranjith said that there would be no Catholic Masses during the weekend. The UK, Germany and Australia issued travel advisories.

The police issued photos of three men and three women who were being sought for questioning.

Reuters reported on April 26 that Sri Lankan police were searching for 140 people believed to have ISIS connections. They had already detained 76 people, including some from Syria and Egypt. They kept the focus of the investigation on local jihadi groups National Thawheed Jama'ut and Jammiyathul Millathu Ibrahim. Police said they had arrested the deputy chief of NTJ.

Investigators established that the terrorists were trained by the "Army Mohideen", and that they were trained in weapons overseas and in Sri Lanka's Eastern Province. Police arrested the operator of a copper factory who had helped Mohideen make bombs and purchase empty cartridges sold by the Sri Lankan military as scrap copper.

The official @SriLankaPolice2 Twitter account was deleted after it misidentified U.S. human rights activist Amara Majeed as a suspected terrorist. Police apologized for the "inconvenience".

Forensic investigators said the recalculation of the number of individuals killed was probably due to original over counting. Numerous body fragments can easily be doublecounted.

On April 26, police tipped off soldiers regarding a safehouse. Troops conducted a gun battle with suspects linked to the attacks after attempting to raid a safehouse in the Sainda-Marudu area of Sammanthurai in Eastern Province. Three explosions went off in the Kalmunai area around 7:15 p.m. Sixteen civilians and six terrorists died. Police found 15 bodies, including six children, at the house. Police found the bodies of an adult woman and a man with their clothes burned off. A woman passing on a rickshaw was killed. Three people were wounded. A woman and a girl were critically injured. Two terrorists escaped; one wounded suspect fled on a motorbike. *CNN* and *AP* reported that troops seized bombmaking equipment, flags, ISIS uniforms, 150 sticks of Gelignite, 100,000 ball bearings, "suicide kits", and a drone camera in a garage a few miles from the shootout.

Police later said that a woman and child, 4, found wounded after the gunfight were the wife and daughter of Mohammed Zahran.

Among the six dead terrorists was Mohamed Niyas, a prominent member of the NTJ and the brother-in-law of Zahran Hashim. *Aamaq* claimed that three ISIS members killed in the battle were Abu Hammad, Abu Sufyan and Abu al-Qa'qa, saying "after exhausting their ammunition, detonated on them their explosive belts".

On April 27, the office of President Maithripala Sirisena said that the National Thawheed Jammath (NTJ) and Jamathei Millathu

Ibraheem (JMI) would be banned by presidential decree, allowing the government to confiscate their property.

On May 1, Sri Lankan authorities said that the terrorists included:

- Mohammed Azam Mohammed Mubarak, who set off the bomb at the Kingsbury Hotel

- Alauvdeen Ahmed Muwath, who bombed St. Anthony's Shrine in Colombo

- Achchi Mohamadhu Mohamadhu Hasthun, who hit St. Sebastian's Church in Negombo

- Inshaf Ibrahim, the son of a prosperous merchant who made his fortune trading spices like pepper and cinnamon, who bombed the Cinnamon Grand Hotel

- Ilham Ibrahim, who targeted the nearby Shangri-La Hotel

- Ilham's wife Fatima, who detonated a bomb at a safehouse, killing three police officers and several children

- Zahran Hashim, radical preacher from Kattankudy and mastermind of the attacks, who bombed the Shangri-La Hotel

- Mohamed Nazar Mohamed Azad, from Kattankudy, lived in a lane around the corner from where Hashim started preaching an extremist version of Islam under the banner of National Thowheed Jamaath.

- Abdul Latheet Jameel Mohammed, had traveled to Britain and Australia to pursue higher education. His original target may have been the luxury Taj Hotel, but he ultimately detonated a bomb outside a small hotel near the zoo in Colombo during the afternoon, killing two other people.

The *New York Times* reported on May 5, 2019 that Arhchi Mohamed Mohamadu Hassthun, who bombed St. Sebastian's Church, was the bomb maker. Investigators found bombmaking manuals on his computer, and that he might have trained in Turkey. He built 11 TATP bombs in a garage south of Colombo. Bomber Abdul Latheef Jamil had traveled to Syria, but might have been radicalized in Australia, where he studied aeronautical engineering.

AP reported on May 6, 2019 that acting police chief C.D. Wickramaratne announced that explosives the ISIS-linked group stacked for use in more attacks had been seized. Police found $140,000 in cash in bank accounts connected to the group and another $40 million worth of assets in land, houses, vehicles and jewelry.

Catholic schools remained closed until further notice after reports said two of their locations were to be attacked the previous weekend.

On June 14, 2019, police spokesman Ruwan Gunasekara said that five suspects in the bombings were extradited from Saudi Arabia after their arrests in an undisclosed Middle Eastern country. They included Hayathu Mohamed Ahmed Milhan, the main suspect in the 2018 murder of two policemen at a checkpoint in eastern Sri Lanka, in an attack blamed on jihadis. Gunasekara said 102 suspects were being held in connection with the Easter suicide bomb attacks.

On July 2, 2019, Police spokesman Ruwan Gunasekara announced the arrests of former Defense Secretary Hemasiri Fernando and police chief Pujith Jayasundara, currently on compulsory leave, for alleged negligence leading to the Easter Sunday bombings that killed more than 250 people at churches and hotels. The duo were arrested at hospitals where they had been admitted. Fernando resigned after the bombings. 19042101

April 22, 2019: Three bombs exploded in a van parked near a church that was bombed on Easter Sunday (April 21), causing no injuries. Police were trying to defuse the devices.

May 5, 2019: *Reuters* reported that police found a 10-acre camp in Kattankudy, where jihadis linked to the deadly Easter attacks practiced shooting and bombmaking. The walled terrain was in a poor residential area on the outskirts of the home town of Zahran Hashim. The compound featured a cinderblock four-storey watchtower, mango trees, a chicken coop and a goat shed. Police found bullet holes in the wall on one side of the grounds, and long tubes suspected of holding bombs. Police arrests two owners of the plot of land.

August 5, 2019: Police spokesman Ruwan Gunasekara announced the arrests in eastern Ampara district of three members of Jamathei Millathu Ibrahim, a banned Islamic organization linked to Easter Sunday suicide bomb attacks that killed more than 250 people and wounded more than 500. He believed they received training at two locations run by ringleader Mohamed Zahran, who blew himself up at a tourist hotel on April 21. Two domestic radical Islamic groups, National Thowheed Jammath and Jamathei Millathu Ibrahim, are accused of having pledged allegiance to ISIS and carried out the blasts.

November 16, 2019: Shots were fired at a convoy of Muslims heading to the northern district of Mannar to vote in the presidential elections. No injuries were reported.

November 25, 2019: A Swiss Embassy worker claimed she was forced into a car and threatened by her abductors to produce embassy information.

TAJIKISTAN

November 6, 2019: *Reuters* reported that 20 armed men wearing masks attacked an outpost on the Tajik-Uzbek border during the night. Tajikistan's National Security Committee said that the terrorists killed a border guard and a policeman before 15 of them were killed by return fire. Authorities captured the surviving five 30 miles southwest of Dushanbe.

THAILAND

January 8, 2019: A bomb went off outside a school and a car bomb went off elsewhere in Songkhla Province, wounding a student, 12, a security guard for teachers, and a police medic.

January 10, 2019: Police Lieutenant Colonel Wicha Nupannoi said that around noon, gunmen dressed like state security personnel approached armed paramilitary territorial defense volunteers guarding a school in Pattani Province and shot four of them to death. The attackers took four HK33 assault rifles before fleeing,

scattering nails and other material on the road to delay pursuers. Jihadis were suspected. Thai Defense Minister Prawit Wongsuwan blamed the Barisan Revolusi Nasional (BRN).

January 11, 2019: A Muslim imam was shot to death.

January 18, 2019: During the night, jihadis on motorcycles were suspected of attacking a Buddhist temple in Narathiwat Province, killing two monks, including the temple's abbot, and wounding two others in their quarters. The New York-based Human Rights Watch blamed the Barisan Revolusi Nasional (BRN), calling the temple attack a war crime.

Also in Narathiwat, a roadside bomb wounded five members of the security forces.

A shootout between paramilitary rangers and five gunmen in Narathiwat killed a gunman; the other four fled.

February 26, 2019: In the morning, a remotely-detonated explosive device killed a paramilitary ranger who was patrolling on foot and injured two others in Yala Province.

During the evening, four black-garbed gunmen kidnapped two police officers from a house in which they were socializing and stole two pistols, a rifle, and a pickup truck in Narathiwat Province, the latter of which they set alight. Their bodies, riddled with gunshots, were later found dead in a ditch. Possible motivations included a personal dispute and the ongoing Muslim separatist insurgency.

April 5, 2019: Police Colonel Pariwat Kwanmanij, chief of Than To police station in Yala Province, said four attackers snuck into a mosque and shot in the head two Border Patrol Police officers who were praying. The attackers escaped. Muslim separatists were suspected.

July 23, 2019: *AFP* reported that in a late-night attack, jihadis hit a military outpost in Pattani Province, throwing grenades and shooting for an hour. Colonel Thanawee Suwannarat said, "Four people were killed including an army sergeant-major, two defence volunteers and a villager." The gunmen stole five machine guns, burned tires and scattered spikes on the road. Two other people were critically wounded.

Four days earlier, rebel suspect Abdulloh Esormusor, 34, was left unconscious and unattended with brain swelling for several hours after being arrested under martial law and taken to the Inkayuth military camp in Pattani for interrogation. Sunai Phasuk of Human Rights Watch speculated that the rebels were retaliating for the treatment of Abdulloh.

August 2, 2019: Bombs went off in six locations in Bangkok, hospitalizing four, as Thailand was hosting a meeting of foreign ministers of the 10-member Association of Southeast Asian Nations (ASEAN) attended by U.S. Secretary of State Mike Pompeo and his counterparts from China and several Asia-Pacific countries. Two bombs hit stations of the capital's elevated Skytrain rail system; others hit a government complex in the suburbs, and near the offices of a company associated with supporters of Prime Minister Prayuth Chan-o-cha's new government.

Police found two fake bombs outside their headquarters in central Bangkok, near the venue of the ASEAN meeting. Police arrested two men hours later on a bus at a police checkpoint and were searching for another four. The duo were from Narathiwat Province. Authorities were in contact with a neighboring country where some of the bombers were believed to be hiding; the media suggested it was Malaysia.

AP reported on August 15 that the Bangkok Criminal Court extended the detention of the two suspects, Wildon Maha and Lu-ai Saengae, accused of planting two small bombs in front of police headquarters in Bangkok. They were charged with cooperating in criminal activity, possessing explosive devices, attempted manslaughter and handling explosive devices in public spaces.

November 5, 2019: *AP* reported that gunmen fired at security personnel at checkpoints in Yala Province, killing 15 Village Defense Volunteers officers and wounding five others during the night. Army spokesperson Col. Kiattisak Neewong suggested that some of the attackers were believed injured, based on blood-stained clothing at the scene. The gunmen stole several weapons from the checkpoints, including an M16 rifle and 3 shotguns. Four of the slain officers were women and one was a doctor. Pol. Col. Thaweesak Thongsongsi, a superintendent in a Yala police station, said nails had been scattered on a highway to disable vehicles entering Yala. A small explosive was found placed near an electrical pole. Several burning tires were left at a school. *Reuters* reported that Muslim separatists were suspected. No one immediately claimed credit. Authorities found bloodied gauze in the home of a local village doctor near the crime scene. An official said, "We suspect around 30 to 40 people were involved."

November 9, 2019: *AFP* reported that authorities arrested six individuals in Yala and Pattani Provinces suspected of involvement in rebel attacks in Narathiwat Province, including one on November 5 that killed 15 people, including Buddhists and Muslims. The suspects were held in the Inkayuth military camp in Pattani Province, the army's biggest detention center in the south.

AUSTRALIA/NEW ZEALAND/ PACIFIC

AUSTRALIA

January 7, 2019: The Argentinian consulate in Sydney was partially evacuated after reports of a suspicious substance. The powder, contained in clear plastic bags within an envelope, was determined to not be dangerous.

January 9, 2019: Seven consulates, including those of India, Germany, Italy, Spain and South Korea in Melbourne and Canberra were evacuated after they received packages containing suspicious substances. Diplomatic facilities of Israel, France, Pakistan, the U.S., UK, Denmark, Egypt, Japan, Pakistan, Thailand and Switzerland also received packages. No one was reported injured. A worker from the New Zealand consulate in Melbourne said the packages were envelopes labelled "asbestos". Suspicious packages were also believed to have been found at the Melbourne diplomatic offices of Greece and Hong Kong. Later that night, police arrested Savas Avan, 49, at his home in Shepparton, Victoria State, after 38 suspicious packages containing a possibly hazardous substance were sent to foreign consulates in Melbourne, Canberra and Sydney. The *Age* newspaper, *al-Jazeera* and *Reuters* reported that the Australian Federal Police said he was charged with sending dangerous articles through a postal service. He faced ten years in prison. Local media reported that the parcels appeared to contain plastic bags of concrete and asbestos, with "asbestos" written on at least one bag. A court hearing in Melbourne Magistrates Court was scheduled for March. 19010901-38

January 16, 2019: At 12:10 a.m., an attacker killed Aiia Maasarwe, 21, an Israeli female student who had been studying at La Trobe University in Melbourne, as she was walking on a city street speaking to her sister in Israel by cell phone via *FaceTime* shortly after she got off a tram in the suburb of Bundoora. She was on her way home from a comedy club. Her body was found at 7 a.m. near the tram stop. Police assumed the attack was random and opportunistic. Her bag was split open and some of its contents were removed. Police recovered a black baseball cap and a gray and black T-shirt that they suspected an assailant discarded after the attack. Her uncle, Abed Katane, told *Haaretz* that she had been studying at Shanghai University and had spent recent months in Melbourne on a study-abroad program. She was buried in her Arab home town of Baqa al-Ghabiyye, Israel on January 23.

On January 18, police in Greensborough arrested Codey Herrmann, 20, an aspiring rapper who performs as M.C. Codez. On January 19, he appeared in the Melbourne Magistrates Court accused of rape and murder. He did not apply for bail. A murder conviction carries a potential maximum penalty of life in prison; rape carries a potential maximum of 25 years.

April 16, 2019: Prime Minister Scott Morrison said Australia was working with the Red Cross to repatriate three children and two grandchildren of slain Sydney-born ISIS fighter Khaled Sharrouf from the al-Hawl camp in Syria. The Sydney grandmother of Sharrouf's children, Karen Nettleton, made three trips to the Middle East in bids to bring them back to Sydney.

The eldest of Sharrouf's three surviving children, Zaynab, 17, said she was pregnant and feared giving birth in a tent. Also in the tent was her sister, Hoda, 16, and brother, Humzeh, 8, plus her two children—Ayesha, 3, and Fatima, 2. In 2017, Sharrouf became the first dual national to be stripped of Australian citizenship for actions contrary to his allegiance to Australia. He left Australia in 2013 on his brother's passport because his own had been canceled due to a conviction for his part in a thwarted terrorist attack plot in Australia. He still had Lebanese citizenship. In 2014, he posted on social media a photograph of his young son brandishing the severed head of a Syrian soldier. Sharrouf's wife, Tara Nettleton, brought their five children from Sydney to Syria in 2014. She died in 2015 of a perforated intestine. Sharrouf and his two eldest sons—Abdullah, 12, and Zarqawi, 11—died in an August 2017 air strike near Raqqa, Syria.

On June 19, 2019, Australian National University counterterrorism researcher Jacinta Carroll said that Zaynab Sharrouf was an ISIS propagandist who could potentially face terrorism charges at home. Carroll said Zaynab became a prominent ISIS propagandist making social media posts supporting atrocities and the activities of her father and her husband Mohamed Elomar, an Australian ISIS fighter who was killed while she was pregnant in 2015.

May 1, 2019: A jury in the New South Wales State Supreme Court convicted Khaled Khayat, 51, of plotting to blow up an Etihad Airways airliner on a flight from Sydney to Abu Dhabi in the United Arab Emirates with a bomb hidden in a meat grinder. Khayat had pleaded not guilty to conspiring in early 2017 to plan a terrorist act. The jury continued deliberating on whether his brother, Mahmoud Khayat, 34, was guilty of the same charge. The plan called for setting off the bomb on a July 15, 2017 flight, but the terrorists scrapped the plan when a bag with the bomb inside was too heavy to be taken aboard as carry-on luggage. The brothers were arrested two weeks later. Khaled Khayat was scheduled for sentencing on July 16, 2019. He faced life in prison.

On May 11, 2019, *AP* reported that a Lebanese military court released on bail Amer Khayat, an Australian-Lebanese dual citizen on trial for an alleged plot to bring down an Etihad flight bound for Abu Dhabi from Sydney in 2017. He was detained in Lebanon in the summer of 2017. Two of his brothers were on trial in Australia for the plot. Mahmoud and Khaled Khayat were accused of planting the bomb, hidden inside a Barbie doll and meat grinder, in Amer's hand luggage. One of the brothers is believed to have earlier traveled to Syria to join ISIS. Australian authorities believed Amer Khayat was an unwitting participant. Lawyer Joceline Adib al-Rai said the military court ordered Amer Khayat's release on bail on May 10.

May 3, 2019: Victoria State Supreme Court Justice Michael Croucher ordered ISIS sympathizer and firebrand preacher Robert "Musa" Cerantonio, 34, to serve at least five years and three months in prison of a seven-year sentence before becoming eligible for parole for being the ringleader of a plot to take six extremists from Australia in a motor boat to the southern Philippines to overthrow the provincial government. Cerantonio had pleaded guilty to engaging in conduct in preparation for hostile activities in a foreign country. He and five other men planned in 2016 to take a 23-foot half-cabin fiberglass power boat off the northeast Queensland coast to encourage others to overthrow the government in the southern Philippines and install Sharia law. Their Australian passports had been canceled due to concerns they would become foreign fighters. They towed the boat with a car 1,900 miles from Melbourne to Laura before police arrested them in May 2016. The other five were earlier sentenced from three years and 10 months to four years in prison. Philippine authorities deported Cerantonio in 2014 because of his suspected links to militants based on *YouTube* videos showing him advocating jihad and urging local Muslims to support extremists in the Middle East. His defense attorney was Jarrod Williams.

July 2, 2019: Authorities arrested three men regarding an ISIS-inspired plot to attack targets in Sydney, including police and defense buildings, courts, churches and diplomatic missions. Australian Federal Police Assistant Commissioner Ian McCartney said that police had monitored for a year a suspect, 20, since he returned to Sydney from Lebanon, where he was known to police. McCartney said the suspect would be charged with preparing for a terrorist act and preparing to enter Afghanistan for the purpose of engaging in hostile activities on behalf of ISIS. The suspect was to go to Afghanistan to join in another plot. He faced life in prison on each charge. A second man, 23, was to be charged with being a member of ISIS and faced a 10 year sentence. A third man, 30, their associate, was to be charged with obtaining financial benefit by deception through fraudulently claiming unemployment benefits and faced a decade in prison. McCartney said that the men had not obtained guns or explosives.

August 13, 2019: Police suggested that a man, 21, with a history of mental illness killed a woman, 21, in a downtown Sydney 4th-floor apartment with a 12-inch butcher's knife before slashing in the back another woman, 41, nearby and trying to stab other people at 2 p.m. while yelling "Allahu akbar". He yelled to police that he wanted to be shot. He jumped onto the hood of a Mercedes Uber; the driver sped up and threw him off. One person was hospitalized. Bystanders grabbed the man before he was arrested. New South Wales state Police Commissioner Michael Fuller said the man had collected information on his computer about mass killings in North America and New Zealand, but "It is not currently classed as a terrorist incident… He is by definition, at the moment, a lone actor. Information was found on him that would suggest he has some ideologies in relation to terrorism, but he has no links to terrorism… There was certainly information found on him about other crimes of mass casualties and mass deaths around the world."

FEDERATED STATES OF MICRONESIA

October 14, 2019: An unknown gunman fired three shots at American attorney Rachelle Bergeron as she pulled up and opened the back of her Subaru hatchback at 7:15 p.m. on Yap island, killing her and her dog. Bergeron was hit in her upper leg and upper chest and was pronounced dead on arrival at Yap Memorial Hospital. She had planned to return to the U.S. soon after serving as acting attorney general of Yap State, a job that began in January 2019. She was part of a human trafficking task force. She was from Wisconsin and moved to Yap in 2015 to take a job as assistant attorney general. She earlier worked in Washington D.C., New York and India. Her husband is a pilot with Pacific Mission Aviation, a Christian missionary organization. The couple was about to celebrate their one-year wedding anniversary and hoped to start a family soon. On October 28, Yap Governor Henry S. Falan announced via the state's website that suspects had been arrested.

New Zealand

March 15, 2019: *Newsweek*, *NPR*, *AP*, and *CNN* reported that at 1:45 p.m., a terrorist wearing tactical gear and a camera fired hundreds of rounds for at least six minutes into two Christchurch mosques, killing 50 and hospitalizing 50, some 20 of whom were in critical condition. (The body of the 50th victim was found by police on March 16.) The congregants were kneeling for Friday midday prayers. *NPR* reported that the gunman was an Australian white nationalist, 28, who left behind a 74-page (other reports said 87-page) manifesto under his name, Brenton Harrison Tarrant, about white genocide and hating immigration. Police found two explosive devices, two semi-automatic weapons, two shotguns and a lever-action firearm in his Subaru Outback, which had a strobe light flashing. Police arrested three armed people, including a woman, charging Tarrant with murder. None of the individuals had criminal records in Australia or New Zealand, or were on security watch lists. Police later said the other two people were not involved, and that Tarrant acted alone. The woman was freed without charge. Another man was arrested on an unrelated firearms charge.

The first attack at the Al Noor Mosque on Deans Road, opposite a large downtown park, killed 41 people. Seven people died three miles away at the Linwood Islamic Center. The 49th person died in the hospital. Mosque member Abdul Aziz, 48, picked up a credit card machine, and ran outside screaming "Come here!" at the

terrorist. Aziz threw the machine, and later an empty gun, at the terrorist, who had returned with another gun, but thought better of it, and sped away in his car. Aziz's four sons were in the mosque. Aziz was originally from Kabul, Afghanistan. He lived as a refugee for more than 25 years in Australia before moving to New Zealand two years ago. He was lauded as a hero who saved lives.

Police crashed into Tarrant's van, then arrested him. It was not immediately clear if one terrorist conducted both attacks. Witnesses at Linwood said a caretaker jumped on the gunman and wrestled away his weapon, forcing him to flee.

The *New Zealand Herald* listed the victims' names on March 16, as did Christchurch's *The Press* on March 22. Those papers, plus *AP*, *CNN*, and a host of other news services provided information on the lives of the victims:

- Husna Ahmed, 44 or 45, had returned to the Masjid Al Noor to look for her husband, Farid, after she got some children to safety. She was killed after the couple split up to go to the restroom. Ahmed later saw the video of his wife being shot. She was from Bangladesh.

- Syed Areeb Ahmed, 26, recently arrived from Karachi, Pakistan to work as a chartered accountant on secondment at PriceWaterhouseCoopers. He was an only son. His cousin was Mohammed Bilal. An uncle, Muhammad Muzaffar Khan, said he prayed five times daily.

- Farhaj Ahsan, 30, moved from Hyderabad, India several years earlier. He earned a master's degree at Auckland University and worked as a software engineer. He left behind a 2-year-old and a 7-month old. His uncle was Idris Ansari.

- Ashraf Ali, 61, moved from Fiji 17 years earlier. He left behind a son and an elder brother, Shabeer Ali.

- Ashraf Ali, 58, ran a taxi company in Suva, Fiji. He visited New Zealand twice/year to visit family. He had arrived in Christchurch a week before dying at Al Noor. His brother, Ramzan, said Ali's wife died six months ago. His first wife, with whom Ali had a daughter, died four years ago. Ramzan hid among the bodies in Al Noor and survived. He spotted his brother's body on Tarrant's video.

- Syed Jahandad Ali, 34, from Pakistan, was a senior dynamics developer for Intergen, a software company, since 2012. Syed Jahandad Ali's wife and children were visiting Pakistan. He left behind a wife, Amna, and children Meesha, 4, Aisha, 2, and Mohammad, 6 months old.

- Ansi Alibava, 25, emigrated from Kerala, India to earn a Master of Agribusiness Management at Lincoln University. She was due to graduate in May. She left behind a husband, Abdul Nazer Ponnath Hamsa. She was a part-time intern at Lincoln Agritech and worked at Kmart Riccarton. She died at Masjid Al Noor.

- Linda Armstrong, 64 or 65, grew up in West Auckland and moved to Christchurch in recent years to be near her daughter and grandchildren. She was survived by nephew Kyron Goose. She died in the arms of a woman who was shot in the arm and survived at Linwood Mosque. She sponsored a boy from Bangladesh.

- Muse Nur Awale, 77, had been in Christchurch for three decades. He was married to Muhubo Ali Jama, and had no children. Until 2018, he was a marriage celebrant for the Muslim Association of Canterbury. He earlier taught religious studies at Hagley School and Al Noor.

- Zakaria Bhuiyan, from Bangladesh, was scheduled to move to Auckland to begin an engineering job.

- Karam Bibi, 63, mother of Zeeshan Raza and wife of Ghulam Hussain. The three died together at Linwood.

- Kamel Darwish, variant Kamel Moh'd Kamal Kamel Darwish, 38 or 39, emigrated from Jordan six months earlier and worked on a dairy farm in Ashburton. His wife and three young children had applied for visas to move to New Zealand. He left behind a brother, Zuhair.

- Atta Elayyan, variant Alayyan, 33, was a futsal goalkeeper for the national and Canterbury men's teams who left behind a wife, Farah, and daughter, Aya, 2. He worked in the local tech industry. He died at Masjid Al Noor. He spent seven years as director of his start-up LWA Solutions. He also worked as a UI/UX designer. He taught a friend how to ski. A Givealittle page was set up to support his family.

- Ali Elmadani, variant al-Madani, 65 or 66, was a retired engineer of Palestinian extraction who died at the Al Noor mosque. He and his spouse, Nuha Assad, emigrated from UAE in 1998. He left behind a daughter, Maha.

- Sheikh Abdukadir Elmi, 78 (or 70), survived the Somali civil war and came to New Zealand with his family a decade ago. He was survived by his wife of nearly 50 years, five sons and four daughters. He was Said Abdukadir's father.

- Mohammed Omar Faruk, 36, a welder, came to New Zealand three years earlier. He was married in Bangladesh in 2017. His wife, three months pregnant, lived in Bangladesh. He shared a flat with Md Mehedi, who said he planned to finish building a house in the country and start a business.

- Ahmed Gamaluddin Abdel-Ghany, 68, and his wife and son emigrated from Egypt in 1996. He had worked in the navy at as a hotel rooms division manager. He worked at a steel company in Christchurch and ran a souvlaki shop with his wife. He also ran the Egyptian Donuts food truck in Cathedral Square. He was survived by his son, Omar.

- Amjad Hamid, 57, was a Senior Medical Officer and Rural Hospital Consultant at Hawera Hospital. His son said he had recently taken up a role in cardiology at Hawera Hospital in south Taranaki. He rotated three weeks working at the hospital with three weeks at his Christchurch home. He earlier was a senior doctor in cardiology, working for Canterbury District Health Board (DHB) and as a locum at other DHBs in New Zealand. *LinkedIn* indicated that Dr. Hamid was a consultant in cardiorespiratory integrated specialist services at Canterbury for 20 years. He spent much of his life in Qatar, and trained in medicine in Syria. He moved from Palestine to Christchurch in 1995, commuting to Hawera. His wife, Hanan, was about to board a flight from Melbourne to Christchurch when the attack occurred. He often brought fresh baklava from a Christchurch bakery to Hawera Hospital. He was survived by Hanan and two sons, including Husam Hamid, 22, and Mohammed Hamid, 20.

- Lilik Abdul Hamid, 58, from Medan, Indonesia, who left behind a wife and two children, worked as an aircraft maintenance engineer for Air New Zealand.

- Mohsin Mohammad al-Harbi, variant Mohammed, 61 or 63, a Saudi citizen who had lived in New Zealand for 25 years, working in water desalination and serving as a part-time imam at the Deans Street mosque, sometimes giving the Friday sermon. His wife, Manal, was hospitalized for a heart attack suffered while she was searching for him. He was survived by son Feras al-Harbi.

- Mojammel Hoq, 30, was scheduled to return to Bangladesh in September to marry and open a dental clinic. He had studied dentistry in Christchurch for more than two years. He was survived by cousin Abdul Hai.

- Ghulam Hussain, 66, father of Zeeshan Raza and husband of Karam Bibi, all three of whom died at Linwood. Hussain and Bibi had traveled to New Zealand to visit Raza in February 2019.

- Mucaad Ibrahim, 3, believed to be the youngest victim. His Somali family had fled their country more than 20 years earlier. He was born in Christchurch. He was at Al Noor with his father and brother, Abdi Ibrahim, who escaped. The family became separated in the panic during the attack. Mucaad ran toward the gunman, possibly thinking it was part of a video game.

- Junaid Ismail, variant Junaid Mortara, 35 or 36, was believed to be the first to die in the attack. He was born and raised in Christchurch. He was with his twin brother, Zahid, who escaped with his wife. He was the cousin of Javed Dadabhai, who said Junaid financially supported his mother, his wife and their three children, ages 1 to 5. He owned the Springs Road Dairy family business. Mortara had inherited his father's convenience store. He was an avid cricket fan.

- Ozair Kadir, 24, was a student pilot at the International Aviation Academy of New Zealand. Hailing from Hyderabad, India, he moved to Christchurch a year earlier.

- Mohammed Imran Khan, 46, originally from India and known as Imran Bhai to family and friends, had three businesses, including the Indian Grill restaurant and takeout in Hills Road, the Macah halal butchery on Hills Road, and a café his wife ran in St. Albans. He died at the Linwood Masjid. He left behind his wife and son, 15. He often shared food from his restaurant, particularly a biryani dish, with his friends at the mosque.

- Mahebook Allarkha Khokhar, 65, was scheduled to return home to Ahmedabad, India, on March 17, but died at Masjid Al Noor.

- Osama Adnan Youssef Kwaik, 37, was the son of refugees. He was born in Gaza and raised in Egypt, studying at the American University in Cairo. He and his wife and two children moved to Christchurch in 2017. They recently had another child, a New Zealand citizen. Kwaik was applying for New Zealand citizenship. He was survived by his brother, Youssef Abu Kwaik, who lives in California.

- Dr. Haroon Mahmood, 40 or 41, was a banker in Pakistan and tutored in economics and statistics at Lincoln University from 2014-2016. He lectured in business at Linguis International in Christchurch from 2014-April 2017. He joined Canterbury College in May 2017. The *New Zealand Herald* said that after earning his doctorate in July 2018 on "maturity transformation risk, profitability and stability in Islamic banking", he served as assistant academic director of the private Canterbury College for English language and business students. *LinkedIn* indicated that he earned master's degrees in finance from Shaheed Zulfikar Ali Bhutto Institute of Science and Technology in Pakistan and then worked in banking in Pakistan. He was survived by his wife and two children, aged 11 and 13.

- Sayyad Milne, 14, grew up in Corsair Bay near Lyttleton and was a Cashmere High School student who died at Masjid Al Noor. Half-sister Brydie Henry said he played goalie and dreamt of being an international soccer player. He and his brother had attended the annual al-Khaadem Youth Camp in Malaysia in 2018

- Hussein Moustafa, 70, from Egypt, was the father-in-law of Nada Tawfeek.

- Hamza Mustafa, 16. The family had arrived from Syria a few months earlier. At the funeral, Hamza's Cashmere High School principal said he was an excellent horse rider who aspired to be a veterinarian.

- Khaled Alhaj Mustafa, 44, a recent refugee from Syria who had brought along his family. He and his son, Hamza, 16, died at the Masjid Al Noor. The family were members of the Circassian community who originated from the area around the Black Sea in eastern Europe. They had hoped to go to America to join that community, but were foiled by President Trump's travel ban. He left behind a wife, Salwa, and a daughter. He worked as a farrier in Syria, and loved horses. Mustafa's wife, Salwa, told *Radio New Zealand* that they were told that New Zealand was "the safest country in the world, the most wonderful country you can go ... you will start a very wonderful life there... But it wasn't."

- Haji Daoud Nabi, variant Hati Mohemmed Doud Nabi, 71, an Afghan refugee of the Soviet-Afghan war who arrived in New Zealand in 1977 with his two sons, Omar and Yama Nabi. He ran the Afghan Associ-

ation in Christchurch. He died at the Masjid Al Noor on Deans Avenue as he tried to shield another person.

- Talha Naeem, 21, died with his father, Mian Naeem Rashid.

- Tariq Omar, 24, had graduated from Cashmere High School in Christchurch.

- Musa Vali Suleman Patel, variant Hafiz Musa Patel, 60, the pesh imam of the Lautoka Jame Masjid in Fiji, had run the mosque for 25 years. He had left Fiji three weeks earlier to spend time with children in Australia. He was visiting his son in Christchurch. Patel led the Fiji Muslim League. He left behind his wife, Saira Bibi Patel, three daughters, and two sons.

- Abdelfattah Qasem, 60, originally from Palestine, was the Muslim Association of Canterbury's former secretary. The IT specialist had worked in Kuwait for much of his life. His family moved to New Zealand in the early 1990s during the first Gulf War, and were looking for a more secure place for their children. He lived on a small farm. His wife and three daughters lived in New Zealand, Australia, and the UK. His Australia-based daughter, Rawan, was due to deliver his first grandchild in April. Dr. Mustafa al-Asaad was a brother-in-law of Rawan. Qasem and four close friends died at Masjid Al Noor.

- Ashraf el-Moursy Ragheb, 54, moved from Cairo in the 1990s. He was survived by his wife and two children.

- Mian Naeem Rashid, 40-something, died in Christchurch Hospital. Pakistani Prime Minister Imran Khan announced on March 17 that Rashid would be given a posthumous national award for bravery, having tried to wrestle the gun from the killer before himself being shot along with his son, Talha Naeem. Former banker Rashid had moved to New Zealand for graduate studies. His wife taught there and their three sons were students.

- Zeeshan Raza, 38, a mechanical engineer, moved from Karachi, Pakistan in 2018, living in Auckland before transferring to

Christchurch for work in December 2018. He and his parents, Ghulam Hussain and Karam Bibi, died at Linwood Masjid.

- Mathullah Safi, 55, came from Afghanistan with a relative via India nine years earlier. He left behind a wife, six sons, and a daughter. He died at Al Noor.

- Muhammed Abdusi Samad, 66, from Bangladesh, was a lecturer at Lincoln University. He often led prayers at Al Noor.

- Mounir Soliman, 68, was a design engineer and quality manager at Scotts Engineering in Christchurch since 1997. He died at Al Noor. He was survived by his wife, Ekram. They had no children. They often traveled to Egypt.

- Shahid Suhail, 35, an engineer from Pakistan, worked as a production manager at the resin manufacturer Hexion in Christchurch. He moved to New Zealand in 2017. He lived in Auckland for a year, then moved to Christchurch. He left behind his wife, Asma, and two daughters, aged five and two and one-half.

- Muhammad Maziq Mohd-Tarmizi, 17, arrived from Malaysia with his family 18 months earlier. He died at Al Noor, where his father, Mohd Tarmizi Shuib, was injured. His mother and younger brother escaped. He was a senior at Burnside High School.

- Hussein al-Umari, 35 or 36, and his family moved from the UAE 22 years earlier. He died at Al Noor. He worked in the travel industry. He was the older brother of Aya al-Umari and son of Janna Ezat and Hazim al-Umari. He had worked in the tourism industry until he recently lost his job.

- Arifbhai Mohamedali Vora, 58, was visiting his son, Ramiz.

- Ramiz Arifbhai Vora (also reported as Vora Ramiz), 28, and his father, Arif, were killed at Masjid Al Noor. Vora hailed from Gujarat, India, but lived and worked in Christchurch. He and his wife had a baby daughter, their first child, a week earlier.

- The name of a child, Abdullahi Hashi, 4, was deleted from the official lists. Abdulrahman Hashi, 60, a preacher at Dar Al Hijrah Mosque in Minneapolis, apparently incorrectly told the *Washington Post* that his nephew was among those killed at Linwood. His brother-in-law, Adan Ibrahin Dirie, was hospitalized. Dirie had been worshiping in Christchurch that morning with his five children when the gunman opened fire. Four of his children escaped unharmed. The family had fled Somalia in the mid-1990s as refugees and resettled in New Zealand.

Victims came from numerous countries.

- Shafiqur Rahman Bhuiyan, honorary consul for Bangladesh in Auckland, said three Bangladeshis were killed and others were wounded. "One leg of an injured [person] needed to be amputated while another suffered bullet injuries in his chest." He identified two of the Bangladeshis as Husna Ahmed, 45, wife of Farid Ahmed, and Mojammel Hoq, 30.

- Two Jordanians, according to Jordan's state-run *Petra* news service. Foreign Ministry spokesman Sufian Qudah said that a Jordanian man was killed and eight others were wounded. By March 16, four Jordanians had died after a man died of his injuries. The Foreign Ministry said five others were being treated for their wounds.

- Syrian refugee family members Khaled Mustafa and his son Hamza, 14 (or 16), were killed and son Zaid, 13, was wounded and underwent a six-hour operation. Ali Akil, the Auckland-based spokesman for Syrian Solidarity New Zealand, said the family settled in New Zealand in 2018. They had been refugees in Jordan for six years.

- The Palestinian Foreign Ministry said six people of Palestinian descent had died, identifying them as Atta Elayyan, Abdel Fattah Qassem al-Dokki, Ali al-Madani, Amgad (variant Amjad) Hamid, Osama Adnan Abu Kowik, variant Kwaik, and Kamal (variant Kamel) Darwish.

- Pakistani Foreign Minister Shah Mahmood Qureshi announced that nine Pakistanis were killed. They included Naeem Rashid, 48 (or 50, reports differed), and his son, Talha Naeem, 21; Sohail Shahid, Syed Jahandad Ali, 34, Syed Areeb Ahmed, 27; a couple, Ghulam Hussain and Karam Bibi, and their son Zeeshan Raza; and Mahboob Haroon, 40, an academician and father of two.

- Egyptian officials announced that four Egyptians, including Mounir Sulaiman, 68; Ahmed Jamal Aldean Abdulghani, 68; Ashraf al-Morsi; and Ashraf al-Masri; were killed.

- The Saudi-owned satellite news channel *al-Arabiya* reported that Mohsen al-Muzaini, one of two citizens of the kingdom wounded in the mosque attack, later died.

- Lilik Abdul Hamid, from Indonesia.

- Ashraf Ali, variant Alie, from Fiji, went to school with his friend, Abdul Qayyum, according to the *Daily Mail Australia*. They often played the game Last Card. They were to go to a gathering in Fiji in a few weeks.

- Mohsen Mohammad al-Harbi, variant Mohammed, 61, a Saudi citizen and New Zealand resident who was also sometimes an imam at the Deans Street mosque.

- Indian nationals Maheboob Khokhar, Ramiz Vora (also reported as Vora Ramiz), 28, Asif (or Asir) Vora, 56, Ansi Karippakulam Alibava, 25, a woman originally from India, and Ozair Kadir.

The injured included:

- A girl, 4, in critical condition

- Adeeb Sami, 52, a Dubai-based father who was in the country to surprise his twins for their 23rd birthday. He took a bullet in his spine while diving in front of his sons to protect them, according to *Gulf News*. His daughter, Heba, said that she lost five family friends, including a 12-year-old boy.

- Adan Ibrahin Dirie, a Somali refugee.

- Yasmin Ali lost a family friend she loved like a grandfather. Several people were in town for her engagement, she told *1 News*.

- Mohammed Elyan, a Jordanian in his 60s who co-founded one of the mosques in 1993, a year after arriving in the country, and his son, Atta, who is in his 30s. Elyan taught engineering at a university and ran a consultancy. He last visited Jordan two years ago.

- The Malaysian government said two of its citizens were hospitalized.

- The Saudi Embassy in Wellington said two Saudis were wounded; one died the next day. The second wounded Saudi, Aseel Ansari, 19, was hit in the knee by a rifle round, but was able to flee.

- India's high commissioner to New Zealand, Sanjiv Kohli, tweeted that nine Indians were missing. Akhtar Khokhur, 58, said her husband, electrical engineer Mehaboobbhai Khokhar, 65, was missing. The couple had traveled from India to spend time with their son Imran, their first visit in the eight years since he moved to New Zealand. They were due to fly out on March 17. Two brothers, Farhaj Ashashan, variant Ahsan, 30, and Ramazvora Ashashan, 31, were missing. Farhaj left his home with wife Insha Aziz, his daughter, 3, and son, 7 months, for prayer. His father, Mohammad Sayeeduddin, lived in Hyderabad, India. Farhaj, a software engineer, earned his master's degree at the University of Auckland in 2010 before moving to Christchurch.

- Turkish President Recep Tayyip Erdogan said three Turkish citizens were wounded. Turkish Foreign Minister Mevlut Cavusoglu said that two victims were Mustafa Boztas and Zekeriya Tuyan.

- *AP* reported on March 11, 2020 that in the attack on the al-Noor mosque, Turkey-born Temel Atacocugu was hit by nine bullets, including one in his upper jaw, four in his legs, and four more times in his left arm and leg as gunman Brenton Tarrant fired into a pile of bodies. Atacocugu underwent four operations that included bone and skin grafts and needed several more surgeries. Within the year, he was limping, but playing soccer. He was trying to sell his stake in a kebab shop and return to painting and decorating.

- Afghanistan's ambassador to Australia and New Zealand said two Afghans were missing and a third person of Afghan origin was treated and released from the hospital.

- Zulfirman Syah and son Averroes, two Indonesians, a father and son, were wounded, according to Foreign Ministry spokesman Arrmanatha Nasir. Alta Marie said on *Facebook* that they were shot at the Linwood Islamic Center. She said Zulfirman was hit multiple times as he shielded his son and had a drain in his lung. "I was recently united with my son, who has a gunshot wound to the leg and backside. He is traumatized, but we are all alive." Alta Marie said the family moved to Christchurch two months earlier. The *New York Times* reported on March 15, 2020 that Zulfirman Syah took bullets in the back, upper thigh, elbow, top of his penis, scrotum, and groin. He, his wife Alta Sacra, and their son Roes Syah were diagnosed with PTSD. She, now 35, was from Delaware. He, now 41, is an artist. He had shielded his son with his body, but, he added, "I saw smoke coming from a hole in his diaper." They were married for three years; they met on a Muslim marriage site.

- Nour Tavis, who was at the mosque and escaped after someone smashed a window in the building's exterior, said he saw the terrorist shoot a friend's 5-year-old daughter.

- Rami's father was hit in the hip and buttocks and underwent nerve reconstruction surgery.

- Pakistani Foreign Ministry spokesman Mohammad Faisal tweeted that four Pakistanis were wounded and five others were missing. Asim Mukhtar, secretary general of the Pakistan Association of New Zealand, said two members of the Pakistani community were wounded and five were missing.

- Muhammad Amin Nasir, 67, and his son, Yasir Amin, 35, were 200 meters from the Al Noor mosque when the killer stopped his car to fire at them. Nasir was hit by three bullets in his shoulder, chest and back, and was placed in an induced coma. Amin had left Pakistan for Christchurch five years earlier. Nasir was a farmer of vegetables, wheat and rice in Pakistan, often visiting his son in New Zealand. Amin was 6 when his mother died. Nasir raised him with his four siblings.

- The Red Cross said at least one Briton was a victim.

- Mark Rangi, a New Zealander who worked in Sydney as a baggage handler and had visited Al Noor mosque for Friday prayers for the first time, was shot in his legs.

- Hazem Mohammed, who migrated from Iraq 41 years ago, played dead as Tarrant fired at him, hitting his shoulder.

Members of the Bangladesh cricket team escaped the mosque without harm. They were arriving by bus at the mosque when the shooting started.

The manifesto was similar to that of Norwegian mass shooter Anders Breivik, whom the gunman said he met briefly to obtain his blessing for the attack. "I have only had brief contact with Knight Justiciar Breivik, receiving a blessing for my mission after contacting his brother knights." Prison officials doubted that there was any physical or written contact. Breivik's name was included in a list of "partisans/freedom fighters/ethno soldiers" who the author said fought against "ethnic and cultural genocide".

The attack was teased before the attack on *Twitter*, announced beforehand on the message board *8chan* and live-streamed on *Facebook* for 17 minutes. The *New Zealand Herald* reported that Tarrant had sent a copy of the manifesto to Prime Minister Ardern's office and many media outlets minutes before the attack. Social media firms scrambled to take down the posting.

The gunman said he was spurred to action by attacks by Muslims in Europe and wanted revenge and to create fear, sparking a race war. He wanted to split Turkey from NATO, polarizing and destabilizing the West. He was particularly motivated by the 2017 attack in Stockholm in which an Uzbek man drove a truck into a crowd, killing five, including Ebba Akerlund, 11, a Swedish girl. Ebba's mother, Jeanette Åkerlund, told the Swedish newspaper *Expressen*, "I find it extremely tragic that Ebba's name is being misused in political propaganda."

He often referred to the Crusades and conflict between Muslims and people of European descent. He said an attack in New Zealand would show that no place was safe and that even New Zealand was subject to mass immigration. He said he was an environmentalist and fascist who believes China aligned with his political and social values. He expressed contempt for the wealthiest one percent. He said American conservative commentator Candace Owens had influenced him the most. He hoped to spur conflict over U.S. gun laws, leading to a civil war and racial separation. "I chose firearms for the affect [sic] it would have on social discourse, the extra media coverage they would provide and the effect it could have on the politics of United States and thereby the political situation of the world."

He railed at seeing immigrants in France. He described in the manifesto a stop in a midsize town in eastern France, "As I sat there in the parking lot, in my rental car, I watched a stream of the invaders walk through the shopping center's front doors. For every French man or woman there was double the number of invaders. I had seen enough, and in anger, drove out of the town, refusing to stay any longer in the cursed place and headed on to the next town.... WHY WON'T SOMEBODY DO SOMETHING? WHY DON'T I DO SOMETHING?"

The manifesto's title was "The Great Replacement", also the title of a 2012 book by far-right French polemicist Renaud Camus and the rallying cry of the torch-bearing protesters who marched in Charlottesville in 2017. He said he was inspired by the atmosphere generated by President Trump.

The gunman claimed he was raised in a working-class Australian family, had a typical childhood and was a poor student. He worked as a personal trainer in Grafton, Australia. Prime Minister Ardern said the terrorist was an Australian citizen who had been living in Dunedin, about 220 miles south of Christchurch. He had traveled through Asia and Europe, including

Bulgaria (on November 9-15, 2018), North Korea and countries with large Muslim populations, including Turkey and Pakistan, according to *AP* and *NBC News*. Turkish officials said he had been to Turkey several times. State broadcaster *TRT* said Tarrant visited Turkey twice in 2016, on March 17-20 and September 13 to October 25. The station released a security camera image of him arriving at Istanbul's Ataturk Airport. Bulgarian chief prosecutor Sotir Tsatsarov said Tarrant rented a car and toured more than a dozen cities, visiting historic sites, focusing on battles between Christians and the Ottoman army.

The suspect said he had not joined any organizations, but donated to nationalist groups. He said he contacted the anti-immigration Reborn Knights Templar. He said he was not a Nazi, but the video showed his rifle with the number 14, a possible reference to the "14 Words," a white supremacist slogan attributed in part to Adolf Hitler's "Mein Kampf". The Southern Poverty Law Center observed that he used the symbol of the Schwarze Sonne (black sun), which "has become synonymous with myriad far-right groups who traffic in neo-Nazi" ideas.

He said his victims were invaders who would replace the white race and that he would feel no remorse for their deaths. He claimed that a video game had trained him to kill.

He narrated the video, which was taken by a bodycam attached to his helmet. At the start of the video, he said, "Let's get this party started." As he approached the mosque, one man said, "Hello, brother." He was then fired on. The video showed Tarrant firing into the mosque, coming back for a new gun, and firing again into the mosque, to the sounds of the 1968 song "Fire" by the English rock band The Crazy World of Arthur Brown. He had also played a Serbian nationalist song and military fife-and-drum music. He fired at victims on the ground to ensure they were dead. Some reports said he also fired at people on sidewalks and in the streets. He then drove to the second mosque, saying, "It was too quick. I should have stayed longer," he said. "There was time for the fuel.... Burn that f---ing mosque to the ground."

Tarrant called on viewers to "subscribe to PewDiePie", the *YouTube* alias of Swedish Nazi sympathizer Felix Kjellberg, who distanced himself from the murders. PewDiePie amassed 86 million followers of his video game commentaries. He had apologized for jokes that were criticized as anti-Semitic and posting Nazi imagery in his videos.

The shooter also hailed Dylann Roof, who killed nine black churchgoers in Charleston, South Carolina, on June 17, 2015, saying Roof's writings inspired him.

He said he started planning an attack in Christchurch three months earlier. New Zealand Prime Minister Jacinda Ardern said the suspect legally started purchasing the guns in December 2017 and had a license acquired in November 2017 to carry the five guns used in the shootings. She vowed that national gun laws would be changed. Ardern said her government was looking into how Tarrant had modified his rifles to make them more deadly. The *Washington Post 202* reported on March 22 that Tarrant had apparently named one of his guns "Turkofagos" (Greek for "Turk-eater").

Attorney General David Parker told an Auckland rally that the government would ban semiautomatic rifles. On March 21, Ardern announced an immediate ban on sales of military style semi-automatic rifles and high-capacity magazines. She said the ban would be followed by legislation to be introduced in April.

In the single day, more people were murdered than are killed in an average year in New Zealand. In 2017, there were 35 murders.

President Trump said in the Oval Office that "I don't, really" believe that the racist movement was a rising threat around the world. Rather, it involved "a small group of people that have very, very serious problems". The *Washington Post* reported that the gunman's 16,000-word manifesto cited Trump "as a symbol of renewed white identity and common purpose? Sure. As a policymaker and leader? Dear god no."

Tarrant said in the manifesto that in addition to attacking mosques in Christchurch and Linwood, he would hit the one in Ashburton if he made it that far. He claimed that he planned and trained for the attack for two years in Dunedin.

Attorneys Charles-Olivier Gosselin and Jean-Claude Gingras, who represented Alexandre Bissonnette, who shot to death six people at a Quebec mosque on January 29, 2017, said he was troubled his name was being associated with the New Zealand carnage.

On March 16, Australian Senator Fraser Anning tweeted "Does anyone still dispute the link between Muslim immigration and violence?" He released a statement saying, "The real cause of the bloodshed on New Zealand streets today is the immigration program which allowed Muslim fanatics to migrate to New Zealand in the first place." He later took a swing at William Connolly, 17, who broke an egg over his head at a Melbourne press conference. Anning faced parliamentary censure in April. The boy was arrested but released without charge.

Australia banned British right-wing commentator Milo Yiannopoulos from touring the nation over his social media response to the shootings. Yiannopoulos posted on *Facebook* that attacks like Christchurch happen because "the establishment panders to and mollycoddles extremist leftism and barbaric, alien religious cultures."

On March 16, Brenton Harrison Tarrant did not enter a plea on one count of murder and made a white power thumb-and-forefinger gesture in Christchurch District Court, presided over by Judge Paul Kellar, who scheduled his next hearing for April 5. Daniel John Burrough, 18, was expected to appear in court on charges of inciting racial hostility or ill will.

The *Sunday Telegraph* reported that Tarrant's father, Rodney Tarrant, then 49, committed suicide nine years earlier while suffering from mesothelioma.

CNN reported on March 17 that *Facebook* had removed 1.5 million copies of the attacker's video.

British authorities arrested four people for racist abuse or comments about the attacks. A taxi driver in Queensway, Rochdale was abused and threatened by people. Greater Manchester Police arrested a man, 33, and a woman, 34, on suspicion of "racially aggravated" offenses. Police separately arrested a woman, 38, in Rochdale for online comments about the attack. Police arrested a man, 24, for a social media post pledging support for Tarrant.

The *New Zealand Herald* reported on March 17 that Tarrant fired his court-appointed attorney, Richard Peters, saying he would represent himself.

On March 18, Australian counterterrorism police raided two houses in New South Wales. One was that of Tarrant's sister in Sandy Beach, halfway between Sydney and Brisbane, and the other was farther north in Lawrence, close to Grafton.

Gun City owner David Tipple said his Christchurch store sold four guns and ammunition to Tarrant via a "police-verified online mail order process".

New Zealand Prime Minister Jacinda Ardern vowed to deny fame to the killer, saying, "He sought many things from his act of terror, but one was notoriety... And that is why you will never hear me mention his name... He is a terrorist, he is a criminal, he is an extremist. But he will, when I speak, be nameless... And to others, I implore you, speak the names of those who were lost, rather than name of the man who took them. He may have sought notoriety, but we in New Zealand will give him nothing. Not even his name."

Turkish President Recep Tayyip Erdogan took a different approach, showing excerpts of the video to denounce what he called rising hatred and prejudice against Islam. One showing was during a campaign rally in Eregli. The excerpts also ran on Turkish television. Erdogan wrote a March 20 op-ed in the *Washington Post* entitled "The New Zealand killer and the Islamic State are cut from the same cloth." He called on Western leaders to learn from "the courage, leadership and sincerity" of Prime Minister Jacinda Ardern and "embrace Muslims living in their respective countries." The West "must reject the normalization of racism, xenophobia and Islamophobia".

Facebook reported that no one flagged the posting of the video to its attention, although 1.5 million postings were recorded.

On March 20, 2019, the United Arab Emirates detained and deported a Transguard Group employee who made comments on his *Facebook*

page under an assumed name celebrating the attacks. Transguard, part of the Emirates aviation group in Dubai, stripped his security credentials, fired him, and handed him over to authorities. The UAE's *National* newspaper said the employee was believed to be a security officer whose *Facebook* post also mentioned a deadly attack on Indian soldiers in Kashmir in February.

Judge Stephen O'Driscoll of a Christchurch court denied bail and ordered Philip Arps, 44, jailed on two charges of distributing the livestream video on March 16 in violation of New Zealand's questionable publications law. Each charge carried a 14 year sentence. He did not enter a plea. His next court appearance was set for mid-April.

The New Zealand government covered the costs of the funerals. Four burials were held the evening of March 20 for Junaid Ismail, Ashraf Ali and Lilik Abdul Hamid. *AP* reported that the fourth victim's name was suppressed by court order.

Tens of thousands of people joined Muslims in Christchurch for Friday prayers in Hagley Park, opposite the Al Noor Mosque, and across the country on national tv and radio broadcasts on March 22. In an open-air ceremony, 20,000 people observed two minutes of silence. In Wellington, hundreds formed a human chain around the Kilbirnie Mosque.

The New Zealand government's Chief Censor, David Shanks, on March 23 banned the manifesto, having earlier banned the livestream.

On April 5, Tarrant was charged with 50 murder counts and 39 attempted murder counts. He appeared via video from Auckland's Paremoremo Prison, New Zealand's only maximum-security prison. He was not asked to enter a plea. He was ordered to undergo a psychiatric assessment before his next hearing of the Christchurch High Court on June 14. He was represented by attorney Shane Tait. Presiding Justice Cameron Mander ordered that no filming or recording take place in the court and that existing images be pixelated. Tarrant faced life without parole if convicted.

Investigators found that Tarrant had made two donations to the European anti-immigrant Identitarian Movement. Romain Espino, a spokesman for the French branch of the group, said that Tarrant sent about 1,000 euros, or about $1,200, in September 2017. In early 2018, Tarrant donated $1,700 to the head of the Austrian Identitarian Movement.

AP reported on April 17, 2019 that New Zealand police claimed that they arrested Tarrant 18 minutes after receiving the first emergency call.

AP reported on April 26 that Christchurch businessman Philip Arps, 44, pleaded guilty to two counts of sharing Tarrant's livestream video of the attack. Sentencing was scheduled for June 14. He faced 14 years in prison. Prosecutors accused him of sending the video to an unknown person and instructing that person to insert crosshairs and to include a kill count. Prosecutors say he forwarded the video to 30 people. By April 26, six people had been charged with illegally sharing the video. Arps and one other person, an 18-year-old, were jailed in March 2019.

AP reported on May 2, 2019 that Turkish Foreign Minister Mevlut Cavusoglu tweeted that Turkish citizen Zekeriya Tuyan died of his wounds in the Christchurch attack, raising the death toll to 51. Tuyan was one of three Turkish citizens wounded. *Anadolu* reported that he was the father of two children and was wounded in the back and the leg.

On May 21, 2019, New Zealand police filed a terrorism charge against Tarrant, adding to earlier murder and attempted murder charges. The terrorism charge included a maximum penalty of life in prison. The New Zealand law defines terrorism as including acts that are carried out to advance an ideological, political, or religious cause with the intention of inducing terror in a civilian population. Police on May 21 charged Tarrant with an additional count of murder, bringing the total number of murder charges against him to 51, and increased the number of attempted murder charges from 39 to 40.

On June 14, 2019, Australian Brenton Harrison Tarrant, 28, pleaded not guilty to all 51 counts of murder and 39 of attempted murder when he appeared in the Christchurch High Court. Prosecutors added an amended charge of murder following the death of Turkish national Zekeriya Tuyan, 46, on May 2, two additional charges of attempted murder and a charge of engaging in a terrorist act under the Terrorism Suppression Act of 2002. He appeared by video link from Auckland's Paremoremo Prison, where he was held in isolation. Justice Cameron Mander said mental health assessments by the prosecutors and defense showed Tarrant to be fit to stand trial, which was to begin on May 4, 2020.

On June 18, 2019, the Christchurch District Court sentenced Christchurch businessman Philip Neville Arps, who livestreamed a video on *Facebook* of worshippers being killed, to 21 months in prison. Arps had described the video as "awesome" and showed no empathy toward the 51 victims. The judge said Arps had compared himself to Rudolf Hess, a Nazi leader under Adolf Hitler. Arps had faced up to 14 years in prison on each count. Arps was represented by attorney Anselm Williams.

On October 16, 2019, Prime Minister Jacinda Ardern presented the 2019 New Zealand Police Association Bravery Award to the two New Zealand police officers who arrested Tarrant. The duo remained unnamed until Tarrant's trial. Tarrant wrote in his manifesto that he planned to attack a third mosque in Ashburton.

Tarrant's trial on charges of terrorism, murder and attempted murder was scheduled to begin in June 2020.

AP reported on March 27, 2020 that Brenton Harrison Tarrant, via a video link from his jail cell in Auckland, pleaded guilty to all charges, including 51 counts of murder, 40 counts of attempted murder and one count of terrorism at the Christchurch High Court. He had previously pleaded not guilty to all charges. He was the first person to be found guilty of terrorism in New Zealand under laws passed after 9/11. Judge Cameron Mander did not set a sentencing date. Tarrant faced life in prison.

Al-Jazeera reported on July 3, 2020 that Justice Cameron Mander announced that the sentencing hearing for Brenton Tarrant would begin on August 24, 2020 in Christchurch District Court.

Al-Jazeera, AFP, Reuters, CNN, the *Washington Post,* and *AP* reported on August 24-27, 2020 that 91 survivors and families of victims confronted Australian white supremacist Brenton Harrison Tarrant, 29, in the High Court in Christchurch during the four-day sentencing hearing. The attacks of March 15, 2019 killed 51 people and injured 49 at the Al Noor and Linwood mosques in Christchurch. He had pleaded guilty in March 2020 to 51 counts of murder, 40 counts of attempted murder, and one count of terrorism in the first terrorism conviction in New Zealand's history. Tarrant had dismissed his attorneys so he could represent himself. Judge Cameron Mander said he had received more than 200 victim impact statements. Prosecutor Barnaby Hawes said Tarrant planned his attacks for several years to maximize casualties. Tarrant planned to burn the mosques and regretted not taking more lives.

Among those in attendance and/or gave testimony were

- Many people who traveled from overseas and went into quarantine for 14 days because of the coronavirus lockdown.

- Sazada Akhter, who likely will never walk again

- Mohammed Alam

- Khaled Alnobani was injured at Al Noor

- Temel Atacocugu, a Turk who was shot nine times at Al Noor

- Mustafa Boztas, an Al Noor survivor

- Wassail Daragmih

- Aden Diriye, whose 3-year-old son was killed

- Janna Ezat, whose son Hussein al-Umari was killed. His body was returned to her on her birthday.

- Gamal Fouda, imam of Al Noor mosque

- Kyron Gosse, nephew of shooting victim Linda Armstrong

- Tony Green

- Mariam Gul, whose parents and sister were murdered

- Che Ta Binti Mat Ludin hid from Tarrant in the women's prayer room. She moved back to Malaysia.

- John Milne, father of son Sayyad, 14, who was killed at Linwood. Sayyad's mother, Noraini Abbas Milne, also testified.

- Ahad Nabi, whose father, Haji Mohemmed Daoud Nabi, 71, was killed at Al Noor

- Ambreen Naeem, whose husband Mian Naeem Rashid was posthumously awarded a medal for bravery by Pakistan. Rashid was killed charging Tarrant at the Al Noor mosque. Their son, Talha Naeem, 21, was also killed.

- Rosemary Omar, mother of mosque shooting victim Tariq Omar, 24

- Sara Qasem, whose father, Abdelfattah Qasem, died

- Farisha Razak, whose father Ashraf Ali was killed at Al Noor

- Maysoon Salama, mother of Atta Elayyan, 33, who was shot dead. Her husband, Mohammed Atta Ahmad Alayan, was shot in the head and shoulder but survived.

- Mohammed Siddiqui was hospitalized for eight days after being shot in the arm at Al Noor

- Nathan Smith, 46, who had held a dying 3-year-old boy in his arms at Al Noor

- Aya al-Umari, whose brother, Hussein, 35, died. Their mother, Janna Ezat, forgave Tarrant.

- Abdul Aziz Wahabzadah, who fought off Tarrant at the Linwood Islamic Center with an EFTPOS credit card machine

- Mirwais Waziri, an Afghan living in New Zealand, who survived the attacks

Tarrant did not testify in his defense, but his court-appointed standby lawyer, Philip "Pip" Hall, said he would make a brief statement.

Prosecutors said Tarrant flew a drone over the Al Noor mosque and researched its layout.

On August 27, Judge Cameron Mander sentenced Tarrant to life in prison without parole, the first time that sentence was given in the country's history.

Australian Prime Minister Scott Morrison said he would be open to allowing Tarrant to serve his sentence on Australian soil, but the victims' wishes would be paramount. New Zealand had not made such a proposal, which was championed by New Zealand Deputy Prime Minister Winston Peters, who wanted to take the cost of Tarrant's enhanced security off New Zealanders. Winston told *Nine Network TV*: "Given this unprecedented circumstance and all the regard to the cost of looking after the victims in our country who survived and their families and also the 50 million New Zealand dollar plus ($33 million) downstream in real terms of providing safety for this terrorist, then the sound, reasonable, logical thing to do would be to ask Australia to step up." The countries do not have a legal framework for prisoner transfers. 19031501

March 27, 2019: *AP* reported on April 3, 2019 that Artemiy Dubovskiy, alias Troy, 54, who apparently killed himself during a standoff with police on March 27, had posed a "significant threat" to the community and supported the actions of Brenton Harrison Tarrant, who killed 50 Muslims at two mosques on March 15. He apparently did not have a direct connection to Tarrant. Canterbury District Police Commander John Price said Dubovskiy sent troubling emails referencing the attacks. Police searched three of Dubovskiy's properties and found guns, ammunition and violent extremist content. Police found Dubovskiy in a vehicle at 12:30 a.m. on March 27, and negotiated with him for three hours before approaching the vehicle and finding him with a mortal stab wound. They also found a knife. Police were investigating two more people. Dubovskiy's father Vlad Dubovskiy told the *New Zealand Herald* that he and his son moved to New Zealand from Russia in 1997. *AP* reported that Vlad said Artemiy was fanatical about weapons and military history, and collected Nazi memorabilia. Artemiy had several previous convictions, including two following a 1999 incident in which he burgled a Russian couple he knew. He was sentenced to four years.

April 30, 2019: Police arrested a man, 33, after finding ammunition and a package containing a suspected explosive device at a vacant property in Christchurch. Police Superintendent John Price said that a defense force bomb squad had rendered the package safe.

EUROPE

EUROPEAN UNION

January 7, 2019: Danish Foreign Minister Anders Samuelsen announced that the European Union "agreed to enact sanctions" and put an Iranian intelligence service and two Iranian nationals on its terror list after Denmark and France alleged Iran was plotting to kill opposition activists on European soil. The French government linked Tehran's Intelligence Ministry's internal security section to the alleged attempt to bomb a rally of opponents on June 30 outside Paris. The Danish government said that Iran in October 2018 was planning to kill in Denmark a member of the group that Tehran blamed for a September 22 attack that killed 25 people. The Dutch government accused Iran of involvement in two assassination plots in the Netherlands and expelled two Iranian diplomats in June 2018. The Dutch AIVD domestic intelligence service said the first incident occurred in Almere, near Amsterdam, in December 2015, when electrician Ali Motamed, 56, was shot at point-blank range by two people. Dutch newspaper *Het Parool* reported that court documents indicated that Motamed was living under an assumed name. His real name was Mohammad Reza Kolahi, who had been sentenced to death in absentia in Iran in connection with organizing a 1981 bombing of the Islamic Republican Party's headquarters in Tehran which killed more than 70 people, including Chief Justice Ayatollah Mohammed Beheshti. The two suspects in his killing were Dutch criminals without connections to the local Iranian community. The second killing occurred in The Hague in November 2017 when Ahmad Mola Nissi, 52, founder of an Arab nationalist movement in the Iranian province of Khuzestan, was shot in front of his home.

February 14, 2019: *Newsweek* reported that the European Union added Saudi Arabia, Panama and Nigeria to its list of countries that lack tight control over money laundering and terrorism financing. If the 28 EU member states ratify the move, European banks would have to institute tighter controls on transactions made with individuals or institutions from those countries.

Albania

October 22, 2019: Police chief Ardi Veliu announced they had thwarted the foreign wing of Iran's Revolutionary Guard that had operated a paramilitary "active terrorist cell" targeting Mujahedin-e Khalq (MEK) exiles in Albania. Police claimed that two senior Iranian security officials commanded the cell from Tehran. Authorities said the group was linked with organized crime groups in Turkey and used a former MEK member to collect information in Albania.

Veliu said a planned attack on MEK in Albania by Iranian government agents was foiled in March during the Sultan Nevruz day festivities.

Austria

April 9, 2019: Authorities searched dozens of homes in several states, seizing weapons and large amounts of banned right-wing propaganda material.

December 6, 2019: Europol announced that Austrian and Moldovan authorities broke up an organized crime ring suspected of attempting to sell "radiological material to an army" for 3 million euros ($3.33 million). Vienna police arrested three people, one of whom has a previous conviction related to such activities in the past.

Belgium

January 9, 2019: Brussels prosecutor's office spokesman Denis Goeman announced the arrest of Illiass Khayari, born in 1991, a man who served jail time on terrorism charges over the theft of a computer hard drive containing autopsy reports about the victims of the suicide bombings in Brussels on March 22, 2016. Police believed he stole the hard drive and other items from a forensic doctor's office at the city's main justice offices on January 3, 2019. Belgian media said Khayari was sentenced to five years in prison on terror charges in 2016 but only served about half his term. He claimed to have beheaded a man in Syria. Authorities traced a mobile phone that Khayari had allegedly stolen.

March 19, 2019: Brussels police temporarily closed a street near the European Union headquarters after a telephoned bomb threat was sent to a consulting company linked to the EU Commission.

April 14, 2019: State broadcaster *RTBF* reported that in the morning, authorities arrested Belgian Islamic convert Jimmy K., 22, on suspicion that he was part of a terrorist group and might have been planning an attack. He was charged with "taking part in the activities of a terrorist group". Police conducted searches in three Belgian towns but found no weapons or explosives. Police arrested him at his grandmother's house in Wavre.

Bosnia-Herzegovina

January 14, 2019: Bosnian prosecutors charged Munib Ahmetspahic, who was born in 1990 in the Bosnian town of Zenica, and who fought alongside Islamic extremists in Syria and Iraq, with "organizing a terrorist group". Prosecutors said he twice went to Syria and Iraq between 2013 and 2018 where he joined ISIS and other extremist organizations. He was detained in Bosnia in 2018.

April 22, 2019: In the nighttime, Slavisa Krunic, 48, a prominent Bosnian Serb businessman who owned several businesses including Sector Security, a private security firm, was shot dead in his vehicle along with his bodyguard in a mafia-style execution that sparked a shootout. The married father of four was approaching his home outside Banja Luka in northern Bosnia. One of the attackers, Zeljko Kovacevic, was killed and Krunic's driver was seriously injured. Krunic was a critic of the ruling Bosnian Serb nationalist party and its hard-line leader, Milorad Dodik, whom Krunic accused of stoking ethnic tensions in Bosnia to divert attention from his corrupt practices. Bosnia media said Kovacevic was a well-known criminal who should have been serving a five-year prison sentence for a string of robberies but was free due to a clerical error. Some pundits blamed the regime for the murders. Dodik was subject to U.S. sanctions for "actively obstructing" the Dayton peace accords, which ended Bosnia's 1992-95 war.

BULGARIA

January 18, 2019: Deputy Chief Prosecutor Ivan Geshev announced that police had broken up a suspected terrorism financing ring and detained 43 people in raids across the country. One suspect was a Syrian citizen permanently residing in Bulgaria who allegedly transferred money to people abroad linked to international extremist groups, saying "the main suspect has been in touch and has financed people who provide logistics to international terrorist groups" by sending money through a hawala. Geshev credited a year-long investigation in several European Union member states.

June 8, 2019: Deputy Prosecutor-General Ivan Geshev said that authorities in Plovdiv arrested a boy, 16, after finding in the high school student's home explosive devices they believed could have been used for a terror attack. Police found a pipe bomb, a device filled with 14 kilograms (31 pounds) of nails, an ISIS flag and Islamist literature. The bomb was similar to one used by a man who was inspired by ISIS and set one off in New York City's Times Square in 2017, injuring only himself, and one sent in parcels to senior Democrats, donors, and journalists in 2018. The device, filled with nails, used the same explosive as that used in terrorist attacks in Belgium, France, and a Bulgarian airport near Burgas on the Black Sea coast. The *New York Times* reported that he was charged with planning a terrorist attack. Geshev said ISIS recruited the boy over social media and *Telegram*. He was released to his family and was to receive psychological counseling.

August 21, 2019: Police investigated several bomb threats emailed to media outlets in Sofia and to major airports in Sofia, Plovdiv, Varna and Burgas, as well as the offices of *Bulgarian National TV* and the newspaper *24 Hours*. No devices were found. The emails used Internet anonymizing tools and online messaging providers based outside Bulgaria. Similar messages were sent on August 20 to airports and later to media organizations in other EU countries.

CYPRUS

March 23, 2019: Government spokesman Prodromos Prodromou announced the arrest on a European warrant of a Turkish Kurd against whom Germany launched criminal proceedings for "terrorist activities". Cyprus had given him political refugee status and local travel documents. Germany requested extradition.

CZECH REPUBLIC

June 10, 2019: Police tweeted that they had received reports of a threat of a shooting attack against schools.

October 9, 2019: Police spokesman Hana Rubasova announced authorities were increasing security measures in the country following the shooting in Germany. Special attention was being paid to synagogues and other Jewish buildings and objects, Prague's international airport and the border.

November 15, 2019: Prague's Municipal Court convicted Slovak national Dominik Kobulnicky, 25, of public endangerment and promoting terrorism and sentenced him to six-and-a-half years in prison. Two years earlier, police found chemicals that can be used to make explosives and videos on how to make them in his Prague apartment. The court held that there was not sufficient evidence to support charges of planning a terror attack in Prague. He converted to Islam four years ago. He admitted he had been planning a terror attack at a bus station in the eastern Slovak city of Presov several years earlier.

DENMARK

January 22, 2019: The trial began in Copenhagen City Court of a Syrian man, 31, charged with planning to set off one or more bombs in Copenhagen and stab random people with kitchen knives on behalf of ISIS. His accomplice, Dieab Khadigah, was sentenced by a German court in July 2017 to six-and-a-half years in prison. Khadigah was arrested in Germany as he tried to enter Denmark with a backpack containing

17,000 matches, 17 batteries, fireworks, two kitchen knives and six walkie-talkies that Moyed al-Zoebi had ordered. Al-Zoebi had lived in Sweden since September 2015. In 2017, he was acquitted of arson of a Shi'ite mosque in Malmo, Sweden. The court found him guilty in April 2019. On May 20, 2019, the Copenhagen City Court sentenced Syrian asylum seeker Moyed al-Zoebi, 32, to 12 years. He appealed the sentence. Following an Internet chat, al-Zoebi and Khadigah planned to meet in Copenhagen on November 16, 2016 for the attack in an unknown place. Danish police arrested al-Zoebi in December 2017. The three judges and the 12-man jury also ruled al-Zoebi should be expelled from Denmark after serving his time.

March 25, 2019: *AP* reported on April 3 that Czech police extradited to Austria two suspects who allegedly formed a terror cell with a man detained by Austrian authorities over unsuccessful attacks on trains in Germany. They said that the two Iraqi citizens, a man, 30, and a woman, 27, were handed over to Austrian officers at the border on April 2. They pleaded not guilty but agreed to be extradited. They were arrested at Austria's request the previous week at after arriving at Prague's international airport. They were identified as Amar Rahim Mahmoud Mahmoud and Riyam Shukri Sali Badri.

An Iraqi, 42, was arrested in Vienna on March 25, on suspicion of carrying out two attacks late in 2018, including one in which a high-speed train hit a steel cable stretched over tracks between Nuremberg and Munich. Nobody was hurt. Iraqi Ammar Raheem Mahmod Mahmod, suspected of terrorism, appeared at the Municipal Court in Prague on March 29, 2019.

April 17, 2019: A man, 19, placed a functioning hand grenade on a square in a Copenhagen neighborhood with a large immigrant population. The grenade did not explode. He also allegedly made a death threat against Rasmus Paludan, an anti-Muslim provocateur who was planning a demonstration in the area. The 19-year-old was jailed for 27 days.

July 5, 2019: Prosecutor Kristian Kirk charged three men, aged 30, under Denmark's anti-terror

laws on suspicion of buying drones and components with the purpose of delivering them to ISIS in Syria and Iraq where they were to be used "in combat actions". Kirk said the trio "deliberately and systematically obtained lots of small parts and components, which together could have become powerful weapons for terrorists… it may sound like shopping lists for a hobby project (but) it is dead serious." Two of them were Danish citizens. Kirk said they purchased "hobby planes, drones and thermal cameras as well as components, tools and accessories" in Denmark between 2013 and 2017. Their trial was set for September 2019 in Copenhagen.

August 6, 2019: A bomb went off during the night outside the Danish Tax Agency office in Copenhagen, slightly injuring a bystander, shattering windows and damaging the building. On August 14, police arrested a Swedish man, 22, and issued an international arrest warrant for another Swedish man, 23. Copenhagen Police Chief Inspector Joergen Bergen Skov said police seized a car believed to have been used in connection with the bombing. On August 22, Swedish police arrested two more men, aged 22 and 27. A fourth suspect was sought on an international arrest warrant. On September 17, 2019, police at Copenhagen's international airport arrested a Swedish man, 23, as a suspect. On September 18, he was ordered jailed for six days while police continued to investigate. Another person remained in custody. Two other detainees were later released.

August 10, 2019: *AP* and *Reuters* reported that an explosion went off in the early morning outside a neighborhood police station in the Norrebro suburb of Copenhagen, damaging the building but causing no injuries. *Ekstra Bladet* said police were searching for a man wearing dark clothes and white shoes seen leaving the area.

November 12, 2019: Prosecutor Sidsel Klixbull told the Copenhagen City Court that Danish citizen and ISIS foreign fighter Ahmad Salem el-Haj was jailed in pre-trial custody for 27 days on preliminary charges of violating Danish terror laws. Turkey had deported el-Haj the previous day. Police arrested him at Copenhagen Airport in the evening. In 2017, Turkey denied his extradition. Turkey had found him guilty of joining ISIS and sentenced him to four years.

December 11, 2019: Flemming Drejer, operative head of the Denmark's domestic Security and Intelligence Service, announced that police had arrested "some 20 people… driven by a militant, Islamist motive" and suspected of involvement in Islamist terrorism in a series of raids across the country. Copenhagen Police Chief Inspector Joergen Bergen Skov said, "some had procured things to make explosives and have tried to acquire weapons", and would be charged under terrorism laws. Six police departments raided 20 addresses. Danish media reported the next day that six men and two women faced pre-trial custody hearings. On December 12, 13 of 22 detainees were released but remained suspects. On December 13, the Copenhagen City Court remanded six people. The six faced potential life prison sentences; however, life sentences' served times average 16 years in Denmark. It remanded two men aged 24 and 25 to custody for allegedly trying to buy guns, silencers and ammunition that was "to be used in connection with one or several terror attacks in Denmark or abroad". The court ordered two 21-year-old men and a woman, 38, to remain jailed for allegedly trying to produce one or several bombs with the explosive tri-acetone tri-peroxide (TATP), nicknamed the "mother of Satan" because of its volatility. A central Denmark court remanded a man, 28, to custody in a hearing held behind "double-closed doors", i.e., no information was made public.

FRANCE

February 13, 2019: A man and a woman were burned by an "unknown liquid", possibly in an acid attack, on the Paris Metro.

February 15, 2019: During morning rush hour, a person was seriously injured by an "unknown liquid" in the Paris Metro near the Bastille station. French media deemed it an acid attack. The person was treated for major burns to the face and hands. The attacker escaped.

February 19, 2019: Authorities in Marseille shot to death a knife-wielding man who injured two pedestrians in the late afternoon.

March 5, 2019: Justice Minister Nicole Belloubet said anti-terror prosecutors were investigating as a terrorist incident a ceramic knife attack by a jihadi inmate who injured two guards at the Conde-sur-Sarthe prison in western France. The prisoner's wife was visiting him before he locked himself in a visiting room after stabbing the guards. No hostages were taken. The Justice Ministry announced that the inmate had convictions for kidnapping leading to death, armed robbery and glorifying terrorism. He was sentenced in 2015 to a 30-year prison term for the murder of an 89-year-old man who had survived Nazi concentration camps. The wife later died of her wounds.

The next day, guards from the CGT union protested the attack, blocking entrances at 18 French prisons, saying prisoners were becoming "increasingly vindictive, aggressive and violent".

April 26, 2019: *BFM TV* reported that the Paris prosecutor's office announced the arrests of several people, including a minor, 17, on suspicion of preparing an attack possibly targeting French security forces in the near future. The investigation of terrorist conspiracy began on February 1. Police held four men for questioning. The minor was arrested in February 2017 at the age of 15 as he was trying to go to Syria to join ISIS. A juvenile court had sentenced him to a three-year prison sentence, with two years suspended.

May 16, 2019: French intelligence services and Spanish Civil Guard agents arrested Jose Antonio Urruticoetxea Bengoetxea, 69, alias Josu Ternera, an Euskadi ta Askatasuna (ETA) leader, near the local hospital in Sallanches in the French Alps. He had been the most wanted ETA member since 2002. Interpol had issued a red alert against him. Spanish authorities accused him of crimes against humanity. Spain's caretaker Interior Minister Fernando Grande-Marlaska said that Spain will ask France to extradite Ternera to stand trial for his alleged crimes, before he completes any possible prison sentences in France. Ternera was one of the two ETA members who read a statement announcing the group's dismantling on audio recordings released May 3, 2018. He was one of the negotiators who sat down with Spanish government envoys for talks to try to end ETA's activities in the mid-2000s. He became a lawmaker in the Basque regional parliament but went into hiding in late 2002 after Spain's Supreme Court summonsed him for his alleged involvement in a bomb attack in the barracks of the Civil Guard in Zaragoza that killed 11 people, including six minors. Investigators named the mission to arrest Ternera "Operation Stolen Childhood". Spanish courts wanted to try him for his alleged part in that massacre, as well as the alleged killing of businessman Luis Maria Hergueta Guinea in 1980, for crimes against humanity, and for belonging to a terrorist organization. Ternera was living near Saint-Gervais-les-Bains, an area popular with winter sports aficionados close to the borders of France, Switzerland and Italy. Ternera, of Ugao-Miraballes, Spain, was in a French jail the next day. He was convicted in absentia in 2017 in France for involvement in a terrorist group and sentenced to eight years in prison. On June 28, Spanish government spokeswoman Isabel Celaa announced after a weekly Cabinet meeting that Madrid would request that Josu Ternera be sent to Spain to stand trial for crimes against humanity and multiple killings.

May 24, 2019: French officials announced that a 5:30 p.m. explosion on a busy pedestrian street near the intersection of Victor Hugo road and Sala road at the bakery chain Brioche Doree in Lyon's central Presqu'ile area, which lies between the Rhone and Saone rivers, had slightly injured 14 people, some in the legs, when it shattered the glass from a refrigerated shop cooler. Soldiers of the anti-terrorist Vigipirate Mission secured the area. French President Emmanuel Macron called it an "attack" during a live interview. The news media suggested a package bomb was involved. Investigators found screws, metallic balls, and a triggering device that can be used remotely. *Reuters* reported that police were searching for a partially masked individual seen on video wheeling a bicycle before leaving behind a paper bag believed to contain a bomb. He appeared to be a European or North African male wearing beige

Bermuda shorts, an army-green scarf or head wrap and dark glasses. Counter-terrorism prosecutor Remy Heitz said an investigation had been opened for "attempted murder in relation with a terrorist undertaking" and "criminal terrorist association". No group claimed responsibility. On May 27, Interior Minister Christophe Castaner tweeted the arrest of a suspect. The prosecutors' office later said two other suspects, including a woman, were detained and formally arrested. Lyon mayor Gerard Collomb, a former interior minister, said one suspect was an IT student who was arrested as he stepped off a bus. Collomb told *BFM TV*, "It's a relief for all Lyon inhabitants. I believe the case has been resolved… If there was a network, it has been identified and will certainly be dismantled." On May 30, Mohamed Hichem M., the male detainee, said he had pledged allegiance to ISIS. His parents and brother were also detained, but released without charge on May 30.

June 11, 2019: French judicial authorities discovered an ultra-right plot to attack a religious venue. In May, authorities arrested two people, one a minor, for criminal terrorist association. Three others were arrested in September in Grenoble. *BFMTV* reported that the targets were Muslim or Jewish.

June 27, 2019: A gunman opened fire in front of Mosquée Sunna de Brest, hospitalizing imam Rachid Eljay and another person, fled in a Renault Clio, then shot himself in the head.

August 31, 2019: An assailant stabbed to death a man, 19, and injured eight others, three critically, near a subway station in Villeurbanne, outside Lyon. Passers-by surrounded and apprehended the attacker before police arrived and detained an Afghan male asylum seeker, 33. An official said the attack did not appear to be terrorism-related. Police were searching for a second suspect. Regional prosecutor Nicols Jacquet said the suspect was in a "psychotic state" of "paranoid delirium", on drugs, and claimed he "heard voices" telling him to kill. The Afghan was living in a French center for asylum-seekers, and held a temporary French residency card. He was first recorded in France in 2009, and subsequently traveled to the UK, Italy, Germany, and Norway before returning to France in 2017. He was "incoherent" at arrest and gave police three different dates of birth. He was not on any radicalism watch list. Jacquet said after a search of the Afghan's residence, "nothing was found showing any kind of radicalization". The suspect had no police record. He had two knives.

September 26, 2019: On October 17, 2019, Interior Minister Christophe Castaner announced on *France 2 TV* the 60th time that French authorities had thwarted a potential terrorist attack since 2013. The DGSI intelligence service on September 26 had detained a young male French resident in his 20s suspected of Islamic radicalism after threatening a 9/11-like plane hijacking and attack. Castaner said the individual was planning an attack and trying to obtain weapons.

October 3, 2019: *CNN*, *AP*, and the *Washington Post* reported that at 1 p.m., Mickaël Harpon, 45, a computer technician who worked at the Paris police headquarters, stabbed to death three officers and an administrator at the headquarters building, across the street from Notre Dame Cathedral on the Ile-de-la-Cité.

Victims included:

- a female police officer, 39
- a police major 50, whose throat was slit
- an officer, 38, who was stabbed in the abdomen
- an administrative employee, 37

A seriously wounded police employee underwent emergency surgery.

Police shot and killed the attacker, who used a ceramic knife. The rookie officer who shot Harpon completed police academy training six days before the attack. *AP* reported that Alliance Nationale police union regional secretary Loïc Travers said the attack started in an office and continued elsewhere in a part of the building not open to the public inside the compound.

BFM-TV reported that Harpon had worked since 2003 for the police force, most recently as a technology administrator in the intelligence unit.

The attack took place a day after police officers protested throughout Paris against the violence they regularly face in their work, police suicides, low wages, and long hours.

Police initially treated the stabbing spree as a murder, but the next day opened a terrorism investigation. *BFM TV* and *France Info* reported that his wife told police her husband, who was deaf and frustrated that the disability was preventing his being promoted, had visions and made incoherent statements during the night before the attack. He did not have a history of psychiatric problems. Police noted that he had been accused of domestic violence in 2009, but received no penalty. He converted to Islam 18 months (other reports said a decade) earlier. Paris prosecutor Jean-Francois Ricard said at a press conference that the killer "had likely contacts with members of the Salafist movement". The *New York Times* reported on October 6, 2019 that he had tried to justify to a colleague the January 2015 *Charlie Hebdo* attack and other jihadi killings. He had posted on *Facebook* a video that imitated throat-slashing. The killer's wife was apprehended after police determined that she had exchanged 33 text messages with her husband about Islam in the hours leading up to the attack. Harpon was born in the French West Indies department of Martinique. A radical imam presided at his mosque, but was nearly expelled from France. He lived in the Gonesse suburb of Paris.

On October 14, *Agence France Presse* and *RTL* reported that French police arrested five people at three locations in the northern suburbs of Paris. Detainees included the imam who preached at the Gonesse mosque Harpon attended, who is on France's "Fiche S" list of potential security risks. The mayor of Gonesse announced that the Muslim association which employed the Salafist imam had fired him.

Harpon had a USB key holding ISIS propaganda videos and details on dozens of officers, raising fears he intended to pass them to jihadis. Although ISIS mentioned the attack in a propaganda statement, it did not claim credit.

The *Wall Street Journal* reported on October 13 that after joining the police, he was living with a Muslim woman from Madagascar. In 2008, she filed a complaint against him for assault. Harpon received an administrative sanction from the police over the accusation. Six years later, he married her.

October 28, 2019: A man, 84, with previous far-right links, fired on a mosque in Bayonne, seriously injuring two men, aged 74 and 78, who grabbed him as he was attempting to set fire to the mosque's door. Police arrested the gunman, who also torched a car before fleeing. *Sud Ouest* reported that the man wrote days earlier to the region's prosecutor saying he wanted to file a complaint against President Macron. *Sud Ouest* said the writer was Claude Sinke, a candidate in 2015 departmental elections for France's far-right National Rally party, then known as the National Front. In 2015, a Claude Sinke ran unsuccessfully in Seignanx. The National Rally said he was kicked out of the local federation for speaking in a way "deemed contrary to the spirit and the political line" of the anti-immigration party.

December 13, 2019: A man lunged at a Paris police patrol with a knife and threatened to kill the officers in the La Defense main business district of Paris. Police shot him to death. The officers were not injured.

Georgia

March 13, 2019: The State Security Service announced the arrest in Kobuleti, on the Black Sea, of two men for possessing 40 grams of uranium-238 that they were planning to sell for $2.8 million.

Germany

January 1, 2019: Shortly after midnight, a German man, 50, crashed his silver Mercedes into a crowd of people in Bottrop, injuring four people, in what appeared to be an intentional attack against foreigners. He initially tried to hit a group of people who jumped out of the way, then drove to the center of the city and crashed into another crowd, hitting Syrian and Afghan citizens, some of whom were seriously injured. The victims included a woman, 46, who suffered life-threatening injuries, and a child. He then sped toward Essen, where he twice tried to hit people waiting at a bus stop before being arrested by police on suspicion of attempted homicide. One person was injured in Essen. He made anti-foreigner comments during his arrest. Police said that there were indications the suspect suffered from mental illness. Angela Luettmann, spokeswoman for the Muenster police, said he came from Essen. Essen prosecutors said on April 15 that he injured 14 people, but could not be held criminally responsible because of his mental illness. They called for him to be kept at a psychiatric hospital.

AP reported on June 7, 2019 that the trial began in Essen regional court of a German man, 50, accused of attempted murder for intentionally driving his car into crowds he believed to be foreigners on New Year's Day, injuring 14 people, including a Syrian woman, 46, with life-threatening injuries. His attorneys claimed that their client suffered from paranoid schizophrenia and believed the people he drove into were about to conduct an attack.

January 3, 2019: *DPA* reported that during the night, a bomb exploded outside the office of the rightwing AfD party in Doebeln, Saxony State, damaging windows and doors but causing no injuries.

January 14, 2019: The left-wing *taz* daily said one of its female employees was attacked by members of a far-right group after she confronted six black-clad people who were piling cobblestones and attempting to put up posters in front of the newspaper's Berlin offices. The far-right Identitarian Movement tweeted photos of members putting up posters in front of the building. The group targeted other media buildings and left-wing politicians' offices. The Identitarian Movement is close to the far-right Alternative for Germany party, whose lawmaker Frank Magnitz was attacked the previous week.

January 16, 2019: Authorities raided 12 properties in Baden-Wuerttemberg State of 17 suspected members of a far-right group calling itself the National Socialist Knights of the Ku Klux Klan Deutschland. Prosecutors and regional police seized membership lists and more than 100 weapons, including air guns, swords, machetes and knives. Some 40 people were under investigation for glorifying Nazism and, in some cases, of harboring "violent fantasies". Investigators found no evidence of links to other Ku Klux Klan groups.

Prosecutors filed terrorism charges against German woman Sabine Ulrike Sch., 32, arrested after allegedly living from late 2013 to August 2017 in a part of Syria controlled by ISIS. She faced charges of membership in a terrorist organization, looting, and violating weapons laws. Prosecutors said she went to Syria in late 2013 and married an ISIS fighter, living with him in houses seized by the group. She allegedly received weapons training between 2014 and mid-2017 and wrote blogs praising life in ISIS-controlled territory. Her husband died in fighting in 2016. Kurdish forces captured her and the wives of other ISIS fighters in September 2017. She returned to Germany in April 2018. On July 5, 2019, the regional court in Stuttgart sentenced her to five years in prison for membership in ISIS. She was earlier convicted of joining a foreign terrorist organization.

January 22, 2019: Prosecutors charged a Syrian man, 29, for joining the Islamist Ahrar al-Sham insurgent group in Syria from 2013 to 2014 and violating the war weapons control law. Frankfurt prosecutors said he volunteered as a fighter and donated 50,000 Syrian lira, then worth about 250 euros (284 dollars) to the group. Authorities seized a Kalashnikov. He had posed for recruiting photos that showed him on pickup trucks using an anti-aircraft gun and a machine cannon. Authorities detained him in February 2018 when he entered Germany for the second time. He first came to Germany as an asylum-seeker in 2015 but left in 2017.

January 30, 2019: A police SWAT team arrested three suspected Iraqi male jihadis—Shahin F. and Hersh F., both 23, and Rauf S., 36—during a morning raid of an apartment building in Meldorf in the area of Dithmarschen, near the border with Denmark on allegations they were planning a bombing and searched properties in three states. Police said the 23-year-olds were suspected of preparing a bomb attack and violating weapons laws; Rauf S. allegedly aided them. Prosecutors said that in December 2018, Shahin F. downloaded "various instructions" on how to

build a bomb, and ordered a detonator from a contact person in Britain. British law enforcement stopped delivery. The two tested 250 grams of gunpowder taken from New Year's fireworks, and asked Rauf S. to obtain a firearm. Prosecutors said he contacted Iraqi Walid Khaled Y.Y., who offered them a Russian semi-automatic Makarov 9mm pistol for 1,200 euros ($1,370) for the weapon. The would-be attackers said it was too expensive. Police searched Y.Y.'s home in the Schwerin area; he was investigated for alleged weapons and drug violations. Shahin F. started taking driving lessons as the potential getaway driver. They did not appear to be ISIS members.

February 7, 2019: *AP* reported that a Frankfurt court rejected a U.S. extradition request for Turkish man Adem Yilmaz, who was indicted under seal in the U.S. in 2015 on charges of participating a decade earlier in attacks on U.S. military forces along the border between Afghanistan and Pakistan, and was convicted of membership in a terrorist organization in Germany in 2010. Frankfurt state court spokeswoman Gundula Fehns-Boeer said his extradition to face trial in the U.S. on terrorism charges would constitute double jeopardy under German law. State Interior Ministry spokesman Marcus Gerngross said that Hesse state officials on February 5 deported Yilmaz to his native Turkey. Yilmaz was charged in the U.S. with giving advice and instructions on military-type training to a man involved in a 2008 suicide bombing in Afghanistan that killed two American soldiers and injured 11 others. He was indicted in the Southern District of New York on charges of providing material support to a terrorist organization and aiding and abetting military-style training. He had served in prison in Germany until October 2018 after his conviction for involvement in a foiled 2007 plot to attack American citizens and facilities in the country, including the U.S. Air Force's Ramstein base. As members of the Islamic Jihad Union, he and three others had stockpiled what they thought was highly concentrated hydrogen peroxide, purchased from a chemical supplier, and planned to mix it with other substances to make explosives equivalent to 1,200 pounds of dynamite. German authorities had covertly replaced the hydrogen peroxide with a diluted substitute that could not have been used to produce a bomb. Upon arriving at Istanbul's Ataturk Airport in Turkey, anti-terrorism authorities detained him.

February 12, 2019: Interior Minister Horst Seehofer banned the publishers Mezopotamien Verlag und Vertrieb GmbH and the MIR Multimedia GmbH because they support the Kurdistan Workers' Party (PKK). Authorities searched the two publishing houses in western and northern Germany.

February 21, 2019: Police searched 16 homes of alleged Islamic extremists in central and western Germany on the suspicion that the extremists were planning an attack. In the morning, authorities raided 15 homes in Ruesselsheim, Biebesheim, and Raumheim in Hesse State and a home in Kerpen in North Rhine-Westphalia.

February 27, 2019: The Stuttgart court acquitted for lack of reliable evidence an Afghan, 22, charged with having belonged to the Taliban in his homeland after he retracted statements made during his asylum proceedings. He had been charged with membership in a terror organization and violating arms control laws. He was accused of having spent six months with the Taliban in 2013, checking cars at a roadblock and being sent to train as a suicide bomber in Pakistan. He later fled to Germany. He claimed that he had invented his Taliban membership and had hoped to secure refugee status by saying he was persecuted.

March 5, 2019: Prosecutors charged Russian national Magomed-Ali C., 31, with plotting an Islamic extremist bombing in Germany with an alleged accomplice arrested in France for involvement in a separate planned attack there. The pair were associates of Anis Amri, a Tunisian who carried out an attack on a Christmas market in Berlin on December 19, 2016 in which 12 people were killed. C. was charged at a Berlin court with preparing an act of violence and preparing an explosion. Prosecutors accused him of storing a "not insignificant" but unspecified amount of the explosive TATP at his Berlin apartment in October 2016, with which C. and alleged accomplice Clement B. were believed to

have planned to carry out an attack in Germany. C. arrived in Germany in late 2011 then spent time at a now-closed radical Berlin mosque. He decided to travel to Syria to join ISIS, but local police discovered his intentions in 2015 and Berlin's office for foreigners barred him from leaving Germany. He met Clement during a visit to Belgium. In late 2015, they met Amri, who joined the bomb plot in October 2016. The duo dropped the plan that month. B. was arrested in Marseille in April 2017 over plans to carry out an attack in France, with several weapons and three kilograms (6.61 pounds) of TATP.

March 15, 2019: *CNN* reported that threatening letters had been sent to Richard Grenell, 52, U.S. Ambassador to Germany, including one threat against his life. A death threat in January told him to leave Germany and was signed by the Society for the New Truth. Two envelopes sent to the embassy included an unidentified white powder and came in suspicious envelopes with no return address. 19031503

March 18, 2019: Federal prosecutors charged three Iraqi men with membership in a terrorist organization on allegations that they fought for ISIS in Iraq, including one suspected of attacks that killed American soldiers. They said Mohammed Rafea Yassen Y., 28, joined ISIS in his hometown of Rutba. He was accused of 13 bomb attacks in Rutba from 2006-2008, causing death and injuries to "U.S. forces, the Iraqi army, local police and civilians". He also faced charges of war crimes and accessory to murder. Muqatil Ahmed Osman A., 29, and Hasan Sabbar Khazaal K., 27, were suspected of fighting for ISIS. They came to Germany in 2015 and were in custody since their arrest in the summer of 2018.

March 22, 2019: *DPA* reported that authorities arrested 11 people in raids on people suspected of planning a jihadi attack using a vehicle and firearms "to kill as many 'infidels' as possible". The main suspects were two 31-year-old brothers from Wiesbaden and a man, 21, from Offenbach, near Frankfurt, all of them German citizens. The group under investigation—aged between 20 and 42, and from Frankfurt, Offenbach, Mainz and Wiesbaden—were suspected of offenses including terror financing and conspiracy to commit a crime. *AP* reported that the suspects apparently hired a large vehicle, contacted weapons dealers, and collected money. Police seized more than 20,000 euros ($22,780) in cash, several knives, small quantities of drugs, and documents in the raids around Frankfurt.

March 26, 2019: *NBC News* reported that police evacuated several buildings in Kaiserslautern, Chemnitz, Rendsburg, Augsburg, Göttingen and Neunkirchen after bomb threats were emailed to city officials in their general email inboxes.

March 29-30, 2019: *DPA* reported that police arrested 11 people in Essen, Duesseldorf, Wuppertal, Moenchengladbach, Duisburg and Ulm on suspicion of planning an ISIS terrorist attack. One suspect was from Tajikistan.

April 2, 2019: A police tactical weapons unit in Wiesbaden arrested a German-Iranian suspect, 18, who tried to buy a gun to carry out a shooting. Officers lured him with a fake firearm. Police were tipped off by "foreign law enforcement agencies" who warned German police that the teen wanted to buy a gun on the Darknet. They said he had "right-wing ideas" and could be mentally ill. He told police he planned to kill people who were "mobbing" him.

April 9, 2019: *Deutsche Welle* reported that the trial in Munich Higher Regional Court began for German Islamic convert Jennifer W., 27, on charges that she let a 5-year-old Yazidi girl she and her husband held as a slave in ISIS-held territory in Iraq die of thirst in the hot sun. She was charged with murder, a war crime, and membership in a terrorist organization, and could face life in prison. *DPA* reported that Seda Basay-Yildiz served as her defense attorney. The girl's mother, a co-plaintiff in the case, was enslaved by the couple and was represented by a team of lawyers that included Amal Clooney and Natalie von Wistinghausen. *Sueddeutsche Zeitung* reported that W. quit school after completing eighth grade. She grew up in Lower Saxony as a Protestant but converted to Islam in 2013. Prosecutors said she made her way to Iraq through Turkey and Syria in 2014 to join ISIS. In 2015, as a member of ISIS's "morality police",

she patrolled parks in Fallujah and Mosul, armed with an AK-47 assault rifle and a pistol as well as an explosive vest, looking for women who did not conform with its strict codes of behavior and dress. That summer, she and her ISIS terrorist husband purchased the young Yazidi girl as a slave. One day when the girl wet her bed, prosecutors claimed the husband chained the girl outside in the 45-degree Centigrade heat of the day and W. did nothing to prevent her dying of thirst. Authorities arrested W. when she tried to renew her identity papers at the German embassy in Ankara in 2016, and deported her to Germany. She was arrested again in June 2018 while trying to return to Syria. *Der Spiegel* reported that W. incriminated herself while talking to an undercover FBI informant in a bugged car. *Sueddeutsche Zeitung* reported her husband is believed to still be living in the Turkey-Iraq border region.

April 10, 2019: The Interior Ministry announced that authorities raided 90 properties across the country associated with an "Islamist network" suspected of helping Hamas under the guise of providing humanitarian aid. The network was headed by two groups based in North Rhine-Westphalia State—WWR Help and Ansaar International.

DPA reported that police raided more than 30 premises linked to suspected far-right extremists in Berlin and three other eastern German states, mainly centered on Brandenburg State and the region around Cottbus. Brandenburg police said that the investigation focused on about 20 people with ties to Germany's hooligan, martial arts, and right-wing extremist scene. Cottbus has a comparatively large neo-Nazi scene affiliated with the city's Energie Cottbus main football team.

April 11, 2019: Railway operator Deutsche Bahn said the ICE train traveling from Berlin to Saarbruecken was hit by unidentified projectiles in the late evening near Mannheim. Police said only the outer panes of double-glazed windows were damaged by the air pistol and no injuries were reported. None of the projectiles got inside the train. Investigators found nine points of impact on four cars of the train. Police believed that several people shot at the moving train, which was carrying 150 people.

April 12, 2019: Federal prosecutors indicted Sivatheeban B., 37, a Sri Lankan man suspected of involvement in killing 15 captured government soldiers while fighting for the Tamil Tigers. He was arrested in August 2018 and accused of membership in a foreign terrorist organization, war crimes, two cases of manslaughter, and 11 cases of attempted manslaughter. Prosecutors alleged that in 2008 he guarded 15 captured soldiers as they were driven to a site where they were executed, and later helped burn their bodies. Prosecutors said that in 2009, he fired on 13 soldiers, two of whom died.

April 17, 2019: Federal prosecutors announced the arrest in Hamburg of Volkan L., 28, a German suspected of joining ISIS in Syria and later helping send another new recruit for ISIS from Germany to Syria. Prosecutors said that he traveled to Syria in November 2013 to undergo military training. He returned to Germany in March 2014 to find new recruits. He was accused of helping organize travel to Syria for a recruit in summer 2014.

May 9, 2019: Authorities closed Frankfurt international airport and halted flights from 7:20 a.m. until 8:20 a.m. after a pilot saw a drone. German federal police searched for the drone and its operator with a helicopter.

May 20, 2019: *DPA* reported that the retrial began of seven men, aged between 27 and 37, accused of posing as a self-styled "Sharia police" in Wuppertal in 2014, on charges of violating rules on wearing uniforms. They had dressed in orange vests bearing the words "Sharia police" and handed out leaflets declaring the area a "Sharia-controlled zone" where alcohol, music and pornography were banned. Five were allegedly part of the patrol and the other two were accessories. They were acquitted in 2016 when judges found that the vests could not be classified as a uniform and were not intimidating. A federal court ordered the retrial. *DPA* reported on May 27 that a court found the seven guilty on charges of violating rules on wearing uniforms and fined them between 300 ($335) and 1,800 ($2,015) euros.

May 22, 2019: Federal prosecutors charged German woman Derya O., 26, with belonging to a foreign terrorist organization and violating arms control laws by attempting to sell a suicide belt online. She left Germany in February 2014 for Syria, where she married an ISIS fighter and lived in ISIS-held territory, living free of charge in buildings that residents had fled. She received training on using automatic weapons and owned a suicide belt, which she tried to sell via an online messenger service. She was arrested in November 2018.

June 1, 2019: Walter Luebcke, an official from German Chancellor Angela Merkel's Christian Democratic Union party who led the Kassel regional administration, was shot dead at his home. Stephan Ernst, 45, a far-right German extremist with a string of convictions for violent anti-migrant crimes, was arrested on June 15 and confessed on June 25. On July 2, he recanted his confession. He was represented by attorney Frank Hannig. *AP* and *Tagesspiegel* reported on August 21, 2019 that authorities found 46 guns in the possession of three men suspected in the killing of Walter Luebcke. Two other men were accused of accessory to murder for allegedly helping Ernst obtain the murder weapon. *AP* reported on September 19, 2019 that Ernst was suspected in the attempted killing of an Iraqi asylum-seeker on January 6, 2016. Ernst's rap sheet included several convictions for violent anti-migrant crimes. He faced attempted murder charges in the Iraqi's attack in which he snuck up behind the man and stabbed him in the upper back, leaving him in intensive care.

AP reported on April 29, 2020 that German prosecutors charged neo-Nazi Stephan Ernst, 46, with Luebcke's murder and a near-fatal stabbing of an Iraqi asylum-seeker in January 2016. Ernst was accused of murder, attempted murder, serious bodily harm and firearms offenses. A second man, Markus H., was charged with accessory to murder and breaking firearms laws for allegedly helping Ernst improve his marksmanship while suspecting that he was considering a politically motivated attack. Prosecutors said Ernst fired a Rossi revolver into Luebcke's head at close distance. Ernst was represented by attorney Frank Hannig.

Reuters reported on June 16, 2020 that the trial began of Stephan Ernst. Markus H. was charged with aiding and abetting the killing. The court announced that "Both defendants are charged with having committed these crimes based on extreme right-wing political convictions." Stephan Ernst initially confessed that he and Markus H. had gone to the house with a gun intending to threaten Luebcke but the gun went off while Markus H. was holding it.

AP, Reuters, al-Jazeera, and *DPA* reported on August 5, 2020 that during his trial at the Oberlandesgericht Frankfurt court house, right wing neo-Nazi extremist Stephan Ernst, 46, admitted to firing the fatal shot that killed politician Walter Luebcke. The defendant was represented by attorney Mustafa Kaplan. Ernst faced charged of murder, attempted murder, serious bodily harm and firearms offenses. He had previous convictions for violent anti-migrant crimes. Defendant Markus Hartmann was charged with being an accessory to murder by helping him train with firearms, including the murder weapon, and breaking firearms laws. Prosecutors said the two defendants attended an October 2015 town hall event where Luebcke defended the German government's decision to allow hundreds of thousands of refugees into the country. Prosecutors had charged Ernst with attempted murder for allegedly stabbing an Iraqi asylum seeker in the back in 2016. Ernst was convicted of an attempted bomb attack on an asylum home in 1993.

June 7, 2019: Federal prosecutors charged German woman Carla-Josephine S., 32, with terrorism for joining ISIS in Syria, with child endangerment resulting in death, and other offenses. Prosecutors said she took her three children to Syria in 2015, joined ISIS, and lived in one of their facilities while her children underwent ISIS ideological indoctrination and her son took paramilitary training before his death in 2018 when their compound was bombed. She could not talk her husband into joining her, so in 2016 she married a Somali ISIS terrorist and took paramilitary training. German officials arrested her when she returned in April 2019.

DPA reported the trial began of Tunisian Sief Allah H., 30, and his German wife, Yasmin H., 43, on charges of preparing a BW attack for ISIS by producing ricin via castor beans they purchased online in their Cologne apartment in 2018. They would have filled the bomb with steel bearings and explosives from illegal firecrackers. Prosecutor Verena Bauer told the court "They planned to detonate a bomb in a crowded place to kill as many unbelievers as possible." The duo tested the ricin on a dwarf hamster, which survived.

June 12, 2019: The federal prosecutor's office said authorities in the Pinneberg area, near Hamburg, arrested Hassan Rejan B., 31, a Kosovo man accused of supporting ISIS by transferring thousands of euros to a fighter and a would-be recruit. He was held on 15 counts of supporting ISIS and 11 of violating German export laws. Prosecutors claimed B. made 11 transfers in 2016 and 2017 to an ISIS fighter in Syria and in 2015 he transferred money to a man from North Macedonia who wanted to join ISIS in Syria. They said he transferred about 15,000 euros ($17,000), in most cases as an intermediary.

June 28, 2019: Federal prosecutors indicted eight far-right German men, aged 21 to 31, on suspicion of planning to start a violent uprising and forming a terrorist organization they called Revolution Chemnitz. They were arrested in 2018 in eastern Germany's Chemnitz area. Several suspects were alleged to have been involved in an attack on a group of migrants in Chemnitz on September 14, 2018. Authorities intercepted communication between them indicating that they were trying to obtain firearms.

July 18, 2019: At 4 a.m., police raided apartments in Dueren of alleged jihadis and detained six people amid suspicions the group may have been planning an attack. Cologne police said the raids included an apartment where the main suspect, a German-Lebanese Islamic convert, 30, had recently moved, joining another radical who already lived there, and on his construction company in Cologne. Police also searched his previous apartment in Berlin. Senior police official Klaus-Stephan Becker explained that the key suspect was investigated as an extremist for six years and tried often to travel to ISIS-controlled territory. Becker said police moved in after the man was heard talking about "planning to ascend to the highest level of paradise of the Muslim faith" which "could be a synonym for a suicide attack".

July 22, 2019: A German gunman, 55, fatally shot himself in the head three hours after he shot and seriously wounded an Eritrean man, 26, in the stomach during lunchtime in Waechsterbach. The suspect, who was found in his car in a neighboring town, apparently had an anti-foreigner motive. Police said the victim appeared to have been chosen at random because of his skin color. The gunman appeared to have acted alone. 19072202

July 30, 2019: Authorities raided the apartments of six suspected members of a potentially violent far-right group and four other people in four German states. The six allegedly founded the "Storm Brigade" in 2018 as a sub-organization of the "Wolf Brigade". Prosecutors said that the group aims for the "reinvigoration of a free fatherland" in accordance with a "Teutonic moral law", and that they suspect it may be prepared to use violence.

July 31, 2019: A man, 36, was fatally stabbed on a street in Stuttgart with a "sword-like object" in the evening. Police arrested a Syrian, 28, who apparently had shared an apartment until recently with the victim. The duo had argued. The attacker escaped on a bicycle. He admitted to the killing. Investigators said the motive was related to his personal relationship with the victim, and they found no indications of an "Islamist or political background". A judge ordered him to be held in custody on suspicion of murder pending possible formal charges.

August 7, 2019: Federal prosecutors arrested German woman Sibel H. on charges of membership in a terrorist organization, allegedly joining ISIS in Syria, war crimes, and weapons infractions. She reportedly traveled to Syria with her husband in 2016 to join ISIS, and moved to Mosul, Iraq. Prosecutors said they lived in homes seized by ISIS. Her husband served as a nurse in an ISIS hospital. They fled through Kurdish-controlled areas in the north and were captured by a militia in 2017.

August 14, 2019: Federal prosecutors charged three Iraqi refugees with planning a jihadi bombing. Shahin F. and Hersh F. were accused of preparing an act of violence and Sarkawt N. of aiding them. Because they were not linked to a specific organization they did not face terrorism charges. They allegedly ordered a detonator from UK but never received it after police there arrested their contact. They could not afford to buy an illegal firearm, then switched to a truck bomb idea. Shahin F. began taking driving theory classes. All were arrested in January 2019.

August 23, 2019: *AP* reported on August 29 that Kremlin spokesman Dmitry Peskov denied media reports that Moscow was involved in the daytime slaying of Tornike K., alias Zelimkhan Khangoshvili, a Russian-Georgian man, 40, in Berlin. The victim was shot by a Russian male cyclist, 48, who was captured shortly afterward. The news media claimed that the victim was an ex-insurgent who fought Russian forces in Chechnya. Moscow had deemed him a "terrorist" for his role in armed conflict with Russia; between 2000-2004, he commanded a Chechen militia and fought with a Georgian unit defending South Ossetia during the 2008 Georgia-Russia war. He survived a 2015 assassination attempt when he was shot four times, and fled to Germany, where he requested asylum. On September 3, 2019, Berlin police published a photo of the Russian and a bicycle and e-scooter he used and asked for witnesses to assist the investigators. *Der Spiegel* and *Bellingcat* reported that the suspect's passport indicated ties to Russian intelligence. The German press said he was shot with a Glock-26 pistol. Police arrested Vadim Sokolov on suspicion of murder; he was traveling on a genuine Russian passport, but possibly in alias.

The *Washington Post* reported on December 4, 2019 that German authorities said they suspected that Russian agents were behind an execution-style killing and expelled two Russian diplomats in connection with the case. The federal public prosecutor said there was "sufficient factual evidence" that the murder was carried out by Russian intelligence agencies or those of Russia's Chechen Republic. The German Foreign Ministry declared two employees of the Russian

Embassy in Berlin "persona non gratae", noting that Russian authorities had not cooperated with the investigation "sufficiently" despite repeated "high-ranking" requests.

Bellingcat reported that Sokolov's real name was Vadim Krasikov, originally subject of an international arrest warrant issued by Russian authorities in 2014 for a murder a year prior in Moscow in which the killer approached the victim on a bicycle.

September 9, 2019: Federal prosecutors arrested Omaima A., a German-Tunisian woman, on charges of being a member of a terror organization and for joining ISIS in Syria, weapons charges, and violating her child-raising obligations. Prosecutors said she traveled with her three minor children to Raqqa, Syria in 2015. She raised her children according to ISIS ideology while her husband, who had traveled to Syria in December 2014, was an ISIS fighter. He died in an air raid. ISIS gave her $1,310 (1,187 euros). She married another ISIS fighter. After disagreements with him, she returned to Germany with her children in September 2016.

September 11, 2019: *DPA* reported that authorities arrested two Syrian men, aged 34 and 37, suspected of being part of a criminal network that earned commissions for sending six-figure sums abroad that might have been used to fund extremist activity. Authorities investigated 11 people. Police and prosecutors searched 16 locations in Schleswig-Holstein, Mecklenburg Western-Pomerania and Hamburg.

September 25, 2019: The Stuttgart state court convicted a German-Tunisian man, 30, of membership in ISIS and Junud al-Sham and sentenced him to two years and five months in prison. The court said he traveled to Syria in late 2013 to join ISIS and received military training. He left ISIS in February 2014 and joined Junud al-Sham. He served two months as a fighter and paramedic before returning to Germany, where he was in custody for a year. Judges ordered his release after taking into account time he spent jailed in Tunisia from June 2015 until January 2018.

September 30, 2019: The Dresden regional court began the trial of eight men, aged between 21 and 32, all suspected far-right extremists accused of forming a terrorist organization calling itself "Revolution Chemnitz" and planning a violent uprising. The leading members of Chemnitz's neo-Nazi, skinhead and hooligan scene sought to obtain firearms and overthrow Germany's democratic order, starting with an attack scheduled for October 3, 2018. They were arrested on October 1, 2018. Several suspects allegedly were involved in a September 14, 2018 attack on a group of migrants in Chemnitz, which days earlier saw far-right protests following the killing of a German man by migrants.

October 7, 2019: A Syrian refugee, 32, was arrested after he commandeered a truck and crashed it into a line of seven cars and a van in Limburg in the late afternoon, injuring eight people, seven of whom were hospitalized. The driver, who was slightly injured, was arrested. The driver lived in the Offenbach area near Frankfurt. He did not use a weapon. Police searched two apartments in the area, seizing cellphones and USB sticks. *ZDF* reported that officials believed he had an extremist background. *NPR* reported that police were investigating a terrorist motive.

October 9, 2019: Bavaria's state criminal police office announced raids on seven properties in connection with 23 threatening far-right emails sent in a two-week period in July to mosques, political parties, the media, and migrant reception centers. Properties in three other states were also searched. The emails threatened bombings, inter alia, and were signed by the "People's Front", "Combat 18", or "Blood and Honor". Seven people were under investigation and six were temporarily detained. They were released once the raids were over.

October 9, 2019: *NPR, AP, CNN,* the *Washington Post, Bild* and *Middeldeutsche Zeitung* reported that police arrested a suspect after two people—one German woman, 40; one man, 20—were shot to death and several injured at 12:15 p.m. in the vicinity of Humboldtstrasse, outside a Halle synagogue and a nearby kabob shop on Yom Kippur. Police spokeswoman Ulrike Diener said that multiple suspects were believed to have fled the scene in a grey Volkswagen Golf en route to Schillerstrasse. Regional public broadcaster *MDR* ran a video of a man wearing a helmet-mounted camera and olive-colored top getting out of a car and firing four shots from behind the vehicle from a long-barreled gun. *DPA* reported that federal prosecutors took over the investigation. The Federal Criminal Office warned that three suspects may be at large. German Interior Minister Horst Seehofer called the incident an anti-Semitic attack and said prosecutors suspected a far-right motive. He said the individual failed to break into the synagogue. *Der Spiegel* reported that the suspect was a 27-year-old man from Saxony-Anhalt State, where Halle is located. Livestreaming site *Twitch* said a 35-minute video of the shooting was broadcast live on its platform, but it "worked with urgency to remove this content" and any account found to be posting or reposting "content of this abhorrent act" would be permanently suspended. *NTV* reported that police conducted an operation in the small village of Wiedersdorf, 8.6 miles east of Halle.

U.S. Ambassador Richard Grenell said ten Americans were among the 80 people inside the synagogue.

Eyewitness Conrad Rössler told *NTV* that he saw a man throw what "looked like a hand grenade with gaffer tape" into the kebab store, but it "bounced back from the door frame and did not land inside the shop and did not explode". The attacker then shot at "least once" into the shop where there were five other customers. *AP* reported that the attacker shouted "The root of all problems are the Jews!" Rössler hid in the restroom.

The Golf was registered to the town of Euskirchen, North Rhine-Westfalia, 263 miles from Halle.

The terrorist wounded two other people in the Queis Landsberg, ten miles away, then abandoned his car and carjacked a taxi. He was arrested 90 minutes later as he got out of the taxi, which had been in an accident.

Authorities said the terrorist had four kilograms of explosives and four firearms, apparently homemade "ghost guns". The guns, including a shotgun, often jammed. During the live stream, he observed, "I have certainly managed to prove how absurd improvised weapons are." Investigators found a 3-D printer at the suspect's residence, and believed some of the gun components were made with the printer. Prosecutors said that the gunman carried several explosive devices, a helmet and a protective vest.

AP reported on October 11 that the attacker was a German, Stephan Balliet, 27, who was held on suspicion of two counts of murder, nine of attempted murder, and other offenses. He had posted an 11-page manifesto online before the attack. He had planned more extensive carnage. In the manifesto, he said his aims were to:

- "1. Prove the viability of improvised weapons.
- 2. Increase the morale of other suppressed Whites by spreading the combat footage.
- 3. Kill as many anti-Whites as possible, Jews preferred.
- Bonus: Don't die."

DPA reported that Balliet admitted to the shooting and to having a right-wing extremist motive. Federal prosecutors said he talked for several hours. Defense attorney Hans-Dieter Weber told broadcaster *Suedwestrundfunk* "it would be pointless to dispute anything, and he didn't do that."

Holger Stahlknecht, interior minister of Saxony-Anhalt State, said Balliet was wounded in the neck in a shootout with police.

On October 14, *DPA* quoted regional lawmakers in Saxony-Anhalt State who said that police lost track of the terrorist for an hour and credited two officers in Zeitz for arresting Balliet.

AP and *DPA* reported that on July 21, 2020, the trial in the eastern German state court in Magdeburg began of Stephan Balliet, 28, for the attack. He faced 13 charges, including murder, attempted murder, bodily harm, incitement to hatred and attempted violent extortion. Forty-three victims and relatives were listed as co-plaintiffs, and 168 people were listed as witnesses.

AP reported on September 27, 2020 that Balliett threw explosives over a wall into a cemetery inside the compound.

NBC News and DPA reported on November 18, 2020 that German prosecutors in a court in Magdeburg called for a life sentence for Balliet, 28, who allegedly posted an anti-Jewish rant before livestreaming his attack on a synagogue in Halle on Yom Kippur, October 9, 2019, killing two people. Prosecutors asked the judges to find him "seriously culpable", thereby barring him from early release after 15 years.

DPA, Reuters, and AP reported on December 21, 2020 that Presiding Judge Ursula Mertens of the Naumburg Higher Regional Court, meeting in the district court in Magdeburg for security and capacity reasons, convicted rightwing extremist Stephan Balliet, 28, of 13 charges, including murder, attempted murder, and incitement, and sentenced him to life in prison. He was effectively barred from early release after 15 years.

October 21, 2019: Prosecutors charged German woman Carla-Josephine S. with membership in a terrorist organization and child endangerment for taking her three minor children to Syria and joining ISIS in 2015 while her husband was on a business trip. ISIS gave the children ideological indoctrination. When her son questioned the teaching, she reported him to ISIS leadership, who punished him. He also underwent paramilitary training and was killed in 2018 when their compound was bombed. She married an ISIS fighter from Somalia in 2016 and underwent paramilitary training. German authorities arrested her upon her return in April 2019.

October 27, 2019: German Green politicians Cem Özdemir and Claudia Roth received email death threats signed by "Atomwaffen Division Deutschland" (AWD), which claimed to have a list of people marked for assassination.

November 6, 2019: Muenster prosecutor Martin Botzenhardt said a gunman shooting from a white vehicle with Netherlands license plates seriously wounded a Dutch male attorney, 43, believed to have been intentionally targeted in a morning attack in Gronau.

November 12, 2019: NPR and AP reported that 170 police raided three apartments in Offenbach, arresting three men believed to be ISIS support-ers planning a bombing against non-Muslims in the Rhine-Main region. One person, 24, a German with Macedonian roots, had obtained bombmaking materials and searched for firearms online. Police confiscated substances and electronic devices at his apartment. The other two were Turkish citizens aged 21 and 22.

November 15, 2019: Federal prosecutors accused German woman Nasim A., with joining ISIS in Syria in 2014 and marrying an ISIS fighter. She was arrested during the evening. Kurdish fighters had detained her earlier in the year and held her at the al-Hawl camp in northeastern Syria. The couple allegedly moved to Tal Afar, Iraq, where they lived in an ISIS-seized house. The woman ran the household, receiving $100/month from ISIS.

November 18, 2019: Der Spiegel, the Guardian and Reuters reported that the neo-Nazi terrorist group Atomwaffen Division (AWD) targeted a U.S. activist in Germany. She told the Guardian that U.S. authorities warned German federal Bundespolizei in November 2018 of "a specific threat to find me and do me harm". She had moved to Germany in part due to threats from the far right in the U.S. American authorities warned about an AWD member who had traveled to Germany with the possible intention of harming her. In mid-November 2019, German authorities denied entry to a suspected American member of AWD.

November 19, 2019: DPA reported that federal prosecutors announced the arrest of a "radical Islamist" Syrian man, 37, and raid on his Berlin apartment over suspicions he was planning an attack to "kill and injure a maximum number of people". He researched online how to build bombs and posted about planning an attack in Internet chats. In January 2019, he allegedly began obtaining material and chemicals, including acetone and hydrogen peroxide, to build an explosive device.

In the evening, a German man, 57, jumped up from the audience at the Schlosspark-Klinik and stabbed to death Fritz von Weizsaecker, 59, son of former German president Richard von Weizsaecker, while he was lecturing about fatty liver disease at a Berlin's Charite Hospital where he worked as a head physician. An off-duty police officer in the audience who tried to stop the attack underwent surgery for serious wounds. The attacker was not a patient at the hospital. Richard von Weizsaecker became West Germany's head of state in 1984 and when the country was unified, became the first president of the new nation, serving until 1994. He died in 2015. Fritz, a member of the Free Democrats party, was one of the ex-president's four children.

November 23, 2019: *DPA* reported that a woman, 30, allegedly an ISIS member, had returned to Germany with her three children via a nighttime flight from Irbil, Iraq, to Frankfurt. *DPA* suggested they were in a detention camp in northern Syria.

GREECE

January 9-10, 2019: Letters containing white powder arrived at 11 university campuses around the country. Four postal workers and five university staff members received medical attention as a precaution. The letters were sent from India. The letters went to administrative offices at campuses on the island of Crete, Lesbos, and Corfu plus Athens and the central mainland city of Volos. Another envelope arrived at a college in Thessaloniki on January 11 as the incident count reached 24; police searched another ten university and college buildings around the country. A dozen people received medical attention. Analysis of the first sample obtained by authorities showed the powder consisted of an industrial adhesive. State-run television reported that the letters contained printed "Islamic material" in English. 19010939-63

February 27, 2019: A council in Volos rejected a 7th furlough for convicted far-left November 17 extremist Dimitris Koufodinas, 61, who was serving multiple life sentences for a string of assassinations. The judges held that he still posed a danger to society and could commit new crimes were he granted a furlough.

March 1, 2019: In the morning, a car explosion seriously injured a man and damaged four cars in a parking lot in the upscale Glyfada area south of Athens. Bomb squad officers were involved in the investigation. Witnesses said the blast occurred after the man started the ignition.

March 22, 2019: During the night, a hand grenade was thrown over the perimeter fence of the Russian Consulate in suburban Athens, causing minor damage and no injuries. Leftist Popular Fighters Group (OLA) terrorists were suspected. Cameras showed two people on a motorbike throwing a small object in the early hours of the morning. No security guard was at the post at the time. A partially burned motorbike was found in the area. *AP* reported on April 18 that the anarchist Revenge Plot Mikhail Zhlobitsky Cell claimed credit, saying the grenade toss was revenge for a suicide bomb attack by Zhlobitsky. A Greek left-wing site said Zhlobitsky was a teen who died in an attack on the Akhrangelsk office of Russia's domestic security agency that injured three people. 19032201

March 25, 2019: Police arrested four suspects after a firebomb was thrown before dawn at the Athens home of Greece's deputy health minister Pavlos Polakis, causing minor damage and no injuries. Three suspects were released; the fourth was held for being in the country illegally and was awaiting deportation.

May 7, 2019: Dimitris Koufodinas, 61, November 17 assassin serving 11 life terms, was hospitalized in Volos following a five-day hunger strike over prison authorities' refusal to grant him temporary leave. Since late 2017 he was granted six furloughs. On May 9, he vowed to continue the strike "until the end". His attorney, Ioanna Kourtovik, said that he would refuse any medical assistance. A council of judges upheld the wardens' decision to reject the furlough request.

During the evening of May 8, some 30 hooded youths protesting the decision smashed the windows of more than 20 shops and two banks in central Athens.

On May 9, anarchists invaded the Athens offices of *Avgi* newspaper, which strongly backed the ruling Syriza party, to protest the ruling.

On May 17, Koufodinas went into intensive care after a 15-day hunger strike. His attorney, Ioanna Kourtovik, said he risked kidney failure "at any moment… His health has deteriorated rapidly, and he is in danger of suffering irreversible damage." He held a two-week hunger strike in the summer of 2018.

On May 21, the Greek Supreme Court began hearing an appeal by Koufodinas against the denial of a temporary leave of absence from prison. Kourtovik claimed on May 23 that the court ordered lower judges in Volo to reconsider his request.

May 21, 2019: Ten members of the Rouvikonas anarchist group threw red paint at parliament and set off a smoke bomb.

June 10, 2019: Before dawn, arsonists poured flammable liquid over two vehicles owned by Turkish citizens, including a diplomat working in the Turkish Consulate and a Turk employed at an international financial institution headquartered in Thessaloniki, parked in front of a block of flats in Thessaloniki. The fire destroyed the two cars and damaged four others. No one claimed credit. 19061001

November 9, 2019: The police counterterrorism squad arrested three people and detained another 15 in a "wide sweep" of 13 houses against suspected left-wing extremists. One person remained at large in the ongoing operation. Two of those arrested, and the one at large, were men in their 40s who faced charges of engaging in terrorist action, illegal possession of firearms and explosives, and forgery. The three allegedly robbed a betting shop in an Athens suburb on October 21. A woman, 39, was arrested for "violating the firearms law". Police found five AK-47 rifles, a submachine gun, two pistols, grenades, explosives and detonators. One AK-47 was used in the betting shop robbery and another was used in 2014, 2016 and twice in 2017. In May 2014, on a European Parliament election day, shots were fired at the offices of the socialist party, then ruling in coalition with the conservatives. In January and November 2017, shots from the AK-47 were fired at riot police guarding the socialist party's offices. A police officer was injured in the first of these attacks. In July 2016, shots were fired at the Mexican Embassy in Athens. In November 2016, a grenade thrown at the French Embassy injured a police officer. The Organization for Revolutionary Self-Defense claimed all of the attacks. One of the arrested men was jailed in 2010 for membership in the Revolutionary Struggle. He was released early in February 2018.

Hungary

March 22, 2019: Authorities detained a Syrian man, 27, suspected of having taken part in beheadings in Homs, Syria of about 20 relatives of a Homs resident who refused to join ISIS. He had refugee status in Greece. He was initially apprehended in December 2018 at Budapest's Ferenc Liszt International Airport when he and a female companion were found to have forged personal IDs. Belgian prosecutors and local officials determined that he joined ISIS in 2016. He was awaiting deportation to Greece. On September 3, 2019, prosecutors charged Hassan F., 27, a Syrian who was suspected of belonging to ISIS, with committing acts of terror, murder, and crimes against humanity in Syria in May 2015. Prosecutors said he participated in the beheading of a religious leader in al-Sukhnah in Homs Province and was involved in the killing of at least 25 people, including six women and children. They sought a life sentence without the possibility of parole. On November 13, 2019, his trial began in the Metropolitan Court in Budapest. Prosecutors said Hassan F. compiled a list of those to be killed, which was then approved by ISIS leaders, and supervised the killings. Hassan F. denied prosecutors' claims that he was a member of a small, armed ISIS unit. His attorney said his client had not been in Syria since 2014 and was in Turkey with his wife at the time of the alleged crimes, during the first half of May 2015. Hassan F.'s father testified that his son had been imprisoned in Syria for refusing to join ISIS. His lawyer said Hassan F. had attempted suicide in prison. Hassan F. obtained refugee status in Greece.

Ireland

February 21, 2019: Flights to and from Dublin Airport were suspended in the morning "for safety reasons" after a "confirmed sighting" of a drone over the airfield.

March 10, 2019: Minister for Justice and Equality Charlie Flanagan said he would make "every effort" to bring home from Syria Lisa Smith, formerly of the Irish Defense Forces, who was believed to have joined ISIS. She was believed to have a young son.

March 22, 2019: A parcel bomb found in the morning at an Irish return mail office in Limerick appeared identical to devices sent to the UK earlier in March. Irish Justice Minister Charlie Flanagan said a stamp on the package was similar to small letter bombs sent to the UK for which an Irish dissident group claimed credit.

ITALY

January 23, 2019: Police in Sicily arrested Giuseppe D'Ignoti, 32, an Italian convert to Islam on terrorism charges for allegedly inciting contacts to participate in a holy war. *ANSA* reported that he converted in 2011 while in jail; after his release he identified himself as Moroccan and used Yussuf as his first name. Investigators said he forced his girlfriend to follow Islam, wear a veil and to watch videos showing executions of "infidels".

January 24, 2019: An Italian anti-terrorism unit investigated graffiti on a wall in Milan inciting violence against Interior Minister Matteo Salvini. Translated, the blue lettering said, "Don't shoot blanks. Shoot Salvini." It bore a red A inside a circle, an anarchist symbol, and Salvini wearing a law enforcement uniform.

March 1, 2019: Italian Interior Minister Matteo Salvini announced the arrest in a farmhouse near Acerra of Algerian Mourad Sadaoui, 45, who fought in Syria for ISIS. He was the first foreign fighter to have gone from Italy to Syria and then be captured after returning to Italian soil. He quietly reentered Italy in 2017. Algeria had issued a warrant on terrorism charges. He had worked as a bricklayer in Italy starting in 2003. He went to Syria via Algeria in 2013.

April 17, 2019: Sicilian prosecutors announced the arrests in northern Italy of Giuseppe Frittatta, alias Yusef, 25, a Sicilian convert to Islam and a Moroccan resident, Ossama Gafhir, 18, who met over the Internet and were preparing to fight with ISIS in Syria. Frittatta had posted on social media selfies of himself holding a knife with a 10-inch blade calling for deaths to "all westerners". Prosecutors said Frittatta induced Gafhir to extremism. Gafhir was following a stringent fitness routine to prepare for combat. Frittatta allegedly was in contact with extremists in Italy and abroad, including an American.

May 20-21, 2019: *ANSA* reported that a nighttime arson killed two people living in apartments above a ground-floor police station in Mirandola, north of Bologna, and injured more than a dozen others, two seriously. The dead included a woman, 74, and her live-in caretaker. Carabinieri arrested a North African; it was not clear if he was a legal resident.

July 3, 2019: A court in Genoa jailed three men who were found guilty of fighting alongside Russian-backed separatists who control a large swathe of Ukraine's Donetsk and Luhansk regions. Italian Antonio Cataldo and Albanian-born Olsi Krutani were sentenced to two years and eight months. Moldovan citizen Vladimir Vrbitchii was sentenced to one year and four months.

July 15, 2019: Turin Digos police detained three men, including one linked to a neo-fascist Italian political party, following an investigation into Italians who took part in the Russian-backed insurgency in the eastern Ukraine. One of the men had in 2001 run unsuccessfully as a Senate candidate for the neo-fascist Forza Nuova party. At his home in Gallarate, police found nine assault weapons, nearly 30 hunting rifles, pistols, bayonets, 1,000 cartridges and antique Nazi plaques featuring swastikas. Two other men were detained after police found a French-made missile at a Pavia airport hangar. The missile did not have an explosive. *La Repubblica* identified the suspects as Fabio Del Bergiolo, 50, a former customs officer who was affiliated with the far-right Forza Nuova party, Swiss national Alessandro Monti, 42, and an Italian, Fabio Bernardi, 51. *Reuters* reported that the suspects attempted to sell the air-to-air missile, believed to be a French Matra Super 530 F, over the messaging service *WhatsApp*. *BBC* reported that the missile came from the Qatari armed forces. On July 20, police said they found another cache of weapons during a search of a second residence of one of the three suspects. Anti-terrorism police confiscated a rifle, a machete, a tripod for a machine gun, mortars and other weapons and ammunition. They also found a framed portrait of Benito Mussolini.

November 28, 2019: The *Guardian* reported that police arrested 19 far-right extremists in various parts of the country who wanted to form a new Nazi party. *AFP* reported that police found weapons, explosives, Nazi plaques featuring swastikas, Nazi flags, and books on Adolph Hitler and Benito Mussolini. Prosecutors in Caltanissetta, Sicily, who led the Black Shadows investigation, said the suspects allegedly wanted to create "an openly pro-Nazi, xenophobic, antisemitic group called the Italian National Socialist Workers' Party". They apparently created a chat group for the military-style training of militants, and contacted other neo-Nazi groups outside Italy, including the UK's neo-Nazi Combat 18 and Portugal's far-right New Social Order. A woman, 50, alias Hitler's Sergeant Major, based in Padua led the organization. She worked in public administration and had no criminal record. Investigators found swastikas and anti-Semitic material at her home. Police also investigated a Sicilian woman, 26, who won an online "Miss Hitler" beauty contest and addressed a far-right conference in Lisbon in August 2019. The group's training chief was a former senior member of the Calabrian mafia 'Ndrangheta who turned informer a few years ago and had since collaborated with the police. He was a former member and contact person in the region of Liguria of the neo-fascist Italian political party Forza Nuova. Police searching the homes of two suspects discovered leaflets insulting two MPs for the centre-left Democratic party: Emanuele Fiano, a prominent figure in the Italian Jewish Community, and Laura Boldrini, a former parliamentary speaker and the victim of persistent online abuse and bogus news reports.

The next day, *ANSA* reported that police arrested a man, 57, from Monza for suspected illegal weapons possession. Police found rifles and revolvers in his home.

December 2, 2019: The Interior Ministry expelled two suspected extremists from Bangladesh and Morocco, including a Bangladeshi imam, 19, who allegedly beat children studying the Quran. He was teaching religion at an Islamic cultural center in Padua, expounding a "radical vision of Islam". The Moroccan, 24, lived in Turin, and allegedly had links to a Moroccan who was convicted of association with the aim of terrorism.

Kosovo

January 22, 2019: A Pristina court convicted M.D., a man, for participating in terrorist groups in Syria and jailed him for five years. The court said he went to Turkey with his wife and son in March 2013 and later crossed into neighboring Syria to join ISIS. He surrendered in August 2017 to Turkish authorities.

The court separately convicted five others to prison terms "for participation in terror groups and other acts related to terrorism" and sentenced them from one to seven years in jail and fined them 600 to 3,500 Euros ($680 to $4,100) each.

April 4, 2019: Prosecutors charged a male suspect, B.E., for illegally spreading information on ISIS in Syria, saying that from August 2018 until January 2019 he had used his social network page to spread photos and other information about the group, "openly supporting their terrorist acts". He also posted a photo threatening Kosovo Prime Minister Ramush Haradinaj. He faced five years in prison.

April 24, 2019: A court in Pristina ordered 19 women who had repatriated from Syria put under house arrest after prosecutors said they were suspected of joining or taking part in the conflict there as foreign militants. The previous day, ten other women were put under house arrest. None were charged with a crime. Four alleged fighters, all men, were arrested the moment they arrived in the country.

November 7, 2019: Prosecutors filed terrorism charges against A.M., a man suspected of fighting with ISIS in Syria. The charge said that in July 2015, A.M. went to North Macedonia, where he obtained a false passport, then went to Syria via Greece and Turkey. He fought for ISIS until Kurdish forces arrested him in July 2017. He was among 110 Kosovo citizens repatriated from Syria in April 2019. He faced 10 years in prison. Kosovo authorities said 30 Kosovars continued to support terrorist groups in Syria.

NETHERLANDS

February 27, 2019: The National Prosecutor's Office announced the arrest of a man, 48, on suspicion of preparing a terror attack. Police found a pistol, hidden in a child's backpack, and ammunition at his home in Groningen. An investigating judge ordered the man detained for 90 days while investigations continued. A Dutch intelligence agency alerted police that he was a supporter of ISIS and that he owned a weapon.

March 18, 2019: *CNN* reported that police were searching for Turkish-born Gökmen Tanis, 37, after he fired an automatic weapon inside a tram in 24 October Square in Utrecht at 10:45 a.m., killing three—two men and a woman—and injuring five (originally reported as nine), three critically. A 4th victim, a man, 74, died on March 28. Among the dead was Rinke Terpstra. Several people kicked out train windows and jumped to safety. The gunman escaped, possibly in a red Renault Clio compact sedan, which was later found abandoned. Police said it could be a terrorist attack. Germany increased border surveillance. Later that day, police arrested an armed Tanis, who had a criminal record that included attempted manslaughter and petty crime in the Utrecht area. Police also arrested a man, 23, and a third man, 27, both Utrecht residents, for possible links to the attack. Two weeks earlier, Tanis was in court on charges of raping a woman in 2017, but was released. Tanis was jailed in that case from August-September 2017 and again from January 4, 2019 to March 1, 2019 and freed after pledging to cooperate with police, according to the official website of Dutch courts, www.recht-spraak.nl. He was convicted in March 2019 of shoplifting and burglary in 2018 and sentenced to four months for the burglary and a week for the shop theft. He had not served time in those cases because the cases can still be appealed. His rape trial was scheduled for July 15, 2019. In 2014, Tanis was acquitted of manslaughter but convicted of illegal weapon possession and attempted theft. Dutch politician Geert Wilders, the anti-Islam head of the Party for Freedom, demanded that Justice Minister Ferd Grapperhaus resign over the release. It did not appear that Tanis knew any of the victims, who included a woman, 19, from Vianen, and two Utrecht men aged 28 and 49. The *Washington Post* reported the next day that police found a note in Tanis's vehicle regarding the motivations behind the attack.

Police released the two other male suspects on March 19. However, later that day, they arrested another male suspect, 40.

Prosecution spokesman Frans Zonneveld said on March 22 that Tanis had confessed and said he had acted alone. Court spokeswoman Els de Stigter said that an investigating judge extended Tanis's detention by two weeks on charges including multiple murder or manslaughter with terrorist intent. *AP* reported on April 4 that a Dutch court extended Tanis's detention by 90 days.

On July 1, 2019, Dutch prosecutors said in Utrecht District Court that Tanis left a handwritten letter in a getaway car that said in Dutch: "I'm doing this for my religion, you kill Muslims and you want to take our religion away from us, but you won't succeed. Allah is great." Tanis was held on charges including multiple murder or manslaughter with terrorist intent for the deaths of three men and a woman. Prosecutors said Tanis was a repeat offender, a drug user and "difficult person".

On March 2, 2020, Dutch prosecutors demanded a life sentence for Gokmen Tanis, 38, a Dutch man of Turkish descent. Tanis was removed from court for showing disrespect to judges and families of his victims and for spitting at his court-appointed lawyer. Psychological tests established that Tanis had a personality disorder and low IQ.

AP reported on March 20, 2020 that presiding judge Ruud van Veldhuisen convicted Tanis of murder with a terrorist motive and sentenced him to life in prison. Tanis was not in court due to restrictions imposed to prevent the spread of COVID-19. 19031801

May 21, 2019: Police in Kapelle, acting on a tip from German police, arrested a Syrian, 47, on suspicion of war crimes and terrorism in Syria where he allegedly was a commander in the former al-Qaeda-affiliated Nusra Front. He had lived in the Netherlands since 2014 on a temporary asylum visa. Police confiscated a computer, smartphone and documents during a search of the suspect's house. Dutch prosecutors said that German police simultaneously searched six homes of suspected members of the Nusra battalion led by the man arrested in the Netherlands. He was scheduled to appear before an investigating judge in The Hague on May 24.

October 29, 2019: Prosecutors demanded a six-year prison sentence for Junaid I., 27, a Pakistani man accused of plotting a terrorist attack on Dutch anti-Islam lawmaker Geert Wilders. Prosecutors said I. came to the Netherlands in August 2018 with "the intention to kill the politician" because of a competition Wilders was organizing featuring cartoons of the Prophet Muhammad. Prosecutors said I. threatened Wilders in a video he posted on *Facebook* in which he said: "I will send that dog ... to Hell." On November 18, the Hague District Court sentenced the Pakistani to 10 years in prison. The judges imposed the higher sentence because of factors including the suspect's ongoing aim to kill Wilders. The defendant traveled to the Netherlands in August 2018.

November 22, 2019: Two trains in the southern Netherlands were hit by gunfire, causing no injuries. Breda police tweeted during the night that a passenger train traveling from Tilburg to nearby Breda, close to the border with Belgium, "could possibly have been shot". Five windows were damaged. A train using the same tracks arrived in Eindhoven with a broken window also possibly caused by gunfire. The next day, Dutch police detained two 15-year-old boys in an investigation into the possible shooting of two trains. The boys had BB pistols with them when they were detained on suspicion of damaging the trains.

November 25, 2019: The National Prosecutor's Office announced that police counterterror officers arrested two men, aged 20 and 34, suspected of plotting a jihadi attack using suicide vests and one or more car bombs around the end of the year. Police searched their homes and found an ax and a dagger concealed above the ceiling in one of the men's homes in Zoetermeer, six miles east of The Hague. The investigation began in October on the heels of a tip to police by the main Dutch intelligence agency that the suspects had the intention of staging an attack using explosives and were seeking training.

November 29, 2019: *NPR* reported that at 7:45 p.m., two 15-year-old girls and a 13-year-old boy were injured in a stabbing in a shopping district in The Hague. *AP* and *Reuters* reported that police arrested an adult homeless man, 35. Police announced that a preliminary description of the suspect as a 45-year-old man in a grey track suit was incorrect. National broadcaster *NOS* reported that an "athletic" man easily jumped over obstacles while escaping. The victims were treated in a hospital and released. They did not know one another. Police said on December 1 that they had not found indications of a terrorist motive.

NORTHERN IRELAND

January 19, 2019: Irish Republican Army dissidents belonging to the New IRA were suspected when a bomb placed inside a hijacked pizza delivery vehicle went off during the night outside a courthouse on Bishop Street in Londonderry. Police had received a warning. No injuries were reported. Police arrested two men in their 20s. By January 21, five men had been arrested.

January 21, 2019: Army bomb-disposal experts conducted a controlled explosion on a hijacked vehicle in Londonderry.

April 18-19, 2019: The dissident New IRA was suspected in the fatal shooting of journalist/author Lyra McKee, 29, during overnight rioting in the Creggan housing complex of Londonderry. Assistant Chief Constable Mark Hamilton of the Police Service of Northern Ireland said a gunman fired at police during the evening, saying, "We believe this to be a terrorist act... We believe it has been carried out by violent dissident republicans." McKee apparently was inadvertently hit. Hamilton said police believed "that the New IRA are most likely to be the ones behind this and that forms our primary line of inquiry". Police arrested two male suspects, aged 18 and 19, on April 20. Police freed the two teens the next day without charging them. On April 23, the Northern Ireland Police Service arrested a woman, 57, under the Terrorism Act in the slaying. The New IRA, which is opposed to the Good Friday agreement, sent a statement to the *Irish News* apologizing that one of its "volunteers" killed McKee "while standing beside enemy forces". *AP* and *NBC News* reported on May 9 that the Police Service of Northern Ireland arrested males aged 15, 18, 38, and 51 in Londonderry under terrorism legislation. On May 11, prosecutors told a court that Paul McIntyre and Christopher Gillen were connected to the New IRA and charged them with rioting in Londonderry on the night McKee was killed, petrol bomb offenses, and the arson and hijacking of vehicles. The duo were refused bail.

On February 11, 2020, *Reuters* reported that Northern Irish police arrested four men, aged 20, 27, 29, and 52, in Londonderry under the Terrorism Act for the April 2019 shooting of Lyra McKee. A mural in Belfast celebrated her life. McKee was named *Sky News* Young Journalist of the Year in 2006. McKee was writing a book on the disappearance of young people during the violence in Northern Ireland. *Reuters* reported on February 12 that Northern Irish police charged a man, 52, with McKee's murder, possession of a firearm with intent to endanger life and with professing to be a member of a proscribed organization. He was to appear at Londonderry Magistrates Court on February 13, 2020. A 29-year-old man was released without charge. The 20- and 27-year olds were freed pending a report to the Public Prosecution Service.

NORWAY

January 17, 2019: Benedicte Bjornland, head of Norway's PST domestic intelligence agency, said police were investigating the stabbing of a wom-

an in her 20s in a Kiwi supermarket in downtown Oslo as a terrorist attack. A detainee told investigators he wanted to kill several people. The suspect was a Russian citizen, 20, who entered Norway via Sweden. The victim was in critical condition. The Oslo District Court ordered the suspect held for four weeks ahead of trial for stabbing the woman and plotting a terrorist attack. PST was investigating the Russian's possible links to jihadis. Defense attorney Ola Lunde told *NTB* that it was believed the suspect acted alone. Norwegian public broadcaster *NRK* said he was from Russia's Bashkortostan region near Kazakhstan. 19011703

February 7, 2019: Daniel Lindblad of the Swedish Maritime Administration announced that a Norwegian Air plane bound for Nice returned to Stockholm after takeoff for security reasons after the airline received a bomb threat at 10.30 a.m. The plane landed safely at 11.14 a.m. at Stockholm airport. The 169 passengers were evacuated.

July 15, 2019: Norwegian PST domestic security agency authorities detained Iraqi-born Najm al-Din Faraj Ahmad, alias Mullah Krekar, 63, on an Italian arrest warrant. An Italian court in Bolzano had found him guilty of planning terrorism, attempting to overthrow the Kurdish government in northern Iraq and create an Islamic caliphate, and sentenced him to 12 years. Italian prosecutors said he was behind Rawti Shax, a European network aimed at violently overthrowing the government in Kurdistan. Krekar's Italian lawyer, Enrica Franzini, planned to appeal. He was represented in Norway by attorney Brynjar Meiling. On July 18, the Oslo District Court declared Krekar a flight risk and ordered him held for four weeks. Norwegian broadcaster *NRK* said an Italian extradition request was expected soon.

August 10, 2019: At 4 p.m., a gunman in his 20s shot and lightly injured a person at al-Noor Islamic Center in Baerum, a western Oslo suburb, in the afternoon. *Budstikka* reported that the shooter, who was taken into custody, wore a helmet, body armor, and a uniform. Three people, including Mohamed Rafiq, 65, a former Pakistani military officer, overpowered the suspect and held him down until police arrived. *CNN* reported that police said the shooter expressed right-wing views online, praising figures like Vidkun Quisling, the leader of Norway under Nazi occupation during World War II. Police were investigating the shooting as a "possible act of terrorism". The gunman was charged with the murder of his step-sister, 17, who was found dead in his home and faced an attempted murder charge in the shooting at the mosque. Police found several weapons—believed linked to the shooter—inside the mosque. Philip Manshaus, 21, with bruises on his face but smiling, appeared in Oslo District Court on August 12. Defense attorney Unni Fries said her client "will use his right not to explain himself for now" in the pre-trial detention hearing. Manshaus was ordered held for four weeks, including two weeks in solitary confinement, while police investigated. Hans Sverre Sjoevold, head of Norway's PST agency, said officials had received a "vague" tip a year earlier about the suspect, but it was not sufficient to act because no "concrete plans" were articulated. *Dagbladet* reported that on August 10, Manshaus posted that he had been "chosen" by "Saint (Brenton) Tarrant," the Christchurch, New Zealand gunman who attacked a mosque with a similar name to the Oslo Islamic center. He posted on *8chan* in English "well cobblers it's my time" and used the Norwegian phrase "valhall venter" (Heaven awaits), according to the *New York Times*. *AP* reported on September 17, 2019 that *NTB* reported that Norwegian police announced that Johanne Ihle-Hansen, 17, stepsister of Philip Manshaus, 22, who was suspected of an attempted terrorist attack on a mosque, was shot three times in the head and once in the chest by a .22-caliber rifle that was later found in his car. She died the same day of the August 10, 2019 attack. Police suspected Manshaus killed her.

BBC reported on May 7, 2020 that the trial began of far-right Norwegian man Philip Manshaus, 22, who allegedly shot dead his stepsister, then fired on the al-Noor Islamic Center. Manshaus yelled racist, homophobic, anti-Semitic and conspiracy theories in court. Although admitting that the facts of the case were true, he pleaded not guilty to terror and murder charges, telling Judge Annika Lindstrom that he was invoking "emergency justice". Under Norwegian law, such a defense holds that the perpetrator had no choice but to commit a crime, and therefore cannot be punished. Police said there was a racist motive to his murder of his step-sister, who was adopted from China at age 2. Her adoptive mother later married Philip's father. Manshaus told the court he was inspired by the Christchurch, New Zealand attack that killed 51 people. He wished he had "planned the attack better", but was "proud to have had the opportunity to fight". Thirty witnesses, including his father and Johanne Ihle-Hansen's mother, were scheduled for the trial.

Reuters reported on June 11, 2020 that the Asker and Baerum district court in Sandvika sentenced Manshaus to 21 years for the racially motivated shooting death of his Chinese-born adopted stepsister Johanne Zhangjia Ihle-Hansen in their family home and attempting to kill worshippers at the al-Noor Islamic Center Mosque. He had earlier expressed anti-immigrant and anti-Muslim views and was unrepentant during his trial. He claimed that the adopted daughter of his father's spouse posed a risk to the family because of her Asian origin. He praised the killing of more than 50 people at two New Zealand mosques in 2019. Manshaus was represented by attorney Unnin Fries. A psychologist found him mentally fit to stand trial. The sentence included a provision that his release could be put off indefinitely should he still be considered a threat to society.

October 22, 2019: A Norwegian gunman, 32, stole a yellow-and-blue ambulance and drove it along a sidewalk in Oslo, injuring two seven-month old twins in a stroller. An elderly couple dove under a parked car. Police shot at the tires and rammed the vehicle, injuring the man, whom they arrested on suspicion of attempted murder. Police found in the ambulance an Uzi submachine gun, a shotgun and "large amounts" of narcotics. Investigator Grete Lier Mettid said the suspect had ties to far-right groups.

POLAND

January 13, 2019: Private broadcaster *TVN24* reported that at 8 p.m., a man with a knife stabbed Mayor Pawel Adamowicz, 53, while he was on stage for the finale of the Great Orchestra of Christmas Charity "Lights to Heaven" fundraising event in Gdansk. Police detained a suspect, 27, identified as a convicted bank robber. The mayor was seriously injured and died the next day. *TVN* reported the assailant shouted from the stage that he was imprisoned under the government of Civic Platform, to which the mayor formerly belonged. He said his name was Stefan and that "I was jailed but innocent... Civic Platform tortured me. That's why Adamowicz just died." Adamowicz was mayor of Gdansk since 1998. *Radio Gdansk* reported that Adamowicz was stabbed in the heart. Police spokesman Mariusz Ciarka said the attacker appeared to have mental problems and gained access to the area with a media badge. He had served 5½ years in prison and was released in late 2018. He was charged with murder.

November 7, 2019: Stanislaw Zaryn, a spokesman for the head of the security services, said the government planned to expel Anton T., a Swedish right-wing radical in his early 20s, who came to Poland for training on weapons similar to those used in the March shooting attack on mosques in Christchurch, New Zealand. The government said he was highly dangerous to public security. He was under arrest pending the expulsion, expected later in the week. Anton T. had been a member of the neo-Nazi Nordic Resistance Movement. In 2017, he was sentenced in Sweden to 18 months in prison for providing components for an unexploded device found near a campsite accommodating migrants.

RUSSIA

January 22, 2019: The National Anti-Terrorism Committee said a drunken man on an Aeroflot flight from Surgut, Siberia, to Moscow, ordered the crew to fly to Afghanistan. The plane landed in Khanty-Mansiysk about 143 miles to the west. It was not immediately clear if the hijacker was armed and what his demands were. Police detained him an hour after landing. Police said he lived in Surgut and had been convicted of property damage. He faced hijacking charges. 19012201

February 5, 2019: *Interfax* and *RIA Novosti* reported that Moscow's emergency services received nearly 300 bomb threats against 130 venues, leading to the evacuation of 50,000 people. No explosives were found. During the week, authorities evacuated shopping malls, schools and official buildings across the country.

March 22, 2019: A court sentenced Ukrainian Pavlo Gryb, 19, to six years in prison for plotting a bombing in a Russian school. Gryb was kidnapped in summer 2017 in Belarus where he had traveled to meet a girl he met online. He later surfaced in a Russian prison. He believed he was having an online romance, but a Russian intelligence officer was messaging him on her behalf shortly before his trip. Investigators claimed that Gryb was messaging the student online and was trying to get her to plant an improvised explosive device in her school in southern Russia. Gryb denied the charges. Gryb had a grave liver condition. Ukrainian Foreign Minister Pavlo Klimkin said, "Instead of urgent surgery that Pavlo needs because his life is in real danger, he has received this idiotic sentence of six years."

April 2, 2019: The *Fontanka* news website reported that four people were injured when an improvised explosive device with the equivalent of 200 grams of TNT went off inside the prestigious Mozhaisky Academy in St. Petersburg in the afternoon. The military academy trains officers for the army's missile defense unit.

June 23, 2019: When police in Grozny stopped a vehicle for a check, a gunman, 21, wounded two officers before he was shot dead. The driver, a Grozny resident, had stabbed one policeman with a knife, then shot a second officer. Police were investigating any ties to extremists. ISIS claimed on *Aamaq* that the attacker killed and wounded a number of guards at the gates of Chechen regional leader Ramzan Kadyrov's residence before being killed.

October 25, 2019: The Russian Defense Ministry announced that soldier Ramil Shamsutdinov, 20, shot to death eight of his comrades, including two officers and six enlisted men and seriously wounded two others at a base in Gorny in the Baikal Lake region of Siberia. He was arrested. Russia's Investigative Committee opened a murder case against Shamsutdinov. The Defense Ministry said he experienced a "nervous breakdown over personal problems unrelated to his military duties".

December 19, 2019: A gunman opened fire at the Moscow headquarters of the FSB state security service. In the shootout, the gunman and an FSB traffic police officer were killed and five people were wounded, two critically. The FSB called it a terrorist attack, saying, "The FSB Public Relations Center rejects some media reports that there were three people who opened fire… the gunman was alone." The *Guardian* and *Interfax* reported that the gunman attacked the reception area of the Lubyanka building before fleeing and barricading himself in a nearby building.

December 27, 2019: *Reuters* reported that President Vladimir Putin thanked U.S. President Donald Trump for a U.S. tip-off that led to Russian thwarting terrorist attacks planned in St. Petersburg. Russian news agencies cited the Federal Security Service (FSB) as saying that two Russians were detained on December 27 on suspicion of plotting attacks during New Year festivities.

SLOVENIA

November 1, 2019: Police treated as a hate crime a 4 a.m. attack on Ljubljana's popular Tiffany Club, which caters to an LGBT crowd. The attackers smashed the entrance door and windows and threatened the staff and visitors. They fled when police arrived. No one was injured. The club is located in a former army barracks.

SPAIN

January 15, 2019: Police in Catalonia arrested 17 people, including five alleged Algerian members of an extremist Islamist cell, in an ongoing anti-terror operation in six venues in and near Barcelona. A Catalan Mossos d'Esquadra regional police spokeswoman said that more arrests were expected on possible terror-related links, theft, drug trafficking and other crimes and that more than 100 agents were involved. Two suspects were arrested in a central neighborhood of Barcelona while another was detained in nearby Igualada. Investigating magistrate Manuel Garcia-Castellon of the National Court, which normally handles terror related probes in Spain, ordered the arrests.

Authorities in Malaga arrested a Moroccan national, 27, whom police suspected could be linked to ISIS. The man had allegedly used several social network profiles to express his violent views and allegiance to ISIS.

April 16, 2019: The Torrespacio skyscraper, a 770-foot 57-storey office tower in Madrid's business district that houses several foreign embassies, including those of the UK, Canada, and the Netherlands, along with offices of several multinational firms, was evacuated due to a mid-day phoned security threat to the Australian Embassy.

June 11, 2019: The retrial at the National Court in Madrid began of Moroccan-born Spaniard Aziz Zaghanane and his Mexican wife Ana Marilú Reyna on charges of helping recruit for ISIS in Madrid. He initially received a six-year prison sentence in his 2018 trial and his wife was sentenced to one year. The National Court ruled that evidence given in the original trial should have included testimony from three others accused in the case, who admitted terror-related crimes and therefore did not take the stand. The Muslim couple argued that their social media activity discussed issues related to ISIS and the war in Syria but rejected violence. The court's verdict was expected later in the week.

September 23, 2019: The Civil Guard arrested nine activists linked to pro-Catalan independence Committees for the Defense of the Republic groups suspected of preparing to commit violent acts, possibly with explosives. The Committees earlier organized street protests and blocked road and rail transport. In ten raids, police seized material and substances they believe could be used to make explosives. *AP* reported on September 26 that seven Catalan separatists were jailed in the case as the National Court continued its investigation. No bail was granted. Some of the activists lived in Barcelona.

SWEDEN

January 7, 2019: *Swedish Radio* reported the beginning of the trial in Stockholm of three men suspected of preparing an extremist attack in Sweden. The prosecutor said the trio had obtained 1,100 pounds of chemicals, knives, gas masks and military equipment. Authorities found photos of potential targets in Stockholm on their cell phones. The trio and three others were accused of financing the Islamic State group in Syria. *SR* said the five Uzbeks and a citizen of Kyrgyzstan communicated via closed chat rooms. The men lived legally in Sweden. The trial was expected to run until February 11.

March 8, 2019: The Solna District Court in Stockholm declared David Idrisson, 46, an Uzbek national who lived legally in Sweden since 2008, guilty of preparing an attack in Stockholm on behalf of ISIS and financing ISIS in Syria, and sentenced him to seven years in jail. He was to be expelled from Sweden after serving his time. The court revealed that he had obtained 1,100 pounds of chemicals, knives, gas masks and military equipment. His cell phone contained photos of potential targets in Stockholm. Two younger male associates were acquitted. They were released from detention earlier in the week.

Six men—five Uzbeks and a citizen of Kyrgyzstan—were also accused of financing ISIS by sending up to 20,000 kronor ($2,135) each. The court found four of them—including Idrisson—guilty of that charge and sentenced them to four to six months. Two were acquitted. All live legally in Sweden and denied wrongdoing.

On June 12, 2019, Judge Ragnar Palmkvist of the Svea Court appeals court acquitted David Idrisson. The court held that there was "not sufficient evidence" against Idrisson and two others that they were planning terrorist offenses. The two other defendants had been acquitted by a lower court. The Svea Court upheld guilty verdicts and prison sentences of between four and six months against the trio for financing ISIS.

May 15, 2019: Seven children of Amanda Gonzales, a Swede, and her Norwegian husband Michael Skramo, who had joined ISIS and were killed in Syria earlier in 2019, returned to Goteborg, Sweden. Their grandfather, Patricio Galvez, told Swedish broadcaster *SVT* that the children, aged between 1 and 8, will be taken care of by social services. The children were living at a refugee camp in northern Syria before being transferred to Irbil, Iraq.

August 14, 2019: Police in Ostersund arrested a man initially suspected of planning a murder and later suspected of conspiracy to commit terrorism. *SVT* reported that police arrested him when he drove into a large flower pot.

November 2, 2019: Police detained three people following an explosion in an apartment in Malmo which broke the building's main door, blew out windows, damaged the entrance level, but caused no injuries. Police spokesman Peter Martin told Swedish news agency *TT* that the explosion apparently was not connected to a blast the previous morning in another Malmo district where a parked car and a nearby building were damaged.

November 9, 2019: A bomb exploded under a car in Malmo, destroying the vehicle and damaging other cars.

Minutes later, at 9 p.m., gunmen on bicycles fired into a pizza parlor in another section of Malmo, killing a 15-year-old boy and critically injuring another teen.

SWITZERLAND

April 22, 2019: Shortly before 3 a.m., two incendiary devices were thrown at the Turkish consulate general in Zurich. A hedge outside the building caught fire. Swiss police arrested three men aged 17, 18 and 19 who tried to flee. 04192201

October 25, 2019: The attorney general's office indicted two men who lived in northeastern Switzerland and were accused of supporting, participating in, and recruiting people for ISIS. The main suspect was a Swiss-Italian dual citizen who allegedly traveled to ISIS-controlled territory in Syria and on his return recruited several people for the group. The other suspect was a dual citizen of Switzerland and North Macedonia. He tried to travel to Syria via North Macedonia, where police stopped him. He allegedly recruited a person for ISIS. Both suspects were accused of spreading propaganda for the group. The case against the first suspect began in February 2015 and was later expanded to include the second suspect.

TURKEY

January 2, 2019: *Anadolu* reported that earlier in the week, police in Bursa Province had detained twelve suspected Islamic State terrorists, including two women who are wanted in France. The detainees included French citizens of Syrian or Algerian descent who settled in Bursa after allegedly carrying out unspecified "acts" on behalf of ISIS in Syria. Five of the suspects were to be deported.

January 17, 2019: The government deported Dutch journalist Ans Boersma, who worked for the *Het Financieele Dagblad* newspaper and other news outlets in Istanbul, claiming it had received information about her from Dutch police who said "that Ms. Boersma had links to a designated terrorist organization", the jihadist group Jabhat al-Nusra. A Dutch prosecutor's office spokeswoman said Boersma was a suspect in an investigation, but not for terrorism offenses. Turkish police had detained her the previous day while she submitted documents at an immigration office to extend her Turkish residence permit.

February 14, 2019: *Anadolu* reported that police in Osmangazi in Bursa Province detained 52 Syrian nationals believed linked to ISIS. *DHA* said police raided five locations at dawn.

March 15, 2019: A Turkish court convicted Australian-born ISIS member Neil Prakash of belonging to a terrorist group and sentenced him to seven years and six months in prison in prison. He could be released in 30 months. He had been

in a Turkish prison since 2016, the year he was arrested near the Syrian border for attempting to cross with fake documents. Prakash expressed remorse. Australia revoked Prakash's citizenship and requested his extradition.

March 26, 2019: Gunshots were heard at the domestic flights terminal of Kayseri Airport in central Turkey. *U.S. News and World Report* and *DHA* reported that two people were hospitalized. The *Independent* and *Hurriyet* reported that at 4:20 p.m., a police officer fired three shots at a colleague during an argument, then turned the gun on himself.

April 25, 2019: The *Washington Post* reported that authorities arrested a suspected ISIS member believed to be planning attacks on Australians and New Zealanders.

April 29, 2019: *Anadolu* reported that police in Ankara detained 22 people—17 Iraqis and five Syrians—suspected of having links to ISIS. They had entered Turkey illegally and had reportedly acted on behalf of ISIS in Syria and Iraq.

May 14, 2019: Police detained two suspected Revolutionary People's Liberation Party-Front (DHKP-C) militants, a woman and a man, who tried to enter Parliament with sharp objects and a hoax explosive device. Presidential communications director Fahrettin Altun called their attempt a "terrorist act against the will and the peace of the nation". *Anadolu* said the suspects tried to take a security official hostage before they were subdued.

May 26, 2019: Kurdish politician Leyla Guyen announced the end of a 200-day hunger strike by 3,000 people in 90 prisons demanding improved conditions for Abdullah Ocalan, leader of the Kurdistan Worker's Party. The Turkish government lifted a ban on lawyer visits to a prison island where Ocalan was serving a life term.

July 3, 2019: *Anadolu* reported that authorities in Akcakale, a border town, detained B.I. and F.B., two Russian women suspected of being ISIS members listed as wanted by Interpol. The duo were trying to enter Turkey illegally from Syria while accompanied by their nine children. They told police that their husbands had been killed in Syria and that they were trying to return to Russia via Turkey. They were to appear in court in Sanliurfa.

July 5, 2019: *Anadolu* reported that a bomb went off in a car in transit 750 yards from a local government office in Reyhanli in Hatay Province near Turkey's border with Syria, killing two Syrians who were inside the vehicle. A third Syrian was seriously injured. The three Syrians were legally registered in Turkey. Turkish President Recep Tayyip Erdogan said the explosion appeared to be terror-linked. 19070501

July 24, 2019: Ankara Governor Vasip Sahin said Belarusian diplomat Alexander Poganshev underwent surgery after being shot by a neighbor who later committed suicide. The incident apparently stemmed from a personal dispute between the two.

September 12, 2019: *DHA* reported that Turkish officials blamed Kurdish rebels for setting off a bomb on a road near Kulp that hit a vehicle carrying villagers returning home after gathering wood, killing four people and wounding 13 others.

September 25, 2019: *Anadolu* reported that a bomb exploded as a riot police bus passed by in Adana, injuring five people, including a police officer.

October 9, 2019: Turkish state media reported that mortar shells were fired into a Turkish town on the Syrian border, causing no casualties.

October 28, 2019: *Anadolu* reported that anti-terrorism police in Ankara detained 20 foreign nationals suspected of links to ISIS. The previous day, the U.S. announced the death of ISIS caliph Abu Bakr al-Baghdadi.

October 29, 2019: *Anadolu* reported that police in Istanbul detained three suspected ISIS terrorists who were allegedly scheming a "sensational" attack in the aftermath of the killing of ISIS leader Abu Bakr al-Baghdadi. The trio was allegedly preparing an attack to coincide with celebrations marking the 96th anniversary of the founding of the Turkish republic.

October 30, 2019: Police Chief Mehmet Aktas said 100 people have been detained in 26 raids against ISIS across 21 provinces; the group was allegedly planning an attack with celebrations marking the 96th anniversary of the founding of the Turkish Republic.

November 3, 2019: Police in Istanbul detained a driver, 33, who rammed his bus into a crowded stop and stabbed people who tried to prevent him from escaping when he jumped into the sea. Thirteen people, including three Iranians and two children, were injured. 19110302

November 10, 2019: *AFP* reported that Aierken Saimaiti, a Chinese businessman-turned-whistleblower with shadowy ties to Kyrgyzstan, was shot to death in Istanbul. Police in Turkey arrested three people in connection with his killing. On November 28, Erkin Sopokov, recently dismissed as Kyrgyz Consul General in Istanbul, was arrested after his car was found near the scene. Hundreds took to the streets of Bishkek, Kyrgyzstan, to demand the arrest of Rayimbek Matraimov, alias Rayim Million, a former customs official that Saimaiti named as a beneficiary of bribery and money laundering schemes. Sopokov has been held in Kyrgyzstan on suspicion of abuse of office for allowing Saimaiti, a Chinese national of Uighur heritage, and other people to use the car which had diplomatic number plates. He was also accused of illegal enrichment.

Radio Free Europe's Kyrgyz service, local outlet *Kloop.kg* and the US-based Organized Crime and Corruption Reporting Project said Saimati had reported an earlier attempt on his life in Kyrgyzstan and told the journalists he feared for his safety.

November 13, 2019: Mohammad Darwis B., 39, a suspected American ISIS member of Jordanian background, was seen in a heavily militarized no man's land between Turkey and Greece for a third straight day. Greek officials said Turkey tried to expel the man to Greece but Athens refused him entry. On November 14, Turkey's Interior Ministry said he would be repatriated to the U.S., which agreed to take him in and would give him travel documents. Turkish Interior

Minister Suleyman Soylu said the man was put on a plane to the U.S. on November 15.

November 14, 2019: The Interior Ministry announced that during a raid in Istanbul, anti-terrorism police detained Mevlut Cuskun, a wanted ISIS suspect, after he illegally crossed into Turkey from Syria.

Turkey deported seven Germans linked to ISIS.

November 15, 2019: *Anadolu* reported that police detained the mayors of Savur, Derik and Mazidagi in Mardin Province and Suruc in Sanliurfa Province along with 20 municipality officials over their suspected links to Kurdistan Workers' Party (PKK) rebels. The mayors, members of the pro-Kurdish People's Democratic Party (HDP), were elected in March 2019.

November 21, 2019: *DISRN.com* and International Christian Concern reported that Christian evangelist Jinwood Kim, who had served as a minister in Turkey for five years, was stabbed three times and killed. Authorities said it was an attempt to steal his cell phone, but others said the attack was religiously motivated. He was married with one child; his wife was expecting. Police arrested a suspect, 16.

A Turkish evangelist received a death threat the next day.

December 9, 2019: The Interior Ministry announced the deportation to France of 11 French nationals suspected of ISIS membership. An Australian accused of being a foreign terrorist fighter was also deported.

December 30, 2019: *NPR* reported that authorities in the capital and five provinces arrested 100 people from Iraq, Syria and northern Africa suspected of ISIS ties.

UKRAINE

July 13, 2019: Authorities said a terrorist attack was involved when someone fired a rocket-propelled grenade at the pro-Russian *Ukraine 112* 24-hour television news network in Kiev, damaging the building. No one was hurt. *Ukraine 112*'s owner, Taras Kozak, is running for parliament on the Opposition Bloc party ticket, organized by Viktor Medvedchuk, who has ties to Putin and was sanctioned by the U.S. in 2014.

November 15, 2019: The Ukrainian Security Service (SBU) arrested Georgian national al-Bar Shishani, one of the top commanders in ISIS near Kiyv. SBU said on *Facebook* that the CIA and the Georgian police participated in the operation. Since 2012, Shishani had served as a deputy to Abu Omar al-Shishani, the "minister of war" in ISIS, who was declared dead in 2016. In 2016, al-Bar Shishani fled to Turkey, and in 2018 arrived in Ukraine, using a fake passport.

UNITED KINGDOM

January 4, 2019: West Midlands Police officers shot to death a man, 31, and detained two others following an "intelligence-led" operation in a residential area north of Coventry's city center.

January 8, 2019: *Reuters* reported that drone sightings led airport officials to temporarily halt flights from London's Heathrow airport.

February 14, 2019: The *Washington Examiner, Times of London* and *AP* reported that former London schoolgirl Shamima Begum, 19, one of the three Bethnal Green students who ran away from the UK in 2015 to join ISIS, wanted to "come home" to give birth. She had married a foreign ISIS fighter and had already given birth to two other children, who had died from illness and malnutrition. She fled in January 2019 and was found in a refugee camp. She believed the other two runaways were still alive, although she had not heard from them since 2015. The *Times* reported that Kadiza Sultana was believed to have been killed by an airstrike in 2016. On February 14, Home Secretary Sajid Javid warned that he would block the return of Britons who traveled to the Middle East to join ISIS. Begum gave birth to a boy on February 17 in a Syrian refugee camp. The family's attorney, Tasnime Akunjee, said on February 19 that the Home Office planned to revoke Begum's citizenship. The next day, the UK revoked the dual national's British citizenship. Her Dutch jihadi husband Yago Riedijk, who was in a Kurdish-run detention center, wanted to return to the Netherlands with Begum and their son. On March 8, 2019, Syrian Democratic Forces spokesman Mustafa Bali confirmed that the infant died at a camp in north Syria.

February 18, 2019: Fatah Mohammed Abdullah, 33, a man living in Newcastle, was charged under Britain's terrorism laws with encouraging another person to crash a car into crowds in Germany, attack people with a meat cleaver, and detonate bombs, "with the aim of killing and/or causing serious injury". The incitement allegedly occurred between April 9 and December 11, 2018.

March 5, 2019: The Metropolitan Police Counter Terrorism Command was investigating three padded A4-sized white mailing bags containing small explosive devices that were found near major transport hubs in London. Police said smaller bags inside the mailers enclosed the devices that "appear capable of igniting an initially small fire when opened". One mailer was found near Heathrow Airport. When it was opened, part of it burned. No injuries were reported. Other mailers were found near London's City Airport and in the mail room at Waterloo Station, a major rail and Underground hub. No arrests were made and no one claimed credit. The envelopes received in London appeared to carry Irish stamps. *AP* and *CNN* reported on March 11 that British police said they were "aware" that a media outlet in Northern Ireland had received a claim of responsibility by Irish dissidents who used an Irish Republican Army (IRA) code word to establish authenticity. The group said five devices were sent, but police had found only four. 19030501-03

March 6, 2019: Police in Scotland said suspicious packages were found at the Royal Bank of Scotland headquarters in Edinburgh and at the University of Glasgow's mailroom. No one was injured.

CNN reported that an item was found inside a courtyard at the British Parliament in the afternoon was later deemed "non-suspicious".

Judge Nicholas Hilliard at London's Central Criminal Court sentenced British Muslim convert Lewis Ludlow, 27, of Rochester in southern England, to life in prison with no opportunity for parole for 15 years for plotting a van attack on crowds in London's Oxford Street shopping district. Ludlow earlier pleaded guilty to preparing acts of terrorism and fundraising for ISIS. Police found ripped-up planning notes for an attack in a garbage bin. Ludlow wrote that the area was "ideal" target because "nearly 100 could be killed". Other "potential attack sites" included Madame Tussaud's wax museum, St. Paul's Cathedral and a Shi'a temple in Romford, east London. Ludlow tried to travel to the Philippines in February 2018 to join IS, but was stopped by police at Heathrow Airport. Police said he set up a *Facebook* account called Antique Collections as a front to send money to militants in the Philippines. He was arrested in April 2018 and charged with the attack plot. He told the court that he had been coerced by a militant in the Philippines to conduct an attack.

March 17, 2019: Police arrested a man, 50, from Stanwell, near Heathrow Airport, on suspicion of attempted murder and racially aggravated public order offenses for attacking a man, 19, with a baseball bat and knife while hurling racist abuse. Police said the attack was a terrorist incident "inspired by the far-right".

March 21, 2019: Windows on five mosques in Birmingham were broken by a sledgehammer. Counter-terrorism officers searched for a motive.

March 21, 27, 2019: *Reuters* reported on April 2 that police were investigating two attempts to disrupt the rail network that they said were linked to Brexit. Rail workers found the devices on tracks in central England on March 21 and 27. A *BBC* reporter said the devices were left near Yaxley in Cambridgeshire and Netherfield in Nottinghamshire. One had a note that said "Leave means leave." The other had a note reading, "We'll bring Britain to a standstill."

April 10, 2019: Police arrested four men from Sri Lanka who arrived on a nighttime flight at Luton Airport. They were held on suspicion of violating the Terrorism Act by belonging to a banned extremist organization. They were question at a police station in Bedfordshire northeast of London.

June 2019: On September 10, 2019, the *Evening Standard* and *www.heraldscotland.com* reported that in June 2019 police arrested ISIS-inspired lone wolf Hisham Muhammad, 25, of Victoria Avenue, Whitefield, Bury, who was planning an attack on the British army or police using a drone, knives, axes, and Japanese "ninja eggs". They told the Old Bailey they found a tomahawk, a machete, bear-claws, two painted eggs containing crushed chilli seeds and shards of glass which were described as Japanese "ninja eggs" at his home. He was making a prototype of a drone attachment using lollipop sticks to drop a projectile or "harmful" device on his target. Police said the Bermudan, who moved to the UK in 2013, had researched police and army bases, including Castle Armoury Barracks in Bury, Greater Manchester, which he visited. He allegedly helped fund his activities with money from a bogus online escort agency scam. Car salesman and landlord Onkar Singh turned him in after he saw "suspicious" items in Muhammad's home, including knives, a tub of wires and a soldering iron. The landlord visited the property after Muhammad and his cousin Faisal Abu Ahmad, 24, had fallen behind with their £600 rent. Prosecutor Anne Whyte QC said Muhammad had steeped himself in "barbarous" ISIS propaganda. On May 21, 2018, he allegedly researched suicide belts, machetes and the Victoria train station which had been part of the scene of the Manchester Arena terror attack a year earlier. Two days later, Muhammad visited an army recruitment event in Bury town center and the nearby Castle Armoury Barracks. He Googled "weak points of the human body for assault" as well as armed police in UK and Manchester. He told police that he had a "gift from god for making things and liked to innovate". Defense attorney Bernard Richmond QC said there had been "no effort to hide" any of the objects.

Abu Ahmad, of the same address, pleaded not guilty to failing to alert authorities of the alleged attack plan. He was represented by attorney Francis FitzGibbon QC.

June 18, 2019: The *BBC*, the *Guardian*, *AP*, *MSN.com* and *The Hill* reported that London Judge Rebecca Poulet sentenced neo-Nazi Polish nationals Michal Szewczuk, 19, and Oskar Dunn-Koczorowski, 18, to prison for spreading self-created right-wing extremist propaganda online and encouraging terrorist attacks against politicians, members of the royal family, racial minorities and white women in interracial relationships. Szewczuk received four years in prison, while Dunn-Koczorowski was sentenced to 18 months. Poulet said the messages were "uniformly violent and threatening", and "the nature of the violence includes rape and execution". Prosecutors said that the duo belonged to the "Sonnenkrieg Division", and used personal accounts with pseudonyms on the social media site *Gab* to encourage violence against members of the public. The duo posted an image of Prince Harry, the Duke of Sussex, with a gun to his head and the caption "See Ya Later Race Traitor" months after his marriage to a mixed-race woman, American actress Meghan Markle, in May 2018. Szewczuk pleaded guilty in April 2019 to two counts of encouraging acts of terror and five counts of possessing documents useful to terrorists. Dunn-Koczorowski, a minor when the crimes were committed, pleaded guilty to two counts of encouraging terrorism in December 2018. Investigators said Szewczuk's residence had bomb-making instructions and a "white resistance" manual, and instructional propaganda on conducting Islamist terrorist attacks while a university student. David Kitson served as defense attorney for Dunn-Koczorowski.

June 21, 2019: Organic farmer John Letts, 58, and ex-Oxfam fundraiser Sally Lane, 56, were found guilty on one charge of funding terrorism but given suspended sentences for trying to send money to their Islamic convert son, Jack Letts, 23, who went to Syria to support ISIS. The Oxford couple had tried to send him 1,723 pounds ($2,188), believing Jack was in mortal danger and trapped in Raqqa, Syria. British media nicknamed him Jihadi Jack. Judge Nicholas Hilliard gave the couple 15 months in prison, but suspended the sentence for 12 months. The parents believed he was on a "grand adventure" to learn Arabic in Jordan in May 2014, then moved to Kuwait and married. In September 2014, Jack phoned Lane from Syria. Police raided the family's home in 2015. Jack later posted on *Facebook* that he wanted to conduct a martyrdom operation against British soldiers. Kurdish authorities held Jack in northern Syria.

July 4, 2019: The South East Counter Terrorism police unit arrested a Swedish woman, 40, at London's Gatwick Airport after arriving on an afternoon flight from Italy on suspicion of violating the Terrorism Act 2000 by preparing acts of terrorism.

July 20, 2019: Police suspected two young men of releasing the irritating CS gas (a component of incapacitating tear gas) on a London subway train that was stopped at Oxford Circus station. Paramedics treated a number of people for coughing and shortness of breath. Police released CCTV images of two suspects.

July 28, 2019: Counterterrorism detectives arrested a 59-year-old man on suspicion of terrorism offenses after grenades, an imitation gun and chemicals were found at a Lowestoft house in eastern England. He was held on suspicion of the "commission, preparation or instigation of acts of terrorism".

August 15, 2019: *CNN* reported that a man was stabbed on London's Marsham Street outside the Home Office building. The interior ministry was locked down. Police detained a man "on suspicion of grievous bodily harm". Police said the incident was not believed to be terrorism-related.

October 1, 2019: In the morning, London police detained a man under the Mental Health Act near the Houses of Parliament after he doused himself with an apparently flammable liquid. He also had a lighter. Police hosed him down with a fire extinguisher. No injuries were reported.

October 11, 2019: At 11:17 a.m., a man, 41, lunged with a knife at shoppers at the Arndale Centre mall in Manchester, injuring four people. Two women and a man were hospitalized; one woman was treated at the scene. Police detained him for "the commission, preparation and instigation of an act of terrorism". Greater Manchester Police's assistant chief constable, Russ Jackson, said the suspect was believed to be a British citizen from the Manchester area. Two unarmed police officers confronted the attacker and called for backup as he chased them.

November 4, 2019: The Joint Terrorism Analysis Centre downgraded the UK's terrorism threat level from "severe" to "substantial", with officials saying the country now sees an attack as "likely" rather than "highly likely". Home Secretary Priti Patel said, "Despite the change in the threat level, terrorism remains one of the most direct and immediate risks to our national security… Substantial…continues to indicate a high level of threat; and an attack might well occur without further warning." Neil Basu, head of counterterrorism policing, said about 800 investigations were underway nationally and 24 attack plots had been thwarted since March 2017. The UK's terror threat was last listed as "substantial" in August 2014. It briefly was listed as "critical" in May and September 2017.

November 14, 2019: The Counter Terrorism Command police at Heathrow Airport arrested a 26-year-old man who landed on a flight from Turkey, hours after Turkey said it deported a British man linked to ISIS. He was held on suspicion of terrorism offenses. Police said the arrest was "Syria-related".

November 29, 2019: *Reuters*, *Sky News*, *NPR*, the *BBC*, *CNN* and *AP* reported that at 2 p.m., British police shot to death Usman Khan, 28, a man wearing a fake explosive vest, after a stabbing incident in the London Bridge area and announced that the incident was being treated "as though it is terror-related". Police said a man and a woman were killed and a man and two women were injured. Bystanders tackled the terrorist, using a fire extinguisher and a narwhal tusk. One bystander sprayed liquid from the extinguisher at Khan. British media reported that one of the several men who subdued Khan was an ex-prisoner, who had served time with Khan. *AP* identified the narwhal tusk-wielder as Darryn Frost, 38, a civil servant in the Justice Ministry. He said another man used a chair as a weapon.

The *Guardian* reported that Metropolitan police identified one of the victims as Saskia Jones, 23, a former Cambridge student from Stratford-upon-Avon. Her family noted, "Saskia had a great passion for providing invaluable support to victims of criminal injustice, which led her to the point of recently applying for the police graduate recruitment programme, wishing to specialise in victim support."

The *Daily Telegraph* reported that Cambridge Learning Together law and criminology course leader Jack Merritt, 25, was also killed.

One of the three people wounded was a member of the Cambridge University graduate program to foster collaboration between graduate students, prisoners, police and Cambridge.

The *Washington Post* reported that politicians questioned the wisdom of giving early release to Khan, who had served roughly half his 16-year sentence issued in 2012 for an earlier jihadi plot to bomb the London Stock Exchange and pubs in Stoke-on-Trent with eight others. Anti-terrorist police raided his home in 2008. Before his 2010 arrest, he belonged to a cell inspired by al-Qaeda. Prosecutors said during his earlier conviction that the group tried to assemble materials to make pipe bombs. They raised funds to construct a madrassa in Pakistan to train terrorists. He was released in December 2018 and was living a two-hour train ride from London. He was born and raised in the UK. Prime Minister Boris Johnson blamed changes in sentencing rules made by the last Labour Party government. Khan apparently had complied with the conditions of his release, including wearing an electronic tracking device on his ankle, which he was wearing during the attack. However, he was still able to conduct the attack. He appeared to be attending a meeting of the Cambridge group to celebrate its fifth year, and held at Fishmongers' Hall beside the bridge. Those who wrestled the burly, bearded Khan to the ground reportedly included James Ford, 42, a convicted murderer who was on a day-release program at the time. Another hero was a Polish immigrant.

Police searched Khan's house in Staffordshire, England.

He was earlier represented by attorney Vajahat Sharif, who told the *Guardian* that Khan "appeared to be rehabilitated and was a model prisoner". He believed jihadis re-radicalized him when he was freed from prison. *ITV* published a letter written by Khan in October 2012, saying "I don't carry the views I had before my arrest and also I can prove that at the time I was immature, and now I am much more mature and want to live my life as a good Muslim and also a good citizen of Britain."

Aamaq reported that ISIS claimed Khan was one of its followers.

Fox News and *Sky News* reported on December 3 that police arrested Islamist and former Khan associate Nazam Hussain, 34, in Stoke-on-Trent as part of the ongoing review of terrorists permitted to leave prison early. He was held on suspicion of preparation of terrorist attacks after a search of his home. Hussain was released early from prison alongside Khan in December 2018. The *Telegraph* reported that the two were close friends growing up in Stoke-on-Trent and had plotted to bomb the London Stock Exchange and other targets in 2010. They planned to travel to a Pakistan-controlled part of the Kashmir region in 2011 to establish a terrorist training camp for jihadis.

The *PA Media* news agency reported that Khan had threatened to blow up Fishmonger's Hall just before 2 p.m. Witnesses said Khan had duct-taped one of his two knives to his hand.

Khan originally came from Pakistan.

On October 18, 2020, *Business Insider* reported that the Queen granted a rare royal pardon to convicted murderer Steve Gallant, who fought off terrorist knife attacker Usman Khan with a 5-foot narwhal tusk on London Bridge on November 29, 2019. Former firefighter Gallant, 47, was serving a 17-year sentence, which was to be reduced by 10 months. He could apply for parole in June 2021. Gallant was arrested in 2005 after killing a former firefighter outside of a pub in Hull. It was the first royal pardon for a convicted murderer in 25 years. The Ministry of Justice told the *BBC* he was pardoned for his "exceptionally brave actions ... which helped save people's lives despite the tremendous risk to his own". The *Guardian* reported that the family of the murdered firefighter, Barrie Jackson, supported the decision.

November 30, 2019: West Midlands Police searched a home and arrested a 34-year-old man in Stoke-on-Trent on suspicion of preparation of terrorist acts. On December 2, he was returned to prison for breaching release conditions.

LATIN AMERICA

ARGENTINA

February 25, 2019: Attackers entered the Buenos Aires home of Rabbi Gabriel Davidovich, 62, and beat him, shouting, "We know you are the rabbi of the AMIA", badly injuring Argentina's chief rabbi. The Argentine Israelite Mutual Association, one of the country's most prominent Jewish groups, was bombed on July 18, 1994, killing 85 people and injuring hundreds. Davidovich suffered several broken ribs and a punctured lung. The assailants stole money and some belongings.

May 9, 2019: *Telam, AFP* and *Reuters* reported that gunmen shot to death Miguel Marcelo Yadón, 58, a coordinator who worked in the fiduciary of La Rioja's federal electric transportation system, and critically injured his friend since their teen years, Héctor Olivares, 61, representative of La Rioja province in Argentina's lower house of congress at 7 a.m. as they were walking near the congressional building in Buenos Aires. He was treated for gunshot wounds that pierced his abdomen and affected vital organs. Olivares was hit three times; Yadón was hit five times. Local media initially said that the victims had been shot from a moving vehicle, but surveillance video of the shooting released by the security ministry showed a parked car waiting for them. Authorities found the car and identified the suspects. Security Minister Patricia Bullrich called the attack "mafia-style". *AP* reported that the two men lived together. Olivares died on May 12.

Olivares was a member of the Radical Civic Union party of the ruling government coalition and sat on the transportation committee in the lower house. Before he was shot, he had been discussing a bill against soccer hooliganism.

The following day, the Policia Federal Argentina arrested six people, including Juan José Navarro in Uruguay with help from Interpol. He was allegedly one of the two gunmen. Also detained was Juan Jesús Fernández, owner of the car used in the attack, as he was en route to the Argentine town of Concepción de Uruguay, 186 miles northwest of Buenos Aires. Minister Bullrich said that Navarro and Fernández will likely be charged with the shooting. Others, including Fernández's daughter, Estefanía Fernández, were arrested for collaborating with the plan or helping cover up the attack. Bullrich suggested that the attack targeting Yadón was for "personal reasons" rather than political ones. Officials in Argentina and Uruguay were working to expel Navarro from Uruguay.

May 13, 2019: Security agents stopped Francisco Ariel Muñiz after he tried to walk into Argentina's presidential palace, the Casa Rosada (Pink House), with an unloaded .44-caliber Taurus revolver inside a briefcase while seeking a meeting with President Mauricio Macri. Presidential security agents stopped him at a subway station. Security Minister Patricia Bullrich said that he would be given a medical exam.

Telam state news agency reported that explosives experts were sent to a building next to the lower house of Congress and the presidential palace following bomb threats. Other bomb threats forced an evacuation of Buenos Aires's two main train stations.

July 18, 2019: The government's Financial Information Unit declared Hizballah a terrorist organization and froze its assets, 25 years to the day after a bombing blamed on the Lebanese-based group destroyed the Argentine-Israelite Mutual Association (AMIA) Jewish community center in Buenos Aires, killing 85 people. The previous day, President Mauricio Macri's government created a list of terrorist organizations.

BOLIVIA

November 11, 2019: Several voting centers were damaged in arson attacks.

Former President Evo Morales, who had resigned, tweeted that his house and the home of his sister were attacked and his ministers had been threatened.

BRAZIL

December 7, 2019: Drive-by gunmen shot at a group of Guajajara indigenous people on the margins of a federal highway near El-Betel village in Maranhao State, killing two. Guajajara forest guardians protect their territory against illegal deforestation.

December 9, 2019: Police in Belo Horizonte arrested three people after home-made bombs were detonated at Mineirão Stadium as Cruzeiro was being relegated to the second division for the first time. Fans suspected of violence were being sought a day after the game. Police said 13 people were hospitalized for injuries inside and outside the stadium after Cruzeiro lost to Palmeiras 2-0. The match was ended early after the first home-made bomb exploded in the stands. Cruzeiro, founded 98 years ago, needed to win in the last round of the Brazilian championship.

December 24, 2019: Individuals posted a video on social media in which three masked people claimed credit for a Christmas Eve gasoline bomb attack of a video production house in Rio de Janeiro that targeted Brazilian humorist group Porta dos Fundos for its Portuguese-language Christmas program on *Netflix* that some critics called blasphemous. The digitally-altered voice said the Command of Popular National Insurgence was responsible. No injuries were reported. "The First Temptation of Christ" depicted Jesus returning home on his 30th birthday and insinuated that he is gay. Two million people signed an online petition calling for the film to be banned.

CHILE

November 21, 2019: A vehicle drove into a group of protesters in Antofagasta Province. It was not clear how many people were injured. Police said the driver had been "delivered to their headquarters". The car sustained several dents and cracks in the windshield.

COLOMBIA

January 14, 2019: Army Commander Nicasio Martinez said the military was attempting to rescue three employees of Brinks, a Richmond, Virginia-based cash transfer company, who were kidnapped the previous week after their helicop-

ter was forced to land during adverse weather in remote North Santander Province while carrying the equivalent of $500,000 in cash.

January 17, 2019: *BBC* reported that at 9:30 a.m., a 1993 Nissan pick-up truck loaded with 80 kilograms of pentolite explosives went off at the General Santander Police Academy in Bogota, killing 21, including a Panamanian and an Ecuadoran, and injuring 68, including three visiting students from Panama and the brother of Lorena Mora, 25, who had a sprained knee.

The *Washington Post* reported that Chief Prosecutor Nestor Martinez said police had identified the bomber as National Liberation Army (ELN) member Jose Aldemar Rodriguez, variant Jose Aldemar Rojas, alias Mocho Kiko, 56. Colombian Defense Minister Guillermo Botero said Rojas, an explosives expert, had lost his arm manipulating explosives for the ELN. He had no criminal record. He died in the attack. Authorities said Rojas, as a member of the hardline Domingo Lain Front, traveled on several occasions to Venezuela to train rebels in the use of explosives. The ELN's central command claimed credit on January 21, deeming the attack a legitimate response to the armed forces' bombing of a guerrilla camp during a recently concluded unilateral cease-fire the rebels declared during the Christmas holiday. The ELN called on President Ivan Duque to resume peace talks to avoid further bloodshed.

The vehicle had its last official inspection sometime in 2018 in Arauca State, along the eastern border with Venezuela.

FARC dissidents and the Usuga drug cartel were earlier suspected.

Chief Prosecutor Nestor Martinez said that in intercepted phone conversations, Ricardo Carvajal recognized his role in the attack. Police arrested him before dawn on January 18 in Bogota, confiscating military uniforms and a rebel combatant manual. He was charged with terrorism and murder.

Defense Minister Botero said the terrorist entered the facility via a side entrance used for deliveries, driving fast through a gate opened to allow the exit of a few motorcycles. He then drove into the heart of the school where the vehicle exploded in front of a red tile-roofed barracks used by female cadets after an honor ceremony had ended. Ten minutes before the explosion, a man had gotten out of the vehicle at a bus stop. The bomb thus might have been remotely detonated. The driver bought the car ten months earlier from Mauricio Mosquera, who was charged earlier for terrorism and rebellion.

Colombian President Ivan Duque on January 18 asked Cuba to arrest ten ELN peace negotiators. In a televised address, Duque said he had revoked a decree suspending arrest orders against ELN leaders. On January 22, Pablo Beltran, chief of ELN's negotiating team, said he did not have advance knowledge of the bombing. The dead included:

- Cesar Ojeda, 22, son of a transit worker from a town in Santander Department.

- Diego Alejandro Molina, 20, a star athlete who was changing out of his honor guard uniform. He had trained with two of Colombia's most popular soccer clubs as a goalkeeper, but was two inches short of the league's height requirement. He entered the school 18 months ago, and rose to the rank of brigadier.

- Jonathan Sucscun, 21, son of a couple selling empanadas in Meta Department. He was a baseball player who won a scholarship to attend the academy.

- Erika Chico, 21, a female Ecuadoran cadet who was at the top of the class.

Reuters reported on July 2, 2020 that authorities captured eight National Liberation Army (ELN) rebels accused of taking part in the car bombing in Bogota that killed 22 police cadets, injured 89 people, and scuttled peace talks with the government. Authorities conducted raids in Bogota, Zipaquira, Manizales, and the La Esmeralda settlement in Arauca Province, which borders Venezuela, seizing equipment and vehicles. The detainees faced sentences between 40 and 50 years on charges of murder and terrorism. Authorities had earlier arrested five others linked to the attack. 19011701

April 9, 2019: *Deutsch Welle* reported that the Colombian government announced that armed groups planned to use a "high-precision weap-

on" in a terrorist attack against President Ivan Duque during a scheduled meeting with indigenous communities and "minga" protestors.

May 4, 2019: Gunmen launched a grenade and shot at a crowd of environmental activists in Santander de Quilichao, injuring two people. Bodyguards battled the attackers. Among the individuals meeting with local leaders was prominent activist Francia Marquez, winner of the 2018 Goldman Environmental Prize for her work fighting illegal gold mining by armed groups in her Afro-Colombian community.

May 17, 2019: Police rearrested former Revolutionary Armed Forces of Colombia rebel leader Seuxis Hernandez, alias Jesus Santrich, moments after his release from La Picota jail by a peace tribunal whose ruling against extraditing him to the U.S. on drug trafficking and conspiracy charges triggered an institutional crisis. The blind rebel was in a wheelchair and his wrists were bandaged from what prison authorities said were self-inflicted wounds that required emergency medical attention. He was sent to a hospital. Colombia's chief prosecutor, Nestor Martinez, resigned to protest the court's decision. An Interpol notice for Santrich's arrest claimed he met with cocaine buyers at his residence on November 2, 2017 regarding a 10-ton shipment to the U.S., after the signing of the 2016 peace agreement. The Supreme Court ordered his immediate release on May 30, ruling that his election gave him limited immunity from prosecution; he was freed that day.

The tribunal recently ordered the capture of former FARC leader Hernán Velásquez, alias El Paisa, for failing to fulfill his commitments under the peace deal and provide testimony about FARC kidnappings.

June 30, 2019: Former FARC rebel Seuxis Hernandez, alias Jesus Santrich, had been elected to the Chamber of Representatives of the Colombian congress in Bogota. United Nations workers assisting in Colombia's peace process said on July 1 that Santrich had gone missing the previous day, raising questions about his safety. Hernandez had abandoned his security detail granted to lawmakers. He was wanted on U.S. drug charges;

he was suspected of shipping 10 tons of cocaine to the United States.

August 29, 2019: A group of former peace negotiators for the Revolutionary Armed Forces of Colombia released a video announcing that they were rearming following what they considered the failure of the 2016 peace deal to guarantee their political rights. Chief negotiator Luciano Marin, alias Iván Márquez, and 20 heavily armed guerrillas, including Jesus Santrich, denounced what he called the failure of President Ivan Duque to uphold the accord. Marquez said the dissidents would coordinate with the National Liberation Army (ELN), "and those comrades who have not folded up their flags". Later that day, Colombia's peace tribunal ordered the arrest of four FARC leaders who appeared in the video. Colombian President Iván Duque accused Venezuelan President Nicolás Maduro of providing safe haven to the group. Duque announced a nearly $1 million reward for the arrest of the insurgents.

August 30, 2019: *AFP* reported that Defense Minister Guillermo Botero said that Colombian troops had killed nine FARC dissidents in a raid in the San Vicente del Caguan region. President Ivan Duque said the operation sent "a clear message" to those who rearmed, calling them "a gang of narco-terrorist criminals who are residuals of what was known as the FARC, and who are part of the criminal structures that seek to challenge Colombia". Duque added, "Colombians must be clear that we are not facing a new guerrilla, but facing the criminal threats of a gang of narco-terrorists who have the shelter and support of the dictatorship of Nicolas Maduro", Venezuela's leader. Duque said the raid killed a FARC unit leader, Gildardo Cucho, "a criminal dedicated to drug-trafficking, kidnapping, intimidation of social leaders and who intended to be part of that threatening structure that yesterday was presented to the country as a new guerrilla, which it is not".

September 1, 2019: Gunmen kidnapped Karina García, 32, an attorney who was campaigning to become the first female mayor of Suarez. Hours later, an explosion went off. Her body and that of her mother, a candidate for city council, and two others were found in an abandoned, burnt-out vehicle. The vehicle had been hit by heavy gunfire and a grenade. On August 24, she posted a video on *Facebook* in which she said, "Please, for God's sake, don't act so irresponsibly", after four armed men told members of her campaign to take down all banners and posters in support of her candidacy. She asked her competitors to stop claiming that she would invite multinational companies and right-wing paramilitary groups to the town. She left behind a young daughter and husband. Peace Commissioner Miguel Ceballos blamed Mayimbu, a FARC commander who refused to demobilize as part of the 2016 peace deal. She was the fifth candidate to be killed ahead of the October 27 elections.

The same weekend, the National Liberation Army (ELN) kidnapped Tulio Mosquera Asprilla, a candidate from García's Liberal Party who was running for mayor in Alto Buado, in western Choco State.

September 23, 2019: Eleven former Revolutionary Armed Forces of Colombia (FARC) rebels testified before the Special Peace Tribunal regarding 522 kidnappings committed between 1993 and 2012. Rodrigo Londoño, alias Timochenko, FARC's former leader, said, "We are reflecting deeply over the acts of war so that we can ask for forgiveness for the errors committed... In the name of the men and women who formed our organization, we assume collective ethical and political responsibility for the harm done."

Many former combatants making the change to civilian life were reportedly killed by unknown assailants.

October 29, 2019: Men in a black vehicle killed five members of the Association of Indigenous Councils of Northern Cauca and wounded six in the late afternoon near Tacueyo, 43 miles from Cali. The gunmen fired at an ambulance tending to the injured. Investigators said it was in retaliation for the capture of three members of a residual front of the former Revolutionary Armed Forces of Colombia. Colombia's indigenous guards do not carry firearms. The Organization of American States identified one of the dead as Cristina Bautista, a spiritual leader with the Neehwe'sx community in southwestern Colombia.

November 22, 2019: The *New York Times* reported that a bomb went off during the night at a police station in Santander de Quilichao in Cauca Province, killing three officers and wounding ten other officers. No group claimed credit.

December 23, 2019: The National Liberation Army released three teens they had kidnapped earlier in the month following mediation by several human rights groups. The rebels claimed that the military had trained the teens to collect intelligence on them. The International Committee of the Red Cross said that the teens were in good health when they were handed over to humanitarian workers in a rural area of Arauca Department.

GUYANA

April 29, 2019: The U.S. objected to the legislative resolution honoring the life and work of Abdul Kadir, a former civil engineer and former politician convicted of plotting to blow up fuel tanks at New York's John F. Kennedy Airport, deeming it an "insensitive and thoughtless act" that disregarded the gravity of his actions. U.S. officials were surprised that "Guyana chose to honor a man who conspired to kill innocent people from across the United States and around the world", adding, "members of Guyana's assembly have left a stain on their legacy as representatives of the Guyanese people and on their commitment to the rule of law." Kadir and three other men were sentenced to life in prison in the U.S. in 2010. Kadir died in 2018 and was buried in the bauxite mining city of Linden, where he had served as mayor. Kadir claimed he was set up by government informants and had no intention of carrying out the alleged plot. Prosecutors said the suspects tried to obtain money and operations support from al-Qaeda terrorists in the Caribbean region and from Jamaat al-Muslimeen, which attempted a coup in Trinidad in 1990.

HONDURAS

May 31, 2019: *CNN* reported that demonstrators set fire to tires and objects in front of the U.S. Embassy in Tegucigalpa, charring some of the building. The fire was extinguished by mid-afternoon. Education and medical professionals were protesting government plans to privatize their sectors.

November 25, 2019: Security spokesman Jair Meza Barahona said television journalist José Arita was shot to death shortly after leaving *Channel 12* in the north coast city of Puerto Cortes during the night. Four men were waiting for Arita outside and shot him at close range. The Inter American Press Association said he was the fourth journalist killed in Honduras in 2019.

MEXICO

February 15, 2019: Janitors found a homemade bomb inside a cigar box inside a rest room in a shopping mall in Tlalnepantla, a Mexico City suburb. The device was housed in a small wooden box and included a battery detonator, analog clock, nuts and screws. State police disarmed the device, which was set to detonate in an hour.

April 6, 2019: Former Mexican President Vicente Fox tweeted that gunmen tried to storm into his house on a large ranch in Guanajuato State, months after President Andrés Manuel López Obrador cut off security for the country's ex-presidents. He added, "I hold President Andres Manuel Lopez Obrador directly responsible for the security of myself, my family and my belongings."

November 4, 2019: *AP, CNN, Reuters, Agence France-Presse*, the *New York Times*, and the *Wall Street Journal* reported that Mexican Public Security Secretary Alfonso Durazo said gunmen from a drug cartel ambushed three SUVs along a rural, dirt road in Sonora State, killing six children and three women, all U.S. citizens living in northern Mexico. The nine LeBarón extended family members belonged to a fundamentalist Mormon offshoot community unaffiliated with the main LDS church. Relatives said the six children were aged from 8-month-old twins to 12 years. Their mothers were Rhonita Maria Miller, 30; Dawna Langford, 43; and Christina Langford Johnson, 30; all were part of a community of U.S.-Mexican dual citizens who have resided in La Mora,

Sonora State, Mexico for decades. Some of the victims were traveling to plan a wedding at Colonia LeBarón in Chihuahua State; Miller was going to the airport in Phoenix to meet her husband. Eight other children were found alive, hiding in the brush; five had gunshot wounds or other injuries. Faith Marie Johnson, 7-month-old daughter of victim Christina Langford Johnson, was found uninjured in her car seat. Security Secretary Alfonso Durazo suggested that the gunmen may have mistaken the SUVs for those of rival gangs. Family members said the attackers knew they were shooting civilians. Investigators found more than 200 shell casings, mostly from assault rifles. President Trump offered to "wage WAR on the drug cartels and wipe them off the face of the earth"—an offer President Andrews Manuel López Obrador declined.

Miller was driving her Chevrolet Tahoe outside San Miguelito in the morning when gunmen shot her and her four children, including the twins, a boy, 11, and a girl, 9, then set the SUV on fire.

Eleven miles east, authorities found a second vehicle, a white Chevrolet Suburban, with the bodies of Dawna Langford and her 11- and 3-year-old sons. Family members said Dawna Langford's son, Devin, 13, watched his mother die and then hid his six surviving siblings in nearby bushes.

A white Suburban was found a mile east of the Chihuahua border. The body of Christina Langford Johnson was found nearby.

Survivors included a 10-month-old boy and a boy, 8, who underwent surgery the next day. A bullet took out much of the latter's jaw.

In 2009, a prominent member of the family, Benjamin LeBarón, 31, and his brother-in-law Luis Widmar were shot dead near their community. Benjamin had publicly denounced the drug traffickers after they kidnapped his younger brother. The family refused to pay a $1 million ransom.

CNN reported on November 6 that authorities had arrested a suspect believed to be part of a newly-formed cartel. Police found two bound and gagged hostages.

AP reported on November 11 that Mexican Security Secretary Alfonso Durazo announced that an unspecified number of arrests had been made.

The *Washington Post* reported on December 1, 2019 that Mexican soldiers, Marines, National Guard and other security forces arrested several people suspected of involvement. *El Universal* reported that three people were arrested in Bavispe, not far from La Mora.

On December 31, 2019, *AFP* reported that Mexican authorities had arrested seven suspects in connection with the murders of the nine Mormon women and children of the LeBarón family. A local police chief suspected of links to organized crime was among the detainees. Three suspects were arrested on December 26 for "probable responsibility" in organized crime. The other four were arrested earlier.

CNN and *AFP* reported on November 5, 2020 that authorities in Ciudad Juarez arrested Alfredo L. in connection with the murder. The government said he was part of a criminal organization. He was charged with homicide and organized crime.

Reuters added on November 25, 2020 that authorities in Chihuahua State captured three members of the criminal organization La Linea, including Roberto Gonzalez, alias "the 32", a gang leader believed to be the "intellectual architect" of the attack.

November 30, 2019: Twenty-one people were killed in a gun battle between the Cartel of the Northeast and security forces in Villa Union in Coahuila State, about 35 miles southwest of Eagle Pass, Texas. The attackers had arrived in pickup trucks and stormed the city hall. At least four police officers died and several municipal workers were missing. Seven attackers were killed at the site; another seven died in raids by authorities. *Zocalo* of Saltillo reported that the gunmen stole several vehicles, including a hearse headed for a funeral.

PERU

April 2, 2019: The burned body of Paul McAuley, 71, a British lay religious activist who faced expulsion from Peru a decade earlier for his work on behalf of indigenous communities, was found at a youth hostel he ran in the Amazon rain forest. He had worked to embolden Peru's historically discriminated tribes in the battle against powerful oil and mining interests. In 2010, the regime failed to deny him his residency for allegedly inciting unrest after he fought attempts to open up the Amazon to drilling. The La Salle Christian Brothers said McAuley had burned to death. Loreto region chief forensic doctor Francisco Moreno said that there was no carbon dioxide in his blood, ruling out burning as the cause of death and indicating that he had died before the body was burned. Authorities questioned six indigenous youth who lived in the hostel he managed in a poor section in Iquitos. In 2004, McAuley, an Oxford-educated philosopher and mathematician, founded the Loreto Environmental Network, which works on behalf of indigenous groups. He and environmentalists opposed then-President Alan Garcia's moves to open up the Amazon to extensive mining and oil exploration and drilling.

April 17, 2019: The *Washington Post* and *CNN* reported that former two-time Peruvian President Alan Garcia, 69, shot himself in the neck as police attempted to arrest him at his Lima home in a corruption scandal. Garcia died soon after in Casimiro Ulloa Hospital of a massive brain hemorrhage. It was a rare case anywhere in the world of peacetime suicide by a former president. The *Post* reported that he allegedly accepted bribes from the Brazilian construction firm Odebrecht in return for massive public works contracts during his second term, from 2006 to 2011. Odebrecht admitted paying nearly $1 billion in kickbacks to politicians from Mexico to Argentina. The U.S. Justice Department fined Odebrecht $3.5 billion in 2016. Garcia's first term ran from 1985 to 1990. Garcia had a recent disapproval rating of around 90 percent.

MIDDLE EAST

February 28, 2019: The *Long War Journal, CNN* and *AP* reported that the U.S. Rewards for Justice Program offered $1 million for information on the whereabouts of Hamza bin Laden, son of Osama bin Laden. Some observers believed that Hamza was being groomed to take over al-Qaeda. The State Department issued a wanted poster showing an image of him from his wedding video. State said that he married the daughter of Mohammed Atta, the lead 9/11 hijacker, although some scholars said that there was no official record of Atta having a child (an unannounced daughter was possible). Also attending Hamza's wedding was Mohammed Islambouli, a senior al-Qaeda figure who hid out in Iran for years after 9/11 and was recently located in Turkey. The U.S. designated Hamza as a terrorist in January 2017. On March 1, Saudi Arabia announced that a November 2018 royal decree had revoked his citizenship. Hamza married the daughter of senior al-Qaeda military leader Abu Mohammed al-Masri while in Iran.

March 18, 2019: The *Long War Journal* reported that ISIS spokesman Abul-Hasan al-Muhajir released a 44-minute audio entitled "He Was True to Allah and Allah Was True to Him" on March 18. He argued that "patience" will lead to "victory". He mentioned the New Zealand attack of three days earlier. "O people, everyone saw the incident of the massacre at the two mosques in Crusader New Zealand. We will reflect on that incident." Some "compare the killing of those worshipers with the Shari'ah-compliant jihad that the sons of the State of Islam are undertaking to establish the religion and repel the aggression of the Safavids, the Crusaders, and the murtaddin and turn them back from the Muslims' lands." He dismissed the comparison, saying ISIS actions are necessary to "establish the religion" and defensive in the face of opposition from the Iranians, the West, and "apostates". He admitted that it "is rare now not to find in the Islamic State a household that did not offer sacrifice and redemption for this religion… Rhetoric fails to describe their sacrifice and redemption in terms of numbers among the killed, captive, and displaced among young, women, and children... entire families refused to abandon Darul-Islam and preferred to die over abandoning Darul-Islam and returning to Darul-Kufr and living under the oppression of the taghut and its rule." He mentioned Mosul, Raqqa and Sirte, arguing that "the epic battles and their effect in the Wilayat [provinces] of the Islamic State are no longer obscured" and the "sons of the Khilafah continue to prove that they are the firm and solid rock on which will break the alliance of kufr." He cited comments made by Brett McGurk (who was the special presidential envoy for the Global Coalition to Counter the Islamic State), CENTCOM Commander Joseph Votel, and National Security Adviser John Bolton who said that ISIS was not dead. He noted that McGurk resigned "in protest over" President Trump's "claim of victory". He said that Trump "quickly denigrated" and humiliated McGurk, "stating that he never knew him [McGurk] before" and that he was part of the Obama administration and its "failed policies". He called Trump "the Roman dog" who complained that "developed countries can not engage in endless wars" and that other countries were not "committing to send enough supplies and soldiers to solidify the bases of the government of the Iranian Rafidah militias in Iraq, in fear of the sudden emergence of the Islamic State and its recapture of the territories from which it was ousted". The "state of the Khilafah has become a reality, the danger of which cannot be ignored or denied... its army, the companies of its battalions touring Iraq, Sham, Khorasan, West Africa, and other Wilayat [provinces], awaiting the hour of decision." He added, "O Sunni people of Iraq, the Islamic State is your lifeboat and your impenetrable fortress against the Iranian Safavids expansion, so repent before it is too late and learn a lesson from others... No matter how long it might take, the Islamic State is coming back to the areas it departed, by Allah's will." He called on fighters to abandon electronic communications that can be monitored and that there is "no harm if a job that can be accomplished with those devices in two days is accomplished without it in one week instead".

March 19, 2019: The *New York Times* reported that ISIS spokesman Abu Hassan al-Muhajir broke a silence since September 2018 by releasing a 44-minute audio that mocked U.S. claims of having defeated ISIS and called for retaliation for the Christchurch mosque attacks. "The scenes of the massacres in the two mosques should wake up those who were fooled, and should incite the supporters of the caliphate to avenge their religion." "Here is Baghuz in Syria, where Muslims are burned to death and are bombed by all known and unknown weapons of mass destruction." He cited a White House "state of confusion and contradiction that make it impossible for any observer to know what is meant by the word 'victory'". He mentioned President Trump's claim not to know Brett McGurk, the American special envoy in the fight against ISIS, who resigned in protest. Regarding Trump's visit to Iraq, he added, "How strange for a victor who can't even announce publicly an official visit to a country he claims to be bringing peace and stability to. He could only come like a frightened and cowardly thief." He claimed ISIS emir al-Baghdadi was alive, adding, "A message of advice from the caliph of the believers regarding communication devices: Be careful, careful of communication devices—even if it slows down work from two days to seven days."

April 29, 2019: *NPR* reported that Abu Bakr al-Baghdadi released his first video in five years on ISIS's *Furqan* channel, in which he outlined the next steps for ISIS. In the 18-minute video, he admitted that ISIS had lost the battle of Baghouz, Syria and praised the Sri Lanka church attacks and affiliates in Libya, Mali, Western Sahara, Pakistan, Khorasan (Afghanistan), and Burkina Faso. The *Washington Post* reported that he sat on a flowered mattress in a bare white room, an AK-74 rifle at his side. He congratulated the Sri Lanka Easter attackers in a separate audio at the end of the video, saying the attacks were revenge for the deaths of ISIS fighters in the battle of Baghouz, and not for the white extremist attack on two mosques in New Zealand in March. "This is part of the vengeance that awaits the Crusaders and their henchmen." "As for your brothers in Sri Lanka, they have put joy in the hearts of the monotheists with their immersing operations that struck the homes of the crusaders in their Easter." He called on them to be "a thorn in the chests of the crusaders". He also mentioned Israeli Prime Minister Benjamin Netanyahu's April 9 election victory, the April 11 coup in Sudan, and the resignation of Algerian President Abdelaziz Bouteflika. He named 13 ISIS members who died in the Baghouz battle, including French brothers Fabien and Jean-Michel Clain. His aides handed him folders with the names of IS provinces, including West Africa, Somalia, Egypt's Sinai, Libya, Central Africa, the Caucasus and Turkey.

May 11, 2019: The *Long War Journal* reported that al-Qaeda's *as-Sahab* media released a video entitled, "Under the Shade of the Islamic Emirate: Paktika – Ambush on the Convoy of Afghan National Army in the Hindi Mountains" advertising the group's role in an ambush on an ANA convoy in Paktika Province. Al-Qaeda underscored its alliance with the Taliban. The video included English subtitles. A narrator observed that the U.S. had been defeated in Afghanistan, saying, "Fifteen years ago from today, if anyone had said that the super power of the time, America, would be defeated in Afghanistan, it would have been hilarious for the world... But today it has become a reality." He said the Americans, NATO and the ANA were an "army besieged in their bases". "By the grace of Allah almighty, today the Islamic Emirate has liberated most areas of Afghanistan from American control." The narrator claimed that the mujahidin "cleansed a major area" of the Wazikhawa (Wazakhwa) district of Paktika "from the filthy presence of the Americans and their allies". The "Islamic Emirate of Afghanistan" (the Taliban) "gained great victories in this area and besieged the district headquarters" in 2014. Jihadists have "enforced a continuous blockade", forcing the "enemy" to "bring its military supplies and even items of food through helicopters". The attack occurred at the "beginning of the winter season".

A jihadist, Abdul Hannan, said the U.S. "does not consider [the] Afghan National Army anything more than human fuel to carry on its war and to keep its soldiers safe, does not even hesitate to use them as scapegoats!"

Text on the screen included, "Under the leadership of the Islamic Emirate of Afghanistan, the Ansar and Muhajir Mujahidin decided to lay an ambush for this convoy." "The first stage of the ambush was to choose a suitable place for the attack. After the help of Allah, the success of an ambush depends largely on choosing the right place."

The video showed Muhammad Farooqi, his face hidden, with the text, "In Guerrilla Warfare, you can lay a successful ambush from a hilltop on the enemy passing below... Between the districts [of] Wazikhawa and Gomal lies the long mountainous range of Hindi, it was the best place to teach this devilish army a lesson." The area is defined by "barren peaks, dangerous and difficult passages" and "violent winds increase the harshness of these mountains." The mujahidin "were only fifteen in number," equipped with "only 6 rockets of RR-82 [Recoil Rifle 82mm (Light Cannon)]", "4 rockets of RPG-7", a "sniper gun", "Kalashnikovs and PK [light] machine guns".

One of the raiders was Yasir Mirza, alias Khalid Qeemti, who was positioned on the mountainside. He was from Rawalpindi, Pakistan, and killed in a U.S. drone strike in Paktika. He and his colleagues shot at the convoy when it "came close", with the "first strike" by an "RR-82 rocket" destroying "the enemy's mine sweeper truck". The "enemy soldiers panicked and started shooting blindly", but "mujahidin kept targeting their enemies calmly."

Abdul Hannan observed that "due to the limited amount of rockets", the jihadists "were unable to finish off all of the vehicles". The video told the "Ummah [worldwide community of Muslims] and its wealthy people" that it is "their duty" to "aid the Mujahidin with your wealth, your lives and your sincere prayers" during this "confrontation with the Kufr (infidels) of the whole world".

Slogans on the screen during a montage of al-Qaeda and Taliban leaders read:

"One home! One body! One soul Emirate! (Of Afghanistan)"

"One voice! One force! One wish! Emirate!"

"One rank! One army! One leader! One path! Emirate!"

"Live! Live! Live! May emirate live!"

"We pray to Allah almighty to strengthen the Islamic Emirate of Afghanistan and shower the blessings...of Jihad and Sharia in the whole region", the text reads over images of a truck flying a Taliban-style banner.

The video ended with: "Shari'ah or Martyrdom".

July 31, 2019: *NBC News, CNN,* the *New York Times,* the *Guardian,* and the *Washington Post* reported that Hamza bin Laden, 30, son of al-Qaeda leader Osama bin Laden, had been killed, possibly by an airstrike in which the U.S. had a role, in the last two years. Earlier in 2019, the U.S. Department of State's Rewards for Justice Program offered $1 million for information about his whereabouts. Official Saudi newspaper *Um al-Qura* had reported earlier in 2019 that the Interior Ministry had revoked Hamza's Saudi citizenship.

August 1, 2019: *CNN* reported that intelligence and a U.N. Security Council monitoring report suggested that al-Qaeda leader Ayman al-Zawahiri, 68, had a potentially serious "heart complaint".

September 11, 2019: Al-Qaeda leader Ayman al-Zawahiri, in a 33-minute, 28-second video released by the as-Sahab Media Foundation, called on Muslims to attack U.S., European, Israeli and Russian targets and criticized "backtrackers" from jihad, such as repentant jihadis who changed their views in prison and called the 9/11 attacks unacceptable because innocent civilians were harmed. "If you want Jihad to be focused solely on military targets, the American military has presence all over the world, from the East to the West. Your countries are littered with American bases, with all the infidels therein and the corruption they spread." He mentioned President Donald Trump's recognition of the Golan Heights as Israeli territory, which was announced on March 25. He urged Palestinians to seek "martyrdom" by attacking Israelis with a suicide vest.

September 14, 2019: *CNN* reported that President Donald Trump confirmed that Hamza bin Laden, late al-Qaeda leader Osama bin Laden's son, was "killed in a United States counterterrorism operation in the Afghanistan/Pakistan region" on an undisclosed date. "The loss of Hamza bin Ladin not only deprives al-Qa'ida

of important leadership skills and the symbolic connection to his father, but undermines important operational activities of the group... Hamza bin Ladin was responsible for planning and dealing with various terrorist groups." Al-Qaeda had yet to issue a eulogy. The U.S. State Department's Rewards for Justice program had earlier reported that he was married to a daughter of Abdullah Ahmed Abdullah, an al-Qaeda leader and Egyptian charged for his role in the August 1998 bombings of the U.S. embassies in Tanzania and Kenya. They had two children, Osama and Khairiah, named after his parents.

September 16, 2019: ISIS caliph Abu Bakr al-Baghdad released a 30-minute audio via *al-Furqan* in which he called upon its membership to do all they can to free ISIS detainees and women held in jails and camps. "How can a Muslim enjoy life?" when Muslim women are held in "prisons of humiliation run by Crusaders and their Shi'ite followers". He said that ISIS fighters should attack interrogators and judges who are questioning ISIS members. Detainees and women should be patient. The *Washington Post* added that he called for "daily operations" across "different fronts" in the Middle East, Africa and Asia. "As for the worst and most important matter—the prisons, the prisons, oh soldiers of the caliphate... Your brothers and sisters, do your utmost to free them and tear down the walls restricting them... Do not hesitate to pay ransom if you cannot free them by force, and attack their butchers." "From [Afghanistan] to Iraq to Yemen, to Somalia to western and central Africa, eastern Asia, northern Africa... Sacrifice your lives if you have to... Revenge the torture."

AFGHANISTAN

January 1, 2019: *Reuters* reported that the Taliban set off explosives planted in a tunnel below an Afghan military outpost in the Maiwand district of Kandahar Province, killing five soldiers and wounding six troops. Taliban spokesman Qari Yousuf Ahmadi said the terrorists had killed or wounded 35 soldiers and destroyed a large cache of weapons and ammunition.

January 2, 2019: A rogue border policeman fired on an Italian military advisor's armored vehicle after he exited a meeting in Herat Province, not far from the border with Iran, wounding a female police officer before being shot dead by nearby police. The advisor was unharmed. Noorullah Qadri, commander of 207 Zafar military corps, said two attackers had infiltrated the border security forces to kill Italians at the base. Qadri said, "The Italian nationals escaped uninjured. One attacker was gunned down immediately and the other was arrested." 19010201

January 3, 2019: The Taliban killed eight police in an attack on their post in the provincial capital of Baghlan Province. Police fought the insurgents for four hours; two police were wounded.

January 4, 2019: Aziz Ahmad Azizi, spokesman for the provincial governor in Kandahar, said gunmen attacked a checkpoint in Kandahar Province's Spin Bolduk (variant Boldak) district, killing seven border police officers and wounding four. Sixteen gunmen were killed and eleven others injured in the late evening attack.

January 6, 2019: Two Taliban attacks in Badghis Province killed eight security force members. Spokesman Jamshid Shahabi said the attacks wounded five security force members. Ten insurgents were killed. However, Abdul Aziz Beg, the head of Badghis's provincial council, said the attacks killed 21 security force members.

January 7, 2019: Nawroz Ishaq, the provincial governor's spokesman, said a roadside bomb in Paktika Province's Jani Khail district killed five civilians and wounded seven. No one claimed credit.

January 9, 2019: Taliban attacks in western and northern Afghanistan killed 21 members of the security forces and wounded another 23 security forces. The Taliban claimed credit for all of the attacks.

Jamshed Shahabi, spokesman for the governor in Badghis Province, says the Taliban overran outposts there, killing six policemen.

Baghlan Provincial Council member Shamsul Haq Barekzai said seven members of the local police force were killed.

Takhar Provincial Council member Ruhollah Raufi said gunmen killed eight policemen.

January 12, 2019: The Taliban attacked a checkpoint in Spin Bolduk district in Kandahar Province, killing five security forces and wounding two. Aziz Ahmad Azizi, provincial governor's spokesman, said seven Taliban were killed and six others were wounded.

U.S. Army Special Operations Command said an Army Ranger, Sergeant Cameron A. Meddock, 26, of Spearman, Texas, died in Landstuhl, Germany, on January 17 of wounds he received from small arms fire during combat operations on January 12 in Badghis Province. Meddock served with Company A, 2nd Battalion, 75th Ranger Regiment, based at Joint Base Lewis-McChord in Washington State. He was on his second deployment with the U.S.-led coalition. 19011201

January 14, 2019: During the night, a Taliban suicide car bomb exploded in the Green Village near the airport in an area frequented by aid workers and contractors in eastern Kabul's Police District Nine (PD9), killing three military personnel and one civilian and injuring 113, including at least 12 women, 23 children and 55 men.

January 20, 2019: A Taliban suicide bomber rammed a government convoy in Logar Province, killing eight bodyguards of the provincial governor, who survived.

January 21, 2019: The Taliban attacked a military base and police and intelligence training center in Maidan in Wardak Province in the morning, killing between 45 and 50, most of them military personnel and intelligence officers, and wounding 70 people, according to initial reports. *AFP* said 65-70 were killed. One provincial security official said he counted 75 dead bodies. *Reuters* reported 126 Afghan security forces were killed. Nasrat Rahimi, deputy spokesman for the interior minister, said a suicide Humvee bomber hit the base; gunmen dressed in uniforms used by Afghan special forces and riding in a Toyota truck entered the base and fired at the Afghan forces, who in turn killed two Taliban fighters. The Taliban had captured the Humvee earlier. Taliban spokesman Zabihullah Mujahid claimed credit, saying it had killed more than 190 people and wounded many more.

Reuters on January 24 quoted the National Directorate of Security (NDS) intelligence agency as saying that its airstrike had killed eight terrorists, including Taliban commander Noman on the night of January 22, claiming that he had orchestrated the attack. The Taliban denied that he was killed.

January 26, 2019: An accidental explosion killed four Taliban, including a local commander, and a civilian, and injured 20 people, including Taliban and civilians, near a volleyball match in an area controlled by the Taliban in Baghlan Province.

A female university student was killed by a sticky bomb attached to a vehicle in Nangarhar Province.

January 27, 2019: Munir Ahmad Farhad, spokesman for Balkh Province's governor, said a woman was arrested on suspicion of attempting to attack the Pakistani consulate in Mazar-e-Sharif after a hand grenade was found in her bag.

January 31, 2019: The Taliban attacked an army checkpoint during the night in the Sozma Qala district of Sari Pul Province, killing six soldiers and wounding seven soldiers. Troops returned fire, killing nine Taliban and injuring 13.

February 4, 2019: During the night, the Taliban attacked a checkpoint in Baghlan Province's Baghlani Markazi district, killing 11 policemen, wounding five policemen, and seizing all weapons and ammunition from the checkpoint.

February 5, 2019: At 2 a.m., the Taliban attacked an army base outside Kunduz, killing 26 members of the security forces, including 23 soldiers and three members of the local police force, and wounding 12 troops during the two-hour battle.

In the morning, the Taliban attacked a local pro-government militia in a village in Dara-I Suf district in Samangan Province, killing ten people, including a woman, and injuring four people.

February 15, 2019: The *New York Times* reported that in the early morning, as border security troops were asleep inside their post in Kandahar Province, a Taliban gunman climbed a guard

tower after a lone sentry had left to awaken his replacement. The gunman shot the replacement. Terrorists then crashed a stolen police Humvee packed with explosives through the base's entrance. They then fired on survivors, killing all 32 men posted at the base in Spin Boldak district. The Humvee driver died.

February 16, 2019: The Taliban attacked a police checkpoint in Balkh Province, killing six police charged with guarding a gas pipeline.

February 17, 2019: A roadside bomb killed three civilians, including a small child, in Kandahar Province. Provincial police chief General Tadeen Khan blamed the Taliban.

February 19, 2019: A roadside bomb exploded under a car in Qarghayi district in Laghman Province, killing six civilians. No one claimed credit. The Taliban was suspected.

A sticky bomb attached to a doctor's vehicle exploded as he returned home from his private clinic in Kabul. ISIS-K claimed credit.

February 27, 2019: A bomb exploded in Mazar-i-Sharif, capital of Balkh Province, wounding six civilians. No one claimed credit.

February 28, 2019: In the morning, the Taliban attacked a security outpost in Balkh Province for five hours, killing five personnel until reinforcements arrived and repulsed the attack. Taliban spokesman Zabihullah Mujahid said six police were killed.

March 1, 2019: Taliban suicide bombers and gunmen carrying grenade launchers assaulted a major army base in the Wahser district of Helmand Province before dawn. A suicide bomber set off his explosives at Shorab camp. Three other suicide bombers blew themselves up; gunmen followed them into the base. During the gun battle, 23 Afghan security personnel and 20 Taliban were killed and 16 soldiers were wounded. Taliban spokesman Qari Yousef Ahmadi claimed the group caused serious damage to a fleet of military helicopters.

Army Colonel David Butler, a U.S. military spokesman in Kabul, said that U.S. Marines living in another part of the base responded to a smaller attack and "mitigated the threat". 19030101

Camp Shorab was previously a British air base known as Camp Bastion.

The Taliban ambushed a convoy of Afghan security forces in the Sangcharak district of Sari Pul Province, killing nine and wounding 12 in a seven-hour gun battle. Four security forces were missing and presumed kidnapped.

March 6, 2019: At 5 a.m., two suicide bombers set off explosives and three gunmen attacked a construction company near the Jalalabad airport in Nangarhar Province, killing 17 people and wounding nine. Among the dead in a five-hour-long shootout were 16 employees of the Afghan construction company EBE and a military intelligence officer.

March 7, 2019: ISIS-K mortar fire hit a mid-morning outdoor memorial service in Kabul attended by numerous Afghan politicians and officials, including Chief Executive Abdullah Abdullah, 58, and former president Hamid Karzai, killing 11 civilians and injuring nearly 100, including presidential candidate Latif Pedram, 55, a liberal politician and member of parliament, and eight guards of another presidential candidate, former national security adviser Hanif Atmar. Two of the people killed were inside a house near the event. The Interior Ministry claimed that the attackers had used another house in the area to launch the mortars at the crowd. Interior Ministry spokesman Nasrat Rahimi said two attackers were killed and a third was arrested. The service marked the anniversary of the 1995 murder by the Taliban of a minority Shi'ite and ethnic Hazara leader, Abdul Ali Mazari. In March 2018, an ISIS-K suicide bomber hit a memorial service for Mazari outside a Kabul mosque, killing ten and injuring 22.

March 9-12, 2019: Jamshid Shahabi, the Badghis provincial governor's spokesman, said the Taliban killed at least 13 Afghan soldiers in battles over three days in western Badghis Province at several army checkpoints. Twelve other soldiers were missing. The fighting began on March 9 in Bala Murghab district. Shahabi said 42 Taliban were killed and 15 troops were wounded in the fighting. Mohammad Naser Nazari, a member of the provincial council, claimed that 20 soldiers were killed and 20 others were missing. Clashes continued into March 12. The Taliban claimed credit.

March 12, 2019: The Taliban attacked an army checkpoint along the main highway in Gulistan district in Farah Province, killing ten soldiers. The Taliban took credit.

March 13, 2019: Afghan *Sabahoon* radio and TV journalist Nesar Ahmad Ahmadi, long the subject of death threats, was seriously wounded in the leg when a sticky bomb attached to his car exploded as he was heading to work in Helmand Province.

Gunmen shot to death Mohammad Salim Farahi, an engineer and the head of the public works department, outside his home in Farah.

March 15, 2019: Two motorcycle-riding gunmen shot to death Sultan Mahmoud Khirkhowa, a journalist with the local *Zhman* TV and radio, in an attack on his vehicle in Khost Province. ISIS-K claimed credit on March 17.

March 16-17, 2019: Overnight Taliban attacks on checkpoints in Faryab Province's Qaisar district killed 22 troops and wounded 20 soldiers in fighting that extended into March 17.

Jamshid Shahabi, the Badghis provincial governor's spokesman, said 16 soldiers were killed and 20 wounded during the ongoing battle in the Bala Murghab district. He claimed that more than 40 insurgents were killed.

March 21, 2019: Three remotely-detonated bombs went off near the Shi'ite Karti Sakhi shrine and cemetery in Kabul during the morning on the holiday of Nowruz, the Persian New Year, killing six and wounding 23, including two children. ISIS-K claimed credit the next day. ISIS-K said its aim was "to spoil the ritual of the polytheists".

March 22, 2019: The *Washington Post* reported that two U.S. troops were killed during an operation in Kunduz Province. The Taliban claimed three Americans and nine Afghan soldiers from the country's commando force were killed in a house raid. Taliban spokesman Zabiullah Mujahid said, "American occupying forces and their local slaves wanted to raid a house but faced tough resistance." The Pentagon identified the soldiers as Spc. Joseph Collette of Lancaster, Ohio, 29, assigned to the 242nd Ordnance Battalion, 71st Explosive Ordnance Group in Fort Carson, Colorado; and Sgt. 1st Class Will Lindsay, 33, of Cortez, Colorado, from the 2nd Battalion, 10th Special Forces Group (Airborne) out of Fort Carson. Lindsay enlisted in the Army in 2004 and was awarded the Bronze Star Medal and the Purple Heart Medal, among other awards. Deployments included tours in Iraq, plus tours in Tajikistan and Afghanistan. They died during a U.S.-Afghan military operation against the Taliban. Afghan troops were also killed.

March 23, 2019: Two Taliban bombs hit a celebration of Farmers' Day in a sports stadium in Lashkar Gah, capital of Helmand Province, killing four people, including provincial official Mohammad Khan Nasrat, the economic director of Helmand, and wounding 31, including provincial council members and provincial security officials.

Gunmen fired on the vehicle of former lawmaker Obaidullah Barekzai in Kandahar, killing him. No one claimed credit.

The Taliban attacked an Afghan army outpost in Helmand Province's Sangin district, killing 26 soldiers and seven policemen and wounding 31 soldiers, according to Helmand council chief Attahullah Afghan. The Taliban claimed credit.

March 24, 2019: An attack in Helmand Province killed five policemen.

March 25, 2019: A bomb wounded six women and children in a clinic in Jalalabad. No one claimed credit.

March 28-29, 2019: In an overnight attack that lasted until morning, the Taliban overran the Arghanj Khowa district headquarters in Badakhshan Province, killing four police and wounding five others. Taliban spokesman Zabihullah Mujahid said the attackers seized large amounts of ammunition and weapons plus two military vehicles.

March 30, 2019: The Taliban attacked a police checkpoint in Andar district of Ghazni Province, killing four students and wounding 17 others, including 15 students and two teachers, when rocket fire apparently hit a nearby school. The students were between 10 and 16 years old. No one claimed credit.

Reuters reported that gunmen attacked the convoy of Afghanistan's vice president, Abdul Rashid Dostum, killing one of his bodyguards and wounding two other bodyguards. Dostum was unhurt. The convoy was en route from Mazar-i-Sharif in Balkh Province to Jawzjan Province.

March 31, 2019: Zabihullah Amani, spokesman for the provincial governor in Sari Pul Province, said that during the night the Taliban attacked a checkpoint in Sozma Qala district, killing five security forces and wounding two troops. The fighting extended into the next morning. The insurgents captured six soldiers. No one claimed credit.

April 1, 2019: Jamshid Shahabi, spokesman for the provincial governor, reported that the Taliban overran an army checkpoint in the Bal Murghab district of Badghis Province, killing three soldiers and wounding four. Two soldiers were missing. Taliban spokesman Qari Yusouf Ahmadi claimed responsibility.

During the evening, the Taliban was suspected in an attack on a checkpoint in Balkh Province's Sholgara district that killed eight members of the security forces and injured another five. The attackers took some casualties.

April 4, 2019: Provincial council member Mohammad Nasir Nazari said that the Taliban attacked a government compound in the district of Balal Murgab in Badghis Province at dawn, killing 20 troops and policemen. The battle continued into a second day, with 12 more troops killed and the rest running out of ammunition, water, and food. Soldiers claimed that 2,000 Taliban were attacking 600 Afghan troops and policemen. The battle continued into a fifth day with the overall death toll passing 40 and dozens of insurgents killed and wounded.

April 6, 2019: The Taliban attacked security checkpoints in Ghazni Province, killing three policemen and wounding seven.

The Taliban attacked a security checkpoint in Sari Pul Province, killing four policemen and wounding five others in the capital's suburbs.

Two bombs exploded in Nangarhar Province, killing three civilians. No one claimed credit.

ISIS-K claimed credit for attacks in Jalalabad on April 6 and 7.

April 8, 2019: *Military Times* reported that U.S. forces announced that three U.S. Marines were killed and three other service members and an Afghan contractor were wounded in a roadside bombing near Bagram Air Base in Parwan Province while conducting combat operations. The Pentagon said the next day that a report that an Afghan citizen contractor had been killed was erroneous; he had been injured. Taliban spokesman Zabihullah Mujahid said a suicide bomber set off his car bomb near the NATO base. Photos showed a destroyed Toyota Land Cruiser. *NBC News* later said a suicide car bomber hit a military convoy. 19040801

Marine Corps Times reported that the Pentagon identified those killed as members of the 25th Marine Regiment, 4th Marine Division, Marine Forces Reserve:

- Staff Sgt. Christopher Slutman, 43, of Newark, Delaware. The Marine reservist had served as a Fire Department of New York (FDNY) firefighter for 15 years and was a veteran of the Kentland, Maryland, volunteer fire department. Oleg Pelekhaty, the Kentland fire chief, posted to *Facebook*: "It is with deep regret that the Kentland Volunteer Fire Department (KVFD), Incorporated announces the tragic passing of Life Member Christopher Slutman (#7194)." The *New York Post* reported that he was awarded the Fire Chiefs Association Memorial Medal for his heroic actions by rescuing a woman from a burning building in South Bronx in 2014. He was survived by his wife and three children.

- Cpl. Robert A. Hendriks, 25, of Locust Valley, New York

- Sgt. Benjamin S. Hines, 31, of York, Pennsylvania

At noon, an Afghan army officer shot and killed two of his fellow soldiers, seized a Humvee and ammunition, and fled to join the Taliban in Dari Suf district.

Zabihullah Amani, provincial governor's spokesman, said a nighttime Taliban attack on a joint base in Sari Pul Province's Sangcharak district killed five members of the security forces and wounded seven other soldiers. Amani said four Taliban were killed.

A roadside bomb killed two people and wounded five in Jalalabad and wounded another five. No one claimed credit.

A nighttime Taliban attack on army checkpoints in Kandahar Province's Shorabak district killed 20 troops and wounded eight. Taliban spokesman Qari Yusouf Ahmadi said the group seized weapons and ammunition.

April 11, 2019: In the morning, the Taliban attacked a security outpost in Ghazni Province, killing seven policemen.

A Taliban attack wounded two policemen in the Waghaz district of Ghazni Province.

Raz Mohammad, head of the provincial council, said the Taliban arrested 60 truck drivers for failing to pay a 7,000 afghanis (about $90) per month tax on trucks passing through Taliban-controlled territory in Samangan Province near the border with Balkh Province. The trucks carry charcoal from local mines.

Provincial council member Mohammad Naser Nazari said that 15 policemen surrendered to the Taliban in Badghis Province.

April 12, 2019: In the afternoon, the Taliban ambushed a police convoy in Ghor Province, killing seven security forces and wounding two police and a civilian. The dead included Faqir Ahmad Noori, head of operations for the provincial police.

During the night, the Taliban attacked checkpoints in Baghlan Province, killing seven police and wounding eight.

Attahullah Khogyani, the governor's spokesman, said that the Taliban attacked a district headquarters in Nangarhar Province, killing two police.

April 13, 2019: After midnight, the Taliban attacked Kunduz, killing six people and wounding more than 50.

April 14, 2019: During the evening, a gunman shot at a wedding ceremony in Tani district in Khost Province, killing three wedding guests and wounding 12 before escaping. No one claimed credit.

April 15, 2019: During the night, a police officer shot at fellow policemen at a checkpoint near Farah, killing four before he was taken into custody in Farah Province. The Taliban was suspected.

April 20, 2019: A suicide bomber and four gunmen stormed the 18-story Ministry of Telecommunications office building in Kabul in the morning. Four attackers entered the building by using a small shrine attached to one wall of the building. Dozens of office workers were evacuated, but others were trapped inside. Seven people, including four civilians and three members of the Afghan security forces, were killed and a dozen were injured. The Minister of Telecommunications said five ministry employees had been killed. The four gunmen were killed during the clash. The Taliban denied involvement. ISIS-K claimed credit. The building was near several other government ministries, a large mosque, a block-long city park and the luxury Serena hotel.

April 24, 2019: The Taliban ambushed a security convoy in Anardara district in Farah Province, killing nine policemen. Council Abdul Samad Salehi said the convoy was en route to defuse a roadside bomb during the afternoon. Other Taliban attacked the district police headquarters, sparking hours-long gun battles.

April 25, 2019: At 10:30 a.m., a bomb believed intended for the private Jahan University in Kabul went off prematurely inside a campus bathroom, killing the suspected terrorist and wounding three students. No one claimed credit.

May 3, 2019: Provincial Councilman Mohammad Naser Nazari said that during the night, the Taliban attacked security checkpoints in Qadis district in Badghis Province, killing seven Afghan policemen and wounding three others.

Two coalition airstrikes in Chapadara district in Kunar Province killed 43 ISIS-K terrorists, including several Pakistani and Uzbek fighters, among them prominent Uzbek leader Ismail, who had previously cooperated with al-Qaeda but had recently joined IS.

May 4, 2019: Gunmen wounded lawmaker Mohammad Afzal Shamil and killed his wife at their home in Kabul. The next day, police said it was unclear whether the attack was due to a personal dispute or a terrorist attack. He represented northeastern Takhar Province in the upper house of parliament.

A roadside bomb killed three children and wounded two children in Herat Province. No one claimed credit.

May 5, 2019: Provincial council head Safder Mohsini said the Taliban attacked a police headquarters in Puli Khumri, capital of Baghlan Province, sparking a six-hour gun battle inside. At noon, a suicide bomber detonated explosives outside the security headquarters, causing police casualties. A Taliban spokesman said the suicide bomber had used a Humvee packed with explosives. Eight terrorists wearing suicide vests rushed in. At least 13 police were killed and 55 people, including 20 civilians, were injured before authorities killed the attackers. Three terrorists set off their suicide vests; guards shot to death the other five. Several people were critically injured.

Coalition forces conducted air strikes against Taliban-run heroin labs in Bakwa district in Farah Province. Dadullah Qaneh, councilman in Farah, said 15 laborers were killed. Mohibullah Mohib, the provincial police chief's spokesman, countered that those killed were all members of the Taliban.

May 5-6, 2019: During the night, the Taliban attacked an army checkpoint in Farah Province's Gulistan district, killing 20 soldiers and kidnapping two.

May 6, 2019: During the night, the Taliban attacked security checkpoints in Takhar Province's Khwaja Bahaudin district, killing three soldiers and five policemen. The Taliban claimed credit.

May 7, 2019: The Taliban attacked police in Laghman Province, killing four police officers, including Arif Sadat, district police chief in Alingar district, when his vehicle exploded near the district police headquarters, according to Asadullah Dawlatzai, the provincial governor's spokesman. Four other officers were wounded.

May 8, 2019: The Taliban attacked the Kabul offices of Counterpart International, a U.S. government-supported group headquartered in Arlington, Virginia in central Kabul's upscale commercial Shahr-e Now district. A suicide car bomber set off explosives outside the office, starting a five-hour gun battle with security forces. Gunmen carrying RPGs and suicide vests entered the building. Two Afghan civilians died and 20, including a foreigner, were hospitalized with injuries. Another 80 people were rescued from the four-story building, which is occupied by the group that promotes leadership, civic engagement and elections in foreign countries. The Interior Ministry said that all assailants were killed and that five fighters may have joined the assault. Taliban spokesman Zabiullah Mujahid said in an email that the group's office was targeted because it was engaged in "harmful Western activities" and had "implemented a dangerous program" that promoted "open intermixing between men and women". 19050801

May 10, 2019: Ziauddinn Akazai, a lawmaker in Badghis Province, said the Taliban attacked two security outposts in Bala Murghab district, killing 15 security personnel and wounding 11 soldiers.

May 11, 2019: Nasrat Rahimi, a spokesman for the Interior Ministry, said that gunmen killed Mena Mangal, a cultural adviser for the lower house of the parliament and former TV presenter, in Kabul as she was on her way to work in the morning. Rahimi said one or possibly more assailants escaped from the scene. No one claimed credit. Kabul police said that it was not clear whether the murder was a terrorist act or related to a personal dispute.

May 12, 2019: Gunmen killed Abdul Ghafour Mahmoud, deputy intelligence director for Baghlan Province, while he was traveling on the outskirts of Baghlan's provincial capital, Puli Khumri, to Kabul. Another intelligence officer was wounded. The Taliban was suspected.

In the nighttime, the Taliban attacked security checkpoints near the provincial capital of Sari Pul Province, killing seven members of the country's security forces, wounding five, and abducting two more. The troops were providing security for fuel wells in the area. Four Taliban fighters were killed.

May 18, 2019: Gelani Farhad, a spokesman for Herat Province's governor, said that in the morning, a remotely-controlled bomb exploded when the district chief's vehicle was passing by the Obe area's main market, killing two people, including a child, and wounding 14. No one claimed credit.

May 19, 2019: An afternoon gun battle between illegal armed groups in Rustaq district in Takhar Province killed nine people and wounded seven others from the armed groups. One of the group leaders, who was on a police wanted list, was killed.

A roadside bombing in the Washer district in Helmand Province killed two police officers and wounded two other policemen. No one claimed credit, but the Taliban was suspected.

May 22, 2019: Taliban in a stolen Humvee packed with explosives conducted a gun battle with police in Ghazni. Police fired warning shots to get the vehicle to stop. Two policemen, two civilians and four Taliban were killed; ten civilians and five police were wounded. Provincial governor's spokesman Arif Noori said officials had received intelligence reports that the Taliban was preparing an attack.

May 23, 2019: A car bomb exploded during the night in Kandahar's posh Aino Mina residential area, wounding 12, including four children. Provincial council member Yousaf Younasi said the bombing targeted insurgents from Pakistan's secessionist Baluchistan Liberation Army.

May 24, 2019: A bomb concealed in the microphone used to deliver the sermon exploded during prayers at the al-Taqwa mosque in Kabul, killing four people, including pro-government prayer leader Maulvi Samiullah Rayan, variant

Samiullah Raihan, and wounding 16. The neighborhood is dominated by ethnic Pashtuns, most of whom are Sunni Muslims. No one claimed credit. Rayan had recently received death threats and traveled in an armored government vehicle.

May 26, 2019: The U.N. Assistance Mission in Afghanistan, after interviewing 13 detainees from a group of 53 rescued from the Taliban on April 25, announced that the Taliban had subjected captives to abuse, ill-treatment, and actions that may amount to torture. The former hostages were mainly members of Afghan forces but also civilians and government officials held in the Khas Uruzgan district in Uruzgan Province. Most of the captives were held since 2018, with three since 2016.

The Taliban set off a roadside bomb in the afternoon, killing ten Afghan soldiers who were driving back to base in a Humvee after picking up their salaries in the Bala Buluk district in Farah Province. The Taliban claimed credit.

The Taliban attacked several checkpoints in Sari Pul Province during the night, killing four members of the security forces and wounding 22. Some 15 Taliban fighters were killed.

Gunmen killed prominent religious scholar Mawlavi Shabir Ahmad Kamawi in Kabul.

May 27, 2019: A sticky bomb attached to a minibus carrying religious affairs ministry employees to work in Kabul went off during the morning, wounding 10 people, one critically. No one claimed credit.

The Taliban attacked a security checkpoint near Feroz Koh in Ghor Province, killing 18 policemen and pro-government militiamen and wounding seven in an hours-long gun battle. No one claimed credit.

Mohammad Naser Ghairat, a provincial councilman, said gunmen attacked an army checkpoint in Baraki Barak district in Logar Province, killing five soldiers and wounding four soldiers. The Taliban captured four others and stole a Humvee and ammunition. They claimed credit for the attack.

May 30, 2019: In the afternoon, an ISIS-K suicide car bomber set off his explosives outside the Marshal Fahim National Defense University,

killing six people and wounding 16 others. Cadets were leaving the hillside campus overlooking Kabul for their weekly two-day break.

May 31, 2019: A Taliban suicide car bomb exploded near a passing U.S. convoy in Kabul, killing four bystanders and injuring four U.S. troops and three bystanders. 19053101

June 1, 2019: Naser Ahmad Faqeri, head of Ghazni's provincial council, said that during the night, a Taliban suicide bomber entered a police compound in a stolen Humvee packed with explosives, killing seven police reserve unit personnel and wounding eight others in Ghazni Province.

Abdul Samad Salehi, a provincial council member, said that the Taliban attacked a checkpoint during the night in Farah Province, killing six members of the border security forces and injuring eight.

June 2, 2019: Three ISIS-K bombs in Kabul killed two people and injured 24 people, including Afghan journalists Ahmad Jawed Kargar and Mohammad Faseh Mutawakil and four women. A bomb attached to a bus carrying university students exploded, killing one person. Twenty minutes later, two roadside bombs injured seven people, including five members of the security forces, who arrived at the scene in a residential area of western Kabul. Kargar, a photographer for the *European Pressphoto Agency*, said he was injured by a secondary explosion. ISIS-K said it set off an improvised explosive device on a bus allegedly transporting minority Shi'ite Muslims, and after security forces and journalists had gathered at the site, it detonated two additional explosives there.

June 3, 2019: The Afghan Ministry of Public Health announced that a bomb exploded on a bus carrying government employees in Kabul, killing five and wounding ten. No one claimed credit.

June 5, 2019: Afghan military spokesman Mohammad Anif Rezaye said troops freed 84 prisoners, mostly security personnel and civilians, from a Taliban-run facility in Faryab Province. Several captive ISIS-K fighters, including four from Uzbekistan, three from Tajikistan and one from Kyrgyzstan, were also found. The ISIS-K fighters were captured in 2018 during a Taliban push to drive them from Jozjan Province.

June 7, 2019: In the evening, the Taliban attacked checkpoints in Ghor Province, killing 14 members of a pro-government militia. Abdul Hai Khateby, spokesman for the provincial governor, said seven other militiamen were wounded, two critically.

June 10, 2019: The Interior Ministry announced that special forces rescued 34 people (17 civilians and 17 members of the security forces, including seven soldiers, seven policemen and three intelligence agents) from a Taliban-run prison in Baghlan Province.

June 11, 2019: Jawad Hajri, spokesman for the governor in Takhar Province, said security forces repelled Taliban attacks on checkpoints in Khoja Ghor district. Three pro-government fighters and 15 gunmen were killed.

June 12, 2019: Provincial councilman Yousof Younosi said six people from a single family—two men, two women, and two children—were killed when a civilian vehicle hit a roadside bomb in Dand district in Kandahar Province. Younosi blamed the Taliban.

June 12, 2019: The government freed 490 Taliban prisoners in jails across the country as a goodwill gesture for the peace process.

June 13, 2019: A suicide bomber walked up to an Afghan police vehicle in Jalalabad in Nangarhar Province and set off his explosives, killing three police and six civilians and wounding 13 people, included police, some seriously. Spokesman Attahullah Khogyani said that security forces were the target. ISIS-K claimed credit on *Aamaq*, saying eight were killed.

June 26, 2019: The U.S. military said two service members were killed in combat. The Taliban claimed credit for an ambush in Wardak Province's Sayad Abad district. *Stars and Stripes* and the *New York Times* reported that the soldiers were members of an army special forces unit in a close-quarters fight with the Taliban in Uruzgan Province.

ABC News reported on June 28 that the victims were Master Sgt. Micheal B. Riley, 32, from Heilbronn, Germany, and Sgt. James Gregory Johnston, 24, from Trumansburg, New York.

Master Sgt. Micheal B. Riley, a Green Beret serving as a communications sergeant, was assigned to 10th Special Forces Group (Airborne). He was on his sixth deployment to Afghanistan. He joined the Army in March 2006 and after completing basic combat training and airborne school, was assigned to the 112th Special Operations Command Europe Signal Detachment. He completed the Special Forces Qualification Course in 2012 and was assigned to 10th Special Forces Group (A). His awards and decorations included the Bronze Star Medal, Meritorious Service Medal, Army Commendation Medal with four Oak Leaf Clusters (4 OLC), Army Achievement Medal, Joint Meritorious Unit Award (OLC), Army Good Conduct Medal (3), National Defense Service Medal, Afghanistan Campaign Medal with three Campaign Stars, Global War on Terrorism Expeditionary Medal, Global War on Terrorism Service Medal, Noncommissioned Officer Professional Development Ribbon (3), Army Service Ribbon, Overseas Service Ribbon (2), NATO Medal, Special Forces Tab, Ranger Tab, Combat Infantryman Badge, Military Freefall Parachutist Badge, Parachutist Badge, Air Assault Badge, Driver and Mechanic Badge, and Marine Qualification Badge Expert-Rifle.

Sgt. James Gregory Johnston was assigned to 79th Ordnance Battalion (Explosive Ordnance Disposal), 71st Ordnance Group. He entered active-duty military service in July 2013 as an explosive ordnance disposal specialist. He was on his first deployment to Afghanistan, arriving in March 2019. His awards and decorations included a Bronze Star Medal, Purple Heart, Army Commendation Medal, Army Achievement Medal, Army Good Conduct Medal, National Defense Service Medal, Afghanistan Campaign Medal, Global War on Terrorism Service Medal, Korea Defense Service Medal, Army Service Ribbon, Overseas Service Ribbon, Combat Action Badge, Senior Explosive Ordnance Disposal Badge and Explosive Ordnance Badge. 19062601

June 27, 2019: An air strike killed the Taliban's shadow governor for Logar Province and two deputies during the night in Charkh district.

Arif Noori, the provincial governor's spokesman, said that during the night, the Taliban attacked Afghan security checkpoints in Dehyak district in Ghazni Province, killing four police officers and wounding three. Seven Taliban fighters were killed.

June 28, 2019: A bomb exploded in a mosque in Aybak, capital of Samangan Province, during Friday prayers, wounding 11 people. The mullah was in critical condition and was being treated in Balkh Province. No one claimed credit.

The Taliban attacked pro-government forces in Baghlan Province's Nahrin area, killing 25 people and wounding eight pro-government fighters.

June 29, 2019: During the night, a Taliban bomb killed four Afghan security officers and eight election officials conducting voter registration in Maruf district in Kandahar Province. Defense Ministry spokesman Fawad Aman added that the Taliban detonated four stolen Humvees full of explosives outside the district's police headquarters, where the election officials were staying. The Interior Ministry announced that security forces killed 25 Taliban fighters. Taliban spokesman Qari Yusouf Ahmadi claimed credit. *AP* reported the next day that suicide attackers using four Humvees on government buildings in southern Kandahar killed dozens of security forces and eight election workers.

Shah Mahmmod Nahimi, a provincial council member, said that the Taliban attacked the police security cordon protecting Farah city during the night, killing four security officers and wounding four other security officers.

Local councilman Abdul Samad Salehi said that the Taliban attacked army checkpoints in the Bala Buluk district of Farah Province, killing five and wounding seven.

July 1, 2019: Taliban terrorists attacked a security compound in central Kabul during the morning, sparking a 10-hour gun battle that killed 40 Afghans, many of them with the security forces, and injured 105 people, including 51 children at two nearby schools, and several journalists working in a nearby building. One student was still clutching his pencil and notebook while being rushed to the hospital. The terrorists set off a suicide truck bomb outside the Ministry of Defense, killing two police, a child, a private security guard and two passers-by. Five heavily armed terrorists, including suicide bombers, then entered the compound. Security officials killed all of the attackers. The Taliban claimed credit. Taliban spokesman Zabiullah Mujahid said the target was the military facility.

July 5, 2019: The Taliban fired mortars into a busy market in Khwaja Sabz Posh district in Faryab Province, killing 14 people and injuring 30 others, including several children. Taliban spokesman Zabihullah Mujahed said the government fired the mortars during a firefight.

In Taliban attacks, one each in Farah and Herat Provinces, 18 Afghan security personnel died.

ISIS-K claimed credit for bombing a Shi'ite mosque in Ghazni Province during Friday evening prayers, killing two people and injuring 20, including eight children. ISIS-K said 40 worshippers were killed or wounded.

July 7, 2019: The Taliban set off a car bomb in the morning near a compound of the national intelligence agency in Ghazni, killing 12 and wounding at least 179, many of them schoolchildren on their way to class. The intelligence agency said two employees were killed and 80 people wounded.

Stars and Stripes reported that the National Director of Security announced the arrest of Mubasher Muslimyar, a lecturer in Islamic studies at the partially U.S.-funded Kabul University, on suspicion of recruiting students to join ISIS-K. NDS also arrested three of his suspected recruits, who were accused of organizing several deadly ISIS-K attacks in Kabul. Two of them were students at the university; the third was related to one of the students. The students included alum Ahmad Farouq and his brother, Ahmad Tariq.

July 12, 2019: *CNN*, *Reuters*, and *AP* reported that a male suicide bomber, 13, hit a morning wedding in the Pachirwa Agham district of Nangarhar Province, killing five people, including Malik Toor, a commander of a pro-government militia who had organized the wedding, and injuring 40 others. The Taliban denied responsibility.

In the evening, *Radio Gardez* newsreader Nader Shah was killed in an attack in Paktia Province.

July 13, 2019: A spokesman for the Resolute Support mission said that a United States service member was killed. Taliban spokesman Zabiullah Mujahid tweeted that two American soldiers were killed and three wounded in a bombing in Wardak Province. *MSN.com* reported on July 14 that U.S. Army Special Operations Command announced that Sgt. Maj. James G. "Ryan" Sartor, 40, a decorated Special Forces company sergeant major, died during combat operations in Faryab Province. He was from Teague, Texas, and was assigned to the 2nd Battalion, 10th Special Forces Group in Fort Carson, Colorado. He joined the Army in 2001 as an infantryman and had deployed numerous times to Iraq and Afghanistan. *Army Times* reported that Sartor deployed to Iraq as an infantryman in 2002. As a Green Beret, he was deployed in 2006, 2007, 2009 and 2010 with 2nd Battalion, 10th Group. He deployed with the 10th to Afghanistan in 2017 and 2019. He received dozens of awards and decorations, including the Bronze Star Medal with three oak leaf clusters, Defense Meritorious Service Medal, Joint Service Commendation Medal, Army Commendation Medal with three oak leaf clusters, Army Achievement Medal, Presidential Unit Citation Award, Joint Meritorious Unit Award, Valorous Unit Award with two oak leaf clusters, Meritorious Unit Citation with one oak leaf cluster, National Defense Service Medal, the Special Forces Tab, Ranger Tab, Combat Infantryman Badge, Senior Parachutist Badge and Special Operations Diver Badge. He was posthumously awarded a Purple Heart and Bronze Star. The Department of Defense said he was injured by enemy small arms fire. 19071301

July 15, 2019: A truck hit a roadside bomb in Kandahar Province's Khakrez district, killing 11, including women and children, and injuring 35

civilians, some critically, during the afternoon. Yousof Younosi, a provincial council member, blamed the Taliban. All the victims were members of one family and their close relatives who were en route to a shrine.

July 16, 2019: Ramez Azimi, director of the local *Samaa* station in Ghazni, announced that he had shut down the station four days earlier after phone threats and written warnings from the area's Taliban commander because three of the station's 16 employees are women. It was the station's third closure in four years.

July 17, 2019: Sonny Mansson, country director of the nongovernmental charity Swedish Committee for Afghanistan, said that the Taliban threatened SCA staff by saying that if they do not close the facilities, "it would have consequences for themselves and their families." The group closed 42 health facilities it ran in Maidan Wardak Province in eastern Afghanistan over the weekend. The next day, the Taliban said it would talk with the NGO.

July 18, 2019: The Taliban attacked police headquarters in Kandahar Province, killing ten people, including police, and wounding 80. A suicide vehicle bomber set off his explosives outside provincial police headquarters, whereupon several other attackers shot at security guards with small arms. Four gunmen were killed.

July 19, 2019: In the morning, a bomb went off outside the gates of Kabul University, killing eight people and wounding 33, several critically. Two vehicles were reported on fire. It was not clear if it was a suicide bomb or remotely detonated. The university compound houses hostels for students who attend classes and work on research projects during the summer. The university is co-ed and has women attending classes. Several lawyers were taking their exams to become judges when the explosion occurred. In recent months, two Kabul University professors with alleged ISIS-K links were arrested.

A roadside bomb killed five people who were riding in a car in Ghazni Province. No one claimed credit.

July 24, 2019: In the morning, a suicide bomber crashed his motorcycle into a military convoy near a military base in Kabul, killing J.B., 27, a Croatian soldier, and wounding two other Croatian soldiers. Croatian Defense Minister Darmir Krsticevic said the soldiers were aged between 27 and 32. 19072402

July 25, 2019: Three bombings in Kabul killed ten people, including five women and a child, and wounded 41.

In the morning, an ISIS-K suicide bomber on a motorcycle hit a bus carrying Ministry of Mines employees. A smaller magnetic explosive device was left by ISIS-K near the scene of the bus attack, but caused no deaths.

A Taliban suicide car bomber targeted coalition forces in eastern Kabul.

A roadside bomb killed six women and a child and wounded four others traveling in a vehicle en route to a wedding party in Nangarhar Province.

July 27, 2019: Ahmad Khan Serat, spokesman for the provincial police chief, said that in the morning, a Taliban suicide bomber hit a district police headquarters in Ab Band district in Ghazni Province, killing three police officers and injuring a dozen police. The terrorist drove a stolen military Humvee in the attack.

July 28, 2019: On the first day of the presidential election campaign, a suicide car bomb exploded at the political office in Kabul of the Afghan president's running mate, former intelligence chief Amrullah Saleh. Several gunmen crashed into the Green Trend party headquarters building and holed up, firing at police, killing 20 people, including a woman, and injuring 50. Several terrorists were killed. Saleh and 85 other civilians were safely evacuated. No group claimed credit.

In the morning, a Taliban suicide bomber attacked a police station in Ghani Province, killing four police officers.

July 29, 2019: *AP* and *CNN* reported that an Afghan army soldier fired on a group of Americans at a military base in the Shah Wali Kot district of Kandahar Province, killing two U.S. service members and wounding a third. Afghan officials said that the shooter was wounded in return

fire and taken into Afghan military custody. The U.S. Army's 3rd Brigade Combat team, 82nd Airborne Division, based in Fort Bragg, North Carolina, posted a tribute on *Facebook* to their slain paratrooper comrades. The Pentagon announced that Pfc. Brandon Jay Kreischer, 20, of Stryker, Ohio, and Spc. Michael Isaiah Nance, 24, of Chicago, were killed in a combat-related incident. 19072901

July 31, 2019: *Reuters* reported that a roadside bomb hit a bus in the Ab Khorma area of Farah Province, killing 35 and wounding 27. Victims included women and children. Authorities blamed the Taliban, although no one claimed credit and the Taliban denied responsibility.

August 1, 2019: A bomb exploded near a police checkpoint in Kabul, killing two policemen and wounding three policemen. No one claimed credit.

Shandand district chief Hekmatullah Hekmat said a shootout between two rival Taliban groups in Herat Province killed two women and a child who were caught in the crossfire.

August 2, 2019: The Taliban attacked a police checkpoint in Day Kundi Province's Patu district, killing ten policemen and injuring 15 policemen. Provincial councilman Ghayrat Jawaheri said 13 policemen were killed in the attack. The governor of Day Kundi, Anwar Rahmati, said that the insurgents also suffered casualties.

Meanwhile, the Taliban also attacked in Kijran district of Day Kundi Province, killing a police officer and wounding another police officer.

Taliban spokesman Qari Yusouf Ahmadi claimed credit for the Patu attack but did not comment on the Kijran assault.

August 4, 2019: A magnetic explosive device attached to a bus carrying media workers in Kabul killed the bus driver and a pedestrian and injured two employees of the *Khurshid TV* station and another pedestrian. ISIS-K claimed credit.

The Taliban claimed credit when a policeman in Kandahar Province fired on his colleagues, killing seven policemen before fleeing.

The Taliban attacked a checkpoint in Jawzjan Province, killing 11 security forces.

August 5, 2019: A gunman killed a female police officer who was traveling in Balkh Province.

August 6, 2019: A bomb hit a van carrying employees of the Interior Ministry's counter-narcotics division in Kabul, killing five people and wounding seven.

The Taliban warned voters to stay away from the September 28 elections.

August 6-7, 2019: The National Directorate of Security (NDS) said that overnight, security forces raided three ISIS-K hideouts in Kabul, killing two terrorists and seizing explosives and bombmaking equipment. Three security force members died.

August 7, 2019: *AP* and *Reuters* reported that during morning rush hour, a Taliban suicide car bomber hit a police station in a minority Hazara Shi'ite neighborhood in southwestern Kabul, killing 65, including four policemen and ten civilians, and wounding 145, including 92 civilians. The Taliban claimed it hit a "recruitment center". Interior Ministry spokesman Nasrat Rahimi said the bomb went off at a checkpoint outside the station. Women and children were among the casualties. Mohammad Jawad said seven members of his family were wounded by flying glass at his house.

A suicide bomber driving a Humvee tried to attack an Afghan base in Baghlan Province but was killed without killing any security forces.

A sticky bomb exploded in Herat, wounding eight people, including women and children.

August 17, 2019: At 11 p.m., an ISIS-K suicide bomber set off explosives near the stage where children had gathered inside the Dubai City wedding hall in western Kabul at which more than 1,200 people were invited. *NPR* and the *Washington Post* reported that 80 people, including 14 members of the bride's family, including her 8-year-old brother, were killed and 182 wounded. The son, 14, of Amanullah died. Mohammad Toofan and the brother of Sakhi Mohammed were among the wounded. The bride and groom (tailor Mirwais Elmi, in his 20s) survived. Elmi told *ToloNews TV* that he lost several relatives including a brother and many friends. Jamshid Alami said a group of his

brothers, cousins and friends in the band were onstage at the Dubai City event when the bomb exploded; five died. Many Shi'ite Hazara live in the area. ISIS-K claimed that a Pakistani, Abu Asim, seeking martyrdom was responsible for attacking "rejecter polytheists", and said that a car bomb was also involved. The Taliban condemned the attack.

August 19, 2019: Ten bombs went off in Jalalabad in Nangarhar Province, injuring 66 people. No one claimed credit.

August 21, 2019: The NATO Resolute Support mission announced that two U.S. service members were killed. *Army Times* reported on August 23 that the U.S. Special Forces soldiers were killed during combat operations in Faryab Province. They soldiers were assigned to 7th Special Forces Group at Eglin Air Force Base, Florida. They were posthumously promoted to master sergeant.

- Master Sgt. Jose J. Gonzalez, 35, from La Puente, California, first arrived at 7th Group's 1st Battalion in 2014.

- Master Sgt. Luis F. DeLeon-Figueroa, 31, of Chicopee, Massachusetts, served more than 13 years in the Army and deployed six times during his career. He deployed as an infantryman to Iraq in 2008, and to Afghanistan in 2010. As a Green Beret, he deployed to South America in 2015 and 2018, and to Afghanistan in 2018 and 2019. He completed the Special Forces Qualification Course and was assigned to 1st Battalion, 7th Group, in 2014—first as a Special Forces communications sergeant (18E), and later as a Special Forces operations and intelligence sergeant (18F). He earned the Bronze Star Medal, the Army Commendation Medal with valor device, the Afghanistan Campaign Medal with two Campaign Stars, the Iraq Campaign Medal with one Campaign Star and the NATO Medal. He also received the Special Forces Tab, Ranger Tab, Combat Infantryman Badge, Expert Infantryman Badge, Military Free Fall Jumpmaster Badge, Parachutist Badge and Air Assault Badge. 19082101

August 23, 2019: *Stars and Stripes* reported that at 11:30 p.m., U.S. troops were targeted in a Taliban suicide car bombing of a convoy of foreign forces in Sar-e-Sayad near Bagram Airfield. Two civilians were wounded, a foreign forces vehicle was damaged, four shops were destroyed, but no troops were injured. 19082301

August 27, 2019: During the night, the Taliban attacked a checkpoint in the Robat Sangi district of Herat Province, killing 14 pro-government militia members and wounding seven. Police chief spokesman Abdul Ahid Walizada said an unspecified number of Taliban fighters suffered casualties.

A university professor died and two others were wounded when a bomb attached to their vehicle exploded in Jalalabad in Nangarhar Province. No one claimed credit.

August 29, 2019: The *Washington Examiner, Military Times,* and *Fox News* reported that Sgt. 1st Class Dustin Ard, 31, a Green Beret from Idaho, was killed in combat operations in Zabul Province. He was survived by his pregnant wife and a young daughter. He died after exiting a helicopter at the start of a joint mission between the U.S. Army Special Forces and Afghan commandos. Ard's father, Bruce, is the former mayor of Ammon, Idaho.

August 31, 2019: Overnight, the Taliban attacked Kunduz, taking hospital patients as hostages. Defense Ministry spokesman Rohullah Ahmadzai claimed that 26 Taliban fighters had been killed in an airstrike. Twenty members of the security forces and five civilians died and 75 people were wounded.

In the early evening, a suicide bomber killed ten people, including police spokesman Col. Sayed Sarwar Hussaini, who was meeting with officials at a roundabout in Kunduz.

September 1, 2019: The *Washington Post* reported that at 2 a.m., 30-40 Taliban attacked Pul-e-Kumri.

September 2, 2019: A suicide bomber hit a police checkpoint in Kunduz Province, killing four officers and wounding 17 people, including 10 civilians, according to provincial health director Esanullah Fazeli.

September 2, 2019: At 10 p.m., a tractor bomb went off in Kabul's Green Village compound, site of several international organizations and guesthouses, killing 16 people, including a Romanian diplomat, three members of the security forces and 13 civilians, wounding 119, and destroying several homes. Interior Ministry official Bahar Maher told *Tolo* news channel that a car bomb exploded. The *Washington Post* reported the next day that 500 protesters gathered outside a compound housing foreign nationals and demanded it be closed. The Taliban said it had targeted "foreign invaders". 19090201

September 4, 2019: In an evening raid, National Directorate of Security (NDS) special forces killed four brothers in Jalalabad for allegedly having links with ISIS-K fighters. One of the brothers was a secretary for a Senate official.

September 5, 2019: *Reuters* and *AP* reported that at 10 a.m., a Taliban suicide van bomber set off the explosives in his Toyota Town Ace van, killing 12 people, including Sgt. 1st Class Elis Barreto Ortiz, 34, of Morovis, Puerto Rico, and Romanian soldier Corporal Ciprian-Stefan Polschi, wounding 42, and destroying cars and shops in an area near a checkpoint on a road near the headquarters of Afghanistan's NATO force and the U.S. embassy. Among the dead was Akbar Fazelyar, subject of a profile in the *New York Times* on September 22. He owned a shop selling and installing computer networking equipment. Single and in his 30s, he enjoyed watching cricket and swimming. He was bringing an invoice to a client, a job usually handled by an employee. Besmellah Ahmadi was wounded, saying his car windows were shattered. Also wounded was Sulaiman Layeq, 89, a Pashto-language poet and former cabinet minister. The Taliban said it targeted three vehicles of "foreigners" as they tried to enter the heavily guarded Shashdarak area.

On September 8, *Reuters* reported that President Donald Trump canceled Afghan peace talks with the Taliban at Camp David because of the bombing that killed an American soldier. Taliban spokesman Zabihullah Mujahid said, "This will lead to more losses to the U.S. Its credibility will be affected, its anti-peace stance will be exposed to the world, losses to lives and assets will increase." U.S. Representative Liz Cheney, a Republican whose father, Dick Cheney, was U.S. vice president at the time of the attacks, tweeted, "Camp David is where America's leaders met to plan our response after al Qaeda, supported by the Taliban, killed 3000 Americans on 9/11. No member of the Taliban should set foot there. Ever." 19090501

A Taliban car bomb went off near a security meeting in Puli Alam in Logar Province, killing four civilians and wounding four civilians. An Afghan official said the bomb exploded in front of an Afghan military base that houses Afghan special forces and that a small number of international forces were in the area.

September 6, 2019: Farah provincial governor Mohammad Shoaib Sabet said the Taliban attacked Farah, killing two civilians and wounding 15. The Taliban seized an army recruitment center near the town's main police headquarters and set it on fire.

September 11, 2019: Minutes after midnight, a rocket exploded at the U.S. Embassy in Kabul, causing no injuries. 19091101

September 12, 2019: *Reuters* and *AP* reported that Fawad Aman, deputy spokesman for the Afghan Defense Ministry, announced that a Taliban suicide minibus bomber hit the entrance of an Afghan Special Forces base in the Chahar Asyab district in Kabul Province, killing four commandos and wounding three soldiers. Taliban spokesman Zabihullah Mujahid claimed credit, saying more than 200 commandos died.

September 14, 2019: *Reuters* reported that Afghan security forces and U.S. air strikes killed two Taliban shadow provincial governors. The Afghan Defense Ministry announced that 85 Taliban fighters were killed in Paktika Province on the night of September 14. The Taliban claimed that seven Taliban were killed and 11 wounded, while more than 20 security forces were killed. The Taliban's shadow provincial governor, Mawlavi Nooruddin, was killed along with four fighters in an air strike in Dara-e-Soof Payeen district in Samangan province on September 14. The Taliban claimed he was alive. Mohibullah Mohib, a spokesman for Farah provincial police,

said that Mullah Sayed Azim, a Taliban shadow governor for Anar Dara district in Farah Province, was killed along with 34 other insurgents in a joint Afghan and foreign force raid.

September 15, 2019: Five civilians, including women and children, died when their vehicle hit a roadside bomb in Farah Province. No one claimed credit.

September 16, 2019: A sticky bomb attached to a mini bus belonging to the university in Ghazni Province exploded, killing the bus driver and wounding five Ghazni University students.

In a battle between the Taliban and security forces in the Mohammad Agha district of Logar Province, a schoolgirl died in the crossfire and another student was wounded.

Army Times reported that NATO's Resolute Support mission announced that a U.S. Green Beret was killed in action. *AP* added on September 17 that U.S. Army Sgt. 1st Class Jeremy W. Griffin, 40, from Greenbrier, Tennessee, was killed in action by small arms fire when his unit was engaged in combat operations in Wardak Province. He served as a Special Forces communications sergeant and was based at Joint Base Lewis-McCord in Washington. He joined the Army in 2004. He was posthumously awarded the Bronze Star Medal and Purple Heart. 19091601

September 17, 2019: A Taliban suicide bomber on a motorcycle hit a morning campaign rally held by Afghan President Ashraf Ghani at an open airfield in a police training compound in the suburbs of Charakar in Parwan Province, killing 26 people, including four Afghan military personnel, and injuring 42, including women and children. Ghani was unharmed. The Taliban said it hit "a rally for the fake presidential election". The rally of 2,200 people continued after the bombing, with Ghani delivering a stump speech.

NPR reported that a second Taliban suicide bomber attacked near Massood Square near the U.S. Embassy, killing 22 people and injuring scores. The Taliban said it was targeting an army base. 19091701

September 18, 2019: Gunmen tried to enter a government office in Jalalabad in Nangarhar

Province, setting off a suicide bombing and gun battle with security forces. No one immediately claimed credit. Ten people, including a woman and a small child, were wounded. *Reuters* added that at least one suicide bomber was involved in the attack outside the building, which is used for the distribution of electronic identity cards.

September 19, 2019: At 6 a.m., a Taliban suicide truck bomber hit a hospital in Qalat, capital of Zabul Province, killing 20 and wounding 97, many critically. Many victims were women and children. Parts of a nearby mosque were destroyed. Taliban spokesman Zabihullah Mujahed tweeted that the target was a nearby intelligence office, which he claimed was destroyed and "tens of intelligence operatives killed/wounded". Provincial council chief Atta Jan Haqbayan said the wall of the National Security Department building was damaged.

September 21, 2019: A roadside bomb went off in the Spin Boldak district of Kandahar Province, killing two children and wounding five others. No one claimed credit.

Children were playing with unexploded ordinance when one of the devices went off, killing a pregnant woman and injuring seven children and two other women in Parwan Province. One child was critically injured.

Two bombs went off during the night in Kabul, causing no casualties. The Taliban claimed credit.

September 22-23, 2019: U.S. and Afghan troops raided al-Qaeda in the Musa Qala district of Helmand Province, detaining five Pakistanis and a Bangladeshi and destroying a "large warehouse of the terrorists' supplies and equipment". U.S. defense officials said civilian casualties may have been involved as its air strike was conducted "against barricaded terrorists firing on Afghan and U.S. forces" and that civilians might have been inside the hideout. U.S. forces said "the majority of those killed in the fighting died from al-Qaeda weapons or in the explosion of the terrorists' explosives caches or suicide vests." Riders on a motorcycle had fired on U.S. and Afghan forces. Local residents said 35-60 civilians were killed. Abdul Majed Akhund, deputy provincial

councilman, said 24 civilians were killed. Attahullah Afghan, head of the provincial council, said most of the dead were women and children attending an evening wedding ceremony, and twelve other people were injured. Omar Zwak, the provincial governor's spokesman, said 14 insurgents including six foreign fighters were killed during the raid.

September 23, 2019: *Military Times* reported that the Taliban tweeted that a member of the Afghan National Civil Order Police fired on a coalition convoy in Kandahar, killing three troops in a green-on-blue attack. U.S. Forces-Afghanistan spokesman Colonel Sonny Leggett said that the three American soldiers sustained non-life-threatening injuries and survived. Resolute Support coalition forces fired back, killing the attacker. 19092301

September 23, 2019: *AP* reported on October 8, 2019 that Afghanistan's National Directorate for Security conducted a raid that killed Asim Omar, a senior al-Qaeda commander who led AQ operations in South Asia, and six other al-Qaeda members in Helmand Province. Among the dead was Raihan, Omar's courier to Ayman al-Zawahiri. NDS said, "They had been embedded inside the Taliban compound in the Taliban stronghold of Musa Qala."

September 28, 2019: A bomb hit a mosque in Kandahar where a polling station was located, injuring 15 people, including a police officer, several election officials, and voters. Three were critically wounded.

October 2019: Unknown gunmen wounded Hassan Haqyar, a mining official during the Taliban regime. No one claimed credit. Soon after, Abdul Shakoor Mutmaen, 46, a former Olympic committee head under the Taliban regime, said that he also was attacked but was unhurt.

October 2019: At a series of peace rallies, the Taliban abducted six activists from the People's Peace Movement of Afghanistan in Logar Province, releasing them hours later.

October 1, 2019: The Taliban attacked the Shortepa district headquarters in Balkh Province in the early morning, killing 11 policemen in a gun battle that lasted several hours.

In the evening, a vehicle hit a roadside bomb in Nejrab district in Kapisa Province, killing six civilians, including women and children, and injuring two other civilians. Interior Ministry spokesman Nasrat Rahimi blamed the Taliban.

October 2, 2019: The Taliban conducted attacks in three districts in the Taluqan area in Takhar Province during the previous three days, displacing more than 4,000 families.

October 7, 2019: A bomb on a rickshaw hit a minibus carrying new army recruits in Jalalabad in Nangarhar Province, killing ten people, including a child, and wounding 27 other people, several critically. Bomb techs defused two other bombs in the area. No one claimed credit.

October 8, 2019: Arif Noori, spokesman for the provincial governor, said that a bomb exploded inside a classroom in Ghazni Province, wounding 19 Ghazni University students, including a dozen women. Two of the wounded were in critical condition. No one claimed credit.

October 11, 2019: Shortly after 7 a.m., a remotely-detonated bomb went off at the house of Suhrab Qaderi, head of the Nangarhar provincial council, wounding a bodyguard. Minutes later, a second remotely-detonated bomb went off nearby, wounding a civilian.

Hours later, a remotely-detonated bomb went off outside a mosque in Jalalabad in Nangarhar Province, injuring three people.

An ISIS-K affiliate headquartered in Nangarhar Province took responsibility for two of the attacks.

The National Directorate for Security killed three insurgents and wounded three others, including their group leader, in a nighttime operation in Chardara district in Kunduz Province.

ISIS-K said it killed and wounded four Afghan police and guards protecting the home of an unidentified Member of Parliament. Provincial council member Azrat said the house belonged to the head of the council.

October 12, 2019: Mohibullah Sharifzai, the governor's spokesman, announced that gunmen

in Kabul killed Raz Mohammad, Jaghatu district chief of Maidan Wardak Province. Taliban spokesman Zabihullah Mujahid claimed credit.

Police chief Mohgoz Walizada announced that gunmen killed a provincial appeals court's prosecutor in Charakar, capital of Parwan Province.

Mohammad Yusouf Olamzada, Dawlat Abad district chief in Balkh Province, announced that during the night, a policeman with links to the Taliban killed three of his fellow police officers at a checkpoint near the district headquarters, then fled with all weapons and ammunition at the checkpoint. Taliban spokesman Zabihullah Mujahid said the attacker joined the Taliban.

October 13, 2019: Police spokesman Adil Shah Adil said gunmen killed a local pro-government cleric in Balkh Province.

October 15, 2019: The U.N. Assistance Mission in Afghanistan (UNAMA) released a special report on election-related violence during September 28 presidential voting. Attacks killed 85 people and wounded 373 others. Among them were 277 civilian casualties, 28 of whom were killed on the polling day. More than one-third of civilian casualties were children. The Taliban had vowed to disrupt the elections.

October 16, 2019: A car bomb exploded near Alishing district headquarters in Laghman Province, killing two security officers and wounding 26 people, including 20 children inside a nearby mosque where they were studying the Quran, and six security forces.

October 18, 2019: *AFP,* the *Washington Post* and *AP* initially reported that a mortar round hit a mosque in Jodari (variant Jawdara) village in the Haska Mina district, some 30 miles from Jalalabad in Nangarhar Province during Friday prayers, killing 73 people and wounding 36. Riazullah, who was wounded, said one of his brothers was killed, as was the village's only doctor, Mohammed Aref, his two brothers and two sons; two teachers; and 23 teenagers or people younger. Attaullah Khogyani, spokesman for Nangahar's provincial governor, said that two bombs were planted inside the mosque and detonated almost simultaneously. Afghan presidential spokesman

Sediq Seddiqi said the attack was carried out by a suicide bomber affiliated with the Taliban. The Taliban countered that it was a "major crime" conducted by ISIS-K or the Afghan government. Locals suspected ISIS-K, which had cut off the village's water upstream eight months earlier.

October 21, 2019: The Taliban attacked a checkpoint in the Ali Abad district of Kunduz Province from several sides during the night, sparking an hours-long gun battle in which 15 policemen died and two officers were wounded.

October 22, 2019: The *New York Times* reported that at 2:50 p.m., a Taliban rocket attack injured five U.S. Marines and another American. *Marine Corps Times* reported on November 6, 2019 that five Marines received Purple Hearts. The award citations noted, "All six casualties were MEDEVAC'd to contingency location Shorab Role II Medical Facility for immediate medical attention and were subsequently transferred to Kandahar Role III Medical Treatment Facility for follow-on care." Four of the Marines involved were on active duty; the fifth was a reservist activated for the deployment. Four of the Marines were assigned to Task Force Southwest; another was assigned to the Marine Corps Forces Central Command's Afghanistan coordination element. They were deployed to a post at Bost airfield outside Lashkar Gah, Helmand Province. The Taliban tweeted that it had fired more than 60 missiles, killing or wounding tens of Americans and Afghans. 19102201

October 25, 2019: Provincial governor's spokesman Attaullah Khogyani announced that a Taliban suicide bomber hit a convoy carrying officials from the intelligence service, killing five people, including a child, and wounding 21, including six security personnel, in Jalalabad in Nangarhar Province. The Taliban claimed credit.

Hours later, a bomb targeted a checkpoint at the entrance to Jalalabad near a bus stand crowded with people heading to Kabul, killing two security personnel and wounding six people.

October 31, 2019: The *New York Times* reported that a gunman fired three rounds into Amanullah Watandost, 42, a government employee who was driving his adopted daughter, Madina,

3, in their Toyota Corolla during the afternoon. They were shopping for groceries in Arghandab district. The government blamed the Taliban. The next day, the Kandahar governor's office announced that intelligence forces had killed the assassin.

November 2, 2019: *AP* reported that a roadside bomb killed eight children near their school in Darqad district in Takhar Province. (The *New York Times* reported that five were killed and three wounded on their way to school.) Provincial police chief Sayed Mehraj Sadat said the victims were from 10 to 15 years old. He said the bomb's intended target was most likely Afghan security forces. No one claimed credit, although Sadat blamed the Taliban.

November 4, 2019: A roadside bomb killed eight civilians and wounded six others in the Dand Shabuddin area outside of Puli Khumri, capital of Baghlan Province. Jawed Basharat, provincial police chief's spokesman, said women and children are among the casualties. The Taliban was suspected.

Pakistan closed its consular services in Kabul, citing unspecified security concerns. The previous day, Pakistan's foreign affairs ministry summoned the Afghan chargé d'affaires to convey concerns "that the officers and staff of the Embassy of Pakistan were being harassed over the past two days", adding that they were blocked while on the road and that embassy vehicles were hit by motorcycles while on their way to the diplomatic mission in Kabul.

November 13, 2019: A car bomb exploded near Kabul Airport during morning rush hour, killing 12 people, including three children, and wounding ten. The bomb may have been targeted against an armored vehicle of GardaWorld, a Canadian security company. Nasrat Rahimi, a spokesman for the Interior Ministry, said at least four of the wounded were foreigners. The dead included the two oldest children of shopkeeper Abdul Saboor Samadi, Dunya, 10, and Hadis, 7 (he celebrated his 7th birthday two days before the bombing), whom he was walking to school along with their friend Mustafa and their cousin, Sana. Mustafa also died and Sana was wounded. Abdul Saboor Samadi was hospitalized with shrapnel wounds in his arm and leg. No group claimed credit. 19111303

Reuters reported that seven people were killed and seven wounded in a car bombing near the Interior Ministry building in Kabul. No one claimed credit.

November 16, 2019: Jamshid Rasouli, spokesman for the national Attorney General's office, said gunmen killed two federal prosecutors and wounded two other prosecutors as they were driving to the prison at Bagram Airfield, which has held top-level Taliban detainees, including Anas Haqqani.

November 18, 2019: Kabul police spokesman Firdous Faramarz said that two suicide bombers attacked at 7:30 a.m., wounding four Afghan national army soldiers and a civilian at the entrance to the Kabul Military Training Center. Interior Ministry spokesman Nasrat Rahimi later said that it was from a pair of hand grenades, not suicide bombers. No one claimed credit.

November 20, 2019: Two American service members were killed when their helicopter crashed in Logar Province while supporting combat operations. The Taliban said the helicopter was shot down, which the U.S. military dismissed as false. Chief Warrant Officer 2s David C. Knadle, 33, of Tarrant, Texas, and Kirk T. Fuchigami, Jr., 25, from Keaau, Hawaii, were assigned to a unit from Fort Hood, Texas.

November 20, 2019: The *Washington Post* reported on December 25, 2019 that Wahid Mozhdah, 66, a prominent political analyst, writer, and onetime diplomatic official for the Taliban regime's foreign ministry, was shot to death by gunmen on a motorbike outside his Kabul home on November 20 as he walked home from afternoon prayers. In the early 1990s, he published several books of poetry in Dari he had written during the anti-Soviet jihad. No one claimed credit. Although never a member of the Taliban religious militia, he was a strict Sunni Muslim who lived an austere family life in Kabul. His two children, including son Ahmad Jahid, 28, graduated from the American University of Afghanistan.

November 24, 2019: Anwar Rahmati, governor of Daykundi Province, said the Taliban attacked a checkpoint in Kajran district, sparking an hourslong gun battle that killed eight Afghan soldiers and wounded four soldiers. Twenty Taliban were killed. Taliban spokesman Qari Yusouf Ahmadi said the insurgents had seized weapons and ammunition.

The *New York Times* reported that a bomb hit a UN-marked vehicle in Kabul's police district 9, killing an American aid worker assisting the UN Development Agency and wounding two Afghan UN workers and three other Afghan civilians. The *Times* reported that the American was assisting UNDA in managing the payroll for Afghan security forces. Authorities believed a sticky (magnetic) bomb was attached to the roof of the vehicle. Secretary of State Mike Pompeo identified the American as Anil Raj. 19112401

The *Times* reported the UN vehicles in Panjshir Province had recently come under fire, but no one was hurt. 19119901

November 27, 2019: Interior Ministry spokesman Nasrat Rahimi said that in the evening, a roadside bomb hit a civilian vehicle going to a wedding in Kunduz Province, killing 15 people, including six women, six girls and two infants, plus the male driver, and injuring two other civilians. The government blamed the Taliban.

November 28, 2019: Mohammad Nooragha Faizi, a police spokesman in Sari Pul Province, announced that in the morning, terrorists in a vehicle carrying explosives were stopped at a checkpoint. The terrorists opened fire, then detonated their explosives remotely, killing a policeman. The government blamed the Taliban.

November 30, 2019: A roadside bomb hit a passing convoy and killed two security personnel, including army border unit commander General Zahir Gul Muqbil, and wounded two other security officials and local *Shamshad TV* network reporter Sardar Mohammad Sarwary, in Marjah district in Helmand Province.

December 2, 2019: Interior Ministry spokesman Nasrat Rahimi said in the early morning, a gunman shot at a vehicle in Kabul's District 9, killing two intelligence officials and wounding three others. No group claimed credit.

December 4, 2019: *AFP* reported that at 8 a.m., gunmen in a vehicle shot to death Dr. Tetsu Nakamura, 73, a Japanese doctor who headed Peace Japan Medical Services (known as Peshawar Kai in Japanese) who spent decades working in Afghanistan, and five Afghans in an attack in Jalalabad in Nangarhar Province. Nakamura was hit on the right side of his chest. He died at Jalalabad airport. The five Afghans killed included three of Nakamura's security guards, a driver and another colleague. The Taliban denied responsibility.

Associates of Nakamura founded Peshawar-kai. He had lived and worked in Afghanistan and Pakistan since 1984 when he went to treat leprosy patients among Afghan refugees. In 2003 the native of Fukuoka won the Philippines' Ramon Magsaysay Award for peace and international understanding—sometimes deemed Asia's Nobel Prize. He came to Afghanistan after a Japanese colleague, Kazuya Ito, was abducted and killed. In April 2019, Afghan President Ashraf Ghani granted Nakamura honorary Afghan citizenship. 19120104

December 9, 2019: Ministry of Defense spokesman Fawad Aman said that a suicide car bomber killed five Afghan soldiers and wounded four others in Helmand Province. Authorities shot to death the attacker before he could reach a checkpoint for an Afghan national army compound; the vehicle then exploded. The Taliban claimed credit.

December 10, 2019: The Taliban kidnapped 45 elderly family members of an Afghan government employee who were attending his funeral. The young men in the funeral were not taken. Payghambarpul Khuram, head of intelligence in Jawzjan Province, said that the Taliban had warned people not to attend the funerals of anyone working with the Kabul government. Khuram said only six family members were taken and that other local elders were negotiating with the Taliban for their release.

December 11, 2019: *Reuters* and *AP* reported that two suicide bombers hit an under-construction medical facility at the southern end of Bagram Air Base, the main American base north of Kabul, killing one person and wounding six

Afghans, one critically. Five terrorists opened fire. Scores more were treated for cuts and bruises from flying glass. Abdul Shukoor Qudosi, Bagram district governor, said one woman was killed and 87 people were injured. The Republic of Georgia's Defense Ministry announced that five of its servicemen were wounded. Several homes belonging to the poor and a mosque were destroyed or badly damaged. Taliban spokesman Zabihullah Mujahid said, "First, a heavy-duty Mazda vehicle struck the wall of the American base… Later several mujahideen equipped with light and heavy weapons were able to attack the American occupiers." Wahida Shahkar, a spokeswoman for the governor of Parwan Province, added that "A 30-minute clash also happened between the attackers, who obviously wanted to enter the base, and foreign forces." 19121101

December 13, 2019: A roadside bomb killed ten civilians, including four women and a child, and wounded six civilians in Jaghato district in Ghazni Province. The civilians were traveling in a minivan from Day Kundi Province to Ghazni. Marwa Amini, spokeswoman for the Interior Ministry, blamed the Taliban.

December 14, 2019: A member of an Afghan militia opened fire on his fellow militiamen in the morning, killing nine, in what Interior Ministry spokesman Fawad Aman called an insider attack in the Karabagh district of Ghazni Province. Taliban spokesman Zabihullah Mujahid claimed the attack was a coordinated assault on the checkpoint where the shooting took place, killing over two dozen militiamen.

December 23, 2019: *CNN, AP,* and *Military Times* reported that the Taliban claimed credit for killing a U.S. service member by setting off a bomb during a raid in Kunduz Province. The Taliban said he was killed in the Chardara district during a joint Afghan-U.S. raid.

The Pentagon identified him as Sergeant First Class Michael J. Goble, 33, of Washington Township, New Jersey. He was assigned to 1st Battalion, 7th Special Forces Group (Airborne), Eglin Air Force Base, Florida. The Pentagon said the Green Beret was a senior intelligence sergeant assigned to Charlie Company. *Army Times* reported that he was on his third Afghan deployment; he had also served in Argentina, Guatemala, Colombia, and South Korea. He was born on January 13, 1986 and raised in Westwood, New Jersey. He enlisted directly into the service as a Special Forces candidate in July 2004. Following basic training and Airborne School, he graduated from Special Forces Qualification Course at Fort Bragg, North Carolina, in February 2007. He deployed to Afghanistan in 2007 and 2008, serving as a weapons sergeant. He was a sniper instructor from 2012 through 2016, before returning to 7th Group as an intelligence sergeant. He attended the Special Forces Sniper Course, basic and advanced Military Freefall Course, Military Freefall Advanced Tactical Insertion Course, Joint Armorer Course, Special Forces Intelligence Sergeant Course, and Special Operations Force Surveillance Operator Course. He earned the Bronze Star Medal with three Oak Leaf Clusters, the Army Commendation Medal with Valor device, the Valorous Unit Award, the Special Forces Tab, Combat Infantryman's Badge, Basic Airborne and Military Free Fall Jumpmaster badges. 19122301

Asadullah Dawlatzai, the provincial governor's spokesman, announced that a bomb exploded during the morning at the funeral of a village elder in Dawlat Shah district in Laghman Province, killing three civilians and wounding seven. He blamed the Taliban. No one claimed credit.

December 24, 2019: The Afghan Defense Ministry said that the Taliban attacked an army checkpoint in Dawlat Abad district in Balkh Province, killing seven Afghan soldiers and wounding three soldiers and three intelligence officers. Taliban spokesman Zabihullah Mujahid said that the attackers killed 20 members of the security forces, injured six, captured four, and seized weapons and ammunition. *Reuters* later reported that 15 members of the security forces were killed.

The Taliban stopped a six-vehicle peace convoy in Bala Buluk district in Farah Province and abducted 27 People's Peace Movement of Afghanistan activists whose convoy was going village-to-village to rally for peace. Tribal elders in the province launched an effort to negotiate

with the Taliban. The Taliban freed the 27 hostages on December 26.

December 26, 2019: A Taliban suicide car bomber hit an Afghan army compound in Balkh Province in the morning, killing six Afghan soldiers and wounding three. Taliban gunmen ran into the compound, setting off an hours-long gun battle.

A roadside bomb hit a police patrol in Khost Province, wounding five policemen.

December 27, 2019: The Taliban set off a bomb at an army checkpoint during the night, then staged an hours-long gun battle in Sangin district in Helmand Province that killed ten Afghan soldiers and wounded four soldiers. Taliban spokesman Qari Yusouf Ahmadi claimed the insurgents also seized weapons and ammunition.

December 28, 2019: Jawad Hajri, spokesman for the governor of Takhar Province, said that during the night the Taliban attacked a local militia commander who escaped unharmed, but killed 17 local militiamen. Taliban spokesman Zabihullah Mujahid claimed credit.

December 29, 2019: A Taliban negotiating team announced that it had agreed to a temporary nationwide cease-fire.

December 30, 2019: The Taliban attacked a pro-government militia compound in Jawzjan Province before dawn, killing 14 members of the Afghan security forces, including 13 members of the pro-government militia and one policeman, and wounding five other militiamen. Two were missing.

December 31, 2019: Taliban attacks on security forces across northern Afghanistan killed 26 people.

During the night, gunmen attacked a police checkpoint in Dashti Archi district in Kunduz Province, killing ten Afghan forces.

The Taliban attacked a police checkpoint in Balkh Province, killing nine police officers. The fate of the other four policemen at the site was unknown.

Ten Taliban and seven security officers were killed in a nighttime gun battle in Darqad district in Takhar Province.

ALGERIA

November 28, 2019: Spanish Defense Minister Margarita Robles told *Cadena Ser* radio that foreign intelligence services operating in the area warned of a possible terrorist attack against Spanish citizens visiting or working in the Saharawi refugee camps in the Western Sahara. IS-affiliated terrorists operate in the region. The camps house 100,000 Saharawis displaced after Morocco annexed the former Spanish colony of the Western Sahara in 1975.

BAHRAIN

July 27, 2019: The government executed Shi'ite activists Ali al-Arab, 25, and Ahmed al-Malali, 24, who were convicted in January 2018 in a mass terrorism trial of 60 men. Attorney General Ahmed al-Hammadi said that the individuals were involved in terrorist operations that killed a security officer in 2017 and an imam in 2018, as well as firing at and wounding security forces, assisting in a prison riot, working with terrorist operatives in Iran and Iraq, possessing explosives and weapons illegally, and being involved in crimes against the state. The two were arrested in February 2017. The *New York Times* reported that the 2018 trial also led to the sentencing of 19 individuals to life, and 37 others for terms of up to 15 years. Prosecutors said that they belonged to a terrorist group trained in using heavy weapons and explosives.

EGYPT

January 5, 2019: During the night, a bomb exploded, killing a policeman who was trying to defuse it near a church in the Nasr City suburb of Cairo. The commander of the bomb squad and another policeman were injured. The device was in a suitcase concealed on the rooftop of a building close to the church. IS was suspected.

January 12, 2019: Security forces killed six Islamic terrorists in a morning raid on their desert hideout south of Cairo in an area between Sohag and Assiut Provinces.

January 14, 2019: Egypt deported a German teen resident of Giessen who was believed to have come to Egypt with the intention of joining Islamic State terrorists fighting security forces in the Sinai Peninsula. Authorities detained him on December 17, 2018 at Luxor Airport when police found maps of Sinai and a compass in his possession. He told police that he subscribed to ISIS ideology and was in online contact with members of the group. The previous week, authorities repatriated a 23-year-old Goettingen resident.

January 16, 2019: Police killed five militants in a shootout on a deserted farm used by the militants as a hideout in el-Arish in the Sinai Peninsula. Police seized explosives and weapons.

January 17, 2019: Jihadis kidnapped Adeeb Nakhlah, 45, a Christian man traveling in a communal taxi in the Sinai Peninsula. Police killed a kidnapper and wounded two others in a firefight, but could not free the hostage. Two policemen were wounded. Nakhlah, a police forensic expert, had lived and worked in el-Arish until 2017 when he fled following a series of attacks against Christians.

January 20, 2019: Security forces killed 14 militants and seized a ton of explosives in an operation outside el-Arish in the Sinai Peninsula. The terrorists had intended to plant roadside bombs in areas between there and the cities of Rafah and Sheikh Zuweyid. Authorities found other weapons caches including explosives in the Sinai's Jabal al-Halal mountain area.

January 22, 2019: Authorities said that seven troops, including an officer, were killed in clashes with militants in recent operations in the Sinai Peninsula. Military forces killed 59 suspected militants and arrested another 142 suspected militants and criminals. Airstrikes destroyed 56 vehicles containing weapons and ammunition in the Western Desert, south and northeastern border areas. The armed forces destroyed six smuggling tunnels leading into the Gaza Strip.

January 27, 2019: An Egyptian air force airstrike on a militant "outpost" killed several militants, including two local commanders, in the Sinai Peninsula.

February 15, 2019: A bomb exploded during Friday prayers near the al-Istaqama mosque in a square in the Giza district of Cairo, hospitalizing three people, including a policeman. The Interior Ministry blamed the Muslim Brotherhood. No group claimed credit.

February 16, 2019: Two hundred gunmen ran from olive groves to attack an army checkpoint in the Sinai at dawn, killing an officer and causing 14 other casualties. The army killed seven terrorists. Two officers said 15 soldiers were killed.

February 18, 2019: Suicide bomber al-Hassan Abdullah, 37, killed three police officers and wounded two policemen and a woman as he was pursued near Cairo's Khan el-Khalili tourist marketplace in the Gamaliya district during the night. Police were moving in to arrest him. He was wanted in the February 15, 2019 bombing near a mosque in Cairo's Giza district. Police had been following him. No group claimed credit. Police found a bomb and bomb-making material in a nearby house.

Security forces killed 16 terrorists and seized explosives and weapons in two raids outside el-Arish in the Sinai Peninsula.

March 7, 2019: In the morning, security forces killed seven members of a militant group with suspected links to the banned Muslim Brotherhood in Cairo shootouts. Authorities killed three gunmen on a highway known as Ring Road in Cairo's district of Giza. Another four died in a firefight when police raided their hideout in Cairo's suburb of Sixth of October. A police officer was injured. Authorities seized weapons and ammunition.

March 11, 2019: The armed forces announced that three troops and 46 suspected jihadis were killed in recent days in the northern and central Sinai Peninsula. Egyptian forces destroyed 15 hideouts and dismantled 204 explosive devices. Troops found weapons caches, including explosives, in Sinai, the Western Desert and southern Egypt.

March 25, 2019: Prosecutors referred to court 28 terrorism suspects in two cases on charges of joining local affiliates of ISIS and al-Qaeda. Authorities said the terrorists had plotted to attack security forces and the headquarters of the high state security prosecution in Cairo. Only 17 of the 28 suspects were in custody.

March 30, 2019: The Cairo criminal court sentenced 18 suspected militants to life in prison for allegedly forming a "terrorist cell" affiliated with ISIS and another 12 defendants to 10 to 15 years on charges that included plotting attacks on the country's Christian minority in Alexandria, assaulting security forces, and disrupting public order.

April 2, 2019: The Ismailia criminal court sentenced more than 70 suspected members of the Muslim Brotherhood to prison on terror-related charges. Nine of the defendants received 15 years in prison; 43 others 10 years; 22 were sentenced to three to seven years; 14 were acquitted. Nearly half of the defendants were tried in absentia. The defendants were accused of burning police vehicles and attacking a coffee shop in 2013.

April 7, 2019: Gunmen got out of their car and fired automatic rifles on police who were inspecting a parked car in Cairo's Heliopolis district, killing two and wounding two before fleeing.

April 9, 2019: The Interior Ministry announced that a suicide bomber attacked police forces who were inspecting a market in the town of Sheikh Zuweid in the Sinai Peninsula, killing four Egyptian policemen, including two officers, and three civilians, including a six-year-old child, and wounding another 26 people. A local affiliate of the Islamic State group claimed credit.

April 10, 2019: A bomb hit an armored vehicle, killing a police officer and two conscripts in el-Arish.

A separate bomb hit an armored vehicle in Rafah, killing a conscript and wounding four others.

No one claimed credit for the overnight attacks. The Islamic State was suspected.

April 11, 2019: The Interior Ministry announced the security forces killed eleven jihadis in a raid on their hideout in el-Arish in the Sinai Peninsula, after several attacks in the last two days that killed eight policemen and three civilians. No casualties were reported among the police, who found weapons, two explosive devices and two explosive belts.

April 16, 2019: The Alexandria criminal court sentenced 36 people convicted of joining the outlawed Muslim Brotherhood to five years in prison and five years of probation. They were arrested in Alexandria in 2017.

April 30, 2019: The Supreme State Security Emergency Court sentenced seven Muslim Brotherhood members, including one of the group's top financiers, to life in prison on charges of joining and funding a terrorist group. The court sentenced three others to 10 years, and acquitted 14. Life sentences went to Hassan Malek, a businessman who owned stores that imported computers and electronics, and his son.

May 7, 2019: The Court of Cassation upheld death sentences for 13 people convicted of terrorism charges for attacks in Cairo in which bombs killed two police officers. The court upheld life sentences for 17 others and lesser sentences for another nine, all on similar charges. The defendants were accused of attempting to kill policemen and civilians by setting off bombs outside a university campus in December 2014 and a presidential palace the following month. The attacks wounded 12 people. The sentences were handed down in 2017. Five others were acquitted.

May 16, 2019: Military spokesman Tamer al-Rifai announced that clashes between soldiers and gunmen killed five soldiers, including an officer, and 47 militants, and wounded four soldiers in the Sinai Peninsula. Police found scores of militant hideouts and ammunition and bombs, which Egyptian forces safely detonated.

May 19, 2019: Egyptian officials said a roadside bomb hit a tourist bus traveling on a road close to the under-construction Grand Egyptian Museum near the Giza Pyramids, wounding 17 people, including South African tourists. The bus was carrying 25 people, most of them South Africans. *Reuters* reported that four Egyptians in a nearby car were injured by broken glass.

No group claimed credit. On May 20, security forces killed 12 members of Hasm, a militant group suspected of Muslim Brotherhood ties, in shootouts in Cairo. Seven militants died in a raid on their hideout in the Sixth of October suburb. The other five were killed after opening fire on police raiding their residences in Cairo's Shorouk suburb. The Interior Ministry said that authorities found explosive devices, weapons and ammunition in the militants' possession. No group claimed responsibility for the attack. 19052001

May 21, 2019: The Interior Ministry said police killed 16 militants in raids on hideouts in el-Arish in the Sinai Peninsula. Police sustained no casualties. Police said the terrorists planned to conduct attacks in the city. Police found weapons, three explosive devices and an explosive belt.

May 22, 2019: The Cairo Criminal Court referred the case of six alleged Muslim Brotherhood members convicted of terrorism to the Grand Mufti, Egypt's top religious authority, for a non-binding opinion on their execution. The six were found guilty of killing three people, including a policeman, among other charges. The case involved 70 defendants.

June 5, 2019: Jihadis attacked a checkpoint in el-Arish in the early morning, killing two police officers and eight conscripts; the Interior Ministry later said eight police were killed. The Egyptian ISIS affiliate, Wilayat Sinai, claimed credit on *Aamaq*. The terrorists stole an armored vehicle to make their getaway but a warplane chased them in the desert, killing five.

June 6, 2019: Security forces killed 14 jihadis while pursuing attackers behind an Islamic State assault on a police checkpoint near el-Arish in northern Sinai that killed ten policemen. The Interior Ministry announced that security forces who were pursuing the attackers found a group of insurgents hiding inside a deserted house in the city. A shootout ensued, killing 14 terrorists who had automatic rifles, bombs and explosive belts.

June 8, 2019: The Interior Ministry announced that security forces killed four jihadis in a shootout in el-Arish the Sinai Peninsula. Police seized automatic rifles, bombs and explosive belts. The four were implicated in an ISIS attack earlier in the week on a police checkpoint in northern Sinai that authorities said killed eight policemen.

June 12, 2019: A military court in Cairo sentenced 32 people to life in prison on terror charges, including plotting to assassinate President Abdel-Fattah el-Sissi. Judges said the defendants attempted the president's assassination twice, including when he was on pilgrimage in Saudi Arabia in 2014. The court sentenced 264 other defendants to three to 15 years in prison for terrorism charges, including attacks in the Sinai. Two were acquitted. One defendant died during the trial. A minor was referred to another court. Nearly half of the defendants were tried in absentia.

June 13, 2019: A remotely-detonated roadside bomb hit a police patrol vehicle near el-Arish in Sinai Province, injuring six policemen. Police said jihadis had set up ambushes along the highway leading to el-Arish where they had kidnapped 14 civilians during the previous 24 hours.

June 22, 2019: The local ISIS affiliate was suspected when gunmen attacked construction workers in el-Arish in the Sinai Peninsula, killing four civilian workers, wounding five workers, and burning two vehicles.

June 25, 2019: Gunmen attacked three police checkpoints in the Sinai Peninsula during the night, killing six policemen and wounding eight other officers. Authorities said four gunmen died, including a suicide bomber who set off his explosives at one of the checkpoints in al-Arish. No group claimed credit; the IS affiliate was suspected.

June 27, 2019: Al-Qaeda said on *as-Sahab* that Egyptian authorities killed jailed former President Mohamed Morsi, who died in a Cairo courtroom during his trial on June 17. The group called on Egyptians to rise against current President Abdel Fattah el-Sissi, observing, "We do not doubt that he (Morsi) was killed, oppressed and humiliated" in jail.

July 1, 2019: Gunmen attacked a post office in al-Rouda village in the northern Sinai Peninsula, stealing circa $6,000 in local currency. No one claimed credit. In 2017, terrorists attacked a mosque in al-Rouda, killing more than 300 people.

July 17, 2019: Terrorists attacked several people in Bir al-Abd in the Sinai Peninsula, beheading four and kidnapping a fifth after accusing them of cooperating with security forces.

July 18, 2019: The local Islamic State affiliate posted on a website that its member Abu Omar el-Seedy set off his suicide vest near a military checkpoint in the Sinai Peninsula at dawn, killing two people, including a civilian, and wounding three. Egyptian security officials said the bomber targeted an armored vehicle near a local market in Sheikh Zuweid, killing a soldier and a civilian and wounding three soldiers.

The next day, security officials said airstrikes targeting jihadis in the Sinai Peninsula had killed 20 insurgents in sorties against more than 100 mountainous hideouts of militant groups in El-Arish and the small town of Bir al-Abd.

July 20, 2019: The *Washington Post, Reuters,* and *BBC* reported that British Airways and Lufthansa canceled all flights to Cairo after the UK government warned of a "heightened risk of terrorism against aviation". The British Foreign Office's travel advisory urged people to avoid "all but essential travel" to the South Sinai governorate and areas west of the Nile Valley and Nile Delta regions, outside of a few specific places. It cautioned against any travel to the governorate of North Sinai "due to continuing criminal activity and terrorist attacks on police and security forces that have resulted in deaths". The UK warned against air travel to and from the resort town of Sharm el-Sheikh.

July 24, 2019: Outside a bus station a few miles from Cairo's Tahrir Square, an Egyptian with psychological problems grabbed a policeman's gun and shot at passers-by, wounding three people before he was arrested. Authorities insisted there was no connection to any terrorist groups. An online video showed the man on a stretcher in hospital being asked why he carried out the attack. "I love the Caliphate," a reference to ISIS.

August 5, 2019: A suicide car bomber driving on the wrong side of the road hit three vehicles before crashing into several others and setting off the vehicle's explosives in front of the National Cancer Institute in Cairo on the busy Corniche boulevard along the Nile River, killing 20 people and injuring 47, some with burns and broken bones. Some 78 patients were evacuated to other hospitals. The government blamed Hasm. The car was stolen in the Nile Delta. The target was apparently elsewhere. President Abdel-Fattah el-Sissi called it a "terrorist incident".

August 8, 2019: Security forces killed 17 suspected Hasm terrorists in raids in Cairo's Shortouk suburb and the town of Atsa in Fayoum Province. Eight terrorists died in a raid on their Atsa hideout. Seven terrorists died in Shortouk. Two, including a brother of the suspected terrorist who was driving the suicide car bomb on August 5 that killed 20, were killed in Cairo. Police arrested another suspect and seized assault rifles.

August 20, 2019: The Interior Ministry said security forces killed 11 suspected militants hiding at a farm in el-Arish in the Sinai Peninsula. The terrorists fired on police, who later found seven rifles, two explosive devices and an explosive belt.

August 29, 2019: Authorities arrested suspected Hasm member Hammad Mohamed Shafei, 25, in Senofar village in Fayoum Province, and were pursuing 80 others for plotting an imminent attack.

September 7, 2019: The Cairo criminal court sentenced 11 Muslim Brotherhood leaders, including its chief, Mohammed Badie, to life in prison on espionage charges for allegedly passing state secrets to Hamas. Badie was sentenced to life in prison the previous week on charges related to mass prison breaks during a January 2011 uprising. Three others received 10-year sentences, two were sentenced to seven years, and five others were acquitted.

September 10, 2019: The Interior Ministry announced that police had arrested 16 suspected Muslim Brotherhood members for smuggling currency out of the country, collaborating with wanted Brotherhood members in Turkey to help smuggle wanted Islamists from Egypt to Europe, and plotting terrorist attacks in Egypt.

September 14, 2019: Jihadis attacked the Majahr checkpoint in el-Arish in the Sinai Province, killing three security officers and wounding two; three gunmen also died. No group claimed credit.

September 18, 2019: The Interior Ministry announced that police killed nine suspected members of the Revolution Brigade, a breakaway faction of the Muslim Brotherhood, in two shootouts as police were trying to arrest them at hideouts in the northeastern Obour district and the southern May 15th City suburb of Cairo. Police found rifles and ammunition at the scene. The dead included a militant leader accused of killing Brigadier General Adel Ragai, commander of the army's 9th armored division, who was shot to death in October 2016 near his home in Obour. The suspected militant leader was also believed behind an attack on a checkpoint in August 2016 in the northern Nile delta province of Menoufia.

Prosecutors ordered activist Kamal Khalil to remain in custody for 15 days pending an investigation into charges of joining a terrorist group and disseminating false news. Police arrested Khalil earlier in the week from his home in Cairo.

September 19, 2019: A remotely-detonated roadside bomb hit an armored vehicle on patrol in Sheikh Zuweid in the Sinai Province, killing a member of the security forces and wounding two others. No one claimed credit.

September 22, 2019: Police killed 15 suspected militants in a shootout during a raid on their hideout west of el-Arish in the Sinai Peninsula. Police seized weapons and explosive materials.

A roadside bomb hit a security force vehicle in Sheikh Zuweid, injuring six security forces.

September 24, 2019: Security forces killed six suspected Muslim Brotherhood members in a shootout in Cairo's Sixth of October suburb. The Interior Ministry said the gunmen were planning terrorist attacks.

September 26, 2019: The Islamic State attacked a checkpoint in Bir el-Abd, killing eight troops and a civilian. Security forces killed 15 terrorists.

September 29, 2019: The Interior Ministry announced that police killed 15 suspected militants in a raid on their hideout in el-Arish in the Sinai Peninsula. No police were injured.

October 10, 2019: *MENA* reported that security forces shot and killed a terrorist who tried to detonate his explosive-laden belt near a checkpoint in el-Arish in Sinai Province.

October 12, 2019: The Giza criminal court sentenced six people to death on terror-related charges for carrying out the January 2016 terrorist attack outside the Three Pyramids Hotel near the Giza Pyramids; no one was hurt. The court sentenced eight defendants to life in prison on similar charges that included attacking security forces, and possession of weapons and explosives. A dozen defendants received a decade in prison. The verdict can be appealed.

October 19, 2019: Shells hit two houses in Sheikh Zuweid in the Sinai Peninsula, killing four civilians, including a child, and hospitalizing 12 people.

October 28, 2019: During the night, gunmen attacked police in Sheikh Zuweid in the Sinai Peninsula, killing a police conscript and hospitalizing three other policemen.

October 29, 2019: Security forces killed 13 suspected terrorists in a raid in el-Arish's el-Obour neighborhood. Police found weapons and explosives in the hideout.

November 9, 2019: A roadside bomb hit an armored vehicle of security forces on patrol in Rafah in Sinai Province, on the border with the Gaza Strip, killing two officers and wounding two. No one claimed credit.

November 17, 2019: A roadside bomb hit an armored vehicle, killing three members of the security forces, including a captain, and wounding four others, including an officer, in Sheikh Zuweid in Sinai Province. The Islamic State claimed credit.

November 25, 2019: The Cairo Criminal Court issued death sentences to seven people convicted of carrying out attacks in Cairo that killed 11

policemen in 2016, including an IS attack that killed eight police in a microbus in Helwan, and sentenced 18 others to 10-15 years in prison for the same charges, including attacking security forces, joining a terrorist group and possession of weapons and explosives. The court acquitted seven others.

November 27, 2019: An Egyptian military court issued a death by hanging sentence to Hisham el-Ashmawi, 40, a former army officer turned jihadi terrorist, for his participation in scores of attacks on government targets. He was captured in Libya by Cairo-allied forces and returned to Egypt in 2018. Authorities said he was involved in a 2013 attempt to assassinate Interior Minister Mohammed Ibrahim and a 2017 ambush that killed 30 Christian pilgrims. He was convicted of leading assaults on security forces near Egypt's desert border with Libya.

December 8, 2019: Jihadis attacked a police checkpoint in Rafah in the Sinai Peninsula in the morning, killing a police conscript and hospitalizing two other conscripts. Security forces killed one terrorist and wounded others. No group claimed credit.

Gaza Strip

January 6, 2019: Hamas fired rockets during the night from the Gaza Strip toward Ashkelon. The Iron Dome defense system intercepted the rockets. No injuries were reported. The Israeli military targeted a militant camp in the northern Gaza Strip the next morning.

March 14, 2019: In the evening, Palestinians fired two rockets from the Gaza Strip toward Tel Aviv. No damage or injuries were reported. No one claimed credit. Hamas and the Islamic Jihad denied responsibility. The next day, Israeli airstrikes hit 100 Hamas targets, among them an office complex in Gaza City, an underground complex that served as Hamas's main rocket-manufacturing site, and a center used for a Hamas drone program. *Haaretz* reported that Israeli defense officials later said that the Gaza rockets apparently were fired by mistake during maintenance work.

March 31, 2019: Five rockets fired from the Gaza Strip landed in Israel in the morning, causing no injuries. No group claimed credit.

May 2, 2019: Terrorists launched incendiary balloons with explosives attached at targets in Israel. The Israeli military responded by striking several Hamas sites in Gaza. Two rockets were fired out of Gaza. There were no injuries on either side.

May 4, 2019: *CNN* reported that Palestinians fired 250 rockets into Israel. Israel responded by airstrikes against 125 targets.

CNN, the *New York Times,* and *AP* reported on May 5 that 600 rockets had been fired, killing three Israelis, including Moshe Agadi, 58, a father of four who died from shrapnel to the chest when a rocket hit his house in Ashkelon, according to Barzilai Hospital. A man, 49, was killed when a rocket hit an Ashkelon factory. A man died when a Kornet antitank missile hit his vehicle near the Gaza border. A man, 35, died when a rocket hit his car in Ashdod. Israeli police said 66 people were wounded, including three who were seriously wounded. The Barzilai hospital was hit by debris from a rocket that was intercepted by an Iron Dome missile.

Islamic Jihad snipers wounded two Israeli soldiers.

Israel had conducted 260 airstrikes, killing four Palestinian militants and two other Palestinian men. Palestinian medical officials said 23 people were killed, including eight gunmen, two pregnant women, and two babies. Palestinians said an airstrike killed a pregnant woman, Filisteen Abu Arar, 37, and her 14-month-old daughter, Sebba Abu Arar; the child's older sister was wounded. The Israel Defense Force attributed the deaths to a Hamas rocket that misfired. Israel killed Hamid Ahmed Abdul Khudri, 34, who was responsible for transferring money from Iran to militant groups inside of Gaza, according to the IDF. The *New York Times* reported that Palestinian militant Emad Muhammad Nasir, 20, was killed; he was part of Hamas's military wing. Khaled Muhammad Abu Qlaq, 25, was hit on his motorcycle. The IDF said it hit 200 militant targets in Gaza, including a tunnel, rocket launcher sites and other military compounds used by Hamas and Palestinian Islamic

Jihad (PIJ), plus a mosque in al-Shati in northern Gaza, which the IDF said was used as a command and control center by PIJ. An airstrike hit a building housing the office of Turkey's state-run *Anadolu* news agency, a building which Israel said is also used by Hamas's military intelligence.

June 25, 2019: Incendiary balloons launched from the Gaza Strip caused fires in southern Israel. Israel retaliated by cutting off fuel shipments to the Gaza Strip, resulting in new power cuts in the territory.

July 8, 2019: The Israeli military announced it had shot down and was examining a drone fired from the Gaza Strip.

August 17, 2019: Three rockets were fired from the Hamas-controlled Gaza Strip into southern Israel. Israeli aerial defense batteries intercepted two of the missiles. Shrapnel from the Iron Dome defense system landed on the patio of a house. No injuries were reported.

August 25, 2019: Gunmen fired three projectiles from the Gaza Strip into Israel. The Israeli military said its missile defense system knocked down two of the missiles during the evening.

August 27, 2019: *NPR* and *Reuters* reported that a Palestinian jihadi set off a bomb at a police checkpoint, then detonated his suicide bomb at a second Hamas police checkpoint, killing three officers and wounding several other Palestinians. The Hamas-run interior ministry declared a state of emergency. It was believed to be the first jihadi suicide bombing against Hamas. The first bomb destroyed a motorcycle with two riders on board as it was passing a checkpoint, killing two policemen and wounding another Palestinian. An hour later, a suicide bomb went off at a police checkpoint elsewhere in the city.

October 31, 2019: Israeli tank and aircraft fire struck two Hamas military posts in northern Gaza in retaliation for a Palestinian rocket attack. There were no immediate reports of injuries from the single rocket that was fired toward Israel from Gaza.

November 25, 2019: The Israeli army announced that a rocket was fired from the Gaza Strip less than two weeks after a cease-fire halted hostilities with Palestinian militants. No injuries were reported.

December 7, 2019: The Israeli military said air defenses stopped two of three rockets fired from the Gaza Strip toward southern Israel. No injuries were reported. No one claimed credit.

December 18, 2019: *AFP* reported that Israeli warplanes attacked an arms plant in the Hamas-controlled northern Gaza Strip after Palestinians fired a rocket at Israel during the night. No casualties were reported in either attack.

IRAN

January 26, 2019: *Fars* reported that police official Ali Ghasempour said that in the morning, the Arab Struggle Movement for the Liberation of Ahvaz shot to death two policemen who were on patrol in the oil-rich Khuzestan Province.

February 2, 2019: Nikshahr prosecutor Mohsen Golmohammadi told the semi-official *Mehr* news agency that two attackers hopped the wall of a Basij paramilitary base in Nikshahr in Sistan-Baluchistan Province and fired on troops, killing Morteza Aliahmadi, a member of the Revolutionary Guard, and wounding five others. The gunmen fled. No one claimed credit. Baluch separatists and drug traffickers were suspected.

February 6, 2019: State television reported that gunmen killed a policeman and wounded a police officer in a shootout in which a stray bullet hit a fuel tanker, causing it to explode near a gas station in Lurestan Province. The assailants fled in a stolen car.

February 13, 2019: *IRNA* reported that the al-Qaeda-linked Jaish al-Adl (Army of Justice, a Sunni extremist group) claimed credit for a suicide car bomb attack during the night on a bus carrying Revolutionary Guard paramilitary force members on a road between the cities of Khash and Zahedan, a mountainous region along the Pakistani border near Afghanistan, killing 27 people and wounding 13 others. On February 19,

Iranian Revolutionary Guard commander General Mohammad Pakpour told Iranian state television that the attacker was a Pakistani named Hafiz Mohammad Ali and a second Pakistani was involved. A woman was arrested over the weekend. Iran had initially blamed Saudi Arabia and the UAE.

July 2, 2019: *Fars* reported that the Revolutionary Guard killed two gunmen trying to infiltrate the country through the border with Turkey. Two Iranian guards were killed in the skirmish in West Azerbaijan Province. Iranian forces confiscated weapons, explosives and communication systems.

July 9, 2019: The semi-official *Mehr* news agency reported that armed members of the Kurdistan Democratic Party killed three Revolutionary Guards and wounded another when they ambushed a Guard vehicle in a village near the Iran-Iraq border town of Piranshahr.

July 10, 2019: The Revolutionary Guard said on its website that it killed five gunmen who crossed into a mostly Kurdish region from Iraq. One Guardsman died in the shootout in Kermanshah Province. Authorities confiscated weapons, explosives and communications equipment. 19071001

July 20, 2019: State TV blamed "terrorists" when gunmen killed two members of the Revolutionary Guard and wounded two others in Sistan and Baluchistan Province near the border with Pakistan.

August 29, 2019: *Fox News* and *AP* reported that the U.S. Department of the Treasury's Office of Foreign Assets Control sanctioned the Lebanon-based Jammal Trust Bank as a global terrorist organization for ties to the Iran-backed Hizballah terrorist group. *AP* reported on October 5, 2019 that the bank later closed.

September 2019: *AP* and *Fars* reported on October 3, 2019 that Iranian authorities foiled an assassination attempt against General Qassim Soleimani, head of the Revolutionary Guard's Quds Force, in September, when he planned to attend a religious ceremony in Kerman Province.

The assassins plotted to plant nearly 500 kilograms of explosives in an underground tunnel under where Soleimani was to be. *Fars* blamed Israeli and Arab intelligence services.

December 7, 2019: *Fars* reported that a soldier shot to death three policemen at a police station near the port city of Bandar Lengeh. He was immediately arrested.

IRAQ

January 6, 2019: The *New York Times* reported that the Syrian Democratic Forces announced the arrest of Americans Warren Christopher Clark, 34, a former substitute teacher from Houston, and Zaid Abed al-Hamid, variant al-Hamed, 35, who were seized alongside other foreign fighters, including citizens of Ireland and Pakistan. Among the documents left behind in a house that had been occupied by ISIS in Mosul, Iraq, were Clark's résumé and a cover letter, which said, "Dear Director, I am looking to get a position teaching English to students in the Islamic State... I was born and raised in the United States and have always loved teaching others and learning from others as well. My work background is largely in English and I consider working at the University of Mosul to be a great way of continuing my career... I believe that a successful teacher can understand a student's strengths and weaknesses and is able to use that understanding to help students build on their understanding of the English language." He claimed he earned a bachelor's degree from the University of Houston and that he served as a substitute teacher in the Fort Bend Independent School District in Sugar Land, Texas, for more than two years. He later moved to Saudi Arabia to teach English and then taught English for three months in Turkey. He identified himself as Abu Muhammad al-Ameriki. Richard Engel of *NBC News* interviewed him on January 15, 2019. The Muslim convert said he saw executions and crucifixions during the three-plus years he spent with ISIS. He said he did not regret joining ISIS, observing, "I wanted to go see exactly what the group was about, and what they were doing. Of course I saw the videos. I think with the behead-

ings, that's execution. I'm from the United States, from Texas. They like to execute people, too. So I really don't see any difference. They might do it off camera, but it's the same." He told Engel, "I wanted to learn more about the ideology. I'm a political science major, global business minor. I like politics. I like travel, world events. That's what I wanted to do... It was a place that was constantly being bombed. You were always on edge. Day and night, just bombs and airstrikes. You sleep in the middle of the day. I spent most of my time living in a mosque. I just remember every day hoping not to get bombed." Clark said he crossed into Syria from Turkey in June 2015.

The name Zaid Abdul-Hamid appeared in a cache of ISIS registration forms indicating that he provided a reference for a recruit from Trinidad and Tobago when that recruit joined the group in 2014.

January 21, 2019: The *Washington Post* reported that Iraqi scientist Suleiman al-Afari, 52, had been forced by ISIS to help make chemical weapons such as sulfur mustard during its 15-month takeover of Mosul. He had earlier served as a geologist in charge of acquisitions in the metallurgical division of Iraq's Ministry of Industry and Minerals. He was now on death row inside the headquarters of the Kurdistan Regional Government's Counterterrorism Department.

February 2, 2019: During the night, gunmen shot to death Iraqi novelist Alaa Mashzoub as he left a literary event and was headed home on his motorcycle. He had written 20 books, most of them about Karbala's history and culture, and about Iraq's once-thriving Jewish minority.

February 3, 2019: Gunmen attacked a bus carrying ten people from Samarra to Baghdad, injuring seven Iranian Shi'ite pilgrims 30 miles north of Baghdad. One woman was seriously injured. No one claimed credit. 19020301

February 14, 2019: A roadside bomb went off on a road in the Makhoul mountains 60 miles north of Baghdad, killing nine members of the Iraqi security forces, including Colonel Ghalib Dawri, head of counter-explosives operations in Salahuddin Province, and eight members of the Saraya al-Salam militia, or the Peace Brigades, including commander Hussein Attiyeh, a commander in a militia headed by populist Shi'ite cleric Muqtada al-Sadr. No one claimed credit. The militia manages security for the holy city of Samarra, home to the Shi'ite al-Askari Shrine.

February 23, 2019: In a morning attack, ISIS killed five fishermen at a camp site near the Therthar lake, 60 miles northwest of Baghdad. Naim Kaoud, head of the Anbar Province security council, said three militiamen were wounded in a subsequent firefight.

February 26, 2019: A roadside bomb exploded near a vehicle carrying construction workers in the Naimiya district of Fallujah, killing three Iraqi workers and injuring three others. No one claimed credit; ISIS was suspected.

February 28, 2019: Two bombs exploded in Mosul, killing one person and wounding 17 others. A road side bomb went off southwest of Mosul near a vehicle belonging to the Popular Mobilization Forces, a coalition of predominantly Shi'ite militias, wounding four. A second bomb exploded near the cultural center, killing one person and wounding 13. ISIS was suspected.

March 6, 2019: During the night, ISIS attacked a bus carrying mainly Shi'ite Popular Mobilization Forces militia near Makhmour, south of Mosul, killing six militiamen and wounding 31 fighters. The bus was en route to Kirkuk.

March 8, 2019: A car bomb exploded during the evening outside a restaurant on Muthana Street in Mosul, killing two people, including a 13-year-old girl, and wounding ten others. There was no immediate claim of credit.

March 19, 2019: Authorities blamed ISIS for an ambush of an army patrol in Tarmiyah that killed three soldiers and wounded five as they were on patrol.

May 9, 2019: A suicide bomber set off his explosive vest during the evening at the Jamila marketplace in Baghdad's Sadr City suburb, killing eight people and wounding 15.

May 12, 2019: The U.S. Embassy tweeted that it was advising U.S. citizens against traveling to Iraq amid what it called "heightened tensions", reflecting worsening strains between Washington and Tehran. Washington deployed the aircraft carrier *USS Abraham Lincoln* and B-52 bombers to the Persian Gulf in response to unspecified "threats" by Iran.

May 15, 2019: *CNN* and *AP* reported that the U.S. Department of State ordered the departure of non-emergency U.S. government employees from Iraq amid increasing tensions with Iran and warned U.S. citizens not to travel to the country, citing a "high risk for violence and kidnapping". Employees working in the U.S. embassy in Baghdad and the U.S. consulate in Erbil were instructed to leave Iraq, and that "normal visa services will be temporarily suspended at both posts". American Citizens Services employees working in the embassy "will continue to provide consular services to U.S. citizens in Basrah". U.S. officials told *CNN* they had "specific and credible" intelligence that suggested Iranian forces and proxies were planning to target U.S. forces in locations including Iraq.

May 19, 2019: The Popular Mobilization Forces, an Iraqi Shi'ite paramilitary group, said a roadside bomb hit a bus carrying its fighters from Basra Province in Balad Ruz, killing seven people and wounding 26. ISIS was suspected.

NPR reported that a rocket landed near Iraq's parliament building inside Baghdad's fortified Green Zone, a third of a mile from the U.S. Embassy, amid escalating tensions with Iran. No injuries or serious damage were reported. No one claimed credit. Shi'ite militias were suspected.

May 23, 2019: A parked car bomb exploded during the afternoon in Karabila near the Syrian border, killing two people and wounding two others. ISIS was suspected.

May 26, 2019: A Baghdad court sentenced three French members of ISIS to death. The trio were among 13 French citizens the U.S.-backed Syrian Democratic Forces handed over to Iraq in January 2019.

A parked car bomb killed five people and wounded eight near a market in Oweinat in Nineveh Province near the Syrian border. The area was once held by ISIS.

May 27, 2019: A Baghdad court sentenced a fourth former French fighter with ISIS, Mustafa Mohammed Ibrahim, 37, to death and postponed the verdict for a fifth man after he testified to being tortured in detention. The Tunisian-origin defendant had lived in Nice and said to Judge Ahmed Mohammed, "I ask for forgiveness from the people of Iraq and Syria and the victims." The judge ordered him to remove his top in order to see if there were any signs of torture on his body. None were visible. Ibrahim claimed that he had worked as a driver in France.

The second man tried in the courtroom was Fadil Hamad Abdallah, 33, of Moroccan origin. Abdallah said he was tortured while in detention and the judge referred him to a medical committee for investigation and postponed his next session until June 2. Judge Mohammed postponed the sentencing of three other Frenchmen until June 3.

May 28, 2019: An Iraqi court sentenced to death two high-profile French members of ISIS—Karam Salam Mohammed el-Harchaoui, 33, and Brahim Ali Mansour Nejara, 32. Nejara helped run one of the networks that sent Europeans to join ISIS and appeared in a video a week after the November 2015 attacks in Paris. The video was titled "Paris has collapsed" and showed a fictitious destruction of the Eiffel Tower. He was from the Meyzieu suburb of Lyon. Authorities believed that he encouraged one of his brothers to carry out an attack in France, possibly on the stadium there. Two brothers were arrested in France.

El-Harchaoui lived in Belgium before he left for Syria in 2014. He was wounded in one of the battles he fought for ISIS in Syria. His second wife, Samira, said he joined ISIS in Syria in 2014, was sent to Iraq to fight, escaped and traveled back to Syria's Shaddadeh, then to Raqqa where he was wounded in an airstrike in 2016. He was jailed for fleeing, then released. The couple married in October 2015, after which he was rearrested.

May 29, 2019: Turkey's *Anadolu* news service reported that a PKK bomb killed two Turkish soldiers during the "Claw Operation" against PKK targets in Mount Khakurk with commando units, airstrikes and artillery.

Judge Abdul Sattar Bayraqdar announced that at Baghdad airport, Iraq handed over 188 Turkish children of suspected ISIS terrorists to Turkish government representatives in the presence of Iraqi government officials and the U.N. children's agency.

The Iraqi Criminal Court in Baghdad's Karkh district sentenced two former ISIS members—one Frenchman and a Tunisian resident of France—to death for joining the group. They were accused of being parties or accomplices to ISIS crimes, and threatening the national security of Iraq. The French man was Yassin Sakkam, 29, who left France in 2014 to fight with ISIS. The Tunisian was Mohammed Berriri, 24, who told the judge he worked as a sentry at an ISIS camp, did not take part in any battles in Syria, and never traveled to Iraq. He said he regretted joining ISIS but did not regret traveling to Syria.

May 30, 2019: Six bombs went off in quick succession after *iftar* (the meal that breaks the daylong Ramadan fast) in a commercial area in Kirkuk that has several malls, cafes and restaurants, killing four and wounding 23. Saad Harbya, head of Kirkuk security operations, told Kurdish *Rudaw TV* that he blamed ISIS.

June 2, 2019: A court in Baghdad sentenced two French citizens—Fadil Hamad Abdallah, 33, of Moroccan origin and Vianney Jamal Abdelqader, alias Abu Mariam, 29. Abdallah the previous week said he was subjected to torture while in detention. He was then referred to a medical committee that later said he lied.

Iraqi authorities handed over 122 Turkish children of suspected ISIS members to Turkey's government representatives in Baghdad.

June 3, 2019: A Baghdad court sentenced to death two French nationals, Murad Mohammed Mustafa, 41, and Bilal Abdel-Fattah, 32, for membership in ISIS.

June 4, 2019: After a roadside bomb hit an army patrol in Tarmiya. Gunmen hiding in nearby fields fired on the officers being evacuated, killing four security personnel and wounding four others. Three terrorists were killed. No one claimed credit. ISIS was suspected.

June 14, 2019: After midnight, terrorists fired three mortar shells into Balad Air Base north of Baghdad where American trainers are stationed, causing no casualties but causing small fires in bushes.

During the night, a rocket hit a home in Baghdad's Jadriyah neighborhood, causing damage.

June 17, 2019: Three Katushya rockets landed near an Iraqi air defense unit in Camp Taji, an installation north of Baghdad used by Iraqi troops and where American trainers were also present. 19061701

June 18, 2019: Late in the day, Iraq's joint operations command said that a Katyusha rocket landed on open ground of a base housing a small contingent of U.S. troops in Mosul, causing no casualties. 19061802

June 19, 2019: The *Washington Post* reported that at dawn, a rocket landed in the Zubair and Rumeila oil fields camp, operated by the Iraqi Drilling company, on the edge of the Burjesia residential compound near Basra housing staff from ExxonMobil. Three Iraqi staffers from a local drilling company were hospitalized with light wounds. No one claimed credit. ExxonMobil evacuated several dozen international staff members from the nearby West Qurna oil field the previous month. An Iraqi intelligence officer said 40 workers for Exxon Mobil were evacuated from an oil-drilling site. 19061901

June 22-23, 2019: Iraqi Counterterrorism Forces special forces conducted a two-day operation near Kirkuk in which they killed 14 ISIS members.

July 5, 2019: Gunmen attacked the mostly Sunni Tribal Mobilization Forces paramilitary fighters in an area north of Fallujah, killing five and wounding ten. ISIS was suspected.

July 17, 2019: *Anadolu* reported that in the afternoon, a gunman in civilian clothes and carrying two weapons fired at a group of Turkish consulate workers shortly after they entered the HuQQabaz restaurant in Irbil, killing deputy general consul Osman Kose, 38, and several members of his entourage. Kurdish security forces reported that a Turkish diplomat and an Iraqi civilian accompanying him were killed and a civilian was wounded. No one claimed credit. On July 20, the Kurdistan Region Security Council said it had arrested the lead suspect in the shooting. The Council identified him as a 27-year-old from Turkey's predominantly Kurdish city of Diyarbakir. On August 8, 2019, *AP* and *Anadolu* reported that an operation the previous week by the Turkish military and its intelligence agency against a vehicle in the semi-autonomous northern Kurdish region killed two more suspects and alleged planners in the assassination. Turkish forces killed other suspected planners on July 18 and July 24. Iraqi Kurdish officials arrested the lead suspect, 27, who hails from Turkey's predominantly Kurdish city of Diyarbakir. 17071702

Turkish airstrikes killed seven PKK members. On July 25, *DHA* and *Daily Sabah* reported that the Turkish air force, acting on Turkish intelligence, on July 18 and 24 attacked two vehicles carrying the alleged Kurdistan Workers' Party (PKK) masterminds of the attack, killing them and their bodyguards.

July 18, 2019: A drone dropped a grenade on a base belonging to Iran-backed paramilitary forces in Amirli, in Salaheddin Province, wounding two. No one claimed credit. The militias blamed ISIS.

August 10, 2019: U.S. Central Command announced that a U.S. service member was killed by small arms fire in Nineveh Province during a combat mission with Iraqi security forces against ISIS. The *Washington Post* reported that Gunnery Sergeant Scott A. Koppenhafer of Mancos, Colorado and a U.S. contractor were killed. Koppenhafer was assigned to the 2nd Marine Raider Battalion, Marine Forces Special Operations Command in Camp Lejeune, North Carolina. *Marine Corps Times* reported on November 26, 2019 that officials with Operation Inherent Resolve announced that Koppenhafer was killed by enemy fire during a firefight near Qanus Island. The Pentagon had attributed his death to friendly fire earlier, but ultimately said he was killed in a combat operation. OIR reported that a U.S.

military contractor died, and another U.S. service member and two members of the Mosul SWAT force were wounded in the attack. Koppenhafer was selected as the Raiders' 2018 Critical Skills Operator of the Year. He earned two Bronze Stars for combat valor in Afghanistan and combating ISIS militants in the Middle East during his decade with the Marine Raiders. He was the honor graduate of a Marine special operations school. 19081002

August 23, 2019: During the night, a motorcycle rigged with explosives detonated on a commercial street near a Shi'ite mosque in Mussayyib, south of Baghdad, killing three people and wounding 34. ISIS said it targeted "gatherings of Shi'ites" near a Shi'ite mosque.

August 25, 2019: *Anadolu* reported that the Turkish Defense Ministry said that three Turkish soldiers were killed and seven hospitalized in clashes with Kurdistan Workers' Party (PKK) fighters in the Sinat-Haftanin region. 19082501

Police said ISIS fired mortar rounds at a soccer field near a Shi'ite shrine in Daquq village in Kirkuk Province, killing six civilians and wounding nine others who were exercising. The area is controlled by Iran-supported Popular Mobilization Forces (PMF) militias.

Two drones killed two Iraqi PMF members in Anbar Province near the Qaim border crossing with Syria. The attack targeted vehicles belonging to the Hizballah (variant Hezbollah) Brigades faction, also known as Brigade 45, which is separate from the Lebanese group of the same name. The vehicles were transporting weapons. No one claimed credit.

September 20, 2019: A bomb went off during the night on a minibus en route to al-Hilla packed with passengers at an Iraqi Army checkpoint outside the Shi'ite holy city of Karbala, killing 12 civilians and wounding five others. ISIS claimed credit via its *Aamaq* news agency. A passenger exited the minibus but left a bag containing explosives under one of the seats. The bomb was remotely detonated. Prime Minister Adel Abdul-Mahdi said security forces detained a man suspected of leaving the bomb.

September 23, 2019: Terrorists fired two rockets into Baghdad's Green Zone during the evening, landing a half mile from the U.S. Embassy.

A bomb exploded at a club in central Baghdad, damaging nearby cars.

October 2020: *Stars and Stripes* reported on November 4, 2020 that US-trained Iraqi CTS counterterrorism forces captured an ISIS child recruiter in Fallujah.

October 5, 2019: Gunmen attacked the Baghdad offices of television stations.

Masked gunmen wearing black clothes drove up in black cars and raided the offices of the Saudi-owned *al-Arabiya* news channel on Abu Nawas Street during the evening, beat up some of the employees, and smashed equipment. Majed Hamid, the channel's correspondent in Baghdad, said several colleagues were injured. The station had been threatened for several days. 19100501

Gunmen attacked the offices of Iraq's privately owned *Dajla* and *NRT* news channels.

October 28-29, 2019: During the night, masked gunmen shot at Iraqi protesters in the Education Square of the Shi'ite holy city of Karbala, killing 18 people, including a 22-year-old female medical student, and wounding hundreds, including 17 students. It was not immediately clear who was behind the attack. Protestors suggested they could have been riot police, special forces, or Iran-linked militias. Provincial governor Nassif al-Khutabi said no protesters were killed, but some security forces were injured. Hundreds of protestors had set up tents for a sit-in at nearby Imam Hussein Shrine. Bullets were fired at them from a passing car. Gunmen in black plainclothes arrived and fired on the protesters.

October 30, 2019: Two Katyusha rockets landed in Baghdad's fortified Green Zone area during the night, killing a soldier manning a checkpoint near a restaurant. One rocket landed 10 yards away from the U.S. Embassy.

November 3, 2019: *NPR* reported that during the night, Iraqi soldiers killed three protestors and wounded 19 who threw firebombs at the Iranian Consulate in Karbala. Seven police were wounded in the violent demonstration. 19110401

November 8, 2019: Seventeen Katyusha rockets were fired at an Iraqi air base in Qayyara that houses American troops 38 miles south of Mosul. 19110810

November 10, 2019: A roadside bomb wounded five Italian military members, three gravely, as they returned from a mission aimed at helping Iraqi troops combat ISIS. The three members of the navy and two of the army were part of a special forces team that was traveling back after a mission aimed at finding ISIS refuges. Some Iraqi armed forces members were also injured in the explosion outside Kirkuk. One Italian soldier lost a leg to amputation due to injuries from the bomb and another suffered serious internal injuries. 19111001

November 26, 2019: Three bombs exploded simultaneously around 8 p.m. in Baghdad, killing five people and wounding 13. One bomb killed three and wounded five in the Baiyaa neighborhood. Another bomb killed two and wounded four in Shaab City. Four people were wounded in Baladiyat. ISIS was suspected.

November 27, 2019: Anti-government protesters burned down the Iranian consulate building in Najaf. Police fired live ammunition, killing a protester and injuring 35 to prevent them from entering the building. The demonstrators replaced the Iranian flag with an Iraqi one. Iranian staff were not harmed and escaped the building from the back door. 19112701

December 3, 2019: *Military Times* reported that several rockets landed outside al-Asad airbase in Anbar Province, which houses American troops. Colonel Myles B. Caggins III, the spokesman for Operation Inherent Resolve, said that no facilities were hit and there were no injuries. The Iraqi military said that five rockets landed on the airbase. No one claimed credit. ISIS was suspected. 19120301

December 5, 2019: Anti-government protesters said 15 people were stabbed in Baghdad's Tahrir Square after political parties and Iran-backed militia groups briefly joined them. There were no fatalities. A protester suggested that the attacks "might have been perpetrated by the parties or someone who wants to ignite problems with the parties".

December 6-7, 2019: Gunmen in cars killed 12 people, including two policemen, and injured 100 in Baghdad's Khilani Square. Video showed seven vehicles speeding away. Attacks continued through the night and into the next morning, raising the death toll to 25 protesters killed and more than 130 people wounded in attacks on Sinak Bridge.

The U.S. Department of the Treasury announced financial sanctions against Qais al-Khazali, the leader of Asaib al-Haq; his brother Laith al-Khazali, a commander in the group; and Husain Falih Aziz al-Lami, security chief for the Popular Mobilization Forces. The Treasury Department named Khamis al-Khanjar, an Iraqi millionaire businessman, for alleged corruption.

The *New York Times* reported that an unmanned drone bombed the home of Shi'ite cleric Moktada al-Sadr in Najaf on December 7, causing no injuries. No one claimed credit.

December 9, 2019: Four rockets fired from a nearby neighborhood hit an army base's barracks for Iraq's elite counterterrorism forces near Baghdad International Airport, wounding six Iraqi personnel, two critically. No group claimed responsibility.

December 12, 2019: A gunman, 16, shot and killed six people, including four anti-government protesters and two shop owners, and wounded eight before an angry mob beat him to death and hoisted the corpse by its feet from a traffic pole in central Baghdad's Wathba Square. The teen was wanted by police on drug-related charges and was running from security forces. Shi'ite cleric Muqtada al-Sadr called the mob "terrorists" and warned that if they were not identified within 48 hours, he would order his militia to leave the square. Members of Saraya Salam (Peace Brigades "blue hats") had deployed in the square to protect protesters.

December 28, 2019: *ABC News* reported that at 7:20 p.m., 30 rockets were fired at the K1 military base outside Kirkuk, killing a U.S. civilian contractor and injuring several service members and Iraqi personnel. *Reuters* added that security forces found a launchpad for Katyusha rockets inside an abandoned vehicle near the base. ISIS was suspected. The next day, the U.S. conducted air strikes in Iraq and Syria against five sites of the the Iranian-backed Iraqi militia Hizballah Brigades (Kataeb Hizballah) believed responsible for the rocket attack. U.S. Air Force F-15 Strike Eagles hit three sites in western Iraq and two in eastern Syria, including weapons depots and the group's command and control bases. The group is separate from the Lebanese Hizballah, and is part of the Popular Mobilization Forces. Iraqi Abu Mahdi al-Muhandis is chief of Kataeb Hizballah and served as deputy head of the Popular Mobilization Forces. The State Department earlier linked him to the Quds Force of the Iranian Revolutionary Guard. The militia vowed retaliation, saying the airstrikes had killed 25 people and wounded 51. U.S. President Trump tweeted, "Iran killed an American contractor, wounding many. We strongly responded, and always will. Now Iran is orchestrating an attack on the U.S. Embassy in Iraq. They will be held fully responsible. In addition, we expect Iraq to use its forces to protect the Embassy, and so notified!"

The *Washington Post* reported on January 7, 2020 that the dead Valiant Integrated Services defense contractor was Nawres Hamid, 33, a naturalized U.S. citizen born in Iraq who lived in Sacramento. He obtained U.S. citizenship in 2017. He left behind a wife, Noor Alkhalili, and two sons, aged 2 and 8. He was an Arabic interpreter for U.S. forces in Iraq. The *Sacramento Bee* reported that Valiant paid for his funeral at the Greater Sacramento Muslim Cemetery. 19122802

CNN and the *Washington Post* reported on December 31 that protesters shouting "death to America" scaled the walls and forced the gates of the U.S. Embassy compound in Baghdad while hundreds demonstrated against the airstrikes. Protestors smashed windows, set items on fire, and threw rocks over the walls. Some of the demonstrators broke into one of the facility's re-ception areas, breaking down fortified doors and bulletproof glass and torching the room. They also smashed security cameras, set alight two guardrooms and burned tires, papers and military MREs (meals ready to eat).

Most demonstrators were from Iraq's Popular Mobilization Units (PMU), a coalition of predominantly Shi'ite militias. Leaders of powerful militia groups were at the protest, including

- Jamal Jaafar Ibrahimi, alias Abu Mahdi al-Muhandis, 56, who was in a Kuwait prison for years for bombing the U.S. Embassy in Kuwait. He died in a U.S. airstrike on January 3, 2020 on Baghdad Airport that also killed Iranian General Qassem Soleimani, head of the Revolutionary Guard Quds Force.

- Hadi al-Amiri, leader of the Badr Organization

- Qais al-Khazali, who runs the Asaib Ahl al-Haq militia and was once imprisoned by the U.S. military

Occupiers began leaving the Embassy grounds on January 1, 2020.

Secretary of State Mike Pompeo told *CBS News* interviewer Major Garrett that the Embassy attack was "state-sponsored terror, this is Iranian-backed terrorism that took place". During the night of January 2-3, 2020, a U.S. drone strike on a two-car convoy killed Iranian intelligence chief and Revolutionary Guards Quds Force commander General Qassem Soleimani, 62, at Baghdad International Airport. Also killed were five other people, including Abu Mahdi al-Muhandis, deputy commander of the Popular Mobilization Forces and founder of Kataeb Hizballah, and al-Muhandis's son-in-law Mohammed Rida al-Jaberi. U.S. Secretary of Defense Mark Esper observed, "Gen. Soleimani was actively developing plans to attack American diplomats and service members in Iraq and throughout the region. This strike was aimed at deterring future Iranian attack plans." *NPR* reported that polls indicated that Soleimani was the most respected figure in Iran.

ISRAEL

February 7, 2019: The stabbed body of Ori Ansbaher, 19, was found in the woods near Jerusalem. Israeli police on February 9 arrested a Palestinian suspect in Ramallah. The suspect came from Hebron.

March 12, 2019: Police closed the entrances to Jerusalem's most sensitive holy site, which Jews call the Temple Mount and Muslims the Noble Sanctuary, after Palestinians firebombed a police station. No injuries were reported. Two Palestinian minors were arrested.

March 25, 2019: A rocket fired from Gaza hit a house on the Mishmeret agricultural community near Tel Aviv, injuring seven members of one Israeli family, including three children. Authorities blamed Hamas. Local media reported that the rocket was fired by accident. No group claimed credit. Israel conducted airstrikes against Hamas targets in Gaza, including the office of Hamas leader Ismail Haniyeh and a multistory building that served as a Hamas military intelligence headquarters.

May 5, 2019: *AP* reported on May 9 that on May 5, the Israel Defense Forces tweeted that "HamasCyberHQ.exe" had been removed "following our successful cyber defensive operation". Israeli fighter aircraft struck a building hosting Hamas cyber operatives engaged in a cyberattack aimed at "harming the quality of life of Israeli citizens".

May 31, 2019: Israeli police shot dead a Palestinian, Yousef Wajih, 19, from a village near the West Bank city of Ramallah, suspected of two stabbings that injured two Israelis near Damascus Gate in Jerusalem's Old City. One Israeli was in critical condition; the second was moderately wounded. Security forces shot Wajih as he ran through the Old City's Muslim quarter.

June 12, 2019: Israeli fighter jets targeted "underground infrastructure in a Hamas military compound" in Gaza after air defenses intercepted a rocket launched from the Gaza Strip into southern Israel overnight.

July 31, 2019: During the night, Israeli soldiers shot and killed Palestinian gunman Hani Abu Salah, a member of the armed wing of Hamas, who had crossed the Gaza perimeter fence and fired on soldiers, wounding three of them. The Israeli Army said a tank "targeted a Hamas military post in Gaza". Abu Salah had lived in Khan Younis in southern Gaza. In 2018, his brother, Fadi, was killed during weekly protests staged by Hamas along the Israel-Gaza frontier.

August 6, 2019: Shin Bet arrested three Palestinians suspected of involvement in a Hamas plot to conduct a bombing in Jerusalem. Hamas operatives in Hebron in the West Bank were also plotting to attack Palestinian President Mahmoud Abbas's Western-backed Palestinian Authority.

August 10, 2019: Israeli troops killed four Palestinians who the army said had tried to carry out a cross-border attack. Hamas said the attack was an "individual act" carried out by youths and was not planned by the group.

August 11, 2019: Authorities killed Marwan Nasser, 26, a Palestinian who exchanged fire with Israeli troops along the perimeter fence surrounding Gaza. The Israeli military says an "armed terrorist" approached the frontier in the morning and shot at troops on the other side. It was not clear if he was a member of an armed group. No group claimed credit.

August 15, 2019: Two Palestinian teens stabbed a policeman, moderately wounding him, outside the Temple Mount/Noble Sanctuary in Jerusalem's Old City. Police fired back at the minors, killing one and seriously wounding another. The Palestinian Red Crescent said a guard from the Islamic Waqf was hospitalized with a gunshot wound.

September 1, 2019: Hizballah fired anti-tank missiles at an Israeli Army base, scoring several direct hits. Israel fired 100 shells toward three villages in southern Lebanon, including Maroun el-Ras village. Hizballah said the missile unit was named after two operatives who were killed in an Israeli airstrike on Syria on August 24. It claimed one unit destroyed an Israeli military vehicle, wounding its occupants.

September 10, 2019: In the evening, the Israeli military intercepted two rockets launched from the Gaza Strip toward Ashdod. The rocket fire interrupted a Likud party campaign rally featuring Prime Minister Benjamin Netanyahu. No injuries were reported. There was no immediate claim of responsibility.

September 18, 2019: Israeli security guards at the Qalandia checkpoint outside Jerusalem shot in the leg and killed a Palestinian woman carrying a knife. Police spokesman Micky Rosenfeld said the woman was armed with a knife and walking in an area reserved for vehicles. "She shouldn't have been there in the first place, which shows clearly that she had intentions of carrying out an attack." The security guards "made a decision at a time when they were in immediate danger and they opened fire according to the danger, the life-threatening situation". She was not carrying an ID.

November 12, 2019: The *Washington Post* reported that an Israeli Defense Forces airstrike at 4 a.m. on a house in the Shejaiya neighborhood in the east Gaza Strip killed Baha Abu al-Ata, variant Bahaa Abu el-Atta, a northern commander of the Iranian-backed Palestinian Islamic Jihad believed to be behind several rocket attacks on Israel and to be planning an imminent strike. Prime Minister Benjamin Netanyahu called Abu al-Ata the "chief terrorist in Gaza". A neighbor said al-Ata's wife was also killed. PIJ announced that the "Al-Quds Brigades, the military wing of the Islamic Jihad movement in Palestine, is mourning its martyr and one of the most prominent members of its military council and the commander of the northern region", calling the attack a "cowardly assassination". "We affirm that the response to this crime will have no limits and will be the size of the crime committed by the criminal enemy and that the occupation will bear the consequences of this aggression." The army and Shin Bet attributed recent rocket attacks on a summer music festival and on Sderot to the faction he led.

Retaliatory rocket fire landed in several Israeli cities, including Tel Aviv, hitting highways, buildings and vehicles. Israeli media said more than 150 rockets were launched, 60 of which were intercepted. Several minor injuries were reported; an 8-year-old girl was in stable condition after losing consciousness.

The IDF announced missile strikes against a rocket-launching site. The Hamas Health Ministry announced that one person was killed and seven injured.

November 26, 2019: The Justice Ministry announced it had charged Bentzi Gopstein, leader of a Jewish extremist group, with incitement to violence and terrorism for inflammatory remarks about Palestinians. The Ministry said he called "for committing acts of violence", published "racially inciting" material and voiced support for Baruch Goldstein, a Jewish extremist who massacred 29 Muslim worshippers at Hebron's Ibrahimi Mosque in 1994. Gopstein is the leader of an anti-assimilation group that harasses Jewish-Arab couples and is a member of the radical Jewish Power party, comprised of hard-line religious nationalists who have cast themselves as successors to the outlawed Kahanist movement, which advocated the forced removal of Palestinians.

JORDAN

November 6, 2019: *NPR, AP, and Reuters* reported that an individual stabbed eight people, including three Mexican tourists, a Swiss woman, their tour guide and three Jordanians, including a policeman, at the popular Jerash archaeological site in northern Jordan. The independent *Ammon* news site said two people were in critical condition. Police arrested the attacker. The Jerash ruins include a Roman amphitheater and a columned road. 19110601

LEBANON

June 3, 2019: The state-run *National News Agency* reported that during the night, a motorcyclist fired on police and army vehicles in different parts of Tripoli, killing two police officers and two soldiers and wounding several others before blowing himself up with an explosive belt when confronted by an elite military intelligence force that stormed an apartment he had broken into the following morning. No one claimed credit. The army identified the gunman as Abdul-Rahman Mabsout. *LBC* said he was a former member of ISIS who fought with them in Syria. He had been detained when he returned to Lebanon in 2016 and was released in 2017.

Mabsout first fired at a branch of the Lebanese Central Bank, then shot at police and later at an army vehicle. A soldier was killed and two others wounded in the shooting at the army vehicle.

Interior Minister Raya el-Hassan said Mabsout was an "individual case" and worked alone.

June 9, 2019: The Jamaa Islamiya political party said gunmen killed Mohammed Jarrar, one of its officials, in a nighttime attack in Chebaa village. The state-run *National News Agency* reported that he was shot in the stomach four times. No group claimed responsibility. JI is the Lebanese branch of the Muslim Brotherhood, a regional Islamist organization. JI is not represented in parliament.

June 30, 2019: Minister of State for Displaced Affairs Saleh al-Gharib told local TV that his convoy came under fire as he was heading to the mountain village of Qabr Shamoun. Two guards were killed and another wounded. His Druze party is allied with Hizballah and supports the Syrian government.

July 2019: *AP* reported on October 5, 2019 that in July 2019, the U.S. Department of the Treasury sanctioned Lebanese Hizballah members of the Lebanese Parliament Amin Sherri and Mohammad Raad as designated supporters of terrorism.

July 18, 2019: Lebanese Hizballah member of Parliament Nawaf Musawi offered his resignation to Parliament Speaker Nabih Berri after a shooting at a police station he was allegedly involved in a few days earlier. A leaked police report indicated that Musawi and a dozen gunmen tried to storm the station where his daughter and her ex-husband had been brought following a high-speed car chase. The group was denied entry, and a gunshot was fired, hitting the ex-husband's wrist. Musawi denied firing. The dispute was apparently over child visitation rights.

LIBYA

January 16, 2019: Fighting between militias in Tripoli killed five people and wounded 20.

February 13, 2019: The Tripoli-based U.N.-backed government announced that joint Libyan and U.S. forces bombed al-Qaeda terrorists in Ubari, 590 miles south of Tripoli. U.S. Africa Command said it was not involved in the raid.

February 14, 2019: The National Commission for Human Rights in Libya said gunmen kidnapped 14 Tunisian workers on their way to work at an oil refinery in Zawiya near Tripoli. The kidnappers demanded the release of an unnamed Libyan man detained in Tunisia on drug-related charges. The Tunisians were released on February 17. 19021401

April 8-9, 2019: Lawmaker Ismail al-Sharif said that during the night, suspected Islamic State terrorists attacked al-Fuqaha, a small town south of Sirte in central Libya, killing at least three people, including the mayor, and torching several houses. Resident Rabie al-Zidani said the mayor and two other security officials were beheaded.

April 17, 2019: The Philippine embassy evacuated to Tunisia three Filipino hospital workers and four Filipino students from Tripoli after Tripoli was hit by rocket fire that wounded a Filipino warehouse worker, Rolando Torres, who was in his living room when two explosions went off outside his house. He ran to another room but another blast sent debris flying, wounding him in the forehead. 19041701

May 4, 2019: Gunmen attacked a training camp for the Libyan National Army near an air base in Sabha, killing nine soldiers. The Islamic State claimed credit.

May 18, 2019: Islamic State terrorists killed three troops in an attack on a checkpoint in Zallah, a desert town. The Libyan National Army said the gunmen captured four soldiers, but troops freed three of them. The Islamic State claimed credit.

May 20, 2019: U.N. spokesman Stephane Dujarric said gunmen attacked the main water distribution station in Tripoli and closed valves supplying Tripoli and cities in the northwest, potentially affecting two million people.

May 28, 2019: Khalifa Hifter's Libyan National Army said on its *Facebook* page that Hisham el-Ashmawi, a prominent Egyptian militant and former army officer captured in October 2018, was returned to Egypt, which wanted him for several attacks, including a 2013 attempted assassination on the interior minister.

June 28, 2019: The Libyan National Army militia forces said that Turkish vessels and interests are "legitimate targets" in its battle to seize Tripoli. LNA accused Turkey of helping rival militias allied with the U.N.-supported government. LNA spokesman Ahmed al-Mesmari said Libya had "come under illegitimate Turkish aggression" in recent weeks. "Turkey has become directly involved in the battle (for Tripoli), with its soldiers, planes, sea ships and all the supplies that now reach Misrata, Tripoli and Zuwara directly." He said the LNA was ordered to target any Turkish ships, strategic sites or companies operating in Libya or its territorial waters, and to arrest any Turkish nationals in Libya. *AP* reported the next day that the Turkish Foreign Ministry said six Turkish nationals were being held and that it would consider Field Marshal Khalifa Hifter's "illegal militia forces" to be "legitimate targets" if the Turks were not released. On July 1, a Turkish Foreign Ministry official said the six Turkish crew members had been released.

July 11, 2019: Two car bombs exploded in Benghazi near leaders of the Libyan National Army militia, killing four people, including two civilians and two soldiers, and wounding 33 others, including civilians, army personnel, and police. The LNA leaders, including the commander of LNA special forces, were to attend the funeral of a senior general. None of the LNA leaders were harmed.

July 17, 2019: The U.N.-backed government based in Tripoli accused forces loyal to LNA commander Khalifa Hifter of kidnapping female lawmaker Seham Siqiwa, who often criticized his military operations. She disappeared from her house in Benghazi.

July 22, 2019: French President Emmanuel Macron said buildings of the U.N. High Commissioner for Refugees in Libya were attacked. 19072201

August 10, 2019: A car bomb exploded outside the Arkan Mall in Benghazi's Hawari neighborhood, where people were shopping a day before Eid al-Adha, killing three U.N. Support Mission in Libya security staff who were in a convoy, and wounding nine people, including a Jamaican staff member and a child, 3. The *Washington Post* reported that two of the dead were from Libya and "Fuji" (sic). No group claimed credit. 19081001

September 19, 2019: U.S. Africa Command announced an airstrike against the Islamic State in Libya, killing eight terrorists near Murziq, 500 miles south of Tripoli. No civilians were killed or injured.

September 24, 2019: U.S. Africa Command announced that an airstrike killed 11 IS in Libya terrorists near Murziq.

September 25, 2019: U.S. Africa Command announced its third airstrike against the Islamic State group over the last eight days, killing 17 militants outside Murzuq in southwest Libya.

September 30, 2019: AFRICOM announced that an airstrike killed seven Islamic State terrorists.

October 11, 2019: Four armed men stopped a humanitarian convoy in Zintan in western Libya and kidnapped four physicians, a nurse and a technician. The six medical workers were released on October 23. Human Rights Watch reported that family members believed that the kidnappers apparently sought to obtain the release of an imprisoned man.

October 16, 2019: Gunmen killed two women and three children from the same family as they were driving on a highway near Tripoli. Abdel Rahman al-Tamimi, his wife, sister and three children were traveling during the evening to Tripoli from their hometown of Aziziya to get vaccinations for the children, ages 3 to 6.

November 10, 2020: *AP, al-Jazeera* and *AFP* reported that gunmen on Road 20, a commercial street in Benghazi, shot to death attorney Hanan al-Barassi, 46, a critic of abuses in the eastern areas controlled by renegade military commander Khalifa Hifter's self-styled Libyan National Army (LNA). She had been livestreaming minutes earlier on *Facebook.* Amnesty International said al-Barassi and her daughter had received death threats. *AP* reported that the masked gunmen had tried to kidnap her. No one claimed credit.

SAUDI ARABIA

April 7, 2019: Authorities announced the killing of two wanted men and arrests of two others after security forces spotted four wanted people in Qatif en route to conduct a terrorist attack. The group fired at security forces and threw a hand grenade into a gas station, sparking a fire. A Bahraini woman who was at the gas station with her family, a Pakistani truck driver, and two security men were wounded. 19040701

April 21, 2019: The state-run *al-Ekhbariya* news channel reported that four gunmen were killed and three security officers were wounded in an attack on a security building in Zulfi, 155 miles north of Riyadh. The attackers had tried to crash a car through the front of an Interior Ministry building but were stopped by security in a shootout against gunmen armed with machine guns and explosives. The Islamic State claimed credit the next day, showing a video in which a martyrdom-seeking man said the Saudi royal family are infidels and the attack aimed to avenge Muslims imprisoned in Saudi Arabia, Syria and Iraq. 19042102

April 23, 2019: Saudi news channel *al-Ekhbariya* reported that the Interior Ministry announced that it had executed by beheading 37 Saudis for terrorism-related crimes. The terrorists came from across Saudi Arabia and had adopted extremist ideologies and formed terrorist cells with the aim of spreading chaos and provoking sectarian strife. *CNN* and the *Saudi Press Agency (SPA)* quoted the Interior Ministry as saying that one of the convicts was crucified.

May 11, 2019: The Interior Ministry announced that security forces raided a suspected jihadi hideout on Tarot Island off the coast of Eastern Province and killed eight alleged terrorists in a shootout in the predominantly Shi'ite eastern region of Qatif. The Ministry accused the terrorists of planning to attack vital installations and security targets.

May 14, 2019: Yemen's Houthi rebels attacked an oil pipeline in Saudi Arabia with drones. Houthis had earlier used Qatef-1 (Striker) Unmanned Aerial Vehicles, which reportedly were "virtually identical in design, dimensions and capability to that of the Ababil-T, manufactured by the Iran Aircraft Manufacturing Industries". They said the new attack was to call on the Kingdom to "stop your aggression". Saudi Arabia said other assaults targeted energy infrastructure elsewhere in the kingdom. Anwar Gargash, UAE Minister of State for Foreign Affairs, threatened retaliation for the attack on Pumping Station No. 8 outside of al-Duadmi. 19051401

May 21, 2019: Yemen's Houthi rebel-run *al-Masirah* satellite news channel claimed the group launched a bomb-laden Qasef-2K drone targeting an airport in Najran, Saudi Arabia that houses a military base, striking an "arms depot" there. The state-run *Saudi Press Agency* quoted Saudi-led coalition spokesman Colonel Turki al-Maliki as saying the Houthis "had tried to target" a civilian site in Najran.

May 26, 2019: The state-run *Saudi Press Agency* reported that in the morning, Yemeni Houthi rebels launched a bomb-carrying drone against Jizan Regional Airport. The Houthis said on their *al-Masirah* satellite news channel it was a Qasef-2K drone. Saudi Colonel Turki al-Maliki said the military intercepted and destroyed the drone. 19052601

June 7, 2019: *AP* reported on June 18 that Saudi Interior Ministry spokesman Maj. Gen. Mansour al-Turki said two Italians were wounded in Jiddah in a premeditated attack targeting their cars. Security forces believed the attack was a criminal act centered around a personal dispute. Investigations indicated that an explosive device was placed under the gas pedals of two cars, causing the vehicles to catch fire and injuring the drivers, but not the other Italian passengers.

June 11, 2019: Yemeni Houthis' *al-Masirah* satellite news channel reported that the group launched at least two Qasef-2K drones to strike the Saudi city of Khamis Mushait, home to an air base. Saudi military spokesman Colonel Turki al-Maliki told the state-run *Saudi Press Agency* that soldiers "intercepted" two drones. 19061101

June 12, 2019: The *Washington Post* reported that Yemeni Houthi rebels fired a missile that hit the arrivals hall of the civilian Abha International Airport in southern Saudi Arabia, injuring 26 people from Saudi Arabia, Yemen, and India, including three women and two children, and causing damage. Eight of the wounded were hospitalized. The Houthis claimed credit on their *al-Masirah* TV network, saying they had fired a cruise missile. Turki al-Malki, spokesman of the U.S.-backed Saudi-led coalition battling rebels in Yemen, said, "Three women, a Yemeni, an Indian, a Saudi and two Saudi children were amongst those injured... authorities are working on identifying the type of missile that was used in this terrorist attack." 19061201

June 17, 2019: The Houthi-owned *al-Masirah* television network reported that Yemeni Houthi rebels claimed to have launched a Qasef-2K drone attack on the Abha civilian airport in southern Saudi Arabia.

The state-run *Saudi Press Agency* quoted military spokesman Col. Turki al-Maliki as saying that the kingdom intercepted two bomb-laden drones launched by Yemen's Iranian-backed Houthi rebels. Al-Maliki said one drone targeted a civilian area near the airport in Abha. The other drone was shot down over Yemen. 19061702

June 19, 2019: During the night, Yemeni Houthi rebels fired a rocket at a desalination plant, causing no injuries or damage. The Houthis said on their *al-Masirah* satellite channel that they targeted a power plant in Jizan. 19061902

June 22, 2019: Yemeni Houthi rebels attacked the airport in Abha after 9 p.m., killing a Syrian resident of Saudi Arabia and injuring seven peo-

ple. Houthi spokesman Yahia al-Sarie said that the rebels had launched drone attacks on Saudi airports in Abha and Jizan. 19062201

June 25, 2019: Saudi military spokesman Col. Turki al-Maliki announced the country shot down a drone launched by Houthi rebels into the kingdom near the southern Saudi city of Khamis Mushait during the night. 19062501

July 2, 2019: The *Saudi Press Agency* reported that Yemeni Houthi rebels fired an armed drone which hit Abha airport in the morning, injuring nine civilians, including an Indian and eight Saudis, none seriously. The Houthis' *al-Masirah* TV said they had launched a "large operation" against the Abha airport. 19070201

July 6, 2019: Yemeni Houthi rebels' *al-Masirah* satellite news channel said rebels launched Qasef-2K drone attacks on Saudi airports in Abha and Jizan, suspending air traffic. 19070601-02

July 16, 2019: During the night, military spokesman Colonel Turki al-Maliki announced the interception of three Houthi drones launched at Saudi cities near Yemen's border. 17071601-03

July 17, 2019: The *Saudi Press Agency* reported that military spokesman Colonel Turki al-Maliki announced that the armed forces intercepted a drone launched at the kingdom's southern border town of Jizan by Houthis in Yemen's Sanaa Governorate. 17071701

August 17, 2019: Yemeni Houthis launched a drone attack on the Shaybah oil and gas field in the Saudi desert, starting a fire but causing no injuries. Production was not affected. The field produces one million barrels of crude oil/day. Yahia Sarie, military spokesman for the Houthis, issued a video claiming the rebels launched 10 bomb-laden drones.

September 14, 2019: Yemeni Houthi rebels claimed they conducted 4 a.m. drone attacks on major Aramco oil installations in Saudi Arabia. The Houthi-run *al-Masirah* news agency said they used ten drones against facilities in Khurais Province and Abqaiq. *CNN Business* reported that the attacks disrupted production of 5 million barrels/day, half of the kingdom's oil capacity, equaling 5% of the world's daily global supply. Iran denied U.S. Secretary of State Mike Pompeo's charges of Iranian complicity. Satellite photos suggested that the drone flights originated in Iran or Iraq, not Yemen, assuming a straight-line flight path. The Saudi government said the attackers used Iranian weapons. Unnamed U.S. officials said cruise missiles were involved. 19091401

November 11, 2019: Two men and a woman performing on stage in a park in Riyadh during the evening were wounded in a knife attack, the first such incident since the kingdom eased restrictions on entertainment. Saudi broadcaster *al-Ekhbariya* reported that police detained a 33-year-old Yemeni male resident of Saudi Arabia. The man had run on stage and attacked the performers from behind as the troupe, dressed in gold ensembles, danced.

On December 29, 2019, the state-owned *al-Ekhbariya* news channel reported that the Specialized Criminal Court sentenced a Yemeni male, 33, residing in Saudi Arabia, to death for attacking with a knife and wounding dancers from Spain and a security guard during a performance. He was also deemed guilty of intimidating the public, creating chaos and terror, attempting to derail entertainment activities in Saudi Arabia, inciting violence, and acting on the orders of an unnamed senior AQAP leader in Yemen. A second suspect was sentenced to 12 and one half years in prison for aiding and abetting the attacker and sending money to AQAP in Yemen. 19111101

SYRIA

January 5, 2019: The Kurdish-run *Rudaw* news agency reported that an ISIS missile attack in Shaafa in Deir el-Zour Province killed a Kurdish fighter and wounded two British soldiers and one Kurdish Syrian Democratic Forces fighter. 19010501

January 6-7, 2019: On January 9, 2019, the *New York Times* and *USA Today* reported that the Syrian Democratic Forces announced the capture of eight foreign fighters during the week, including a 16-year-old American boy fighting on behalf

of ISIS. *USA Today* identified him as Soulay Noah Su, alias Abu Souleiman al-Amriki, who was captured near Hajin. The Kurdish People's Protection Units (YPG) said they were "Daesh terrorists of American, Russian, Ukrainian, German, Kazakh, Tajik and Uzbek origin". YPG said YPG Special Operations Team captured them on January 6 and 7, identifying them as

- Adil Rahimov, (Abu Amina Uzbeki), 58, Uzbekistan

- Farhad Qaderov (Abu Bilal Uzbeki), 28, Uzbekistan

- Mohammad Dawlat (Abu Moshab Tajiki), 22, Tajikistan

- Askar Zarmanbetov (Abu Dawoud Nougha), 27, Ukraine

- Sattibek Oshibaev (Abu Rouqaya), 30, Kazakhistan

- Bimuraev Begjan (Abu Sara), 30, Russia

- Soulay Noah Su (Abu Souleiman al-Amriki), 16, USA

- Lucas Glass (Abu Ibrahim al-Almani), 31, Germany

Other American teens were earlier found in ISIS-controlled territory.

- A girl, 15, from Kansas was repatriated from Syria, after her father forced her to travel to Syria, where she was forced to marry an ISIS fighter; she was pregnant at the time of her capture.

- Zakaryia Abdin, then 16, was accused in South Carolina of plotting an attack against soldiers on behalf of ISIS. He pleaded guilty to a firearms offense and was sentenced to a year in a juvenile facility. Following his parole, at age 18 he went to Syria; the U.S. Department of Justice charged him with providing material support to a foreign terrorist organization.

- Santos Colon, 17, pleaded guilty in New Jersey in 2017 to participating in a plot to kill Pope Francis during a Mass in Philadelphia in 2015. He was released to a halfway house pending sentencing; he faced up to 15 years in prison.

January 16, 2019: The *Washington Post, New York Times,* and *Military Times* reported that ISIS claimed credit for a suicide bomb that killed 14 people, including four Americans—two U.S. service members, a Department of Defense civilian, and a contractor—eight civilians and two fighters from the U.S.-backed Syrian Democratic Forces, and injured three other U.S. service members, one critically, at the popular Palace of the Princes restaurant in Manbij. The suicide bomber was on foot. Hours later, U.S. Vice President Mike Pence echoed President Trump's belief that ISIS had been defeated during his address to the Global Chiefs of Mission Conference at the State Department. ISIS said one of its fighters used a suicide vest. The UK-based Syrian Observatory for Human Rights said 16 people, including nine civilians and five U.S.-backed Syrian Democratic Forces fighters, were killed and others were wounded.

The dead included:

- Army Chief Warrant Officer 2 Jonathan R. Farmer, 37, a Green Beret from Boynton Beach, Florida. He was assigned to 3rd Battalion, 5th Special Forces Group (Airborne) at Fort Campbell, Kentucky. The U.S. Army Special Operations Command said he joined the Army in 2005, later serving on six overseas combat tours, including in Iraq, Afghanistan and Syria. He served in Operation Iraqi Freedom in 2007 and 2009, Operation New Dawn in 2010, Operation Enduring Freedom in 2012 and Operation Inherent Resolve in 2018 and 2019. Awards included a Bronze Star with two Oak Leaf clusters, a Purple Heart and a Global War on Terrorism Expeditionary Medal. He left behind a wife, four children, and his parents.

- Navy Chief Cryptologic Technician (Interpretive) Shannon M. Kent, 35. She was a sailor assigned to Cryptologic Warfare Activity 66, based at Fort George G. Meade, Maryland. She graduated from Stissing Mountain Junior/Senior High School in Pine Plains in upstate New York in 2001. Principal Tara Grieb remembered her as an honor student. She enlisted in the Navy in 2003. U.S. Fleet Cyber Command/US 10th Fleet reported that her awards included the Navy/Marine Corps Commendation Medal, the Army Commendation Medal and the Iraq Campaign Medal. New York Gov. Andrew Cuomo said Kent had followed in the footsteps of her father, New York State Police Colonel Stephen J. Smith, by joining the military. Commander Joseph Harrison, commanding officer of CWA-66, observed, "She was a rock star, an outstanding chief petty officer and leader to many in the Navy Information Warfare Community." Dutchess County Legislature Chairman Gregg Pulver said she spoke seven languages fluently. She was the first female service member killed by enemy fire in more than three years.

- Scott A. Wirtz, 42, a Defense Department civilian from St. Louis. In 1997, he enlisted and served in the U.S. Navy and as a Navy SEAL until 2005. Awards included the SEAL Insignia, Navy and Marine Corps Achievement Medal and the Secretary of Defense Medal for the Global War on Terrorism. He began working with the Defense Intelligence Agency in 2017 as an operations support specialist, collaborating with troops in Syria to collect information about security and adversaries in the area. He had completed three deployments in the Middle East. He competed in mixed martial arts in 2009, winning a bout in the Battles for Fame.

- Ghadir Taher, 27, a civilian contractor from East Point, Georgia, working with the Army as an interpreter for defense contractor Valiant Integrated Services. She and her brother, Ali Taher, moved to the United States from Damascus, Syria in 2001. She graduated from Tri-Cities High School and attended Georgia State University for two years before earning an associate degree through an online school. She held multiple jobs at one point and started her own business. She was survived by her parents and three siblings. 19011602

Stars and Stripes reported on January 22 that the wounded included Captain Jonathan Turnbull, 32, of Gaylord, Michigan. He was deployed with Apache Troop, 3rd Squadron, 7th U.S. Cavalry to Combat Outpost Shir Khan, Afghanistan. He was reported in serious condition at Landstuhl Regional Medical Center in Germany. He sustained a broken pelvis and a fractured skull.

Reuters and *CNN* reported on March 19, 2019 that U.S.-backed Syrian Democratic Forces in Manbij detained five ISIS fighters linked to a January 2019 suicide attack in Manbij.

January 18, 2019: A bomb went off outside an office of the al-Qaeda-linked Hayat Tahrir al-Sham (HTS, Levant Liberation Committee) in rebel-held Idlib, killing 11 people, including seven HTS members, and wounding several others.

January 20, 2019: A bomb went off on a bus in Afrin, killing three people and wounding nine.

January 21, 2019: An ISIS suicide bomber hit a joint convoy of U.S. and allied Kurdish forces at a checkpoint on the edge of Shaddadeh in the Hassakeh Province, on a road used by local Kurdish fighters near the Iraqi border. The Kurdish *Hawar* news agency said two Kurdish fighters were lightly wounded. The UK-based Syrian Observatory for Human Rights said five were killed and others were wounded. 19012101

January 10, 2019: The *Guardian* reported on February 7, 2019 that ISIS leader Abu Bakr al-Baghdadi survived a coup attempt on January 10, 2019 in his eastern Syria hideout in a village near Hajin in the Euphrates River valley and that jihadis had placed a bounty on the head of ringleader Abu Muath al-Jazairi, believed to be a veteran foreign fighter. Al-Baghdadi's bodyguards reportedly exchanged gunfire with the foreign fighters involved in the insurrection. Two people were believed killed. The *Guardian* reported that al-Baghdadi was a diabetic with high blood pressure.

January 29, 2019: *AP* reported on February 11, 2019 that Muhammad Saifuddin, alias Abu Walid, an Indonesian ISIS executioner, was killed by shrapnel on January 29 in Deir Ezzor Province in a battle with U.S.-backed forces. He appeared in several videos, including one in 2016

in which he and two terrorists from Malaysia and the Philippines killed three foreigners, including Japanese journalist Kenji Goto.

February 1, 2019: The Kurdish-led Syrian Democratic Forces said they had captured three foreign members of ISIS, including a German jihadi who had adopted a jihadi alias, a Saudi Arabian and an Egyptian.

February 8, 2019: *SANA* reported that a mine left behind by militants (probably ISIS) killed seven civilians and wounded another in agricultural land east of Salamiyeh in Hama Province.

February 18, 2019: Two bombs went off within seconds of each other in Idlib's Qusour neighborhood during afternoon rush hour, killing 13 and wounding 25. The opposition's Syrian Civil Defense, a group of volunteer first responders, said one of its members was wounded. Idlib is controlled by the al-Qaeda-linked Hayat Tahrir al-Sham.

February 20, 2019: The Kurdish-led Syrian Democratic Forces repatriated 150 Iraqi ISIS prisoners back to Iraq.

February 20, 2019: Local media reported that an airstrike in Baghouz village had killed French ISIS member Fabien Clain, a key figure in the 2015 attacks in Paris; he claimed responsibility in the name of ISIS for the attack. *AP* added on February 28, 2019 that coalition spokesman Colonel Sean Ryan confirmed that the strike on Baghouz occurred on February 20. Clain was born in Toulouse in 1978 and raised in Normandy. He converted from Catholicism in his early 20s, and talked his future wife, his younger brother Jean-Michel, his half-sister and his mother to join Islam. In 2009, he was sentenced to five years in prison for sending recruits to fight with jihadis in Iraq. Five years later, he was believed to have left for Syria with his extended family to join ISIS.

On December 28, 2018, he issued a diatribe addressed to France's yellow vest protesters, calling on them to turn against their government, "which spends your money indiscriminately", particularly on wars.

Two suicide bombs went off in the evening in Shahil, six miles from the al-Omar Oil Field base in Deir el-Zour Province, killing 14 people. Two suicide bombers stopped their cars and detonated the vehicles in the market. The Syrian Observatory for Human Rights reported that a car bomb that was remotely detonated as a convoy of workers and technicians who work at the oil field was passing by, killing 20.

February 24, 2019: *SANA* reported that in the morning, a van ferrying workers to pick desert truffles hit an ISIS mine in Salamiyeh, killing 20.

February 28, 2019: A suicide bomber fired on diners, then set off his explosives inside a restaurant in Idlib, killing eight people, including six jihadis.

March 4, 2019: Mark Taylor, *Twitter* handle Kiwi Jihadi, a New Zealand man who joined ISIS, was captured in Syria. He told the *Australian Broadcasting Corporation* he regretted not being able to afford a slave and expected to return home. In 2014, he forgot to turn off *Twitter*'s geotagging function, alerting outsiders to the location of ISIS fighters. He claimed that he worked as an ISIS guard for five years, but fled in December 2018 and surrendered to Kurdish forces because life had become unbearable. He said there was no food or money and basic services had collapsed.

March 5, 2019: Jean-Michel Clain, a French member of ISIS, died in a mortar strike during the weekend while trying recover from wounds suffered in a February 20 airstrike on Baghouz village that killed his jihadi brother, his French wife Dorothee Maquere, 38, said. She added that another French ISIS woman, Hayat Boumeddiene, was killed in another strike the previous week that hit a safe house known as the "French House", where many French nationals were staying. Boumeddiene had been wanted by French police as a suspected accomplice in a January 2015 attack on a kosher supermarket in the Paris region by her now-deceased husband, Amedy Coulibaly. Maquere said her daughter, 7, was killed and her other daughter wounded by an explosion two weeks earlier. Two other sons were killed earlier in a mortar attack and Syrian government fire. She had five surviving children. Maquere said Boumeddiene had "started a new life" and remarried, sans children.

March 9, 2019: Sharfan Darwish, of the Kurdish-led Manbij Military Council, said that a suicide bomber set off his explosives in the afternoon near a military vehicle in Manbij, wounding eight people, including seven civilians and a U.S.-backed fighter. A military car and several civilian vehicles were passing by.

March 11, 2019: A 90-second ISIS recording called on supporters across the world to stage attacks in their defense, saying that men, women and children in Baghouz were being subjected to a "holocaust by the Crusaders". Muslim "brothers, in Europe and in the whole world" should "rise against the Crusaders and ... take revenge for your religion." "Crusaders warplanes" and "Kurdish atheists" were attacking.

March 23, 2019: A day after President Trump proclaimed that ISIS had lost all of its territory, U.S.-backed Syrian Democratic Forces spokesman Mustafa Bali declared military victory over the ISIS caliphate by taking over the village of Baghouz. Still undetermined was the location of ISIS leader Abu Bakr al-Baghdadi and the location of foreign hostages, including John Cantlie.

April 24, 2019: *SANA* reported that a bomb in a car killed a civilian driver and wounded five others in the Nahr Aysheh district in southern Damascus. No one claimed credit. The target was an intelligence official.

An explosion in insurgent-controlled Jisr al-Shughur killed 16 people, including four children, and destroyed a building. A car bomb was suspected. The town is controlled by such radical groups as the Turkistan Islamist Party, foreign fighters from the Uighur Muslim minority.

May 20, 2019: Mustafa Bali, spokesman for the Kurdish-led Syrian Democratic Forces, said an ISIS suicide bomber set off his explosives on a road near Shaddadeh, targeting a joint convoy belonging to the force and the U.S.-led anti-IS coalition. The bomb caused material damage but no casualties. ISIS claimed the bomber killed or wounded eight people in the convoy.

June 2, 2019: A car bomb went off during the night near the Maytam mosque in Azaz, a northern town held by Turkish-backed fighters, killing 14 people, including four children, and wounding dozens. The explosion went off after the *iftar* meal that breaks the day's Ramadan fast.

June 7, 2019: The *Washington Post* reported that ISIS claimed credit for a series of crop fires in tens of thousands of acres of eastern farmlands stretching from the Iranian border in the east to near the Mediterranean coast in the west. Scorch marks were visible from satellites. The ISIS *al-Naba* newsletter called on supporters to set more fires, observing, "the harvest season is still long, and we tell the soldiers of the Caliphate: you have before you millions of dunams of land planted with wheat and barley, which are owned by apostates." Some 20,000 acres of wheat and barley were incinerated in Syria, while in Iraq, fires broke out across 134,000 acres of land, destroying 20,000 acres of crops. Not all of the fires were attributed to ISIS; several were believed to be over disputes regarding farm ownership.

June 30, 2019: U.S. Central Command said an airstrike hit an al-Qaeda leadership and training facility in northern Syria near Aleppo Province where attacks threatening Americans and others were being planned. The UK-based Syrian Observatory for Human Rights reported that the strike killed eight members of the al-Qaeda-linked Horas al-Din (Guardians of Religion). The dead included six commanders: two Algerians, two Tunisians, an Egyptian and a Syrian.

July 3, 2019: During the night, a booby-trapped motorcycle exploded in Sweida Province, killing three people and hospitalizing another.

July 11, 2019: *Anadolu* reported that a bomb in a fuel truck exploded at the entrance to Afrin, Syria, which is controlled by Turkish forces and allied Syrian fighters, killing nine people and wounding 35. The UK-based Syrian Observatory for Human Rights said 11 died.

July 18, 2019: *CNN* reported that the U.S. transported an alleged U.S. citizen ISIS fighter back to the U.S. to face trial. He had been held by the Syrian Democratic Forces, a Kurdish anti-ISIS militia. *NPR* reported the next day that prosecutors charged Kazakh-born U.S. citizen Ruslan Meritovich Hussainov with material support to a terrorist group by becoming a sniper for ISIS and later providing weapons training to other ISIS members.

August 1, 2019: *CNN* reported that a federal grand jury in Dallas indicted dual Turkish-American national Omer Kuzu, 23, on charges of traveling to Syria and conspiring to provide material support to ISIS. The U.S. had transported him back from Syria to face trial. Kuzu was born in Dallas. In 2014, he and his brother went from Houston to Istanbul en route to Syria. He received weapons and other training in Mosul, Iraq. He returned to Syria, where he was issued weapons and was paid the equivalent of $125 a month to maintain and repair communications equipment for front-line ISIS fighters. The Federal Public Defender's Office in Dallas represented Kuzu. He had been held by the US-backed Syrian Democratic Forces.

August 4, 2019: The *Washington Post* reported on August 9 that Hisham al-Mohammed, 21, a Syrian refugee whom Turkey had deported back to Syria's Idlib Province in June 2019, was shot and killed on August 4 while trying to illegally cross the border to get back to his wife and three young children in Istanbul. He had stopped to pray a few hundred yards from the border wall, and had been walking with a group of Syrian refugees. It was unclear who fired the shots. He had worked as a tailor.

August 9, 2019: The Turkish Defense Ministry announced that the Syrian Kurdish People's Protection Units (YPG) fired an anti-tank missile at a Turkish base in a Turkish-controlled area in Afrin in northern Syria, wounding two Turkish soldiers. Turkish soldiers in fire support vehicles returned fire at YPG targets. 19080901

August 18, 2019: Canadian Public Safety Minister Ralph Goodale expressed disappointment that the UK government withdrew the British citizenship of Jack Letts, 23, alias Jihadi Jack, a British-Canadian man who is imprisoned in Syria. Goodale said, "Canada is disappointed that the United Kingdom has taken this unilateral action to off-load their responsibilities." In 2015, Letts said on *Facebook* that he wanted to conduct a "martyrdom operation" against British soldiers. The man's parents, organic farmer John Letts, 58, and ex-Oxfam fundraiser Sally Lane, 56, received a suspended sentence after they were found guilty in 2019 of sending him money.

September 13, 2019: The UK-based Syrian Observatory for Human Rights said a car bombing in Afrin near the offices of a Turkey-backed rebel faction wounded 25 people. Two mortar shells wounded two people.

September 17, 2019: *CBS News* reported that Abdelhamid al-Madioum, 22, from Minneapolis, Minnesota, told them in a prison for foreign ISIS fighters run by the U.S.-allied Syrian Democratic Forces in northern Syria that he had been recruited to ISIS via a contact on *Twitter*. He said he entered ISIS territory in 2015, aiming to become a doctor. "They gave me a blank check to buy whatever I wanted… Here's the thing. People like me that see this, don't really believe the news." He claimed he lost his arm in a U.S. airstrike. Al-Madioum said FBI agents interrogated him, and said he could face 15 years in prison in the U.S. "Fifteen years is a very long time for mistakes you made coming to Syria."

Lirim Sylejmani told *CBS News* that he left his home in Chicago in 2015 to live under ISIS. He remained unrepentant and "just wanted to live under Islamic law… The choices that I made, in somebody's eyes, the wrong choices, so I face jail time." "Of course. I'm gonna die soon here. I'm sick."

Another prisoner told *CBS News* that he was a U.S. citizen, 17, from New York City. He said his parents brought him to join ISIS.

October 9, 2019: *AP* reported that the U.S. military was taking custody of two of the ISIS "Beatles"—El-Shafee Elsheikh and Alexanda Kotey—two British men accused of involvement in ISIS killings of American and other Western hostages, including the beheading of journalist James Foley. The duo were being held in a Kurdish-led Syrian Democratic Forces-run detention center in Rmeilan, Syria as of August 4, 2019. The U.S. military took them to Iraq.

Third "Beatle" Mohammed Emwazi, who killed Americans James Foley, Steven Sotloff, Peter Kassig and other hostages in 2014, was killed in a drone strike in 2015. A fourth American, Kayla Mueller, was killed while being held hostage by ISIS. The fourth "Beatle", Aine Davis, was convicted in Turkey of membership in a terrorist organization and sentenced to seven years in prison. *AP* reported on October 22 that independent public British Crown Prosecution Service prosecutors were reconsidering earlier opposition to trying Kotey and Elsheikh.

October 10, 2019: Two Iraqi intelligence officials said the U.S. would hand over to Iraqi authorities nearly 50 ISIS members who were transferred from Syria in recent days.

October 24, 2019: *SANA* reported that a car bomb exploded in Tal Abyad, outside the headquarters of a Turkish-allied militia of Syrian fighters, wounding four people. No one claimed credit.

October 26, 2019: The UK-based Syrian Observatory for Human Rights reported that the U.S.-led coalition launched at least one airstrike in western Aleppo targeting Abu Hassan al-Muhajer, variant Muhajir, an aide and spokesman for ISIS caliph Abu Bakr al-Baghdadi. The Observatory said he was traveling in a convoy of an oil tanker and a sedan. Kurdish commander Mazloum Abdi said al-Muhajer died near Jarablus during the night, hours after al-Baghdadi died. ISIS soon announced that his replacement was Abu Hamza al-Qurashi.

October 26, 2019: During a two-hour raid by American Special Operations soldiers, ISIS caliph Abu Bakr al-Baghdadi, 48, set off his explosive vest in a dead-end tunnel near Barisha in al-Qaeda-infested Idlib Province, killing himself, some adults, and three of his six children and wounding Conan, a male Belgian Malinois K-9 who had chased him. Special forces had blasted through the walls of the compound, avoiding booby-trapped doors. Two of Baghdadi's wives, who were wearing explosive vests, were killed. Two U.S. service members were lightly wounded. *The Hill, Stars and Stripes* and the *Washington Post* reported that Delta Force and the Army's

75th Ranger Regiment captured two male ISIS terrorists. Nearly a dozen children were removed from the site. *The Hill* reported that Joint Chiefs of Staff Chairman General Mark Milley said U.S. forces fired air-launched cruise missiles, guided bombs and Hellfire missiles to destroy al-Baghdadi's compound. *CNN* reported that Conan suffered some electrocution injuries, but recovered.

The *Daily Mail* reported that social media critiqued the *Washington Post*'s initial obituary headline referring to al-Baghdadi as "terrorist-in-chief", then an "austere religious scholar", and finally "extremist leader". Satiric postings using the hashtag #WaPoDeathNotices soon populated *Twitter*.

President Trump offered a different take in a televised announcement from the White House, announcing that al-Baghdadi "died like a dog" in a "dangerous and daring" nighttime operation. "Last night the United States brought the world's Number One terrorist leader to justice. He was a sick and depraved man, and now he's gone... Baghdadi was vicious and violent, and he died in a vicious and violent way, as a coward running and crying... screaming, crying, and whimpering."

CNN noted highlights from the President's colorful and detailed description of the takedown:

- "He died after running into a dead-end tunnel, whimpering and crying and screaming all the way."

- "The thug who tried so hard to intimidate others spent his last moments in utter fear, in total panic and dread, terrified of the American forces bearing down on him."

- "As you know, last month we announced that we recently killed Hamza bin Laden, the very violent son of Osama bin Laden, who was saying very bad things about people, about our country, about the world."

- "Baghdadi has been on the run for many years, long before I took office. But at my direction, as commander-in-chief of the United States, we obliterated his caliphate 100% in March of this year."

- "Baghdadi was vicious and violent. And he died in a vicious and violent way, as a coward, running and crying."

- "He died like a dog. He died like a coward."

- "I don't want to say how, but we had absolutely perfect -- as though you were watching a movie. It was -- that -- that in -- the technology there alone is -- is really great."

- "Russia treated us great. They opened up. We had a fly over certain Russia areas, Russia-held areas. Russia was great."

- "Turkey -- we dealt with them. They knew we were going in. We flew over some territory. They were terrific. No problem. They were not a problem."

- "We flew very, very low and very, very fast."

- "They had the gunfire terminated immediately, meaning they were shot from the air ships."

- "And we would kill terrorist leaders but they were names I never heard of, they were names that weren't recognizable and they weren't the big names. Some good ones, some important ones, but they weren't the big names."

- "You know, they use the Internet better than almost anybody in the world, perhaps other than Donald Trump."

- "And what they've done with the Internet through recruiting and everything -- and that's why he died like a dog, he died like a coward. He was whimpering, screaming and crying."

- "He didn't die a hero. He died a coward: crying, whimpering, screaming and bringing three kids with him to die."

- "I've been looking for him for three years. I've been looking for him."

- "We were going to notify them last night, but we decided not to do that because Washington leaks like I've never seen before."

- "This is the biggest one perhaps that we've ever captured, because this is the one that built ISIS and beyond, and was looking to rebuild it again."

- "That was to notify you guys that you have something big this morning, so you wouldn't be out playing golf or tennis or otherwise being indisposed." (A reference to his 9:23 p.m. October 26 tweet "Something very big has just happened!")

- "The Kurds have worked along incredibly with us, but, in all fairness, it was much easier dealing with the Kurds after they went through three days of fighting, because that was a brutal three days."

- "Now, Russia likes us being there for two reasons, because we kill ISIS. We kill terrorists. And they're very close to Russia."

- "Now, maybe they can get here, but we have done very well with homeland security and the ban, which, by the way, is approved by the United States Supreme Court, as you know."

- "But it's many thousands of miles away, whereas Russia is right there. Turkey is right there. Syria is there. They're all right there."

- "Excuse me. Iran is right there. Iraq is right there. They all hate ISIS."

- "The European nations have been a tremendous disappointment, because I personally called, but my people called a lot, take your ISIS fighters. And they didn't want them."

- "They can't walk to our country. We have lots of water in between our country and them."

- "If you read about the history of Donald Trump, I was a civilian. I had absolutely nothing to do with going into Iraq and I was totally against it."

- "Our K9, as they call -- I call it a dog, a beautiful dog, a talented dog -- was injured and brought back, but we had no soldier injured."

- "By the time those things went off, they had a beautiful big hole and they ran in and they got everybody by surprise."

- "And as I said, they brought body parts back with them, et cetera, et cetera. There wasn't much left. The vest blew up, but there are still substantial pieces that they brought back."

- "Osama bin Laden was very big, but Osama bin Laden became big with the World Trade Center. This is a man who built a whole, as he would like to call it, a country, a caliphate, and was trying to do it again."

- "When we use our intelligence correctly, what we can do is incredible. When we waste our time with intelligence that hurts our country, because we had poor leadership at the top, that's not good."

- "And it's really a deserving name, intelligence. I have dealt with some people that aren't very intelligent having to do with intel. But this is the top people."

- "There's a lot of Syrian people with lots of guns."

- "But he was screaming, crying and whimpering. And he was scared out of his mind."

- "And then I also wanted Hamza bin Laden, because he's a young man, around 30, looks just like his father, tall, very handsome, and he was talking bad things just like his father."

- "I wrote a book. A really very successful book. And in that book, about a year before the World Trade Center was blown up, I said there's somebody named Osama bin Laden, you better kill him or take him out, something to that effect, he's big trouble."

- "And I'm writing a book. I think I wrote 12 books, all did very well."

- "And I'm saying to people, take out Osama bin Laden, that nobody ever heard of."

- "We had nobody even hurt. That's why the dog was so great."

- "He was an animal. And he was a gutless animal."

Trump and Defense Secretary Mark Esper said some 100 Delta special forces used eight CH-47 helicopters and underwent firefights before and after the takedown, which occurred about four miles south of Turkey's border. The military took DNA samples from Baghdadi's remains, which were buried at sea within 24 hours in accordance with the rules of armed conflict and Muslim custom.

Trump tweeted a Photoshopped photo of him giving Conan the Medal of Honor. The original photo was of him giving the medal to James McCloughan, now 73, who earned it during a days-long firefight in Tam Ky, Vietnam in May 1969 in which he saved 10 soldiers. The star of the medal was replaced by a paw print. McCloughan was the first to receive the Medal of Honor from Trump.

The *Washington Post* said that the Delta Force team was supported by the CIA and the Kurdish-led Syrian Democratic Forces (SDF). It noted that the DNA material used to identify al-Baghdadi was voluntarily provided by one of his daughters. A senior Iraqi intelligence official said the arrests and interrogation of people close to al-Baghdadi yielded his location.

The Pentagon named the operation after Kayla Jean Mueller, 26, an American on a humanitarian mission who was kidnapped in August 2013 and died in February 2015 as an ISIS hostage whom Baghdadi repeatedly raped.

Military Times reported that the Malinois, whose name had been classified because he served with a classified unit, recovered and returned to service. President Trump tweeted his name, Conan, on October 31, saying he would visit the White House.

Baghdadi was born Ibrahim Awwad Ibrahim al-Badri in Samarra, Iraq on July 28, 1971. He was raised in a devout Sunni family that included several clerics and claimed to descend from the prophet Muhammad. Al-Baghdadi graduated from the University of Baghdad in 1996 and obtained a master's degree in Koranic recitation from the Saddam University for Islamic Studies in 1999. By 2003, at age 31, he was en route to a doctorate and a full professorship. But after U.S. troops invaded Iraq, he joined a local resistance movement. He was arrested in Fallujah, Iraq in 2004, and held at Camp Bucca prison, where he became further radicalized. He became an adherent of Musab al-Zarqawi, leader of al-Qaeda in Iraq. In 2007, he returned to school to defend his dissertation on Koranic recitation. Upon the death of AQI leaders, he took the mantle of leadership and in 2014 declared

the caliphate from a mosque in Mosul, Iraq after taking over extensive territory in Iraq and Syria.

Many of his adherents initially refused to believe reports of his death, noting that similar earlier claims came up short. In following days, terrorists grew to accept his passing, and moved to a jihad-as-usual status, vowing revenge.

Several officials quietly noted that some of the details released by the White House were wrong, while others were too sensitive to release. President Trump said he thanked officials in Russia, Turkey, Syria and Iraq for their assistance, but did not inform leaders on Capitol Hill, fearing leaks. Speaker Nancy Pelosi (D-California) said the House "must be briefed on this raid, which the Russians but not top Congressional leadership were notified of in advance..."

President Trump and senior U.S. military officials said that U.S. troops would remain in the area to deny ISIS access to Syrian oil resources.

NBC News said a Kurdish informant had direct access to al-Baghdadi during the summer and provided the ISIS leader's used underwear and a sample of his blood. General Mazloum Abdi of the Syrian Democratic Forces said his intelligence service had a source—one of al-Baghdadi's security advisers—in al Baghdadi's inner circle who described a room-by-room layout of the compound, including the number of guards, floor plan and tunnels. *NBC News* quoted Abdi as saying, "I think he was under a lot of pressure from his family... His relatives were subjected to harsh treatment by ISIS and he no longer believed in the future of ISIS. He wanted to take revenge on ISIS and Baghdadi himself." One source reported that ISIS had killed a family member. Abdi said the source was on location during the raid and left with U.S. forces. *CNN* identified the source, a relative through marriage, on October 28 as Mohammed Ali Sajet, who joined ISIS in 2015. Iraqi authorities arrested him two months before the raid in the Baghdad suburbs. Sajet provided information about Baghdadi's possible location, and about a courier. A senior official said, "We followed the courier, a raid killed him and that is how we got his wife. He had documents that led to his wife." The courier's wife led the Iraqis to another location where they found more documents.

Sajet told the Saudi-owned *al-Arabiya* TV station, "We didn't expect this to happen. Even he didn't expect to be killed due to his security measures... I met him in an area close to the Syrian-Iraqi border. His security was good. They were tending and herding sheep. He was there, hiding underground and there was a tent above him... Their movement was hard due to the tight grip of security forces on the area I saw him in... He was talking about deteriorating security status due to the security forces. He wanted to change his location and didn't know how to... He was in an 8-meter-long underground tunnel with a width of 5 to 6 meters. It had a library, religious books, and the Quran and things of that sort. It had lights and various things so the hiding situation was good," he said. Sajet said that another ISIS member claimed he found a location in Idlib for al-Baghdadi.

Sajet was found after the interrogation of six captured ISIS members six months earlier in Anbar. Some were related to Sajet by marriage. He was exfiltrated with his family and stood to receive the $25 million bounty for al-Baghdadi.

Military Times reported that the commando raid was launched from al-Asad Air Base in Iraq's Anbar Province and had rehearsed in Erbil, using concrete T-walls to practice breaching.

Political jockeying for position among possible successors began during the early mourning period, with no obvious heir on the horizon. Most of al-Baghdadi's Iraqi cohorts are dead. *AP* reported that U.S. authorities were searching for six senior advisors to al-Baghdadi. Few had international name recognition. Among those who might be in the running were:

- Amir Muhammad Sa'id Abdal-Rahman al-Mawla, alias al-Haj Abdullah Qardash, variant Kardash, alias Hajji Abdullah al-Afari, a Turkmen from Tal-Afar, Iraq, who was imprisoned with Baghdadi by the U.S. military in Camp Bucca over a decade ago and was one of his closest companions. Born in the 1970s, he apparently was a Baathist officer who went underground after the coalition invasion of Iraq. The U.S. Department of State reported that he "helped drive and justify the abduction, slaughter, and trafficking of the Yazidi religious minority in north-

west Iraq". In August 2019, the Rewards for Justice Program was offering $5 million for his capture. ISIS defectors reported that he was a leader of the Delegated Committee, ISIS's executive body, with daily hands-on control of ISIS.

- Abu Saleh al-Jazrawi, alias Abu Othman al-Tunisi, a Saudi citizen despite his kunya, one of two aides who appeared alongside Baghdadi in a video he released in 2019.

- A leader of a local franchise who might have a vision of expanding his scope of operations to a regional or worldwide theater.

A more visible and approachable leadership style than that of the reclusive al-Baghdadi might help a successor patch together the wounded ISIS, but make him vulnerable to attacks by the anti-ISIS coalition as well as rival groups and contenders within ISIS for the throne of the caliphate. Baghdadi's tendency to hide ensured that the group was not dependent upon a single leader, but also made it difficult for a successor to rally troops to the cause.

The ISIS *al-Furqan Foundation* media group announced in an audio that ISIS's Consultative Council chose the successor to be Abu Ibrahim al-Hashimi al-Qurayshi, variant Abu Ibrahim al-Hashimi al-Qorashi (a likely alias or kunya). "Hashimi" denotes a descendant of the Banu Hashim clan of the Prophet Muhammad's Quraysh tribe. The new ISIS spokesman, Abu Hamza al-Qurayshi, also confirmed the death of his predecessor, Abu Hassan al-Muhajir. He added, "So don't rejoice America for the death of Sheik al-Baghdadi. Don't you know America that the state (IS) today is at the doorstep of Europe and is in Central Africa? It is also expanding and remaining from east to west... Do you not see how you have become the laughingstock of the nations... your destiny ruled by an old fool who goes to sleep with one opinion and wakes with another?" The group vowed to exact retribution.

October 31, 2019: *Anadolu* reported that a refrigerator truck bomb exploded in a vegetable market in Afrin, killing eight people and wounding 14. *SANA* reported that nine were killed and 20 wounded when the blast ignited a nearby patrol station and damaged surrounding homes and shops. No one claimed credit.

November 2, 2019: A car bomb exploded in Tal Abyad, which is held by Turkish-backed opposition fighters, along the border with Turkey, killing 13 and wounding 20. The Turkish Defense Ministry blamed Syrian Kurdish fighters, who in turn blamed Turkey. There was no immediate claim of credit.

November 3, 2019: Mustafa Bali, a spokesman for the Kurdish-led Syrian Democratic Forces, and the UK-based Syrian Observatory for Human Rights reported that Turkish-backed opposition fighters struck the international medic group Free Burma Rangers, killing one of its Asian members near Tal Tamr. The Free Burma Rangers (FBR) is a multi-ethnic humanitarian service movement working in Burma, Syria, Iraq and Kurdistan. 19110301

November 4, 2019: Turkey announced that it had captured Kasmiya Awad, 65, the elder sister of deceased ISIS caliph Abu Bakr al-Baghdadi, in northwestern Syria, calling her an intelligence "gold mine". She was grabbed during the night in a raid on a trailer container she was living in with her family near Azaz in Aleppo Province. She was with her husband, daughter-in-law and five children.

November 10, 2019: A car bomb in Tal Abyad killed eight civilians and wounded 20. The Turkish government blamed Syrian Kurdish fighters for "massacring innocent civilians".

November 11, 2019: *SANA* reported that three car bombs exploded in Qamishli near the border with Turkey, killing six people.

November 12, 2019: Syrian state media reported that an Israeli rocket attack struck the house of Akram al-Ajouri, a Palestinian Islamic Jihad leader living in Damascus. He was not injured but his son and one other person were killed and 10 others were wounded. Israel declined to comment on the reports.

November 13, 2019: Turkish Interior Minister Suleyman Soylu said that Turkish forces captured an "important" ISIS figure in Syria. Tur-

key earlier said it captured several members of the family of the slain ISIS caliph Abu Bakr al-Baghdadi, including one of his wives, his sister and a daughter. On November 22, *Hurriyet* reported that Soylu identified the ISIS suspect as Yusuf Huba, alias Abu Jihad al-Din al-Nasır Ubeyde, whom Soylu alleged planned and ordered a bomb attack in Russia in 2018 and an attack at a supermarket in Germany. In a 2017 attack in Hamburg, Germany, a Palestinian man, 26, killed one person and wounded six others in a stabbing spree at a supermarket. Soylu said Huba was being questioned in Syria.

November 16, 2019: *NPR* reported that a car bomb exploded near a bus station in al-Bab, a northern Syrian town controlled by Turkish-backed opposition fighters, in Aleppo Province, killing 19 people and wounding several others. Turkey blamed Kurdish People's Protection Units militia. No one claimed credit.

November 23, 2019: Turkey's Defense Ministry announced that a car bomb exploded in the industrial neighborhood of Sinaa in Tal Abyad, a Turkish-controlled northern Syrian town on the border, killing at least three people and wounding more than 20. The UK-based Syrian Observatory for Human Rights put the death toll at nine, saying four of them were from the same family.

November 26, 2019: *Reuters* reported that Turkey's Defense Ministry said a car bomb went off in Tal Half, near the city of Ras al-Ayn in a Turkish-controlled area of Hassakeh Province in northeastern Syria, killing 17 people and wounding more than 20 others. The Turkish Defense Ministry blamed Syrian Kurdish YPG fighters.

December 5, 2019: Turkey's Defense Ministry said a car bomb in Ras al-Ayn in a Turkish-controlled area of northeastern Syria killed two civilians and injured 10 other people. The ministry blamed Syrian Kurdish fighters.

TUNISIA

February 26, 2019: Tunisian defendant Adel Ghandri, 33, suspected of several extremist attacks, assaulted a judge with his gavel during his trial at a Tunis military court. Ghandri and several other suspects were accused of attacking a military station in Ben Guerdane, near the border with Libya. Ghandri hit the judge on the head. He was suspected of involvement in the Ben Guerdane attack and two other attacks in Tunisia that killed 60 people, mainly tourists, in 2015.

June 27, 2019: A suicide bomber hit a commercial district in Tunis near the French Embassy around 11 a.m., apparently targeting a police patrol. One officer died; one policeman and three bystanders were injured.

A second suicide bomber hit an entrance to the anti-terrorism brigade in the Tunis suburbs, hospitalizing four officers.

Interior Ministry spokesman Sofiane Zaag announced on July 4 on *Radio Mosaique* that another passerby had died.

On July 2, Sofiane Selliti, a spokesman for anti-terrorism prosecutors, said that police in al-Intilaka, near Tunis, shot and killed Aymen Smiri, 23, a man wanted being the alleged "brain" behind the two suicide bombings. The suspect was killed when his explosive belt detonated during the nighttime police chase. The Islamic State claimed credit on *Aamaq*, saying that Smiri was one of its fighters.

September 2, 2019: In a clash between national guard officers and army troops against jihadis in the Kef mountains near Hydra in the Kasserine region near the Algerian border, a Tunisian national guard chief and three extremists were killed on the first day of Tunisia's presidential campaign.

United Arab Emirates

May 15, 2019: The State Security Court sentenced Lebanese man Abdulrahman Chouman, 39, to life in prison on terrorism charges. Two others were sentenced to 10 years. Five others were ordered released. Chouman was charged with being one of the leaders of a terrorist cell with links to Lebanese Hizballah. The eight men, Shi'ites and long-time residents of the Emirates, were detained more than a year earlier. Chouman had trained Emirati airline staff on security and safety.

West Bank

January 30, 2019: Israeli police officers shot and killed a female Palestinian, 16, who allegedly attempted to stab security personnel at a West Bank checkpoint near Jerusalem. No Israelis were wounded.

February 4, 2019: Israeli troops killed a suspected Palestinian attacker, 21, and wounded another at a northern West Bank checkpoint after the duo threw an explosive device at the troops. No soldiers were wounded.

March 4, 2019: Before dawn, a Palestinian vehicle targeted Israeli troops on a highway near Ramallah in the West Bank, seriously injuring an Israeli officer and wounding a border policeman. Troops opened fire, killing two Palestinians inside. The Palestinian health ministry identified the two dead Palestinians as Amir Daraj and Yusuf Anqawi, both 20, residents of villages near Ramallah. A third Palestinian inside the car was wounded and detained. The Palestinian suspects had thrown firebombs at a nearby highway earlier in the night. Hamas leader Ismail Haniyeh called them "heroes".

March 12, 2019: Israeli troops shot to death a man, 37, who lunged at them with a kitchen knife near a military post in Hebron. His father, Fawzi Sheaki, denied his son Yasser was trying to stab anyone and was merely at his job in the city's Islamic court.

March 17, 2019: A Palestinian gunman, 19, fired at two locations in the West Bank, killing Israeli Staff Sergeant Gal Keidan, 19, and seriously wounding two others. The gunman initially assaulted an Israeli soldier with a knife, stole his weapon, and fired on passing vehicles at a busy intersection. He carjacked a vehicle and sped away. Hamas and Islamic Jihad deemed the attack "heroic". The next day, a second Israeli, Ahiad Ettinger, 47, an ordained rabbi and father of 12, died of his wounds in Beilinson Hospital. Ettinger lived in a West Bank settlement and headed a religious seminary in Tel Aviv. He fired a few shots from his personal sidearm before he was shot. Keidan was buried on March 18 in Beersheba. On March 19, Israeli Army troops killed Palestinian suspect Omar Abu Leila, 19, when he fired on soldiers trying to arrest him in a building near Ramallah. There were no Israeli injuries.

March 20, 2019: The Israeli military shot and killed two Palestinians, Raed Hamadan, 21, and Zeid Nouri, 20, who threw explosive devices at soldiers securing Jewish worshippers at Joseph's Tomb in Nablus.

April 3, 2019: An Israeli civilian shot and killed a Palestinian who he said tried to stab him with a knife near Nablus. Another Palestinian was moderately wounded. The Israeli said the Palestinian "jumped on the car with a knife and tried to open the door".

June 11, 2019: During the night, Israeli and Palestinian forces engaged in a rare shootout in Nablus that injured a Palestinian. Israeli soldiers identified a group of armed suspects that they realized only later were Palestinian security. The soldiers opened fire mistakenly.

August 8, 2019: The body of soldier Dvir Sorek, 19, with stab wounds, was found on the side of a road near a Jewish settlement near a pre-military Jewish seminary. Israeli troops raided Beit Fajar, a Palestinian village. Prime Minister Benjamin Netanyahu denounced the terrorist attack. Sorek, who lived in the West Bank settlement of Ofra, north of Jerusalem, was a student at the seminary in the Gush Etzion settlement bloc, south of Jerusalem. Army spokesman Lt. Col. Jonathan Conricus said that Sorek was neither armed nor in uniform when his body was found. Hamas issued a statement praising the killing of the soldier, saying, "We salute the hero fighters, sons of our people, who carried out the heroic operation which killed a soldier of the occupation army." Islamic Jihad deemed the killing as "heroic and bold". Rabbi Shlomo Wilk, head of the yeshiva, told *Israel Radio* that Sorek had gone to Jerusalem to buy presents for the school's faculty. Sorek's father, Yoav, edits a Hebrew language Jewish history magazine and the *Shiloach Journal of for Policy and Thought*. Dvir Sorek's grandfather was the prominent religious nationalist rabbi Benjamin Herling, one of the forerunners of the settlement movement, who was killed by a Pal-

estinian gunman near Nablus in the West Bank in 2000.

On November 28, 2019, the Israeli military demolished the homes in the West Bank village of Beit Kahil of four Palestinians suspected of being involved in the fatal stabbing of Cpl. Dvir Sorek in August. Aref Asafrah, father of one of the suspected killers, said he and his ten children were left homeless.

August 16, 2019: A Palestinian crashed his car into a crowd near the Gush Etzion settlement bloc in the West Bank, severely injuring a man and moderately injuring a woman. The victims were 17 and 19. The Israeli military shot and killed the driver.

August 23, 2019: Palestinians set off a bomb at a water spring near Dolev settlement in the West Bank, killing an Israeli girl, Rina Shnerb, 17, seriously wounding her brother, 21, and moderately injuring her father, 46. On September 28, 2019, Shin Bet announced the arrest of three members of the Popular Front for the Liberation of Palestine who lived in the area of Ramallah. The terrorists used a hidden explosive device, a tactic rarely used by Palestinian terrorists in the West Bank. Authorities said the terrorists were planning other attacks. Police found another bomb. The next day, Mahmoud Hassan, attorney for Samir Arbeed, one of the three detainees, said his client "suffered broken ribs and kidney failure" and was in severe condition under a respirator at Hadassah Hospital, suggesting he was harmed under interrogation.

October 18, 2019: Security personnel shot and killed a knife-wielding Palestinian at the West Bank's Te'enim checkpoint near Tulkarem city after the attacker neglected calls to stop. No Israeli forces were hurt.

October 30, 2019: Police shot a Palestinian woman who attempted to stab troops outside a contested holy site in Hebron, announcing that she "drew a knife with the aim of carrying out a stabbing attack" on Israeli forces outside the site known to Muslims as the Ibrahimi Mosque and to Jews as the Tomb of the Patriarchs. Israeli paramedics treated the woman, who was hospitalized in critical condition.

YEMEN

January 10, 2019: *AP* reported that Shi'ite Houthi rebels sent an Iranian-made Qasef drone against the al-Anad Air Base outside Aden, dropping a bomb from 82 feet in the air into a military parade involving 8,000 soldiers, two governors, and high-ranking military officials in Yemen's internationally recognized government. Army spokesman Mohammed al-Naqib was delivering a speech from a podium when the drone exploded, killing six people and wounding Major General Mohammad Saleh Tamah, head of Yemen's intelligence service (he died of his wounds on January 13), senior military commander Mohammad Jawas, Lahj governor Ahmed al-Turki, a soldier, and a journalist. The Houthis claimed the attack via their *al-Masirah* satellite news channel, saying they targeted "invaders and mercenaries" at the base in the southern province of Lahj, leaving "dozens of dead and wounded". Houthi media said the drone was a new variant of its Qasef (Striker) drone, a Qasef-2K, designed to explode from a height of 65 feet in the air and blast shrapnel down on its target. The U.N. had reported in 2018 that the Houthis' Qasef-1 drone "is virtually identical in design, dimensions and capability to that of the Ababil-T, manufactured by the Iran Aircraft Manufacturing Industries". The Ababil-T drone can deliver a 100-pound warhead up to 95 miles away.

January 17, 2019: Gunmen in Hodeida fired on the vehicle of retired Dutch Major General Patrick Cammaert, head of the U.N. mission in Yemen charged with monitoring a cease-fire and withdrawal of rival forces, and his staff. No one was injured. Houthi rebel spokesman Yania Sarie denied involvement, saying workers tried to remove barricades to allow Cammaert's team to cross into the part of Hodeida controlled by government forces when they came under fire. 19011702

January 20, 2019: The MASAM Demining Project said five foreign demining specialists—two South Africans, a Croatian, a Bosnian and a Kosovar—transporting mines and explosives to be destroyed in Marib Province were killed in an accidental explosion. A Briton was wounded.

January 26, 2019: U.N. Human Coordinator for Yemen Lise Grande said shelling of a camp for displaced people in Hajjah Province's Haradh district killed eight civilians and wounded 30. No one claimed credit.

January 28, 2019: *WAM* news agency reported that a bombing in Yemen killed six people in Mokha, including Ziad al-Sharabi, a cameraman for the Abu Dhabi capital's state television channel, and wounded reporter Faisal al-Dhahbani. *WAM* and Abu Dhabi media officials blamed Yemen's Houthi rebels.

April 26, 2019: Al-Qaeda in the Arabian Peninsula (AQAP) posted on jihadi websites that the Saudi beheadings of 37 defendants killed "noble children of the nation just to appease America" and that it would "never forget about their blood and we will avenge them". The body of one of the Sunni defendants was pinned to a pole in public.

April 27, 2019: A bomb went off in Qataba district in Dhale Province, killing seven members of the same family, including two women. Houthi rebels claimed that an airstrike by a Saudi-led coalition hit the family vehicle, while the internationally recognized government said Houthi shells killed the family.

June 3, 2019: On June 25, Saudi Colonel Turki al-Maliki, spokesman for the Saudi-led coalition, said that Saudi special forces in cooperation from Yemeni special forces on June 3 captured Abu Osama al-Muhajir, leader of the Islamic State branch in Yemen, during a 10-minute raid on a house that was under surveillance. Authorities also captured the group's chief financial operator in Yemen and other unnamed suspects. Yemeni tribal leaders said the raid took place in Mahfad district in Abyan Province. Authorities seized weapons, ammunition, laptops, cash, and GPS and communication equipment.

June 21, 2019: AQAP was suspected when gunmen attacked a military checkpoint in Coton in Hadramawt Province, killing three soldiers and wounding four. No one claimed credit.

June 24, 2019: Local tribal leaders said suspected U.S. drone strikes killed five alleged AQAP members in Dhi Naim district in Bayda Province.

June 29, 2019: The *Saudi Press Agency* reported that spokesman Colonel Turki al-Maliki said that the military intercepted two drones launched by Yemeni Houthis, which caused no damage or casualties. 19062901

July 19, 2019: Gunmen armed with hand grenades and an RPG launcher attacked a police checkpoint in Abyan Province, killing five policemen and wounding three. The attackers torched an armored vehicle and stole police machineguns. Authorities blamed AQAP.

August 1, 2019: Suicide bombers driving a car, a bus and three motorcycles killed 11 people and wounded 29 at the Sheikh Othman police station in Aden's al-Mokhtar neighborhood during morning roll-call.

Reuters and *al-Masirah* reported that Houthis claimed credit for firing a drone and a medium-range ballistic missile at a military parade at the al-Galaa military camp in Aden's Breiqa neighborhood, killing 40 people and wounding dozens. Doctors Without Borders said dozens of people were hospitalized. The attackers targeted the Security Belt, a local force trained and supported by the United Arab Emirates. Brig. Gen. Munir al-Yafei, variant Monier, aka Abu al-Yamama, variant Aboul Yamama, a commander of the Security Belt, was killed. A journalist said the attack occurred during a graduation ceremony at the base.

A Yemeni health official said that 51 were killed and 56 were wounded.

August 1-2, 2019: At midnight, AQAP attacked a military camp in Abyan Province, killing 20 troops in hours-long clashes that lasted into the early morning. The terrorists fired rocket-propelled grenades at the camp belonging to members of the Security Belt. The gunmen overran the camp, seizing equipment and weapons, before setting it on fire.

August 3, 2019: Yemeni officials and tribal leaders said security forces pursued AQAP through the mountainous areas of al-Mahfad district in Abyan Province, killing seven terrorists. One soldier died.

August 10, 2019: Southern separatists overran the Fourth Brigade camp, pushing out forces loyal to the internationally-backed government in Aden. During the overnight fighting, 45 people, including combatants and civilians, died. Five civilians were killed in the surrounding Dar Saad neighborhood. The separatists also captured a military camp in the Khormaksar neighborhood.

August 20, 2019: Houthi rebel military spokesman Yahia Sarie said Houthi air defenses downed a U.S. MQ-9 drone over Dhamar. U.S. Central Command said it was aware of claims that an American MQ-9 Reaper drone had been shot down over Yemen.

September 18, 2019: A roadside bomb hit a government military convoy in Hadramawt Province, killing six Yemeni troops and one Saudi Arabian officer, the representative of Saudi troops in Hadramawt, Lt. Col. Bandar Murid al-Otaiby, and wounding 13 soldiers, many of them Saudi. No group claimed credit, but AQAP was suspected. 19091801

September 28, 2019: *Reuters* and *AP* reported that the Houthis claimed to have killed or wounded 500 coalition fighters and captured 2,000 soldiers in an attack near the border with the southern Saudi region of Najran. There was no immediate confirmation from Saudi Arabian authorities. A Houthi military spokesman said that the group captured "thousands" of enemy troops and hundreds of vehicles.

October 7, 2019: During the night, a bomb exploded in Wadi Nakhla, near Hodeida, killing four children and wounding two other children. All of the victims were from one family. The government blamed Houthi rebels.

October 29, 2019: A large explosion hit the convoy of Defense Minister Mohammed al-Maqdishi of the internationally recognized government while it was inside a complex of buildings used as the ministry's interim headquarters in Marib Province. Two guards died and four others were wounded. It was not immediately clear if an explosive device or a projectile was involved. No group claimed credit.

November 6, 2019: Wadah Dobish, spokesman for government forces on Yemen's western coast, said Houthi rebels fired four missiles and conducted drone attacks on warehouses used by the Giants Bridges allied force in the port town of Mocha, killing eight people, including three civilians, wounding a dozen people, mostly fighters, and causing large fires. Air defenses intercepted three other missiles. Attackers also hit a refugee camp and a hospital run by Doctors Without Borders in Mocha. 19110601

November 12, 2019: Government forces repelled an attack by Houthi rebel forces south of Hodeida, killing four Houthi fighters.

November 13, 2019: The internationally recognized government announced that a missile attack killed five soldiers and wounded 12 soldiers at a military camp in Sahn al-Gin district in Marib Province. No group claimed credit.

Sudanese officials said Iran-backed Houthi rebels killed six members of the Sudanese paramilitary Rapid Support Forces (RSF) fighting in Yemen. Three RSF members were wounded. The RSF grew out of the Janjaweed militias. 19111301

The United Arab Emirates said an attack on the Saudi-Yemen border killed one of its soldiers. 19111302

November 17, 2019: The state-run *Saudi Press Agency* and *CNN* quoted coalition spokesman Col. Turki al-Maliki as saying that Iran-aligned Houthi rebels hijacked a Saudi Arabia tugboat towing a South Korean drilling rig south of the Red Sea. A Houthi leader, Mohammed Ali al-Houthi, tweeted that Houthi forces seized a South Korean vessel in Yemeni waters and would release it. The Houthi-run *al-Masirah* news agency reported that the ship was among three vessels seized within three miles off Uqban island and taken to the Salif port in western Yemen. Kim In-chul, a spokesman for South Korea's Ministry of Foreign Affairs, said two South Koreans were among those captured. Saudi military spokesman Al-Maliki called the seizure of the ship a "terrorist operation". On November 20, the South Korean Foreign Ministry said the Houthis released three hijacked foreign vessels

seized earlier in the week south of the Red Sea and freed 16 crew members. Two vessels were South Korean, one was Saudi. They were en route to Jizan, Saudi Arabia. 19111701

November 24, 2019: Abdel Mohsen Tawoos, a leader of the Iranian-backed Houthi rebels, claimed the group detained a number of U.N. humanitarian workers on suspicion of spying, including two Jordanians who were since released. Tawoos said aid organizations conspire to "secretly target" Yemenis. The two Jordanians were transferred to Sana'a. 19112402

November 26, 2019: Colonel Turki al-Maliki, spokesman for the Saudi-led coalition, said the group released 200 Houthi rebels to advance a U.N.-brokered deal aimed at ending the war. Rebel leader Mohammed Ali al-Houthi welcomed the move, calling on the coalition to release "all war prisoners".

December 22, 2019: Gunmen fired rocket-propelled grenades at three aid organizations in Dhale Province over the weekend, wounding a security guard and damaging several office buildings. The New York-based nonprofit International Rescue Committee said that grenades went off in its office and women's center during the night of December 22. Terrorists also hit the Dhale office of UK-based Oxfam. A dozen humanitarian organizations suspended their operations. AQAP was suspected. 19122201-02

December 29, 2019: A ballistic missile hit during the end of a military parade in Dhale for the Resistance Force, a Yemeni southern separatist group backed by the United Arab Emirates, killing six troops and three children and wounding more than 20 people. The separatists were celebrating new recruits at a soccer field. Houthi rebels were suspected.

NORTH AMERICA

CANADA

January 25, 2019: Royal Canadian Mounted Police Superintendent Peter Lambertucci said police charged a minor with a terrorism-related offense of "knowingly facilitating a terrorist activity" and "counselling a person to deliver, place, discharge or detonate an explosive" in a public place with intent to injure and cause death. In December, the FBI had warned the RCMP about an attack plot. Police found elements of an explosive device. Police also arrested an adult male, Hussam Eddin Alzahabi, 20, in Kingston, Ontario, but did not charge him. The family arrived in Canada two years earlier leaving Syria for Kuwait. Their home in Syria was destroyed and their father was once imprisoned for not joining the ruling political party.

March 22, 2019: *CNN* reported that a man, 26, stabbed several times Father Claude Grou, 77, rector of St. Joseph's Oratory at Mount Royal, Canada's biggest church, in Montreal's culturally diverse Côte-des-Neiges neighborhood during a televised 8:30 a.m. Mass for 60 people in the church. Police tweeted, "Today's event is an individual act committed by one individual", and was not a terrorist attack. Police detained the suspect, Vlad Cristian Eremia, who was known to them. A hearing was scheduled at the Quebec Court Criminal Room about 1:30 p.m. on March 23. Eremia was charged with attempted murder and assault with a weapon.

March 25, 2019: A judge ruled that former Guantanamo Bay prisoner Omar Khadr's sentence had expired. He was released in 2015 pending an appeal of his guilty plea. His sentence would have ended in October 2018, but he was freed on bail.

October 12, 2019: Prime Minister Justin Trudeau wore an armored vest and was accompanied by a heavy security detail at a major election rally by 2,000 supporters. The nature of the threat against him was not disclosed.

UNITED STATES

January 7, 2019: *ABC News* reported on June 21, 2019 that high school student Ismail Hamed, 18, an ISIS follower, was shot after throwing rocks at and wielding a knife at a police officer in metro Phoenix on January 7, 2019. *ABC News* reported that authorities released documents on June 14 indicating that he had texted to a friend terrorist propaganda, including links to Osama bin Laden's declaration of jihad, a video of U.S.-born militant cleric Anwar al-Awlaki and a photo of the gunman in the 2016 Florida Pulse nightclub massacre with a message saying, "Never forget Orlando". Other texts alluded to the Columbine High School shooting in 1999, effects of Western secularism on Islam, and accounts of Guantanamo Bay prisoners. He became radicalized in the four months before the attack outside a sheriff's substation in Fountain Hills, 30 miles northeast of Phoenix. In mid-December 2018, he texted a friend that the afterlife was all that mattered and that he did not need anyone but Allah to survive. On January 7, he told a 911 operator that he pledged allegiance to ISIS, was armed with rocks and a knife, wanted to meet face-to-face with an officer, and wanted to protest suffering in the Middle East. Hamed ignored a warning to drop the knife after he had thrown rocks at a sheriff's sergeant, who shot him. Hamed pleaded not guilty to aggravated assault and terrorism charges. His defense attorneys included Mark Mendoza. The Maricopa County Sheriff's Office said that Hamed was self-radicalized and was not in contact with terrorist recruiters.

January 16, 2019: Georgia man Hasher Jallal Taheb, 21, was charged in federal court in Atlanta with plotting a terrorist attack on the White House by means of fire or an explosive, after he allegedly told an undercover FBI agent he "wanted to do as much damage as possible" and hoped to be a martyr. The FBI began investigating Taheb in March 2018, when an unidentified citizen told law enforcement officials that he had "become radicalized". He told an FBI informant and an undercover FBI agent that he planned to "blow a hole in the White House" so that the trio could then enter and attack the people inside with guns and grenades. He was arrested when the trio met in a parking lot in Buford, Georgia, to exchange their cars for rifles, an antitank weapon and explosives. The weapons were all rendered inert. For the past three weeks, the undercover agent and the other agents on the case had not been paid, because of the partial government shutdown that meant no paychecks for Justice Department employees, including FBI agents.

January 22, 2019: *CNN* reported that flights in and out of New Jersey's Newark Liberty International Airport were disrupted after reports from the flight crew of a Southwest flight and of a United flight of a drone flying near Teterboro Airport.

NPR reported that three men and a 16-year-old were arrested on weapons and conspiracy charges for planning to bomb the 200-person community of Islamberg, three hours outside Rochester, New York. The oldest was 20 and two of the suspects were high schoolers. Police chief Patrick Phelan from Greece, N.Y., said the suspects assembled an arsenal including more than 20 firearms and three improvised explosive devices. Alt-right conspiracy theorists believed Islamberg residents stockpiled weapons and were conducting ISIS training.

February 15, 2019: Agents with the FBI Baltimore field office and the Coast Guard Investigative Service arrested self-proclaimed white nationalist U.S. Coast Guard Lieutenant Christopher Paul Hasson, 49, on charges of illegally possessing weapons and drugs for planning a mass terrorist attack on politicians and journalists. Authorities seized 15 weapons and more than 1,000 rounds of ammunition from his Silver Spring, Maryland home. He had called for "focused violence" to "establish a white homeland" and observed, "I am dreaming of a way to kill almost every last person on the earth", according to court records filed in U.S. District Court in Maryland. He had built up his arsenal since 2017, and had developed a "hit list" spreadsheet that included House Speaker Nancy Pelosi (D-Calif.). Prosecutors found an e-mail draft that read, "Please send me your violence that I may unleash it onto their heads… Guide my hate to make a lasting impression on this world."

Prosecutors reported that he purchased steroids and narcotics to increase his ability to carry out his alleged plan.

A magistrate judge ordered the federal public defender's office to represent Hasson. Hasson's Internet searches included:

- "what if trump illegally impeached"
- "best place in dc to see congress people"
- "where in dc to congress live"
- "civil war if trump impeached"
- "social democrats usa"
- "are supreme court justices protected."

In the raid on Hasson's apartment, police found a locked container of more than 30 vials of what appeared to be human growth hormone. He had ordered more than 4,200 pills of the narcotic Tramadol since 2016, plus synthetic urine to allegedly bypass possible random drug screenings at work. His hit list included such politicians as

- House Speaker Nancy Pelosi (D-Calif.)
- Senate Minority Leader Chuck Schumer (D-N.Y.)
- "gillibran", presumably Senator Kirsten Gillibrand (D-N.Y.)
- "poca warren", presumably Senator Elizabeth Warren (D-Mass.)
- Senator Cory Booker (D-N.J.)
- Senator Kamala Harris (D-Calif.)
- "Sen blumen jew," presumably Senator Richard Blumenthal (D-Conn.)
- Beto O'Rourke, former Representative (D-Texas) and Democratic Party Presidential hopeful
- Representative Maxine Waters (D-Calif.)
- Representative Sheila Jackson Lee (D-Texas)
- Cortez, probably freshman Representative Alexandria Ocasio-Cortez (D-N.Y.)
- Angela Davis
- John Podesta, Hillary Clinton's 2016 campaign chairman

and news media anchors and commentators such as

- Chris Cuomo, *CNN*
- Van Jones, *CNN*
- Don Lemon, *CNN*
- JOEY, probably former Representative Joe Scarborough (R-Fla.), now of *MSNBC*
- Ari Melber, *MSNBC*
- Chris Hayes, *MSNBC*

Hasson had read the 1,500-page manifesto of right-wing terrorist Fjotolf Hansen, nee Anders Behring Breivik, who conducted two attacks in 2011 that killed 77 people in Norway. Prosecutors wrote, "The defendant is a domestic terrorist, bent on committing acts dangerous to human life that are intended to affect governmental conduct."

The *Washington Post* reported on February 22 that prosecutors told the federal court in Greenbelt, Maryland that he spent hours on work computers in planning the attacks studying the manifestos and activities of mass killers (including the Unabomber, the Virginia Tech shooter and the Olympic Park bomber), how to carry out sniper attacks, and whether rifle scopes were illegal. He was part of a project to replace some aging cutters in the fleet. Hasson was represented by federal public defender Julie Stelzig. Presiding judge Charles B. Day gave the government 14 days to bring additional charges before Stelzig could file an appeal for his possible release. *CNN* added that Stelzig argued that it was not a crime to think negative thoughts about people.

He served in the U.S. Marine Corps from December 1988 to 1993, serving as an F/A-18 aircraft mechanic and becoming a corporal. In June 1994, he joined the Virginia Army National Guard, becoming an infantryman with Alpha Company, 1st Battalion, 183rd Infantry Regiment. In September 1995, he moved to the Arizona Army National Guard and left in March 1996 with the same rank as when he joined. Hasson joined the Coast Guard in March 1996 as an enlisted electronics technician. He became a chief warrant officer in 2012 and a lieutenant in 2015. He worked at the U.S. Coast Guard head-

quarters in Washington since 2016. He moved frequently in his military career, including stints in Arizona, California and Virginia. In 2007, he bought a house in Currituck, North Carolina, living there with his wife and children. *Navy Times* reported that prosecutors called the alleged violations "the proverbial tip of the iceberg... The defendant is a domestic terrorist, bent on committing acts dangerous to human life."

On March 11, 2019, *AP* reported that USCG Lieutenant Christopher Hasson pleaded not guilty to drug and weapons charges in U.S. District Court in Maryland. He was represented by federal public defenders Elizabeth Oyer and Julie Stelzig. Magistrate Judge Charles B. Day granted the government's motion to keep Hasson detained during trial. The government had added two new weapons charges. He faced 31 years in prison on charges of possession of firearms and ammunition by an unlawful user of a controlled substance, unlawful possession of Tramadol, and two counts of unlawful possession of silencers. Prosecutors said the silencers lacked serial numbers and had not been registered.

On April 25, 2019, *CNN* reported that Judge Charles Day ordered Christopher Hasson released from detention. He had pleaded not guilty in March to weapons and drug charges including unlawful possession of two improperly registered silencers, possession of a narcotic opioid and possession of 17 firearms as an unlawful user and addict of a controlled substance. Elizabeth Oyer, his public defender, noted that he did not face charges related to terrorism or attempted murder, arguing that his detention was unlawful. There was no federal domestic terrorism statute under which he could be charged.

The *Washington Post* reported on January 31, 2020 that a federal judge sentenced former Coast Guard Lieutenant Christopher P. Hasson, 50, who pleaded guilty in 2019 to drug charges and for stockpiling 15 guns and other weapons in his Maryland home as part of an alleged plot to kill people in support of white nationalism, to more than 13 years in prison. Authorities said his targets would have been liberal politicians on Capitol Hill and prominent on-air figures at cable news networks. Assistant U.S. Attorney Thomas P. Windom had requested a 25-year sentence. Hasson was a Marine Corps aircraft mechanic in the first Gulf War and joined the Coast Guard in 1996 after serving in the Virginia National Guard. Defense attorneys Elizabeth G. Oyer and Cullen Macbeth said he was a victim of opioid abuse. Hasson pleaded guilty to one misdemeanor charge of possessing Tramadol, a painkiller, without a prescription; one felony count of possessing firearms while being an illegal narcotics user; and two felony charges of possessing silencers to suppress gunfire noise.

Hasson was stationed at Coast Guard headquarters in Washington, D.C. before being arrested on February 15, 2019. He admitted stockpiling guns, bullets, knives, smoke grenades and tactical gear in his Silver Spring, Maryland apartment. He read bombmaking and sniper manuals, racist and anti-Semitic tracts and the right-wing manifesto of Norwegian extremist Anders Behring Breivik, who killed 77 people in and near Oslo in 2011. FBI found six handguns, seven rifles, two shotguns and more than 1,000 rounds of ammunition in Hasson's basement apartment. He also had 30 vials of a human growth hormone and five vials of testosterone, among other steroids, and had purchased thousands of opioid Tramadol pills on the Internet. Software used by the Coast Guard to identify internal threats flagged suspicious activity on his work computer, such as an Excel spreadsheet with references to targets, including 12 prominent Democrats in Congress and a half-dozen hosts of *MSNBC* and *CNN* news programs."

February 21, 2019: *CNN* reported that Ahmed Ali Muthana, father of Hoda Muthana, 24, of Hoover, Alabama, who traveled to Syria five years earlier to join ISIS, was suing the Trump administration to restore her U.S. citizenship and allow her to return to the U.S. *NPR* reported that she was born to a Yemeni diplomat who was serving in the U.S., and the administration said that *jus soli* did not apply to her. Secretary of State Mike Pompeo said that Muthana is "not a U.S. citizen and will not be admitted into the United States. She does not have any legal basis, no valid U.S. passport, no right to a passport, nor any visa to travel to the United States."

March 12, 2019: *Military Times* reported that authorities in Richmond County, Georgia took into custody Kim Anh Vo, 20, on one count of conspiring to provide material support to a designated foreign terrorist organization (ISIS). The Department of Justice said she was to create "kill lists" of U.S. service members. In 2016, she allegedly joined the United Cyber Caliphate (UCC), an ISIS-loyalist group dedicated to carrying out cyber attacks against Americans. That April, UCC doxxed (posted) the names and addresses of more than 3,600 people in the New York City area, with the message, "List of most important citizens of #New York and #Brooklyn and some other cities ... We Want them #Dead." In 2017, UCC issued a graphic video of a beheading and another kill list that contained identifying information for more than 8,000 people across the U.S., saying, "We have a message to the people of the U.S., and most importantly, your president Trump. Know that we continue to wage war against you, know that your counter attacks only makes stronger. ... We will release a list with over 8000 names, addresses, and email addresses, of those who fight against the US. Or live amongst the kuffar. Kill them wherever you find them!" For a year after joining UCC, she used such aliases as "F@ng", "SyxxZMC", "Zozo", "Miss.Bones", "Sage Pi", and "Kitty Lee" and, according to the DOJ, tried to recruit others to help launch such cyber attacks. She faced 20 years in prison.

March 14, 2019: The *Washington Post* reported that federal prosecutors brought terrorism and other serious charges against five people arrested in 2018 living with 11 children on a New Mexico compound. A superseding indictment said that the group was gathering weapons and training to kill FBI and military personnel, conspired to provide material support to terrorists, and kidnapped a child who later died. The indictment said the group talked of engaging in jihad and dying as martyrs.

The defendants were identified as Jany Leveille, 36; Siraj Ibn Wahhaj, 40; Hujrah Wahhaj, 38; Subhanah Wahhaj, 36; and Lucas Morton, 41. Officials found 11 guns on the compound in Amalia, near the state's border with Colorado, as well as 11 children they said were neglected and the body of Ibn Wahhaj's son, Abdul-Ghani, 3. An earlier indictment said Leveille, an undocumented immigrant from Haiti who was considered the group's leader, wanted to perform an exorcism on the child. Amy Sirignano, Morton's attorney, said, "All of our clients will be pleading not guilty at the arraignment next week."

March 28, 2019: On April 8, 2019, *NBC News, CNN* and the *Washington Post* reported that the FBI on March 28 arrested U.S. citizen Rondell Henry, 28, a computer engineer from Germantown, Maryland, who planned to ram into crowds at MGM National Harbor in Maryland's Prince George's County in an ISIS-inspired attack on the shopping and entertainment compound outside of Washington, D.C. Henry stole a U-Haul Chevy van, plate BE 3625K, from a mall parking garage in Alexandria, Virginia, two days earlier because he believed his four-door sedan was not large enough to conduct a mass casualty attack similar to the Nice attack that killed 86 people in 2016. Unsealed documents filed in U.S. District Court for Maryland said he harbored "hatred" for "disbelievers" who did not practice Islam and confessed to the plot. He spent nearly two hours at Washington Dulles International Airport in Virginia on March 27, but determined that the crowds were not large enough to provide sufficient targets and that security was too tight. Prosecutors charged him with transporting a stolen vehicle, alleging that he stole the van to "commit mass murder". The government's detention memo added that, "He had no escape plan, intending to die while killing others for his cause." Charging papers said Henry told the FBI, "I was just going to keep driving and driving and driving. I wasn't going to stop." The detention memo said that Henry sought out videos of terrorists beheading civilians and fighting overseas. Thomas Mooney represented him regarding charges filed by Prince George's County. The Office of the Federal Public Defender in Maryland represented Henry in the federal case. The FBI arrested Henry at National Harbor after discovering the stolen van and setting up a stakeout to catch the thief when he returned. Henry had broken into a boat near the National Harbor and hid there overnight. Law enforcement committed him to a hospital for emergency psychiatric services and took him into federal custody when he was cleared from the hospital on April 3.

Prosecutors said Henry left his job in Germantown on March 26 "determined to walk down the extremist path". The family told police they were concerned for his "physical and emotional welfare". Montgomery County police reported Henry as a "critical missing person" on March 27 in a lookout notice.

Court documents indicated that Henry drove around the Washington area looking for a vehicle to steal and threw away his cellphone along an interstate highway to "destroy evidence of the inspiration behind his attack". Law enforcement agents found the phone, which included images of armed ISIS fighters, the ISIS flag and the Pulse nightclub shooter.

Prosecutors said Henry shadowed a U-Haul van to the parking garage of a mall in Alexandria and stole the vehicle on March 26. The driver who had leased the van called police to report it stolen and said that he had noticed a blue BMW following the U-Haul off Interstate 395 and parking next to the van. Police traced the BMW to Henry.

April 8, 2019: The *Washington Post* reported that the U.S. Department of State designated the Iranian Revolutionary Guard Corps as a foreign terrorist organization, the first time Washington had branded a foreign government entity a terrorist group. The designation was to take effect on April 16. *Reuters* reported that Iran's Supreme National Security Council responded by naming the U.S. Central Command (CENTCOM) a terrorist group and called the U.S. Government a sponsor of terrorism. *Reuters* reported that the U.S. published the designation in the *Federal Register* on April 15. The next day, the Iranian majlis (parliament) approved a bill by a vote of 204-2-1 submitted by Defense Minister General Amir Hatami labeling U.S. forces in the Middle East as terrorist. *Instagram* suspended accounts believed to belong to four Guard commanders, including its commander, General Mohammad Ali Jafari; the leader of the Guard's foreign wing (Quds Force), Qassem Soleimani; Chief of General Staff of Iranian Armed Forces Major General Mohammad Hossein Bagheri; and one of his deputies, General Musa Kamali. On April 23, Iranian lawmakers voted 173-4-41 to deem all U.S. military forces as terrorist. Parliament requested Iran's intelligence agency provide a list of all CENTCOM commanders within three months so that Iran's judiciary could prosecute them in absentia as terrorists.

April 17, 2019: *CNN, CBS,* and the *Washington Post* reported that around 7:55 p.m. New York City Police counterterrorism officers arrested college philosophy professor Marc Lamparello, 37, who tried to enter St. Patrick's Cathedral with more than four gallons of gasoline, two bottles of lighter fluid and butane lighters which he had taken from his minivan parked nearby on Fifth Avenue. The incident came two days after an accidental fire gutted the 850-year-old Notre Dame de Paris cathedral. No injuries or damage were reported. NYPD Deputy Commissioner John Miller said the man told the officers he had been cutting through the cathedral to get to Madison Avenue because his car had run out of gas, but the van had plenty of fuel. The Deputy Commissioner said Lamparello, who is from New Jersey, is "known to police" and that authorities are "looking into his background". St. Patrick's Cathedral opened in 1879. He had been arrested at the Cathedral Basilica of the Sacred Heart in Newark, New Jersey earlier in the week and had booked a $2,800 5:20 p.m. flight to Rome. He faced charges of attempted arson and reckless endangerment. His attorney said it was part of a psychotic episode.

April 23, 2019: Phoenix Police Sergeant Tommy Thompson announced that police arrested a student, 15, at Pinnacle High School after a classmate saw him carrying "several pounds" of potassium nitrate in a plastic bag and the classmate overheard him saying he wanted to "blow up a Muslim church".

The *Washington Post* reported on April 28 that Army veteran Isaiah Joel Peoples, 34, was arrested after he drove his car into a group of eight people crossing an intersection in Sunnyvale, California, during the evening, injuring seven, including a 13-year-old in critical condition with a broken pelvis and severe brain swelling, according to the *Sacramento Bee*. Others suffered broken bones. He was charged with eight counts of attempted murder and held without bail in Santa Clara County. The *San Francisco Chronicle* reported that Sunnyvale Police Chief Phan Ngo announced that Peoples "intentionally targeted the victims based on their race and his belief that they were of the Muslim faith". Attorney Chuck Smith represented Peoples. Peoples's mother told the *Sacramento Bee* that he had debilitating post-traumatic stress disorder since returning from Iraq and experienced seizures and blackouts.

April 25, 2019: *CNN* ran a long feature on Palestinian-born Jordanian Vallmoe Shqaire, 51, a former jihadi who spent years in an Israeli jail for attempting to bomb a bus in 1988 "acting on the direction" of a cell of the Palestine Liberation Organization, and later became a U.S. citizen. He remained in the U.S. for nearly a decade. Federal authorities became aware of his prison time in 2010, having fingerprint evidence conclusively linking him to the terrorist act, since early 2016. He had used the name Mahmad Hadr Mahmad Shakir. He took the U.S. citizen's oath of allegiance on November 6, 2008. Prosecutors charged him in September 2018 with illegally obtaining U.S. citizenship by intentionally withholding his criminal record and past associations. He was free on bond in Los Angeles, awaiting sentencing. He was represented by attorney Mark Werksman, a former federal prosecutor in Los Angeles, who said his client had worked as a parking valet in Southern California for years. Shqaire claimed his 13 family members were in a refugee camp following the war among Israel, Egypt, Jordan and Syria. He was recruited by the PLO in the 1980s, joining its "Shabeba" cell, according to confessions obtained by Israeli military officials. He trained with rifles and grenades and learned how to build bombs. Court records indicated that in December 1988, Shqaire and an accomplice built a pipe bomb, which the accomplice placed along the route of an Israeli bus. Shqaire was a lookout. The bomb exploded, causing no injuries. Shqaire claimed his confessions were coerced. Israel sentenced him to a decade in prison in 1991. A military appeals court reduced the sentence to seven years. Shqaire was released after serving four years following the 1993 Oslo peace accords and subsequent agreements. He came to the United States on a visitor's visa in 1999, then married a U.S. citizen. The woman told investigators they met on their wedding day, and she was paid $500 in a "green card marriage". They divorced in 2002. He married a second time, obtaining PRA status. In 2008, he did not tell an immigration officer of his PLO status or past conviction. In 2010, he was questioned about repeated money transfers to Ramallah and was characterized in court records as a "subject of interest" to the Joint Terrorism Task Force in Los Angeles in 2011. He was convicted of grand theft that year for involvement in credit card fraud, but given a suspended sentence of five years in state prison. He spent four months in county jail, and was placed on probation for five years. In January 2019 he entered into a plea agreement subjecting him to the possibility of prison time, and agreeing to the loss of his citizenship and removal from the country.

April 26, 2019: *NPR* and *CNN* reported on April 29 that the FBI foiled a plan to carry out attacks in Los Angeles, California, arresting on April 26, 2019 Mark Steven Domingo, 26, a former U.S. Army soldier who served in Afghanistan. Prosecutors alleged that he planned to set off bombs containing nails over the weekend at a rally in Long Beach that was organized by a white nationalist group. U.S. Attorney Nick Hanna announced that he was arrested during the night after he took receipt of what he thought were pressure cooker bombs. Hanna said the suspect sought to "seek retribution for attacks against Muslims" and also considered attacks on Jewish people, churches and law enforcement. He was accused of targeting "Jews as they walked to synagogue, police officers, a military facility, and crowds at the Santa Monica Pier". The Department of Justice said on March 2 that he posted a video citing his Muslim faith and observing, "America needs another Vegas event" like the mass shooting in Las Vegas in October 2017 in which more than 50 people died. He was a recent Muslim convert. Following the New Zealand attacks, he posted, "there mustbe (sic) retribution". Domingo asked an FBI informant to find someone to construct a bomb, then met with the informant and came armed with an AK-47-style rifle.

April 27, 2019: At 11:30 a.m. on the last day of Passover, John Earnest, 19, fired an assault rifle in the Chabad of Poway synagogue in Poway, California, 20 miles north of San Diego, killing a woman and injuring a girl and two men. The shooter posted a manifesto citing the attack on the Tree of Life synagogue in Pittsburgh six months earlier and the attacks in March on New Zealand mosques. San Diego County Sheriff William D. Gore said that the assault weapon might have malfunctioned. An off-duty border patrol agent fired at Earnest when he was fleeing, but missed. San Diego police Chief David Nisleit said Earnest called in to police to say he was involved in the shooting and gave his location. He jumped out of his car and surrendered to a K-9 team. Earnest had no earlier contact with law enforcement. He is a California State University San Marcos dean's list nursing student. He was held on suspicion of murder and attempted murder.

The online manifesto, posted on *8chan*, described plans to kill Jews, calling himself an "anti-Semite" and "white supremacist". He called Jesus Christ and Adolf Hitler role models. He expressed no remorse. He admitted setting fire to a mosque in Escondido, California, a month earlier, and dedicated the arson to the New Zealand shooter, Tarrant. He said he would live-stream the attack, but *8chan* blocked the profile. He mentioned the misogynistic "red pill" movement regarding men's rights, anti-feminism and the alt-right.

Lori Kaye, 60, was killed when she jumped between the shooter and the rabbi. She had gone to the synagogue to pray for her late mother, who died in November 2018. She left behind a husband—a physician—and a daughter, 22.

The injured included:

- Rabbi Yisroel Goldstein, 57, who underwent surgeries to both hands. He will likely lose his right index finger.

- Noya Dahan, 9, who was injured by shrapnel in the leg and face. She was with her two sisters. The family had moved from Israel eight years earlier, seeking a safer community after the parents were injured by rockets. A few years earlier, their home was sprayed with swastikas.

- Almog Peretz, 34, Dahan's brother-in-law, was injured by shrapnel while trying to protect his niece. He was visiting from Israel.

- The FBI learned of threatening postings five minutes before the shooting.

- Prosecutors said Earnest had 50 unfired bullets. He also had a tactical vest and helmet.

- During his first hearing, the judge scheduled a status hearing for May 30 and denied bail.

CBS News reported on May 14, 2019 that John Earnest pleaded not guilty to federal hate crime charges in front of Magistrate Judge Michael Berg. He agreed with his court-appointed attorney, Kathryn Nester, in her decision to not seek bail. Assistant U.S. Attorney Peter Ko said that the government had not decided whether to seek the death penalty. Ko reaffirmed plans to try Earnest separately and simultaneously with a state charge of murder. Earnest pleaded not guilty to state and federal charges of trying to burn a mosque in Escondido. 19042701

May 8, 2019: FBI, Justice Department and Homeland Security officials testified before Congress that the FBI had opened more than 850 investigations into domestic terrorism.

May 20, 2019: *CNN* reported on May 20, 2019 that "American Taliban" John Walker Lindh, inmate number 45426-083, 38, was due to be released from the Terre Haute Federal Correctional Institution prison in Indiana on May 23, 2019 after serving 17 years and five months of a 20-year sentence for supporting terrorists who harbored al-Qaeda during its 9/11 planning. His ultimate destination was unclear. He was captured in November 2001 and gave a California address. Kevin D. Lowry wrote in the *Journal for Deradicalization* in 2018 that some 500 federal prisoners had been sentenced for terror-related crimes, and about a fifth will be released within five years; 62 of them are U.S. citizens.

Many observers questioned whether he had become deradicalized, citing recent calls for violence. *Foreign Policy* noted in 2017 that the National Counterterrorism Center said he "continued to advocate for global jihad and to write and translate violent extremist texts". *NBC*

News reported that Lindh had written to a network affiliate in 2015 and said he believed ISIS was "doing a spectacular job". *NBC* said he sent three letters to the station and in one said ISIS was "very sincere and serious about fulfilling the long-neglected religious obligation to establish a caliphate through armed struggle, which is the only correct method".

Lindh was represented by attorney Bill Cummings, who confirmed on May 23 that his client had been given supervised release, which included monitoring software on his Internet devices; requiring his online communications be only in English; that he undergo mental health counseling; and that he could not own or view extremist material, a passport of any kind, or leave the U.S. Defense attorney Tony West said Lindh planned to obtain a college degree and doctorate. Defense attorney William Cummings said Lindh must reside in the Eastern District of Virginia to comply with probation.

May 22, 2019: Jonathan Xie, 20, of New Jersey, was scheduled to appear in a Newark court on charges of attempting to provide material support to a designated terrorist organization (Hamas), making false statements, and transmitting a threat in interstate commerce. *AP* reported that he threatened to "shoot everybody" at a pro-Israel march. The U.S. attorney's office said he posted on *Instagram* that he wanted to bomb the Israeli embassy and Trump Tower in New York City.

June 6, 2019: Federal authorities arrested Ashiqul Alam, 22, a Bangladeshi citizen and lawful permanent U.S. resident who lived in Queens, New York who they allege praised terrorist organizations including ISIS and plotted an attack in Times Square. Prosecutors in a Brooklyn federal court said he spent months trying to obtain guns and grenades. He was arrested after he and an FBI undercover agent bought weapons with their serial numbers removed. They claimed he feared being deemed the Looney Tunes Terrorist or the Blind Terrorist if his glasses fell off and he could not shoot straight. He had worked with the FBI agent since August 2018, praising ISIS and al-Qaeda leader Osama bin Laden, musing about using a suicide vest in New York City's

Times Square or in Washington, D.C., or killing law enforcement officers with an AR-15. The duo surveilled Times Square and went to a Pennsylvania shooting range in early 2019. The duo bought two Glock pistols for $400/each from another FBI undercover agent. The charging papers indicated that Alam said he wanted to purchase an enhanced driver's license so he could "walk on to a military base" and "blow it up".

June 16, 2019: The *Washington Post* ran a long article on the response of the Forsyth County, Georgia Saddlebrook subdivision to the January 2019 arrest on terrorist charges against a neighbor, Hasher Jallal Taheb, 21, on the corner of Horseshoe Creek Lane and Walking Horse Trail. He was charged with plotting to blow up the White House, Washington Monument, Lincoln Memorial, and a synagogue in what he told undercover agents was a "martyrdom operation". Authorities said he tried to purchase grenades and a shoulder-fired antitank rocket when he was arrested in the parking lot of a Lowe's store. He was held without bond on a charge of attempting to damage and destroy a federal building "by means of fire and an explosive".

June 19, 2019: *ABC News* reported that federal authorities arrested Mustafa Mousab Alowemer, 21, a Syrian refugee accused of plotting to attack a Pittsburgh church, the Legacy International Worship Center, "to support the cause of ISIS and to inspire other ISIS supporters in the United States". Alowemer was born in Daraa, Syria and entered the U.S. as a refugee in August 2016. The Department of Justice said he gave an undercover FBI agent posing as an ISIS supporter "multiple instructional documents" on how to build improvised explosive devices, and posted his plans and support for ISIS and jihad in social media communications. DOJ added, "Alowemer also distributed propaganda materials, offered to provide potential targets in the Pittsburgh area, requested a weapon with a silencer, and recorded a video of himself pledging an oath of allegiance to the leader of ISIS, Abu Bakr al-Baghdadi." DOJ said he had written a "10-point handwritten plan" related to a plot to bomb the church, and printed out copies of satellite maps from Google which he provided to an FBI source and

to an undercover FBI employee. He recently purchased nails for shrapnel, batteries, and consumer products that contained chemicals that could be used in bomb-making. He allegedly planned to conduct the attack in July 2019.

July 2019: The U.S. repatriated from Syria Rulan Asainov, who was arraigned in federal court in Brooklyn, New York, and charged with support to ISIS. He did not enter a plea.

July 26, 2019: *CNN* reported that authorities at JFK Airport arrested Delowar Mohammed Hossain, 33, of the Bronx, for attempting to provide material support for acts of terrorism. The US Attorney's Office for the Southern District of New York said he planned to join the Taliban in Afghanistan and kill American forces. Michael McGarrity, the FBI assistant director of counterterrorism, said that in recorded conversations with a confidential informant in September 2017, Hossain said he wanted to join the terror group and fight American forces. Hossain attempted to recruit a confidential FBI source to travel with him to Pakistan then cross the border into Afghanistan. He planned to fly to Bangkok, then Pakistan en route to Afghanistan. He purchased walkie-talkies and trekking gear, and told the informant to save money for weapons after arrival in Afghanistan. He faced 15 years in prison.

The *Washington Examiner* reported male Somali refugees Ahmed Mahad Mohamed and Abdi Yemani Hussein were arrested on July 26 after trying to fly from Tucson International Airport in Arizona to Egypt to join ISIS. Mohamed had obtained permanent resident status.

The duo were surveilled by an undercover FBI agent who was pretending to be an ISIS supporter. Mohamed allegedly started talking to the undercover agent on an unnamed social media platform in August 2018, continuing the conversation with another undercover agent in December 2018, telling him, "I love jihad so much… If I go to Syria I want to be the beheading person… I want to kill them so many I am thirsty their blood."

On June 24, the duo met with an undercover employee in Tucson, where Hussein allegedly said that he will "kill so many people" and that he sought "to be on the front line". They were charged with conspiring to provide material support to ISIS.

July 28, 2019: At 5:40 p.m., Santino William Legan, 19, randomly fired an SKS rifle at people attending the annual Garlic Festival in Gilroy, California, killing Stephen Romero, 6; a girl, Keyla Salazar, 13; and a man in his 20s; and wounding 12 victims, ranging in age from 12 to 69. He shared neo-Nazi white supremacist propaganda on *Instagram* before shooting people. *CNN* reported on July 30 that he legally purchased his rifle in Nevada on July 9. Three officers on the scene fatally shot Legan within a minute. Witnesses reported seeing a second individual. Legan had cut through a fence to avoid security and metal detectors. *AP* reported on August 7, 2019 that Legan's computer contained a target list of religious institutions, courthouses, federal buildings and both major U.S. political parties. He used a Romanian-made AK-47-style rifle. His *Instagram* account indicated that he was Italian and Iranian.

He set up the *Instagram* account four days earlier. One message included a photo of attendees at the festival, with the comment, "Ayyy garlic festival time Come get wasted on overpriced sh**." His second posting included a photo of Smokey the Bear and a sign saying "Fire Danger High Today", with the caption "Read Might is Right by Ragnar Redbeard. Why overcrowd towns and pave more open space to make room for hordes of mestizos and Silicon Valley white tw**s?" *Might is Right*, published in the late 1800s, is a white supremacist text that promotes anarchy and vilifies Christianity. The book calls Jesus the "true Prince of Evil" and says that white men must rule over those of color.

Leban was a sophomore at Gilroy High School.

CNN reported on July 31 that police found extremist material from competing ideologies during a search of a Walker Lake, Nevada home they believed Leban once rented. Police had earlier seized several weapons accessories, computer hardware, an empty bottle of the anxiety medicine diazepam (Valium), a bulletproof vest, gas mask, rifle box, empty ammunition boxes, a pocket knife, a bag containing pamphlets about guns, a sack of ammunition casings, three hard drives, three thumb drives, and a computer tower. His social media activity suggested he had xenophobic/racist views.

August 3, 2019: At 10:39 a.m., a gunman killed 22 and wounded 26 inside the Cielo Vista mall in El Paso, Texas, starting in the Walmart parking lot. Victims ranged in age from 15 to 90. *CNN* reported that the U.S. Attorney for the Western District of Texas was treating the incident as "domestic terrorism". U.S. Attorney John Bash said the Justice Department was "seriously considering" bringing federal hate crime and federal firearm charges, which carry a possible penalty of death, against Patrick Crusius, 21, of the Starcreek neighborhood of Allen, Texas, 650 miles away. Bash said the shooting "appears to be designed to intimidate a civilian population, to say the least". El Paso County District Attorney Jaime Esparza said Crusius faced capital murder charges and "We will seek the death penalty." Authorities looked into a racist, anti-immigrant and anti-Latino 2,300-word "manifesto" they believe was posted by Crusius 20 minutes earlier on *8chan*. The poster observed, "I'm probably going to die today." The poster blamed immigrants and first-generation Americans for taking away jobs and complained of a "Hispanic invasion". The manifesto also mentioned the Christchurch, New Zealand attack. Texas Governor Greg Abbott called the attack a "hate crime". The FBI began a domestic terrorism investigation.

Thirteen of the dead were U.S. citizens, eight were Mexican nationals and one was a German man married to a Mexican woman and living in Ciudad Juarez, Mexico. Mexican President López Obrador said seven Mexicans were killed and seven wounded, including a girl, 10. Mexican Foreign Minister Marcelo Ebrard said Mexico would take action under international law. Mexican officials said it might charge Crusius in Mexican courts. Mexico's ambassador to Washington, Martha Bárcena, tweeted "The intentionality of the attack against the Mexicans and the Latino community in El Paso is frightening. NO to hate speech. NO to xenophobic discourse."

Ebrard identified the dead Mexican citizens as

- Jorge Calvillo García, 61, of Torreón, shielded his granddaughter and her teammates from the bullets outside Walmart. He was visiting his son, Ever Calvillo Quiroga, and granddaughter, Emily. The three were outside the Walmart raising money for Emily's soccer team. Calvillo, a coach for the soccer team, was also shot and was in critical condition. Jorge brought food and water for the collection event. Mexican newspaper *Vanguardia* reported that he hailed from Gómez Palacio in Durango State but had spent years in Ciudad Juarez. He recently moved to El Paso and worked as an accountant. His son, critically injured, underwent four surgeries. Jorge had three children: Ever, Jorge and Alberto. His ashes were taken to Juarez.

- María Eugenia Legarretta Rothe, 58, of Chihuahua City, a full-time homemaker who came from a prominent business family, doted on her four children. She was going to the El Paso airport to pick up her youngest child, a 16-year-old girl, who was returning from a trip to Europe. She stopped in Walmart to shop.

- Gloria Irma Márquez, 61, of Ciudad Juarez, was born in Sinaloa State and moved to the U.S. more than two decades ago. Her first two children were born in Mexico; the other two were U.S.-born. She also was a grandmother. John Ogaz was her companion for 11 years. She was a health care assistant for elderly patients. Ogaz, an El Paso-born U.S. citizen, was living in a trailer but she helped him move into a home. They considered each other their spouse but never formally married. He had been waiting for her at McDonald's; she had gone to the ATM. One of her Mexican daughters had difficulty getting into the U.S., but was granted a visa to attend Marquez's funeral.

- Elsa Mendoza, 57, of Yepomera in Chihuahua State, was a special education teacher and the principal of the Club de Leones y Rafael Veloz primary school in Ciudad Juarez, across the border from El Paso. The newspaper *Reforma* said she was killed while in Walmart's supermarket section. Her husband and son were waiting in the car. Her husband, Antonio de la Mora, was a professor at the Autonomous University of Ciudad Juarez.

- Ivan Filiberto Manzano, 45, of Ciudad Juarez, had a wife and two children, aged 5 and 9, and worked in sales and marketing for years. He and a colleague at Megaradio, a broadcasting firm in Juarez, founded Grupo IVER, a marketing firm. He also had a business selling medical equipment. He held jobs in Argentina and in Monterrey, Mexico. He enjoyed running marathons.

- Sara Esther Regalado, 66, of Ciudad Juarez and her husband, Adolfo Cerros Hernández, 68, of Aguascalientes, were a married couple who lived in Ciudad Juarez.

- Teresa Sanchez, 82

- Other killed in the shooting included:

- Alexander Gerhard Hoffman, 66, a German citizen

- El Paso couple Jordan, 25, and Andre Anchondo, 24, shopping for school supplies, were killed trying to shield Paul, their two-month-old son. They recently celebrated their first year of marriage. They had dropped off their daughter, 6, at cheer practice before going shopping. They had another child, 2. Andre owned a mechanic shop, Andre House of Granite and Stone, in El Paso. Jordan was from Odessa, Texas. Paul suffered broken fingers. Andre had recently finished building his family's house. Jordan was a stay-at-home mother. The 6-year-old and 1-year-old daughters were from earlier relationships, and she had Paul with Andre.

- Arturo "Nino" Benavides, 60, was running an errand with his wife, Patricia, 63. They were paying for groceries at a Walmart register when the gunman started firing. Someone pushed Patricia into a bathroom stall and she was unhurt. The *Washington Post* reported that Arturo lived for his family, his Husky mix named Milo, and pineapple upside-down cake. They had been married more than 30 years. He had retired two years ago as a bus driver for Sun Metro, the city's public transit service. He had served in the Army.

- Leo Campos, 41, and Maribel Hernandez, 56, an El Paso native, dropped their dog off at the groomer before going to Walmart, where they died. They had been married for 16 years. He worked in a call center; she worked in the home. Campos was training to get certified as an elementary school sports coach; his wife helped him with his essays. He often wrote her long letters and gave her large bouquets of flowers. They vacationed in South Padre Island on the Gulf Coast. Campos grew up in Hidalgo County in the Rio Grande Valley. He was a gregarious football and soccer player and Mexican folkloric dancer. His dance troupe performed in parks, schools and nursing homes.

- Angie Englisbee, 86, went to nearby St. Pius Roman Catholic Church every Sunday and lived in her home for more than 50 years. She was in the check-out line at Walmart. After her husband died of a heart attack, she raised seven children as a single mother.

- Raul Flores, 83, and Maria Flores, 77, were married for 60 years, rarely spending a day apart. The U.S. citizens met in Ciudad Juarez as young adults, then raised their family around the hills of San Gabriel Valley in California. In 1959, their 2-week-old infant, Alejandra, died of pneumonia. They retired two decades ago to their El Paso house. They had three children, 11 grandchildren, and 10 great-grandchildren, with another on the way. Raul was scheduled to have open-heart surgery on August 5. The couple was at Walmart buying airbeds for relatives who were visiting for the surgery. Raul was born in Jiménez, Mexico and was a painter. Maria was born in Tlahualilo and loved to cook, listening to Elvis Presley and Marco Antonio Solis.

- David Johnson, 63, an Army veteran who was in the Walmart checkout line with his wife Kathy and granddaughter, Kaitlyn, 9. He fell toward them to protect them from the gunman, who was two feet away. They

escaped. He enjoyed watching golf tournaments and NASCAR races and helping Kaitlyn with science experiments.

- Luis Alfonzo Juarez, 90, a U.S. citizen who had immigrated to the U.S., bought a home, and had a career as an iron worker. He and Martha, 87, his wife of 70 years, had seven children, 20 grandchildren, 35 great-grandchildren and eight great-great-grandchildren. He helped erect many buildings in El Paso and Los Angeles and worked on the country's railroads and locomotives. She was injured in the attack.

- Margie Reckard, 67 (or 63), wife of Antonio Basco for 22 years and mother of Dean Reckard. She was affiliated with San Antonio In-Home Health Care.

- Javier Amir Rodriguez, 15, was a rising Horizon High School sophomore who loved playing soccer.

- Juan de Dios Velazquez, 77, who held U.S. and Mexican citizenships, was shot in the parking lot as they arrived to shop for groceries. He jumped in front of his wife, Nicolasa (variant Estela), 65, who was shot in the stomach and was recovering in the hospital. Granddaughter Daisy Fuentes told *KTSM* that the couple had six children and 15 grandchildren. They had just parked their car when they were shot. The retired couple had moved from Juarez to El Paso six months earlier after obtaining U.S. citizenship. He grew up in Sombrerete in Zacatecas State. He was shot three times in the back and underwent three operations, but died.

Texas authorities filed a capital murder charge against Crusius on August 4. Federal charges would not supersede any charges brought by local prosecutors, but would operate as a parallel prosecution.

Walmart is one of the world's largest gun retailers.

The *Washington Post 202* reported on August 5 that Crusius's parents divorced in 2011 and sold the house in 2018. His father had a four-decade drug addiction. While at Plano High School in 2017, Crusius studied law enforcement and calculus. He attended Collin College from fall 2017 to spring 2019. He often muttered to himself in chemistry lab.

CNN and the *Washington Post* reported on August 9 that Crusius told police that he had come to El Paso to target Mexicans.

AP reported on October 10, 2019 that Crusius pleaded not guilty to a single charge of capital murder in a court appearance in El Paso. District Judge Sam Medrano scheduled the next hearing for November 7. Crusius was represented by attorneys Mark Stevens of San Antonio and Joe Spencer of El Paso.

CNN reported on February 6, 2020 that Patrick Crusius was indicted on 90 federal charges, including hate crimes resulting in death, hate crimes involving an attempt to kill, use of a firearm to commit murder and in relation to a crime of violence, and use of a firearm during and in relation to a crime of violence.

AP reported that Guillermo "Memo" Garcia died in April 2020, nine months after he was shot in the WalMart in El Paso by gunman Patrick Crusius, becoming the 23rd death from the shooting. 19080301

August 3, 2019: Thirteen hours after the El Paso shooting, at 1:07 a.m., Connor Betts, 24, a gunman wearing body armor, fired an assault rifle and shot to death nine people and injured 37 while making his way toward the Ned Peppers bar in a popular nightclub district on East Fifth Street of downtown Dayton, Ohio's Oregon District. A pedestrian grabbed the barrel of Betts's .223 high-capacity rifle, but Betts grabbed a handgun and kept shooting until six police officers killed him within 30 seconds of the beginning of the attack. Betts was about to enter a bar, where a bouncer was injured by shrapnel. No officers were injured. Mayor Nan Whaley said he had additional magazines with him. Betts had gotten off 41 shots within 30 seconds.

Among the dead were four women and five men, aged from 22 to 57. Six of them were African-American.

- Connor Betts's sister, Megan K., 22, who, along with a friend, had driven the family's 2007 Toyota Corolla to the historic Oregon District, apparently for a night on the town. Her male companion was injured. Megan was a tour guide in the wilds of Missoula County, Montana, according to her former supervisor at the Smokejumper Visitor Center. Her internship was run by the Student Conservation Association. Megan was a student at Wright State University studying earth and environmental sciences.

- Monica E. Brickhouse, 39, from Springfield, Ohio, recently lived in Virginia Beach, Virginia, worked as a recovery specialist for the Anthem health insurance company and ran a design, event planning, and catering business called "Two Good Girls". She attended Springfield South High School and the College for America at Southern New Hampshire University. She had returned to her native state a year ago, having moved to Virginia in the 1990s. She and her husband, Anthony Brickhouse, and son, 6, settled in Dayton. She had purchased a record player for her son's upcoming birthday and compiled a collection of vinyl for him.

- Nicholas P. Cumer, 25, a graduate student in the master of cancer care program at St. Francis University in Loretto, Pennsylvania. He spent the summer living in Columbus, commuting an hour each morning to the health alliance's treatment center, completing an internship program with the Maple Tree Cancer Alliance. He was a week away from completing the internship. University President Malachi Van Tassell said, "He was recognized at the 2019 Community Engagement Awards among students who had completed 100+ hours of service. In addition he was a graduate assistant with the university marching band." He and three other interns were standing in line at the Ned Peppers bar when the shooter fired, injuring two of them and killing Cumer, according to Tyler Erwin, 27, who was unhurt. It was Cumer's first visit to downtown Dayton. He had an offer for a full-time job running two of the cancer organization's new offices. He enjoyed going to the gym.

- Derrick R. Fudge, 57, of Springfield, Ohio, was survived by five siblings, his extended family, and his dog, a Labrador mix named

Lucy Lu. He was having a night out with his son, Dion Green, 37, and Dion's fiancée. Derrick died in his son's arms. Green thinks he spoke to Megan Betts as she died. Fudge lived 26 miles away from Dion. He volunteered for the Salvation Army and enjoyed fishing and playing cards. In grade school, he was hit by a train while riding a bike, losing several toes. Through hard work, he regained his ability to walk.

- Thomas J. "TeeJay" McNichols, 25, a father of two daughters and two sons, aged 2 to 8. He lived in Dayton with his aunt. He attended Dunbar High School and worked at a Dayton factory. He was in the Oregon District with a cousin.

- Lois L. Oglesby, 29, a nurse's aide who had a baby in July and had an older child. She had recently returned to work from maternity leave. She worked in a day care center.

- Saeed Saleh, 38, left Eritrea as a refugee and spent time in Sudan, Libya and Malta before coming to the United States three years ago with his wife Zaid Eseyas Nuguse and daughter Randa, 5. He worked seven days a week, often 12-16 hours/day, and had taken one day off to spend time with a friend downtown. He was the father of three children. He worked to support his wife and daughter in Dayton plus two other children in Eritrea and a brother in Egypt.

- Logan M. Turner, 30, a resident of Springboro, Ohio, was a machinist at Thaler Machine Company. He was celebrating his birthday with friends. He graduated from Sinclair Community College and the University of Toledo, where he majored in engineering. He had attended Wright State University for awhile.

- Beatrice Nicole Warren-Curtis, 36, lived in Carrollton, Virginia and was friends with Brickhouse. She hailed from Wilmington, Delaware, attending Delcastle Technical High School, and enjoyed auto shop. She was unmarried and had no children.

Those injured included

- Hannah Martin was shot in the leg.

- Kelsey Colaric was shot in the abdomen.

WHIO reported that Betts grew up in the Bellbrook neighborhood and was quiet. *CNN* quoted police as saying that police had arrested Betts, then a sophomore, from a school bus. Four classmates, including Spencer Brickler, said Betts had put together a hit list of men he wanted to kill and women he wanted to rape. The four said Bellbrook High School officials told them they were on the hit list, as was Betts's sister and Brickler's sister. David Partridge, 26, who also attended Bellbrook, said the list included a member of his family. Betts graduated in 2013. He studied psychology at a local community college and worked at a Chipotle restaurant. He apparently had no felony record as an adult.

Police were still searching for a motive for the mass shooting. Police said he wore a mask, bulletproof vest and hearing protection. He was carrying 100-round drum magazines of ammunition. Police also found a shotgun in his car.

On August 5, the *Washington Post* reported that Betts parked west of the scene, then shot his first victim in the alley beside Blind Bob's pub. He then walked to Fifth Street, killing eight more people. He was killed in front of Ned Peppers bar.

President Trump initially said, "May God bless the memory of those who perished in Toledo, and may God protect them… May God protect all of those from Texas to Ohio, may God bless the victims and their families, may God bless America." Toledo Mayor Wade Kapszukiewicz said the city is "happy to accept his prayers, even if they were meant for Dayton". Dayton Mayor Nan Whaley said, "I've heard that he's coming Wednesday, but I've not gotten a call. And you know, he might be going to Toledo. I don't know."

President Trump blamed video games, media coverage, and mental illness, saying "in one voice, our nation must condemn racism, bigotry and white supremacy… These sinister ideologies must be defeated. Hate has no place in America." At one point, he sought to link immigration legislation to gun control.

Former President Barack Obama posted that the nation should "soundly reject language coming out of the mouths of any of our leaders that feeds a climate of fear and hatred or normalizes racist statements".

CNN reported on August 6 that Betts appeared to have tweeted extreme leftist and anti-police views, posted support for Antifa, and had an ongoing interest in violence. The final tweet on the @iamthespookster account on August 3 reposted, "Millenials have a message for the Joe Biden generation: hurry up and die." His bio read "he/him / anime fan / metalhead / leftist / I'm going to hell and I'm not coming back" and used the hashtag #HailSatan. High school classmates said he was in the "pornogrind" band Menstrual Munchies with extremely graphic, violent lyrics. Authorities searching his family home found writings that expressed an interest in killing people, but did not include any racial or political motive.

CNN added on August 6 that Adelia Johnson, who began dating Betts after meeting in January in a social psychology class at Sinclair Community College, said he was fascinated by mass shootings, wanting "to know what led a person to do those things". On their first date, Betts showed her video of a mass shooting. They shared notes about their mental problems. He talked of having bipolar disorder, and she had depression, generalized anxiety and attention deficit disorder.

CNN reported on August 12 that shortly after the attack, agents with the FBI and the Bureau of Alcohol, Firearms, Tobacco and Explosives visited the home of Ethan Kollie, 24, in nearby Kettering. He admitted that earlier in the year he bought body armor, an upper receiver for an AR-15, and a 100-round double drum magazine used by Betts in the attack. An affidavit noted that in a search of Kollie's home, agents smelled marijuana and saw a water pipe, commonly used to consume cannabis, and a Draco pistol. At a followup interview at his workplace, Kollie told agents he had done hard drugs, marijuana, and LSD with Betts several times a week between 2014 and 2015. He also claimed that he had smoked marijuana every day for the past decade. But when he filled out ATF paperwork to obtain the Draco pistol in May 2019, he checked the "no" box when asked whether he had been a regular user of drugs. Agents arrested Kollie on

August 9 on charges of possession of a firearm by someone who illegally uses or is addicted to a controlled substance, and making false statements with respect to information required by the federal firearms code. He was represented by attorney Nick Gounaris. Kollie was taken to Montgomery County Jail. He faced 15 years in prison.

NPR reported on August 15 that the coroner found cocaine, an antidepressant, and alcohol in the killer's system. Betts was hit by more than two dozen police bullets, and had 50+ entry and exit wounds.

August 5, 2019: Venezuela and Uruguay issued travel warnings regarding the United States. Venezuelan Foreign Minister Jorge Arreaza said travelers should "take extreme precautions or postpone their travels in the face of the proliferation of acts of violence and hate crimes… These growing acts of violence have found echo and sustenance in the speeches and actions impregnated with racial discrimination and hatred against migrant populations pronounced and executed from the supremacist elite that hold political power in Washington." The Uruguayan foreign ministry warned of "growing indiscriminate violence, mostly for hate crimes" and "the indiscriminate possession of firearms by the population". Travelers were counseled not to take children to theme parks, shopping centers, arts festivals, religious activities, food fairs and cultural or sporting events and other places that attract crowds. Uruguay also suggested staying out of Baltimore, Detroit and Albuquerque, listed by the *CEOWorld Magazine* 2019 index of the 20 most dangerous cities in the world. Venezuela suggested staying away from Atlanta, Buffalo, Cleveland, Memphis, Oakland, St. Louis, Birmingham, Alabama, and Stockton, California.

In recent years, the Bahamas, Canada, Germany, Ireland, Japan and New Zealand had also issued travel advisories regarding the U.S.

August 7, 2019: *CNN* reported that an explosion leveled a home in Sterling in Wayne County, Ohio, south of Cleveland. Police found racial slurs and a swastika spray-painted on a garage at the scene. Authorities believed the fire was intentionally set and were investigating the incident as a possible hate crime. *WOIO* reported that an interracial couple, Brad and Angela Frase, lived for 23 years at the home, which was unoccupied at the time of the explosion. The home was being renovated after a fire in July.

August 8, 2019: At 4 p.m., Dmitriy Andreychenko, 20, of Springfield, Missouri, walked into the Springfield Walmart carrying a rifle, wearing body armor, and taking selfies of himself pushing a cart before a manager pushed a fire alarm and an armed off-duty firefighter stopped him until police arrived. *CNN* reported that he told police that it was a "social experiment" and that "I wanted to know if that Walmart honored the Second Amendment." A probable cause document indicated that his rifle had a loaded magazine, but a round was not chambered; a handgun was loaded with a round in the chamber. The police department tweeted that he faced a charge of making a terrorist threat in the second degree; he faced a $10,000 fine and four years in prison. Missouri is an open carry state. Police Lieutenant Mike Lucas said, "He's lucky to be alive still, to be honest." On November 1, 2019, Andreychenko pleaded guilty to a lesser amended misdemeanor charge of making a false report after the terrorist-related felony was dropped. The plea agreement called for him to serve 48 hours of shock incarceration and two years of probation and receive firearm training. He was represented by attorney Dee Wampler.

August 8, 2019: *KTNB, CNN* and *NBC* reported on August 10 that the FBI said that Las Vegas security guard and white supremacist Connor Climo, 23, plotted attacks on a mosque, a synagogue and an LGBTQ bar near Fremont Street. He was arrested on a federal charge of possessing "destructive devices" by having bomb-making materials. He also had two rifles. The criminal complaint filed against him stated that he chatted online with white supremacists, quoted Hitler, and drew a sketch for the attacks. The *New York Times* reported that the complaint said he used derogatory racial, anti-Semitic and homophobic slurs in encrypted online conversations. The complaint said he had discussed with an FBI informant making Molotov cocktails and bombs. He faced up to 10 years in prison

and a $250,000 fine. Climo in 2016 patrolled his neighborhood with a semi-automatic rifle, wearing a full vest of magazines. Police said he was unsuccessful in recruiting a homeless person to surveil targets. Allied Universal, based in Santa Ana, California, said he had been suspended.

August 9, 2019: *NBC* reported that the Florida Department of Law Enforcement arrested Richard Clayton, 26, of Winter Park on August 9 after he posted a threat on *Facebook* that said "3 more days of probation left then I get my AR-15 back. Don't go to Walmart next week." Investigators said he had a history of posting threats using fake *Facebook* accounts, and appeared to believe in white supremacist ideology. He was booked into the Orange County Jail. He was held on a $15,000 bond.

August 13, 2019: The *Washington Post 202* and the *Washington Examiner* reported that at 3 a.m., shots were fired at the ICE field office in San Antonio, Texas. One shot penetrated a window. Police arrested a man believed to have fired from across the highway.

August 16, 2019: Authorities in Indianapolis arrested Thomas Matthew McVicker, 38, a truck driver who threatened to "shoot up" a church in Memphis and was haunted by "spiritual snakes and spiders" people put in his bed. An FBI special agent said McVicker made "credible threats to conduct a mass shooting and suicide" on August 22.

August 16, 2019: The FBI in Seattle arrested Eric Lin, 35, of Clarksburg, Maryland after he made a series of social media threats via *Facebook* between May and August against several Hispanic women in Miami. He was charged in a Seattle federal court on August 19 on a charge of interstate transmission of threatening communication. Lin did not enter a plea. He had sent messages to a female acquaintance from Spain, threatening her and her family, expressing support for Adolf Hitler and calling for the extermination of Spanish-speaking people and other ethnic groups. He wrote to her in June, "I will stop at Nothing until you, your family, your friends,, your entire WORTHLESS LATIN RACE IS RACIALLY EXTERMINATED."

She worked in a restaurant he frequented. In July, he allegedly wrote, "By the Authority of ADOLF HITLER AND GOD I HEREBY DECLARE SPANISH AND SPANISH ALL SPANISH SPEAKING PEOPLE ILLEGAL." Three days later, he called her "Spaniard" and told her he would cut out her heart and eat her flesh "like eating a Steak". The *Miami New Times* and *AP* reported that he contacted "Chris" on *Facebook* and planned to wire a man $10,000 to beat up the Hispanic woman. Three days later, he plotted to kidnap her, move her from Miami to Seattle for $25,000, keep her captive inside a plastic bin, and vowed to kill the entire Hispanic population of Magic City. He allegedly told Chris, "I don't care if I have to Pay you a Million Dollars or More I want this Done!" On August 8, he allegedly wrote, "The time will come when Miami will burn to the ground—and every Latin Man will be lined up against a Wall and Shot and every Latin Woman Raped or Cut to Pieces." *The Miami New Times* added that Lin superimposed his face atop an image of Adolf Hitler's body with the caption: "Composite of my face with the Führer and Reichskanzler Deutschland". *Lawandcrime.com* and *AP* reported that the neo-Nazi wrote, "I Thank God Everyday Donald John Trump Is President and that he will launch a Racial War and Crusade to keep the N*****s, S**cs, and Muslims and any dangerous non-White or Ethnically or Culturally foreign group 'In Line.' By 'in Line' it is meant that they will either be sent to 'Concentration Camps' or dealt with Ruthlessly and Vigorously by the United States Military." *AP* reported that he sent one South Florida woman more than 150 pages of messages of racist threats of violence and murder. He had earlier written in all-caps, "I FOLLOW ONLY ADOLF HITLER AND THEN GOD. THEY ARE ONE AND THE SAME." He was represented by federal public defender Gregory Geist. Lin maintained two *Facebook* accounts using the pseudonyms "Jake Howard" and "Eric A Schopenhauer".

August 16, 2019: *CNN* reported that three rice cookers were found in Manhattan in the morning, sparking fears that the suspicious packages were bombs. Police issued still photos from a video of a young white man pushing a shopping cart and placing rice cookers in the Fulton subway complex; a third was found next to a garbage can in Chelsea. Police took the man into custody in the Bronx the next day. He was hospitalized. The *New York Times* reported on August 18, 2019 that a West Virginia sheriff's office identified the man as Larry K. Griffin II, 25, a former resident of Bruno, West Virginia. He had been arrested three times in the past eight years on charges of possession of a controlled substance involving weapons and use of obscene material to seduce a minor. He had an active warrant for failure to report and for missing drug screens. He had a history of mental illness and homelessness.

August 16, 2019: The *Washington Post 202* reported that authorities arrested Tristan Scott Wix, 25, of Daytona Beach, Florida, in a Winn-Dixie parking lot after he texted his ex-girlfriend threats to commit a mass shooting, observing "A good 100 kills would be nice." He added, "A school is a weak target.. id be more likely to open fire on a large crowd of people from over 3 miles away.. I'd wanna break a world record for longest confirmed kill ever." He wrote that he wanted to die and "have fun doing it". During a search of his apartment, police confiscated a .22-caliber hunting rifle and 400 rounds of ammunition. He had initially told investigators he did not own any firearms but was fascinated with mass shootings. Wix faced charges of making written threats to kill or do bodily injury. He was held without bond at the Volusia County Branch Jail.

August 17, 2019: The *Washington Post 202* reported that police in Ohio arrested James Patrick Reardon, Jr., 20, for threatening a shooting at a Youngstown Jewish community center. New Middletown Police Chief Vincent D'Egidio said that Reardon's *Instagram* account included a video of a man firing a gun. Andy Lipkin, executive vice-president of the Youngstown Area Jewish Federation, said the post with the username "ira_seamus" was captioned, "Police identified the Youngstown Jewish Family Community shooter as local white nationalist Seamus O'Reareadon". Other postings contained anti-Semitic and white nationalist content, plus images of Reardon or someone else firing guns. *WFMJ* reported that police found a cache of weapons, including knives, two assault rifles, and a large amount of ammunition, along with a gas mask and bulletproof armor in a search of his parents' home. Reardon was booked into the Mahoning County Jail on one count of telecommunications harassment and one count of aggravated menacing. Bail was set at $250,000. Arraignment was scheduled for August 19. *WFMJ* reported that Reardon took part in the 2017 Charlottesville "Unite the Right" rally and was interviewed for a documentary about his views, claiming membership in the alt-right and wanting "a homeland for white people".

August 18, 2019: The *Washington Post 202* reported that the FBI and Norwalk Police Department announced the arrest in Connecticut of Brandon Wagshol, 22, after he expressed interest on *Facebook* in committing a mass shooting. He faced four charges of illegal possession of large capacity magazines, and was being held on a $250,000 bond. A court hearing was scheduled for September 6. Authorities were tipped off that he was trying to buy large capacity rifle magazines from out of state. Investigators discovered that he was trying to build his own rifle. *CNN* reported that police found a handgun, a rifle, a rifle scope with a laser, numerous rounds of ammunition, body armor, a ballistic helmet and other tactical gear in his home. Some of the weapons were registered to Wagshol's father.

August 20, 2019: The *Washington Post 202* and the *New York Times* reported that Joseph Rubino was arrested with 17 guns, a grenade launcher, and Nazi paraphernalia in New Jersey. He was charged in federal court with unlawful possession of a firearm, along with several drug offenses. Officers pulled him from the wreckage of a car accident, where they found a stockpile of weapons and ammunition. The *Times* reported that officials found marijuana, methamphetamine, and boxes of bumper stickers and clothing with "common white Supremacist and Nazi symbols" in Rubino's home.

August 21, 2019: *CNN* reported that police arrested Marriott Long Beach hotel cook Rodolfo Montoya, 37, at his Huntington Beach, California home for allegedly planning a mass shooting of his coworkers and guests. Police seized firearms, hundreds of rounds of ammunition and tactical gear, including high-capacity magazines and an assault rifle, which are illegal to possess in California. Long Beach Police Chief Robert Luna said "Suspect Montoya had clear plans, intent, and the means to carry out an act of violence that may have resulted in a mass-casualty incident." A court appearance was scheduled for August 22. He was booked on manufacturing and distributing assault weapons, possession of an assault weapon, and making a criminal threat and was held on a $500,000 bail at the Long Beach City Jail. *CNN* said he was reportedly disturbed about a human resources issue.

August 23, 2019: *CNN* reported that Delaware state troopers arrested Delaware man Brian Knight, 26, at his home in Newark, Delaware, after he allegedly assaulted a supervisor and threatened mass violence at the Elkton, Maryland food distribution warehouse where he worked. He was charged with threat of mass violence, second-degree assault and malicious destruction of property. Troopers were called to the warehouse on August 22 about "an irate individual ... damaging property and threatening to kill everyone in the building", according to the state police.

CNN reported that the US Attorney's Office of the Eastern District of New York announced that Asia Siddiqui, 35, and Noelle Velentzas, 31, both U.S. citizens and residents of Queens, New York City, pleaded guilty to "teaching and distributing information pertaining to the making and use of an explosive, destructive device, and weapon of mass destruction, intending that it be used to commit a federal crime of violence" after plotting to build a bomb for a terrorist attack in the United States. They faced 20 years in prison. U.S. Attorney Richard Donoghue added, "In an effort to implement their violent, radical ideology, the defendants studied some of the most deadly terrorist attacks in U.S. history, and used them as a blueprint for their own plans to kill American law enforcement and military personnel." The duo had pleaded not guilty in 2015. Authorities said the women discussed making a bomb between 2013 and 2015; taught each other chemistry and electrical skills; researched how to make a car bomb; and bought materials to make an explosive device. They had looked into devices used in Boston, Oklahoma City, and the 1993 World Trade Center bombings and were looking at law enforcement and military targets. Assistant Attorney General John Demers explained that the women were "inspired by radical Islam". Velentzas praised the 9/11 attacks and said being a martyr through a suicide attack guaranteed entrance into heaven. During the arrests, police found propane gas tanks, soldering tools, car bomb instructions, jihadist literature, machetes, and several knives in their homes.

August 29, 2019: *CNN* and *NBC News* reported that NYPD officers and agents with the FBI, Homeland Security Investigations and other federal agencies in the Joint Terrorism Task Force arrested Awais Chudhary, 19, of East Elmhurst, Queens, who was born in Pakistan, after he texted undercover agents that he planned to conduct a stabbing or bombing terrorist attack in the name of ISIS in Queens. He was arrested at the SkyView shopping center in Flushing when he went to pick up a knife through an undercover law enforcement officer. According to a criminal complaint filed in the Eastern District of New York, Chudhary hoped to attack the pedestrian bridges over the Grand Central Parkway to the Flushing Bay Promenade and the New York World's Fair Marina. Chudhary intended to record the attack during the late afternoon because "this is when it's most crowded." He asked an undercover agent how he could avoid leaving finger prints, DNA, or any traces of evidence behind. He asked if the agent could teach him how to build a "bucket bomb", which he could throw over the bridge onto cars passing below. Chudhary lived on Butler Avenue in Queens. At arraignment in a Brooklyn federal court the next day, Judge James Orenstein ordered a permanent order for detention and no bail. The next court date was set for September 13. Chudhary faced 20 years in prison.

August 31, 2019: In the afternoon, a woman walked into the office of a U.S. Citizenship and Immigration Services office in Oakland Park, Florida, and threw a bottle filled with gasoline and a lit fuse in the lobby. No one was injured after the fuse disconnected from the bottle and

failed to ignite. Court records showed that Cellicia Hunt was charged with maliciously attempting to damage or destroy a government building by fire.

August 31, 2019: A gunman killed seven people and injured 22 others before police shot him to death in Midland, Texas. Troopers with the Texas Department of Public Safety tried to stop him for failing to use his turn signal on Interstate 20 at 3:17 p.m. He fired an AR-type assault rifle at them, hitting one officer, and sped away in his gold Honda on Highway 191 and the streets, shooting randomly at residents and passing cars. Driving into West Odessa, he fired through the city and at shopping centers. He carjacked a U.S. Postal Service truck and drove to Odessa, 20 miles away. Police rammed the truck, surrounded him in the Cinergy movie theater parking lot, and killed him in a shootout. The injured included a 17-month-old girl and three law enforcement officers—a trooper from the Department of Public Safety and two from the Midland and Odessa police departments. Odessa Police Chief Michael Gerke said the gunman was a white male in his 30s. A neighbor said the shooter threatened her with a rifle.

On September 1, *CNN* reported that law enforcement officials said the shooter was Seth Ator, 36, a truck driver who had a criminal record. He was arrested in 2001 for criminal trespass and evading arrest, both misdemeanors. Adjudication was deferred. Ector County court records noted a 2018 traffic citation for a federal motor carrier safety violation. The *New York Times* and *CNN* reported that he had been fired from his trucking job hours before the shooting spree.

The dead included victims aged between 15 and 57 years old.

- Letter carrier Mary Granados, 29, worked for a year for the United States Postal Service, according to USPS Inspection Service spokeswoman Silvia Torres. She left behind a twin sister, Rosie, who was on the phone when she heard her scream.

- Edwin Peregrino, 25, had been visiting his parents in Odessa when he heard gunshots outside. He ran into the yard to investigate, just as Ator was driving by, killing Peregrino outside the home he had moved out of weeks earlier. Eritizi Peregrino, Edwin's sister, said her husband also was shot and was recovering. Her brother was telling them about his new job and life in San Antonio. Edwin was an uncle to two nephews and a niece and wanted to start his own family.

- Leilah Hernandez, 15, an Odessa High School student, bled to death after leaving a dealership where her brother, Nathan, 18, had just picked up the keys to his new truck. She celebrated her quinceañera in May. Nathan was in the Intensive Care Unit. The teens were walking out of the dealership when the gunman fired. Leilah's grandmother Nora Leyva's daughter pushed her 9-year-old son under a car. Nathan wrapped his arms around Leilah, taking a bullet in his right arm. The next shot went through Leilah's left shoulder, near her collarbone. Leilah enjoyed playing volleyball, looked forward to catechism classes, and was figuring out what she wanted to do in life.

- Joseph Griffith, 40, a former seventh-grade math teacher at Goddard Junior High School in Midland, was shot while sitting at a traffic light with his wife and two children, according to his oldest sister, Carla Byrne. He worked six days/week to support his family.

Parents Kelby and Garret Davis said that Anderson, their wounded 17-month-old daughter, was treated in the University Medical Center in Lubbock and was expected to make a full recovery. Her front teeth were knocked out and she had a hole through her bottom lip and tongue. She had surgery to remove shrapnel from her chest.

The trooper was in serious condition and the officers were in stable condition.

Police searched 15 separate crime scenes and multiple cars.

September 5, 2019: The Volusia Sherriff's Office arrested U.S. Army veteran Leo Arong, Jr., 45, of Daytona Beach, Florida on charges of making written threats to commit a mass shooting or act of terrorism after he posted a threat on *YouTube* during a *PBS News Hour* live video to "murder as

many people as I can". Several of the posts were anti-Semitic and referred to the El Paso shooting.

September 5, 2019: *CNN, AP,* and the *Miami Herald* reported that American Airlines mechanic Abdul-Majeed Marouf Ahmed Alani, 60, was arrested on charges of "willfully damaging, destroying, disabling, or wrecking an aircraft, and attempting to do so". He was accused of trying to damage or disable the B-737's air data module (ADM) system, which reports aircraft speed, pitch and other critical data, on July 17, shortly before it was set to take off from Miami International Airport for the Bahamas with 150 people on board. No one was injured. The criminal complaint said Alani "admitted that he accessed the ADM" and that he "inserted a piece of foam into the ADM's inlet where the line connects and that he applied super glue to the foam so as to prevent the foam from coming off… Alani stated that his intention was not to cause harm to the aircraft or its passengers." He was angry over a contract dispute between union workers and the airlines, and the dispute had cost him money. He wanted to get overtime working on the plane. He faced 20 years in prison.

On September 18, Magistrate Judge Chris McAliley denied him bond and he was ordered held in custody until trial. No terror-related charges were filed. U.S. Attorney Maria Medetis said Alani had downloaded an ISIS video on his phone and sent it to an unnamed individual. Medetis also said Alani had traveled to Iraq earlier in 2019 and that he sent a $700 payment to someone in Iraq around July 2019. He claimed he was visiting his brother, an ISIS member, in Iraq. Alani's roommate told prosecutors that Alani traveled to Iraq because his brother had been kidnapped. Someone had sent Alani an article that mentioned the Lion Air crash, citing the plane's ADM system. American Airlines fired Alani. He worked for Alaska Airlines from January to August 1990, and from June 1998 to July 2008. In a lawsuit Alani filed in 2010, he said Alaska fired him in 2008 for shoddy work. He was born in Iraq, and became a U.S. citizen in 1992.

September 16, 2019: *Military Times* reported that the FBI arrested U.S.-Jordanian dual citizen

Nayef Qashou of Auburn, Alabama on charges of lying to the FBI and destroying records. He had told agents he would execute a U.S. soldier if ordered to do so by ISIS. The FBI said Qashou arrived in the U.S. through Atlanta's airport in 2015, planning to study nursing at an Opelika, Alabama, community college. The FBI interviewed him more than a dozen times since then. He used encrypted phone apps to communicate with suspected terrorists who said he should conduct an attack in the United States. He told the FBI that although he did not believe in violence, he was willing to "drive fuel trucks, feed troops, and use a gun to defend against U.S.-led attacks against ISIS". He said he would like to join ISIS fighters in Syria because "ISIS is fighting a humanitarian war that will benefit all Muslims in the Middle East." He added, "it was his duty as a Muslim to inform the interviewing agents that he thinks the Boston Marathon bomber, Dzhokhar Tsarnaev, is innocent and the FBI should reopen the case to examine all the evidence". Qashou was raised in Saudi Arabia. He was held in a detention facility in Montgomery.

September 19, 2019: The Office of Public Affairs of the U.S. Department of Justice, the *New York Times*, and the *Cipher Brief* reported that authorities in Manhattan federal court unsealed a nine-count indictment of Alexei Saab, 42, alias Ali Hassan Saab, Alex Saab, and Rachid, of Morristown, New Jersey, a U.S. citizen since 2008, on terrorism-related crimes and participating in a sham marriage to help an unnamed conspirator obtain citizenship. Hizballah's Islamic Jihad Organization trained him in bomb-making and intelligence gathering. He took years to scout sites like Times Square, New York's airports, tunnels, and bridges as potential targets. U.S. District Judge Paul G. Gardephe was to hear the case.

Assistant Attorney General for National Security John C. Demers said that "while living in the United States, Saab served as an operative of Hizballah and conducted surveillance of possible target locations in order to help the foreign terrorist organization prepare for potential future attacks against the United States... Such covert activities conducted on U.S. soil are a clear threat to our national security and I applaud the agents,

analysts, and prosecutors who are responsible for this investigation and prosecution."

Geoffrey S. Berman, the United States attorney in Manhattan, said that "Alexei Saab allegedly used his training to scout possible targets throughout the U.S... Even though Saab was a naturalized American citizen, his true allegiance was to Hizballah, the terrorist organization responsible for decades of terrorist attacks that have killed hundreds, including U.S. citizens and military personnel. Thankfully, Saab is now in federal custody, and faces significant prison time for his alleged crimes."

The Department of Justice complaint explained that "The Islamic Jihad Organization (IJO), which is also known as the External Security Organization and '910,' is a component of Hizballah responsible for the planning and coordination of intelligence, counterintelligence, and terrorist activities on behalf of Hizballah outside of Lebanon.

"Saab joined Hizballah in 1996. Saab's first Hizballah operation occurred in Lebanon, where he was tasked with observing and reporting on the movements of Israeli and Southern Lebanese Army soldiers in Yaroun, Lebanon. Among other things, Saab reported on patrol schedules and formations, procedures at security checkpoints, and the vehicles used by soldiers.

"In approximately 1999, Saab attended his first Hizballah training. The training focused on the use of firearms, and Saab handled and fired an AK-47, an M16 rifle, and a pistol, and threw grenades. In 2000, Saab transitioned to membership in Hizballah's unit responsible for external operations, the IJO, and he then received extensive training in IJO tradecraft, weapons, and military tactics, including how to construct bombs and other explosive devices. In 2004 and 2005, Saab attended explosives training in Lebanon during which he received detailed instruction in, among other things, triggering mechanisms, explosive substances, detonators, and the assembly of circuits.

"In 2000, Saab lawfully entered the United States using a Lebanese passport. In 2005, Saab applied for naturalized citizenship and falsely affirmed, under penalty of perjury, that he had never been 'a member of or in any way associated with ... a terrorist organization.' In August 2008, Saab became a naturalized U.S. citizen.

"While living in the United States, Saab remained an IJO operative, continued to receive military training in Lebanon, and conducted numerous operations for the IJO. For example, Saab surveilled dozens of locations in New York City—including the United Nations headquarters, the Statue of Liberty, Rockefeller Center, Times Square, the Empire State Building, and local airports, tunnels, and bridges—and provided detailed information on these locations, including photographs, to the IJO. In particular, Saab focused on the structural weaknesses of locations he surveilled in order to determine how a future attack could cause the most destruction. Saab's reporting to the IJO included the materials used to construct a particular target, how close in proximity one could get to a target, and site weaknesses or "soft spots" that the IJO could exploit if it attacked a target in the future. Saab conducted similar intelligence gathering in a variety of American cities. The FBI recovered photographs from Saab's electronic devices reflecting his surveillance activities, including photographs of New York City landmarks.

"In addition to his attack-planning activities in the United States, Saab conducted operations abroad. For example, Saab attempted to murder a man he later understood to be a suspected Israeli spy. Saab pointed a firearm at the individual at close range and pulled the trigger twice, but the firearm did not fire. Saab also conducted intelligence-gathering for Hizballah in Istanbul, Turkey.

"Finally, unrelated to his IJO activities, in July 2012, Saab married another individual (CC-1) so that CC-1 could apply for naturalized citizenship in the United States based on their marriage. On March 13, 2015, Saab and CC-1 jointly filed a petition seeking to obtain naturalized citizenship for CC-1. In doing so, Saab and CC-1 falsely claimed under penalty of perjury that their marriage was 'not for the purpose of procuring an immigration benefit.'

"Saab is charged with

- providing material support to a designated foreign terrorist organization, which carries a maximum sentence of 20 years in prison;

- conspiracy to provide material support and resources to a designated foreign terrorist organization, which carries a maximum sentence of 20 years in prison;

- receiving military-type training from a designated foreign terrorist organization, which carries a sentence of 10 years in prison or a fine;

- conspiracy to receive military-type training from a designated foreign terrorist organization, which carries a maximum sentence of five years in prison;

- unlawful procurement of citizenship or naturalization to facilitate an act of international terrorism, which carries a maximum sentence of 25 years in prison;

- marriage fraud conspiracy, which carries a maximum sentence of five years;

- citizenship application fraud, which carries a maximum sentence of 10 years;

- naturalization fraud, which carries a maximum sentence of five years; and

- making false statements, which carries a maximum sentence of five years. (Editor's note: bullets by Ed, not DOJ.)

"The maximum potential sentences in this case are prescribed by Congress and are provided here for informational purposes only, as any sentencing of the defendant will be determined by a judge.

"This prosecution is being handled by the Office's Terrorism and International Narcotics Unit. Assistant U.S. Attorneys Michael K. Krouse and Jason A. Richman are in charge of the prosecution, with assistance from Trial Attorneys Bridget Behling and Alexandra Hughes of the Counterterrorism Section."

September 21, 2019: *NPR, ABC News,* and *CNN* reported that the FBI on September 21, 2019 arrested Army Spc. Jarrett William Smith, 24, an infantry soldier stationed at Fort Riley, Kansas, who allegedly planned to fight with the paramilitary neo-Nazi Azov Battalion in Ukraine. The Justice Department charged him with one count of distributing information related to explosives and weapons of mass destruction over social media. He faced up to 20 years in federal prison.

The FBI began looking into his activities in March 2019, after determining that he had given bomb-making lessons over *Facebook*. He wrote to an extremist, "To fight is what I want to do." Before joining the Army in Conway, South Carolina in 2017, he was active in the far right for several years. He was initially stationed at Fort Bliss, Texas. He moved to Fort Riley in July 2019. The military said he was promoted in June 2019 to specialist. He had not deployed.

In 2016, he corresponded on *Facebook* with mentor Craig Lang, a U.S.-based extremist who traveled to Ukraine to fight with Right Sector far-right militants. The duo met at least once in person, in El Paso, Texas. Smith wrote to Lang that if he could not get to Ukraine by October 2016, he planned to join the U.S. Army. Lang replied that he would put Smith in touch with a militant who vetted volunteers, noting "You may also be asked to kill certain people" who fall into the "bad graces of certain groups". Authorities said that in December 2018, Smith led a *Facebook* group chat in which he boasted about his skill at making homemade bombs, observing, "Oh yeah, I got knowledge of IEDs for days… We can make cell phone IEDs in the style of the Afghans. I can teach you that." He posted a DIY guide for building a cellphone detonator and how to make explosive material out of match heads.

On August 19, 2019, Smith began chatting with an FBI confidential source posing as a fellow far-right extremist. Smith allegedly talked about killing members of the far-left group Antifa and about targeting cell towers or a local news station. He later advocated car bombing the headquarters of a major news network. He suggested remotely detonating a "large vehicle bomb. Fill a vehicle full of [explosives] then fill a ping pong ball with [commonly available chemical] via drilling then injection. Put the ball in the tank of the vehicle and leave. 30 minutes later, BOOM."

Smith talked with an undercover FBI employee via *Telegram*. The FBI officer called Smith "brother", requesting assistance in building a car bomb that would be stable enough to transport from Oklahoma to Texas. Smith responded with instructions for what he called "a Middle

East-style bomb" that could damage or destroy U.S. military vehicles. "Most of the time it can obliterate civilian vehicles and people nearby." The operative told Smith the target was "TX politician", preferably federal government and congressional targets. Smith offered instructions on building "a quick and cheap gas grenade" with "One hell of a wallop and it leaves behind a toxic chlorine gas". When asked on September 20 for suggested Texas targets, Smith replied: "Outside of [Presidential candidate] Beto [O'Rourke]? I don't know enough people that would be relevant enough to cause a change if they died." The FBI arrested Smith on September 21.

Smith admitted to an FBI agent that he often shared his bomb-making expertise "even with individuals who tell him they intend to use the information to cause harm to others". He wanted to cause "chaos".

ABC News reported that Lang faced federal charges in Florida, North Carolina and Arizona in separate cases with alleged ties to a murdered couple in Florida, the terrorist group al-Shabaab, and groups fighting against the Venezuelan government. Court documents indicated that in 2017 Lang met another Army veteran, Alex Jared Zwiefelhofer, in Ukraine, where they fought with the Right Sector. In June 2017, the duo traveled to Kenya because they wanted to fight al-Shabaab there. They were stopped when they tried to enter South Sudan and expelled to the United States. Because Lang had failed to pay outstanding child support payments, his passport was canceled. In April 2018, Lang and Zwiefelhofer allegedly killed a husband and wife in Lee County, Florida, during an armed robbery to fund travel to Venezuela, where they wanted to fight against the Venezuelan government. Court documents indicated that in August 2018, Lang met three others at a Roxboro, North Carolina hotel, where they planned to have Lang give one of the men guns and money in exchange for using his personal information and documents to obtain a passport in that man's name. On September 11, 2018, Lang provided the man a suitcase with four pistols, a military smoke grenade and about $1500 in cash. A week later, Lang bought a flight to Ukraine using the man's identity. Lang then used an altered version of his original revoked passport to obtain a Mexican visa. In late September 2018 he went to Mexico and then Bogota, Colombia. On November 23, 2018, he left Colombia for Madrid, Spain. The court suggested he then entered Ukraine, where he currently resides.

Lang was indicted in Arizona on one count of misuse of a passport. He and three alleged co-conspirators were indicted in the Eastern District of North Carolina on nine counts of identity theft- and fraud-related charges. He and Zwiefelhofer were indicted in the Middle District of Florida on four counts for the armed robbery that left two people dead.

Smith was scheduled to appear in a federal court in Topeka, Kansas on September 26 for a detention hearing.

September 23, 2019: U.S. Magistrate Judge Thomas Wilson denied bond and ordered Daniel McMahon to continue to be jailed on charges of cyberstalking and making racist threats against a black activist in Virginia. The judge cited Wilson's mental instability, ability to obtain firearms, and praise of mass killings in Pittsburgh and Charleston, South Carolina, indicating that he remained a threat to the community.

October 3, 2019: *CNN* reported that the FBI's New York Field Office announced that blue lasers had been pointed at incoming planes near New York's JFK International Airport. Pilots reported eye injuries from the lasers, which appeared to originate from Roslyn, New York, a town on Long Island. Pointing lasers at aircraft is a felony punishable by up to five years in prison, up to a $250,000 fine, or both. The FAA said there were 147 reported laser strike incidents in 2018 and 92 in 2019 through September 7 for the metro New York and New Jersey area. There were 6,754 laser strikes in the U.S. in 2017, a 250 percent increase since 2010.

CNN and *AP* reported that Hillsborough County Sheriff Chad Chronister announced that Michelle Louise Kolts, 27, of Tampa Bay, Florida, was arrested shortly after midnight on 24 counts of making a destructive device with intent to harm or property damage, a second-degree felony carrying a 15-year sentence. Her parents tipped deputies after finding "what appeared

to be a significant amount of pipe bombs, other bomb-making materials and numerous weapons", including smokeless pistol powder, axes, bows and arrows, 23 knives, fused material, two hatchets, two BB pellet type rifles, six BB pellet type handguns, nunchucks and "dozens of books and DVDs about murder, mass killing, domestic terrorism and bomb making" in her bedroom. Each pipe bomb was filled with nails or metallic pellets. Police said it would have taken "less than 60 seconds per device to add the powder and fuse materials she already possessed to detonate each bomb". Kolts admitted to making the bombs and said they were meant to hurt people. Investigators found no concrete plans to use the bombs. She was arrested at her place of work.

October 15, 2019: *CNN* and *KTVH* reported that a homemade bomb exploded on the playground of Rossiter Elementary School in Helena, Montana, shortly after a school official found it. No children were injured. The bomb consisted of a soda bottle with duct tape around it.

November 1, 2019: *CNN* reported that a man was videotaped throwing acid in the face of U.S. citizen Mahud Villalaz, 42, a welder, at 8:30 p.m., causing second-degree burns. The two men were arguing over how Villalaz had parked his car at 13th and Cleveland in a bus lane near a Mexican restaurant. Milwaukee Police Public Information Officer Sgt. Sheronda Grant announced the arrest of a 61-year-old man who told Villalaz to "go back to (his) country". The District Attorney's Office was expected to file charges later in the week. *WISN* reported that Villalaz said his attacker called him an "illegal" before throwing acid in his face, adding, "I believe (I) am a victim of a hate crime because (of) how he approached me." Villalaz was originally from Peru. He had been in the U.S. for 19 years. The *Milwaukee Journal-Sentinel* reported that the attacker said "Why did you come here and invade my country?"

Villalaz became a U.S. citizen in 2013.

The *Washington Post* reported on November 7 that a Milwaukee white male, Clifton Blackwell, 61, was charged with first-degree reckless injury in a hate crime using a dangerous weapon. He faced 25 years in prison and $100,000 in fines. The Prosecutors' decision to pursue hate crime and dangerous weapon enhancements meant Blackwell could face 10 more years' imprisonment. In a search of Blackwell's home, police found hydrochloric acid, four bottles of sulfuric acid, and two bottles of drain opener made of lye. Bond was set at $20,000 on the condition that he wear an electronic monitoring device. He was banned from contact with acids or large batteries. Blackwell was earlier convicted of false imprisonment and pointing a gun at a person.

November 1, 2019: *ABC News, NPR* and *AP* reported that during the night, FBI officials arrested Richard Holzer, 27, of Pueblo, Colorado, a self-described skinhead and white supremacist who was allegedly planning to bomb Colorado's second-oldest synagogue, the Reform Jewish Temple Emanuel in Pueblo. The arrest affidavit alleged that he told an undercover FBI agent that he hoped to poison members of the synagogue and claimed he had paid off a "Mexican cook to hex and poison" attendees by putting arsenic in the water pipes as part of a "racial holy war". Investigators deemed the plot a hate crime and an act of domestic terrorism. The FBI detained him after he picked up what he thought was a bundle of pipe bombs and dynamite from undercover agents—the two pipe bombs and 14 sticks of dynamite were inert. FBI Special Agent John W. Smith wrote in the filing that Holzer was wearing a Nazi armband during the meeting and carrying a copy of Mein Kampf. On November 4, Holzer was charged with attempting to obstruct people from exercising their religion through force and attempted use of explosives and fire. He faced 20 years in prison. He was assigned a public defender. Earlier in the year, Holzer had posted hate-filled, anti-Semitic rants on social media. An undercover agent posing as a white supremacist contacted Holzer on *Facebook* in late September 2019 after being tipped off about his online comments. Holzer replied with photos of himself holding guns and wearing swastikas and other white supremacist paraphernalia. Holzer bragged that he had tried to "hex and poison" the water at the Temple Emanuel synagogue in 2018. He told the agent that he paid a cook to put arsenic in the water pipes and that he intended to do it again on Hallow-

een. He wanted to "make them know they're not wanted here" and said he was "getting ready for RAHOWA", a white supremacist acronym for "racial holy war". He allegedly posted "I wish the Holocaust really did happen... They need to die." In other postings, he claimed he hated Jews "with a passion" and spoke about how he wanted to "die in a cop Shoot out". He allegedly told the undercover agent he was a former member of the Ku Klux Klan.

CNN reported on October 16, 2020 that Holzer pleaded guilty in federal court to federal hate crime and explosives charges. The Justice Department announced that "Holzer pleaded guilty to intentionally attempting to obstruct persons in the enjoyment of their free exercise of religious beliefs...and with attempting to maliciously damage and destroy, by means of fire and explosives, a building used in interstate commerce... The actions Holzer admitted in the plea agreement meet the federal definition of domestic terrorism, as they involved criminal acts dangerous to human life that were intended to intimidate or coerce a civilian population." Sentencing was scheduled for January 20, 2021. He faced 20 years in prison for the hate crime charge and 20 years for the explosives charge, plus a fine of up to $250,000 and a term of supervised release.

November 15, 2019: *News4Jax.com* and the *Florida Times-Union* reported that the FBI in Roanoke, Virginia, arrested Romeo Xavier Langhorne, 30, who has addresses in Rocky Mount, Virginia, and St. Augustine, Florida, for attempting to provide material support to ISIS. He was held at the Western Virginia Regional Jail in Salem, Virginia. A federal complaint said Langhorne had been directing an undercover FBI agent since February 2019 in the production of a video intended to provide instructions on how to acquire materials and create TATP, an explosive. Langhorne came to the attention of law enforcement in 2014, when he posted pro-ISIS images on *Facebook*. He posted an image captioned "SEEKING TO KILL AND BE KILLED" and a picture of himself with his face covered in a red Arab headdress. He had conversations with an FBI agent until November 7. He had lived at a mobile home park off Francis Street in Roanoke. He faced 20 years and a fine.

November 19, 2019: The *Washington Post* reported that police in northern Georgia arrested a white 16-year-old girl who was plotting to kill parishioners at the mostly black Bethel African Methodist Episcopal Church in Gainesville. She was charged with attempting to commit murder after students at her high school told administrators she had a notebook filled with "detailed plans" to kill. Sgt. Kevin Holbrook of the Gainesville Police Department said that the alleged plot was "definitely racially motivated". The notebook included "manifesto-type" language that discussed how she wanted to assault black parishioners with butcher knives and other sharp-edged weapons. "There were many writings and drawings, different depictions, and a lot of hateful messages in it… As far as the details go, they were down to very specific information." She researched African American churches online, choosing Bethel AME Church because it is small. Investigators believed she went to the church earlier in November, possibly to carry out the attack, but the building was empty.

November 25, 2019: *WSVN Channel 7* and the *Washington Post* reported that the U.S. attorney's office in Southern Florida announced the arrest of Salman Rashid, 23, of North Miami Beach on charges of soliciting another person to commit a crime of violence. Rashid "solicited confidential human sources" he believed could connect him with ISIS but who were working with the FBI. He wanted to attack deans at two Florida colleges where he had been suspended or expelled. The 22-page federal criminal complaint said he wanted to find ISIS members who would conduct the bombing for him. He initially planned to hit a religious building or a nightclub with explosives "as big as possible" before settling on the college deans. He was denied bond. He was assigned a public defender. Rashid faced 20 years in prison. The complaint detailed Rashid's litany of violent, misogynistic and extremist social media posts and messages to individuals. Miami Dade College suspended him in December 2018 for threatening a female classmate; one message stated "In the hereafter, we will meet once again. But things will be a little different :). You will not have excuses, will not be given a choice and will have to come close to me …," In February 2019,

he posted, "Feminists are a Cancer on Earth. If I had Authority, I Would Strip their skin from Flesh and Hang their Bodies in the Sun to Rot." Broward College expelled him in May 2019 for failing to disclose the disciplinary matter at MDC. In April 2018, the FBI began an investigation when Rashid posted on *Facebook* that he "advocated for the violent overthrow of democracy and the establishment of Islamic law". An FBI source reached out to him to "establish an online friendship" and "build rapport". His next court appearance was scheduled for November 27, 2019.

December 2, 2019: *CNN* reported that the FBI offered $5 million for information leading to the arrest of Jehad Serwan Mostafa, alias Ahmed Gurey, alias Ahmed, alias Anwar, alias Abu Anwar al-Muhajir, alias Abu Abdallah al-Muhajir, 37, a U.S. citizen on the Bureau's Most Wanted Terrorist List. An unsealed federal indictment accused him of providing material support to al-Shabaab. US Attorney for the Southern District of California Robert Brewer said, "We believe this defendant is the highest-ranking U.S. citizen fighting overseas with a terrorist organization… Al-Shabaab's reign of terror threatens U.S. national security, our international allies and innocent civilians. Today we seek the public's assistance in capturing Mostafa and disrupting al-Shabaab." San Diego special-agent-in-charge Scott Brunner said Mostafa was believed to be in Somalia. He was linked to the use of improvised explosive devices in attacks in Somalia. He grew up in San Diego, California, attending high school and college there before traveling to Yemen and Somalia in 2005. While in Somalia, he fought against Ethiopian forces and later joined al-Shabaab. In 2009, he was indicted on three counts of providing support to a terrorist organization. The superseding indictment included alleged activities in support of al-Shabaab that took place from March 2008 to February 2017. FBI Special Agent Erin Westfall said, "Over the past decade, Mostafa has held positions within al-Shabaab's explosives department, media wing, and training camps… We believe he will continue to play an active role in terrorist acts that al-Shabaab commits until he is stopped."

December 3, 2019: U.S. District Court in Manhattan sentenced naturalized U.S. citizen Ali Kourani, 35, a native of Lebanon and member of Lebanese Hizballah, to 40 years in federal prison for gathering intelligence on potential sites for terrorist attacks in New York City. He became the first member of the Islamic Jihad Organization, an arm of Hizballah, to be convicted and sentenced in the United States. He was under investigation when he sought out the FBI in 2017 and offered to work as an informant in support of the Bureau's counterterrorism efforts. He misled investigators. A jury convicted him on several terrorism counts in May 2019 after an eight-day trial. He was part of the IJO's efforts to scout possible vulnerabilities at various sites, including John F. Kennedy International Airport, a military armory in Harlem and the federal building in Lower Manhattan, which houses a day-care center in addition to 7,000 federal employees and 30 agencies. He tried to procure weapons and went to China to find chemicals that could be used to make explosives. He joined the IJO when he was 16 and moved to the United States legally in 2003. He was a member of the terrorist group when he applied for citizenship in August 2008. He earned a biomedical engineering degree in 2009, as well as an MBA in 2013. His wife divorced him and took the children to Canada.

December 4, 2019: *Navy Times, CNN, KGMB/KHNL* and the *Washington Post* reported that Rear Admiral Robert B. Chadwick II, commander of Navy Region Hawaii, said an active duty sailor shot to death two people and injured another before committing suicide in a shooting spree near the Los Angeles-class attack submarine *U.S.S. Columbia*, which was undergoing repairs while in dry dock in Pearl Harbor Naval Shipyard and Intermediate Maintenance Facility, Hawaii. The shooter was assigned to the *Columbia*. He hit three Department of Defense civilian workers near the shipyard's Dry Dock 2 around 2:30 p.m. *Navy Times* reported that the three men were members of the International Federation of Professional and Technical Engineers Local 121. *AP* identified the shooter as Machinist's Mate Auxiliary Fireman Gabriel Antonio Romero, 22, a watchstander on the *Columbia*. He

fired his service rifle at the victims, then killed himself with his service pistol. Vincent Kapoi, Jr., 30, was killed, according to his wife, Tara. Kapoi grew up in Waianae, in western Oahu. *Navy Times* reported on December 10 that Roger Nakamine, 36, a civilian apprentice injured in the shooting, was released from the hospital.

December 6, 2019: The *Washington Post* and *USA Today* reported that at 6:45 a.m., a shooter firing a Glock 45 9mm handgun killed three people and injured others at Naval Air Station Pensacola before being killed by Florida law enforcement. Two Escambia County sheriff's deputies were wounded. One officer was hit in the arm; the other was shot in the knee and underwent surgery. Baptist Health Care said it had received eight patients from the shooting. *Marine Corps Times* reported that a Marine reservist was wounded.

The dead students were identified as

- Ensign Joshua Kaleb Watson, 23, of Enterprise, Alabama, was a recent graduate of the U.S. Naval Academy. His brother, Adam Watson, said that Joshua suffered multiple gunshot wounds but fled the building to seek help and warn of the attack, according to *NPR*.

- Airman Mohammed Sameh Haitham, 19, of St. Petersburg, Florida, who joined the Navy after graduating from high school in 2018

- Airman Apprentice Cameron Scott Walters, 21, of Richmond Hill, Georgia

The three victims were posthumously awarded the naval aviator and aircrewman Wings of Gold.

The *New York Times* reported on December 8 that the injured included Ryan Blackwell, a Navy airman and assistant high school wrestling coach, who was wounded in his right arm and pelvis.

Federal and state authorities later confirmed that the gunman was a Saudi Arabian military pilot training in the United States. *NBC News* identified the gunman as Second Lieutenant Mohamed Saeed al-Shamrani, 21, who arrived in August 2017 for a scheduled three years of English, basic aviation, and initial pilot training.

Shamrani attended language school at Lackland Air Force Base in San Antonio for six months and was assigned to the training program in Pensacola in the past week.

CNN and *SITE* reported that a *Twitter* account with the handle @m7MD_SHAMRANI included a message to the American people praising Osama bin Laden and quoting Anwar al-Aulaqi (variant Awlaki). The posting declared hate for Americans because of "crimes" against Muslims. "American as a whole has turned into a nation of evil", quoting the words posted by al-Aulaqi in March 2010. "You will not be safe until we live it as reality in pleastain [sic], and American troops get out of our lands."

The *Twitter* account was created in 2012. The *Twitter* account @M7MD_SHAMRANI re-tweeted a *Military Times* post about a November 2019 fatal crash at Vance Air Force Base in Oklahoma. The @M7MD_SHAMRANI *Twitter* account retweeted at least one news article alleging Israeli mistreatment of Palestinians. The penultimate tweet was a retweet of a *Times of Israel* tweet from December 2017 containing the "Full Text of Trump's speech recognizing Jerusalem as capital of Israel".

AP reported that the shooter and three other pilot trainees watched videos of mass shootings at a dinner party al-Shamrani hosted for them earlier in the week. One of the attendees videotaped outside the building while the attack was occurring. Two other Saudi students watched from a car. The trio were held on base; several others were unaccounted for.

The *Washington Post* reported on December 10 that al-Shamrani's personality appeared to have changed after a trip to Saudi Arabia earlier in 2019. Acquaintances said the gifted student was sullen and seemed "angry at the world". The *New York Times* and *Washington Post* noted that he filed a formal complaint in April 2019 against an instructor for humiliating him by calling him by a derogatory nickname in front of other students.

Al-Shamrani legally purchased the murder weapon in Florida from a licensed dealer on July 20, 2019. He qualified for an exception to laws prohibiting foreign nationals from having a gun because he had a valid Florida hunting license, according to the FBI.

Al-Shamrani had visited New York City, including Rockefeller Center, days before the attack.

WOKV and the *Pensacola News Journal* reported on December 10, 2019 that the Navy had suspended flight training for more than 300 Saudi students at Naval Air Stations, including 175 at NAS Pensacola, 35 at NAS Whiting Field and 128 at NAS Mayport, Florida.

AP reported on February 2, 2020 that AQAP released an 18-minute video in which it claimed credit for the shooting. AQAP claimed that he had planned for years to attack a U.S. base. It provided a will written by al-Shamrani to his family in September 2019, saying he wanted to attack the U.S. for religious reasons. AQAP leader Qassim al-Rimi (believed killed in a drone strike the previous week) said in the video that AQAP claimed "full responsibility" for the attack, calling the killer "the hero, the courageous knight".

CNN reported on May 18, 2020 that Al-Shamrani was in touch with an al-Qaeda operative. The connection was found after the FBI broke the encryption on his two iPhones. AQAP had claimed responsibility and that it was in touch with him. FBI Director Christopher Wray said that Al-Shamrani began his AQAP contacts in 2015 and talked with them the day before the attack. Government officials complained of a lack of support from Apple Computer in obtaining evidence from the phones. Al-Shamrani had damaged one of the phones with a bullet before he was killed. 19120601

CNN reported on December 9 that Pensacola, Florida, Mayor Grover Robinson told *WEAR* that the city was experiencing a cyber "incident" since late December 6 and had disconnected several city services until the issue could be resolved. The issue affected city emails and phones; 311 customer service and online payments, including Pensacola Energy and Pensacola Sanitation Services; 911 and emergency services were not affected. It was not clear whether the attack was related to the shooting. Since March 2019, some 140 local governments, police stations and hospitals had been held hostage by ransomware attacks. Victims included the cities of Atlanta, Baltimore, and Albany.

The *Pensacola News Journal, USA Today,* and *Florida Times-Union* reported that a 267-page U.S. Navy investigation into the attack concluded that the shooter had self-radicalized while in the U.S. A Delware Resource Group civilian contractor calling him Pornstache added to his sense of grievance.

December 9, 2019: The *Washington Post* and the *New York Times* reported on December 21 and 22, respectively, that Nicole Marie Poole Franklin, 42, was charged with attempted murder after she allegedly ran over Natalia Miranda, 14, on the sidewalk in Clive, Iowa with her Jeep Grand Cherokee SUV on December 9 because she was "a Mexican". Miranda's injuries—a concussion and bruises—kept her out of Indian Hills Junior High School for a week. Clive Police Chief Michael Venema said Franklin had confessed to being behind the wheel and made derogatory comments about Latinos. Franklin was arrested in an unrelated incident an hour after she sped off. The *Des Moines Register* reported that Franklin allegedly drove to a West Des Moines gas station 90 minutes later and called an employee and customers a racial slur before she threw items at the employee. She had pocketed some items before the clerk questioned her. She told police that she had smoked meth within the previous five hours. Franklin had a police record. She was charged with assault, operating under the influence, theft and public intoxication. *CNN* reported on December 24 that Franklin was charged with another attempted murder after she intentionally hit a 12-year-old African American boy 60 minutes before she hit Miranda on December 9. Police said her SUV jumped the curb, ran over his leg, and sped away. The Des Moines Adult Public Defender's Office withdrew from her case. A district judge was to appoint her a new attorney during her preliminary hearing on her first attempted murder charge on December 30. She was held on a $1 million bond on the attempted murder charge.

December 10, 2019: *CNN* and *USA Today* reported that at 12:21 p.m., two shooters got out of a stolen white U-Haul van, then opened fire on Hasidic Jews while entering the Jersey City Kosher Supermarket at 223 Martin Luther King,

Jr., Boulevard. The gunmen killed Leah Minda (Mindy) Ferencz, 31, the store's co-owner with her husband; Moshe Hirsch Deutsch, 24, a customer; and Douglas Miguel Rodriguez Barzola, 49, a store employee who had recently emigrated from Guayaquil, Ecuador, in the store. Another man was shot but ran out of the store. The attackers had killed Police Detective Joseph Seals in Bay View Cemetery, a mile away, at noon. The *New York Times* reported that one gunman was a former member of the anti-Semitic Black Hebrew Israelite movement. Jersey City Department of Public Safety Director James Shea said, "There were many other (potential) targets available to them that they bypassed to attack that place." New Jersey Attorney General Gurbir Grewal said police killed gunmen David N. Anderson, 47, the driver and Black Israelite, and Francine Graham, 50, the van's passenger, during a three hour shootout. Anderson was armed with a rifle. Several Orthodox Jews were next door at a small synagogue.

Detective Seals, a father of five, was a 15-year veteran of the department and member of the Cease Fire Unit aimed at limiting gun crimes through community outreach and the confiscation of illegal weapons.

The gunmen were prime suspects in the murder of a Jersey City man who was found beaten to death in the trunk of a car in Bayonne on December 7.

The mayors of Jersey City and New York City said the attack was a hate crime against the Jewish community.

Black Israelites believe that African Americans are the true descendants of biblical Jews. Some members have expressed anti-Semitic sentiments.

Police found a note in the stolen U-Haul truck that contained anti-Semitic and anti-police writing. The shooters had posted similar sentiments on social media. Newark FBI Special Agent in Charge Gregory W. Ehrie said police found an operable pipe bomb in the back of the U-Haul. Police found an AR-15-style rifle, a 12-gauge Mossburg shotgun and two other guns in the store and one in the van. The Mossburg and a .22 caliber Ruger pistol were purchased in Ohio in spring 2018.

Graham lived in Elizabeth in the Elizabeth-port suburb's Waters Edge town house complex. Neighbors said she was unfriendly.

On December 14, the FBI arrested pawn-shop owner Ahmed A-Hady, 35, on one count of being a felon in possession of a firearm after they found a note with his phone number and business address in Anderson's back pocket. Searches of A-Hady's home and store in Keyport, New Jersey, turned up three "AR-15-style assault rifles" similar to one of the weapons used in the attack, three other rifles, a shotgun, three hand-guns, and 400 rounds of ammunition, including a "large number" of hollow point bullets. Prosecutors said A-Hady had legally purchased a .44 caliber Smith and Wesson, in June 2007, but was no longer allowed to own firearms because of a 2012 drug-related conviction. He faced up to 10 years in prison if convicted.

AP reported on January 14, 2020 that federal and state law enforcement authorities said that the two killers had planned the attack for months and left notes at the scene and in online posts. They were equipped to cause greater destruction. 19121001

December 13, 2019: *CNN* reported that New Orleans Mayor LaToya Cantrell declared a state of emergency after the city was hit by a cyberattack at 5 a.m. Ransomware was detected.

December 13, 2019: *NBC News* reported that the FBI charged Saudi man Hassan Alqahtani, 28, who is enrolled at the University of New Mexico's school of engineering, with illegal possession of a firearm by a person admitted to the U.S. under a non-immigrant visa. An FBI search of his home found a .380-caliber Cobra handgun. The Bureau opened its investigation on August 8 when a student called a tip line to warn that he was "creating a list of people who he wants to kill before he leaves the U.S.", which included the tipster and University of New Mexico professors. The *Albuquerque Journal* reported that a judge ordered him held through the weekend; a detention hearing was scheduled for December 16. He was represented by defense attorney Joel Meyers. Alqahtani faced 10 years in prison.

December 15, 2019: The *Houston Chronicle* reported that prosecutors in the Harris County 183rd District Criminal Court in Houston, Texas, charged Christopher Lee Melder, 19, with stealing mercury and spilling it at several locations. Charges included burglary and unlawful disposal of hazardous material around the intersection of Westview Drive and the West Sam Houston Parkway. Nearly 60 people were decontaminated. Houston Fire Chief Sam Peña said that a pregnant woman was the only person hospitalized. The FBI said Melder broke into a Houston-area lab and stole the mercury. A "concerned citizen" who works in the chemical industry reported a white silvery substance on the ground at 11:15 a.m. in the 10700 block of Westview near the parkway. Firefighters found the chemical outside the nearby Walmart, Sonic Drive-In and a Shell gas station. Melder was also arrested on an unrelated drug-related warrant.

December 28, 2019: The *Washington Post, CNN,* and *AP* reported that at 10 p.m., a man with a machete walked into Orthodox Rabbi Chaim Rottenberg's home on Forshay Road in Monsey, New York during a Hanukkah celebration and stabbed five Hasidic Jews, two critically. Rottenberg's son was among the victims. One hundred people were in the home while the rabbi was "lighting the candle" on the seventh night of Hanukkah. The attacker tried to run into a nearby synagogue, but someone closed the doors. Police found a silver Nissan and apprehended a tall black man, Grafton E. Thomas, 37, of Orange County, New York. He faced five counts of attempted murder and one count of burglary. New York leaders called the attack domestic terrorism. *NPR* reported that friends said he had mental difficulties. The *Washington Post* reported that he had been arrested seven times since 2001 for assault, resisting arrest, killing or injuring a police animal, driving while under the influence, possessing controlled substances and menacing a police or peace officer. He was jailed in 2013 for possession of a controlled substance. He pleaded not guilty to five counts of attempted murder and one count of burglary during a court appearance. Bail was set at $5 million. He was represented by Kristine Ciganek of the Rockland County public defender's office.

December 29, 2019: The *Washington Post*, *CNN* and *KTVT* reported that at 10 a.m., two parishioners, including Antony "Tony" Wallace, 64, of Fort Worth, and Richard White, 67, of River Oaks, both members of the church's security team, were shot to death at the West Freeway Church of Christ in White Settlement, Texas, a suburb west of Fort Worth. Video showed that volunteer church guard Jack Wilson, 71, a firearms instructor, shot to death the murderer, Keith Thomas Kinnunen, 43, of River Oaks. Several other congregants also pulled their weapons. The gunman had sat with the congregants before standing up with a long gun, confronting deacon Tony Wallace, and firing. Wilson was running for commissioner in Hood County. Kinnunen often was given food at the church, but became angry when denied cash. Church members said he showed up wearing a fake beard, wig, hat, and long coat, drawing their suspicion, before he fired.

2020 CHRONOLOGY

WORLDWIDE

May 27, 2020: Peter Maurer, President of the International Committee of the Red Cross, told the United Nations Security Council that there had been 208 COVID-19-related attacks against health workers and installations in 13 countries since March, adding that it was "likely the actual numbers are much higher than what we calculated". The ICRC said 23% were physical assaults including arsons, another 20% were discriminatory-related attacks on health workers, and the rest involved failing to provide or denying assistance, verbal assaults and threats, and a disregard for health personnel protective measures.

August 27, 2020: Peter Maurer told the UN Security Council that cyber attacks were increasing against hospitals, electricity and water supplies, and other critical civilian infrastructure, including a petrochemical plant. "If hospitals cannot provide life-saving treatment in the middle of a health crisis or an armed conflict, whole communities will suffer... If electricity supply is interrupted, there is a real risk that water, health care, and other essential services will be disrupted... And if even nuclear facilities are not considered off limits, we risk seeing severe and widespread humanitarian consequences."

December 9, 2020: The International Federal of Journalists announced that 42 journalists and media workers were killed while doing their jobs during 2020. In the past three decades, 2,658 journalists had died. Mexico logged 13 killings in 2020, topping the list for four of the last five years; Pakistan had five; Afghanistan, India, Iraq and Nigeria tallied three.

UNITED NATIONS

April 30, 2020: The U.N. announced that Secretary General Antonio Guterres's March 23 call for a global cease-fire was positively received by 16 armed groups, "114 governments, diverse regional organizations, religious leaders and more than 200 civil society groups spanning all regions". The armed groups hailed from Yemen, Myanmar, Ukraine, Philippines, Colombia, Angola, Libya, Senegal, Sudan, Syria, Indonesia and Nagorno-Karabakh.

June 29, 2020: The U.N. Security Council voted 15-0-0 to extend the mandate of the 15,600 peacekeeping force in Mali for a year to support implementation of Mali's 2015 peace agreement signed by three parties: the government, the Coordination of Movements of Azawad that includes ethnic Arabs and Tuaregs who seek autonomy in northern Mali, and a pro-government Platform militia.

July 15, 2020: The Pakistani Foreign Ministry announced that the United Nations had released "expense" money for several men designated as terrorists at the request of the Pakistani government, including one with a $10 million U.S. bounty on his head. Hafiz Saeed, the founder of Lashkar-e-Taiba and alleged mastermind behind the 2008 attack in Mumbai, India that killed more than 160 people, was on the list. Saeed was on India's most wanted list. The Ministry explained that the money was to cover basic expenses and did not entail restoration or unfreezing of bank accounts. "These exemptions are being enforced and monitored as per law." Pakistan did not disclose the number or names of designated terrorists who were on the list sent to the U.N. or how much money was released or the nature of the expenses for which the terrorists needed the money.

August 31, 2020: The United States vetoed a U.N. resolution introduced by Indonesia calling for the prosecution, rehabilitation and reintegration of all those engaged in terrorism-related activities, objecting that it did not call for the repatriation from Syria and Iraq of foreign fighters for ISIS and their families which is "the crucial first step". U.S. Ambassador Kelly Craft deemed the resolution "a cynical and willfully oblivious farce". Due to COVID-19, the Security Council voted by e-mail, 14-1-0.

November 12, 2020: The U.N. Security Council voted 13-0 with Russia and China abstaining to prevent the sale or shipment to Somalia of components of improvised explosive devices if there is "significant risk" they may be used to manufacture bombs being used in attacks by al-Shabaab. The UNSC urged the Somali government "to continue working with Somali financial authorities, private sector financial institutions and the international community to identify, assess and mitigate money laundering and terrorist financing risks" that U.N. experts estimate raised over $21 million in 2019. The UNSC reaffirmed the arms embargo on Somalia and banned the resale or transfer of any weapons or military equipment sold or supplied to help develop Somalia's National Security Forces and security sector.

Africa

January 8, 2020: Mohamed Ibn Chambas, U.N. envoy for West Africa and the Sahel, told the U.N. Security Council that deaths from terrorist attacks in Burkina Faso, Mali and Niger had increased from 770 deaths in 2016 to more than 4,000 in 2019. Deaths in Burkina Faso rose from 80 in 2016 to more than 1,800 in 2019.

Benin

February 9, 2020: At dawn, gunmen armed with rifles and machetes attacked a police station in Mekrou-Djimdjim near the border with Burkina Faso, killing a policeman and wounding a second. The terrorists torched the building. Jihadis were suspected.

Burkina Faso

January 21, 2020: Terrorists burned a market in Sanmatenga Province, killing 36 people and wounding several others.

January 27, 2020: Colonel Salfo Kabore, governor of Sahel region, announced that motorcyclists fired on a vehicle, killing a nurse who was traveling with three others on her way to her post in Kelbo.

January 28, 2020: A military vehicle struck a roadside bomb in the east, killing six soldiers. Seven others were missing.

February 16, 2020: The *Independent* and *AP* reported that 20 "armed terrorists" attacked a Protestant church in Pansi in the Yagha region. They separated the women from the men before killing 24, including the pastor, wounding 18, and kidnapping three young people. Christians and Muslims were killed. The attackers torched the church. The terrorists stole oil and rice from shops and forced the three hostages to help transport the booty on their motorbikes.

The previous week, gunmen killed a retired pastor and kidnapped another pastor in Yagha Province.

March 9, 2020: Gunmen attacked Dinguila and Barga villages in Yatenga Province, killing 43 people. The military took six injured people to the central hospital in Ouahigouya. Fulani herdsmen live in the villages and had been attacked by local defense groups for their ties to local jihadis.

April 15, 2020: The *Washington Post* reported that on the same day that the country had its first coronavirus death, militants killed four men in a northwestern village.

A few evenings later, the same day that four government ministers tested positive for COVID-19, gunmen set fire to a national park office and kidnapped a forest ranger. Days later, gunmen killed several soldiers, abducted a rural town's head nurse, and stole military gear. Jihadis were reportedly blocking food, water and medicine trucks while attempting to annex territory in the north and east.

May 9, 2020: *AP* reported that jihadis had raided a gold mine, forbid everyone from smoking and drinking, and later returned to level the site, kill people and burn homes. Some observers estimate that jihadis controlled 20 small mines in the east, using them as hideouts and financial sources.

May 11, 2020: Authorities arrested 25 people on suspicion of being extremists in Tawalbougou village in the Fada N'Gourma commune. Judicael Kadeba, the prosecutor of Faso in the Eastern region, announced that, "Twelve among them died in the same night in the cells where they were detained."

May 28, 2020: The armed forces destroyed a terrorist camp in the north, killing ten gunmen. One soldier died.

May 29, 2020: *AP* and *Reuters* reported that jihadis attacked a convoy of traders escorted by a local defense group in Loroum Province, killing 15 people, including children, and wounding others. Several people were missing. Authorities believed the defense group was the target. Government spokesman Remis Fulgance Dandjinou said the attack was in response to army efforts to halt growing violence.

May 30, 2020: Gunmen fired on a cattle market in Kompienga Province, killing 25 people. One survivor blamed the Burkinabe military and claimed that more than 50 people were killed.

Gunmen fired on a convoy in Sanmatenga Province, killing five civilians and five security forces. Several people were missing.

June 3, 2020: *AP* reported that jihadi attacks in villages in the north and the western breadbasket in the Boucle du Mouhoun region had forced thousands of farmers from their lands, abandoning a year's worth of crops. Food rotted in storage. Farmer Adama Drabo reported that a roadside bomb killed his son, 20. Coronavirus and jihadi attacks threatened to increase food insecurity, endangering millions. In 2020, five roadside bombs went off in Boucle du Mouhoun, versus only two in 2019, according to the Armed Conflict Location and Event Data Project.

June 23, 2020: *AFP* reported that security forces claimed they had destroyed two jihadi bases in the north and east of the country and arrested two suspects near the border with the Ivory Coast. The Armed Forces Chief of Staff said in a weekly bulletin that on June 20, a gendarmerie unit "dismantled a terrorist base" near the eastern town of Tanwalbougou. In a separate operation in the north, soldiers in the five-nation G5 Sahel force, supported by a company of soldiers from Niger, destroyed a terrorist base in a drilling zone 40 kilometers from Oursi, seizing eight motorbikes, phones and other equipment.

On June 20, Burkinabe and Ivorian forces arrested two "suspects" near Alidougou near where ten Ivorian soldiers were killed in a jihadi attack on a frontier post on June 11.

August 7, 2020: Gunmen fired on a cattle market in Namoungou village, killing 20 and injuring many others. Jihadis were suspected. Jihadis killed a cattle breeder in a village 15 kilometers away earlier in the week.

October 4, 2020: *AFP* and *AP* reported that during the night, gunmen ambushed a convoy five miles from Pissila, identified themselves as jihadis, separated the women and children from the men, killed 25 men, and fled in Burkina Faso's Center-North region. Three women said the terrorists explained that they were retaliating for the village having volunteer defense fighters. *Al-Jazeera* added that the convoy was carrying dozens of displaced civilians hoping to return to their homes in Wintokuilga and Tang-kienga in Sanmatenga Province. One man left for dead survived.

October 14, 2020: *AFP* reported that government spokesman Remis Fulgance Dandjinou said that jihadi gunmen killed 20 people in attacks on the villages of Demniol, Bombofa and Peteguerse in northern Seno Province. Several people were injured; others were missing.

November 6, 2020: In the evening, an attacker threw a flammable bottle into a mosque in Ouagadougou, wounding six people. A note left on the ground nearby read: "Close the mosque or we'll launch grenades at you."

November 11, 2020: Government spokesman Remis Fulgance Dandjinou said gunmen ambushed a military convoy from the Tin-Akoff area of the Sahel region in Oudalan Province, killing 14 soldiers and injuring others. A plane evacuated three severely injured people to Ouagadougou.

Twenty jihadis on motorbikes burned a bar in the nearby town of Gorom Gorom.

CAMEROON

February 14, 2020: Some 22 people, including small children, died in clashes between separatists and the military in the Anglophone North West and South West regions. A fuel tank exploded, burning homes and killing a woman and four children. Bruno Ngeh, 38, a teacher, said that he lost his wife's aunt and her eight children in a battle in Ngarbu in North West.

March 8, 2020: Anglophone separatists attacked a security post in Galim village in the western French-speaking region, killing seven people, including officers and civilians.

A bomb went off in the English-speaking northwestern town of Bamenda, causing no deaths or injuries. Authorities suspected separatists who had vowed to disrupt International Women Day activities.

April 4, 2020: The *Washington Post* and *BBC* reported that the Southern Cameroons Defense Forces rebel group declared a pause in fighting as a "gesture of goodwill".

July 27, 2020: *AFP* and Human Rights Watch reported that since May, separatist groups killed six civilians, including a humanitarian worker and a teacher, in the minority anglophone Northwest and Southwest regions. In mid-May, separatists shot to death a teacher at the University of Bamenda who had refused to stop teaching, in line with their demands to boycott education. In June, terrorists fired a grenade into a hospital courtyard in Bali. Gun battles between the army and separatists killed one person and wounded four. In early July, gunmen killed a Cameroonian aid worker with Doctors Without Borders (MSF). 200729901

August 2, 2020: *CNN* reported that Boko Haram was suspected when a grenade went off in a camp for internally displaced people in Nguetchewe village during the morning, killing 15 and wounding five. The terrorists had snuck across the Nigerian border around midnight. 20080201

October 24, 2020: *Reuters* and *CNN* reported that at midday, 12 gunmen riding four motorbikes and wearing civilian clothes attacked the Mother Francisca International Bilingual Academy, a private school in Kumba in South West Region, and fired indiscriminately, killing seven children and wounding eight while they were studying French. One of the terrorists had a rocket launcher. Some children were injured jumping from second storey windows. Isabel Dione's daughter, 12, was shot in the stomach. The UN Office for the Coordination of Humanitarian Affairs said eight children were killed, some by machete, and that 12 were injured. Local education official Ahhim Abanaw Obase said six children between age 12 and 14 were killed. Government officials blamed anglophone secessionists, who denied involvement. Boniface Tamungwa, a pastor in Kumba, said his son, 11, was killed. *Reuters* reported that the next day, a seventh child, Renny Ngwane, 12, daughter of carpenter Claude Ngwane, 36, died. Blessing Mbeng, 13, son of Edwin Ojong Ayuk Mbeng, was hospitalized. *CNN* reported that Cameroonian Prime Minister Joseph Dion Ngute said that nine students had died. No group claimed credit.

November 3, 2020: *AFP* reported that gunmen kidnapped between six and 11 teachers from a Presbyterian primary and secondary school in Kumbo in the Northwest Region.

AFP reported on November 5 that the 11 teachers were freed and in good health after local residents visited the separatists' camp three times to call for their release.

The government had announced on November 3 that three other schools in the anglophone regions had been attacked since November 2.

Six students in Fundong in the Northwest Region were kidnapped but were released several hours later.

November 5, 2020: *AFP* reported that gunmen briefly kidnapped Archbishop Emeritus Christian Tumi, 90, a retired cardinal, on a road near Kumbo in the Northwest Region. He and his driver were released the next day. Ten other hostages, including Sehm Mbinglo, chief of the Nso people, seized with them remained captives. Local leaders were negotiating for their release.

December 6, 2020: *Reuters* reported that separatists in the anglophone Northwest region killed a voter during the elections to appoint regional councils.

Gunmen wounded a priest and a seminarian driving to Mass in Akum in the Northwest region.

CENTRAL AFRICAN REPUBLIC

March 7, 2020: Civilians found the bullet-ridden body of a U.N. peacekeeper from the U.N. mission in Ndele in Ouaka Province. The government blamed the Popular Front for the Renaissance in the Central African Republic (FPRC), an ex-Seleka faction. 20030702

March 15, 2020: Members of the mainly Christian anti-Balaka militia under the command of Dimitri Ayoloma fired on the homes of the mayor and regional officials in Grimari. UN peacekeepers in Grimari in Ouaka Province intervened and were fired on. A peacekeeper from Burundi was killed. 20031502

In a separate attack, two suspected rebel groups attacked a UN patrol on the Ndele-Birao

axis in northern Bamingui-Bangoran Province, injuring a Pakistani peacekeeper. 20031503

December 25, 2020: *AFP* reported that the six-group rebel Coalition of Patriots for Change (CPC) called off its three-day ceasefire ahead of the weekend's general election and would continue its march on the capital, Bangui. Two of the groups—the 3R and the Popular Front for the Rebirth of Central Africa (FPRC)—confirmed the announcement.

Reuters and *AFP* reported that later that day, three U.N. peacekeepers from Burundi were killed in Dekoa in Kemo Prefecture, 125 miles north of Bangui. Two other MINUSCA peacekeepers were injured. 20122501

Gunmen attacked peacekeepers in Bakouma in Mbomou Prefecture. 20122502

CHAD

January 20, 2020: A female suicide bomber set off her explosives during the night in a crowd in Kaiga-Kindjiria in Fouli Department in Lake Chad Province, killing nine people and injuring two. Boko Haram killed five people in the town in August 2019. 20012001

March 23, 2020: *Reuters* reported that Boko Haram terrorists killed 92 Chadian soldiers and wounded 47 more in an attack on the island village of Boma in the Lake Chad zone. 20032301

April 2-9, 2020: On April 10, *AP* reported that Chad Army spokesman Colonel Azem Bermandoa announced that during eight days of fighting in an operation on the islands of Lake Chad, soldiers killed some 1,000 Boko Haram jihadis. He added that 52 soldiers were killed and 196 others were wounded.

April 19, 2020: *BBC* and *AFP* reported that Chad's public prosecutor announced that 44 suspected Boko Haram terrorists died in detention from apparent poisoning. They were part of 58 suspects captured during a recent major army operation around Lake Chad. Four autopsies showed a lethal substance had killed them. The terrorists killed nearly 100 Chadian troops on March 23 during a seven-hour attack on an island base in Lake Chad. The prisoners were found dead the morning of April 16. Public prosecutor Youssouf Tom said that "Forty of them were buried and the other four were taken to a pathologist, whose report revealed that a lethal substance was consumed, leading to heart problems in some and severe asphyxiation amongst others." One detainee recovered, according to the Minister of Justice.

July 8, 2020: *AFP* reported that eight soldiers died and several others wounded when their vehicle hit a landmine planted by suspected jihadis at Kalam in the Lake Chad region, three miles from the border with Nigeria. Various sources said eight or nine people were killed and between 11 and 21 wounded. A Nigerian security source blamed the Islamic State West Africa Province (ISWAP), a splinter group of Nigeria's Boko Haram. One of the dead was a gendarmerie commander.

Congo

January 28, 2020: Beni administrator Donat Kibwana said that during the night, Allied Democratic Forces rebels attacked four villages, including Manzingi and Maleki, in Beni territory, going door to door and killing 36 people in their homes. The terrorists also stole goats, chickens, and other valuables. The ADF originated in Uganda.

January 29, 2020: In a morning attack, a church leader was killed in Bunake village. Soldiers drove off the terrorists.

February 17-18, 2020: Allied Democratic Forces rebels attacked Alungupa village, 15 miles outside Beni, during the night, killing 12 civilians and a soldier.

April 24, 2020: The Democratic Forces for the Liberation of Rwanda was suspected when gunmen killed 17 people, including 12 rangers, a driver, and four civilians in Virunga National Park. Two civilians and four rangers were injured, one critically. The rangers were en route to the park but spotted a civilian vehicle that had been attacked. Responding to the crime scene, they

were ambushed at 11 a.m. near Rumangabo village. The park is a UNESCO World Heritage site.

May 27, 2020: The Allied Democratic Forces and the ISIS-linked MTM killed 40 people in Samboko, Bandavilemba and Walese-Vukutu in Ituri Province. The rebels used machetes and stole food and other valuables. The Centre for the Promotion of Peace, Democracy and Human Rights (CEPADHO) claimed that the ADF had killed 627 civilians since October 30, 2020; 515 of them in the Beni area.

June 3, 2020: *AFP* reported that the government blamed the ethnic militia Cooperative for the Development of the Congo (CODECO) for attacking Mambisa village in Djugu territory in Ituri Province during the night and killing 16 civilians, including seven women, four men, and five children under age 5, via knives and gunfire. CODECO consists primarily of Lendu farmers, who often clash with the Hema community of traders and herders. AFP reported that nearly 300 civilians had been killed in 2020 in CODECO attacks.

July 3, 2020: The army claimed it had killed seven fighters of the ethnic militia Cooperative for the Development of the Congo (CODECO).

July 4, 2020: *AFP* reported that gunmen attacked two vehicles coming from Bunia, capital of Ituri Province, in Matete village, killing eleven people, including the deputy territorial administrator in charge of economy and finance, an accountant, three policemen and four soldiers. The government blamed the ethnic militia Cooperative for the Development of the Congo (CODECO), which claims to defend the interests of the Lendu farming community.

July 8, 2020: *AFP* reported that before dawn, gunmen attacked the village of Djugu, north of Bunia, killing 20 civilians. The government blamed the Cooperative for the Development of Congo (CODECO) militia, which is of Lendu ethnicity.

July 16, 2020: While being pursued by the Mai Mai rebels, Ngumino gunmen attacked the village of Kipupu in South Kivu Province, killing

43 people, including many women and children. Another 40 people disappeared and houses were torched in other villages.

August 5, 2020: *AFP* reported that a UN Joint Human Rights Office (UNJHRO) report indicated that armed groups had killed 1,315 people, including 267 women and 165 children, in the first half of 2020, tripling the 416 deaths in the first half of 2019.

August 13, 2020: *AFP* reported that the UN's Joint Human Rights Office found that 135 rebel groups were active.

August 17, 2020: *Reuters* reported that some 500 fighters of a faction of the NDC-R rebel group loyal to Gilbert Bwira Shuo surrendered to the government in Kashuga, North Kivu Province, after attempting to overthrow the group's leader, Shimiray Guidon, who is the target of UN sanctions, on July 9. Group spokesman Desire Ngabo Kisuba said, "Today we think it's time for us to surrender, lay down our arms and take part in the pacification of the country."

September 8 and 10, 2020: *AFP* reported that 58 people died in attacks in the Tshabi forested area. The government blamed the Allied Democratic Forces, which used knives and guns on the Nyali community. Provincial Interior Minister Adjio Gidi said 23 people died in Irumu territory in southern Ituri on September 8, followed by another 35 on September 10. ADP originated in the 1990s as a Ugandan Muslim rebel group. Another 17 people were missing and believed kidnapped.

September 16, 2020: *Reuters* reported that gunmen attacked a World Vision convoy returning from a mission to deliver food in North Kivu Province, killing an aid worker and taking two hostages for 18 hours. 20091601

October 20, 2020: *Reuters* and *AFP* reported that in the early morning, gunmen raided a military camp and a nearby prison, freeing more than 1,300 prisoners from Kangbayi central prison in Beni. The government blamed jihadis belonging to the Allied Democratic Forces (ADF), which originated in Uganda. Only 110 of 1,456 inmates, including some militia fighters, remained.

Amaq claimed credit for the Islamic State Central African Province. Two inmates died in the 4:30 a.m. raid. By midday around 20 prisoners had returned.

October 21, 2020: Police blamed the ADF when gunmen attacked a jail in Beni, freeing hundreds of prisoners. The Islamic State's Central Africa Province claimed credit.

October 28, 2020: The ADF was suspected in a nighttime attack on the remote Baeti village in which 19 people were killed and the church and 40 homes were torched. The Islamic State's Central Africa Province claimed credit.

October 30, 2020: *AFP* reported that four people, including two aid workers, returning from the Mulongwe refugee camp were kidnapped for ransom in the Mutambala area of South Kivu Province's Fizi region on the edge of Lake Tanganyika, according to Jean Lundimu, head of the Adventist Development and Relief Agency International (ADRA), the humanitarian agency of the Seventh-day Adventist Church. Two Congolese aid workers, a supplier, and a Burundian were taken hostage. The driver was released. Lundimu reported that negotiations had begun. 20103001

Local official Moutard Wa Mlendela said that in mid-October a driver for another international organization was kidnapped before being released after a ransom was paid. 20109901

October 31, 2020: *AFP* reported that the ADF was suspected of attacking a rival Congolese militia before killing 21 villagers in Lisasa in the Beni territory's Buliki area of North Kivu Province. The Cepadho NGO said 15 women were killed and other people were kidnapped. A health center was ransacked, homes were torched, and a Catholic church was desecrated.

November 17, 2020: Rebels killed 35 people in the Beni region during the week. Residents found the bodies of 29 people in Kavuyiri in Virunga National Park; it was unclear when they were killed. On November 17, an attack killed six civilians elsewhere in Beni. The provincial government blamed the Allied Democratic Forces for attacks "perpetrated by men without faith or law".

November 30, 2020: *AFP* reported that during the night, nine people were killed in Djugu territory in Ituri Province. Civil society head Jules Tsuba said five women and four children died, while the UN radio station *Okapi* said three women and six children were killed. Bangladeshi troops in the UN peacekeeping force took three other women seriously injured to a hospital. The government blamed the armed political-religious sect Cooperation for the Development of Congo (CODECO), which claims to defend the rights of ethnic Lendu farming communities.

December 29, 2020: The Allied Democratic Forces were believed responsible for a nighttime attack that killed three civilians and a soldier.

December 31, 2020: *AFP* and *AP* reported 25 people were killed, many by beheading, and others were kidnapped when Allied Democratic Forces rebels attacked farmers in fields in the village of Tingwe in Beni territory.

ERITREA

November 28, 2020: U.S. Embassy diplomats reported hearing six explosions in Asmara during at 10:13 p.m. *AFP* reported that rockets had been launched from Ethiopia's Tigray region toward Asmara's airport and military installations. The Ethiopian government had announced victory against the Tigray People's Liberation Front (TPLF), which had deemed Asmara a legitimate target because Ethiopia was enlisting Eritrean military support for its campaign in Tigray.

ETHIOPIA

June 29, 2020: *AP* and *Reuters* reported that popular Oromo singer Hachalu Hundessa, variant Haacaaluu Hundeessaa, 34, was shot to death in his car during the night in the Addis Ababa suburbs. He died in a local hospital. The gunmen fled. Prime Minister Abiy Ahmed blamed foreign and domestic enemies of democracy. Initial reports indicated that 50 people died in clashes with protestors and security forces the next day; hundreds of cars were burned or damaged. *AP* on July 2 increased that number to more than 80;

AFP ratcheted it to 90. *FANA* reported that police arrested three people for Hundessa's death. *AFP*, *Reuters* and the *Oromo Broadcasting Network* reported that he was buried in an Orthodox church in Ambo on July 2. *AFP* reported that soldiers fired on mourners, killing two and injuring seven. The U.S. Embassy said that eight people were killed, including two Ethiopian Federal Police officers. *Reuters* reported on July 5 that the government announced that 156 people were killed during the protests. By July 10, some 239 people had died in the violence. The *New York Times* reported on July 12 that the government had arrested 5,000 people for the demonstrations and shut down local access to the Internet.

AP reported on July 10 that Ethiopian Attorney General Adanech Abebe announced the arrest of two people for Hundessa's murder; a third remained at large. He said that the duo had confessed that a splinter of the Oromo Liberation Army had instructed them to kill the victim, with the goal of inciting anti-regime feelings and causing ethnic tensions between the Oromos and Amharas.

Reuters reported on October 2, 2020 that Ethiopia filed terrorism charges against four suspects and added that authorities had arrested more than 9,000 people, including politicians, activists, and journalists. The last week of September, prosecutors charged 2,000 people in connection with the violence. Defendants included media mogul and Oromo opposition politician Jawar Mohammed, who faced charges of violating anti-terrorism, telecom fraud and firearms laws. The state-run *Ethiopian Broadcasting Corporation* claimed that the terrorism defendants were working with other suspects still at large to assassinate prominent individuals, to create chaos and oust the government.

June 30, 2020: Three explosions went off in Addis Ababa, with an unreported number of injuries and deaths. A policeman was killed in the city. Gunfire was reported throughout the Oromia region the next day.

October 8, 2020: Gashu Dugaz, chief of security in Western Benishangul-Gumuz region, said a militia attack on ethnic Amhara and Agaw minorities earlier in the week killed 14 civilians and hospitalized eight. One person was a foreigner. Security forces killed 14 militia members in Dangur district. Two attackers were captured alive. Authorities sized five Kalashnikovs. Two recent attacks killed several dozen people. 20100801

The previous month, the Ethiopian Human Rights Commission said an attack in the region on September 6 and then from September 7 to 13 killed civilians and displaced over 300 people.

November 2020: *Reuters* reported on December 3, 2020 that four Ethiopian aid workers affiliated with two foreign organizations were killed in Tigray in one of four camps for Eritrean refugees.

November 1, 2020: *AP* reported that officials announced that several civilians, including children, were "massacred" in an evening terrorist attack in West Wollega's Guliso area in the Oromia region. Getachew Balcha, the region's spokesman, blamed the Oromo Liberation Army. *CNN* and *Reuters* reported that Elias Umeta, administrator in the Oromiya region, blamed the Oromo Liberation Front Shane splinter group. Some reports said 60 terrorists were involved. Survivors told the *Amhara Mass Media Agency* that ethnic Amharas were targeted. One survivor said, "The armed group gathered 200 people for a meeting around 5 p.m., and then started shooting at them. Several people were killed" and a school and 120 houses were burned. Local media, *Reuters and al-Jazeera* reported that several dozen were killed. *AP* reported that survivors counted 54 corpses. The head of the Oromia region police commission, Ararsa Merdasa, said 32 died. Daniel Bekele, the commission's chief commissioner, said, "They were dragged from their homes and taken to a school, where they were killed." One survivor said he found the bodies of his brother, sister-in-law and three children in the schoolyard with bullet wounds.

December 11, 2020: Four workers for humanitarian organizations were reported killed.

December 20, 2020: *Reuters* and the *Ethiopia News Agency* reported that an abandoned bomb exploded in the Lideta area near the center of Addis Ababa, killing three homeless people and injuring five others.

December 23, 2020: *AFP* and *Reuters* reported that at 6 a.m., gunmen attacked Bekoji village in Bulen County in the Benishangul-Gumuz region's Metekel zone, killing more than 100 people, many of them still sleeping in their beds. The attack continued into the afternoon. Some 38 people sustained bullet, knife, and arrow wounds. The terrorists also torched crops. Belay Wajera, a farmer in the western town of Bulen, said his wife and five of his children were shot dead. He was shot in the buttocks. His four other children escaped and were missing. Gunmen shot resident Hassen Yimama in the stomach. A five-year-old child died while being transferred to a clinic.

December 29, 2020: The Dutch aid group ZOA International claimed one of its staffers, 52, was "murdered" at the Hitsats refugee camp in the Tigray region. At least five humanitarian workers were killed during the two months of unrest in the region. Hitsas is part of the camp network hosting circa 100,000 refugees from Eritrea. ZOA did not name those responsible.

The Danish Refugee Council said three staffers who worked as guards at a project site that supports Eritrean refugees were killed. The DRC did not specify the date.

IVORY COAST

June 11, 2020: On June 20, 2020, the Ivory Coast announced it captured the leader of the June 11 jihadi raid on a frontier post at Kafolo, on the border with Burkina Faso, that killed ten Ivorian soldiers and arrested a "very large" number of his subordinates. A source in Burkina Faso said the attack was carried out by the Group to Support Islam and Muslims (GSIM), which has ties to al-Qaeda. On July 2, *AFP* reported that the death toll had reached 14. In a ceremony in Abidjan, the soldiers were posthumously made knights of the national order. Among the dead was Marshal Lansine Bamba, husband of Salimata Doumbia. *AFP* said 30 people, including the jihadi leader, who was from Burkina Faso, were arrested.

November 3, 2020: *AFP* reported that two government supporters were killed in a clash near Equipment Minister Amede Koffi Kouakou's home in Toumodi. Elsewhere, gunmen fired at the convoy of Communication Minister and government spokesman Sidi Tiemoko Toure, causing no casualties. The country was divided over President Alassane Ouattara's contested re-election.

KENYA

January 2, 2020: Jihadis were suspected when gunmen fired on two passenger buses, killing four.

Attackers hit one bus in the Nyongoro area of Lamu County, killing three men and wounding two passengers.

In a second attack, gunmen fired on a Simba bus heading from Mombasa to Lamu County, killing the conductor.

January 5, 2020: In its first attack against U.S. forces in Kenya, at 5:30 a.m., al-Shabaab set off a car bomb at Manda Bay Airfield near Simba military base in Lamu County, which is used by U.S. counterterror forces, destroying U.S. aircraft and vehicles. *CNN* reported that a U.S. service member and two DOD civilian contractors were killed. The *New York Times* identified the contractors as Dustin Harrison, 47, and Bruce Triplett, 64, pilots with L3 Technologies. Four terrorists were killed and five were arrested. A Kenyan police report said a U.S. Cessna and a Kenyan Cessna, two U.S. helicopters, and several U.S. vehicles were destroyed.

The *NBC* affiliate in Chicago said the dead included U.S. Army Specialist Henry "Mitch" Mayfield, Jr., 23, from the Chicago suburb of Hazel Crest. He was part of Operation Octave Shield.

Marine Corps Times reported on January 22 that a dozen Marines from the 3rd Marine Raider Battalion, based out of Camp Lejeune, North Carolina, led Kenyan commandos in the response against al-Shabaab terrorists who conducted the attack. One Marine Raider was injured.

Military Times reported on March 9, 2020 that a February 22 AFRICOM air strike near Saakow, Somalia killed senior al-Shabaab leader Bashir Mohamed Mahamoud, alias Bashir Qoorgaab, who was suspected of involvement in the January 5, 2020 attack on U.S. and Kenyan forces in Manda Bay, Kenya. His wife, an al-Shabaab member, was also killed. He had been an al-Shabaab member for more than a decade, coordinating al-Qaeda activity within Somalia. The U.S. Department of State had offered a $5 million reward for information leading to his capture. 20010501

A villager had claimed on January 3 to have seen 11 suspected al-Shabaab members entering the county's Boni forest. They were not found. Locals said that farmer Mwalimu Chengo Ponda, in his 30s, was hit by six gunshots in Chomo village.

Reuters reported that police arrested three male "terrorist suspects" who tried to break into the British Army Training Unit in Laikipia County at 5 p.m.

The *BBC* reported that on September 16, 2020, a Somali military court sentenced jihadi Farhan Mohamud Hassan to life in prison for his role in the attack and for membership in al-Shabaab. Hassan told Somali state television that he had transported explosives in jerry cans to Kenya, noting, "I was with 70 men on this side [Somalia]. There were about 115 on the other side [Kenya]." He said he joined al-Shabaab in 2010 and participated in numerous attacks in southern Somalia. 20010502

January 7, 2020: Al-Shabaab attacked a telecommunications mast in Garissa County. Four small children, students at Saretho primary school, trying to take refuge at the Saretho police post were shot dead, as was a teacher, during the morning attack. Police officers killed two terrorists. Two other students were wounded. Some injured attackers escaped. Police seized bomb-making materials. 20010701

January 13, 2020: In a 2 a.m. attack, al-Shabaab killed three non-Muslim teachers and kidnapped a Muslim teacher from a primary school in Kamuthe in Garissa County, torching a police post and destroying a telecommunication mast. The terrorists spared the life of a female nurse because of her gender. Another teacher was wounded. Al-Shabaab claimed credit on its Shahada website. 20011301

February 19, 2020: Al-Shabaab members in police uniforms were suspected of killing three people they had pulled from a Moyale Raha bus heading to Nairobi from Moyale, a market town on the Ethiopian border in Mandera County. The terrorists got in front of the bus, but the driver and passengers knew there was no police roadblock in the area, and kept on going. The terrorists fired, injuring the driver and hitting the front and back tires. The driver lost control and the bus crashed into a ditch. The terrorists killed one Muslim and two non-Muslims. 20021901

September 24, 2020: Al-Shabaab was suspected when gunmen kidnapped three non-Muslim bus passengers 18 miles from Lafey in Mandera County. The attackers forced the 54 people from the bus and chose three passengers, ordering the rest to leave. The bus lacked a mandatory police escort. 20092401

December 27, 2020: Special forces raided an al-Shabaab camp in Lamu County, killing seven terrorists.

December 29, 2020: Gunmen ambushed an ambulance carrying a pregnant woman and killed her husband, then torched the vehicle before midnight in Mandera County. Other passengers in the ambulance were slightly injured.

MALI

January 26, 2020: *Reuters* reported that at 5 a.m., gunmen attacked an army camp near Sokolo in central Mali, killing 19 soldiers and wounding five soldiers.

February 13-14, 2020: *AFP* reported that 30 gunmen conducted an overnight attack on Ogossagou village, inhabited by Fulani (Peul) people, killing 20. Another 28 villagers were missing. The government blamed a traditional Dogon hunters' group.

February 14, 2020: A soldier was killed in a suspected jihadi attack on a military camp in Mondoro.

March 19, 2020: Al-Qaeda-linked jihadis were suspected when gunmen attacked a Malian army

camp in Tarkint in the Gao region, killing 29 soldiers and wounding five people.

March 26, 2020: Gunmen kidnapped Soumaila Cissé, 70, the leader of Mali's political opposition Union for the Republic and Democracy party, and members of his campaign team in the Niafounke circle area near Timbuktu where he was campaigning for the March 29 legislative elections. His bodyguard died from injuries sustained during the abduction and two others were injured. No one claimed credit. Cissé was the runner-up in the 2018 presidential election. On April 7, the UN Security Council called for "the swift liberation" of Cissé. On August 21, *AFP* quoted the Red Cross as saying that Cissé had sent letters to his family in their first contact. Al-Qaeda affiliates are active in the area. He was educated in Senegal as a computer engineer. He was a presidential aide in the early 1990s, then served as finance minister for seven years under then-leader Alpha Oumar Konare. After the elections, he ran the commission of the eight-nation West African Economic and Monetary Union (UEMA) currency and customs agreement. He lost in the presidential elections in 2013 and 2018, won by Ibrahim Boubacar Keita, who was overthrown in a military coup on August 18, 2020. International Committee of the Red Cross chief delegate in Mali, Klaus Spreyermann, said, "the ICRC is not taking part in negotiations".

April 2, 2020: Gunmen on motorcycles attacked Army troops in the Tillaberi region near Mali; four soldiers and 63 jihadis died.

April 6, 2020: Army spokesman Colonel Major (a Malian rank) Diarran Kone said gunmen attacked an army camp in Bamba in the Gao region, killing 25 soldiers and wounding six. Al-Qaeda- or ISIS-linked terrorists were suspected.

June 3, 2020: French Defense Minister Florence Parly announced that French troops had killed Abdelmalek Droukdel, variant Droukdal, 50, leader of al-Qaeda in the Islamic Maghreb, during a joint operation with West African partners in northern Mali. He was believed responsible for hundreds of civilian deaths in recent years. Parly added that he died with "several of his close collaborators". U.S. Africa Command spokesman Colonel Christopher Karns said that the U.S. military provided intelligence for the mission. He had a university degree in mathematics. The *New York Times* reported that the Algerian-born Droukdel had fought the Soviets in Afghanistan, then returned to Algeria in the 1990s to participate in its civil war, joining the Salafist Group for Preaching and Combat. He became the group's commander in 2004. To reignite the group's operations, he contacted the head of al-Qaeda in Iraq, Abu Musab al-Zarqawi, pledging allegiance to the group in 2006. The group moved from battling Algerian soldiers to a campaign of suicide bombings and expanding its targets to foreign nationals, including the headquarters of the UN in Algiers. The group, now AQIM, also conducted operations outside Algeria, conducting activities in Mauritania, Mali, Niger, Tunisia and Libya. Through ransom kidnappings, in five years the group made $91 million and was able to finance the 2012 takeover of northern Mali, setting up a caliphate. After the French threw AQIM out of Mali a year later, in 2017 Droukdal opened the JNIM, led by ethnic Malian Tuareg Iyad Ag Ghali. *AFP* reported on June 19, 2020 that AQIM confirmed Droukdal's death.

July 1, 2020: *AP* and *al-Jazeera* reported that Moulaye Guindo, the mayor of Bankass, told the media that self-described jihadi gunmen wearing uniforms rolled up on motorcycles and pick-up trucks and killed men returning from their fields in the farming villages of Gouari, Djimdo, Pangadougou and Dialaikanda in the central Mopti region, killing 33 people—including women, children, and the elderly—and wounding five. He claimed 15 were killed in Djimdo, 16 in Gouari and two in Pangadougou. No group claimed credit, but observers suspected Fulani armed groups, possibly linked to ISIS and al-Qaeda, who have been targeting Dogon farmers. Youssouf Tiessogue, an elder from Gouari, told *AFP*, "From 3 to 9 p.m., nobody came to our rescue. I deplore the inaction of the army. It is always late and never confronts the bandits even if we tell them where they are." Some people were reported missing.

July 12, 2020: Defense lawyers for alleged jihadist leader Al Hassan Ag Abdoul Aziz Ag Mohamed Ag Mahmoud told the International Criminal Court in The Hague, Netherlands, that he was suffering from post-traumatic stress disorder and was unfit to stand trial on charges of running the brutal Ansar al Dine regime in Timbuktu. He was charged with involvement in crimes including rape, torture, enforced marriages and sexual slavery from April 2012 through January 2013. Defense attorney Nicoletta Montefusco said that judges should appoint an expert to determine his client's ability to stand trial. He added that the defense team could not meet their client in person for four months because of COVID-19 restrictions.

August 22, 2020: Four soldiers died when their vehicle hit a roadside bomb in central Mali.

August 27, 2020: Jihadis killed four Malian soldiers and wounded a dozen near Mopti. Soldiers returned fire, killing 20 gunmen. The army sustained major equipment losses.

September 3, 2020: *Al Jazeera*, *AP*, and *AFP* reported that during the night, jihadis on motorcycles killed ten Malian soldiers, including a senior officer, in Guire near the Mauritanian border. The attackers set fire to four vehicles. It was the largest attack on the military since its August 18 coup by the National Committee for the Salvation of the People against President Ibrahim Boubacar Keita, 75.

In an attack the previous week, gunmen ambushed an anti-pouching unit 15 miles from Konna, killing four soldiers and wounding a dozen.

September 5, 2020: *AFP* reported that two French soldiers in the anti-terrorist Barkhane force were killed and a third was wounded when their armored vehicle hit a roadside bomb in the Tessalit Province of Kidal region. The two dead soldiers were members of a paratroop regiment based in Tarbes in southwest France. 20090501

October 6, 2020: Gunmen kidnapped 10 villagers near the Burkina Faso border.

October 13, 2020: *AFP* reported that jihadi attacks killed 23 people. During the night, gunmen raided a military outpost in Sokuora, near the Burkina Faso border, killing nine soldiers. Reinforcements were ambushed and hit a roadside bomb the next morning, killing two soldiers and wounding ten. A dozen civilians, including two women and a baby, traveling in a minibus to a weekly market in Bankass were also killed in the attack.

The military said 13 terrorists were killed and warplanes destroyed two vehicles.

The previous week, jihadis killed five villagers in Farabougou.

October 15, 2020: *AFP* reported that an Egyptian UN peacekeeping contingent's vehicle hit a roadside bomb 30 miles south of Kidal in northern Mali, killing an Egyptian peacekeeper and seriously wounding a second. The Egyptians had been protecting a supply convoy. 20101501

Gunmen fired at the UN camp in Timbuktu, injuring a peacekeeper from Burkina Faso. 20101502

October 30, 2020: *AFP* reported on November 2 that French airstrikes killed more than 50 Qaeda-linked Ansarul Islam jihadis in central Mali near the borders of Burkina Faso and Niger. Thirty 30 motorcycles were destroyed. Two Mirage jets and a drone fired missiles. Military spokesman Colonel Frederic Barbry added that four terrorists were captured. Authorities found explosives and a suicide vest.

November 4, 2020: *AFP* reported that security officers found a decapitated body of a man in his 50s in Fana, the ninth in two years. He was married with four children. The body was found in his bedroom. Residents suspected ritual murder, although authorities had not identified a motive.

November 12, 2020: *AFP* reported that French Barkhane mission soldiers killed 30 Group to Support Islam and Muslims (GSIM) jihadis after several hours of ground combat near Niaki. The army captured or destroyed 20 motorbikes and weapons. Barkhane forces killed GSIM military commander Ba Ag Moussa.

November 26, 2020: *Reuters* reported that terrorists killed six rice farmers and wounded another near Farabougou. Another villager was

reported missing. Suspected jihadis began attacking the village in October and by November 26 had killed 23 villagers and burned crops.

November 30, 2020: Jihadis were suspected when terrorists armed with mortars and rockets attacked military camps housing international forces in Kidal, Gao and Menaka, which are several hundred kilometers from each other. Kidal resident Souleymane Ag Mohamed Ali reported more than 10 explosions coming from the direction of the camp for U.N. peacekeepers and soldiers for the French Operation Barkhane. In the morning, rockets hit the camp in Kidal. No group claimed credit. *AFP* reported that no casualties were announced. 20113001-03

December 28, 2020: *Reuters* reported that Jama'at Nusrat al-Islam wal-Muslimin (JNIM), al-Qaeda's North Africa branch, claimed credit or killing three French Operation Barkhane soldiers when an improvised explosive device hit their armored vehicle. 20122801

MOZAMBIQUE

February 7, 2020: ISIS-affiliated jihadis beheaded seven people in the Quissanga district during the week. The terrorists had attacked homes, 76 schools, and five health clinics. Since the attacks began in October 2017, nearly 500 people had been killed, many by beheading. A handwritten letter from the Armed forces of Ali Xababe (al-Shabaab) was posted on social media, saying the terrorists would continue to move south as far as the Mieze high security prison outside Pemba. France's Total and American ExxonMobil, which operate two onshore gas liquefaction projects, asked the Maputo government to send more troops to protect their installations.

April 24, 2020: *Time* reported that the government acknowledged an ISIS presence; police had reported a "massacre" of 52 villagers in Cabo Delgado region. A local ISIS affiliate claimed credit.

May 14, 2020: The government announced that its armed forces killed 50 ISIS-affiliated jihadis during the week in two battles in the country's north where the insurgents had launched 11 attacks in May, a noteworthy increase in extremist violence in gas-rich Cabo Delgado Province. Jihadis on April 7 killed 52 young men in Xitaxi village.

June 4, 2020: *AFP* reported that the UN Office for the Coordination of Humanitarian Affairs (OCHA) announced that since 2017, 300 jihadi attacks had led 211,485 people, most of them women and children, to flee their homes in northern Cabo Delgado Province. Attacks included burning huts, decapitating villagers and killing more than 1,100 people, according to the Armed Conflict Location and Event Data Project (ACLED). The terrorists are known locally as al-Shabaab—no relation to the same-named Somali jihadis.

June 27, 2020: *AFP* reported that five suspected jihadi gunmen wearing military fatigues similar to those used by government forces ambushed and killed eight employees of a private construction firm working on the multi-billion-dollar liquefied natural gas project in the north. Fenix Constructions Service Lda, which is subcontracted by French oil company Total, operates in Palma. The attack occurred four kilometers north of Mocimboa da Praia in Cabo Delgado Province, some 50 kilometers from the Total LNG site in Palma. Three of the 14 occupants in the vehicle survived. As of early July, the other three were missing.

Meanwhile, jihadis attacked and temporarily occupied the small town of Mocimboa da Praia for the second time in 2020. The Islamic State Central African Province claimed credit.

August 12, 2020: *AFP* and the *Moz24Horas* website reported that at dawn, the Islamic State Central Africa Province (ISCAP) took over the port of Mocimboa da Praia in the gas-rich north after several days of attacks on surrounding villages. During the attack, a rocket-propelled grenade sank a boat owned by former president Armando Guebuza.

August 23, 2020: The premises of the private-owned newspapers, the weekly *Canal de Mozambique* and the daily *CanalMoz*, were firebombed during the night. *Zitamar* news agency

reported that a container of gasoline was found at the site. Days earlier, *Canal* had reported about bribery and the efforts of prominent Mozambicans to win control of part of the fuel retail business worth millions of dollars. Erik Charas, founder of the newspaper *A Verdade*, tweeted that the attack was "a premeditated criminal act", that the door to the building had been sabotaged earlier in the day.

November 4, 2020: *Lusa, Mediafax* and *Zitamar News* reported that 40 people fleeing jihadi violence in the northern part of Cabo Delgado Province drowned when their boat sank after hitting rocks near Ibo Island. They had left from Palma, a coastal town near the border with Tanzania. The boat picked up most of its 74 passengers near Namandingo. The overloaded boat normally carries 30 people.

November 6-9, 2020: *Al-Jazeera*, the *Mozambique News Agency, Pinnacle News, Newsweek* and *AFP* reported that ISIS-linked al-Shabaab (the Mozambique version has no relation to the Somali al-Qaeda affiliate) terrorists beheaded more than 50 people at a soccer pitch turned into an "execution ground" in Muatide village. Another two people were beheaded in Nanjaba village during the night. The villages are in the Miudumbe and Macomia districts of Cabo Delgado Province. The terrorists kidnapped women and children and torched homes. *AP* reported that the bodies of 15 boys, who were participating in a male initiation ceremony, were found among the dead.

December 7, 2020: *AFP* reported that jihadis attacked government soldiers, torched homes, and occupied the northern village of Mute in Cabo Delgado Province, near a giant LNG gas project. Soldiers retook the village on December 10.

December 11, 2020: *AFP* reported that the U.S.-based Armed Conflict Location and Event Data (ACLED) group announced that insurgents had conducted 711 attacks since 2017, claiming more than 2,400 lives and displacing a half million people.

December 29, 2020: *AFP* reported that IS-affiliated al-Shabaab gunmen attacked Monjane, a small village close to a huge natural gas project in Cabo Delgado Province. Residents fled to nearby Senga, three miles away.

NIGER

January 9, 2020: *Reuters* and *AP* reported that the Islamic State was suspected when terrorists attacked the army's Chinagodrar Advanced Military post on the border with Mali, killing 25 soldiers and wounding six. Niger's Defense Ministry said 63 jihadis also died. On January 13, authorities reported that the death toll of victims had risen to 89, and that 77 terrorists were killed.

March 15, 2020: The army claimed that during an overnight attack by Boko Haram fighters on the eastern Toumour Province, air and ground forces killed 50 Boko Haram terrorists and destroyed several vehicles. One soldier was injured. 20031501

May 9, 2020: The Ministry of National Defense announced that gunmen on motorcycles attacked three villages in western Niger's Anzourou area, near its border with Mali, killing at least 20 people, shooting at residents, robbing shops and taking food and cattle before fleeing toward Mali.

May 11, 2020: Niger's defense ministry announced the soldiers had killed 75 Boko Haram terrorists in two operations over the weekend. Soldiers killed 25 on May 12 after Boko Haram attacked military positions over the weekend. Nigerien forces destroyed several bombs in Diffa region.

Meanwhile, forces from Niger, Nigeria, Chad and Cameroon conducted air raids on islands in Lake Chad sheltering Boko Haram fighters, killing 50 terrorists in Nigerian territory.

Days earlier, jihadis with another extremist group attacked three villages in western Niger near its border with Mali, killing at least 20 people.

May 31, 2020: UNHCR reported that dozens of gunmen on motorcycles attacked Intikane, a western town that had hosted 35,000 displaced people (20,000 from Mali and 15,000 from else-

where in Niger), killing three and cutting off the community's water supply. UNHCR tried to provide water for hand-washing in the face of Covid-19. ISIS-linked terrorists were suspected. Two victims were leaders within the local refugee communities. The terrorists torched relief items and destroyed mobile phone towers, cutting off communications.

June 24, 2020: *Al-Jazeera* and *AFP* reported that in the afternoon, gunmen on a motorbike drove into a village in the Tillaberi region and kidnapped 10 Action and Impact Progress (APIS, a UN World Food Program partner) humanitarian aid workers distributing food in southwestern Niger. 20062401

August 9, 2020: *Reuters, Fox News, AFP,* and *AP* reported that in the morning, gunmen on motorcycles killed six French citizens, a Nigerien driver, and a Nigerien guide who riding in a vehicle belonging to the French humanitarian organization ACTED and were visiting a wildlife park that features the Kouré Giraffe Reserve in the Tillaberi region. Jihadis were active in the area. *AP* reported on September 17 that the Islamic State in the Greater Sahara in its *al-Naba* newsletter claimed credit, saying that a security detachment carried out a "blitz attack with firearms" in the Koure area. It showed a photo of two of the hostages still alive. The victims worked for the Paris-based NGO ACTED and Geneva-based IMPACT Initiatives. 20080901

October 27, 2020: *CBS News,* the *Washington Post, AP,* and *AFP* reported that six gunmen armed with AK47s kidnapped an American missionary from his farm on the outskirts of Massalata, 250 miles east of Niamey and six miles from the Nigerian border. The gunmen left on three motorcycles, heading for the border. No one claimed credit, but jihadis were suspected. Bruce Walton told local *Radio Niyya* that his son Philip Nathan Walton, 27, had been kidnapped from his home overnight. Bruce Walton observed that "during the night six men, possibly Fulani, came on foot… They were looking for money in the house but there was not enough. There were only 20,000 CFA francs ($35, 30 euros). After that, they left with him." He noted that the six spoke Hausa and some English. Philip had lived in the area with his wife and a child for two years. *AP* reported that the gunmen demanded a $1 million+ ransom from Bruce, who lives a half mile away. They threatened to otherwise sell him to extremists.

The *Washington Post, CNN, Bloomberg, Politico, CBS News,* and *ABC News* reported on October 31 that Navy SEAL Team Six rescued Walton overnight in northern Nigeria, killing six of the seven kidnappers. The *New York Times* reported that the rescuers tracked the attackers' phones to a hideout. Some 30 commandos parachuted in, then hiked three miles to the lair. No soldiers were injured. No ransom was paid. 20102701

December 12, 2020: *AFP* reported that the day before municipal and regional elections, Boko Haram killed 34 people and burned 1,000 homes and the central market in Toumour in the Diffa region. BH claimed credit on December 16.

December 21, 2020: *AFP* reported on December 24 that on December 21, the Defence Ministry said that seven troops and 11 suspected jihadis died in an ambush by gunmen on motorbikes and other vehicles on an army patrol in the Taroun area in Tillaberi region in the west, ahead of weekend elections. Two other soldiers and a civilian were injured.

Nigeria

January 4, 2020: Major General Olusegun Adeniyi said that Boko Haram conducted an attack near Jakana, 28 miles away from Maiduguri in Borno State, killing six soldiers.

January 6, 2020: *Reuters* reported that a bomb exploded at 5 p.m. on a bridge in Gamboru in Borno State, killing 30 people and injuring 35. The Islamic State West Africa Province (ISWAP) was suspected.

January 7, 2020: In the late evening, the Islamic State West African Province set off a suicide bomb and ambushed a convoy under military escort near a military checkpoint at the entrance to Monguno, killing eight Nigerian soldiers. Soldiers repelled terrorists who attempted to invade

the town. A rocket-propelled grenade landed in the camp, burning 300 shelters built by the International Committee of the Red Cross.

January 17, 2020: The Islamic State's West Africa Province released a video that showed a hooded child firing a pistol, executing a Christian man.

January 20, 2020: Boko Haram killed the Reverend Lawan Andimi, a Christian pastor who had pleaded for his life in a video released on January 17. He was kidnapped earlier in January in the Michika local government area, where he chaired the local chapter of the Christian Association of Nigeria.

January 21, 2020: Osai Ojigho, director of Amnesty International in Nigeria, said that Boko Haram attacked his hometown in the Chibok local government area of northeastern Borno State.

February 9, 2020: The *New York Times, CNN,* and *BBC* reported that Boko Haram was suspected of attacking Auno on a major highway on Borno State, killing 30 people, including a pregnant woman and a baby, and abducting women and children. Travelers were burnt to death while sleeping in their vehicles during an overnight stop. At 10 p.m., the terrorists drove up in trucks mounted with heavy weapons and destroyed 18 vehicles, including trucks carrying food. Most of the victims were en route to Maiduguri.

March 1, 2020: *AFP* reported that armed "bandits" attacked villages in Kaduna State, killing 50 people.

March 21, 2020: Boko Haram killed 50 Nigerian soldiers in an ambush at the Gorge area near Goneri in Yobe State. The terrorists fired rocket-propelled grenades and guns, attacking from the rear.

May 18, 2020: After sundown, when villagers were preparing to break their Ramadan fast, Boko Haram terrorists attacked Gajigana, entering on the opposite side of the village where Nigerian soldiers were posted. The terrorists killed 20 people and wounded 25. Many were too weak to flee after fasting all day in the 108 degree Fahrenheit heat.

June 2020: On July 22, 2020, *AP* and *CNN* reported that Boko Haram was suspected of releasing a video showing the execution of five Nigerian men who had been kidnapped in June in northeastern Nigeria. Nigerian President Muhammadu Buhari said the victims were staff members of Nigeria's State Emergency Management Agency and the international charities France-based Action Against Hunger, Rich International and New York-based International Rescue Committee. They had been delivering food, water, and medical supplies and were traveling on the main road to Maiduguri from Monguno when they were stopped at a roadblock. Terrorists had killed four aid workers in December 2019 on the same highway. Authorities said the kidnappers wanted a ransom. In the video, a person speaking Hausa said, "This is a message to the infidels who are using you to cheat and turn our people into unbelievers." One of the dead aid workers was Luka Filibus, a child protection assistant from northern Nigeria. He had earlier fled his home. Victim Abdurahman Bulama, who worked for the Borno State relief agency, was about to wed. Another victim was a security personnel member working with the team. The video showed the hostages kneeling, with red blindfolds, in front of five terrorists wearing military fatigues and face-covering scarves. The terrorists shot them. 20069901

June 9, 2020: *AFP* and *AP* reported that the Islamic State West Africa Province (ISWAP) terrorist faction attacked people watching over their cattle at a watering hole in an open field outside the village of Felo (variant Foduma Kolomaiya village in the Gubio area of Borno State), using their vehicles and motorcycles to run over men, women and children and shooting others, killing 69, wounding many others, and stealing 1,200 cattle. Still others were reported missing. Local leaders suggested that the jihadis were avenging the death two months earlier of two terrorists by a self-defense group trying to stop cattle rustling. ISWAP broke from Boko Haram in 2016. Defense group leader Malam Bunu said the terrorists returned on the morning of June 10 to kill a surviving herdsman and torch the village. An air force fighter jet fired at the fleeing terrorists.

The previous week, terrorists kidnapped five people, including a regional chairman for the Borno State Regional Emergency Services. On June 7, terrorists kidnapped but later released civil servants and teachers.

The *Washington Post* added on June 10 that 81 people had died in the two-hour attack. Those were more deaths than those from Covid-19 in three months in Borno State. Modu Ajimi, 42, a local civil servant in Gubio district, lost four cousins—Ari, Mamman, Ibrahim, and Maina—who were fetching water to wash their hands to prevent Covid-19 from spreading. Artistan Umar Ashami, 37, lost his sister, 30.

June 13, 2020: Islamic State West Africa Province conducted three attacks in Borno State, killing more than 40 people.

The terrorists attacked Monguno, where 150,000 displaced civilians reside; a United Nations office and a Nigerian military base are also located there. Mohammed Ibrahim, a member of Monguno's community safety force, said some attackers were from Chad and Niger, and added that three civilians and several soldiers were killed. A second witness added that the terrorists used 13 vehicles, including heavily armed trucks. The fighters dropped letters written in English, Hausa and Arabic warning people to stay away from the military and humanitarian organizations.

Residents said terrorists killed 40 people in the Nganzai area's Usmanti village and burned down several homes.

Terrorists also attacked Zuwo village in the Gubio area.

June 26, 2020: *AP* reported that the Islamic State in West Africa Province, a Boko Haram splinted, warned that it would target civilians who help the military or humanitarian organizations. During a single week earlier in June, it had killed more than 120 people, including 40 in Monguno, which houses 150,000 displaced people. The International Crisis Group estimated that the ISWAP has 5,000 members.

July 4, 2020: Suspected jihadis shot at a U.N. aid helicopter in northeastern Nigeria, killing two civilians, including a child, 5, in Borno State. There were no aid workers on board the U.N.

Humanitarian Air Service helicopter. The crew members were unhurt. President Muhammadu Buhari blamed Boko Haram. 20070402

July 18, 2020: *Bloomberg* reported that Defense headquarters spokesman Benard Onyeuko announced that Nigerian troops battled gunmen in the Jibia district of Katsina state. Three soldiers and 17 cattle rustlers and kidnappers were killed. He questioned news reports that said that 23 soldiers died. The Ansaru faction of Boko Haram is active in the area.

August 18, 2020: *Al-Jazeera* reported that the Islamic State West Africa Province (ISWAP) attacked Kukawa in Borno State, seizing hundreds of returning residents who had fled their homes in November 2018. Two days later, the Nigerian Army said it was "in full control" of the town. Three soldiers and eight terrorists were killed and two soldiers were wounded in the gun battle. The residents had returned home on August 2 under military protection after living on camps in Maiduguri.

September 3, 2020: Gunmen attempted to kidnap residents in Dukku in the Rijau local government area. Some gunmen and 17 local defense fighters were killed.

Also that week, gunmen shot to death five people, including a woman and a policeman, and wounded eight other people, during a failed bank robbery in the same area.

September 25, 2020: *Al-Jazeera* reported that gunmen attacked a security convoy taking displaced people back to their homes, killing 11 people. ISIS said on its *Amaq* website that it had killed 30 police officers and soldiers on a road leading to the fishing town of Baga in Borno State. Borno State police said eight police officers and three members of a pro-government militia were killed and 13 people were wounded in the noon attack. Two soldiers, a police officer, and a militia member told *Reuters* that four soldiers were also killed. *AFP* reported that Borno Governor Babagana Umara Zulum, who was traveling with the convoy, was unharmed. In July 2020, ISIS's West Africa Province (ISWAP) attacked his convoy outside Baga, forcing him to cancel his visit.

November 1, 2020: Terrorists killed 12 people and abducted nine women and young girls in the morning in Takulashi village, less than 12 miles from Chibok in Borno State.

November 28, 2020: *AFP* reported that Boko Haram claimed credit after terrorists on motorcycles killed 43 farm workers and injured six in rice fields in Koshobe near Maiduguri by tying them up and slitting their throats. *AFP* later reported that dozens, including ten women, were reported missing. The laborers from Sokoto State had traveled to the area to find work. *AFP* increased the tally to 110 dead the next day.

In two separate incidents in October, Boko Haram killed 22 farmers working on their irrigation fields near Maiduguri.

December 8, 2020: Amnesty International charged that at least 10,000 civilians had died in Nigerian military custody since 2011 after being detained in connection with the Boko Haram insurgency. Many died at the "infamous Giwa Barracks", where Amnesty found "severe overcrowding, scarce food and water, extreme heat, infestation by parasites and insects, and lack of access to adequate sanitation and health care".

December 11, 2020: *AP, CNN, Reuters, al-Jazeera,* and *Business Insider* reported that hundreds of gunmen riding motorcycles and firing AK-47s attacked the Government Science Secondary School in Kankara in northwestern Katsina State around 9 p.m. Police fired back during a 90-minute clash. One student reported that a gunman wounded a policeman guarding the school. Some 1,200 students attend the school, although many had gone home after exams. The gunmen demanded money from the students and stole belongings from their lockers. Hundreds of students scattered; some 400 of them were reported missing and possibly kidnapped two days later. President Muhammadu Buhari said that the armed forces, supported by airpower, located the "bandits'" enclave in Zango/Paula forest in the Kankara area, exchanging gunfire with the kidnappers, who may have been seeking ransoms. Some blamed Fulani herders or jihadis. The boys were later reported in the Rugu forest. The *Washington Post* reported on December

15 that Boko Haram leader Abubakar Shekau in an audio claimed credit for kidnapping more than 300 boys outside its usual area of operation, saying it was discouraging "Western education". "What happened in Katsina was done to promote Islam and discourage un-Islamic practices." The hostages included student Muhammad Bello, 14; Shamsu Ibrahim; two sons of Salisu Masi; Usman Mohammad Rabiu, son of Murjanatu Rabiu; Annas Shuaibu, 16, son of retired health worker Shuaibu Kankara; and the son of Marwa Hamza Kankara. The Katsina governor told local reporters that he had made contact with the abductors but did not provide details. The state's governor said 333 remained missing as of December 16. One of the surviving students said the terrorists had split the hostages into several groups.

AFP reported on December 16 that Boko Haram recruited three local gangs, led by local crime chiefs Awwalun Daudawa, 43, Idi Minorti and Dankarami, in northwest Nigeria to kidnap the schoolboys. A security source told *AFP* that Daudawa is "an armed robber and a cattle rustler before he turned to gun-running, bringing in weapons from Libya, where he had received training, and selling them to bandits... Over time, he forged an alliance with Boko Haram and became their gunrunner, taking weapons the group seizes from the Nigerian security forces in raids and ambushes and selling them to bandits for a cut... Awwalun Daudawa was spotted in the forest in the Kankara area where he recently relocated and there were reports that he was planning something but it was not clear what it was." Another *AFP* source reported that the children were taken into Zamfara State.

Reuters reported on December 17 that a video purportedly released by Boko Haram showed some of the kidnapped schoolboys in a wood begging security forces to leave the area. *Reuters, CNN, Bloomberg, AP, NTA,* and *UPI* reported later that day that security forces rescued 344 of the kidnapped schoolboys. No ransom was paid. Abdu Labaran, spokesman for state governor Aminu Bello Masari, claimed that bandits masquerading as Boko Haram were responsible. The kidnapping would have marked a geographic expansion of BH's area of operations.

Reuters added on December 20 that freed hostage Annas Shuaibu said the gunmen had beaten the boys, who received scant food, forcing them to eat leaves and drink from pools of water in the forest.

December 19, 2020: During the night, gunmen kidnapped 84 Islamic school students in Dandume in Katsina State, some 40 miles from Kankara, where gunmen had kidnapped 344 schoolboys. Authorities and a local community self-defense group freed the hostages after a gun battle. The gunmen had kidnapped four people and stolen 12 cattle before taking the schoolchildren, who were en route home from a celebration.

December 24, 2020: *CNN* and *UPI* reported that Boko Haram attacked the majority-Christian village of Pemi in Borno State on Christmas Eve, killing seven people, kidnapping another seven, including a pastor, burning ten homes, and looting food supplies that were meant to be distributed to residents to celebrate Christmas. Kachallah Usman, secretary of the Chibok local government area, added, "They also burned down a church, a dispensary and several houses." The church was later identified as the Evangelical Church of the Brethren. An eyewitness said a Christian youth organization was holding a Christmas parade when the attack began.

December 27, 2020: Boko Haram was suspected when gunmen attacked schools, shops, and places of worship in four villages in Borno State, killing ten people. Gunmen hit government offices and burned down a police station in Azare, killing a soldier, officer, and a local self-defense fighter. Terrorists attacked Shaffa, killing an uncle and a friend of local resident Ibrahim Buba, and five other people. The terrorists stole thousands of bags of farm products recently harvested by farmers and emptied shops and market stalls.

RWANDA

June 26, 2020: Rwanda Defense Forces spokesman Innocent Munyengango said three of its soldiers were wounded in a nighttime attack in Nyaruguru district conducted by gunmen who crossed over from Burundi. The attackers fled back toward the border, one kilometer away, leaving behind four dead gunmen and military equipment, including weapons and radios. The Army said, "The attacking force originated and retreated back to Burundi through Burundi Defense Force position at Gihisi in Bukinanyana commune, Cibitoke Province." Munyengango said the attackers planned to harm people inside a model village for internally displaced people. 20062602

SOMALIA

January 8, 2020: *Reuters* and *AP* reported that al-Shabaab claimed credit for a car bomb that went off in the morning in Mogadishu's Maka al-Mukarama Street at the Sayidka junction security checkpoint near the presidential palace and other government buildings, killing three people and wounding 11, including three women. Mayoral spokesman Salah Omar said the bomb was attached to a vehicle that soldiers were searching and was remotely detonated. The dead included two government officials, including an advisor to the parliament speaker and a Ministry department director.

January 11, 2020: The *AFIO Weekly Intelligence Notes,* citing *Anadolu,* reported that al-Shabaab gunmen killed Dhayow Osman, national Intelligence and Security Agency (NISA) chief for Qoryoley, in Mogadishu. He was shot in the chest several times.

January 18, 2020: An al-Shabaab suicide car bomber hit a construction site alongside a highway near Mogadishu, killing two people and wounding more than 20, including six Turkish nationals, two seriously. Somali police Col. Abdi Abdullahi said that the Turkish construction workers appeared to be the bomber's target. The workers were building a highway between Mogadishu and Afgoye. 20011801

February 18, 2020: A U.S. air strike killed three people near Wadajir.

February 22, 2020: *CNN* reported on February 25 that a February 22 U.S. AFRICOM airstrike in the Saakow area killed an al-Shabaab leader who had a role in "planning and directing terrorist operations," including a January 5 attack on Manda Bay, Kenya, that killed two American defense contractors and a U.S. soldier. His wife, an al-Shabaab member, was also killed. Another al-Shabaab member was injured.

February 23, 2020: *Bloomberg* reported that U.S. Africa Command bombed an al-Shabaab compound near Dujuuma, wounding three terrorists.

February 25, 2020: A U.S. AFRICOM airstrike killed Mohamud Haji Sirad, 55, a local manager of Hormuud, Somalia's largest telecom company, when two missiles struck his farm on the outskirts of Jilib. AFRICOM and the Somali government said the airstrike killed a member of al-Shabaab.

March 7, 2020: A U.S. AFRICOM airstrike killed four al-Shabaab terrorists in the Gandarshe area.

March 9, 2020: *GaroweOnline* reported on March 11 that Fahah Yasin, head of the NISA intelligence service, claimed that Muse Moalim, who had run al-Shabaab's Amniyat intelligence service, was believed to have been killed by his fellow terrorists near Buale in the Middle Juba region the night of March 9.

March 25, 2020: A suicide bomber walked into a Mogadishu tea shop and set off his explosives, killing two people.

April 2, 2020: The *BBC* and *Daily Exclusives of Uganda* reported that al-Shabaab had warned the coronavirus was spread "by the crusader forces who have invaded the country and the disbelieving countries that support them".

May 4, 2020: *AFP, AP* and *BBC* reported that a Kenyan-registered twin-engine African Express plane crashed during the afternoon on approach to Bardale under unclear circumstances. The plane was carrying coronavirus medical supplies in Somalia. Two Kenyans and four Somalis were killed. The flight originated in Mogadishu with a stop in Baidoa. The Somali transport ministry deemed the crash "a terrible accident". Ahmed Isaq, an official with the Southwestern State regional administration, said a missile fired from the ground hit the plane as it approached the airstrip in Bay region. The airstrip is a base for the Ethiopian military under the multinational African Union mission. *Reuters* reported that a witness at the airfield told former Somali defense minister Abdirashid Abdullahi Mohamed that the plane appeared to have been shot down. The Kenyan Civil Aviation Authority lost contact with the plane at around 4:20 p.m.

May 17, 2020: An al-Shabaab suicide bomber set off his explosives on a motorized cycle-taxi in Galkayo in Puntland's Mudug region, killing Ahmed Muse Nur, 70-something governor of the region, and three of his bodyguards who were in a vehicle outside the regional administration's headquarters.

May 31, 2020: Police officer Abdullahi Ahmed said that in the morning, a minibus hit a roadside bomb in the Hawa Abdi area near Mogadishu, killing eight civilians and seriously wounding several passengers. Al-Shabaab was suspected.

June 12, 2020: Al-Shabaab announced that it had opened a COVID-19 isolation and care facility, featuring a 24/7 hotline, in Jilib, in a building previously used by UNICEF. *Radio Andulus*, the group's propaganda branch, broadcast a speech by Sheikh Mohamed Bali, a senior al-Shabab official and a member of the group's ad hoc COVID-19 response committee, in which he said "I am urging people with the disease symptoms to come to the medical facility and avoid infecting other Muslims."

June 20, 2020: *Reuters* and *Press TV* reported that a bomb exploded in front of the house of a military official in Wanlaweyn during the night, killing four people, including soldiers and civilians. Wanlaweyn police officer Mohamed Nur said, "First we heard a blast at the house. The military officer was absent by then. Guards and residents came to find out what caused the blast, and then a second blast went off." Al-Shabaab was suspected.

June 21, 2020: *Press TV* reported that three suicide car bombers set off their car at a checkpoint in Bacadweyn in Galmudug State, killing three

soldiers and wounding two others, according to Major Abdullahi Ahmed in Galkayo. Al-Shabaab was suspected.

June 23, 2020: An al-Shabaab suicide bomber set off his explosives inside a Turkish military training base as new cadets were doing their morning drills in Mogadishu, killing two people, including a Somali citizen and wounding another person. The Turkish Defense Ministry denied that any Turks were harmed and added that there was no damage to the Camp Turksom barracks. *Anadolu* reported that Turkish Ambassador Mehmet Yilmaz and Somali army chief General Odowa Yusuf Rage said at the last minute, Somali guards spotted the terrorist and shot him outside the main gate, foiling the attack. Al-Shabaab claimed credit via its *Radio al-Furqan* affiliate. 20062301

June 30, 2020: Three mortar rounds hit inside and around Mogadishu Stadium during the evening. Al-Shabaab was suspected. The rounds went off after President Mohamed Abdullahi Mohamed attended the opening ceremonies that included a soccer game.

July 2, 2020: *Reuters* reported that eight years after a suicide bomber destroyed the building, the renovated National Theater in Mogadishu reopened.

July 4, 2020: *NPR* and *AP* reported that a suicide car bomber set off his explosives at the gates of the motor vehicle imports duty authority headquarters near the port in Mogadishu's southwestern Hamar Jajab district. He had driven through the first security checkpoint, whereupon police officers fired. Five police officers and another person were wounded. The bomber was killed before he could reach the collection center.

A land mine was remotely detonated in the morning in a restaurant in the suburbs of Baidoa, killing five people and wounding 10 others.

July 8, 2020: *Reuters* reported that a bomb went off in a road in Hodan district in Mogadishu, killing two policemen, injuring two civilians, and destroying a police car.

July 13, 2020: An al-Shabaab suicide car bomb targeted the convoy of Army chief General Odowa Yusuf Rage in Mogadishu, killing a pedestrian and the bomber. The bomber tried to ram his vehicle into the convoy; his bodyguards opened fire, setting off the car's explosives. Several people, including some of the bodyguards, were injured, some seriously. Shops and businesses were damaged. The convoy was en route to a military camp.

July 21, 2020: *The Hill* reported that U.S. Africa Command forces conducted an airstrike against ISIS after the terrorists attacked partner forces in a remote location near Timirshe in the northeast, killing seven terrorists.

August 8, 2020: *NPR, Reuters,* and *AP* reported that an al-Shabaab car bomb exploded at the gates of the 12th April Army Brigade base near the newly-reopened sports stadium in the Warta-Nabadda district of Mogadishu, killing eight soldiers and wounding 14 others. Soldiers opened fire after the explosion. Army Major Abdullahi Mohamud said "It must be a suicide car bomb." Al-Shabaab military operations spokesman Abdiasis Abu Musab said: "We conducted a successful martyrdom operation on a major apostate military base in Mogadishu. The enemy suffered many casualties and wounded, military vehicles destroyed."

August 10, 2020: During the evening, an inmate grabbed an officer's gun and began firing, starting a riot in the heavily-fortified Mogadishu Central Prison in the old Hamar Jajab neighborhood. Several inmates, including some al-Shabaab members jailed on terrorism charges, picked up the guns of fallen guards. Fifteen prisoners and four guards died and eight people were wounded. *Garoweonline* reported that Mubarak Ibrahim Idle, an al-Shabaab prisoner, escaped. He was serving a 10-year sentence issued in 2014 for terrorism offenses. On August 17, police spokesman Abdiqani Mohamed Qalaf announced that the government suspended Brigadier General Aden Hussein Kulmiye, the prison's warden.

August 16, 2020: A suicide car bomb exploded and gunfire was heard during the afternoon at the new Elite Hotel on Lido Beach in Mogadishu.

The *Washington Post* reported that the gun battle with state security forces continued into the evening. Abdirizak Abdi, a member of the Information Ministry, and Defense Ministry employee Dahir Ali Gawl, were killed. Aamin Ambulance Services said it transported 43 people to hospitals. *AFP* reported that others were taken hostage. Two of the four gunmen were killed at the hotel's gate; the other two remained inside, firing automatic rifles. Al-Shabaab claimed credit on its *Radio Andalus. AP* reported that after a five-hour siege, security forces took back the hotel, rescuing 205 people who were trapped. Sixteen people, including the five attackers, were killed. The hotel is owned by parliamentarian Abdullahi Mohamed Noor, a former Minister of Finance.

August 17, 2020: *Reuters* reported that al-Shabaab conducted a suicide car bomb and gun assault on a Somali military base in the Goofgaduud area, about 30 kilometers from Baidoa in Somalia's southwest. A suicide car bomb crashed into the base's gate, killing three soldiers. Soldiers fled and al-Shabaab entered the base, planting a booby-trap bomb on one of the dead men. When soldiers came back to investigate, the bomb killed another two soldiers. Al-Shabaab military operations spokesman Abdiasis Abu Musab claimed that eight soldiers, including the base commander, died.

September 7, 2020: *CNN, ABC News,* and *AP* reported that an al-Shabaab suicide bomber attacked a vehicle carrying U.S. and Somali forces in the vicinity of Jana Cabdalle, killing two Somali soldiers and injuring three Somali soldiers and an American service member. U.S. Africa Command said the terrorists used "a vehicle employed as an improvised explosive device and mortar fire". The suicide bomber was stopped at a checkpoint en route to attacking the military compound. One al-Shabaab terrorist died. 20090701

September 9, 2020: A suicide bomber set off his explosives vest outside a restaurant near a security checkpoint close to the presidential palace in Mogadishu during the evening, killing three civilians, including a young boy, and injuring seven people. Al-Shabaab was suspected.

September 11, 2020: A suicide bomber set off his explosives at the end of Friday prayers near the gate of a mosque in Kismayo, killing two people and injuring six as they left after services. Local official suggested the main target was the head of the regional chamber of commerce, who was wounded. Al-Shabaab was suspected.

October 14, 2020: *Reuters* reported that a UN sanctions panel indicated that al-Shabaab had moved millions of dollars through the formal banking system and invested its "significant budgetary surplus" in businesses and real estate in Mogadishu. The report mentioned two bank accounts held at Salaam Somali Bank, founded in 2009 as part of the Hormuud group of companies. The report said nearly $1.7 million moved through one of the accounts during a 10-week period until mid-July 2020. A second account appeared to handle fees levied on businessmen using Mogadishu port. The account had $1.1 million moved through it from mid-February until the end of June 2020. The two accounts processed more than 128 transactions exceeding the $10,000 threshold that should trigger automatic reporting to the Financial Reporting Centre. One road checkpoint made between $1.8 million and $2.4 million per year.

Al-Shabaab's 2019 expenditure was believed to be $21 million, with a quarter allocated to the Amniyat intelligence organization.

October 14, 2020: Al-Shabaab ambushed a military convoy traveling between the towns of Afoye and Wanlaweyn in Lower Shabelle region, killing eight soldiers. Two other soldiers were reported missing. Al-Shabaab claimed it had killed 25 soldiers. *Al-Jazeera* reported that 13 Somali troops were killed. A military spokesman said the army had killed four gunmen.

Somalia's intelligence agency said it arrested several smugglers and seized circa 80 tons of sulfuric acid, an explosives precursor, preventing the chemical from being smuggled into al-Shabaab turf.

November 6, 2020: On December 4, 2020, the *New York Times*, *Business Insider* and *The Guardian* reported that a member, 54, of the CIA's Special Activities Center and four Somalis were killed by a car bomb on a mission in Gendershe

to capture al-Shabaab's senior bombmaker and leader of its media wing, Abdullahi Osman Mohamed, alias Engineer Ismail, a Specially Designated Global Terrorist. The *Intercept* reported that the CIA officer died at a German military hospital.

November 17, 2020: A suicide bomber set off an explosive belt at a restaurant frequented by police near the police academy in Mogadishu, killing five people and injuring eight. Al-Shabaab was suspected.

The U.S. Department of State added senior al-Shabaab members—explosives expert and media chief Abdullahi Osman Mohamed and Jaysh Ayman unit commander Maalim Ayman—to the list of Specially Designated Global Terrorists.

November 30, 2020: *UPI* and the *Voice of America* reported that the Ministry of Information said al-Shabaab attacked a military base in Ba'adweyene in the morning, killing four soldiers and 11 civilians. Information Minister Osman Dubbe said government forces killed 51 al-Shabaab terrorists, including the mastermind of the attack. Al-Shabaab said it killed 53 troops in the attack and seized military vehicles and weapons.

December 10, 2020: *UPI* reported that two U.S. Africa Command airstrikes coordinated with Somalia's federal government killed eight al-Shabaab explosives experts "known to play important roles in producing explosives for al-Shabaab, to include vehicle-borne improvised explosive devices" that target civilians. The strikes came on the heels of the Trump Administration's announcement that it was withdrawing the majority of U.S. troops from Somalia.

December 18, 2020: An al-Shabaab suicide bomber attacked the entrance to a sports stadium in Galkayo in Galmudug State, killing 15 people, including some senior members of the army, and injuring others before the arrival of Prime Minister Mohamed Hussein Roble.

South Africa

July 11, 2020: *AP, Reuters, Fox News, ABC News*, and *CNN* reported that gunmen took 200 men, women and children hostage at 3 a.m. at the International Pentecostal Holiness Church in Zuurbekom in Gauteng Province, west of Johannesburg. The South African Police Service and National Defense Force found found four people "shot and burned to death in a car" and a security guard shot in another car. Six other people were hospitalized. It appeared that the 200 were living in the church. Police found rifles, pistols, a baseball bat and boxes of ammunition, including one marked "law enforcement". Police seized 25 firearms. National Commissioner of Police Khehla John Sitole said 40 people were arrested, including members of the police, defense forces and correctional services. *eNCA TV* reported a leadership dispute at the church. Authorities did not believe a terrorist group was involved, suggesting the incident "may have been motivated by a feud between conflicted parties of the church".

South Sudan

May 28, 2020: The *Washington Post* reported that in mid-May, raiders with machine guns attacked remote villages in the Jonglei region, killing hundreds, in apparent retaliation for attacks in February and March on rival cattle-herding communities in ongoing disputes between Dinkas and the Murle subtribe of the Nuers. Doctors Without Borders said one of its medics was killed in the attack; the United Nations said two other aid workers were killed. Their nationalities were not released.

Sudan

January 20, 2020: A grenade exploded during a wedding party in the Shegla neighborhood in Khartoum's al-Haj Youssef district, killing seven people, including three children, and injuring two dozen adults and children. During a fight between two people at the party, one threw a grenade.

March 9, 2020: *Reuters* reported that car bombers failed to assassinate Prime Minister Abdalla Hamdok in a morning attack on his convoy near the Kober Bridge over the Nile River connecting Khartoum with its northern suburbs. One member of his entourage was slightly injured. No group claimed credit.

July 24, 2020: *AFP* reported that remnants of the Janjaweed militia were suspected when gunmen in pickup trucks fired machine guns, killing 20 farmers, including two women and children, and wounding another 20, some seriously, in their fields in Aboudos in South Darfur Province.

October 19, 2020: The *Washington Examiner* and *AP* reported that U.S. President Donald Trump tweeted that Sudan would be removed from the U.S. list of state sponsors of terrorism, contingent on Sudan paying $335 million to U.S. terrorism victims and their families affected by the 1998 al-Qaeda bombings of the U.S. embassies in Kenya and Tanzania and the 2000 bombing of the *USS Cole*. Iran, Syria, and North Korea remain on the list. The *New York Times* reported that Sudan might soon normalize relations with Israel; President Trump announced that the two countries resumed diplomatic relations on October 23

December 14, 2020: The U.S. Embassy in Khartoum announced that the administration had removed Sudan from the list of state sponsors of terrorism. The *Washington Post* noted that Sudan was designated as a state sponsor of terrorism in 1993, in part for its support of militant Palestinian organizations such as Hamas, as well as for harboring al-Qaeda leader Osama bin Laden. North Korea, Iran, and Syria remained on the State Department list of terrorism sponsors, which precludes them from receiving American aid or defense deals and from engaging with the World Bank and the International Monetary Fund. Sudan's government agreed to pay $335 million to settle claims by victims of the 1998 bombings of U.S. embassies in Kenya and Tanzania and the bombing of the *USS Cole* off Yemen's coast in 2000. Negotiations with the families of the 9/11 victims and Congress remained in the works.

TANZANIA

October 22, 2020: An affiliate of the Islamic State that had been conducting terrorist attacks in Mozambique claimed credit when 300 gunmen assaulted Kitaya, a riverside border village in the Mtwara region the previous week. The Inspector General of Police, Simon Sirro, said some people were arrested.

ASIA

Azerbaijan

October 15, 2020: *Al-Jazeera* reported gunmen attacked three people visiting a cemetery in Tartar, killing three and wounding five.

BANGLADESH

June 26, 2020: Police killed four suspected members of a Rohingya group allegedly involved in kidnapping for ransom. Police Inspector Pradeep Kumar Das explained that police were searching for Abdul Hakim, the gang's leader, in a forest near the Myanmar Rohingya refugee camps at Cox's Bazar. Inspector Morzina Akhter said the suspects shot at police, starting a gun battle. Police confiscated 40,000 drug pills and locally made guns. Local media reported that the group kidnapped many locals for ransom and killed those whose families failed to pay. Hostages included seven Bangladeshis over the last two months; three of them were killed. Hakim remained at large. 20062601

July 29, 2020: A bomb hidden inside a weight machine-like object went off during the morning in the Pallabi police station in Dhaka, injuring five people, including four police. Police arrested three suspects and rejected an ISIS claim of responsibility, countering that criminals were involved. Dhaka Metropolitan Police Additional Commissioner Krishna Pada Roy said police confiscated two loaded firearms and another weight machine-like object.

CHINA

June 4, 2020: The state-run *Global Times* tabloid, *Reuters* and *CNN* reported that Li, 50, an elementary school guard in Cangwu County in Guangxi region went on a knifing rampage at 8:30 a.m., slashing 39 people, including 37 children and two adults. Two adults were severely injured. The Shanghai-government-based *Paper* newspaper reported that he worked in Wangfu. Authorities arrested him. A nearby parent told the *Paper* that many of the children were 6-year-olds. Students attending the school are between 6 and 12 years old.

December 27, 2020: *UPI*, state-run *CCTV, Beijing News, CGTN,* and *CNN* reported that police officers arrested a man, Yang, suspected of stabbing to death seven people near a bath house in Kaiyuan in Liaoning Province in the morning. Another seven people were injured, including a police officer who was part of the arresting team.

INDIA

January 11, 2020: Inspector General Vijay Kumar announced that during the night, police in Indian-controlled Kashmir intercepted a speeding car and arrested a long-serving counterinsurgency officer—police deputy superintendent Davinder Singh—and two militants and their civilian aide for allegedly having ties with rebels fighting against Indian rule in Kashmir. Police seized weapons and ammunition. Kumar said one of the rebels was Naveed Baba, second in command of Hizbul Mujahideen, who had deserted police ranks in 2017 with four weapons. Singh had been a longtime member of the police's Special Operations Group and was working in the anti-hijacking unit at Srinagar's airport. He was once injured in an anti-rebel operation and received the Indian president's gallantry award.

January 23, 2020: Assam state police chief Bhaskar Jyoti Mahanta announced that 644 insurgents belonging to eight different rebel groups surrendered to Indian authorities, giving up assault rifles, grenades, bombs and other weapons. More than 300 were members of the National Liberation Front of Bengalis. Others were from the Adivasi Dragon Force, and the United Liberation Front of Asom, a faction headed by Paresh Baruah.

May 2, 2020: Five members of the army and police raided a rebel hideout where gunmen were holding hostages. Five Indian troops and two terrorists were killed in the evening gun battle in Kashmir's northwestern Handwara area. The army said it "successfully extricated the civilians", although it was not clear how, as all of the raiders, including an army colonel, a major, a police officer and two soldiers, were killed. Special forces reinforcements shot dead the two terrorists, but two others fled.

May 3, 2020: A bomb went off a few kilometers from the Handwara hostage site, injuring eight civilians, including three young children and a teenage boy.

May 6, 2020: Police and army soldiers, acting on a tip that gunmen were hiding, conducted an operation in Awantipora, south of Srinagar in Indian-controlled Kashmir, killing Riyaz Naikoo, chief of operations of Hizbul Mujahideen for nearly eight years, and his aide. Naikoo, a former math teacher, had recruited dozens of Kashmiris to fight against India. He became prominent following the 2016 public uprising following the killing of HM's leader, Burhan Wani. The troops deployed earth movers to dig up several patches of land, including a school playground, looking for possible underground hideouts.

May 17, 2020: A separatist gunman and a soldier were killed in a shootout in the remote Doda area of Kashmir.

May 19, 2020: Acting on a tip, scores of counterinsurgency police and paramilitary soldiers cordoned off a congested neighborhood in Srinagar's old quarters and battled Kashmiri separatist rebels for 12 hours, killing Hizbul Mujahideen commander Junaid Ashraf Sehrai and his aide. Junaid was the son of senior separatist political leader Mohammed Ashraf Sehrai. Junaid joined the group in early 2018 after graduating in business management from the region's main university. Three soldiers and a police official

were injured and more than a dozen homes were damaged.

July 11, 2020: State police chief R.P. Upadhayay said security forces killed six separatist National Socialist Council of Nagaland (Isak-Muivah) gunmen in a clash with paramilitary soldiers and police officers in a morning raid of a hideout in a forest in Arunachal Pradesh State, bordering Myanmar. One soldier was injured. Authorities confiscated six assault rifles, 500 bullets and two homemade bombs.

September 24, 2020: *Al-Jazeera* reported that during the evening, two gunmen shot to death Babar Qadri, a prominent lawyer-activist, in his home in Srinagar in Indian-administered Kashmir. The two gunmen had posed as his clients. They shot him outside his home. He was in his late 30s. He often called for Kashmiri self-determination on TV news shows.

October 19, 2020: The *Times of India* reported that two anti-terrorist operations in South Kashmir killed five terrorists. Three Lashkar-e-Taiba gunmen died in Pulwama's Hakripora within 24 hours of attacking a CRPF party in Tral. A CRPF jawan was injured in the Trail attack. Another two terrorists were gunned down during the evening in Shopian's Melhoora, IGP (Kashmir Zone). The army and police seized arms, including three AK-47 rifles, and ammunition at the first site.

October 20, 2020: The *Times of India* reported that the National Investigation Agency filed charges at an NIA special court at Mohali in Punjab against ten people, including the slain senior Hizbul commander Riyaz Naikoo and Punjab-based drug traffickers, in the Hizbul Mujahideen (HM) narco-terror case. The case involves smuggling of heroin into India by Pakistan-based HM commanders, with proceeds sent back to Pakistan through hawala or to HM terrorists based in Jammu and Kashmir. The financing scheme was run by Khurshid, financial head of HM in Pakistan. The 14,000 page charge sheet including three Kashmiri HM terrorists—Riyaz Naikoo (who was killed in May), Hilal Ahmed Shergojri (arrested) and Zafar Hussain Bhat (at large)—and seven members who were part of a

Punjab-based drug trafficking group, including Bikram Singh, Maninder Singh, Ranjit Singh, Jaswant Singh, Ranjit Singh, Gagandeep Singh (all arrested); and Iqbal Singh (at large). They were charged under the NDPS Act, UAPA Act and IPC, besides Section 12(1)(b) of the Indian Passport Act. Authorities said, "Investigation revealed that the accused had received at least six consignments of heroin through Attari border in the garb of importing rock salt granules from Pakistan. Of these, money proceeds of five consignments were partly sent back to Pakistan through hawala operators, while a substantial portion was channelized to HM terrorists in Kashmir through a network of overground workers and other associates." A sixth consignment of around 532 kg of heroin was seized in July 2019 at Attari border. NIA raided 15 locations in Punjab, Haryana and Jammu and Kashmir, seizing Rs 98.5 lakh in cash, eight vehicles and three kg of heroin.

October 27, 2020: The *Times of India* reported that the home ministry listed 18 terrorists based in Pakistan, adding to an earlier 13 listed terrorists. The Ministry named as "designated terrorists" under Schedule 4 of the Unlawful Activities (Prevention) Act key 26/11 (a reference to the November 26 Mumbai attacks) attack conspirators, Indian Mujahideen leaders, and Dawood Ibrahim aides wanted for 1993 Mumbai blasts. Individuals named included

- Abdul Rauf Asghar, Jaish e Mohammad No. 2, an alleged key conspirator behind the 2001 Parliament attack and more recently the Pulwama attack
- Syed Salahuddin, Hizbul Mujahideen chief and head of the United Jihad Council
- Dawood aide Chhota Shakeel, wanted in 104 criminal cases. He looks after all criminal and underworld operations of D-Company, and was an aide of Dawood Ibrahim.
- Shahid Mehmood Rehmatullah, deputy chief of the proscribed LeT arm Falah-i-Insaniyat Foundation (FIF)
- Riyaz Bhatkal, founder of Indian Mujahideen wanted for a series of bombings between 2008 and 2010, who had escaped to

Pakistan in March 2009 with ISI's help

- Sajid Mir, one of the main planners behind the 2008 Mumbai siege
- Yousuf Muzammil Butt, commander of LeT operations in J&K
- Abdur Rehman Makki, LeT chief Hafiz Saeed's brother-in-law and head of LeT political affairs. The U.S. earlier listed Mir and Makki as Specially Designated Global Terrorists.
- Ibrahim Athar and Yusuf Azhar, both involved in the Kandahar hijacking
- Ghulam Nabi Khan, alias Saifullah Khalid, Hizbul chief Syed Salahudeen's deputy
- Zaffar Hussain Bhat, alias Khursheed, Hizbul's finance head
- Shabandri Mohammad Iqbal, alias Iqbal Bhatkal, Indian Mujahideen terrorist based in Pakistan

Three other aides of Dawood Ibrahim:

- Mohammad Anis Shaikh who supplied arms, ammunition and hand grenades and was involved in 1993 blasts
- Tiger Memon, who hatched the 1993 bombing conspiracy
- Javed Chikna

Those wanted for the 2002 Akshardham temple attack included

- Farhatullah Ghori
- Shahid Latif, JeM's Commander of Sialkot sector involved in launching of JeM terrorists into India including those behind a 2016 Pathankot attack.

October 28, 2020: *Mid-Day* reported that the National Investigation Agency (NIA), assisted by local police and paramilitary troopers of the Central Reserve Police Forces, conducted several raids in Srinagar in Jammu and Kashmir, including the office of a prominent English daily newspaper as part of its ongoing investigation into funding of terrorism. Sites included the office of Greater Kashmir on Residency Road area, offices of the local NGO Athroat, a houseboat named

H.B. Hilton in the Dal Lake, the residence of human rights activist Khuram Parvaiz and two other places in the old city areas. Earlier that day, J&K Police raided a terror funding module for Lashkar e Taiba from North Kashmir's Bandipore district, arresting Irshad Ahmad Sheikh, a resident of Chittibandy Aragam, Mohammad Junaid Wani, a resident of Nageen Bagh Sopore, and Raj Mohammad Khan, a resident of Lolab Kupwara. Police seized cash worth Rs 4 lakh.

November 10, 2020: *Mid-Day* reported that security forces killed two gunmen in Kutpora in South Kashmir's Shopian district.

INDONESIA

January 16, 2020: *AP* reported on January 21 that Indonesian authorities announced that Abu Sayyaf on January 16 had kidnapped five Indonesians in the southern Philippines. Eight Indonesians had been in a Malaysian fishing boat that was fishing in Malaysian waters before it was seen entering Philippine waters. When the boat returned, the remaining trio said the gunmen had kidnapped the other five, including the captain. In a September 30, 2020 clash between troops and the terrorists, La Baa, one of five remaining Indonesian hostages, was killed in Patikul in Sulu Province. Police said the terrorists were led by Majan Sahidjuan, alias Apo Mike. 20011601

March 7, 2020: Nearly 2,000 villagers had fled during a clash that began on February 29 in Tembagapura near the Grasberg copper and gold mine in Papua Province between security forces and rebels believed affiliated with the West Papua Liberation Army, the military wing of the Free Papua Organization. A police officer was killed and three others were injured near the world's largest gold mine. Nearly half of the mine is owned by U.S. Freeport-McMoRan and is run by PT Freeport Indonesia. The battle began when WPLA gunmen ambushed a police patrol from a hill, killing one officer and injuring two others. On March 3, gunmen fired on a police car, injuring another officer. Lekagak Telenggen, a National Liberation Army of West

Papua commander, said "We will keep fighting until PT Freeport Indonesia stops operating and closes." 20030701

March 25, 2020: National Police spokesman Argo Yuwono said a police anti-terrorism squad shot and killed one suspect and arrested two others in a nighttime raid in Subah in Batang district in Central Java Province on Java island, seizing weapons including two machetes, a sword, and a bayonet blade and bomb-making chemicals. The dead man had been resisting arrest by brandishing a long sword. Police linked the suspects to the ISIS affiliate Jama'ah Anshorut Daulah, a banned militant organization responsible for recent attacks on police.

March 30, 2020: Local police chief Gusti Gde Era Adhinata said that eight gunmen attacked a parking lot in the Kuala Kencana office area in Timika in Papua Province, killing New Zealand miner Graeme Thomas Wall, 57, from Ngaruawahia and wounding six other employees of PT Freeport Indonesia near the world's largest gold mine. Wall was hit in the chest and died; two Indonesian miners were in critical condition with gunshot wounds. The other four miners sustained minor injuries. The West Papua Liberation Army, the military wing of the Free Papua Organization, claimed credit. Police said security forces had been battling the WPLA since February near the Grasberg copper and gold mine. Spokesman Sebby Sambom warned mine employees to leave PT Freeport areas that the group declared in 2017 to be part of their battle zone, observing "We will keep fighting until Freeport stops operating and talks for the independence of Papua begin." Nearly half of the mine is owned by U.S.-based Freeport-McMoRan and is run by PT Freeport Indonesia. On April 11, 2020 Indonesian security forces announced that they had shot to death three separatist rebels who were suspected in the attack. Local police chief Era Adhinata said on April 9, security forces raided a house owned by a PT Freeport Indonesia security guard who quietly supported the rebels. They shot to death two suspected rebels in a gunfight, arrested the owner, and seized weapons and a "morning star" flag of the WPLA. Police said the two dead rebels had been involved in killing the New Zealander and his colleagues. In a second shootout on April 10 in the Mount Botak of Tembagapura mining district, authorities killed a third rebel and seized an assault rifle and ammunition. WPLA commander Lekagak Telenggen confirmed the police claim and called on the U.S. and Indonesia to stop the gold mine operations in Papua. 20033001

April 15, 2020: During a gunfight in Kayamanya village in the mountainous Poso district of Central Sulawesi Province, security forces shot to death two alleged male members of the East Indonesia Mujahideen suspected of attacking and critically wounding a policeman in front of a bank on Sulawesi island earlier in the afternoon. A video showed two attackers wearing helmets shooting the policeman and then escaping on a motorbike when the officer tried to shoot back. Police said the suspects fired on police when cornered in their hideout, where police found weapons and the motorbike. They defused two bombs found in the house.

June 1, 2020: National Police spokesman Ahmad Ramadhan said that in the morning, police shot to death a suspected jihadi terrorist with a samurai-style sword who fatally slashed a police officer. The terrorist tried to attack two other policemen at the South Daha police station in South Kalimantan Province. The terrorist died en route to the hospital. Police suspected that he was an ISIS supporter. Police seized the sword, an ISIS-style flag and a small Quran. South Kalimantan police spokesman Mohammad Rifai said the terrorist burned a police car at the station, then attacked the officers.

August 16, 2020: Troops shot to death Hengky Wanmang, a Free Papua Organization separatist leader, as he was trying to escape during a morning raid by security forces on the group's apparent headquarters in the mountain village of Kalikopi near the world's largest gold mine in Indonesia's easternmost Papua region. Three other rebels were injured but escaped into the jungle near the mining town of Tembagapura with several other Papuan fighters armed with military weapons, axes and arrows. Security forces seized an assault rifle, two guns, seven air rifles, 19 cell phones, two

telescopes and 22.4 million rupiah ($1,500) in cash. Two thousand villagers fled to safety during the gun battle. The West Papua Liberation Army is the military wing of the Free Papua Organization. Police claimed Wanmang was behind recent attacks near the Grasberg gold and copper mine, operated by PT Freeport Indonesia, that began February 29 in which two security personnel and four rebels died. Authorities also said he was responsible for the March 30 fatal shooting of a New Zealander when he and six employees of PT Freeport Indonesia were in a parking lot at the company's office. He also had led ambushes on the road to the mine in July 2009 that killed eight people, including Australian miner Drew Nicholas Grant, and wounded 37 others.

November 27, 2020: National Police spokesperson Awi Setiyono said the East Indonesia Mujahideen were suspected when ten individuals, three armed, killed four people and burned seven houses in Leban Tongoa village of Sigi District in Central Sulawesi Province. Witnesses said three of the terrorists were members of the group. One of the buildings burned was a Christian church.

December 10, 2020: During the evening, Indonesian counterterrorism police raided a house in East Lampung district on Sumatra island and arrested biologist Aris Sumarsono, alias Zulkarnaen, believed to be the military leader of the al-Qaeda-linked Jemaah Islamiyah network who had been at large since 2003. National Police spokesperson Ahmad Ramadhan said Zulkarnaen was suspected of involvement in making bombs used in several attacks, including the 2002 Bali bombings that killed 202 people, mostly foreign tourists, and a 2003 attack on the J.W. Marriott Hotel in Jakarta that killed 12. Zulkarnaen had trained in Afghanistan. He was accused of harboring Upik Lawanga, another bomb maker and a key JI member. Counterterrorism police in Lampung arrested Lawanga the previous week. He had eluded capture since 2005 after being named as a suspect in an attack that killed more than 20 people at a market in Poso on Indonesia's Sulawesi island. Police were tipped off to Zulkarnaen's location in raids after interrogating several suspected militants arrested in November. Since May 2005, Zulkarnaen was on an al-Qaeda sanctions list by the U.N. Security Council for being associated with Osama bin Laden or the Taliban. The Security Council said Zulkarnaen led the Laskar Khos (Special Force), whose members were recruited from among 300 Indonesians who trained in Afghanistan and the Philippines. He became JI's operations chief after the 2003 arrest in Thailand of his predecessor, Encep Nurjaman, alias Hambali. *Reuters* reported on December 16, 2020 that Indonesian authorities transferred 23 jihadis to Jakarta for questioning.

MALDIVES

February 4, 2020: *NPR, AP* and *AFP* reported on February 6 that Maldives police arrested three suspected jihadis for stabbing two Chinese men and an Australian in separate outdoor attacks on Hulhumale Island on February 4. The three victims were in stable condition as of February 6. ISIS released a video showing a masked man claiming that local sympathizers were responsible. By February 7, six suspects were being held. 20020401

April 2020: *Time* reported on April 29 that ISIS's weekly *al-Naba* magazine reported that "soldiers of the caliphate" torched several boats in a warning to the Indian Ocean archipelago's "apostate" government.

MYANMAR

April 20, 2020: *Newsweek, AFP,* and *Reuters* reported that gunmen ambushed Pyae Sone Win Maung, a driver for the World Health Organization (WHO) who was driving a vehicle transporting COVID-19 samples in Rakhine State, and wounded a Myanmar government health worker on a bridge near Minbya Township during the evening. The duo were en route from Sittwe, capital of Rakhine State, to Yangon, the country's largest city, in support of the Ministry of Health and Sports. Arakan Army rebels were suspected; they denied responsibility and blamed the military. 20042001

May 29, 2020: The website of the Office of the Commander-in-Chief of Defense Services claimed that at 2 a.m., 100 members of the Arakan Army attacked a police post in Rakhine State's Rathedaung township. The site said ten members of the paramilitary Border Guard Police and three of their family members, including a child, were missing. The rebel group, founded in 2009, claim to represent the Buddhist ethnic Rakhine minority. The military said the gunmen used heavy and light weapons to overrun the base, but were fought off by police from another station.

NEPAL

September 28, 2020: *AFP* reported that the government established heavier penalties for acid attackers and restricted production and use of corrosive liquids. Acid attacks disfigure and blind their mostly female victims. Police logged 20 attacks in the past seven years. Jail terms were included from eight years to 20 years and compensation to victims could reach one million rupees ($8,494).

PAKISTAN

January 10, 2020: *Reuters* reported that a bomb planted at a mosque inside the Dar-ul-Aloom Shariah seminary in Quetta exploded during Friday evening prayers, killing 15 people, including senior police officer Haji Amanullah (whose son was killed in December), and injuring more than 20, many seriously. The Islamic State said it had targeted an Afghan Taliban seminary. 20011001

Police said that earlier in the week, Rawalpindi police had killed a suicide bomber after he shot and killed two policemen who died overnight in the hospital. Six people remained in critical condition.

January 30, 2020: *AP* reported that Pakistani research firms, including the Islamabad-based Pakistan Institute for Peace Studies and the Pakistan Institute for Conflict and Security Studies, determined that terrorist attacks in the country dropped by more than 85% over the previous decade, from nearly 2,000 in 2009 to fewer than 250 in 2019. Work remained to be done on stopping terrorist financing.

February 2, 2020: A mortar shell was fired from Afghanistan, hitting a home in Bajur district in Khyber Pakhtunkhwa Province and killing seven members of a Pakistani family, including four children, two women, and a man. Other civilians were wounded. 20020201

February 12, 2020: A Lahore court sentenced radical cleric Hafiz Saaed to five years for terrorism financing. Indian and U.S. authorities wanted him for his alleged role in the November 2008 Mumbai attacks that killed 166 people in India. The U.S. Department of State issued a $10 million bounty for his arrest. The Pakistani court charged that his charity organizations, Jamaat-ud-Dawa and Falah-e-Insaniat, were fronts for funding Lashkar-e-Taiba. Saeed was also sentenced to six months in a separate case in Punjab Province. Four Saeed associates were also sentenced to five and one half years for terrorism financing.

February 16, 2020: *SkyNews* and *al-Jazeera* reported that a suicide bomber on a motorcycle killed ten people and wounded 25, eight seriously, at a Sunni rally organized by the Ahle Sunnat Wal Jammat party in central Quetta. Local police chief Abdul Razzaq Cheema said that police ordered the terrorist to stop, but, "Instead of stopping, [the attacker] attempted to continue going forward... They struggled with him, toppling him and stopping him. As he fell, he detonated himself, which killed two of our men, those who had stopped him ... and [others]."

April 10, 2020: A roadside bomb went off near a Pakistani paramilitary vehicle in Baluchistan Province, killing two soldiers and injuring two who were clearing the area for fencing the Chaman border with Afghanistan. No one claimed credit.

May 2020: The Balochistan Liberation Army claimed credit when a roadside bomb killed six soldiers, including an army major. Pakistan said that troops, searching for smuggling routes and militants, were returning to camp from a mountainous border district.

May 18, 2020: *AFP* and *AP* reported that during the night, a remotely-detonated roadside bomb hit a vehicle in a convoy on routine patrol that was protecting an oil and gas facility, killing six Frontier Corps paramilitary soldiers and wounding four near Pir Ghaib in the hilly areas of Bolan district in Balochistan Province. The troops were returning to camp. Mureed Baloch, spokesman for the United Baloch Army, claimed credit, saying that the group was targeting soldiers protecting engineers at the oil and gas site.

In a separate gun battle with terrorists in Balochistan, a soldier died.

A roadside bomb killed an 8th soldier in the northwest. A roadside bombing in North Waziristan killed one soldier and wounded three as their vehicle was traveling through Mir Ali.

June 2020: The separatist Sindhudesh Revolutionary Army claimed credit for setting off three bombs that killed four people, including two soldiers.

June 18, 2020: A court in Lahore sentenced two associates of radical cleric Hafiz Saaed to five-year terms on charges of terror financing; two others received one-year sentences for the same charge. The four were linked to the Jamaat-ud-Dawa, a front for Saeed's banned Lashkar-e-Taiba group.

June 25, 2020: The *Washington Post* reported that Pakistani Prime Minister Imran Khan told Parliament that the United States "martyred" Osama bin Laden, a term mainly used for honorable figures slain in battle. He added that Pakistan's partnership with the United States in the war on terror was a mistake. "The way we supported America in the war on terror, and the insults we had to face in return. ... They blamed us for every failure in Afghanistan. They openly held us responsible because they did not succeed in Afghanistan." *Deutsche Welle* noted that the speech was consistent with Khan's Islamist views. *Reuters* reported that Pakistani opposition parties criticized the speech. Meanwhile, the Foreign Ministry criticized the new U.S. State Department Country Reports on Terrorism that accused Pakistan of providing safe haven to "regionally focused terrorist groups".

June 29, 2020: *CNN* and *AP* reported that terrorists attacked the Pakistan Stock Exchange in Karachi, killing five people, including a police sub-inspector and two private security guards. A third security guard was in critical condition. Seven people were injured, including three police officers, two security guards, a stock exchange employee and one other person. Abid Ali, director of the Pakistan Stock Exchange, told *Geo News* "There were four attackers who came from the parking lot, they threw a grenade at the main entrance of the KSE (stock exchange) and then started firing indiscriminately… The attackers were wearing uniforms that looked like police uniforms, all four have been killed and the situation is currently under control." The Majeed Brigade of the Baluchistan Liberation Army claimed credit, saying it was targeting "Pakistan's economy" and "Chinese economic interests" in Baluchistan. The paramilitary Rangers quickly secured the building. Policeman Rizwan Ahmend said police found food supplies on the bodies of the gunmen, indicating they may have planned a long siege. Pakistani police and Rangers found more than a dozen hand grenades, boxes of ammunition, several automatic rifles, and a silver Toyota Corolla the terrorists used. *AFP* added on June 30 that Pakistani Prime Minister Imran Khan, in an address to Parliament, said, "Our security forces fought and thwarted a huge tragedy which was planned by our neighboring country India", without offering evidence.

July 12, 2020: *Fox News* and *AP* reported that four soldiers and four gunmen died in a shootout during a morning raid on a hideout in North Waziristan near the Afghan border.

August 5, 2020: *Reuters* reported that the separatist Sindhudesh Revolutionary Army claimed credit for throwing a grenade into a rally in Karachi, injuring 30 people, one critically. The group had announced an alliance with the Balochistan Liberation Army.

August 10, 2020: A bomb attached to a motorcycle and targeting an anti-drug force went off in a busy market in Chaman near the Afghan border, killing five people, wounding ten, some critically, and damaging shops and vehicles. No one claimed credit.

August 21, 2020: Pakistan imposed financial sanctions on members of the Afghan Taliban, including dozens of individuals, such as the Taliban's chief peace negotiator Abdul Ghani Baradar and several members of the Haqqani family, including Sirajuddin, the current head of the Haqqani network and deputy head of the Taliban. Other groups, among them al-Qaeda, Tehreek-e-Taliban, anti-Indian groups, and an ISIS affiliate, were also sanctioned in an effort to avoid blacklisting by the Financial Action Task Force (FATF), which monitors money laundering and terrorist activities. In 2019, FATF grey listed Pakistan. Iran and North Korea are black listed.

September 3, 2020: A roadside bomb set by the Pakistani Taliban hit a military vehicle in North Waziristan in Khyber Pakhtunkhwa Province, killing three soldiers and wounding four. Troops were protecting road construction teams in the area. Two Pakistani intelligence officials told the *AP* that the bomb went off in South Waziristan.

October 5, 2020: Muslim Professor Farooq Maad and another gunman shot to death Professor Naeem Khattak from the Ahmadi minority, as he was driving to his college in Peshawar. The previous day, the two allegedly quarreled over a religious matter.

October 8, 2020: Counter-terrorism police arrested two people in Muzaffargarh district in Punjab Province on charges of collecting funds for radical cleric Hafiz Saeed's outlawed Jamaat-ud-Dawa and Falah-e-Insaniat charities, suspected of being fronts for Lashkar-e-Taiba. Saeed is wanted by the U.S. for his role in the 2008 Mumbai attacks. Saeed has been serving 5 1/2-years since February 2020 for financing terrorism.

October 14, 2020: The military said six soldiers were killed in North Waziristan and another soldier died and a second was wounded at a border security post in Bajur district, a former tribal region of Khyber Pakhtunkhwa Province, from fire from across the Afghan border.

October 15, 2020: Gunmen ambushed a convoy of Oil and Gas Development Company workers escorted by paramilitary troops in Ormara in

Baluchistan Province, near Gwadar Port, being developed by China, killing 15 people, including seven oil and gas employees working as security guards and eight members of the Frontier Corps. The secessionist Baluchistan Liberation Front initially claimed credit, as did a year-old BRAS umbrella organization that includes the group. BRAS said in an English-language statement that it rejects all agreements Pakistan has signed with China and would attack any "enemy" working to advance those deals with "iron fists".

October 25, 2020: A bomb planted on a motorcycle went off during the afternoon in a vegetable market in Quetta, killing three people and injuring two. No one claimed credit.

October 27, 2020: *CNN* and *Reuters* reported that a five-kilogram bomb exploded during the morning's first lecture by Sheikh Rahimullah at the Jamia Zubairia madrassa (religious seminary) along Peshawar's ring road, killing eight people and injuring 123, five critically. The *Express Tribune* reported that 40-50 children were present at the madrassa. Peshawar Police Chief Mohammad Ali Gandapur said an IED with 5-6 kilograms of explosives was hidden in a plastic bag. No one claimed credit. The Pakistani Taliban condemned the blast. Tariq Burki, director of the city's Lady Reading Hospital, said four children were wounded and all the dead were adults. Among the injured was Sheikh Rahimullah and the 27-year-old cousin of local resident Abdul Rahim. *Mid-Day* and *Dawn* added on October 29 that the Rapid Response Force, Ladies Police and Bomb Disposal Unit in Dir Colony arrested 55 people for their suspected involvement. No group claimed credit.

November 22, 2020: A soldier and four gunmen died and two soldiers were injured during a raid in the Spinwam area of North Waziristan in Khyber Pakhtunkhwa Province.

December 26, 2020: A bomb exploded near a soccer field in Panjgur district in Baluchistan Province, killing two spectators and wounding six. No one claimed credit.

December 27, 2020: Gunmen attacked a paramilitary Frontier Corps checkpoint in Harnai

district in Baluchistan Province in the morning, killing seven Pakistani soldiers. Senior police officer Shawli Tareen said six paramilitary troops and two private guards were killed and six other troops were critically wounded. The attackers fled into the mountains. No one claimed credit.

PHILIPPINES

January 20, 2020: Philippine forces rescued Muhammad Farhan, an Indonesian who was held hostage by Abu Sayyaf in the southern jungles of Sulu Province for nearly four months. He was the last known Indonesian being held hostage by Abu Sayyaf. 19999901

April 4, 2020: The *Washington Post* reported that the Communist Party of the Philippines ordered the New People's Army to halt fighting rebel groups until April 15.

April 17, 2020: *Time* reported on April 29 that ISIS-linked gunmen fired on a military convoy in Sulu Province, killing 11 troops conducting an operation against the leader of ISIS in the Philippines. He had masterminded the deadly Cathedral bombing in January 27, 2019 in Jolo in Sulu Province.

June 26, 2020: *AP* reported that Metropolitan Manila Police Chief Debold Sinas said suspected ISIS-linked terrorists fired on police and intelligence officers serving a search warrant at a house in Paranaque in suburban Manila. The police killed four terrorists during the morning raid. An officer was hospitalized with a gunshot wound to the leg. Philippine National Police (NCRPO) seized pistols, an M16 assault rifle, two grenades, ammunition, suspected bomb parts, money transfer records and two black flags similar to those of ISIS. Police identified the dead terrorists, including a woman, as Merhama Abdul Sawari, Bensaudi Sali, Rasmin Hussin and Jamal Kalliming. Chief Sinas said they handled funds for Daulah Islamiyah and that Sawari facilitated funds for Philippine-based militants from Indonesia's Sulawesi region.

June 29, 2020: Military officers were irate when Philippine National Policemen shot to death four army intelligence officers, including a major and a captain, who were trying to locate a foreign suicide bomber believed to be with local Abu Sayyaf terrorists in Jolo. The police thought the group were criminals when they stopped the soldiers' SUV at a police checkpoint in Jolo. A police van tailed the soldiers. The driver stopped their SUV and one of the officers got out with both of his hands up. The police then opened fire, according to the military. The police claimed that Jolo policemen and narcotics agents were on patrol in Jolo's Bus-Bus village when they spotted the SUV. Police directed them to go to the local police station, but the foursome fled, then got out of their car and pointed their guns at the police.

July 3, 2020: Philippine President Rodrigo Duterte signed the unpopular Anti-Terrorism Act. Observers claimed it could be used against human rights defenders and quash dissenters. Opponents vowed to challenge its constitutionality in the Supreme Court. The law permits detaining suspects for up to 24 days without charge and empowers a government anti-terrorism council to designate suspects or groups as suspected terrorists who could then be subject to arrest and surveillance. It replaces the 2007 anti-terror Human Security Act.

August 13, 2020: National police chief General Archie Gamboa announced during the night that Abu Sayyaf commander Anduljihad Susukan, who was linked to beheadings of hostages, including two Canadians and a Malaysian, surrendered after being wounded in battle in Davao city. Police served warrants for 23 cases of murder, six for attempted murder and five for kidnapping. Security officials have blamed Susukan and his men for cross-border kidnappings of tourists and other victims from the Malaysian state of Sabah on Borneo island, including a Malaysian citizen, who was beheaded in 2015 in Sulu Province on the day when Malaysia's then-Prime Minister Najib Razak arrived in Manila to attend the Asia Pacific Economic Cooperation summit. Susukan helped finance the kidnappings in the south of two Canadian men, who were separately beheaded in Sulu in 2016.

A military officer claimed that Abu Sayyaf terrorist Ben Yadah murdered the two Canadians and was at large. Susukan surrendered to Muslim rebel chief Nur Misuari after his M203 rifle grenade accidentally exploded in a clash with troops in Sulu severed his left arm.

August 17, 2020: *Al-Jazeera* reported that Zara Alvarez, 39, former education director of the human rights alliance Karapatan, was shot to death in Bacolod when a gunman fired six shots into her during the evening as she was en route home after buying food for dinner. Witnesses chased the gunman, who escaped with an accomplice on a motorcycle. She was the 13th Karapatan member killed in a "war against dissent" since mid-2016, when President Rodrigo Duterte was inaugurated. She had accused the police of involvement in deadly attacks against farmers on Negros island. The government said it would investigate, including looking into her affiliation with "leftist groups" as a possible lead.

August 24, 2020: *AP, Deutsche Welle, Reuters* and *DPA* reported that around noon, two bombs in Jolo in Sulu Province killed 14 people, including five soldiers, and wounded between 75 and 78 military personnel, police, and civilians. The first bomb was set off by a motorcyclist near two parked army trucks in front of a grocery store and computer shop. It killed most of the victims, including children. The second bomb went off an hour later, killing a suicide bomber who had walked out of a sandwich shop and approached soldiers who were securing a Roman Catholic cathedral. She killed herself, a soldier, and a police commando and wounded several others. Police found an unexploded bomb in a public market. The area had been under tight security after threats by Abu Sayyaf. The military blamed Abu Sayyaf commander Mundi Sawadjaan. Military officials suggested the attacks might have been in retaliation for the detention of surrendered Abu Sayyaf leader Abduljihad Susukan, who faced multiple murder and kidnapping charges. The next day, Philippine Army commanding General Ciriliot Sobejana clarified that both explosions were set off by suicide bombers. The military tried to determine whether the suicide bombers were the widows of Abu Sayyaf terrorists Talha Jumsah, alias Abu Talha (who was killed by troops in November 2019 in a shootout on Jolo) and Norman Lasuca (who died in a suicide attack on a Sulu army camp in June 2019, becoming the country's first suicide bomber). *AFP* reported on August 26 that General Sobejana confirmed that the bombers were Nanah and Inda Nay, widows of Abu Sayyaf terrorists. Nanah, possibly an Indonesian, was Lasuca's wife. Inda Nay was the wife of Talha Jumsah.

October 10, 2020: The Army's Western Mindanao Command said that police and troops arrested suspected Indonesian suicide bomber wannabe Rezky Fantasya Rullie with two Filipino women, who were suspected to be the wives of Abu Sayyaf terrorists, in a house in Jolo in Sulu Province where they found an explosive vest and bomb components. The army believed she was involved in a "very imminent" plot to attack Jolo. The military added that Rullie's husband Andi Baso, who is wanted in the Philippines and Indonesia for his alleged involvement in bomb attacks, had been killed in an August 29 clash near Sulu's Patikul town. Her parents conducted a suicide attack that killed more than 20 people and wounded more than 100 others during Sunday Mass in the Jolo cathedral. Baso had been blamed for a 2016 explosion that killed a child and wounded three others in a church in East Kalimantan Province in Indonesia. He died in a clash with troops in Sulu in August 2020.

One of the women arrested with Rullie was Inda Nurhaina, wife of Abu Sayyaf commander Ben Yadah, alias Ben Tatoo, main suspect in the 2016 beheadings in Sulu of two Canadian tourists who were taken hostage by ransom-seeking Abu Sayyaf gunmen. He remained at large and was linked to recent kidnappings in Sulu.

November 10, 2020: *Al-Jazeera* reported that two gunmen on a motorcycle shot to death radio journalist Virgilio Maganes, 62, outside his home during the morning. Maganes had survived an assassination attempt on November 8, 2016. Maganes lived northwest of Manila. He was hit with six bullets.

THAILAND

February 8, 2020: Royal Thai Police spokesman Krissana Pattanacharoen said that at 3:30 p.m., Thai Army Sub. Lt. Jakrapanth Thomma, 32, from the Second Army Regional Command shot to death 30 people and wounded 58, ten critically. He fled to the popular seven-story Terminal 21 shopping mall in Nakhon Ratchasima Province (also known as Korat) in northern Thailand. He had initially shot dead his commanding officer, Colonel Anantharot Krasae, 48, another soldier and the officer's mother-in-law, 63, and wounded a third person at the officer's home. The shooter was stationed outside the city. He drove from the base to the mall, shooting at civilians en route, then taking hostages. *CNN* reported that Thai Army said the shooter was an ammunition battalion officer working for the 22nd Ammunition Battalion. Lt. Gen. Kongcheep said the gunman, angry over a land dispute, shot to death his superior, then took his superior's gun and shot his colleagues. He stole guns, including a machine gun, and a military Humvee. He shot a doctor who was helping an injured person. By midnight, police said that they had secured the mall, although *CNN* was reporting that Lt. General Thanya Kiatsarn and police Colonel Krissana Pattanacharoen suggested that the shooter, still at large, remained in the mall. Dozens of shoppers were safely evacuated. The *Washington Post* said the shooter, carrying an assault rifle and wearing camouflage, a balaclava, and a helmet, partially live-streamed the shooting on *Facebook*, where he also posted "Getting wealthy from cheating and taking advantage of others… Do they think they can take their money to use in hell?" The *New York Times* reported that the video was available on *4chan*. He shot a motorcyclist. *CBS News* reported that he posted other videos and photos on *Facebook* during the siege, observing "no one can escape death" and asking whether he should "give up", citing his exhausted trigger finger. Police had brought in his mother from Chaiyaphum Province to help negotiate; she suggested it was pointless, as he had depression and an extremely bad temper. The *Washington Post* reported that authorities killed the shooter the next day at 9 a.m. after a 17-hour siege at the mall. Major General Jirapob Puridet said the gunman had a stolen machine gun, 800 rounds of ammunition, and two short guns. One officer was killed and three others wounded during the rescue operation. Trapped shoppers had said that they were inside a freezing room where the oxygen level was waning.

Among the dead were

- Ratchanon Karnchanamethee, 13, a middle school student who was riding his motorbike when the shooter, en route to the mall, killed him

- Papatchaya Kualraksa, 33; her husband; and son, 2

- Wanchai Watchawan, who was working at a store on the mall's second story

Army Chief General Apirat Kongsompong said the shooter was not treated fairly in a land purchase deal involving the commander and the mother-in-law who was a real estate dealer who marketed to local soldiers and that the Army would compensate those affected by the incident.

Buddhist monk Phra Manaswin, 24, said that the shooter stopped by Wat Pa Sattharuam Buddhist temple in Nakhon Ratchasima for 10 minutes, killing nine people, including Rachanon Kanchanamethi, a 13-year-old boy riding a motorbike home, and injuring more at the forest monastery. The killer fired at a woman and a child in a sedan, and killed everyone in an SUV except for the front-seat passenger, who was shielded by the driver's slumped body. He fled when police arrived.

Authorities arrested two people who threatened online to conduct similar shootings. One was a former soldier who said he was drunk and arguing with his girlfriend. The *Bangkok Post* reported that a 16-year-old said he posted the threat for fun. Both faced charges of violating the Computer Crime Act and causing public fear, and could be sentenced to five years and one month.

March 17, 2020: *Reuters* reported that two bombs went off in front of the Yala Province office of the Southern Border Provinces Administrative Center (SBPAC), a government body that oversees the administration of three mostly Malay-Muslim majority provinces of Narathiwat, Pattani and Yala, wounding 18 people. The organization was hosting a government meeting on the region's response to the coronavirus. Military regional security spokesman Colonel Pramote Prom-in said, "The first bomb was a grenade thrown to the area outside the SBPAC office fence to draw people out... Then a car bomb about 10 meters from the first explosion went off. This was hidden in a pick-up truck where the perpetrators parked near the fence. Eighteen are wounded and no one died." He said the car bomb exploded ten minutes after the first explosion. The wounded included five reporters, five police officers, two soldiers and other bystanders. No one claimed credit.

VIETNAM

April 2020: A Vietnamese court jailed a man for terrorism regarding a bombing of a tax office.

AUSTRALIA/NEW ZEALAND/ PACIFIC

NEW ZEALAND

March 4, 2020: *AFP* reported that police arrested a man, 19, for making an "abhorrent" threat against one of the Christchurch mosques targeted in a mass shooting on March 15, 2019. The message was posted on an encrypted app and showed a man wearing a balaclava sitting inside a car outside the al-Noor mosque. The note included a threatening text and a gun emoji.

August 6, 2020: Would-be thieves set off two bombs at a mall ATM at 3:45 a.m. and left five other bombs behind outside the Chartwell Shopping Centre in Hamilton. Police found several devices, including the two devices that apparently exploded, damaging the ATM of the ANZ bank branch and the immediate area but causing no injuries. A witness saw two people wearing black running across the parking lot. No cash was stolen. The bombs were about a foot long and not sophisticated or powerful. A military team disposed of the five unexploded devices.

EUROPE

EUROPEAN UNION

May 13, 2020: European Union Counter-Terrorism Coordinator Gilles de Kerchove warned that the extremists, such as jihadis and right-wing extremists, were using the coronavirus pandemic to spread their message and might exploit it to conduct attacks. He warned that extremists "could view attacks on medical personnel and facilities as highly effective, because these would generate a massive shock in society". *Politico* added that conspiracy theorists, white supremacists, anti-vaxxers, and other far-right extremists were using the pandemic to bolster their propaganda to fascist, anti-EU, anti-government, anti-5G and anti-refugee groups across Europe and the United States in an "infodemic".

AUSTRIA

July 4, 2020: *Fox News, Kurier,* and *Radio Free Europe/Radio Liberty* reported that Austrian police suspected a political hit when Chechen separatist Mamikhan Umarov, 43, a critic of Russian President Vladimir Putin's friend and Chechen strongman Ramzan Kadyrov, was shot to death in a parking lot outside a shopping center in Gerasdorf, a Vienna suburb. Authorities captured a Russian suspect, 47, a few hours later and 125 miles away in Linz. *RFE/RL* said Umarov had claimed to be a former mercenary who worked as a security service official in the former de facto independent Chechen state of Ichkeria. Regional anti-terrorism authorities were investigating. Lower Austria police representative Sonja Stamminger said that a second person was detained. Russian website *Kavkazski Uzel* said Umarov ran a *YouTube* channel containing critical commentary about Chechnya under Kadyrov. 20070401

August 22, 2020: *Reuters* reported that an individual attacked the Graz Jewish community's president, Elie Rosen, with a wooden club at their synagogue, which had been vandalized twice in the past week. Graz escaped to his car and was unhurt. The attacker fled. Styria Province police searched for the suspect.

November 2, 2020: *AP, CBS News, Reuters, Puls 24, Newsweek, New York Times, Washington Post, Business Insider, CNN,* and *ABC News* reported that police believed that at 8 p.m., gunmen armed with semi-automatic rifles fired on six locations, including near the closed Stadttempel synagogue (also known as Seitenstettengasse Temple) in Vienna, killing five people and injuring 22, seven critically. Shots were reported on Vienna's Morzinplatz, Salzgries, Feishmarkt, Bauermarkt and Graben streets. People had gathered at bars and restaurants in the Innere Stadt area to get in one more outing before the next day's coronavirus lockdown. Harald Sörös, spokesman for the interior ministry told Austria's *APA* news agency that a police officer, 28, was among those seriously injured.

NPR and the *Washington Post* reported that police killed gunman Kujtim Fejzulai, 20, an Austrian-North Macedonian dual national who had been sentenced to 22 months on April 25, 2019 after unsuccessfully attempting to go to Syria to join ISIS. He had been released early, on December 5, 2019. He was armed with an assault rifle, machete, and fake suicide belt. Florian Klenk, editor of Vienna's *Falter* newspaper, tweeted that Fejzulai was born in Austria to ethnic Albanian parents from North Macedonia, and known to domestic intelligence agencies as one of 90 Austrian Islamists who planned to travel to Syria.

AFP reported that a second attacker was on the run. *BBC* reported that Czech police would monitor travel between the two countries. The *Washington Examiner* reported that police arrested a gunman.

After reviewing video, police believed that there was only one shooter. Some 35 police sifted through 20,000 sent in by the public.

On November 3, police made 14 preliminary arrests and searched 18 residences, including Fejzulai's apartment, in Vienna and Niederoesterreich. *ANA, APA, ORF, CNN, Kurier,* and *Reuters* reported that police arrested two men, aged between 20 and 25, from the shooter's home town of St. Poelten, capital of Niederoesterreich State, the next morning. *ORF* and *CNN* reported that one had North Macedonian roots; the other was a Chechen.

A Swiss-Turkish national was arrested.

The dead included an elderly man, elderly woman, a young passerby, and a waitress.

The *Washington Examiner* reported on November 3 that ISIS claimed credit but did not provide proof. *Amaq* said on *Telegram* that the attacker was Abu Dagnha al-Albani, hailing the "death and injury of 30 'crusaders' at the hands of a 'soldier of the caliphate,'" according to the *Independent*. ISIS claimed that he used two guns, including one machine gun, and a knife.

Reuters and the *St. Galler Tagblatt* newspaper's website reported on November 3 that Swiss police in Winterthur, near Zurich, arrested two men, aged 18 and 24, who Swiss Justice Minister Karin Keller-Sutter deemed "obviously friends" of Fejzulai. The duo were the subject of two criminal cases being prosecuted by the Swiss attorney general's office (OAG) and which were opened in 2018 and 2019.

Attorney Muna Duzdar said a Palestinian man, Osama Abu el-Hosna, helped rescue a police officer who was injured during the operation. "He could have run away, but he stayed, and he dragged the policeman behind a cement barrier so that he's not in the line of fire any more... The paramedics didn't dare to drag him out and to get right into the barrage of gunfire, so that's when he ran back to get the officer out of there, and then the two guys from Turkey helped because he couldn't have done it by himself... Together, they dragged him to the ambulance." *Reuters* and *Anadolu* earlier reported that two Austrian mixed martial arts (MMA) fighters of Turkish descent had helped save a police officer and two women during the attack.

Business Insider, the *Guardian, Kleine Zeitung* and the *Times of London* reported that the shooter had been released under juvenile law from the Derad deradicalization program after pretending to renounce jihadism. Interior Minister Karl Nehammer said Fejzulai "managed to deceive the judiciary's deradicalization program".

Reuters reported on November 6 that opposition parties argued that the government mishandled intelligence from Slovakia indicating that the shooter tried to purchase ammunition there in July.

Reuters reported on November 6 that German BKA criminal police searched the homes and businesses in Osnabrueck, Kassel and in the district of Pinneberg near Hamburg of four people believed linked to the shooter.

Reuters reported on November 13 authorities were investigating 21 people as possible accomplices. Vienna prosecutors' office spokeswoman Nina Bussek said ten people were in custody.

December 10, 2020: *Reuters* reported that Interior Minister Karl Nehammer announced that Austrian police seized a huge cache of 25 semi-automatic and fully automatic weapons, explosives and hand grenades intended to arm right-wing extremist groups in Germany. Police arrested five people during house searches. Officers from Bavaria and North Rhine-Westphalia were involved in the inquiry into the links between organized crime and the rightwing extremists. Michael Mimra from the state criminal police office in Vienna said that the weapons, including Uzi sub-machine guns, AK-47 assault rifles, and Scorpion machine guns, were believed to have been bought with the proceeds of drug trafficking. More than 100,000 rounds of ammunition were found in a warehouse in lower Austria. In all of the raids, police confiscated 76 automatic and semi-automatic weapons, 14 handguns, ammunition, six hand grenades, detonators and explosives. Some had been packed for transportation. German authorities arrested two people and seized drugs.

DENMARK

June 26, 2020: *AP* reported that the Roskilde city court, west of Copenhagen, found a Norwegian man, 40, of Iranian descent guilty of spying for Iran and accessory to attempts to commit murder on Danish soil. The court said he "collected information about an exiled Iranian in Denmark" from September 25-27, 2018 and provided it to a person working for an Iranian intelligence service with whom he had online chats. He faced six years in prison for assisting Iranian intelligence. The court also held that he must have known his activities helped the Iranian intelligence service prepare for an attempted murder, making him an accessory to attempted murder. The defendant had pleaded not guilty and did not speak during the in camera trial.

The case was linked to a 2018 police operation targeting an alleged Iranian plot to kill one or more opponents of the Iranian government. Three male members of the separatist Arab Struggle Movement for the Liberation of Ahwaz (ASMLA) were accused of spying in Denmark for an unnamed Saudi intelligence service. The trio were arrested in February in Ringsted and were believed to be the target of the plot by the Norwegian.

Al-Jazeera added that the defendant was arrested in October 2018.

ESTONIA

April 8, 2020: *AP* reported on April 11 that authorities had arrested a 13-year-old boy who had called himself "Commander" online and led Feuerkrieg Division, an international neo-Nazi group linked to plots to attack a Las Vegas synagogue and detonate a car bomb at a major U.S. news network. Harrys Puusepp, spokesman for the Estonian Internal Security Service, said that the service "intervened in early January because of a suspicion of danger" and "suspended this person's activities in" Feuerkrieg Division. "As the case dealt with a child under the age of 14, this person cannot be prosecuted under the criminal law and instead other legal methods must be used to eliminate the risk. Cooperation between several authorities, and especially parents, is important to steer a child away from violent extremism." Online the individual mentioned being from Saaremaa, Estonia's largest island. Estonian weekly newspaper *Eesti Ekspress* reported he allegedly was running FD operations out of a small town in the country. The newspaper said the group has a "decentralized structure", and the Estonian teen cannot be considered the organization's actual leader but was certainly one of its key figures. The Anti-Defamation League said FD envisions a race war and promotes some of the most extreme "accelerationist" views of the white supremacist movement. It was formed in 2018 and had some 30 members who communicate via the *Wire* online platform. The ADL said "Commander" was linked to the gaming plat-

form *Steam*, which listed his location as a village in Estonia and his URL as "HeilHitler8814".

Other FD cases include:

- In April 2019, the FBI Joint Terrorism Task Force/Las Vegas opened an investigation of Conor Climo, 24, who was in touch over *Wire* with FD members. He told an FBI source about plans to firebomb a synagogue or attack a local Anti-Defamation League office. Climo pleaded guilty in February 2020 to felony possession of an unregistered firearm.

- In February 2020, U.S. Army soldier Jarrett William Smith, 24, pleaded guilty to providing information about explosives to an FBI undercover agent while stationed at Fort Riley, Kansas, in 2019. An FBI affidavit said he talked about targeting an unidentified news organization with a car bomb. *CNN* reported that it was the target. The Anti-Defamation League said Smith was associated with FD when arrested. FD expressed "consternation" with the arrest on its *Telegram* channel.

FRANCE

January 3, 2020: *CNN, Reuters,* and *BFM-TV* reported that Loïc Travers, the Secretary of the National Police Alliance for the Ile-de-France region, said that at 2 p.m., an individual stabbed several people in a park in the Parc des Hautes-Bruyères area of Villejuif, a commune south of Paris, killing one person and gravely injuring two other people. Two women who were injured were released from the hospital on January 4. French prosecutors initiated a probe into "murder and attempted murder in relation to a terrorist undertaking". The French Police Prefecture said the male attacker was "neutralized", i.e., shot to death. Investigators said that the attacker, 22, with a serious psychiatric history, had been radicalized and had prepared the attack in Villejuif, in the southern suburbs of Paris. He had converted to Islam between May and July 2019 and shouted "Allahu akbar" several times during the attack. Police found a letter and several books about Islam in the attacker's bag. Some were about Salafism.

February 2020: Imran Aliyev, who ran a *YouTube* channel criticizing Chechen leader Ramzan Kadyrov, was found stabbed to death in a hotel in Lille.

February 3, 2020: *Reuters* reported that a man with a knife attacked officers inside a police barracks in Dieuze, near Metz, before they shot and wounded him. *AFP* reported that prosecutor Christian Mercuri said "We must relate the facts to a call received by the operational center of the gendarmerie shortly before, in which an individual declared that he was a soldier, that there was going to be carnage in Dieuze and that he was a member of Islamic State." Several hours later, no one had claimed credit. One officer was wounded in the hand.

April 4, 2020: At 11 a.m., a man with a knife attacked shoppers on a commercial street in Romans-sur-Isere south of Lyon, killing two people and wounding five, one critically. Police arrested him minutes later as he was on his knees on the sidewalk, praying in Arabic; they also detained an acquaintance. The *New York Times* and *France Bleu* reported that he first slit the throat of a man in his 40s in front of his companion and his son outside a bakery. He then went after two workers and a customer inside a tobacco store, then attacked people in a butcher shop. The Sudanese asylum-seeker in his 30s claimed to have been born in 1987. Police found in his home a complaint about living in a "country of unbelievers". *AP* reported the next day that a third person had been detained; all three suspects were Sudanese. The French media reported that the attacker had yelled "allahu akbar". 20040401

April 15, 2020: *Reuters* reported that at 2:30 p.m., police shot to death a man who attacked police officers on bike patrol with a knife in La Courneuve, a northern suburb of Paris.

July 29, 2020: *AFP* reported that a Paris appeals court decided to release from La Santé Prison Jose Antonio Urrutikoetxea Bengoetxea, alias Josu Ternera, 69, former leader of the Basque separatist Basque Nation and Liberty (ETA), and place him under house arrest in Paris for a minimum of six months. He had been held in France since May 2019 after being at large for 16 years. Spain had requested extradition and he was subject of a European arrest warrant. He was freed on July 30 and was to wear an electronic monitoring bracelet. He had been convicted in 2010 in absentia on charges of associating with terrorists after his fingerprints were found in an apartment known to be used by ETA operatives in Lourdes in southern France. He was sentenced to seven years in prison. In 2017, he was sentenced to eight years when convicted in absentia of participating in a terrorist organization. In May 2019, police arrested him at a hospital in Sallanches in the French Alps where he was scheduled to have an operation. Spanish authorities had sought him since 2002; he was wanted for a 1987 attack on a police barracks in Zaragoza that killed 11 people, including five children. He led ETA from 1977 to 1992 and was believed to have orchestrated complex car bomb and shooting attacks in the 1980s. The court banned Ternera from leaving mainland France during his house arrest.

September 11, 2020: *AFP* reported that al-Qaeda in its English-language publication *One Ummah* threatened French satirical weekly *Charlie Hebdo* with a repeat of the 2015 attack on its staff after it republished "contemptible caricatures" of the Prophet Mohammed, saying the first attack was not a "one off".

September 23, 2020: The *Daily Mail* and *AP* reported that the Eiffel Tower in Paris's 7th arrondissement was evacuated in the morning after an anonymous telephoned bomb threat.

September 25, 2020: *CNN, BFM TV, Washington Examiner, Newsweek, France 2, The World, BBC, NBC News, France Info TV, NPR, AP, Reuters, CBS News* and *AFP* reported that before noon, an individual armed with a cleaver stabbed and seriously wounded two people in the Richard Lenoir section of Paris, near the former offices of *Charlie Hebdo*, while the trial continued of 14 suspected accomplices in the January 2015 attack on the satirical magazine. Le Parisien said three people were in serious condition. *Newsweek* said four people were wounded. The police soon arrested a suspect near the Place de la Bastille in Paris's 11th arrondissement. Police opened a terrorism investigation. A national anti-terrorism prosecutor said two suspects were detained, observing, "The main perpetrator has been arrested and is currently in police custody, the second individual was placed in custody for his relations with the main perpetrator." The two victims—a man and a woman—were on a cigarette break. They worked for the French documentary production company Premières Lignes. The main suspect was a man, 18, of Pakistani origin and known to police. *BBC* reported that four other people were arrested. Law enforcement authorities confiscated a meat cleaver near a metro station.

AP reported that a suspect package was found nearby.

Earlier in the week, *Charlie Hebdo* director Laurent "Riss" Sourisseau said she had been forced to leave her home after receiving death threats. She had been injured in the 2015 attack. Al-Qaeda had recently called for attacks against the newspaper.

Road repairers said "a dark-skinned man randomly hit a lady with a big butcher's knife" in front of a memorial mural to the 2015 victims. Police arrested him on the steps of the Bastille Opera.

AP reported on September 26 that police had arrested the suspect a month earlier for carrying a screwdriver. He was not known to them as an Islamic radical. He had arrived in France as an unaccompanied minor three years earlier. Prosecutor Jean-Francois Ricard said the attacker did not know his victims.

Reuters, AFP, and *CNN* reported the next day that the suspect said he had targeted *Charlie Hebdo* because it had reprinted cartoons of the Prophet Mohammad and did not know that it had moved its offices to a secret location. *Reuters* reported that he wanted to burn down the office. Prosecutor Jean-Francois Ricard said the suspect carried three bottles of white spirit, a flammable paint thinner. The attacker had surveilled the area on three separate days, and had purchased the meat cleaver the day of the attack.

A suspected accomplice was released, but another associate, possibly his former roommate, was arrested in a hotel north of Paris. By September 26, seven people, including the suspect,

were in custody. A judicial source said five people were arrested in an apartment "likely to have been used by the main suspect". As of September 28, five people, including three former flatmates of the attacker, his brother Ali Murtaza, 16, and an acquaintance, remained under arrest. Another five were released, including Youssef, 22, an Algerian who claimed he was trying to stop the attack, telling *TF1*, "I wanted to be a hero; I ended up behind bars."

AFP reported on September 28 that the suspect identified himself to investigators as Pakistan-born Hassan A., 18. He had earlier said in a confessor video that he was Zaheer Hassan Mehmood and that "Today, Friday September 25, I will condemn" *Charlie Hebdo.* Investigators found a photo ID of his passport on his phone of a man by that name who was 25 years old. Authorities said "Hassan A." was a young man born in Mandi Bahauddin, Pakistan. *AFP* reported that he spoke some French, but needed a translator during questioning.

Prosecutor Ricard said on September 29, "In his telephone, we found a three-minute video in Urdu, in which he announces his plan, saying that 'here in France they make caricatures about our pure and great Prophet Mohammad. Today...I will revolt against this.'"

Interior Minister Gérald Darmanin told the media that authorities had foiled 32 terrorist attacks during the previous three years.

AP reported on October 8, 2020 that suspect Ali Hassan, born August 10, 2020, second youngest of nine siblings, grew up in Kotli Qazi, Punjab Province, Pakistan, which he had left for Europe three years ago. A friend said Hassan traveled through Iran, Turkey and Italy before reaching France in August 2018. He initially was listed as an unaccompanied minor and put in housing in Cergy.

UPI and *Reuters* reported on December 18, 2020 that police arrested four people of Pakistani origin as part of an investigation into a knife attack in Paris on September 25 in which two journalists were wounded in Paris's Rue Nicolas-Appert. Authorities charged one of them with a terrorism-related offence and placed him in custody in the southwestern Gironde region. The main suspect in the attack was a man, 18, from Pakistan, who was arrested soon after the stabbing. *Le Parisien* reported that the four had allegedly encouraged the attacker to act.

October 16, 2020: *CBS News, New York Times, Le Monde, Le Parisien, BBC, AP, CNN, Reuters,* and *ABC News* reported that after 5 p.m., Samuel Paty, 47, a middle/high school history and geography teacher, was beheaded with a knife in the street in front of his school after allegedly showing two caricatures of the prophet Muhammad to his students in the Paris suburb of Conflans-Saint-Honorine. He had used the caricatures in a discussion of the *Charlie Hebdo* attacks. French police shot to death Moscow, Russia-born Chechen suspect Abdullah Anzorov, 18, in nearby Éragny-sur-Oise (variant Éragny in the Val d'Oise) after he refused to put down his weapons (*Newsweek* said that shooting took place 600 yards from the murder scene.). The national anti-terrorism prosecutor opened an investigation for "murder in connection with a terrorist enterprise" and "criminal terrorist association". *BFM TV* reported that parents had complained on *Twitter* on October 9 about a teacher showing the caricatures as part of a lesson on freedom of expression. A man tweeted that his Muslim daughter was offended. Paty subsequently received threats. Witnesses heard the attacker shout "Allahu Akbar". *AP* reported that he posted a claim of responsibility minutes after the attack, showing a photo of the decapitated head and observing, "I have executed one of the dogs from hell who dared to put Muhammad down." He also indicated that he owned the *Twitter* account under the name Abdoulakh. Anzorov was unknown to intelligence services. He had been granted a ten-year residence in France as a refugee in March 2020. Police said he was carrying a knife and an Airsoft gun, which fires plastic pellets. His half-sister joined ISIS in Syria in 2014. *Newsweek* and *AP* reported that authorities arrested nine people, including Anzorov's grandfather, parents and brother, 17, and two parents of pupils at the College du Bois d'Aulne, where Paty taught. Authorities said Anzorov had been asking students to identify the teacher when he left the building. The headmaster had received threatening phone calls. A man claiming to be

the father of a student tweeted that Paty had shown an image of a naked man, telling the students it was "the prophet of the Muslims". The hashtag #JeSuisSamuel trended.

AFP reported that Nordine Chaouadi, a parent of a student, said that Paty had taken the Muslim children out of the class before showing the caricatures. "My son told me that it was just to preserve them, it was out of pure kindness, because he had to show a caricature of the prophet of Islam and simply said to the Muslim children: 'Go out, I don't want it to hurt your feelings,' that's what my son told me." Some 20 parents had contacted Cecile Ribet-Retel, president of PEEP de Conflans, the local chapter of a national parents association, regarding the lesson.

Reuters added on October 18 that authorities had arrested a 10th suspect on October 17, and an 11th person on October 18. Among those held was Moroccan-born Abdelhakim Sefriuoi, who was known to the intelligence services. *Reuters* reported on October 19 that police raided Islamic associations and foreigners suspected of extremist religious beliefs. The *Washington Examiner* and *AFP* reported on October 20 that authorities arrested five of Paty's students who may have helped the suspect identify Paty for money. Interior Minister Gerald Darmanin said that an arrested jihadi and the father of one of the students issued a *fatwa* against Paty. *AFP* reported on October 21 that Anzorov had been in *WhatsApp* contact with a parent leading an online campaign against Paty. By October 22, seven people, including the two teens who identified Paty to the killer, were charged with complicity in a "terrorist murder"; six other people were released.

Reuters and *BFM TV* reported on October 20 that Education Minister Jean-Michel Blaquer announced that Paty would posthumously receive France's highest award, the Legion d'Honneur.

AFP reported on October 20 that French authorities announced the closure for six months of the Grand Mosque of Pantin known for radical Islam.

President Macron announced the dissolution of the pro-Hamas Cheikh Yassine Collective for being "directly implicated" in the murder.

Police detained the group's founder, Abdelhakim Sefrioui, for publishing a video on *YouTube* insulting Paty.

Paris prosecutors opened an investigation into a French neo-Nazi website hosted abroad that republished the photo of Paty's decapitated corpse Anzorov had tweeted.

Al-Jazeera and *Le Parisien* reported on October 22 that Anzarov had been in contact with a Russian-speaking fighter whose IP address indicated he was in Idlib, Syria, which is controlled by the Hay'et Tahrir al-Sham (HTS), formerly al-Qaeda's Syrian branch. 20101601

October 19, 2020: The back-to-back terrorism trials in Paris began of Josu Urrutikoetxea, 69, alias Josu Ternera, the last known head of the separatist Basque Nation and Liberty (ETA). He had been at large for 17 years. He apologized and told other separatist movements not to engage in violence. He was battling cancer. He faced life in prison. He was staying with a friend in Paris while studying for his college diploma. He had an electronic monitoring bracelet. He joined ETA in 1968 and led the group in the late 1980s. He served 11 years in French and Spanish prisons. He was charged with "criminal association with a view to preparing a terrorist act" for alleged attack plots in the 2000s and 2010s. He was earlier convicted in absentia in both cases and sentenced to 15 years. When the French trials end, France has agreed to extradite him to Spain for crimes against humanity, multiple killings and belonging to a terrorist organization.

October 27, 2020: *Reuters* reported that police evacuated the areas around the Arc de Triomphe and Eiffel Tower after a bomb alert and discovery of a blue bag with different kinds of ammunition in the Paris Champ de Mars park around the Tower.

Police noted that there had been a bomb hoax the previous week in the Lyon rail station.

October 29, 2020: The *Washington Post* and *Le Monde* reported that an attacker with a knife killed three people near Nice's Basilica of Notre-Dame de L'Assomption on the Avenue Jean Médecin shortly after 9 a.m. An undisclosed number of people were injured. The attack came on the Mawlid (the Prophet Muhammad's birthday). The attacker shouted about cartoons (probably a reference to the *Charlie Hebdo* cartoons of the Prophet) and yelled "Allahu Akhbar". French police shot the terrorist several times, arrested him, and took him to a hospital, where he was reportedly in critical condition. Mayor Christian Estrosi called the attack "Islamo-fascism".

Police reported that the terrorist had two bags, containing four knives, two cell phones, a Quran, and his belongings.

The attack took 28 minutes.

Business Insider, Le Parisien, AFP, BFM-TV, and *Nice-Matin* identified the victims as:

- Vincent Loquès, 54, a French citizen from the Saint-Etienne-de-Tinée neighborhood of Nice, who had been the church sexton since 2013. He died two days short of his 55th birthday. He was found in the church, his throat slit. He was divorced and left behind two daughters, aged 21 and 25.

- Simone Barreto Silva, 44, a care worker, mother of three, and worshipper, moved to France 30 years earlier from Salvador, Brazil, according to Brazilian *G1 News*. She moved to France to join a dance group led by her sister. Her last words were "Tell my children I love them", as she died of multiple stab wounds in the restaurant where she sought shelter and warned others. *Correio Braziliense* quoted Brazilian President Jair Bolsonaro as calling the murder "Christophobia".

- Nadine Devillers, 60, who was found "almost beheaded" at the holy water font, according to *Le Figaro, BBC, Reuters,* and *Business Insider*

CNN reported that French national police identified the suspect as Brahim Aouissaoui, variant Ibrahim Issaoui, a Tunisian born in 1999. He arrived in Europe on the Italian island of Lampedusa on September 20. Upon reaching Italy, he was on a coronavirus quarantine ship with 800 other emigres, then briefly harvested olives. Italy issued an expulsion order on October 9, while he was in Bari. He was not classified as being a terrorist by security and judicial authorities.

He phoned his family the night before the attack, saying he had arrived in France.

French President Macron vowed to protect free expression, including the right to caricature the Prophet, roiling the Muslim community and sparking anti-French protests in Muslim nations. Turkish President Recep Tayyip Erdogan and Pakistani Prime Minister Imran Khan criticized Macron. Former Malaysian Prime Minister Mahathir Mohamad, 95, tweeted, "Muslims have a right to be angry and to kill millions of French people for the massacres of the past." In Islamabad, 2,000 protestors tried to march on the French Embassy but were stopped by police firing tear gas. Several demonstrators were wounded. In Lahore, 10,000 followers of the Islamic Tehreek-e-Labbaik party took to the streets. Kuwait, Qatar and Jordan saw boycotts of French products.

ABC News reported that French anti-terrorism prosecutors began an investigation on "counts of assassination in relation to a terrorist enterprise", attempted assassination in relation to a terrorist enterprise and "terrorist association of criminals".

CBS News and *NPR* reported on October 30 that authorities arrested a third suspect, a 35-year-old man who met with Ibrahim Issaoui in Nice. Another man, 47, already in custody had been in contact with Issaoui the night before the attack. By November 1, police had questioned six suspects who were between 25 and 63 years old and were spotted on video surveillance or detained in homes in Nice and Grasse. *Reuters* reported on November 3 that another four people were detained.

AFP reported that Issaoui's family, who lives in Sfax, Tunisia, was shocked by his actions. His mother, Houssem Zouari (also reported as Gamra), said he turned to religion two years earlier, isolated himself. She noted, "He prayed... (and) went from home to work and back, not mixing with others or leaving the house." She said that previously, "he drank alcohol and used drugs. I used to tell him, 'we are poor and you're wasting money?' He would reply 'if God wills it, he will guide me to the right path, it's my business.'" He was one of 11 children. He dropped out of high school and worked as a motorcycle mechanic, later opening an unlicensed gas station. He was involved in common law cases for violence as a teen.

Tunisian antiterrorism authorities investigated an online claim of responsibility by a previously-unknown al-Mehdi of Southern Tunisia extremist group.

Nice imam Otmane Aissaoui condemned a "terrible act of terror, of savagery, of human insanity that plunges us into sadness, shock and pain... (the attacker) hit brothers and sisters who were praying to their lord... It's as if a mosque was touched... I am deeply Christian today."

CNN and *ABC News* reported that the terrorist waited at the Nice train station for 90 minutes, then walked 400 meters to the church, arriving at 8:30 a.m.

ISIS called on sympathizers to attack French companies in Muslim countries. Jihadis on social media posted an Osama bin Laden quotation: "If your freedom of expression respects no boundaries, be prepared to face our freedom of action." 20102901

October 29, 2020: Police arrested a man near a church in Sartrouville before he could conduct a stabbing attack. He said he was inspired by the Nice attack.

October 29, 2020: Police in Montfavet, near Avignon, shot to death a man who had been threatening a trader with a North African background with a gun (conflicting reports said it was a knife). Some reports said he yelled "Allahu Akbar", although others said that he had claimed to be a member of the far-right Génération Identitaire and gave a Nazi salute. He had a history of psychiatric treatment.

Le Monde reported that police in Lyon arrested an Afghan man, 26, wielding a foot-long knife near the Perrache train station. 20102902

October 31, 2020: *CNN* and *AP* reported that at 4 p.m., a lone gunman with a hunting rifle (later reported to be a sawed-off shotgun) shot Greek Orthodox priest Nikolas Kakavelakis, 45 (also reported as 52 years old), a Greek citizen and father of two, who was closing the rear door of a church near Lyon's Jean-Macé quarter in the 7th district, seriously wounding him. He was hit twice in the abdomen and hospitalized with life-threatening injuries. The shooter, who ran away, was dressed in a long black coat and a black beanie. The Lyon prosecutor opened an investigation for attempted murder. Police interrogated and released a suspect resembling the attacker's description, and were searching for other potential suspects. *CNN* and *AFP* reported that French investigators were leaning toward the "personal dispute" theory. French media reported that Kakavelakis had a long-running legal dispute with a former monk who was convicted of defamation. Parishioner and former monk Jean-Mchel Dhimoila, who was seen on video scuffling with Kakavelakis two years earlier, said police raided his home at 8 a.m. on November 2 and took him in for questioning, though not as a suspect. He was later released. *AP* reported on November 7 that Lyon authorities ruled out a terrorism motive, saying that the detainee was a man, 40, whose wife was having an affair with the priest. The man confessed during police questioning. The priest was hit twice in the abdomen.

November 4, 2020: The French Cabinet banned the Turkish ultranationalist Grey Wolves, the militant wing of the Nationalist Movement Party (MHP), led by Devlet Bahceli, accusing the group of "extremely violent actions, disseminating "extremely violent threats" and creating "incitement to hatred against authorities and Armenians". Government spokesperson Gabriel Attal noted that an Armenian memorial near Lyon was defaced the previous weekend. The memorial honors victims of the 1915 Armenian genocide. Vandals had written "Grey wolf" and "RTE" (a reference to Turkish President Recep Tayyip Erdogan) on it.

GERMANY

February 14, 2020: *AFP* reported that police arrested twelve German men, including a German police officer, in raids on 13 locations in six German states during an investigation of a far-right terrorist group. Federal prosecutors said that four key suspects planned to set off "a civil-war-like situation... via as yet undefined attacks on politicians, asylum seekers and people of Muslim faith". Another eight allegedly agreed to "financially support the group, provide it with weapons

or take part in future attacks". The officer was earlier suspended over suspicions he had links to the far-right. The group was founded in September 2019, aiming "to shake the state and social order in Germany and in the end to overturn it", according to prosecutors. Prosecutors said meeting were held by Werner S. and Tony E. The group used messenger apps. *Der Spiegel* reported that police found several weapons, including a self-made "slam gun" similar to the one used in an attack in Halle.

February 19, 2020: *CNN* and *Reuters* reported that starting at 10 p.m., Tobias Rathjen, 43, shot to death nine people, including five Turkish citizens, and injured six, one seriously, in two shisha bars (also known as hookah bars, which serve flavored tobacco in water pipes) in immigrant neighborhoods of Hanau. The licensed gun-holder initially attacked the Midnight shisha bar in a Turkish community, killing three people, then drove his dark car to the Arena Bar and Café in the Kesselstadt area west of the town center, firing on patrons five minutes after the first attack. Police traced him to his apartment in Helmholtzstrasse, where they found his body and that of his mother, 72, both dead of gunshot wounds, at 5 a.m. His father was outside and unharmed. Prosecutors believed he had a far-right background, although he did not have a criminal record. Prosecutors deemed the attack a "suspected terroristic act of violence".

The family of Can-Luca Frisenna runs one of the bars.

Among the dead were

- Gokhan "Gogo" Gultekin, 37, who worked at a drink and tobacco kiosk and took care of his frail parents.

- Vili Viorel Paun, 23, who left school in Singureni, Romani at age 16 to work in Germany to pay his mother's medical bills. He drove a silver Mercedes for a delivery company.

Iskander M. told Turkish television that he was shot in the shoulder. Customers hit the floor. "The boy underneath me had a bullet hole in his neck... He told me, 'I can't breathe, and I can't feel my tongue.' I told him he should say a prayer, which is what he did."

YouTube shut down Rathjen's account the next morning, saying it will remove material that "promotes terrorism or violent extremism". A video posted on February 14 contained xenophobic views. He left a 24-page letter that included xenophobic and racist statements, noting that he had an "aversion" to certain ethnic groups, including Turks, Moroccans, Lebanese and Kurds. Federal prosecutor Dr. Peter Frank said the website included a "kind of manifesto" which included "confused thoughts", "conspiracy theories", and a "deeply racist attitude".

The *Washington Post* reported that a posted video showed a man offering a "message" to Americans, "Your country is under control of invisible secret societies", warning about "mind control" and the "mainstream media". U.S. citizens should "fight now". The nine-minute video ended with a twist on an Adolph Hitler quotation: "I don't believe that the people who are laughing today will be laughing in the future." He claimed to have been watched by the government since birth.

One document the shooter left behind read, "Not everyone who has a German passport is purebred and valuable... I can imagine cutting the population in half", according to the International Centre for the Study of Radicalisation at King's College London. The group said he wrote "strategies" for combat operations in Iraq and Afghanistan. In a second video filmed in his bedroom, he worried that the white race was being "replaced". He summed up with "Wahrheit macht frei" ("the truth sets you free"), a play on the Nazi slogan on the gates of Auschwitz, "Arbeit macht frei" ("work sets you free").

The *Washington Post* reported that his screed added, "The following people must be completely exterminated: Morocco, Algeria, Tunisia, Libya, Egypt, Israel, Syria, Jordan, Lebanon, the complete Arabian Peninsula, Turkey, Iraq, Iran, Kazakhstan, Turkmenistan, Uzbekistan, India, Pakistan, Afghanistan, Bangladesh, Vietnam, Laos, Cambodia and the Philippines." He warned Americans of subterranean military bases where "they abuse, torture and kill little children".

The *Washington Post* reported that the victims, between ages 22 and 44, included foreign and German nationals. *Deutsche Presse-Agentur*

(DPA) reported that some of the victims had migrant backgrounds. *Bild* reported that Kurdish immigrants were killed. 20021901

February 24, 2020: *CNN, BBC, Bild, RTL* and *NBC News* reported that at 2:45 p.m., a silver Mercedes Benz crashed into a crowd at a Rosenmontag (Rose Monday) carnival parade in Volkmarsen, injuring 52 people, including 18 small children. The German driver, 29, from Volkmarsen was arrested on suspicion of attempted homicide. He was among the 30 people treated for injuries. *Der Spiegel* claimed he was drunk. Frankfurt police chief Gerhard Bereswill said a second person was arrested; German media said he was filming behind the car. Witnesses said the driver accelerated toward the crowd and apparently targeted children.

April 15, 2020: *Reuters* and *AP* reported that in the early morning, special forces raided properties near Essen and Duesseldorf in North Rhine-Westphalia State and arrested four suspected ISIS members from Tajikistan who were believed to be planning attacks in Germany. A fifth suspect had been in detention since 2019. The five were believed to be in contact with leading ISIS members in Afghanistan and Syria, who provided instructions. Prosecutors said, "Targets for the attacks were supposed to be institutions of U.S forces in Germany or even individual people... In particular, they planned a murder attack on one person who had made public comments that they viewed as being critical of Islam." Prosecutors suggested that the suspects had surveilled the individual and were obtaining weapons, ammunition and components for a bomb. Authorities named the suspects as Azizjon B., Muhammadali G., Farhodshoh K. and Sunatullokh K.; the earlier detainee was Ravsan B., whom prosecutors claimed had instructions for making bombs and had procured some of the necessary bomb-building materials online. He was also accused of agreeing to a contract killing in Albania for $40,000 to finance the plot; the killing was not carried out. The five were accused of joining ISIS in January 2019, having planned to go to Tajikistan to conduct jihad, but instead went to Germany. German authorities said money for the group was funneled via agents in Turkey.

April 24, 2020: The *New York Times*, *AFP* and *AP* reported that the trial began before a five-judge panel in Frankfurt's Higher Regional Court of Taha al-J., 27, an Iraqi ISIS member on charges of genocide, crimes against humanity, war crimes, and human trafficking, and murdering a child, Rania, belonging to the Kurdish-speaking Yazidi minority whom he had enslaved. His wife, German citizen Jennifer Wenisch, 28, a Muslim convert who quit school in the 8th grade, had been on trial for a year in a Munich court on charges of murder, war crimes, and membership in a terrorist organization. She was charged with murdering the girl by letting the Yazidi girl die of thirst in Fallujah, Iraq in 2015. Wenisch converted in 2013, after being raised in Lower Saxony as a Protestant. She arriver in Iraq via Turkey and Syria in 2014 to join ISIS. Court documents indicated that al-J. joined ISIS in March 2013, eventually being in its leadership in Raqqa, Syria, and Iraq and Turkey. Prosecutors said that the couple bought a woman, Nora, and Rania, 5, as slaves at the end of May or start of June 2015. Al-J. chained the girl to the window of a house as punishment for wetting the bed. She died of thirst in 122 degree temperatures. The mother and daughter were kidnapped in Sinjar, Iraq in the summer of 2014 by ISIS. Greek police arrested al-J. in May 2019, then extradited him to Germany in October 2019. Lebanese-British lawyer Amal Clooney and Yazidi activist Nadia Murad, a survivor of ISIS sexual slavery and a 2018 Nobel Peace Prize winner, represented the Yazidi mother at Wenisch's Munich trial.

April 28, 2020: *Reuters* and *Focus Online* reported that police detained two suspects after four people were stabbed by five to seven men in Hanau during the evening. The detainees were 23 and 29 years old.

April 30, 2020: *Reuters* reported that the Interior Ministry designated Hizballah a terrorist organization and banned all Hizballah activity on its turf. Police raided mosque associations in Dortmund and Muenster in the western state of North Rhine-Westphalia, Bremen and Berlin, including the el-Irschad center in Berlin.

May 13, 2020: *CNN* and *RTL* reported that in the morning, officers from the Dresden State Criminal Police Office in Saxony found a hidden cache of weapons, including an assault rifle and plastic explosives, in the home of a Bundeswehr sergeant major, 45, who was a member of the KSK special forces commandos. The Ministry of Defense announced that he was arrested for violating the Weapons of War Control Act. The Military Counterintelligence Service had been investigating members of the special forces. Dresden State Criminal Police Office said that the search was based on a tip-off from the intelligence agency. The man is no longer allowed to wear his uniform and was banned from entering German military property. The *New York Times* reported on its front page on July 5, 2020 that the nickname of Sergeant Major Philipp Sch. was Little Sheep, a suspected neo-Nazi. Police found that he had buried in his garden two kilograms of PETN, a detonator, a fuse, an AK-47, a noise suppressor, two knives, a crossbow, and thousands of rounds of ammunition, possibly stolen from the military. Police also confiscated an SS songbook, 14 editions of a magazine for former members of the Waffen SS, and much Nazi memorabilia. He was a member of the KSK unit that Defense Minister Annegret Kramp-Karrenbauer disbanded.

June 3, 2020: Eberhard Zorn, Inspector General of the Bundeswehr, and German Defence Minister Annegret Kramp-Karrenbauer announced that the government had agreed on a bill to speed up the dismissal of soldiers involved in extremism or serious crimes if their continued presence would "seriously threaten the military order or the reputation of the Bundeswehr" and they have served less than eight years. The bill moved on to Parliament.

June 23, 2020: *Al-Jazeera* reported the Interior Ministry announced that it had banned the neo-Nazi group Nordadler (Northern Eagle). Police conducted raids in North Rhineland-Westphalia, Saxony, Brandenburg and Lower Saxony. The group reportedly used social media channels including *Telegram*, *Instagram* and *Discord* to spread its ideology, recruit new members and praise far-right attacks. The Ministry said its anti-Semitic members pledge themselves to Adolf Hitler and other high-profile Nazis and use Nazi-era symbols and language. Its leader praised the 2019 attack on a synagogue in Halle in a public group on *Telegram*. The Ministry had banned two other neo-Nazi groups—Combat 18 and United German Peoples and Tribes, in 2020.

July 1, 2020: Defense Minister Annegret Kramp-Karrenbauer (CDU) ordered the disbanding of a company of the Army's elite anti-terrorist Special Forces Command (Kommando Spezialkraefte, KSK) over concerns of right-wing extremist activities. Some of the 70 troops were to be sent to the KSK's other three combat companies; other more problematic soldiers would be forced out of the KSK. The media reported in 2017 that at a going-away party, several troops used the Heil Hitler salute and played right-wing extremist music. Authorities found a cache of weapons, explosives and munitions at the Saxony home of one of the suspected extremists.

July 3, 2020: *Al-Jazeera* reported that the trial began of Lorin I., 30, a German-Syrian woman, on charges of membership in a terrorist organization and violating Germany's war weapons control act for allegedly arranging marriages for ISIS and owning two assault rifles and a hand grenade while in Syria. She told the court in Celle that she had travelled to Syria with her husband in 2014. Her attorney said that the rumored "sister network" of would-be ISIS brides did not exist. Prosecutors presented *WhatsApp* messages showing her encouraging women to join ISIS and praising ISIS martyrs. She faced 10 years in prison.

July 9, 2020: Horst Seehofer (CSU), Federal Minister of the Interior, Homeland and Construction, presented the 2019 Report on the Protection of the Constitution at the Federal Press Conference in Berlin. The report indicated that the tally of right-wing extremists had risen to 32,080 in 2019, up from 24,100 recorded in 2018. The number of far-left extremists rose by 1,500 to 33,500 in 2019. Some 28,020 people had tendencies toward Islamic extremism, up from 26,560 in 2018.

July 24, 2020: The *Washington Post* reported that 27 German public figures in eight states had received 69 threats by apparent neo-Nazis during the previous two years. Some investigators believed a police officer was involved; investigators noted that police computers in Frankfurt and Wiesbaden were used to pull information on left-wing politician Janine Wissler and attorney Seda Basay-Yildiz, who later were threatened. Victims included German comedian/actress Idil Baydar, 45, and numerous left-wing and minority politicians, journalists and lawyers. Most of the threatening emails came from the same address and were signed "NSU 2.0", a reference to the neo-Nazi National Socialist Union that killed ten people in Germany between 2000 and 2007. Baydar received texts from "S.S. Ostubaf," referring to a senior Nazi rank held by figures including Adolf Eichmann. *AP* reported on July 27 that Frankfurt prosecutors announced that on July 24, they had temporarily detained a former Bavarian police officer, 63, and his wife, 55, and searched their Landshut home as part of the investigation of the threats. *DPA* reported that he had a record of previous far-right criminal offenses. The duo were released following the search of their home. In 2018, threatening messages signed NSU 2.0 were sent to a Frankfurt lawyer representing victims' families in the trial of the original NSU's only surviving member.

August 18, 2020: *ABC News, New York Daily News, AP, AFP*, and *Reuters* reported that an Iraqi-born male migrant, 30, was arrested on three counts of attempted murder after he deliberately crashed his black Opel Astra into several vehicles on inner city highway A100 between Wilmersdorf and Tempelhof in Berlin's Tempelhof-Schoeneberg district, injuring six people, three critically, around 6:30 p.m. A motorcyclist was among the injured. After causing three accidents, the driver stopped his wrecked car and put an old ammunition box (or tool box, reports differed) on its roof and warned it was a "dangerous object". *Bild* reported that he yelled "Nobody come any closer or you will all die." Police opened the box using high-pressure water jets and found only tools, not explosives. Berlin's public prosecutor said the incident had a potentially Islamist motive and might have involved "psychological instability". Witnesses said he was yelling "Alla-hu Akbar". Police said he appeared to be target-ing motorcyclists, ramming other cars, two mo-torcycles, and a scooter. Some 300 people were stuck in the resulting traffic jams, with the high-way closed down for several hours. He did not appear to have direct links to a terrorist group and appeared to have acted alone. Police said he had not been on the security services' watch lists, although police said he was earlier detained for assault and resisting officers. In one of the inci-dents, he forced a motorcyclist to crash into a car, injuring three car occupants; the motorcyclist sustained life-threatening injuries. A firefighter was also injured. *DPA* reported that the attacker had published clues on social media, including *Facebook*, that he was planning an attack, posting photos of his car and religious slogans. He was held in a psychiatric jail.

Prosecutors said the next day that the de-fendant was born in Baghdad in 1990 and came to Germany seeking asylum several years ago. A Berlin prosecutor said that the driver might suffer from "bizarre, religious delusion". The lo-cal media identified the driver as Sarmad A., whose asylum request was turned down in 2017. 200081801

August 20, 2020: The *New York Daily News* and *AP* reported that German citizen Zeynep G., an ISIS bride, was forced to sell her wedding gift AK-47 after experiencing financial difficulties in Syria. She was indicted on counts of partici-pating in the activities of a terrorist organization, committing a war crime, and breaching arms control laws. She was married to a Chechen fighter who died. She remarried in 2015 a Ger-man ISIS member. They moved to Raqqa, taking over the home of someone who had fled from ISIS; in international law, this is viewed as loot-ing or pillaging. He died in 2017. She allegedly used social media to call on others to join ISIS. Kurdish fighters detained her in 2019, but she escaped. Turkish authorities arrested her in Feb-ruary 2019 and extradited her after three months to Germany.

August 23, 2020: *AFP* reported on October 4, 2020 that on October 7, a trial would begin of Russian man Vadim Krasikov, alias Vadim S., for shooting to death Georgia national and former Chechen commander Tornike K., 40, in Kleiner Tiergarten park in Berlin on August 23, 2019, allegedly at Russian behest. Krasikov grew up in Kazakhstan when it was part of the USSR, then moved to Siberia. *Bellingcat.com* reported that the FSB intelligence service trained him. The murder weapon was a suppressed Glock 26.

September 16, 2020: Authorities in North Rhine-Westfalia suspended 29 police officers for participating in neo-Nazi chat groups that shared images such as swastikas and a depiction of refugees in a gas chamber. The individuals shared more than 100 images with content pun-ishable by law in five *WhatsApp* chat groups pre-dominantly used by police officers. The officers handed in their badges and weapons. At least 25 of them worked for the same police force in Es-sen. Fourteen officers were expected to be fired. Police raided 34 homes and offices during the morning. One of the chat rooms was created in 2012; a second, in 2015.

October 2, 2020: *AP, Deuetsche Welle,* and *DPA* reported that the Hamburg State Court sen-tenced Omaima A., 36, widow of German-born rapper Denis Cuspert, alias Deso Dogg, who joined ISIS in Syria and was killed in an air-strike, to three years and six months in prison for membership in a terrorist organization, failing to properly care for her children, weapons vio-lations, and aiding and abetting the enslavement of a Yazidi girl, 13. She was born in Hamburg and of Tunisian heritage. She followed her first husband to Syria in 2015 and lived in Raqqa with their three children. Her first husband died in 2015. She later married his friend, Cuspert, whom the U.S. designated a "global terrorist". ISIS announced he died in an airstrike in Ko-bane, Syria in 2018. By then, she had returned to Germany. She was arrested earlier in 2020 when her cell phone was discovered and a war reporter in Syria chronicled her activities listed on 36 gi-gabytes of data.

Meanwhile, federal prosecutors said Kim A., a German woman, had been arrested at Frankfurt airport on her return from Syria on allegations she had joined ISIS. She was charged with membership in a terrorist organization and other crimes. She allegedly traveled to Syria with husband Onur E., in 2014; both joined ISIS. He underwent military training and fought against the Syrian regime. He allegedly taught her how to use an assault rifle. ISIS gave them homes they had seized from their owners. She fled Syria in 2016 and returned to Germany on October 1 on a flight from Turkey.

October 4, 2020: *Reuters* reported that a man, 29, swung a shovel and seriously injured a Jewish citizen in the head at a Hamburg synagogue as the Jewish community celebrated Sukkoth. The attacker was accused of causing grievous bodily harm. He appeared to have acted alone and was wearing military garb similar to that of neo-Nazi attacker Stephan B. in October 9, 2019, who shot two bystanders in Halle.

AFP reported on October 22 that a knife attack in Dresden on October 4 that killed a male tourist, 55, and seriously injured another tourist, 53, was being treated as a terrorist attack by prosecutors. On October 20, authorities arrested a Syrian man, 20, with an Islamist background, according to federal prosecutors in Karlsruhe. The tourists had traveled together from North Rhine-Westphalia. The suspect's long criminal record included charges of soliciting support for a foreign terrorist organization, obtaining instructions to commit a serious act of violence endangering the state, bodily injury and threats. *Der Spiegel* reported that he arrived in Germany in 2015 as a Syrian migrant and became increasingly radicalized since 2017, when police classified him as dangerous. He was living in Germany under "tolerated" status—his asylum request was rejected, but he could not be deported. He was released from a juvenile detention center on September 29. *Bild* reported that his DNA was found on a knife near the scene of the attack. His DNA was already in police databases. 20100401

October 24-25, 2020: *Reuters* reported that several individuals threw incendiary devices at the Robert Koch Institute for infectious diseases overnight, causing mild damage to the building. No one was hurt. The arsonists escaped. Berlin police announced it will investigate whether the attack was politically motivated.

October 26, 2020: *Deutsche Welle* reported that prominent Holocaust denier Horst Mahler, 84, was freed from a Brandenburg prison. Authorities issued a new arrest warrant for the erstwhile far-left terrorist turned neo-Nazi. He was jailed in 2009 after being sentenced to ten years for repeated incitement to racial hatred and for Holocaust denial. Prosecutors in Cottbus were pursuing charges for further incitement to racial hatred, based upon his online postings. He was temporarily released from prison in 2015 for medical reasons, but spent months appearing at neo-Nazi rallies, denying the WWII systematic killing of Jews and existence of gas chambers. He fled to Hungary in 2017 and requested political asylum. He was extradited back to Germany and imprisoned that year.

In the 1960s and early 1970s, he was an attorney representing prominent leftists in West Germany and later founded the Red Army Faction with Andreas Baader, Gundrun Ensslin, Ulrike Meinhof and others. He participated in some of the group's criminal activities, including bank robberies and kidnappings. After his conviction for RAF activities, he became a right-wing extremist while in prison, joining the far-right scene in the 1990s. He joined the extreme-right National Democratic Party (NPD) in 2000.

December 1, 2020: The *Washington Post, N-TV, CBS News, NBC News, AP, DPA*, and *CNN* reported that at 1:48 p.m., a German man, 51, crashed and zig-zagged a silver SUV with Trier license plates at high speed through a pedestrian street in Trier, killing five people—including a 9-month-old girl; woman, 25; a 45-year-old man from Trier, 25; and a 73-year-old woman—and seriously injuring 15, including the baby's mother, who was hospitalized. Police overpowered the Trier-born man after he drove more than a half mile then resisted arrest. The man was reportedly from the Trier-Saarburg area in Rhineland-Palatinate State, near the Luxembourg border. He had no fixed address and was living in a loaned Land Rover, which he used in the attack. Mental illness and drunkenness was suspected. A former neighbor said the driver had mental issues, money worries, and problems with his father. Police said they had no evidence of possible political, religious or terrorist motives.

UPI reported that German Interior Minister Horst Seehofer announced a ban against the neo-Nazi Wolf Brigade 44 (Wolfsbrgade 44) for attempting to re-establish a national socialist state by violent means, if necessary and re-strengthen "a free fatherland" under "Germanic moral law". Police raided the homes of nearly a dozen group members in the states of Hesse, Mecklenburg-Western Pomerania and North Rhine-Westphalia, confiscating Nazi symbols. The group was founded four years earlier as Storm Brigade 44.

GREECE

February 6, 2020: Police arrested five Greeks and two foreigners between the ages of 17 and 24 during the night outside the Moria migrant camp and were searching for two minors—a Greek and a foreigner—on suspicion of planning or carrying out attacks on migrants on the Aegean island of Lesbos. Police seized homemade wooden bats, a metal rod and a full-face hood.

June 3, 2020: *Reuters* reported that during a demonstration of 3,000 people protesting the police murder of George Floyd in Minneapolis, someone threw firebombs at the U.S. Embassy in Athens. Police responded by firing rounds of tear gas.

October 7, 2020: *AFP, Reuters,* and *The Daily Beast* reported that at the end of a five-year trial that featured 453 hearings, more than 200 witnesses, and 60 lawyers, Presiding Judge Maria Lepenioti ruled that neo-Nazi party Golden Dawn founder and leader Nikos Michaloliakos and seven other senior members were guilty of running a criminal organization. They faced 5-to-15-year sentences. Those convicted included Eurodeputy Yiannis Lagos, who defected from the party in 2019; the party's former spokesman Ilias Kassidiaris; and a dozen other senior party members elected to parliament in 2012. Magda Fyssa, the mother of murdered rapper Pavlos Fyssas, hailed the verdict. Pavlos, 34, was killed during the night in September 2013 when a mob of Golden Dawn thugs stabbed him to death in front of a café in the Athens suburb of Keratsini. His killer, former truck driver Yiorgos Roupa-

kias, confessed to murder, possession and use of a weapon. He was convicted with the other defendants and faced a life sentence. Some 68 Golden Dawn members were tried, including 18 former Golden Dawn Members of Parliament. The court also issued guilty verdicts in the case of an Egyptian fisherman left with broken teeth and head injuries after being beaten with clubs and metal bars in June 2012 as he slept, and in the 2013 case of Communists putting up posters who were attacked with nail-studded clubs. Presiding judge Maria Lepenioti on October 14 sentenced party leader Nikos Michaloliakos and seven other former lawmakers to 13 years in prison, nearly the maximum penalty. Another 11 former parliamentarians received sentences of between five and seven years for membership in a criminal organization. A party associate was given a life sentence for the Fyssas murder.

The *New York Times* reported on December 20, 2020 that Ioannis Lagos, who had been sentenced to 13 years in prison for setting up the party, had moved to Brussels, immune from extradition as an elected member of the European Parliament. Greece asked the Parliament to waive his immunity so that Belgian authorities could arrest him and send him to Greece to serve his sentence. Meanwhile, Lagos appealed the verdict. Of the main seven Golden Dawn leaders who were sentenced to 13 years, only five were in prison. Christos Pappas remained at large. Lagos was collecting more than 13,000 euros ($16,000) monthly in salary and expenses.

ITALY

July 1, 2020: *CNN* and *CBS News* reported that police in Salerno seized three containers holding 14 metric tonnes (15.4 US tons) of amphetamines which they claimed ISIS made in Syria. The 84 million pills have a market value of one billion Euros ($1.12 billion). The "Captagon"-logoed drugs established them as the "drug of jihad". They were hidden inside paper cylinders for industrial use, according to the Guardia di Finanza financial police, who said it was the largest amphetamine bust in the world. GdF said "It is known that ISIS/Daesh finances its terrorist activities in large part with the trafficking of synthetic drugs produced largely in Syria, which has become the leading world producer of amphetamines in recent years… The hypothesis is that during the lockdown, due to the global epidemiological emergency, the production and distribution of synthetic drugs in Europe has practically stopped and therefore many traffickers with different organized crime groups have turned to Syria, where it does not seem to have slowed down." The original, legal, now erstwhile Captagon medication contained the synthetic stimulant fenethylline. United Nations Office on Drugs and Crime (UNODC) chief Yury Fedotov told a June 2015 press conference that "(Islamic State) and al Nusra Front are also believed to facilitate the smuggling of chemical precursors for the production of Captagon." The new Captagon pills contain amphetamine. Authorities believed ISIS fighters used the drug in combat.

September 29, 2020: Carabinieri arrested Alice Brignoli, an Italian ISIS fighter, as she and her four children returned home from the al-Hol displaced persons camp in Kurdish-controlled territory. In 2015, Brignoli, her Moroccan-born husband Mohamed Koraichi, and their three young children drove their car from their home north of Milan to ISIS-controlled territory, where they had a fourth child. The children were now aged 11, 8, 6, and 4, and were placed in foster care pending a ruling by an Italian juvenile court. She was to go on trial on terrorism charges. The Carabinieri said she had contributed to radicalizing the children, turning them against West and "thereby embracing the cause of global jihadism". Carabinieri Lt. Col. Andrea Leo said Brignoli voluntarily returned to Italy, "convinced it was the best choice after the conditions she had lived in over the last 5 years". Koraichi died from an intestinal infection in September 2020 while being held as a prisoner in the al-Hol camp. Authorities said he had received training, participated in fighting and was prepared to carry out suicide attacks. He also held Italian citizenship. He helped others receive authorization to travel to ISIS territory, and aided in the recruitment and radicalization of at least two suspects who were arrested in April 2016 before they could leave Italy.

NETHERLANDS

February 13, 2020: *Reuters* reported that police found and disarmed a letter bomb at an office of Unisys, a U.S. information technology firm, near Utrecht. The bomb was delivered to Unisys Payment Services in Leusden. No injuries were reported. Several such devices had been received at businesses around the country; the sender demanded a ransom to be paid in Bitcoin. 20021301

Two similar letter bombs went off earlier in the week at mail rooms of the Dutch bank ABN Amro and Japanese printer company Ricoh. 20029901

Other letter bombs were sent to two hotels, a gas station, a real estate agent, a car dealership, and other businesses in early January. None of them detonated and no injuries were reported.

November 12, 2020: Bullets hit the white façade and several windows at the Saudi Embassy in The Hague in the morning, causing no injuries. Prosecutors said on November 16 that the shooter had a "terrorist" motive. An investigating magistrate ordered that a male suspect, 40, be held for another 14 days on suspicion of crimes "with a terrorist motive" including attempted murder or manslaughter of an embassy guard and "violence toward the building of an internationally protected person". He was earlier fined for defacing the building. 20111201

December 8, 2020: *AP* and *NOS* reported that two Polish Biedronka supermarkets in Aalsmeer in North Brabant Province were badly damaged by 3 a.m. explosions. No injuries were reported. The supermarkets are not part of a large network of budget stores of the same name in Poland.

NORTHERN IRELAND

January 31, 2020: *MSN.com* reported on February 7, 2020 that investigators were looking into a potential dissident republican plot to bomb a lorry on a ferry crossing to Scotland on Brexit Day (January 31, when the UK left the European Unon). Authorities found a bomb attached to a heavy goods vehicle in the Silverwood Industrial Estate in Lurgan in County Armagh in the first week of February. An initial police search had missed the bomb, but a re-search of 400 vehicles turned up the bomb, which was rendered safe by Army bomb disposal officers. The bomb was in the trailer unit of a lorry owned by a haulage company that specializes in transporting frozen goods across the UK, Ireland and Europe.

August 24, 2020: *Deutsche Welle* reported that authorities charged seven suspected members of a New IRA splinter group with terrorism following police raids the previous week. Ten former IRA members were arrested. The *Belfast Telegraph* said that MI5 was involved with the Operation Arbacia electronic monitoring of the suspects. Five suspects were due in a Belfast court; two appeared on videolink on August 22. One was accused of conspiracy to possess Semtex explosives. The Police Service Northern Ireland (PSNI) said two women, aged 45 and 49, were charged "on suspicion of a wide range of offences", including preparing acts of terrorism, such as attending meetings in Omagh, where a 1998 Real IRA car bombing killed 29 people.

NORWAY

March 26, 2020: Norwegian Justice Minister Monica Maeland announced the extradition of Iraqi-born Mullah Krekar, nee Najm al-Din Faraj Ahmad, 63, to Italy, where he was sentenced in July 2019 to 12 years in jail for planning terrorist attacks, attempting to overthrow the Kurdish government in northern Iraq and create an Islamic caliphate. Krekar was represented by Norwegian lawyer Brynjar Meiling. Italian prosecutors said Krekar ran Rawti Shax, a European network aimed at violently overthrowing the government in Kurdistan.

July 14, 2020: *Reuters* reported that police arrested a man after three women were stabbed in several locales in Sarpsborg during the night. One died from critical injuries. Police believed the individual acted alone; the motive was not clear.

July 17, 2020: *Bloomberg* reported that Ryanair flight FR 1392 that had received a bomb threat was safely evacuated after landing in Oslo's Gardermoen Airport at 12:25 p.m. The flight originated from the UK's Stansted Airport. Norwegian police arrested a British man, 51. On July 13, a separate Ryanair flight from Krakow to Dublin made an emergency landing at London's Stansted airport after receiving a hoax bomb threat. Police arrested two men for making threats to endanger an aircraft.

October 3, 2020: *Newsweek, NTB, NRK,* and *AFP* reported that the body of Dan-Eivind Lid, a prominent member of the far-right Stop Islamisation of Norway (Sian) group was discovered in an apartment in Kristiansand. Police launched a murder investigation.

RUSSIA

April 6, 2020: U.S. Secretary of State Mike Pompeo and his counterterrorism coordinator Nathan Sales announced that the Trump administration had designated the white supremacist Russian Imperial Movement (RIM) a "specially designated global terrorist" organization and imposed sanctions on its members. The administration placed individual sanctions on its leaders — Stanislav Anatolyevich Vorobyev, Denis Valliullovich Gariev and Nikolay Nikolayevich Trushchalov. The Movement allegedly provides paramilitary training to neo-Nazis and white supremacists in Russia and elsewhere from two camps it runs in St. Petersburg. In 2016, it allegedly trained two Swedish neo-fascists who later carried out a series of terrorist attacks in Gothenburg, Sweden, including bombing a cafe and attempting to bomb a campsite housing refugees. The Swedes were imprisoned in 2017 for the bombings. RIM claims to be a Russian Orthodox monarchical movement, and often posts anti-Semitic and anti-LGBTQ messages, complaints about incompetent and corrupt Russian elites, and warning of a coming clash of civilizations.

Igor Girkin, alias Igor Strelkov, senior military figure in the "Donetsk People's Republic" in eastern Ukraine, congratulated RIM for being named by the Trump administration as a terrorist group. Dutch authorities had charged Girkin, a former Russian intelligence officer, with murder for shooting down Malaysian Airlines Flight

17 on July 17, 2014, killing all 283 passengers and 15 crew. The U.S. and European Union had sanctioned him. He was commander and defense minister in the separatist Ukrainian region of Donetsk. He posted, "I take the opportunity to congratulate my esteemed comrade-in-arms of RID {the Russian acronym for RIM} on receiving a high award — official recognition of their 'terrorist organization' by the enemies of Russia and the Russian people."

October 30, 2020: *AFP* and *Newsweek* reported that just after midnight, police shot dead a boy, 16, in Kukmor the Muslim-majority Tatarstan region after he threw two Molotov cocktails at a local police station and stabbed thrice a police officer with a knife when police tried to arrest him. Russia's Investigative Committee opened a criminal terrorism case into an "attempted terrorist act" and "encroachment on the life of a law enforcement officer".

November 23, 2020: *Newsweek, Moscow Times, NGS24.ru,* and *Baza Telegram* news channel reported that prosecutors accused three Siberian teens, 14, with terrorism for plotting to blow up a regional Federal Security Service (FSB) which they had made on the brick-building video game *Minecraft.* The trio were arrested in June 2020, described by authorities as "underage supporters of anarchist views" who read "forbidden literature", watched videos on the manufacture of explosives, and trained in terrorist activities in an abandoned house, wastelands and on construction sites. Two of the youths had posted leaflets around Kansk in Krasnoyarsk region expressing support for Azat Mifstakhov, a mathematics student and anarchist from Moscow on trial for involvement in a group act of vandalism resulting in a broken window on a building belonging to the pro-Kremlin political party United Russia. One of the boys faced 10 years in jail.

December 11, 2020: *Interfax* reported that in the morning, a suicide bomber set off his device outside a local office of the Federal Security Service in Uchkeken in the Karachayevo-Cherkessiya region in the North Caucasus, injuring six Russian law enforcement officers who had gathered to investigate why another explosive had gone off minutes earlier.

SPAIN

April 20, 2020: The National Police announced the 3 a.m. arrest in a rented apartment in Cerro de San Cristóbal, a historic neighborhood in Almería, of a suspected Egyptian-born ISIS "dangerous extremist" and two other people who are being investigated for possible links to religious extremist groups. Former London rapper Abdel-Majed Abdel Bary stopped his career shortly after his father's 2012 extradition to the U.S. to face terrorism charges in al-Qaeda's 1998 bombings of two U.S. embassies in Tanzania and Kenya. His Egyptian father Abdel Abdul Bary was convicted of the charges in New York and sentenced in 2015 to 25 years in prison. Police said the man had gone from Europe to fight in Syria and Iraq, deeming him "one of the most sought terrorists in Europe, both because of his criminal trajectory in the ranks of Daesh (Islamic State) and because of the high danger that he represented". Police said he arrived by sea from northern Africa. The trio were to be sent before a National Court judge in Madrid on April 22. They declined to answer questions.

Abdel Bary, 29, grew up in London and used the rap name Lyricist Jinn and L Jinny. His raps mentioned drug use, violence and his family's experience as asylum-seekers in the UK. In 2013 he posted to *Facebook*, "I have left everything for the sake of Allah." In August 2014, a photo of him holding a man's severed head was tweeted. He was initially suspected of being Jihadi John, who was later identified as Mohammed Emwazi. The UK stripped Abdel Bary of his British citizenship when he joined ISIS in 2013; he retained his Egyptian citizenship. In 2015, he posted that he had left ISIS and fled to Turkey.

In 2015, Spanish woman María de los Ángeles Cala Márquez was arrested at an airport terminal in Madrid when she tried to travel to Turkey with a fake passport in order to marry Abdel Bary, with whom she had chatted on-line. In mid-2018, she was sentenced to two years of imprisonment with reprieve.

AP reported on April 23 that one of Bary's companions was Abdeizerrak Seddiki, 28, an Algerian known to Spanish law enforcement as a human trafficker.

Sweden

February 2020: Chechen dissident Tumru Abdurakhmanov was attacked.

Switzerland

September 2020: *Reuters* reported on November 4, 2020 that the Office of the Attorney General announced that it was investigating a fatal stabbing of a Portuguese man in September in the town of Morges, in western Switzerland for a possible "terrorist motive". Authorities arrested a Swiss-Turkish national.

November 24, 2020: Swiss Fedpol federal police said a Swiss woman, 28, suspected of stabbing and injuring two women in Lugano had formed a relationship online with a jihadi in Syria, and had attempted to travel there in 2017 but was prevented by Turkish authorities. Fedpol tweeted, "The woman was suffering from mental health problems at this time... After returning to Switzerland, she was admitted to a psychiatric clinic... Since 2017, the woman has not come to fedpol's attention in any investigations related to terrorist activities." The Swiss federal prosecutor's office opened criminal proceedings against the woman on charges of attempted premeditated homicide, serious bodily harm and being in violation of a ban on extremist groups such as al-Qaeda and ISIS.

Turkey

June 19, 2020: *Reuters* and Turkish media reported that genetics professor Mehmet Kanter, the father of NBA center Enes Kanter, 28, an outspoken critic of Turkish President Tayyip Erdogan's human rights record, was acquitted of charges that he was a member of a terrorist group who supported U.S.-based cleric Fethullah Gulen. Turkey indicted Enes Kanter in 2018 on charges of belonging to an armed terrorist group. He was awaiting U.S. citizenship, having lived in the U.S. for more than a decade.

September 1, 2020: *Deutsche Welle, Anadolu, Namex News, Middle East Eye, See.news, gotravel-*
blogger, and *NPR* reported that Turkish Interior Minister Suleyman Soylu tweeted the capture of ISIS's Turkey emir, Mahmut Ozden, in Adana and seized plans for attacks on businesses and the kidnapping of politicians. *Anadolu* reported that police used information obtained from an Istanbul raid the previous week that netted a suspect believed conducting reconnaissance for a potential attack. Police found an assault rifle in the suspect's hotel room and determined that he reported to Ozden. Intelligence and counter-terrorism police caught Ozden in Adana, then brought him to Istanbul, where he was formally arrested. Soylu said police found computer data on plans to kidnap Turkish political figures and take them to Syria. "The [evidence] seized in Mahmut Ozden's computer has indicated that he had been receiving orders from Iraq and Syria and he would take action by creating groups of 10-12 individuals... [Police] also seized plans to kidnap politicians and statesmen to take them to Syria and for acts against groups that could harm the Turkish economy." Ozden was also known as the Adana emir.

Anadolu reported that Ozden was in pre-trial custody until January 2020. In 2017, police determined that Ozden and his associates planned to attack Incirlik air base in Adana. Ozden had ordered the suspect in the previous week's raid to conduct a bombing in Istanbul.

October 23, 2020: *The Hill, CBS News, Business Insider, Washington Examiner, AP, CNN* and *ABC News* reported that the U.S. Embassy warned American citizens of "credible reports of potential terrorist attacks and kidnappings against US citizens and foreign nationals in Istanbul, including against the US Consulate General, as well as potentially other locations in Turkey". U.S. citizens should "exercise heightened caution in locations where Americans or foreigners may gather, including large office buildings or shopping malls". The Embassy temporarily suspended citizen services and visa processing at all of its facilities, including the embassy in Ankara, the U.S. Consulate General-Istanbul, U.S. Consulate-Adana, and the U.S. Consular Agency-Izmir.

December 13, 2020: *AP* reported that Iran was suspected of kidnapping exiled Iranian opposition figure Habib Chaab, leader of the Arab Struggle Movement for the Liberation of Ahvaz (ASMLA) separatist group, who had traveled from his home in Sweden to Turkey on October 9, 2020. He went to a gas station in Istanbul's district of Beylikduzu to meet with Saberin S., a woman waiting in a van. She had traveled from Iran on a forged Iranian passport. He was jumped by a kidnap team, who apparently worked with a drug trafficker and human smuggler to get Chaab into Iran. Two days after his disappearance, Iranian state media reported that he had been arrested and confessed to his involvement in a deadly attack on a military parade in 2018 in Iran. In December, Turkey arrested 11 Turkish men on charges including "using weapons … to deprive an individual of their liberty through deceit".

UKRAINE

May 29, 2020: *Reuters* reported that nearly 100 people, some carrying hunting rifles and some from Vynnytsya, which is outside the region, clashed during the morning in Brovary, a residential suburb of Kyiv, in Zhytomyr Region. Three people were wounded. National Police of Ukraine officers detained 20 men. *Reuters* reporters counted 40 shots fired. The Interior Ministry said the conflict involved representatives of companies involved in passenger transportation.

July 21, 2020: *AP* and *ABC News* reported that a gunman took circa 20 hostages on a bus in the city center of Lutsk in the northwest. Police said he was carrying explosives. Deputy Interior Minister Anton Gerashchenko said on *Facebook* that the gunman phoned the police at 9:25 a.m., identifying himself as Maksim Plokhoy. The DIM said a Maksim Plokhoy had posted a book, *Philosophy of a Criminal*, describing a man's experience in prison. "For 15 years they've been correcting me, but I haven't been corrected, on the contrary — I've become even more who I am." Witnesses heard several gunshots. He told police he had planted a bomb elsewhere in the city and could remotely detonate it. Evgeny Koval, deputy head of Ukraine's National Police, walked up to the bus repeatedly to negotiate. The national

newspaper *Ukrainskaya Pravda* added that police found posts online from the man complaining about his "dissatisfaction with the system in Ukraine". He had posted on social media "Happy Anti-System Day" and called the state a terrorist. "Plokhoi" translates to "bad" in Russian. The gunman freed three women, who walked to safety with Koval. *ABC News* reported that evening that the gunman surrendered and all 13 hostages were freed. The siege ended after Ukraine President Volodymyr Zelenskiy talked on the phone for 15 minutes with the gunman and fulfilled one of his demands by posting a video in which he called on people to watch the 2005 documentary film *Earthlings*, directed by Shaun Monson and narrated by Joaquin Phoenix, which showed human exploitation of animals. The gunman had also demanded that senior Ukrainian officials, Orthodox church leaders and prominent oligarchs make video statements in which they would call themselves "terrorists". The posts were immediately deleted after the gunman was in custody.

Police identified the gunman as Russian-born Maksym S. Kryvosh, 44, whose parents had lived in Lutsk. The Interior Ministry said a court had convicted him in 1994 and 2005 of serious crimes, including fraud and illegal possession of arms and explosives. He served 10 years in prison.

Hours after the hostage-taking began, police in Kyiv said they had disarmed two bombs at a market. Local media noted that serveral other bomb threats were called into public buildings in Kyiv and Kharkiv. Police said the explosives in Kyiv were not connected to the Lutsk incident.

UNITED KINGDOM

February 2, 2020: *SkyNews*, *AP* and *CNN* reported that London Metropolitan police shot to death Sudesh Amman, 20, who had stabbed several people on High Road, the main commercial street in the southern Streatham neighborhood, at 2 p.m. in a "terrorist-related incident" believed to be "Islamist-related". Police said two people were injured with stab wounds; another was hit by glass after a police weapon fired. Witnesses heard three gunshots. Gulled Bulhan, 19, a student from Streatham, told *PA* news agency that the attacker had a "machete and silver canisters on his chest". Police called it a "hoax device". Amman was released from prison days earlier after serving roughly half of a three-year sentence for possession and distribution of extremist material. He was freed with strict licensing conditions, including a curfew, and was kept under surveillance. *Reuters* reported that ISIS claimed credit via *Amaq*, saying, "The perpetrator of the attack in Streatham district in south London yesterday is a fighter of Islamic State, and carried out the attack in response to calls to attack the citizens of coalition countries." *Fox News* added that Sudesh had posted pro-ISIS messages, supported raping Yazidi women, and suggested to his girlfriend that she behead her parents.

February 7, 2020: Shamima Begum, 20, one of three east London teen Bethnal Green Academy schoolgirls who traveled from Gatwick Airport to Istanbul and on to Syria in 2015 to join ISIS, lost a court challenge to restore her UK citizenship, which former Home Secretary Sajid Javid revoked on national security grounds. She surfaced at a refugee camp in Syria in 2019. She showed no remorse for her actions. The tribunal deemed her "a citizen of Bangladesh by descent," and thus not rendered stateless. Her family said she never had a Bangladeshi passport. She was represented by attorney Daniel Furner. She said she married Dutch Muslim convert Yago Riedijk ten days after arriving in ISIS territory; her mother Doron Blum said the decision did not breach the Home Office's "extraterritorial human rights policy." School friends also reportedly married foreign ISIS fighters. She had three children, all of whom died.

February 20, 2020: *CNN* reported that London's Metropolitan Police arrested a man, 29, in a red hoodie on suspicion of attempted murder after a male prayer caller (muezzin) in his 70s was stabbed on the right side of his neck at the London Central Mosque near Regent's Park during 3 p.m. Asr Prayer. Several of the 100 worshippers helped pin the attacker to the ground. Some said the attacker had attended services in recent weeks. The *Washington Post* and the *Guardian* reported that the muezzin had served there for 25

years, calling the prayer five times/day. He was hospitalized with non-life-threatening injuries. Police and Imam Chokri Majouli suggested that the attack was not terror-related and that the perpetrator was mentally ill.

February 21, 2020: The *Daily Mail* reported that female ISIS supporter Safiyya Amira Shaikh, 36, of Hayes, West London, told the Old Bailey that she planned a suicide bombing on St. Paul's Cathedral after leaving another bomb in a London hotel to "kill herself and as many people as possible" and to the disseminate of terrorist propaganda via *Telegram*. While staying in an unnamed hotel, she surveilled the landmark as a target. Between August and October 2019, she drafted a pledge of fealty to ISIS. She tried to contact a bombmaker online and asked them to build two bombs. She later met with her contact, handing him two bags for the bombs, not realizing he was an undercover officer. Mr. Justice Sweeney remanded her to custody at HMP Bronzefield until her sentence on May 11. The judge ordered that any psychiatric reports be delivered by April 3.

The formal charges against her read:

1) one count of preparation of terrorist acts, contrary to section 5(1) of the Terrorism Act 2006, namely, on and between 19 August 2019 and 10 October 2019, with the intention of committing acts of terrorism, she engaged in conduct in preparation for giving effect to that intention, namely: Made contact with a person she believed to be able to assist in preparing explosives; researched methods and decided on a plan to carry out a terrorist act; travelled to central London and stayed at a hotel in order to conduct reconnaissance; selected the hotel as a target for an explosive device; attended St Paul's Cathedral to scope it, for security and for the best place to plant a second explosive device; met a person and supplied her with two bags, with the intention and belief that explosive devices would be fitted into the bags; prepared the words of a pledge of allegiance to Daesh, also known as Islamic State.

2) one count of dissemination of terrorist publications, contrary to section 2(1) of the Terrorism Act 2006, namely, on various dates between 19 August 2019 and 10 October 2019, she provided a service to others that enabled them to obtain, read, listen to or look at terrorist publications via 'Telegram', intending an effect of her conduct to be a direct or indirect encouragement or other inducement, or to constitute the provision of assistance, to the commission, preparation or instigation of acts of terrorism, contrary to section 2 (1) and 2 (2) (d) of the Terrorism Act 2006.

March 8, 2020: In the nighttime, police shot to death a man who was waving two knives near Trafalgar Square in Westminster in central London. The Metropolitan Police said the incident was not terrorist-related.

June 9, 2020: *Newsweek* reported that the West Midlands Police announced that Alice Cutter, 24, partner Mark Jones, 25, Garry Jack, 24, and Connor Scothern, 19, were convicted in March of being members of the National Action neo Nazi group. She met Jones when she participated in a Miss Hitler pageant as Buchenwald Princess. Then-Home Secretary Amber Rudd banned the group in December 2016 for being "racist, anti-Semitic and homophobic". The four were jailed on June 9, 2020. Cutter and Jones, both of Sowerby Bridge near Halifax, West Yorkshire, were sentenced to three years and five-and-one-half years, respectively. Jack, of Birmingham, was sentenced to four and one half years. Scothern, of Nottingham, was given 18 months. They were to serve at least two-thirds of their sentence before they were eligible for parole. She had sent messages regarding gassing synagogues and using a Jewish person's head as a football. Police said, "They held secret meetings to discuss their ambitions for a race war whilst recruiting other young people to the group, sharing intensely shocking images mocking the Holocaust and glorifying Hitler." Detective Chief Superintendent Kenny Bell, head of the West Midlands Counter Terrorism Unit, said, "We have seen a significant increase of right-wing referrals to our Prevent program and we will investigate the threat as robustly as we would any other terrorist group, as well as training our officers on the signs to look out for and working with communities to increase awareness. Terrorists and extremists use this kind of ideology to create discord, distrust and fear among our communities and we strive to counter this. I would encourage people to report hate crime to us and it will be taken seriously."

June 20, 2020: The *New York Times, Reuters, Newsweek, USA Today, The Hill, NBC News, AP, AFP, Fox News,* and *CNN* reported that at 7 p.m., an individual wielding a five-inch knife stabbed to death three people and seriously injured three others hours after a peaceful Black Lives Matter protest in the Forbury Gardens park in Reading's town center. The next day, Chief Constable John Campbell of the Thames Valley Police said "Deputy Assistant Commissioner Dean Haydon, Senior National Coordinator for the Counter Terrorism Policing network, has this morning declared the incident a terrorist incident, and CTPSE will be taking over the investigation." The individual stabbed people in the neck and under the arms. Witness Lawrence Wort, 20, said the man's eyes "looked like he was on some sort of drugs" and that he had shouted something unintelligible. A security source said mental health was considered to be a factor. The protestors had left the area before the attack began.

Police arrested a Reading man at the scene on suspicion of murder, having "rugby-tackled" him to the ground. They later re-arrested him under Section 41 of the Terrorism Act of 2000. British media and *CNN* reported that the detainee was a Libyan refugee from the country's civil war, Khairi Saadallah, 25, who arrived in the UK years earlier. The UK media said he came to the attention of MI-5 in 2019. *NPR* reported on June 22 that Saadallah had attempted to obtain terrorist training.

The *Washington Post, BBC, CBS News,* and *Philadelphia Inquirer* identified one of the dead as American citizen Joe Ritchie-Bennett, 39, of northeast Philadelphia. He was a friend of fellow victim James Furlong, 36, head of history, government and politics at The Holt School in Wokingham. Ritchie-Bennett moved to the UK

15 years earlier to work at a London law firm and for the past decade worked at a Reading-based Dutch pharmaceutical firm. He was planning an annual summer vacation in Greece. Furlong was a former student at St. Francis Xavier's College in Liverpool. Martin Cooper, chief executive of Reading Pride, said the two victims were both "great supporters" and members of the LGBT community. He met them at the Blagrave Arms pub in Reading, where they were regulars. A friend of the duo, David Wails, 49, a scientist at a chemical company, was also killed.

AFP added on June 23 that counter-terrorism police were given a warrant of further detention until June 27 to question Saadallah. Police had interviewed more than 50 witnesses.

AP reported on June 27 that British counter-terrorism police charged Saadallah with three counts of murder and three counts of attempted murder. He made his first court appearance on June 29; he did not enter a plea. Prosecutor Jan Newbold said Saadallah shouted "words to the effect of 'Allahu akbar'" during the attack.

AFP reported on November 11, 2020 that Libyan refugee Saadallah, 26, pleaded guilty at a pre-trial hearing in the Old Bailey court to three murders and three attempted murders. Judge Nigel Sweeney told the court Saadallah had denied being motivated by an ideological (terrorist) cause. Prosecutor Alison Morgan called for a "whole life" term in prison. Sentencing was scheduled for December 7. Saadallah had six previous convictions for 11 crimes, including racially aggravated assault, knife offences, and criminal damage, between June 2015 and January 2019. He was detained in November 2018 under the Mental Health Act. The media reported a history of debt, homelessness, PTSD, depression, a personality disorder that made him "aggressive and unpredictable", and alcohol and substance misuse. He was released early from prison in June 2020 after an earlier sentence was reduced on appeal. 20062001

June 26, 2020: *Reuters, CNN,* and *Sky News* reported that police shot to death a man who stabbed three people to death and injured six men in the stairwell of the Park Inn Hotel on West George Street in Glasgow, Scotland at 12:50 p.m. David Hamilton, Chairman of the Scottish Police Federation, said a male police officer, 42, had been stabbed and critically injured. The other hospitalized men were aged 17, 18, 20, 38 and 53. Police said the incident was not being treated as terrorism. Radisson Hotel Group said its hotel was being used for temporary housing for asylum seekers during the pandemic.

July 3, 2020: The *Cipher Brief* and *The Guardian* reported that Justice Sweeney sentenced Muslim convert Safiyya Amira Shaikh, nee Michelle Ramsden, 37, of Hayes, West London, to life in prison for planning a suicide bombing at London's St. Paul's cathedral. The ISIS supporter admitted in court to the plan and to sharing terrorist publications, but said that she did not conduct it because she was "too stoned". She would have to serve 14 years before being eligible for parole. She gave the jihadi single-finger salute to journalists in the courtroom.

She had converted in 2007 after being inspired by the kindness of a local Muslim family, but rebelled against a mosque's moderate Islam.

She had been under police and MI-5 surveillance since 2016. She was referred to the Prevent deradicalization program thrice between 2016-2018, but each time she left. She was never sent to the counter-extremism program Channel. She had chatted online with undercover officers regarding targeting a hotel in the City of London and blowing herself up on the underground. She ran a social media channel on *Telegram* called GreenB1rds, which offered pro-ISIS propaganda and advocated attacks in the UK and overseas, particularly against churches. On occasion, she posted as a man. Detectives said she was so sure of her eventual martyrdom that she was working on a succession plan for someone to inherit her *Telegram* account. She initially planned her St. Paul's attack for Christmas, but moved it to Easter. An undercover officer provided her with the alleged explosives.

She was represented by attorney Ben Newton. Justice Sweeney noted her mental health issues, but said: "There are a number of aggravating factors – communication with known extremists, deliberate use of encrypted communications, use of multiple social media platforms, significant volumes of terrorist publications published and attempting to disguise your identity... I had already reached the sure conclusion in the original evidence that your claim of doubt to the police and others was a lie. Your intention had been – and remained throughout – strong." A prison phone call to one of her friends confirmed his suspicions that she intended to conduct the attack, and had not gotten cold feet, just bad drugs.

She told an undercover team posing as husband and wife that she had surveilled St. Paul's, sending pictures to one of them of the dome, saying: "I would like to do this place for sure. I would like to bomb and shoot 'til death … I really would love to destroy that place and the kafir [a derogatory Arabic term for infidel or unbeliever] there." She gave a second undercover officer a pink Nike holdall and a backpack, hoping that these would become explosive devices.

On August 18, 2019, authorities at Luton Airport stopped her from flying to Amsterdam. Yousra Lemouesset, a Dutch-based ISIS supporter who was later convicted of terror offences, had purchased her ticket.

She was in contact with Anjem Choudary, a convicted British jihadist, and had listened to recorded sermons of Anwar al-Awlaki.

Authorities arrested her on October 10, 2019, after she cancelled a meeting with undercover officers.

July 9, 2020: *AFP* reported that Judge Andrew Lees of the Woolwich Crown Court sentenced to life in prison Uber driver Mohiussunnath Chowdhury, 29, of Luton, for plotting a gun and knife rampage at London tourist sites. He had earlier been acquitted of planning a terrorist attack at Buckingham Palace. In February 2020, a court found him guilty of planning to target popular attractions, including an open-top sightseeing bus, the annual gay Pride march in 2019 and Madame Tussaud's wax museum, using a gun, knife and van. He had shared his plans with undercover police posing as fellow extremists. In December 2018, a jury had acquitted him of slashing police with a sword while yelling "Allahu Akbar" outside Queen Elizabeth II's London residence, believing his claim that he was attempting suicide by cop and did not intend to hurt anyone. Police kept him under surveillance upon his release. He began posting extremist messages within a week of his release, and told

undercover officers that the jury believed his lies. Police arrested him three days before the Gay Pride parade. Chowdhury was to serve a minimum of 25 years.

August 22, 2020: *RTE*, the Republic of Ireland's Dublin-based broadcaster, reported that a 62-year-old resident of Scotland was arrested at London's Heathrow airport and flown to Northern Ireland during raids on suspected IRA dissidents. Scottish police searched a property in Edinburgh's Blackhall area.

September 6, 2020: *AFP, Reuters,* and *NBC News* reported that a male slasher killed a man, 23, and critically injured a man and a woman, aged 19 and 32, during a "random" stabbing spree between 12:30 a.m. and 2:30 a.m. in four locations in Birmingham. Five other people were hospitalized with minor injuries. One of the attacks took place in the Arcadian Centre area of restaurants, nightclubs, and bars. West Midlands police ruled out a hate crime, gang violence, and terrorism. *Reuters* reported that the first stabbing was in Constitution Hill, followed by Livery Street, Irving Street, and Hurst Street in the Gay Village area. *AFP* reported on September 7 that police had arrested a man, 27, in the Selly Oak area around 4 a.m. on charges of murder and attempted murder.

October 12, 2020: Justice Mark Warbury sentenced sheep farmer Nigel Wright, 45, to 14 years in prison for plotting to use baby food laced with metal shards to blackmail Tesco, one of Britain's biggest supermarket chains. The Hertfordshire Constabulary confiscated a jar of Heinz baby food that was laced with fragments of a craft knife by Wright. Wright planted jars of the contaminated baby food in Tesco stores and sent dozens of letters and emails to the supermarket company in a bid to extort 1.4 million pounds ($1.8 million) in bitcoin between 2018 and February 2020. Tesco issued a product recall after two mothers reported discovering pieces of metal in jars of Heinz baby food. No babies were harmed. Some 42,000 jars of Heinz baby food were recovered. Wright was accused of masterminding the plot in the name of farmers who were angry at the low price of milk. He was convicted of two counts of contaminating goods and three counts of blackmail. Justice Warby compared Wright's actions to terrorism and called him remorseless, observing, "You chose to use threats of a particularly blood-curdling nature, deliberately designed to exploit the vulnerability of children, and the consequent vulnerability of a supermarket concerned for its business."

October 13, 2020: *CNN* reported that Ken McCallum, head of the MI5 domestic security service since March, announced that eight of the 27 late-stage disrupted terrorist plots since 2017 were the work of far right extremists.

November 3, 2020: The government raised the terrorism threat level to severe, the second-highest on the country's scale.

LATIN AMERICA

BRAZIL

March 31, 2020: The bullet-riddled body of Zezico Guajajara, a teacher and member of the Guajajara indigenous group known for its forest guardians who fight illegal deforestation in their territory, was found on a road near his village in Maranhao State's Arariboia Indigenous Territory. It was the fifth murder of a Guajajara tribesman since November 2019.

June 12, 2020: *AP* reported on June 27 that illegal gold prospectors shot to death two members of the Yanomami indigenous ethnic group inside the Yanomami territory in Brazil's Amazon rainforest in Roraima State. Júnior Hekurari Yanomami, president of Condisi-Y, the local health council, identified the victims as Original Yanomami, 24, and Marcos Yanomami, 20. The Hutukara association, which represents Yanomami communities in Brazil, confirmed the reports of the murders. Yanomami members were following the trespassing prospectors, who shot Original first. The bodies were left in the forest, consonant with Yanomami custom. The Hutukara association added, "We fear that the family of the Yanomami murdered will decide to retaliate

against the prospectors following the justice system of the Yanomami culture. That can lead to a cycle of violence that will result in tragedy."

COLOMBIA

January 12, 2020: Colombian authorities announced that they thwarted a planned attempt to kill Rodrigo Londono, FARC peace negotiator.

January 17, 2020: During the night, five people were found shot to death in the Jamundi municipality in southwestern Colombia. Two vehicles were incinerated. Two bodies were under a bullet-riddled vehicle; three were farther up a dirt road. Police suspected rival drug gangs or splinters of the former Revolutionary Armed Forces of Colombia were involved.

March 2020: The *Washington Post, AP, AFP,* and *CNN* reported that two dissident members of the FARC on motorcycles kidnapped two travelers, Swiss citizen Daniel Max Guggenheim and Brazilian José Ivan Alburneque (or Albuquerque) García Matias, and their Pomeranians Preto and Fifi, from a restaurant in Corinto, Cauca Department. The rebels took their car's keys and rifled their suitcases. They demanding tens of millions in pesos; Guggenheim had $3,600. The rebels phoned his daughter, demanded more. The men were held in 11 locations. Colombia's Rapid Deployment Force No. 4 rescued the hostages and their dogs in Popayan, Colombia, on June 18, 2020, from the Dagoberto Ramos Mobile Column, formerly the FARC's Sixth Front. The Investigative Technical Corps of the Colombian Prosecutor's Office and Colombian soldiers captured their male guard. 20039901

March 5, 2020: *AP* reported that Astrid Conde, a former FARC fighter, was shot four times in the chest and killed while walking her German shepherd in Bogota.

March 31, 2020: *BBC* reported that the National Liberation Army (ELN) announced, "We declare an active unilateral ceasefire for a month, from 1 to 30 April in a humanitarian gesture of the ELN with the Colombian people, who're suffering from devastation because of the coronavirus" pandemic. By March 31, more than 700 people in Colombia had tested positive for the virus and ten had died.

April 4, 2020: Human Rights Watch reported that the ELN was believed responsible for killing farmer José Rubiel Muñoz Samboní, after he arrived from a nearby community to meet friends. A prosecutor suggested that the ELN killed him for failure to comply with the group's COVID-19 lockdown.

April 14, 2020: Carlos Ruiz Massieu, U.N. envoy for Colombia, said that 22 former FARC combatants were making face masks at a textile cooperative to respond to the coronavirus pandemic; eight other former FARC fighters' cooperatives were doing similar work. However, three social leaders and three former combatants were killed in recent weeks.

April 26, 2020: Human Rights Watch reported that members of the Jaime Martínez mobile column, a FARC dissident splinter group, killed three civilians identified as Armando Montaño, Weimar Arará, and Humberto Solís and injured four others in a public park in Cauca State for failing to comply with a COVID-19 lockdown.

May 2020: The *Washington Post* reported that early in the month, gunmen torched a medical transport responding to a call after a rebel-imposed coronavirus curfew, killing its driver and a patient.

May 29, 2020: *Reuters* reported that Pablo Beltran, head of the peace negotiating team of the National Liberation Army (ELN), said that the group would be willing to participate in a global three-month ceasefire being discussed at the United Nations to contain the spread of coronavirus. U.N. Secretary General had called for the ceasefire on March 23. The ELN called a unilateral ceasefire during April. Beltran said no ELN member had been infected.

May 30, 2020: Human Rights Watch reported that the Dagoberto Ramos mobile column attacked four Venezuelan migrants in the Toribío municipality, killing Johan José Ibáñez Hernán-

dez and Yonier Alexis Matute Solano, and injuring Anayibe del Carmen Guerrero Loyo and Erick Alexander Torrealaba Arismendi. The foursome had been drinking alcohol in a cellphone repair shop in defiance of the group's ban on such activities to prevent the spead of COVID-19. Fifteen Venezuelans fled the area.

Human Rights Watch reported that gunmen wearing civilian clothes from the FARC splinter Oliver Sinisterra Front fired on a private silver SUV transporting two prosecutors on a road near Tumaco. Two grazed the head of a prosecutor; Lorena Paredes, 28, was hit three times in the legs. Paredes was returning from a doctor's appointment. The victims drove to get help, but local residents locked themselves in their homes and one said that they were forbidden to help them. Judicial and human rights officers suggested that they were attacked for not abiding by the group's 4 p.m. curfew.

June 17, 2020: *AFP* reported that the Colombian army announced that six soldiers died in a gun battle with a rebel faction.

June 18, 2020: *AFP* and *AP* reported that the U.S. Department of State's Rewards for Justice Program offered up to $10 million for the arrest and conviction of Revolutionary Armed Forces of Colombia (FARC) dissidents Luciano Marin, alias Iván Marquez, and Seuxis Hernandez, alias Jesus Santrich. Marquez had been FARC's deputy chief and the group's lead peace negotiator. Secretary of State Mike Pompeo accused them of involvement in drug trafficking and that they are supported by Venezuelan leftist leader Nicolas Maduro. Marquez and Santrich had been given seats in Colombia's parliament. Hernández was jailed in 2018 after prosecutors in New York ordered his arrest on drug charges. He disappeared a month after Colombia's Supreme Court ordered him freed while the charges were investigated. The duo reappeared in August 2019 in a video showing them in olive-green uniforms with several dissidents.

September 28, 2020: The U.S. deported to his native Colombia paramilitary leader Rodrigo Tovar, 69, alias Jorge 40, after he served 12 years in U.S. prisons for drug trafficking. He had earlier served as a government official in Valledupar. Colombian prosecutors said he was behind several mass killings in rural areas, including El Salado, where paramilitary fighters killed and dismembered 60 civilians they accused of supporting a rebel group. He faced 35 arrest orders in Colombia.

October 14, 2020: U.N. envoy for Colombia Carlos Ruiz Massieu told the U.N. Security Council that former combatants continued to be killed "in alarming numbers" since the 2016 peace accord. Secretary-General Antonio Guterres's latest report to the Council logged 19 killings of former combatants from the Revolutionary Armed Forces of Colombia (FARC) in the three-month period ending September 25. Among the victims was former FARC commander Jorge Iván Ramos, who became a FARC political party leader, who was killed on August 28. FARC had openly charged the National Liberation Army (ELN) with killing Ramos. Since 2016, the U.N. tallied 297 attacks on former FARC fighters, including 224 killings, 20 disappearances and 53 attempted homicides.

October 25, 2020: *AFP* reported that President Ivan Duque announced that a military operation against the jungle commune of Novita in Choco Department killed Andres Vanegas, alias Commander Uriel, 41, one of the main leaders of the leftist National Liberation Army (ELN). He was accused of being an organizer of a January 2019 car bomb attack on a police academy in Bogota that killed 21 recruits. Duque said Uriel was behind kidnappings, murders and recruiting minors for the Marxist guerrillas.

CUBA

May 13, 2020: *AFP* reported that the United States added Cuba to a blacklist of countries that do not fully cooperate on counterterrorism, and denounced the presence of Colombian ELN rebels. The U.S. also did not certify Iran, Syria, North Korea and Venezuela under a counterterrorism law that affects defense exports. Cuba was last not certified in 2015. The Trump administration was also considering adding Cuba to the list of state sponsors of terrorism.

December 30, 2020: The *New York Times* reported that U.S. Secretary of State Mike Pompeo was considering relisting Cuba on the list of state sponsors of terrorism.

HAITI

August 28, 2020: During the night, Monferrier Dorval, head of the Port-au-Prince Bar Association, was shot and killed at his home.

HONDURAS

September 27, 2020: *AFP* reported that two gunmen on a motorcycle shot to death Honduran journalist and government critic Luis Almendares, 35, who was visiting a store in Comayagua, 40 miles north of Tegucigalpa. He had complained to the police and the National Protection System about receiving death threats.

December 26, 2020: Masked gunmen shot to death Félix Vásquez, a longtime environmental activist from the Lenca indigenous group, in front of relatives in his home in Santiago de Puringla. Vásquez was seeking the nomination of the opposition Libre party to run for congress in the national elections scheduled for March. He had fought against hydroelectric projects and land abuses for years. Honduras's National Human Rights Commission had requested protective measures for Vásquez in January 2020, but they were ignored. Rafael Alegría, coordinator of the nongovernmental organization Via Campesina in Honduras, said Vásquez had filed complaints and reported threats since 2017.

December 27, 2020: The bullet-riddled body of Jose Adán Medina, a member of the Tolupan Indigenous group, was found in a remote location in the El Volcan community in the west.

MEXICO

January 4, 2020: Gunmen killed a U.S. citizen, 13, and wounded four relatives in a nighttime attack on two vehicles on a little-used two-lane stretch of highway near the Texas border in Ciudad Mier. One SUV of the attackers cut them off, causing them to collide. The vehicles had Oklahoma license plates. One of the wounded was ten years old. The family had spent the holidays in San Luis Potosi State. Photographs showed the Northeast cartel's Spanish initials CDN on the back window of one of the vehicles.

June 26, 2020: Dozens of gunmen fired 50-caliber weapons and threw grenades at a Chevrolet Suburban carrying Omar García Harfuch, 38, Mexico City's secretary of public security, on Mexico City's Paseo de la Reforma boulevard in the upscale Lomas neighborhood, injuring him. Two police officers guarding him and a woman driving by were killed. Police detained a dozen people, including 11 Mexicans and one Colombian. García Harfuch tweeted that the Jalisco New Generation Cartel (CJNG) was responsible, noting, "This morning we were cowardly attacked by the CJNG, two colleagues and friends of mine lost their life, I have three bullet wounds and several shards." Garcia Harfuch was hit in the shoulder, collar bone and the knee. The Jalisco drug cartel broke from the Sinaloa Cartel around 2010.

Later that day, capital police arrested José Armando Briseño, alias "Cow", an alleged head of the Jalisco New Generation hitmen in Tonala in Jalisco, suggesting he could have been the mastermind.

Ulises Lara, the spokesman for the Mexico City prosecutors' office, said 28 gunmen, organized into four cells, were hired three weeks earlier, and three ambush points were set up. One point was a block from the Independence Monument. They were given ski masks and weapons the evening of June 25. They went to their ambush points at 4 a.m. to set up. The hit team jumped from a truck and fired on Garcia's convoy.

The 11 Mexican detainees were from Mexico City and the states of Jalisco, Guerrero, Nayarit, Chihuahua and Michoacan.

July 1, 2020: *Reuters, NBC News* and *AFP* reported that six or seven gunmen drove up in two vehicles, one red, broke into a two-storey unregistered drug rehabilitation center in Irapuato in Guanajuato State, and shot to death 24 people while wounding seven, three seriously. The gunmen shot every male at the center, letting the females go. No abductions were reported. Governor Diego Sinhue Rodríguez Vallejo said drug gangs apparently were involved. *Fox News* and *AP* reported on July 2 that he death toll had reached 26. Among the dead were three adult sons of Rosa Alba Santoyo, who said a female addict at the center said the gunmen told the women to leave. Santoyo said two of her sons, construction workers aged 29 and 39, had problems with drugs. Her youngest son, 27, had recovered and was visiting his brothers.

November 9, 2020: *CNN* reported that Mexican journalist Israel Vázquez, 31, was shot to death as he was about to go live on air. He worked for digital news outlet *El Salmantino*. The Guanajuato State attorney general's office tweeted that the victim was covering a "discovery of human remains" in Salamanca.

VENEZUELA

March 26, 2020: The U.S. Department of Justice unsealed indictments in New York and Florida against Venezuelan President Nicolás Maduro, 57, and 14 officials, including members of his inner circle and individuals on narcoterrorism charges including money laundering, drug trafficking and narcoterrorism. The administration offered a $15 million reward for information leading to Maduro's capture or conviction and a $10 million reward for four of the others. U.S. Attorney General William P. Barr alleged that Maduro worked with Colombian guerrillas to make Venezuela a transshipment point for moving cocaine into the United States. Barr accused Maduro of "deploying cocaine as a weapon" against the United States, observing, "Maduro and the other defendants expressly intended to flood the United States with cocaine in order to undermine the health and well-being of our nation." The charges carry sentences of between 50 years in prison and life.

The U.S. also charged the head of Venezuela's National Constituent Assembly, a former director of military intelligence, retired General Cliver Alcalá Cordones, Defense Minister Vladimir Padrino López, and chief justice of the Supreme Court Maikel Moreno. *AP* reported that Padrino and Moreno were involved in plotting a military uprising against Maduro in 2019, but failed to act.

New York-based prosecutors accused Maduro and Diosdado Cabello, socialist party leader and head of the constitutional assembly, of conspiring with FARC and the military to "flood the U.S. with cocaine". The Department of Justice said the group helped smuggle 250 metric tons of cocaine/year.

Miami-based prosecutors charged Supreme Court Chief Justice Maikel Moreno with laundering $3 million in illegal proceeds from case-fixing in Venezuela.

In May 2019, Washington-based prosecutors charged Defense Ministry General Vladimir Padrino with conspiracy to smuggle narcotics.

Prosecutors claimed that Maduro and other Venezuelan officials ran the Cartel do los Soles (Cartel of the Suns) since at least 1999, working with the Revolutionary Armed Forces of Colombia (FARC).

AFP and *El Tiempo de Bogota* reported on March 28, 2020 that retired Venezuela General Cliver Alcalá Cordones, 58, surrendered to Colombian authorities on March 27; Colombia passed him on to U.S. authorities, who put him on a flight to New York. Alcalá had lived in Barranquilla, Colombia, for the last two years. He retired in 2013 after Maduro took over the government from Hugo Chavez, who died of cancer.

Maduro called U.S. President Trump a "wretched" man who "will go down in history as the most harmful and most irrational of American presidents".

May 27, 2020: *ABC News, Tribune News Service,* and the *Miami Herald* reported that the U.S. Attorney's Office in Manhattan charged Adel El Zabayar, 56, a former member of the Venezuelan National Assembly, with narco-terrorism offenses, including "conspiracy" to commit "narcoterrorist" acts, "conspiracy to import cocaine", and two weapons-related offenses. He faced sentences ranging from ten years to life in prison. Prosecutors said El Zabayar, who is of Syrian descent, was a member of disputed Venezuelan President Nicolas Maduro's Cartel de Los Soles (Cartel of the Suns) that sought support from the FARC, Hizballah and Hamas to "flood" the U.S. with cocaine. DEA acting Administrator Timothy J. Shea added that "Today's charges against Adel El Zabayar for trading arms for cocaine, and recruiting extremists, further demonstrates the corruption inside the Maduro regime." Prosecutors identified El Zabayar as among the cartel members who received a planeload of military weapons, including rocket-propelled grenade launchers, AK-103s, and sniper rifles, from Lebanon. U.S. Attorney for the Southern District of New York Geoffrey Berman added that, "We further allege today, for the first time, that the Cártel de Los Soles sought to recruit terrorists from Hizballah and Hamas to assist in planning and carrying out attacks on the U.S., and that El Zabayar was instrumental as a go-between." El Zabayar is the president of the Venezuelan Federation of Arab Associations and Entities.

MIDDLE EAST

January 21, 2020: The *AFIO Weekly Newsletter* reported that the *Middle East Monitor* and *The Guardian* said that two intelligence services confirmed that one of the founding members of ISIS had been named in October 2019 as its new caliph, to succeed Abu Bakr al-Baghdadi. The Iraqi Turkmen was born in Tal Afar in northern Iraq as Amir Mohammed Abdul Rahman al-Mawli al-Salbi. He used the kunyas Abdullah Qardash and Hajji Abdullah al-Afari. He was detained in 2004 by U.S. soldiers in the Camp Bucca prison in southern Iraq, where he met al-Baghdadi. He graduated in Shariah legal studies from the University of Mosul. He was among the people that gave a fatwa for ISIS to assault and enslave Iraq's Yazidi sect in 2015, and oversaw international operations. The U.S. Department of State had issued a $5 million bounty for him. He was the first non-Arab ISIS leader. In Turkey, his brother Adel al-Salbi heads the Turkmen Iraqi Front political party.

January 27, 2020: ISIS released an audio saying it would conduct a new phase of attacks focusing on Israel and condemned the Trump administration's Israel-Palestine peace plan.

January 28, 2020: A crackdown coordinated by Europol shut down thousands of ISIS propaganda outlets and communication channels and forced its news agency off the *Telegram* system.

April 2, 2020: *AP* reported that al-Qaeda and ISIS saw the virus as punishment for non-Muslims and called on followers to repent and take care of themselves. Al-Qaeda said that non-Muslims should use their quarantine time to learn about Islam. The mid-March edition of ISIS's *al-Naba* newsletter called for followers to show no mercy and launch attacks during the crisis.

June 23, 2020: Brian Glyn Williams, Professor of Islamic History at University of Massachusetts-Dartmouth wrote in MSN.com's *The Conversation* that an ISIS follower posted the hashtag "#AmericaBurning" in a discussion on *Telegram* in early June, and another posted "You are waking up this morning to news of the destruction of America, the dismantling of its States, and civil war." Another ISIS website posted, "Destruction, fragmentation. America is burning," and an ISIS supporter posted photos in the same *Telegram* forum of the riots, adding "O Allah, burn them like they burned the lands of the Muslims."

November 17, 2020: The *Voice of America* reported that al-Qaeda leader Ayman al-Zawahiri, 69, was rumored to have died from illness.

AFGHANISTAN

January 8, 2020: The *New York Times* reported that a U.S. drone strike in Herat Province killed Mullah Nangyalay, commander of a Taliban splinter group. He had split with the main Taliban two years earlier.

January 11, 2020: *Newsweek, CNN,* the *New York Times* and *AP* reported that two U.S. service combat engineers died and two others were injured when their vehicle hit a roadside bomb in the morning. Taliban spokesman Qari Yousouf Ahmadi said the bomb went off in Kandahar Province. An Afghan official said the attack occurred in the province's Dand district. *Fox News* and *WBBM-TV* of Chicago reported that one of the service members was Private First Class

Miguel Villalon, 21, from Joliet, Illinois. He had graduated from East Aurora High School, and was serving in the U.S. Army. *CBS News* reported that the other soldier was Staff Sergeant Ian McLaughlin, 29 of Newport News, Virginia. *Newsweek* added that both soldiers were assigned to the 307th Brigade Engineer Battalion, 3rd Brigade Combat Team, 82nd Airborne Division, Fort Bragg, North Carolina. *Newsweek* noted that McLaughlin joined the Army in 2012 and was assigned to the 62nd Engineer Battalion at Fort Hood, Texas as a Horizontal Construction Engineer. In 2016, he was assigned to the 307th Airborne Engineer Battalion, later becoming a Squad Leader. His awards and decorations include the Purple Heart, the Bronze Star Medal and the Army Commendation Medal with "C" Device. Villalon joined the Army in 2018 and was assigned to the 307th Airborne Engineer Battalion as a Combat Engineer. His awards and decorations include the Purple Heart, the Bronze Star Medal and the Army Commendation Medal. It was the duo's first combat deployment. 20011101

January 18, 2020: Afghan officials said that the Taliban executed six members of the same family, including an infant girl, in a remote village in Andkhoy district, but the Taliban said it was a personal dispute. The Taliban accused the family of working in prostitution. Jawed Bedar, spokesman for Faryab Province's governor, said the Taliban sentenced them to death for immoral acts, then attacked the house and fired. The infant girl's mother and twin sister survived. Both of the child's legs had to be amputated. The next day, the Taliban attacked rescuing troops; three Taliban, involved in the family's killing, died in the ensuing gun battle. Andkhoy district chief Sultan Mohammad Sanjer said residents of the village said that a member of the slain family was a former Taliban member who recently joined the peace process.

January 27, 2020: The *Washington Post* reported that the Taliban claimed credit when a U.S. Bombardier E-11A surveillance plane crashed in Taliban-controlled territory in Ghazni Province's Deh Yak district. The U.S. said the Taliban was not responsible. U.S. forces recovered the bodies of two U.S. service members from the site. *Air Force Times* on identified the two airmen as Lt. Col. Paul K. Voss, 46, of Yigo, Guam, and Capt. Ryan S. Phaneuf, 30, of Hudson, New Hampshire.

Voss, call sign Tabs, was an 11M mobility pilot assigned to Air Combat Command (ACC) headquarters at Joint Base Langley-Eustis in Virginia. He was commissioned in November 2001 after graduating from Officer Training School. Decorations included the Meritorious Service Medal, the Aerial Achievement Medal, the Air Medal, the Air Force Commendation Medal, and the Air Force Achievement Medal. Voss was on a voluntary deployment to Afghanistan, supporting the 455th Air Expeditionary Wing at Bagram, when he died while piloting the E-11A. Voss was a prior-enlisted airman who served 25 years total on active duty. He had been stationed at Langley-Eustis for four years and was serving as chief of exercises within ACC's directorate of operations. He deployed to Bagram in 2010.

Phaneuf, an 11B bomber pilot, was assigned to the 37th Bomb Squadron at Ellsworth Air Force Base in South Dakota. He flew the B-1B Lancer. He entered active duty in June 2012 after being commissioned through ROTC. Decorations included the Air Force Commendation Medal.

The E-11A communications aircraft was assigned to the 430th Expeditionary Electronic Combat Squadron, and operated out of Kandahar Airfield. It carried the Battlefield Airborne Communications Node, known as "WiFi in the sky".

Taliban spokesman Zabiullah Mujahid claimed that the crash killed "high-ranking CIA officials on board", but a U.S. official said that "there was no one senior" aboard the plane.

January 28, 2020: In a late night raid, four helicopters carrying 50 Afghan special forces commandos led by Major Sayed Rahimullah landed outside a Taliban prison compound in Bala Murghab district in Badghis Province and rescued 62 hostages. The raiders killed eight Taliban and detained five.

During the night, the Taliban killed six Afghan security forces in Kunduz Province. Kun-

duz lawmaker Muhammaddin Hamdard put the death toll at 13 Afghan troops.

In another nighttime attack, the Taliban claimed credit for raiding a police base on the outskirts of Puli Khumri, capital of Baghlan Province, possibly with the assistance of a policeman who opened a door for them, killing 11.

January 31, 2020: The *Washington Post* reported that the U.S. Special Inspector General for Afghanistan Reconstruction's quarterly report indicated that the Taliban and other insurgents conducted more than 8,200 attacks against Afghan troops, U.S. forces and civilians in the last quarter of 2019, more than any other fourth quarter since 2010.

Newsweek and *NPR* reported on February 6 that the Haqqani Network was suspected of kidnapping American contractor Mark R. Frerichs, 57, of Lombard, Illinois, in Khost Province on January 31. The former U.S. Navy diver was managing director for International Logistical Support. He worked as a civil engineer in Iraq and Sudan during the previous decade. He regularly traveled to Afghanistan since 2012. No one claimed credit.

AP reported on April 30, 2020 that SEALs had been unsuccessful in finding U.S. citizen and Navy veteran Mark Frerichs, 57, a commercial contractor from Lombard, Illinois, who was kidnapped by the Haqqani Network in January 2020. The SEALs had tracked his phone and detained suspected Haqqani Network members in a raid on a village on February 3. *AP* reported that U.S. officials believed that Frerichs had been held in Khost Province and might have been moved to Quetta, Pakistan. The Taliban did not acknowledge Frerichs's capture. No demands were made.

On May 10, 2020, *AP* reported that Taliban leaders, including members of the Haqqani Network, announced that they are not holding Mark R. Frerichs, a U.S. Navy veteran turned contractor who disappeared in Afghanistan on January 31. The U.S. requested Pakistan's help in locating Frierchs. 20013101

February 3, 2020: *Task and Purpose* reported that the Special Inspector General for Afghanistan Reconstruction indicated that members of

Afghanistan's security forces fired on their colleagues in 33 insider attacks during the fourth quarter of 2019, resulting in 90 casualties. This averaged one attack every four days. For all of 2019, there were 82 insider attacks that killed 172 and wounded 85.

February 8, 2020: An individual in an Afghan uniform fired a machine gun at Afghan and U.S. service members in Nangarhar Province's Sherzad district, killing two U.S. soldiers and an Afghan Army soldier and wounding six other people, including three Afghans. *ABC News* reported that it was being investigated as an insider attack. The Pentagon said the two dead Americans were:

- Sgt. 1st Class Javier Jaguar Gutierrez, 28, of San Antonio, Texas. He was born in Jacksonville, North Carolina and enlisted in the Army as an infantryman in 2009. He was stationed at Fort Bragg. He was assigned to the 2nd Battalion, 504th Parachute Infantry Regiment. In 2012, he attended the Special Forces Assessment and Selection, and was chosen to attend the Special Forces Qualification Course. He graduated in 2015 as a special forces communications sergeant, assigned to Eglin Air Force base.
- Sgt. 1st Class Antonio Rey Rodriguez, 28, of Las Cruces, New Mexico.

Both soldiers were assigned to 3rd Battalion, 7th Special Forces Group (Airborne), and were posthumously promoted after the attack.

Afghan officials said the attacker's identity was known and he was a soldier from Nangarhar. He was killed during the shootout. The deputy head of the provincial council said two other soldiers were detained for questioning. 20020801

February 11, 2020: A suicide bomber set off his explosives in the morning outside a military academy in Kabul, killing two civilians and four military personnel and wounding 12.

February 16, 2020: *NPR* reported that a Taliban attack killed four soldiers.

February 29, 2020: The *Washington Post* reported that U.S. envoy Zalmay Khalilzad and Taliban deputy leader Mullah Abdul Ghani Baradar

signed a peace agreement in Doha, Qatar. The Taliban agreed to begin talks with the Afghan government and not harbor terrorists. The U.S. would being drawing down to 8,600 troops "within months".

March-April 2020: The *Washington Post* reported on May 1, 2020 that the Afghan National Security Council claimed that the Taliban conducted an average of 55 attacks/day since March 1.

March 4, 2020: A U.S. airstrike targeted Taliban fighters in southern Afghanistan hours after President Trump spoke by phone to Taliban political leader Abdul Ghani Baradar. The Taliban had attacked an Afghan security force outpost in Helmand Province. Interior Ministry spokesman Nasrat Rahimi said that the Taliban "conducted 30 attacks that killed four civilians and 11 security force members and wounded 18 others" within the previous 24 hours.

During an overnight rocket attack, eight soldiers were killed in Kunduz Province.

March 6, 2020: *Reuters* and *AP* reported that before noon, two ISIS-K gunmen fired machine-guns and rocket-propelled grenades and threw hand grenades from a multistory building onto a noontime ceremony of hundreds of people commemorating revered Shi'ite martyr Mazari in southwestern Kabul, killing 32 and wounding 81, including women and children. Senior political opposition leader Abdullah Abdullah escaped unharmed. The gunmen held off Afghan police for five hours before the last one was killed. ISIS-K claimed credit. The Taliban denied involvement.

March 9, 2020: Three mortar rounds and gunfire disrupted Afghan President Ashraf Ghani's swearing-in ceremony as he was delivering a speech in the central garden of the presidential palace in Kabul. Ghani was unhurt.

March 20, 2020: *AP* and *AFP* reported that before dawn, suspected Taliban sympathizers conducted an insider attack at a joint military and police base near Qalat in Zabul Province, killing 25 police and army personnel. Zabul provincial council chief Ata Jan Haq Bayan said that 14 soldiers and ten policemen were killed and another four Afghan security forces were missing. Provincial council member Assadullah Kakar claimed that the Taliban carried out the attack with the help of Afghan police and army personnel inside the base. Taliban spokesman Zabihullah Mujahed said he would look into the allegation but did not claim credit. The terrorists stole weapons and ammunition, then fled in two military Humvees and a pickup truck.

March 25, 2020: *AP* and *AFP* reported that at 7:45 a.m., ISIS-K attacked a temple used by Sikh and Hindu minorities in Kabul, killing 32 worshipers, including a 6-year-old child, and wounding 15. A terrorist threw grenades and fired his automatic rifle into the crowd at the Gurdwara, a Sikh house of worship. Security forces rescued 80 people after a six-hour gun battle. The Taliban denied involvement. Sikh parliamentarian Anarkali Honaryar said that children were among the casualties. Casualties also included Mohan Singh, who was hospitalized after parts of the ceiling fell on him. ISIS-K claimed credit via *Aamaq*, saying the gunman was an Indian named Abu Khalid al-Hindi, who was avenging the plight of Muslims in Kashmir, India's only Muslim-majority state. India's External Affairs Ministry announced that the dead included Indian national Tian Singh. 20032501

A vehicle hit a roadside bomb in Helmand Province, injuring eight civilians. No one claimed credit.

Insurgents fired on a vehicle in Kapisa Province, killing three civilians and a security officer.

March 26, 2020: A bomb disrupted the funeral service for the 25 Sikhs who were killed by ISIS-K the previous day in Kabul. No one was hurt in the explosion, which went off near the gate of a crematorium.

March 29, 2020: The *New York Times* reported on March 29 that the Taliban conducted attacks in Kunduz, Faryab and Badakhshan Provinces earlier in the month.

In Kunduz Province, the Taliban attacked the Ali Abad district, killing two police officers. Skirmishes were also reported in the Kunduz suburbs.

In Badakhshan, the Taliban controlled much of Yamgan district and inflicted heavy casualties on defense forces in Jurm district. In the Yamgan district, hundreds of Taliban attacked after dawn, capturing all five checkpoints of the district center after a three hour gun battle. In Jurm, 30 soldiers were unaccounted for and dozens of soldiers were killed; 20 of the missing soldiers later showed up at the district center. Public health officials said that the Taliban conducted more than 300 attacks in the past week in the dozen provinces that had reported coronavirus cases.

March 29, 2020: The Defense Ministry announced that the Taliban attacked a military checkpoint in Argandab in Zabul Province during the night, killing six troops.

The government said the Taliban attacked a checkpoint outside Pulikhomri in Baghlan Province, killing five security force members and injuring six.

The Taliban did not claim credit.

March 30, 2020: Firdaus Faramraz, a spokesman for the Kabul police chief, said that a sticky bomb attached to a vehicle went off in Kabul, wounding four people.

April 1, 2020: The Taliban announced its willingness to declare a cease-fire in areas it controlled if they were hit by a coronavirus outbreak. Taliban spokesman Zabihullah Muajhed said, "If, God forbid, the outbreak happens in an area where we control the situation then we will stop fighting in that area." It also said it would guarantee the security of health and aid workers traveling to their areas offering assistance to prevent the spread of COVID-19. It was unclear how many cases would trigger a cease-fire.

April 3, 2020: *Stars and Stripes* reported that the National Directorate of Security arrested Abdullah Orakzai, alias Aslam Farooqi, head of ISIS-K, and 19 other jihadis, in southern Afghanistan. *AP* reported on April 10 that Pakistan asked Afghanistan to extradite Farooqi, a Pakistani national wanted for IS attacks in Pakistan. Afghanistan accused Farooqi of involvement in the March 25 attack on a Sikh Gurdwara (house of worship) in Kabul that killed 32 people.

April 9, 2020: *Fox News* and *The Hill* reported that ISIS-K claimed credit for firing five rockets at Bagram Air Base in Kabul in the early morning, causing no injuries or damage. *Reuters* reported that the Taliban denied involvement. 20040901

April 12, 2020: *AFP* and *AP* reported that Taliban spokesman Suhail Shaheen tweeted that it would release 20 prisoners to representatives of the International Committee of the Red Cross in Kandahar.

April 16, 2020: During the night, a gunman on a motorcycle killed six local workers from Bagram Air Base and wounded three others. The nine Afghan cleaning service workers were on their way home when the gunman fired on them a quarter mile from the base before escaping. The Taliban denied involvement. ISIS-K was suspected. 20041601

April 19, 2020: *AFP* and *AP* reported that Taliban attacks on checkpoints around the country killed 23 members of the security forces and nine civilians.

During a morning attack in Balkh Province's Sholgara district, the Taliban killed seven and wounded a child who was caught in the crossfire. Five Taliban died. District governor Sayed Arif Iqbali said the Taliban killed nine civilians who resisted a Taliban extortion attempt.

In the morning, the Taliban hit an army checkpoint in Badghis Province, killing three soldiers and wounding ten. Governorate spokesman Mohammad Jawad Hejri said 19 died.

In a nighttime clash, 16 soldiers and two policemen died in Khwaja Ghor district in Takhar Province. The Taliban fled when reinforcements arrived.

A Taliban attack on a police checkpoint near Tarin Kot, capital of Uruzgan Province, killed five policemen and injured three.

April 29, 2020: The Taliban was blamed when a suicide bomber hit an Afghan special forces base in the Chahar Asyab district outside Kabul, killing three civilians and wounding 15. No one claimed credit. The previous day, Defense Minister General Assadullah Khalid and U.S. General Scott Miller, commander of U.S. forces

in Afghansitan, had visited Army Commando Corps base.

A sticky bomb attached to a vehicle exploded in Kabul, wounding three civilians. No one claimed credit.

May 6, 2020: *Reuters* reported that Afghan security forces arrested eight members of a network grouping Islamic State and Haqqani terrorists behind bloody attacks in the capital including on Sikh worshippers.

May 11, 2020: *Reuters* and AFIO reported that police and NDS special forces in the Kart-e-Naw area in PD8 of Kabul arrested three senior South Asia Islamic State members, including the group's regional leader. *Tolo News* reported that the General Directorate of National Security (NDS) and Interior Ministry identified them as the group's head of South Asia, Abu Omar Khorasani, alias Zia-ul-Haq, the group's spy chief Abu Ali, and a public relations officer named Saheeb. IANS reported that the operation was launched after four other senior members of the group confessed while in NDS custody.

Four roadside bombs exploded in Kabul, wounding four civilians, including a child. ISIS-K claimed credit.

Gun battles in Laghman Province between the Taliban and security forces killed six security forces and wounded five. The Ministry of Defense reported that the Taliban suffered casualties as well.

May 12, 2020: The *Washington Post* reported that three terrorists wearing police uniforms set off a bomb and attacked a maternity ward run by Doctors Without Borders in Kabul Barchi National Maternity Hospital at 10 a.m., killing 24 people, including nurses, pregnant women, ten mothers of newborns, two newborns, and a security guard, and injuring 16 people. The *Washington Post* reported that gunmen shot twice in the abdomen Hajar Sarwari, who was in labor with her second child, killing her and her unborn child, who remained in her womb. Doctors Without Borders said that it had "indications" that one of its staffers was killed. Authorities believed that nurse Maryam Noorzada, 35, was killed. In a four-hour operation, special forces rescued more than 100 patients, including mothers and babies. The hospital is in the capital's minority Shi'ite Hazara community's neighborhood. An obstetrician treated a wounded woman during the gun battle. Observers noted that although ISIS-K did not immediately claim credit, the hospital is located in the Shi'ite-dominated Dasht-e-Barschi area of Kabul where ISIS-K has carried out several attacks. Many of the survivors, including a newborn with a fractured bone, were taken to the separate Ataturk Children's Hospital in Kabul. Doctors Without Borders said the attackers went immediately to the maternity ward to kill mothers. *The World* reported on July 30, 2020 that the surviving newborn, Ameneh Sharifi, was still recovering from leg wounds. Her parents had not even named the eleven-hours-old child when the attack began. Her father, Rafiullah Sharifi, also survived; mother Nazia, 27, did not. Ameneh underwent several surgeries at the French Medical Institute for Mothers and Children, a nonprofit hospital run jointly by the governments of France and Afghanistan, the Aga Khan Development Network, and the French NGO La Chaîne de L'Espoir (Chain of Hope). She was discharged from the hospital on July 26. Ameneh has a sister, 3, and a brother, 5. By July 30, no group had claimed credit. Meanwhile, Doctors Without Borders ended its operations with the Dasht-e-Barchi hospital.

Sarwari's husband, Mohamad Hussain Yaqoobi, said at her funeral, "There's no humanity left in this country... The attackers had no conscience. How can they justify shooting dead innocent newborns and their mothers?"

NPR and *AP* reported that hours later, a suicide bomber set off his explosives in the center of hundreds of people attending the funeral of a local police commander who had died of a heart attack in the Khewa district of Nangarhar Province, killing between 32 and 40 (reports differed) people and wounding 133, including Amir Mohammad. Among the dead was provincial council member Abdullah Lala Jan; his father, lawmaker Noor Agha, was wounded. ISIS-K claimed credit.

The Taliban denied involvement in the attacks. On May 15, U.S. Ambassador Zalmay Khalilzad blamed ISIS-K, which had not claimed credit for the maternity ward attack.

May 13, 2020: Interior Minister Tariq Aryan announced that the Taliban had conducted 3,712 terrorist attacks across the country during the previous two and half months, killing or wounding 1,450 civilians.

May 14, 2020: A suicide bomber apparently failed to reach his target of a military compound in Paktia Province, killing five civilians and wounding 29, including civilians and military personnel. The Taliban said it was retaliating for statements on May 12 by Afghan President Ashraf Ghani blaming the Taliban for the maternity ward attack, which the group had condemned.

May 18, 2020: *AFP* and *AP* reported that a Taliban suicide bomber in a stolen military Humvee hit the main gate at an intelligence service base near Ghazni in the morning, killing nine and wounding 40, eight critically.

May 19, 2020: *AFP* reported that the Taliban attacked several outposts of Afghan forces in the Kunduz suburbs at 1 a.m., starting a firefight that lasted several hours. The government claimed that with air support, the troops killed 11 Taliban and wounded eight. The gunmen briefly captured an army post and killed a soldier.

May 24, 2020: The government and Taliban agreed to a three-day ceasefire to celebrate Eid-al-Ftr, the end of Ramadan.

May 26, 2020: *CBS News* reported that the government released more than 900 Taliban prisoners from Bagram Prison, inter alia, as a goodwill gesture to get the Taliban to extend the three-day ceasefire.

May 27, 2020: *Al-Jazeera* reported that the Taliban attacked checkpoints in the Syagird district of Parwan Province during the night and elsewhere in Farah Province, killing 14 security forces.

May 28, 2020: The Taliban attacked an army checkpoint in Paktia Province, killing 14 military personnel and wounding three others what it deemed a "defensive action". The Taliban accused the Afghan government of carrying out an airstrike the previous day that killed several civilians. The government said it targeted Taliban fighters. Meanwhile, since the February 29 agreement between the U.S. and the Taliban, the government had released 2,000 Taliban prisoners and the Taliban had freed 347 captives.

May 29, 2020: *AFP* reported that a roadside bomb in central Kabul hit a white minibus carrying 15 employees of the private *Khurshid TV* channel, killing a TV journalist and a driver and wounding four other station employees, two critically. ISIS-K claimed credit for the afternoon attack, saying the station was "loyal to the Afghan apostate government". The bombing occurred on the station's eighth anniversary. In August 2019, a *Khurshid TV* van was hit by a sticky bomb that killed two passers-by.

May 30, 2020: A mortar shell hit a home in Parwan Province's Siagred district in the morning, killing three small children who lived there. Wahida Shahkar, a spokeswoman for the provincial governor, blamed the Taliban, which denied involvement.

June 1, 2020: *Foreign Policy* reported that senior Taliban military official Moulawi Muhammad Ali Jan Ahmed said that Afghan Taliban supreme leader Mullah Haibatullah Akhunzada had contracted COVID-19. It was unclear whether Akhunzada was (being) treated in Pakistan, Russia, or elsewhere. Three Taliban figures in Quetta, Pakistan suggested that he might have died during treatment. An Afghan official said that numerous Taliban leaders, including many in Doha, Qatar, who negotiated a bilateral deal with the United States on February 29, were also ill with COVID-19. *Foreign Policy* reported on May 29 that other Taliban leaders were ill, including

- Akhunzada's deputy, Sirajuddin Haqqani, the leader of the jihadi Haqqani Network
- Mullah Nooruddin Turabi, head of the Taliban's prisoners commission who was the Minister of Vice and Virtue during the Taliban's 1996-2001 regime
- Mohammad Nabi Omari, a Doha-based member of the team that negotiated with the U.S. Omari was held at Guantánamo

Bay for nearly 12 years and was one of the Taliban Five who were prominent in the group's pre-9/11 administration and released in 2014 in a prisoner swap for U.S. Army Sgt. Bowe Bergdahl.

Taliban officials reported that the group was being run in the interim by the son of its late founder, Mullah Mohammed Omar, identifying him as Mullah Mohammad Yaqoob, who took over administrative, operational, and military command.

June 2, 2020: *Reuters* reported that a planted bomb exploded at a mosque in a heavily-fortified area of central Kabul during the night, killing two people, including prominent scholar Ayaz Niazi, who served as the outspoken imam of the Qazir Akbar Khan mosque. He often railed against the Taliban, which denied involvement. No one claimed credit.

June 3, 2020: A roadside bomb hit a vehicle in Kandahar Province, killing nine civilians and wounding five.

June 5, 2020: Terrorists set off a roadside bomb and ambushed a police convoy in Zabul Province, killing ten policemen and destroying several police vehicles. Four gunmen died in the ensuing shootout. The next day, the Taliban claimed credit.

June 6, 2020: A roadside bomb hit a security vehicle responding to attacks on checkpoints in the Khash district of Badakhshan Province, killing 11 security force members. A local commander was killed, as were four terrorists.

The Taliban was suspected when gunmen attacked a police checkpoint in Kabul's Gul Dara district, sparking a gun battle that killed three police officers.

The government blamed the Taliban. No one initially claimed credit.

June 12, 2020: *Reuters* and *al-Jazeera* reported that a bomb went off in West Kabul's Shir Shah-e-Suri mosque during Friday prayers, killing four people, including the mosque's mullah, Azizullah Mofleh, and wounding many more. No group claimed credit. ISIS-K was suspected.

June 26, 2020: The *New York Times,* followed by the *American Military News, Forbes,* the *Washington Post, Wall Street Journal, NBC News, Fox News,* and the *Boston Globe,* carried a report citing American intelligence that Russian GRU Unit 29155, linked to assassination attempts and other covert operations in Europe, had secretly offered bounties to Taliban-linked terrorists for killing American and British troops and other coalition military members in Afghanistan in 2019. Jihadis and armed criminals linked to them were believed to have collected some of the bounties although the number of attacks and level of the bounties was unclear. The *Associated Press* said that some of the conclusions were based on interrogations of captured Afghan militants and criminals.

The *Guardian, The Hill, AFP, AP,* and *CNN* added on June 28 that President Trump denied that he had been briefed in March on the bounties. He tweeted: "Nobody briefed or told me, [vice president Mike] Pence, or chief of staff Mark Meadows about the so-called attacks on our troops in Afghanistan by Russians, as reported through an 'anonymous source' by the Fake News @nytimes. Everybody is denying it & there have not been many attacks on us…… …Nobody's been tougher on Russia than the Trump Administration. With Corrupt Joe Biden & Obama, Russia had a field day, taking over important parts of Ukraine - Where's Hunter? Probably just another phony Times hit job, just like their failed Russia Hoax. Who is their 'source'?" The *Times* reported that the National Security Council met about the issue in late March and that the written February 27 edition of the *President's Daily Brief* included the report. The *New York Times* also reported that an assessment of the reporting ran in the CIA's *World Intelligence Review* on May 4, 2020.

The *Wall Street Journal* reported on June 30 that the National Security Agency disagreed with the report. Representative Michael McCaul (R-Texas), the senior Republican on the Foreign Affairs Committee, explained that "There was intelligence reported on the allegation that the Russians were offering a bounty to the Taliban to kill Americans, but at the same time there was a very strong dissenting view from another agen-

cy within the Intelligence Community… This happens where you get one agency that does, say, human intelligence and another one does signals intelligence, and you'll have a difference in opinion as to the accuracy and credibility of the intelligence. It's got to be accurate and credible intelligence for them to present it to the president and for him to be able to make a decision on what action to take." He added that there is a "massive scrub within the Intelligence Community to try to find out the veracity of this reporting."

The *Washington Post* reported on June 28 that intelligence assessments indicated that the bounties had led to the deaths of several American troops. The assessments were based on U.S. Special Operations military interrogations of captured militants. Later that day, President Trump tweeted "Intel just reported to me that they did not find this info credible, and therefore did not report it to me or @VP… possibly another fabricated Russia Hoax… Fake News … wanting to make Republicans look bad!!!"

The *Washington Post 202, Military Times,* and *AP* reported on June 30 that the White House had been aware of the Russian bounties program since earlier 2019 and that then-National Security Advisor John Bolton told colleagues he briefed the President on the issue in March 2019. The *Daily Beast* reported that intelligence and national security leaders did not brief the President orally and in person because they are reluctant to give him information he will resist. *CNBC* reported that Felicia Arculeo, mother of Marine Corporal Robert Hendriks, wanted an investigation into report that he and two other Marines may have been the targets of Taliban bounty hunters in an attack in April 2019. *AP* reported that the Defense Department identified the victims as Marine Staff Sgt. Christopher Slutman, 43, of Newark, Delaware; Sgt. Benjamin Hines, 31, of York, Pennsylvania; and Cpl. Robert Hendriks, 25, of Locust Valley, New York, as the Marines killed in April 2019. The Marine infantrymen were assigned to 2nd Battalion, 25th Marines, a reserve infantry unit headquartered out of Garden City, New York. Three other U.S. service members and an Afghan contractor were wounded in the Taliban attack.

Officials were also looking at green-on-blue insider attacks.

Director of National Intelligence John Ratcliffe said leaks about the matter were a crime and that the Intelligence Community was "still investigating the alleged intelligence referenced in recent media reporting and we will brief the President and Congressional leaders at the appropriate time. This is the analytic process working the way it should."

The *Washington Post* added on June 29 that Republican lawmakers said a U.S. response should await a thorough Intelligence Community review of the material, some of which had been briefed to members of Congress (in separate briefings for each party's contingent) in the White House. CIA Director Gina Haspel added "When developing intelligence assessments, initial tactical reports often require additional collection and validation." In general, such information that may assist in force protection "is shared throughout the national security community — and with U.S. allies — as part of our ongoing efforts to ensure the safety of coalition forces overseas... Hostile states' use of proxies in war zones to inflict damage on U.S. interests and troops is a constant, longstanding concern. CIA will continue to pursue every lead; analyze the information we collect with critical, objective eyes; and brief reliable intelligence to protect U.S. forces deployed around the world."

White House press secretary Kayleigh McEnany said in a media briefing on June 29 that "there is no consensus within the Intelligence Community on these allegations... In effect, there are dissenting opinions from some in the Intelligence Community with regards to the veracity of what's being reported, and the veracity of the underlying allegations continue to be evaluated."

The Russian Embassy in Washington, D.C. said that Russian diplomats in the U.S. and UK had received death threats.

USA Today and *AP* reported that members of the Naval Special Warfare Development Group, SEAL Team Six, raided a Taliban outpost and recovered roughly $500,000 in early 2020.

Business Insider reported that three NATO officials said they had been briefed by American officials on the bounties, two of them a week earlier. One NATO military intelligence official said, "There is no indication that our troops — or any non-US NATO troops — have been targeted in these attacks, but all NATO services with casualties in Afghanistan over the past two years are currently checking for any connections."

The *Huffington Post* reported on June 29 that VoteVets, a group of veterans opposed to President Trump, released a video charging, "Putin owns Donald Trump," and coining the #TRE45SON hashtag. They added in the video, "Intelligence reports on his desk. He says nothing to his master. Takes no action to protect us... If you're going to act like a traitor, you don't get to thank us for our service."

The *Washington Post 202* reported on July 1 that intelligence suggested that the bounties program began in 2018.

The *New York Times, Business Insider,* and *Washington Post 202* reported on July 1-2 that an Afghan construction contractor, former drug smuggler Rahmatullah Azizi, circa 40, served as a middleman, handing out Russian cash. He was believed to be hiding in Russia. During a raid on one of his Kabul homes, authorities found $500,000 in cash. *BI* and the *NYT* reported that the bounties sometimes reached $100,000.

Military Times and *AP* reported on July 7 that General Frank McKenzie, head of U.S. Central Command, said he did not believe that the bounties led to U.S. military deaths. "I found it very worrisome. I didn't find that there was a causative link there."

June 27, 2020: *AP* and the *New York Times* reported that in the morning, a sticky (magnetic) bomb exploded on the car of an employee of the Afghanistan Independent Human Right Commission in Kabul, killing two employees: Fatima Khalil, 24, a donor liaison officer, and Jawid Folad, 41, a driver. They were en route from home to their office. Khalil had recently completed a degree from the American University of Central Asia in Kyrgyzstan. No group claimed credit.

The *New York Times* also reported that the Taliban was contracting out assassinations and targeted killings to criminal networks in cities. In one case, criminals shot to death five prosecutors with the Afghan Attorney General's Office who were en route to Bagram prison to help release

Taliban prisoners. The *Times* added the bombs that exploded outside Kabul mosques killed two prominent religious scholars. A bomb hit the family of Afghan writer/poet Assadullah Walwaliji, killing his wife Anisa and teen daughter Alteen.

June 29, 2020: At 9 a.m., a car bomb and mortar shells went off in a busy market in Helmand Province's Sangin district, killing 23 civilians, including several children, and injuring 15 people, including a boy. The local governor's office said two Taliban were killed. The government blamed the Taliban. The Taliban blamed the army. On July 1, the U.N. Assistance Mission in Afghanistan said that the military probably mistakenly fired the "mortars in response to Taliban fire, missing (the) intended target".

July 7, 2020: Soldiers repelled Taliban attacks on army checkpoints in Khogyani district in Nangarhar Province, killing 20 Taliban insurgents, including their group leader. The Taliban did not claim credit.

July 8, 2020: A Taliban suicide truck bomber hit a police district headquarters in Kandahar Province, killing three officers. Guards fired on the truck before it got to the building, setting off the explosives.

A roadside bombing killed three police officers, including Dayak district police chief Habibullah and his two bodyguards, and wounded 14 policemen and civilians in Ghazni Province's Shah Wali Kot district in the morning. The Taliban claimed credit.

July 12, 2020: The Interior Ministry announced that gunmen conducted 44 attacks or bombings in 21 provinces, including Nangahar, Paktika and Daikundi, killing 21 security forces. An ambush in Baghlan Province killed five soldiers and wounded four police. Many of the attacks were on checkpoints with few casualties.

July 13, 2020: The *Washington Post* reported that a Taliban suicide bomber and gunmen attacked a National Directorate of Security intelligence agency compound in Aybak, capital of Samangan Province, killing 11 Afghan intelligence officers and wounding 60 civilians. The gunmen then attacked the next-door city hall building, injuring scores of civilians, including children. The Interior Ministry claimed that the Taliban conducted 30 ground assaults and remote bombings in 17 provinces, killing another 19 people. The attacks included an assault on a prayer ceremony in Faryab Province and another on a district headquarters in Balkh Province.

The Afghan Independent Human Rights Commission reported that during the first six months of 2020, 1,213 civilians were killed and 1,744 were injured. Some 48 percent of the casualties were attributed to the Taliban.

July 21, 2020: *AFP* and *Fox News* reported that during the previous week, Afghan teen Qamar Gul, circa 15, took her family's AK-47 and shot to death two Taliban terrorists who had killed her parents in Ghor Province. Local police chief Habiburahman Malekzada said that the Taliban had targeted her father, a village chief and government supporter. The gunmen dragged Gul's parents outside of their home before killing them. Gul killed the two murderers and injured several others. Other terrorists returned to attack her home, but other villagers and pro-government militiamen fired back and chased them off. Afghan security forces escorted Gul and her younger brother to a safer location.

July 30, 2020: A suicide bomber hit a police checkpoint in Logar Province's Pul-e-Alam capital, killing nine, including six policemen and three civilians, and injuring 40. A provincial council chief said 15 had died. Several children were hurt. No one claimed credit. The Taliban denied responsibility, nothing that it had ordered a three-day ceasefire during the Eid al-Adha (Feast of the Sacrifice) holiday. Taliban spokesman Zabihullah Mujahid blamed "those intelligence circles that want the continuation of war in Afghanistan".

August 1, 2020: Afghan special forces killed a senior ISIS-K commander in Jalalabad.

August 2, 2020: A suicide car bomber attacked a prison in Jalalabad, capital of Nangarhar Province, killing three people and injuring 24 during an hours-long gun battle. ISIS-K claimed credit. The Taliban denied involvement. *AP* added on

August 3 that the gun battle continued into a second day, with 29 people, including civilians, prisoners, guards, and Afghan security forces, killed and 50 wounded. The prison was believed to hold hundreds of ISIS-K prisoners. Defense Ministry spokesman Fawad Aman announced that the government had retaken the prison in the afternoon. ISIS-K gunmen continued to shoot at Afghan security forces from a nearby neighborhood. Authorities found the bodies of three Taliban prisoners, apparently killed by ISIS-K. The terrorists had killed five prisoners. Some of the 1,500 prisoners escaped, including nearly 400 ISIS-K terrorists; authorities recaptured 1,000 escaped prisoners. Some 430 prisoners, including Azizullah, stayed in their cells or hid during the gun battle. *Military Times* reported on August 4 that ten gunmen were killed. Among the prisoners who escaped with the ISIS was the shadow governor for neighboring Kunar Province.

A United Nations report released in July noted that two senior Islamic State commanders, Abu Qutaibah and Abu Hajar al-Iraqi, had recently arrived in Afghanistan from the Middle East.

August 14, 2020: The government released the first 86 of a final 400 "hard-core" Taliban prisoners from Pul-e-Charkhi prison, a prelude to intra-Afghan negotiations expected to be held in Qatar. *Reuters* added on August 15 that France asked the Afghan government not to free Taliban terrorists convicted of killing French citizens, including soldiers and humanitarian workers.

AP, AFP, and *Reuters* reported that in the afternoon, gunmen tried to assassinate former parliamentarian Fawzia Koofi, 45, a female member of Afghanistan's 21-member peace negotiating team, lightly wounding her right hand as she was returning from a visit to Parwan Province. Koofi and her sister Maryam Koofi were in a market in Kabul's Qarabagh district when they were attacked. A Taliban spokesman denied involvement. Koofi is a prominent women's and girls' rights activist. She had survived an assassination attempt in 2010 following an International Women's Day event. Terrorists had threatened her for wearing nail polish. She is a widowed mother of two daughters. She was the first woman to serve as deputy speaker of parliament.

August 17, 2020: *CNN* reported that US intelligence agencies assessed that Iran paid bounties to the Haqqani Network for attacking U.S. and coalition troops in Afghanistan. The report cited payments tied to six attacks in 2019, including a suicide bombing at the U.S. Bagram Air Base on December 11, 2019 that killed two civilians and injured more than 70 people, including four American personnel. *Military Times* reported on August 19 that Iranian Foreign Ministry spokesman Saeed Khatibzadeh said the claims were "entirely false". *Reuters* added on August 20, 2020 that President Trump said he would retaliate ("We would hit them so hard, your head would spin.") if such stories about foreign governments paying bounties were true.

August 18, 2020: *Al-Jazeera* reported that 14 rockets fired from two vehicles from the northern and eastern part of Kabul landed in the main diplomatic district during Independence Day celebrations. One missile landed in the compound of the presidential palace. *Reuters* reported that several embassies went into lockdown. One rocket landed near a mosque. The previous day, the government announced that it would not free the last 320 Taliban prisoners until armed groups freed more captured Afghan soldiers. Taliban spokesman Zabihullah Mujahid said he was not aware of the attack. ISIS-K claimed credit the next day, saying it fired 16 shells. Most of the shells hit residences. *Al-Jazeera, AFP, AP* and *Reuters* reported that the mortars killed three people, including two members of President Ashraf Ghani's honor guard, and wounded 16, including six members of the honor guard, four children and a woman.

August 19, 2020: *Al-Jazeera* and *AP* reported that a bomb placed in a car killed its owner, Abdul Baqi Amin, director of the Scientific Council of the Ministry of Education, in Kabul. He was also part of the Afghan negotiating team that had met several times with the Taliban in Doha, Qatar. Taliban spokesman Suhail Shaheen condemned the attack by "the enemies of the Islamic system, prosperity and peace".

Another sticky bomb attached to a police vehicle in Kabul killed a police officer and wounded two other people. Taliban spokesman Zabiullah Mujahid said he was not aware of the Kabul bombings.

A bomb targeted a vehicle belonging to the provincial intelligence department in Puli Khumri, capital of Baghlan Province, killing two and injuring 11, among them military and civilians.

Gunmen ambushed the vehicle of the intelligence chief in Tarin Kowt in Urozgan Province, killing him and wounding two other service members.

August 25, 2020: *Reuters* and *AP* reported that a Taliban truck bomb exploded among Afghan army commandos, killing six people and wounding 41 in Mazar-i-Sharif in Balkh Province. The Defence Ministry said six commandos were killed and six wounded; the other casualties were civilians, mostly women and children. Dozens of civilian homes were damaged or destroyed.

Gunmen attacked a checkpoint of pro-government forces in Shahrak district in Ghor Province, killing eight troops and wounding five during a five-hour gun battle. The government blamed the Taliban, although no group claimed credit.

A roadside bomb killed a police officer in Kabul.

In a morning attack, gunmen wounded a policewoman, one of her two guards, and her driver in Kabul. Saba Saher, variant Sahar, a well-known actress/tv director and high-ranking policewoman, was in stable condition with four bullet wounds in the abdomen. She had spent 20 hours in a coma. Saher was a ten-year police veteran who oversaw gender issues. Five people were in her car, including one of her children, who was unharmed. No one claimed the Kabul attack. *CBS News* reported that the Taliban denied involvement.

The *New York Times* logged 17 explosions and assassinations in Kabul during the week.

September 9, 2020: *NBC News, Deutsche Welle, Reuters, ABC News, AFP,* and the *Washington Post* reported that a bomb hidden in a cart by the roadside hit the convoy of First Vice President Amrullah Saleh, killing ten civilians, many who worked in the area, and wounding 31 people, including Saleh and his bodyguards, in Kabul in the morning. The Taliban denied responsibility. The convoy was passing through an area with shops that sell gas cylinders for use in heating homes and cooking.

September 17, 2020: The U.S. Embassy warned that unspecified "extremist organizations continue to plan attacks against a variety of targets in Afghanistan, including a heightened risk of attacks targeting female government and civilian workers, including teachers, human rights activists, office workers, and government employees." Taliban spokesman Zabihullah Mujahed announced that the "Taliban don't have any plans to carry out any such attacks."

September 22, 2020: *AFP* reported that Kabul police confiscated a cache of 48 cylindrical, single-shot "pen guns" used by criminals and jihadis for targeted assassinations against peace activists, academics, and government employees. The armory included "sticky bombs"—magnetic devices that are attached to vehicles and detonated remotely or via timer. The Criminal Investigation Department said that more than 40 people were killed in targeted assassinations in Kabul during the previous six months. Government officials blamed Taliban-linked groups. The Taliban denied involvement.

September 22-23, 2020: Overnight attacks by the Taliban at security checkpoints killed 28 Afghan policemen. The attacks began the night of September 22 in Uruzgan Province. Taliban spokesman Qari Mohammad Yousuf Almadi said the Taliban attacked after policemen in the area refused to surrender. Provincial government spokesman Zelgay Ebadi said the Taliban killed policemen who had surrendered. The Taliban seized weapons before fleeing.

September 29, 2020: *AFP* reported that a minibus hit a roadside bomb, killing 14 civilians, including seven women, five children, and two men in Daikundi Province as they were traveling to a shrine. Another three children were wounded. Interior Ministry spokesman Tareq Arian blamed the Taliban. No group claimed credit.

October 2, 2020: The Ministry of Interior tweeted that during the night, security forces killed a key member of the Taliban and arrested five others in Balkh Province.

October 3, 2020: *Reuters* reported that a truck bomb killed 15 people and wounded 52, including a child, in the Ghani Khel district of Nangarhar Province. No group claimed credit. Ministry of Interior spokesman Tariq Arian blamed the Taliban, claiming that in the previous fortnight, they had conducted 650 attacks, killing 69 civilians and wounding 141.

October 13, 2020: *AFP* reported that during the night, two military helicopters evacuating wounded soldiers fighting against Taliban attacks in Lashkar Gah in Helmand Province collided, killing nine Afghan crew.

October 18, 2020: *AFP* and *AP* reported that a suicide car bomber killed 16 people and wounded 154 others, including five children, nine women, and 26 members of the security forces, near the entrance of the provincial police chief's office and other nearby government buildings in Ghor Province's Feroz Koh capital. The bomb damaged and partially destroyed government building, including the police chief's office, the women's affairs department and the provincial office for refugees. No one claimed credit. The government blamed the Taliban.

October 20, 2020: *Al-Jazeera* and *Reuters* reported that during the night, the Taliban ambushed security forces in Takhar Province's Baharak district, killing 37 security personnel, including the province's deputy police chief, and wounding eight others. *DPA* reported that local politicians said 42 people died.

October 21, 2020: *Stars and Stripes* reported that a roadside bomb hit a NATO Resolution Support patrol in Kandahar Province, injuring Romanian soldiers Sgt. Adrian Ioan Czifrak and Cpl. 2nd Class Iosif Ioan Reman, who were traveling in a convoy of Mine Resistant Ambush Protected vehicles.

A vehicle hit a roadside bomb in Lashkar Gah in Helmand Province during the night, killing two civilians and three police officers. No one claimed credit.

October 22, 2020: The Ministry of Defense blamed the Taliban when rockets destroyed several houses in the Sharin Tagab district of Faryab Province, killing four civilians and injuring 14. No one claimed credit.

October 24, 2020: A roadside bomb went off in the morning beneath a minivan full of civilians, killing eight civilians and a police officer and wounding others in Ghazni Province. A second roadside bomb hit the vehicle of policemen responding to the attack, killing two policemen and wounding others. No one claimed credit, but provincial police blamed the Taliban.

A suicide bomber hit outside the Kawsar e Danish education center in the Shi'ite neighborhood of Dasht-e-Barchi in western Kabul, killing 24 and wounding 57, including school children. Security guards stopped him from entering the center. ISIS-K claimed credit. The Taliban denied responsibility.

The Afghan National Directorate of Security intelligence service tweeted that special forces killed propagandist Husam Abd al-Rauf, alias Abu Muhsin al-Masri, deputy commander of al-Qaeda in the Indian Subcontinent (AQIS), in an operation the previous week in Kunsaf in Ghazni Province's Andar district. The FBI had listed him as among the most wanted terrorists in December 2018, accusing him of providing support to a foreign terrorist organization and conspiracy to kill U.S. citizens. Special forces, led by the intelligence service, raided an isolated home and killed seven suspected terrorists, including the Egyptian, believed to have been born in 1958. An AQIS-issued biography said he was a mujahideen who battled the USSR in 1986. He served for years as al-Qaeda's media chief, issuing audios and written articles.

October 25, 2020: *Military Times* reported that a nighttime U.S. air strike killed five Taliban gunmen attacking Afghan security forces in Nerkh, Wardak.

October 27, 2020: *AP* and *AFP* reported that a suicide car bomber attacked near a police special forces base in Khost Province, sparking a nearly nine-hour-long gunfight with police that featured two more suicide bombings. Five police and seven terrorists died and nine civilians and 25 military personnel were wounded. General Ghulam Daud Tarkhail, Provincial Police Chief, said the terrorists, including the three suicide bombers, were killed by Afghan security forces. No one claimed credit.

A sticky bomb attached to a vehicle exploded near Kabul's airport, killing three and wounding ten. No one claimed credit.

The United Nations Assistance Mission in Afghanistan (UNAMA) reported that the first nine months of 2020 produced the lowest number of civilian casualties since 2012, although between January 1 and September 30, there were 2,117 civilians killed and 3,822 civilians wounded. More than 40% of civilian casualties were children or women.

October 28-29, 2020: Eight inmates died in a nighttime prison riot in Herat. Eight inmates and four guards were wounded. The prisoners had swallowed "poisonous" pills stolen from the jail's clinic. Guards had been confiscating drugs and knives from cells. A spokesman said "One of the prisoners was killed in direct police fire while seven others swallowed poisonous pills confiscated from inside the jail's clinic and they died."

November 2, 2020: *Reuters, CNN, CBS News,* and *The Hill* reported that after setting off a bomb at the gates, three gunmen broke into Kabul University at 11 a.m., conducting a six-hour siege that killed 19 and wounded 22. *Bloomberg* and *AP* put the death toll at 22. Thousands of students fled. The *Washington Post* reported that the terrorists took dozens of students and some professors hostage. Mohammad Aziz, a political science student at Kabul University, told *Tolo News*, "The assailants were shooting at anyone facing them… They stormed my classroom, and the moment they entered they started shooting at the students and I saw blood everywhere." Hostage Qaseem Kohestani, a fourth-year student at the university's public policy school, posted to *Facebook*, "God give patience, my classmates martyred and wounded in front of my eyes, and I am taken hostage." Authorities killed the terrorists, freed the hostages, and rescued hundreds of students who were unable to flee the campus. Vice President Amrullah Saleh tweeted about

an "intelligence failure" and blamed the Taliban, which denied involvement. Saleh claimed Pakistan harbored the Taliban terrorists. ISIS-K claimed credit.

November 7, 2020: A sticky bomb attached to the vehicle of former *Tolo TV* news anchor Yama Siawash went off in the morning, killing him and two other civilians near his home. No group claimed credit. Siawash was working with Afghanistan's Central Bank and was in a bank vehicle along with another senior employee, Ahmadullah Anas and the driver, Mohammad Amin, who also died.

A suicide attack in Zabul Province killed two civilians and wounded seven. Police spokesman Hikmatullah Kochai said that police acting on intelligence reports intercepted the vehicle which was detonated by the bombers inside.

A flatbed carrying several farmers hit a roadside mine, killing five and wounding two in Kandahar Province.

November 10, 2020: *Al-Jazeera* reported that the National Directorate of Security announced the death of Pakistani bombmaker Mohammad Hanif, a close aide to Asim Omar, erstwhile leader of al-Qaeda in the Indian Subcontinent (AQIS). NDS said Hanif, who was from Karachi, had trained Taliban terrorists in making car bombs and improvised explosive devices. He initially was a member of the Taliban, but joined al-Qaeda in 2010. NDS said it detained two Pakistani women in the operation that killed Hanif.

November 21, 2020: *Reuters, AFP,* and *AP* reported that ISIS-K claimed credit for firing 23 mortar shells before 9 a.m. from two cars in Kabul, killing eight people and wounding 31, including employees of a bakery. Some of the shells landed in the upscale Wazir Akbar Khan area. Another landed in the Iranian Embassy's compound's courtyard; some shrapnel hit the main building, damaging windows and equipment but causing no casualties. The walls and windows of the Sana Medical Complex were damaged. The Taliban denied responsibility. Authorities found a burning truck with launch tubes in its bed. 20112101

Hours earlier, a sticky bomb attached to a car killed a policeman and wounded three others in eastern Kabul.

The Interior Ministry claimed that during the previous six months, the Taliban conducted 53 suicide bombings and another 1,250 bombings that killed 1,210 civilians and wounded 2,500 civilians.

November 24, 2020: Two roadside bombs went off in Bamiyan in the late afternoon, killing 13 civilians and a traffic policeman and injuring 45 people. The Taliban denied involvement. ISIS-K was suspected.

November 29, 2020: *CNN* and *AP* reported that a Humvee laden with explosives and gunmen attacked an army base in the Deh Yak district of Ghazni Province, killing 40 soldiers and wounding 24. The gunmen shot dead the guards to the security compound, clearing a way for the Humvee to enter. No group claimed credit.

A bomb in Zabul Province targeted the convoy of a senior provincial official, killing one person and injuring 23. Haji Ata Jan Haqbayan, head of the provincial council of Zabul, sustained minor injuries. No one claimed credit. Haqbayan was an outspoken critic of the Taliban.

December 15, 2020: *Reuters, Anadolu, CBS News,* and the *Washington Post* reported that a sticky bomb exploded on the armored vehicle of Mahboobullah Mohebi, deputy governor of Kabul, as he went to work in the morning, killing him and his assistant and wounding two guards.

A sticky bomb exploded on the car of deputy provincial council leader Abdul Rahman Atshan in Feroz Koh in Ghor Province, killing him and wounding a council member and a driver.

A police officer was shot dead and two others wounded in an attack on their checkpoint in eastern Kabul.

No one claimed credit for any of the attacks.

The previous week, gunmen killed a government prosecutor while he was en route to his work in Kabul. A female news anchor was shot dead in Jalalabad that week.

December 18, 2020: A suspected rickshaw bomb killed 15 civilians, including 11 children, in Ghazni Province.

December 19, 2020: Five rockets hit Bagram Airfield in Parwan Province, causing no casualties. Police defused seven other rockets that were in the back of a pickup truck. ISIS-K claimed credit. 20121901

A civilian vehicle hit a roadside bomb in Balkh Province, killing four people. The government blamed the Taliban.

December 20, 2020: *AP* and *Reuters* reported that a car bomb went off during the morning, killing ten people and wounding 50, including women, children, and a member of Parliament, Khan Mohammad Wardak, as his convoy was passing through an intersection in Kabul's Khoshal Khan neighborhood. Several vehicles were reported on fire and nearby buildings and shops were damaged. No one claimed credit.

Soldiers shot to death a would-be suicide car bomber at an army checkpoint in Nawa district in Helmand Province. Two soldiers were slightly wounded. No one claimed credit.

Bombs went off in Logar, Nangarhar, Helmand, and Badakhshan Provinces, killing and injuring several people.

The Interior Ministry charged that during the previous three months, the Taliban had killed 487 civilians and injured 1,049 others in 35 suicide attacks and 507 bombings across the country.

December 21, 2020: Gunmen shot to death Afghan journalist Rahmatullah Nekzad in Ghazni. He had contributed to *AP* since 2007 and had also worked with *al-Jazeera.*

A Taliban car bomb severely damaged a bazaar and caused several casualties in Dawlat Abad district in Faryab Province.

December 22, 2020: *Reuters* and *AFP* reported that the Taliban denied responsibility when a sticky bomb attached to their vehicle killed four prison doctors and health workers and a passer-by and wounded two people in Kabul en route to Pul-i-Charkhi prison which holds hundreds of prisoners, including scores of Taliban. Masooma Jafari, a spokeswoman for the Ministry of Health, noted that three doctors, two of them women, working to control the spread of COVID-19 in the sprawling jail were killed.

The Taliban attacked two checkpoints in Kunduz Province.

December 23, 2020: *AP* and *ABC News* reported that a bombing and a shooting in Kabul killed three people, including the head of an independent elections watchdog. In the morning, gunmen killed Mohammad Yousuf Rasheed, executive director of the non-governmental Free and Fair Election Forum of Afghanistan. *Tolo News* reported that Rasheed was headed to his office when the gunmen fired on his vehicle. The driver was wounded. No one claimed credit. A sticky bomb hit police vehicle in eastern Kabul, killing a police officer and wounding two others.

December 24, 2020: *France2* and *AFP* reported that gunmen on a motorbike in the Kohistan district of Kapisa Province north of Kabul killed Freshta Kohistani, 29, a women's rights activist, and her brother, near her home. No group claimed credit. Kohistani was survived by her husband and one child. She had noted on *Facebook* that she had asked for protection from the authorities after receiving threats. She had tweeted in November: "Afghanistan is not a place to live in. There is no hope for peace. Tell the tailor to take your measurement (for a funeral shroud), tomorrow it could be your turn."

December 26, 2020: *ABC News* reported that several bombs exploded during the morning in Kabul, killing four people, including two police officers, and wounding four other people. A sticky bomb attached to a police vehicle killed the four people and wounded two civilians. A second sticky bomb injured two other police officers. A third sticky bomb in eastern Kabul caused no casualties. Two other explosions were reported in Kabul. No one immediately claimed credit.

Mohammad Tareq, the garrison commander of the army brigade in Balkh, died when his vehicle hit a roadside bomb in Sholgara District in Balkh Province.

December 30, 2020: *The Hill* and *Axios* reported that the Trump administration was declassifying unconfirmed intelligence from Trump's December 17 briefing indicating that China paid non-state actors in Afghanistan to attack U.S. soldiers.

BAHRAIN

September 20, 2020: Saudi state television reported that Bahrain foiled an Iran-backed terrorist plot to attack diplomats and foreigners days after Bahrain had normalized relations with Israel. Television footage showed assault rifles and explosives. A TV reporter said that the attackers wanted to avenge the January killing of Iranian General Qassem Soleimani.

December 15, 2020: *Reuters* reported that the United States designated the Bahrain-based Saraya al-Mukhtar (Mukhtar Brigades) group as a terrorist organization, saying it is backed by Iran and plotted attacks against U.S. personnel in the Gulf Arab state. Secretary of State Mike Pompeo said "The group has plotted attacks against U.S. personnel in Bahrain and has offered cash rewards for the assassination of Bahraini officials."

EGYPT

January 27, 2020: The Cairo Criminal Court sentenced eight people to life in prison after convicting them for joining a local ISIS affiliate that was active in the Sinai Peninsula from 2015 to early 2018. The court sentenced 29 others to prison terms ranging from one to 15 years in prison, and acquitted seven others, including a soccer player. The defendants were accused of plotting attacks on the Christian minority and their churches, assaulting security forces and disrupting public order by attacking public institutions.

In a separate case, the court referred three Hasm members facing terrorism charges to the Grand Mufti for a non-binding opinion on whether they could be executed. Eleven people, including the trio, were accused of conducting a terrorist attack in of Alexandria in March 2018 that killed two policemen and injured five others in a bombing intended to assassinate the city's police chief, Major General Mostafa Al-Nemr. The verdict was scheduled for March 31.

February 2, 2020: Jihadis were suspected when six masked terrorists set off explosives under a natural gas pipeline in Bir al-Abd in the northern Sinai Peninsula. The pipeline transfers gas to el-Arish, and a cement factory in central Sinai. No group claimed credit.

March 2, 2020: The Cairo Criminal Court sentenced to death 37 defendants, including Hisham el-Ashmawi, one of the country's most high-profile jihadis, following their conviction of terrorism-related charges, including membership in an ISIS affiliate. Former army officer el-Ashmawi, a co-founder of Ansar Beit al-Maqdis (now Welayet Sinai), was captured in Libya in 2018 by Libyan General Khalifa Hifter's forces. He had founded al-Mourabitoun while in Libya; it conducted attacks in Egypt's remote Western Desert. A military court sentenced el-Ashmawi to death in November 2019 for involvement in scores of anti-government attacks. The court sentenced 61 defendants to life in prison, and 85 others to 5 to 15 years in prison.

April 14, 2020: The Interior Ministry announced that security forces raided a suspected terrorist safehouse in Cairo's Amiriyah district and killed seven suspected militants in an hours-long shootout in which a police officer, Lt. Col. Mohammed el-Houfi, also died and three police agents, including an officer, were wounded. Forces confiscated weapons and ammunition. The Ministry said the terrorists planned to attack Coptic Christians during the upcoming Holy Week and Easter Sunday on April 19.

May 30, 2020: Colonel Tamer el-Rifai announced that the military killed 19 terrorists during the previous week in raids and airstrikes in Bir al-Abed, Rafah, and Sheikh Zuweid in the Sinai Peninsula. Two officers, including a colonel and a lieutenant, and three conscript soldiers died when a bomb hit their vehicle during the clashes. Soldiers defused five bombs and destroyed two four-wheel drive vehicles and a storehouse. A Sinai ISIS affiliate claimed credit.

August 28, 2020: *Al-Jazeera, al-Youm al-Sabaa,* and *Reuters* reported that security forces arrested acting Muslim Brotherhood leader Mahmoud Ezzat, 76, in an apartment in the Fifth Settlement District, a residential area east of Cairo, on charges of leading a terrorist group and receiving illicit funds. The Interior Ministry said arresting officers seized encrypted communication equipment. He was earlier given two death sentences in absentia as well as a life sentence on charges including participation in the management of a terrorist organization, collaboration with armed terrorist groups, and endangering the foundations of the state. He joined the Brotherhood in the 1960s. He was imprisoned during the administrations of Gamal Abdel Nasser and Hosni Mubarak. He became the group's acting leader, again, in 2013 upon the arrest of MB leader Mohamed Badie, and was viewed as a hardliner. Authorities suspected him of overseeing assassinations and attempted assassinations as well as a bombing. He was entitled to retrials now that he had been detained.

September 23, 2020: Four male prisoners convicted of terrorism charges and awaiting their death sentences killed three Egyptian police officers in an attempt to escape Cairo's Tora Prison. The Interior Ministry announced that security forces killed the four convicts. Three of the terrorists were convicted in 2014 for the killing and attempted killing of several members of the Egyptian security forces. They were among over 20 defendants charged with conducting jihadi attacks following the military's 2013 overthrow of President Mohammed Morsi of the Muslim Brotherhood. The other man, an ISIS supporter, was convicted and sentenced to death in 2018 for stabbing to death a Coptic Christian doctor at his Cairo clinic in 2017.

October 25, 2020: Security and medical officials announced that during the previous fortnight, 14 civilians, including women and children, were killed and ten were wounded by bombs laid down in their homes in the Sinai Peninsula by IS jihadis. The terrorists had attacked several villages in Bir al-Abd in July, forcing people to flee their homes. Once the military secured the villages in August, they permitted residents to return. But the terrorists had left booby-traps in their homes. Six people from the same family were killed on October 24.

December 7, 2020: The armed forces announced it had killed at least 40 militants, arrested two dozen suspects, destroyed 440 hideouts and weapons depots, and dismantled 160 explosive devices, six four-wheel-drive vehicles, and 32 motorcycles over the past three months in raids and airstrikes against a jihadi insurgency in the northern part of the Sinai Peninsula; there were six casualties among its troops. Among the dead terrorists was Abdel-Qader Sweilam, 46, an Islamic State leader in Rafah, and two of his associates in a raid on his hideout east of el-Arish. Authorities said he masterminded an attack on a mosque in Sinai's al-Rawdah village in November 2017 that killed more than 300 worshippers.

December 17, 2020: Two roadside bombs exploded near separate checkpoints in Sheikh Zuweid in the Sinai Peninsula during the night, killing three members of the security forces and wounding ten. No one immediately claimed credit.

The first bomb killed one person and wounded seven; the other killed two and wounded three.

The Egyptian armed forces conducted raids in Sheikh Zuweid, killing four terrorists.

December 24, 2020: *ABC News* reported that an explosion at a natural gas pipeline in el-Arish during the night caused a fire but no casualties. Security officials said militants planted explosives on the pipeline before fleeing. No group immediately claimed credit.

December 30, 2020: A roadside bomb went off in a village near Rafah, on the border with the Gaza Strip, killing a member of the security forces and wounding three others. The Islamic State on January 1, 2021 claimed credit for the bombing and three other attacks.

GAZA STRIP

January 15, 2020: *AFP* reported that four rockets were fired at Israel from Hamas-controlled Gaza. The military reported that the Iron Dome defense system knocked down two of the rockets.

January 30-31, 2020: *AFP* reported that Israeli aircraft struck Hamas targets in the Gaza Strip on the morning of January 31 in response to three

rockets that were fired overnight from Gaza. The Iron Dome air defense system intercepted two of the missiles. No injuries were reported.

February 23, 2020: Some 21 rockets were fired during the night into Israel, hours after the Palestinian news agency *al-Hadath*, based in Ramallah, West Bank, released a video of an Israeli army bulldozer dragging the body of Mohammed al-Naem, a member of Palestinian Islamic Jihad, who the military said was killed while placing an explosive device along the border. An Army tank accompanied the bulldozer. The Iron Dome aerial defense system knocked down 13 projectiles over Ashkelon and Sderot. PIJ took credit, saying it was responding to Naem's killing.

March 7, 2020: *AP* reported that masked Palestinians attached gas canisters to booby-trapped balloons on February 10 and other dates, then released them near Gaza's Bureij refugee camp along the Israel-Gaza border fence, in hopes that the bombs would reach Israel. Sometimes the balloons included messages such as "I Love You" and "Happy Birthday" along with small improvised explosives dangling by a string. Others had notes in blue paper with writing in Hebrew and Arabic that read, "Zionist, you have no place in the country of Palestine. We will send you to your death." As of March 7, none of the balloons had caused death or injury, and most had landed in the countryside. *AP* identified one of the balloon makers as alias Abu Malek, 30, of Gaza, who said there were at least ten cells sending the balloons, which were fashioned of sheets of taped plastic, rubber gloves or bouquets of inflated condoms. Some bombmakers had been injured assembling them.

August 20, 2020: In the evening, gunmen fired two rockets that landed near the Israeli security fence. Israel airstrikes attacked targets linked to Hamas in the Gaza Strip, including a "concrete manufacturing site used for underground infrastructure and tunnel construction, belonging to the Hamas terror organization". In recent days, Hamas affiliates had launched incendiary balloons across the frontier, aimed at Israeli farmland.

September 15, 2020: During the night, rockets were fired from the Gaza Strip toward Israel, lightly wounding two Israelis. Five projectiles landed in open areas, the others were intercepted. The next day, the IDF attacked ten Hamas sites, including a weapons and explosives manufacturing factory, underground infrastructure, and a military training compound. The rocket attack came as Bahrain and UAE were signing normalization agreements with Israel at the White House.

November 15, 2020: *UPI* reported that at 2 a.m., two rockets were fired from the Gaza Strip into Israel, activating incoming rocket sirens in Ashdod and in communities in the Shfela region of central Israel, including Kibbutz Palmachim about 37 miles from the Gaza Strip. No damage or injuries were reported, although shrapnel from an Iron Dome interception missile fell on Bat Yam, south of Tel Aviv. Israeli Air Force jets, attack helicopters and Israel Defense Forces tanks retaliated by attacking "underground infrastructure and military posts of the terror group Hamas in the Gaza Strip". No one claimed credit.

November 21, 2020: *UPI* and *Jerusalem Post* reported that a rocket was launched from the Gaza Strip into Ashkelon, Israel. An Israeli air strike hit two rocket ammunition manufacturing sites, underground infrastructure and a Hamas military compound in Khan Younis the next morning. No one claimed credit.

IRAN

May 28, 2020: *Press TV* and *IRNA* reported that three Iranian border guards were killed in a gun battle with terrorists at a border post near Sardasht in West Azarbaijan Province on the border with Iraqi Kurdistan. *IRNA* said several terrorists were killed. No one claimed credit. *Press TV* noted that border posts had earlier been attacked by the Kurdistan Free Life Party (PJAK) offshoot of Kurdistan Workers' Party (PKK). Guards also seized weapons, ammunition and telecommunication systems.

June 25, 2020: *The Guardian* reported that Iranian authorities were investigating a large explosion near the Parchin military base outside Tehran believed to have played a role in past nuclear testing activities. *AFP* reported that the government said it was a gas tank explosion. Iranian State *TV IRIB* showed an orange fireball from a midnight gas tank explosion. *Fars* reported that "a number of social media users reported seeing an orange light" east of Tehran. Defence Ministry spokesman Brigadier General Davoud Abdi said two leaking gas tanks exploded in the Parchin public area. *Breaking Defense* reported that Israel denied involvement. Some observers suggested that a "kinetic cyber" weapon was used in the recent Parchin explosion. *BD* noted that the gas storage area is part of the Khojir missile facility. The explosion extensively damaged the Shahid Bakeri Industrial Group, which makes solid-propellant rockets, according to Israeli media.

June 30, 2020: *Bloomberg, Tasnim,* and the *Iranian Students' News* agency reported that a loud explosion went off at a clinic in the busy Tajrish neighborhood of northern Tehran.

July 2, 2020: *AP, Business Insider, New York Times,* and the *New York Daily News* reported that the Atomic Energy Organization of Iran announced that a 2 a.m. fire damaged an "industrial shed" in the northwest corner of the Natanz uranium enrichment facility in Isfahan Province. Officials said it did not affect operations at the Iran Centrifuge Assembly Center or release radiation. The previously-unknown Cheetahs of the Homeland posted a video and told *BBC*'s Persian service that it was responsible. It used language of several exiled Iranian opposition organizations, including the Mujahedeen-e-Khalq exile group. The video and a written statement called Supreme Leader Ayatollah Ali Khamenei "zahhak", a monster in Persian folklore. Observers suggested Mossad involvement, noting that the video referred to the Kashan nuclear site, vice Natanz. Kashan is a nearby city once home to a large, historic Jewish community. *CNN* reported that there was major damage to the site, with a roof charred by fire, broken doors and blown out windows. *Tasnim* said no casualties were reported. The *Times* reported that a Middle Eastern intelligence official explained that the blast was the result of an explosive placed in a part of the facility where centrifuges are balanced before going into operation. The Cheetahs told *BBC* it was an "underground opposition with Iran's security apparatus". *Breaking Defense* reported that Israel denied involvement. Some observers suggested that a "kinetic cyber" weapon was used in the recent Parchin explosion. Natanz was hit by the Stuxnet virus in 2009.

November 27, 2020: The *Washington Post*, *AP*, Iranian *INSA* state television and *CNN* reported that prominent Iranian nuclear scientist and professor Mohsen Fakhrizadeh-Mahavadi, 60, was killed during an attack on his security detail in Damavand. The *Washington Post* said he was a driving force behind Tehran's disbanded Amad Plan to build a nuclear weapon, which was halted in 2003. No one claimed credit. Iranian Foreign Minister Javad Zarif suggested Israeli involvement. The *Washington Post* reported the next day that Iranian President Hassan Rouhani blamed the "usurper Zionist regime" for causing turmoil before President-elect Joe Biden takes office and that Tehran would respond at the "right time". *Sepah Cybery*, a social media channel affiliated with Iran's Islamic Revolutionary Guard Corps, suggested that 12 attackers were involved, in addition to Fakhrizadeh's four bodyguards, two of whom it reported were in serious condition with gunshot wounds. *FARS* reported that a car bomb sent debris flying 300 meters away and damaged an electricity tower. *FARS* and the semi-official Iranian Students News Agency later reported that the killers used a remote-controlled machine gun operating out of another car. *FARS* said Fakhrizadeh was traveling with his wife in a bulletproof car, guarded by three security personnel vehicles. He heard what sounded like bullets hitting a vehicle, and got out of the car to investigate. A remote-controlled machine gun then opened fire from a Nissan stopped about 150 meters from Fakhrizadeh's car. Fakhrizadeh was hit at least three times; his bodyguard was also shot. The Nissan then exploded. *Islamic Republic of Iran Broadcasting* claimed the explosion happened first, followed by gunfire.

December 23, 2020: *Reuters* reported that the FBI and the Department of Homeland Security's Cyber and Infrastructure Security Agency announced that "highly credible information" indicated Iranian "cyber actors" almost certainly were responsible for creating a website earlier in December featuring death threats aimed at U.S. election officials. The apparently since-dormant site criticized election officials who did not support President Trump's claims of election corruption, and showed "an ongoing Iranian intent to create divisions and mistrust in the United States and undermine public confidence in the U.S. electoral process".

IRAQ

January 2-3, 2020: During the night, a U.S. drone strike on a two-car convoy killed Iranian intelligence chief and Revolutionary Guards Quds Force commander General Qassem Soleimani, 62, at Baghdad International Airport. Also killed were five other people, including Abu Mahdi al-Muhandis, deputy commander of the Popular Mobilization Forces and founder of Kataeb Hizballah, and al-Muhandis's son-in-law Mohammed Rida al-Jaberi. U.S. Secretary of Defense Mark Esper observed, "General Soleimani was actively developing plans to attack American diplomats and service members in Iraq and throughout the region. This strike was aimed at deterring future Iranian attack plans." *NPR* reported that polls indicated that Soleimani was the most respected figure in Iran. Al-Muhandis was survived by his Iranian wife and two daughters. Iranian state television claimed ten people were killed, including five Revolutionary Guards. U.S. President Donald Trump said that Soleimani was planning four attacks against U.S. embassies. On January 10, the Islamic State said the death "pleased the hearts of believers".

The U.S. announced it was sending nearly 3,000 more soldiers to the Middle East and urged American citizens to leave Iraq "immediately".

Iranian Supreme Leader Ayatollah Ali Khamenei announced that Soleimani's successor to lead the Qods Force was Soleimani's deputy, Major General Esmail Ghaani.

Iran lobbed a dozen missiles at two military bases in Iraq on January 7, causing no injuries to Americans.

CNN and *FARS* reported on June 29, 2020 that Iran issued an arrest warrant for U.S. President Donald Trump for the January 3, 2020 drone strike. Iranian Attorney General Ali Alqasi Mehr said Trump was at the top of the list of 36 Americans wanted in the case. Mehr said Trump would be prosecuted on "murder and terrorism charges" after his presidential term ends. *ISNA* reported that Iran asked Interpol to issue a Red Notice for these 36 individuals. A spokesman for Iran's judiciary, Gholam-Hossein Esmaili, earlier announced that Iranian citizen Seyed Mahmoud Mousavi Majd had been sentenced to death for allegedly sharing the whereabouts of Soleimani with U.S. intelligence officers. *AP* reported that Interpol rejected the request.

AP reported on July 20, 2020 that Iran executed Mahmoud Mousavi Majd, who was convicted in June 2020 of spying on Major General Qassem Soleimani. Iran claimed Majd provided CIA and Mossad with sensitive information on IRGC operations in Syria. Iranian officials said Majd was arrested in October 2018 and he was thus not directly linked to Soleimani's killing. The judiciary's official *Mizan Online News Agency* said that CIA recruited Majd, an Iranian national, in Syria. Mizan claimed he shared with Mossad intelligence on personnel movements, weapons, base locations and telecommunications equipment. Mizan said Majd moved to Syria with his family in the 1990s because of his father's business. Majd was an interpreter for Iranian forces in Syria.

On August 20, 2020, *Business Insider*, *West Asia News Agency* and *Reuters* reported that Iran unveiled the Martyr Qassem Soleimani intermediate-range surface-to-surface ballistic missile system and the Abu Mahdi al-Muhandis cruise missile.

January 3, 2020: An airstrike killed five members of an Iran-backed militia north of Baghdad. The Iran-backed Popular Mobilization Forces said it hit one of its medical convoys near the stadium in Taji, north of Baghdad. A U.S. official said the attack was not an American military attack.

January 4, 2020: *AFP* reported that during the night, two mortar rounds hit Baghdad's Green Zone and two Katyusha rockets hit Balad Air Base housing US troops. 20010401

January 6, 2020: *Military Times* reported that ISIS killed two Iraqi troops and wounded three in the Tal Diab village in the Daquq district of Kirkuk. Three Katyusha rockets landed in Baghdad, including two inside the Green Zone and one near the al-Shuhada Establishment.

January 8, 2020: *CNN* and the *Washington Post* reported on January 16 that 11 U.S. service members were injured when Iran fired 16 missiles in an attack on al-Asad air base in retaliation for the airstrike that killed IRGC General Qassem Soleimani earlier in the month. *Military Times* reported on January 22 that they were treated for possible traumatic brain injuries, neurological conditions and concussions. President Trump, speaking during the World Economic Forum in Davos, Switzerland, minimized the severity of their head injuries, observing, "I heard they had headaches and a couple of other things ... and I can report it is not very serious... No, I don't consider them very serious relative to other injuries I've seen," such as "people with no legs and no arms. I've seen people that were horribly, horribly injured in that area, that war... No, I do not consider that to be bad injuries, no."

CNN reported on January 24 that Pentagon spokesman Jonathan Hoffman said that 34 U.S. service members had been diagnosed with traumatic brain injuries following the Iranian missile attack. Seventeen service members had since returned to duty in Iraq; 16 of them were treated locally in Iraq. Nine service members were being treated in Germany. Another eight service members who had been flown to Germany were sent to the United States for additional treatment at Walter Reed National Military Medical Center or at hospitals in their home bases.

CNN added on January 28 that the number of U.S. military personnel with diagnosed concussions and TBIs had increased to 50. *Military Times* reported on January 31 that the tally had risen to 64. *WOKV* reported on February 10 that the Pentagon had announced that 109 service members had been treated for mild TBI; 76 had returned to duty. The *New York Times* cited brain injury experts as indicating that science lacks a reliable way to diagnose brain injuries. *The Hill* reported on February 22 a 110th soldier had a TBI.

On May 4, Navy Captain Bill Urban announced that U.S. Central Command awarded Purple Hearts to six Army soldiers who were injured in a ballistic missile attack in Iraq on January 8. Another 23 were approved for the award and were to receive them later in the week. Lt. Gen. Pat White, senior U.S. commander in Iraq, approved the awards. Some 110 U.S. service members were diagnosed with traumatic brain injuries after the Iranian attack at al-Asad Air Base. Eighty of them were considered for the Purple Heart.

January 12, 2020: Six rockets hit Balad air base 50 miles south of Baghdad, injuring an Iraqi air force officer and three enlisted men. No one claimed credit. Balad hosts U.S. trainers, advisers and a company that provides maintenance services for F-16 aircraft. Some rockets hit a restaurant inside the airbase. The Iraqi Army's media office said two officers were wounded when eight rockets hit the base.

January 14, 2020: ISIS conducted a cross border attack from Syria, killing an Iraqi officer. 20011401

January 15, 2020: ISIS attacked Iraqi troops in the Salaheddine region, killing two soldiers and wounding five.

January 16, 2020: The *Middle East Monitor* reported that an elite Iraqi SWAT team in the Nineveh regiment in Mosul arrested morbidly obese ISIS mufti Shifa al-Nima, alias Abu Abdul-Bari, who advocated enslavement, rape, torture and ethnic cleansing. He weighed more than 135 kilograms (roughly 300 pounds), too heavy for a police car and thus placed on the back of a pick-up truck. He was ISIS's top religious authority in issuing fatwas, especially regarding destroying Mosul's cultural heritage, such as the ancient mosque and mausoleum of the Prophet Yunus. Thecipherbrief.com reported that he was also known as Jabba the Jihadi and weighed 560 pounds.

January 17, 2020: A car bomb killed an Iraqi intelligence major north of Baghdad.

January 20, 2020: *CNN* reported that Jeanne Der Agopian, press relations officer, and Ben-

jamin Blanchard, director general of the French charity SOS Chretiens d'Orient (Christians of the Middle East) told a press conference in Paris on January 24 that three French nationals and an Iraqi were missing in Baghdad since January 20. The four SOS employees went missing near the French embassy. The NGO said that the charity workers were conducting "administrative tasks", including a visit to a new school opening. They did not show up for an afternoon appointment. There had been no ransom demands.

January 21, 2020: *Reuters* reported that three Katyusha rockets launched from Zafaraniyah district outside Baghdad landed inside Baghdad's Green Zone which houses government buildings and foreign missions. Two rockets landed near the U.S. embassy. 20012101

January 26, 2020: *CNN* and the *Washington Post* reported that three rockets hit the U.S. Embassy compound, injuring one person and causing minor damage. One rocket hit a dining facility, two others landed close by. The injured person, whose nationality was not disclosed, returned to duty. The *Washington Post* reported that preliminary information suggested that the person was a U.S. contractor. No one claimed credit. 20012601

February 13, 2020: A mortar shell landed at the K1 military airbase in Kirkuk Province, causing no casualties. The base hosts U.S. troops. Iraqi soldiers searching the base perimeter found a launching pad and 11 unused missiles. 200213002

February 15, 2020: *Reuters* reported that small rockets hit a military coalition's Baghdad headquarters before dawn, causing no casualties. The Iraqi military said three Katyusha rockets hit the fortified Green Zone, and a fourth hit a neighboring logistics base for Iraqi paramilitary groups. 20021501

March 2, 2020: *Reuters* reported that in the morning, two Katyusha rockets fell inside the Green Zone in Baghdad, causing no casualties. One missile hit near the U.S. Embassy.

March 4, 2020: The *Washington Post* reported that the Justice Department charged Mariam

Taha Thompson, 61, formerly of Rochester, Minnesota, a contract linguist assigned to a U.S. Special Operations task force in Iraq, with espionage following allegations that she turned over the names of human informants and other classified data to a Lebanese man with ties to Hizballah. She was charged with one count of conspiracy and one count of delivering defense information to aid a foreign government. Prosecutors alleged that she had a romantic interest with the individual. The FBI arrested her on February at a U.S. military facility in Irbil, Iraq, site of an elite U.S. Special Operations counterterrorism program.

Thompson had a top secret clearance. Starting December 30, 2019, she reportedly accessed classified information in Pentagon computer systems for which she had no need to know. The next day, protesters stormed the U.S. Embassy following U.S. airstrikes against Iranian-backed forces in Iraq. The FBI arrest affidavit said she accessed 57 files regarding eight human intelligence sources, including names, photographs, personal identification and background data, and cables detailing information they had provided. When authorities searched her living quarters on February 19, they found a handwritten note in Arabic under her mattress containing classified information naming three sources and including a warning for a Pentagon target affiliated with a designated foreign terrorist organization with ties to Hizballah. She allegedly used a video-messaging app on her phone to give information contained in the note to her unidentified co-conspirator. She knew the co-conspirator's nephew worked for Lebanon's Interior Ministry.

March 8, 2020: *Marine Corps Times* reported that the Pentagon announced that during the evening, enemy forces killed two members of a Marine Corps Forces Special Operations Command (MARSOC), known as Marine Raiders, team while "advising and accompanying Iraqi Security Forces during a mission to eliminate an ISIS terrorist stronghold" in a cave complex in the Qara Chokh Mountains near Makhmur, 45 miles south of Irbil. It took reinforcements six hours to recover their remains because of difficult terrain. The Iraqi military said that 25 ISIS fighters were killed and that nine tunnels and a training camp were destroyed. Four other Americans were wounded in the clash. The duo were assigned to 2nd Marine Raider Battalion, a Special Operations force with headquarters at Camp Lejeune, N.C.

- Captain Moises "Mo" A. Navas, 34, of Germantown, Maryland, a Special Operations officer who had a wife, daughter and three young sons. He was born in Panama and grew up in southern Maryland. He enlisted in the USMC in 2004, became a sergeant, then earned his officer commission via the Marine Enlisted Commissioning Education Program. Navas was trained as a scout sniper, martial arts instructor and combat diver, and recently was selected for promotion to major. He joined the Marine Raiders in 2016. From 2016-2020 he was a team commander and company executive officer. Awards included a Purple Heart, the Joint Service Commendation Medal, the Navy and Marine Corps Commendation Medal, the Navy and Marine Corps Achievement Medal, Combat Action Ribbon, two Good Conduct Medals, the Military Outstanding Volunteer Service Medal, the Humanitarian Service Medal, the National Defense Service Medal, the Global War on Terrorism Expeditionary Medal, the Global War on Terrorism Service Medal, and four Sea Service Deployment Ribbons.

- Gunnery Sgt. Diego D. Pongo, 34, of Simi Valley, California, a critical skills operations officer who regularly finished first in individual training events. He had a young daughter. He joined the USMC in 2004 as an 0311 rifleman. He completed the Sniper Basic Course in 2008 and was a sniper team leader I Afghanistan with the 1st Battalion, 5th Marines. He joined the Marine Raiders in 2011, deploying to Iraq and Aghanistan. He was trained as a foreign weapons instructor and a combat marksmanship leader, and was fluent in several languages. Awards included a Bronze Star Medal with Combat Distinguishing Device, a Purple Heart, two Navy and Marine Corps Commendation Medals, the Navy and Marine Corps Achievement Medal, two Combat Action

Ribbons, the Army Valorous Unit Award, four Good Conduct Medals, two Humanitarian Service Medals, the National Defense Service Medal, the Global War on Terrorism Expeditionary Medal, the Global War on Terrorism Service Medal, and four Sea Service Deployment Ribbons. 20030801

March 11, 2020: *CNN* and *AP* reported that 30 Katyusha rockets were fired from a pickup truck at the Taji military base at 7:35 p.m. Some 18 rockets landed, killing two Americans and a Briton and wounding several other people. The Iraqi military found a Kia Bongo truck with a rocket launcher and three rockets in the chambers. The Usbat al-Thayireen militia claimed credit. On March 12, the U.S. conducted airstrikes against weapons facilities belonging to Kataib Hizballah in Iraq. Iraq's military said the airstrikes killed three Iraqi army commandos, two federal police officers, and a civilian and wounded five militia members of the Popular Mobilization Units. The Iran-backed Shi'ite militia Harakat Hizballah al-Nujaba vowed "eye for an eye" vengeance.

Air Force Times reported on March 16 that the Americans were identified as

- Army Spc. Juan Miguel Mendez Covarrubias, 27, of Hanford, California, who was assigned to 1st Battalion, 227th Aviation Regiment, 1st Air Cavalry Brigade, 1st Cavalry Division, Fort Hood, Texas.

- Air Force Staff Sgt. Marshal D. Roberts, 28, of Owasso, Oklahoma, who was assigned to 219th Engineering Installation Squadron of the Oklahoma Air National Guard's 138th Fighter Wing. The Oklahoma Air National Guard said he enlisted in May 2014, and was the first Oklahoma Air Guardsman to be killed in action since 9/11 and the 20th Oklahoma National Guardsman who has died while deployed since then.

Air Force Times added that the Briton was U.K. Lance Corporal Brodie Gillon, 26. 20031101

March 14, 2020: *NPR* and *AP* reported that 25 107mm rockets crashed into Taji military base at 11 a.m., some landing in the area where coalition forces are based, injuring three American soldiers

and two Iraqi soldiers. Other rockets hit air defense units. Another 24 unlaunched rockets were found in seven platforms in the Abu Azam area north of Baghdad. 20031401

March 16, 2020: During the evening, two rockets hit the Basmaya training base near Baghdad, where a Spanish contingent of the U.S.-led coalition and NATO trainers were present. The projectiles landed in an area with agricultural land and a factory. No one claimed credit. 20031601

March 17 and 18, 2020: *Newsweek* reported that the Iraqi Shi'ite Usbat al-Thayireen (League of Revolutionaries) militia released two videos in which it claimed it could attack Israel. The group had earlier claimed credit for a series of Katyusha rocket attacks against U.S. and coalition forces. A camouflage-wearing gunman said "It is the least of the power that we can use against them... [its] victorious, blooming, prideful and dignified arsenal has far longer-range weapons that can kill you in the land of your spoiled child, Israel." He told President Donald Trump "to leave vertically before we force them to leave horizontally". In a second video, the group said it was "a martyrdom project whose mission is striking the American occupation forces, striking its bases, striking the occupations' embassy and avenging the martyred leaders and their companions... The Islamic resistance of Usbat al-Thayireen vows to strike the occupation forces' bases and embassy in the coming days and will continue striking the occupation until it exits the country, and the matter will be taken further if the occupier does not leave... We say to the hypocrites who are collaborators at the evil embassy: Your days are numbered and you will face your fate very soon."

March 26, 2020: *AP* and *Reuters* reported that two Katyusha rockets landed inside Baghdad's Green Zone near the Baghdad Operations Command, which coordinates Iraq's police and military forces, and a few hundred yards from the U.S. Embassy. No casualties were reported. No one claimed credit. 20032601

April 1, 2020: During a security operation against ISIS, a federal police officer was killed and a battalion commander and brigadier general wounded in the Makhoul mountain range in Diyala.

April 3, 2020: An IED attack targeted a patrol of a commando regiment of the Diyala Operations Command in the outskirts of Maadan.

April 6, 2020: *NPR* and *AP* reported that in the morning, five rockets landed near a Halliburton facility working in the Zubair oil field, which is operated by the Italian ENI, in the Burjesia area in Basra Province. Authorities found a rocket launcher and 11 unused—and later defused— missiles on the Zubair-Shuaiba road. There was no significant damage. No one claimed credit. 20040601

April 28, 2020: A terrorist threw a grenade and set off his suicide vest at the gate of the Intelligence and Counter-Terrorism Directorate in the Qadisiyah neighborhood in Kirkuk, wounding three security personnel. The government blamed ISIS. Security forces had spotted the bomber and a driver approaching the gate. The driver sped away.

May 2, 2020: The *BBC* reported that ISIS killed ten members of the Shia-dominated Popular Mobilization Forces militia in a nighttime ambush in Mkesheefeh village in Salahuddin Province that also wounded several militiamen. The militiamen had no night-vision goggles and were taken by surprise. A federal police unit usually stationed nearby had been redeployed to enforce the public health lockdown during the coronavirus pandemic. The attack involved a car bomb and several waves of attackers.

May 6, 2020: In the morning, three Katyusha rockets landed near the military sector of Baghdad's airport, causing no casualties. Security forces soon discovered the launching pad for the rockets in the al-Barkiya area, west of Baghdad. No group claimed credit. One rocket struck close to Iraqi forces at the military airport, another near Camp Cropper, once a U.S. detention facility where Saddam Hussein had been held, and the third near to where U.S. forces are stationed. 20050601

May 13, 2020: *AP*, Norway's *VG* newspaper, and *Military Times* reported that Norway's top military official in Iraq, Lt. Colonel Stein Grongstad, said that Iraqi terrorists "reside in agricultural areas and are thus not particularly susceptible to the virus infection…", and were attacking Iraqi forces "that are not currently coordinated to the same extent as before the virus struck". On the other hand, U.S. Army Lt. General Pat White argued that curfew had a negative effect on ISIS abilities to conduct attacks and "move above ground". *The Hill* reported that al-Qaeda's *as-Sahab* news service called coronavirus "God's smallest soldier".

May 20, 2020: *Military Times* reported that a Katyusha rocket hit an empty house in Baghdad's Green Zone in the morning, causing minor damage. It apparently was fired from the nearby al-Idrisi neighborhood on Palestine Street.

May 28, 2020: *AP* reported that ISIS released an audio by chief spokesman Abu Hamzi al-Qurayshi in which it deemed new Iraqi Prime Minister Mustafa al-Kadhimi, a former intelligence chief, an American agent and called for daily attacks in Syria, Iraq, and elsewhere. It blasted the closure of the shrine in Mecca to combat the coronavirus, hinting that Muslims are immune. Al-Qurayshi called al-Kadhimi "intelligence's pointed sword" on the heads of Muslims.

June 13, 2020: Two Katyusha rockets hit Camp Taji, an Iraqi military base frequented by U.S. troops north of Baghdad, during the night. No casualties were reported.

June 15, 2020: The military announced that three rockets fired from the al-Makaseb neighborhood landed after midnight near Baghdad airport.

June 18, 2020: *Military Times* reported that after midnight, four rockets hit Baghdad's Green Zone near the U.S. embassy, causing no damage or injuries. No one claimed credit. Security forces found a Katyusha rocket launching platform near the al-Rashid camp south of Baghdad.

June 20, 2020: *Fox News* reported that coalition aircraft destroyed three ISIS camps in Wadi al-Shai in Kirkuk Province.

The U.S. Department of State Rewards for Justice Program offered a $3 million bounty for information on the whereabouts of Muhammad

Khadir Musa Ramadan, a senior ISIS leader responsible for the organization's use of propaganda and beheading videos. State announced earlier that "Muhammad Khadir Musa Ramadan is one of ISIS's longest-serving senior media officials. Ramadan oversees the group's daily media operations, including the management of content from ISIS's dispersed global network of supporters."

June 25, 2020: *AP* and *Military Times* reported that in a nighttime raid, the Counter Terrorism Service arrested 14 men in Baghdad's Dora neighborhood believed linked to an Iran-backed Kataib Hizballah militia who were suspected of several rocket attacks in the Green Zone against the U.S. presence in Iraq. The military said intelligence reports indicated another plot targeted the Green Zone. The Service found two rocket launching pads. *Al-Jazeera* added that the Counter Terrorism Service seized at least 10 rockets. *A-J* added that "Subsequently, dozens of armed Kataib Hizballah fighters arrived in the Green Zone and laid siege to one of the buildings belonging to the Counter Terrorism Service, demanding the release of the detainees, claiming they were arrested illegally without an arrest warrant." *Reuters* reported that three commanders of Kataib Hizballah, including an Iranian, had been detained. *AFP* noted on June 29 that Iraq handed the detainees over to the Hashed al-Shaabi umbrella organization of paramilitary groups and an Iraqi judge ordered the case dropped due to lack of evidence.

July 4, 2020: The Iraqi military announced that a rocket launched from the Ali Al-Saleh area of Baghdad and aimed at Baghdad's fortified Green Zone hit a house close to a local TV channel during the night, injuring a child in the head and damaging the house. Iraqi officials said that the U.S. Embassy's C-RAM air defense system may have attempted to intercept the rocket.

Iraqi security forces thwarted an attack in the Umm al-Azam area aiming to hit Camp Taji, a training base used by U.S.-led coalition forces.

July 6, 2020: During the night, gunmen on a motorcycle shot to death Hisham al-Hashimi, 47, a leading expert on ISIS and other armed groups, in the front seat of his car outside his home in the Zeyouneh area of Baghdad. A family member heard five shots fired. He had been threatened by Iran-backed militias, including Kataib Hizballah. He appeared often on Iraqi television as an expert commentator. No one claimed credit. Hours later, authorities fired the top police officer for Zeyouneh. The *Washington Post* added on July 25 that al-Hashimi was close to the inner advisory circle of Iraqi Prime Minister Mustafa al-Kadhimi.

July 9, 2020: *Military Times* reported that extensive human remains were recently uncovered from a suspected mass grave in Humeydat, part of former ISIS territory. The gravesite covered hundreds of meters, filled with bones, skulls, clothing and shoes. The remains were believed to be those of Shi'ite prisoners who were executed in June 2014. The graves may have contained 400 bodies.

July 20, 2020: *AP* and *DPA* reported that gunmen in a pickup and a van kidnapped German woman Hella Mewis, who was prominent in the Iraqi art community and supported mass anti-government protests, at 8 p.m. outside Baghdad's Beit Tarkib arts center on Abu Nawas Street, where she worked. She had lived in Baghdad for seven years, running an arts program for young Iraqis. No one claimed credit. She often bicycled down Karada Street. *AP* reported on July 24 that Iraqi security forces freed her during a 6:25 a.m. raid in Baghdad's southeastern suburbs. She had been blindfolded. Brigadier General Khaled al-Muhanna said the kidnappers had not been arrested and were being sought. 20072001

August 9, 2020: A bomb targeted a coalition convoy in Dhi Qar Province, causing minor damage. 20080902

August 11, 2020: The apparently newly-formed Iraqi Shi'ite Ashab al-Kahf (Companions of the Cave) group issued an 11-second video during the night in which it claimed that its bomb destroyed "equipment and vehicles belonging to the American enemy" at a border crossing south of Basra at the border with Kuwait. Iraq and Kuwait denied that an attack had occurred.

August 11, 2020: *AP* and *Reuters* reported that a roadside bomb hit a U.S.-led coalition convoy in the Taji area north of Baghdad, causing minor fire damage to a container on one of the vehicles. No injuries were reported. No one claimed credit.

August 14, 2020: Activist Tahseen Osama was killed inside the headquarters of a local Internet company, following the escalating protest movement in the province and demands for basic services. The murder sparked street demonstrations for three days. Security forces fired live bullets at protestors, who threw rocks and Molotov cocktails at the governor's house.

Gunmen severely injured activists Ludia Raymond and Abbas Subhi in Basra.

August 19, 2020: *Al-Jazeera* reported that gunmen on a motorcycle fired an assault rifle at a car, killing prominent female activist Dr. Reham Yacoub and injuring two other women, in Basra. She had been active since 2018 in organizing women's marches. She received death threats when she participated in training courses run by the U.S. consulate in Basra in 2017 and 2018.

August 24, 2020: UN counterterrorism chief Vladimir Voronkov told the UN Security Council that more than 10,000 ISIS fighters remained active in Iraq and Syria.

August 29, 2020: *Reuters* reported that a Katyusha rocket landed in Baghdad's heavily fortified Green Zone, damaging an empty building but causing no casualties.

September 14, 2020: A roadside bomb targeted a convoy of vehicles carrying equipment for Americans on the main highway in Babylon Province, south of Baghdad. 20091401

Two rockets were fired during the evening at the Green Zone, causing no casualties. A U.S. Embassy C-RAM defense system intercepted one of the missiles. 20091402

September 15, 2020: A roadside bomb targeted a British diplomatic convoy on a Baghdad highway near the Umm al-Tabool Mosque, causing no injuries. No one claimed credit. 20091501

September 16, 2020: *Military Times* reported that a Katyusha rocket launched from Baghdad's Amel neighborhood landed inside the Green

Zone near a residential building in the al-Qadisiya complex, causing no casualties or damage. The building was empty. No one claimed credit.

September 18, 2020: In the morning, a bomb damaged the façade of the American Institute for English Learning in Najaf but caused no casualties. The facility is not formally affiliated with any institutions in the United States and no Americans are employed there.

Earlier that morning, a roadside bomb hit an Iraqi convoy transporting equipment headed for the U.S.-led coalition.

September 28, 2020: *AP* and *AFP* reported that a Katyusha rocket launched from the al-Jihad neighborhood hit a home near Baghdad's airport, killing five civilians, including three children and two women from the same family, and severely wounding another two children, and destroying the house. No group claimed credit.

September 30, 2020: *CNN, DPA, DW, AP,* and *Reuters* reported that during the evening, six rockets fired from Sheikh Amir in Nineveh Province landed near Erbil International Airport in the semiautonomous Kurdistan region. Three rockets hit a base housing U.S. troops; the other three landed outside the base. No U.S. injuries or damage were reported. The Defense Ministry said the missiles were fired from a modified Kia four-wheel vehicle carrying a rocket launcher. 20093001

October 2020: *Stars and Stripes* reported on November 4, 2020 that US-trained Iraqi CTS counterterrorism forces captured an ISIS child recruiter in Fallujah.

October 27, 2020—Iraq—*Al-Monitor* reported that terrorists beheaded an anti-ISIS sheikh from the Bani Kaab tribe near Khailaniyah in the Muqdadiyah area of Diyala, killed four of his relatives, then rigged his body with explosives. He had initially been reported to have been a shepherd or buffalo herder who had been kidnapped and killed. ISIS posted a video showing its three fighters pointing guns at the back of the head of a gagged, elderly man. On November 2, the Interior Ministry announced it had arrested two male suspects.

Al-Monitor reported that during the final ten days of October, ISIS

- attacked a village with mortars and snipers in the Jalawla subdistrict
- fired mortars on Sunni tribal Popular Mobilization Units (PMU) in the Sherwan area
- killed four Iraqi intelligence officers and wounded two others near Muqdadiyah
- killed three "Shi'ite militants" at a fake checkpoint set up east of Jalawla
- bombed eight barracks and watchtowers operated by Iraqi SWAT teams in the Waqf area of Diyala Province
- set off a roadside bomb under a vehicle carrying Sunni tribal PMU fighters in the al-Wahda village in the outskirts of al-Azim

In late October, security forces killed ISIS member Abu Hassan al-Kurdi near Mandali, in Diyala Province.

November 17, 2020: Four rockets landed in Baghdad's Green Zone during the night, killing a child and wounding five people, including two Iraqi security forces, following the Trump Administration's announcement of a troop withdrawal. Three rockets landed outside the Green Zone; one near Baghdad Medical City Hospital, one at the gate of a public park, and one exploded in the air. The Ashab al-Kahaf group said it had fired six rockets. One of the rockets hit near the National Security Service, 2,000 feet from the U.S. Embassy. The U.S.-installed C-RAM air defense system knocked down some of the rockets.

November 29, 2020: *Reuters* reported that ISIS claimed credit for firing two Katyusha rockets at the small Siniya oil refinery, causing a fire at a fuel storage tank and a pipeline network and forcing a complete shutdown of operations. No casualties were reported. The facility is managed by the state-run Northern Refineries Co. The Siniya refinery has refining capacity of 30,000 barrels per day.

December 9, 2020: *Reuters* reported that the Oil Ministry announced that two North Oil Com-

pany wells in the small Khabbaz oilfield, southwest of Kirkuk, was set alight by explosives in a "terrorist attack" that did not affect overall production. ISIS claimed credit on *Telegram*. One bomb went off at 1:30 a.m., the other 30 minutes later.

December 20, 2020: *AP* and *Reuters* reported that the Iraqi military announced that at 8:30 p.m., "an outlawed group" launched eight Katyusha rockets at the U.S. Embassy in Baghdad's Green Zone, injuring an Iraqi soldier manning a checkpoint and damaging a residential complex, the embassy compound, and a few cars. The Embassy said its C-RAM defense system, which is used to destroy missiles in mid-air, diverted the rockets. No Americans were hurt. The *Wall Street Journal* reported on December 23 that the commander of U.S. Central Command said 21 missiles were fired. 20122001

ISRAEL

February 6, 2020: Shortly before 2 a.m., a Palestinian rammed his car into Israeli troops outside the First Station, an historic Ottoman-era railway terminus that is a Jerusalem cultural and entertainment center with bars and restaurants, injuring 14 people, including a soldier who was severely injured and hospitalized. The attacker fled. Public radio reported that the soldiers were new recruits en route to an induction ceremony at Jerusalem's Western Wall. Hamas called the attack a "practical response" to the Trump Administration's Middle East peace plan. Hamas spokesman Hazem Qassem said the attack was part of the "resistance operation" but did not claim credit.

Israeli forces shot to death Yazan Abu Tabikh, 19, and injured seven in Jenin in the West Bank. The army announced that troops had "identified a number of armed terrorists who hurled explosive devices and fired towards them. The forces responded with riot dispersal means."

Israeli aircraft hit Hamas positions in the Gaza Strip after Palestinians fired rockets and mortars and launched incendiary balloons at Israel.

February 22, 2020: Israeli police shot to death a man in blue jeans and a black jacket who tried to stab a soldier at the Lion's Gate outside the eastern side of Jerusalem's Old City. A shot wounded a woman, 42, in the leg. A Palestinian was suspected.

May 25, 2020: Police shot and wounded a man who tried to stab an officer in east Jerusalem.

May 30, 2020: *AFP* reported that Israeli police in the alleys of the walled Old City near Lions' Gate in east Jerusalem shot to death a Palestinian with special needs whom they mistakenly thought had a pistol. Police found no weapon. The Palestinian official news agency *Wafa* identified the dead man as Eyad Hallak, who lived in the mainly Palestinian Wadi Joz enclave of east Jerusalem. The *Washington Post* added that police said they believed he had a pistol. When they confronted him, he ran away from the Border Police. They identified him as Iyad Elkhalak, 32, an autistic man en route to the Elwyn El Quds School for people with disabilities, where he was a student and employee in the kitchen.

August 2, 2020: The *Washington Post* reported that at around 11 p.m., the Israeli army spotted terrorists based in Syria planting explosive devices adjacent to the security fence in the Golan Heights on the border with Syria. Troops and aircraft fired on the terrorist cell, "identifying a hit" and killing the four terrorists, whose affiliation was undetermined. *Newsweek* credited two 20-year-old female IDF soldiers, Corporal S. and Corporal K., for thwarting the attempted attack. They had been drafted into the military months earlier and were part of an all-female field observation team stationed in the Golan Heights. They tipped off an Israeli Maglan commando unit, who opened fire. Soldiers found a bomb and a weapon among the bodies. The IDF suspected that the terrorists planned to hit an unmanned Israeli military post used during the Syrian civil war.

Rocket fire from the Gaza Strip damaged the Israeli town of Sderot, but caused no injuries.

August 25, 2020: The IDF reported that Hizballah fired at Israeli troops along the Lebanese border during the night, sparking an exchange of gunfire in which no one was hurt in the IDF. The next morning, Israeli helicopters and aircraft attacked Hizballah border observation posts.

August 27, 2020: *Reuters* reported that Palestinians in Gaza had sent dozens of helium balloons laden with incendiary material into Israel, causing 460 brush fires that damaged open areas and nature reserves. The Balloon Unit terrorists had used party balloons, condoms, and large plastic bags to make the fire balloons which sometimes were strapped with explosives.

October 19, 2020: Chief Palestinian negotiator Saeb Erekat, 65, was on a ventilator and in critical condition in a coronary care unit with COVID-19 at a Tel Aviv hospital, then transferred to Jerusalem's Hadassah Ein Karem Medical Center. He has a history of respiratory illness and underwent a lung transplant in the U.S. for pulmonary fibrosis in 2017. Since 2015, he had served as secretary general of the Palestine Liberation Organization Executive Committee. He was a member of Fatah.

LEBANON

March 22, 2020: Gunmen armed with a suppressed pistol shot to death retired policeman Antoine Hayek, 58, a former member of an Israeli-backed Lebanese militia. Hayek was hit by several bullets inside his grocery store in Mieh Mieh, near Sidon. He had been a warden at the Khiam prison run by the South Lebanon Army militia during Israel's 18-year occupation of southern Lebanon, which ended in 2000. Hayek had been sentenced to 18 months in jail for his prison activities during the occupation. No group claimed credit for his death.

The attack took place three days after Amer Fakhoury, 57, of Dover, New Hampshire, a jailed Lebanese-American man who belonged to the same militia, was released in Beirut and flown to the U.S. Fakhoury had faced decades-old murder and prison torture charges. Hizballah leader Hassan Nasrallah called his release a "blatant violation" of Lebanese sovereignty and law. Fakhoury obtained U.S. citizenship in 2019.

April 1, 2020: Hizballah mobilized 24,500 members and volunteers for a campaign against to the coronavirus pandemic, sending paramedics and volunteers via trucks and on foot to spray disinfectants on shops and buildings and care for virus patients. Many had blamed the organization for inadvertently bringing the virus into the country. Hizballah leader Sayyed Hassan Nasrallah countered by giving regularly televised speeches on COVID-19 responses, observing, "We should feel that we are in a battle and we should fight this battle." Hizballah's Islamic Health Society planned to open testing centers.

April 4, 2020: Gunmen shot and stabbed to death Ali Mohammed Younes, a member of Hizballah whose body was found next to his car during the evening near Nabatiyeh. The body had four bullets in the chest and two stab wounds. The state-run *National News Agency* reported a suspect was detained. *FARS* called him a Hizballah commander who was involved in counterintelligence.

April 10, 2020: *AFP* reported that the U.S. offered a $10 million reward for "any information on the activities, networks and associates" of Muhammad Kawtharani, a Lebanese Hizballah commander accused of playing a key role in coordinating pro-Iran groups in Iraq. The U.S. Department of State said he "has taken over some of the political coordination of Iran-aligned paramilitary groups formerly organized by Qassim Suleimani", leader of Iran's Revolutionary Guard, who was killed in early January 2020 in a U.S. airstrike targeting him in Baghdad, Iraq. The U.S. had put Kawtharani on its list of specially designated international terrorists in 2013, saying he "facilitates the actions of groups operating outside the control of the Government of Iraq that have violently suppressed protests" or "attacked foreign diplomatic missions".

June 27, 2020: Judge Mohamad Mazeh in Tyre barred local and foreign media from interviewing U.S. Ambassador to Lebanon Dorothy Shea, calling a recent interview to the Saudi-owned *al-Hadath* tv station in which she criticized Hizballah "insulting to the Lebanese people", seditious, and a threat to social peace. Mazeh,

a Shi'ite, said violators would be suspended for a year. *LBC TV* said it would appeal the ruling. *Reuters* reported on June 28 that Lebanese media, including broadcaster *MTV*, aired interviews with the U.S. ambassador that day, ignoring the judge's ruling. The state-owned *National News Agency* said media that violate the ban would be fined $200,000. Information Minister Manal Abdel Samad tweeted that "no one had the right to prevent the media from covering news, or to curb press freedoms". *NNA* added that Foreign Minister Nassif Hitti summoned Ambassador Shea to the ministry for a June 29 meeting. Hizballah legislator Hassan Fadlallah deemed Shea's comments "a flagrant aggression on the sovereignty of our country and its national dignity". *Reuters* reported on June 29 that Shea told the media that "We turned the page on this unfortunate distraction so we could all focus on the real crisis at end, which is the deteriorating economic situation in Lebanon."

August 4, 2020: *CNN, Bloomberg, AP, NBC News, Reuters,* Lebanese state *National News Agency,* and the *Washington Post* reported that at 6:08 p.m., a fire set off stored fireworks, which in turn detonated two massive explosions, apparently involving flammable materials, 2,750 tons of unsafely-stored confiscated ammonium nitrate stored in a warehouse in Beirut, killed 190 people, wounded nearly 6,000, and displaced 300,000. By September 4, 191 people had died. Some 1,500 of the wounded needed special treatment, and 120 were in intensive care a week later. Beirut Governor Marwan Abboud told Saudi TV station *al-Hadath* that losses could reach $10 billion to $15 billion in damage. As of August 11, forty people were missing. Four hospitals, already stretched thin with COVID-19 patients, were put out of service by the damage. The St. George University Hospital in Beirut's Achrafieh neighborhood and the Roum Hospital were badly damaged and the port was leveled. Hizballah maintains a facility at the port, which was destroyed; many criticized Hizballah for its role in the storage situation. Some 1,000 families lost their homes. Germany's GFZ geosciences center reported that the explosion registered as a 3.5 magnitude earthquake. The blast was felt in Cyprus, 180 miles away. The *Washington Post 202* reported that a silo that stores most of Lebanon's wheat was ripped open. Damage was reported at the Baabda Presidential palace (the official residence), the South Korean Embassy, the Australian Embassy, the headquarters of former Prime Minister Saad Hariri, *CNN*'s Beirut office, 90% of Beirut's hotels, and homes six miles away.

Abbas Ibrahim, chief of Lebanese General Security said the explosion might have been caused by highly explosive ammonium nitrate that was confiscated from a ship in 2014 and stored at the port. *LBC TV* said it was sodium nitrate. The *Daily Beast* reported that the Lebanese government ignored Thailand-based Russian maritime analyst Mikhail Voytenko's public warning in July 2014 that there was a Russian "floating bomb" at the port, a reference to the Russian-owned yet Moldova-flagged *Rhosus* that came into port in Beirut in September 2013, listing its official cargo as "agricultural commodities"—2,750 metric tons of ammonium nitrate that could be used for fertilizers or high power explosives. (The 1995 Oklahoma City bomber used less than two metric tons of ammonium nitrate.) The ship was believed to be going from Batumi, Georgia to Mozambique. The maritime monitoring website *Fleetmon* reported that Beirut authorities blocked it from leaving and the dangerous cargo was offloaded and stored in Hanger 12 in the port in 2014. The crew members were not permitted to leave the ship due to their immigration status. The owner, reported by *Business Insider* to be Igor Grechushkin, a Russian living in Cyprus, abandoned the ship. Lebanese customs officials echoed Voytenko's concerns about the safety of the materials.

Military Times reported that President Trump called the explosions a "terrible attack", saying "It would seem like it based on the explosion. I met with some of our great generals and they just seem to feel that it was. This was not a — some kind of a manufacturing explosion type of a event. ... They seem to think it was an attack. It was a bomb of some kind, yes." Military officials said that they had not made a determination about the cause of the explosions. *CNN* reported that three Department of Defense officials said that there was no evidence of an attack. *CNN* added that two State Department officials said that Lebanese officials raised concerns with U.S. diplomats about the use of the word "attack ".*AP* reported on August 5 that President Trump stuck with the attack theme, saying "Whatever happened, it's terrible, but they don't really know what it is... Nobody knows yet." "How can you say accident if somebody left some terrible explosive-type devices and things around perhaps — perhaps it was that. Perhaps it was an attack," Trump told reporters during a White House briefing. "I don't think anybody can say right now. We're looking into it very strongly right now... Some people think it was an attack and some people think it wasn't. In any event, it was a terrible event and a lot of people were killed and a tremendous number of people were badly wounded, injured. And we're standing with that country... But whether it was a bomb intentionally set off—it ended up being a bomb... But no, I've heard it both ways. It could have been an accident and it could have also been something that was very offensive."

Israeli bomb expert Boaz Hayoun, owner of the Tamar Group, suggested that fireworks could have set off the bigger explosion.

Among the dead were Nazar Najarian, secretary-general of the Kataeb political party; the sister of Omar Kinno, a Syrian (Another sister's neck was broken. His mother and father were hospitalized.); Nicole al-Helou; an American citizen, according to *NBC News*; a German diplomat; 43 Syrians; two Philippines citizens, according to the Philippine Embassy; an Egyptian; four Bangladeshi migrant workers; French architect Jean-Marc Bonfils; and an Australian citizen, according to *Channel 7 Sunrise*. *NBC News* reported that by August 20, Alexandra "Lexou" Najjar, 3, the first young child to die, had become the face of the tragedy. Her father, Paul, was injured. *AP* reported that Greek Orthodox philanthropist Lady Yvonne Sursock Cochrane, 98, founder of the Association for Protecting Natural Sites and Old Buildings in Lebanon, died of her wounds on August 31.

The injured included scores of Bangladeshi workers; 21 French citizens; *New York Times* reporter Vivian Yee and other Americans; eight Filipinos, including one critically injured (Among the injured were two Filipino seafarers); a Japanese citizen; some Australian Embassy staffers, who suffered cuts and scratches, according to Australian *Channel 9's Today* show; six Turkish citizens; a Chinese citizen; an Indonesian citizen; United Nations Interim Forces in Lebanon (UNIFIL) navy peacekeepers, some seriously. *CNN* reported that a maritime task force ship was damaged.

Hundreds of people, including eleven Filipino seamen, ten Beirut municipal firefighters and many children, were missing, according to Save the Children and Lebanese Health Minister Hamad Hassan.

Leaders from Israel, the UK, France, Turkey, UAE, Jordan, Kuwait, Qatar, Russia and Spain offered support and humanitarian medical assistance. Egypt, Qatar, Iraq, Kuwait, Oman, and Jordan set up emergency field hospitals.

The U.S. Embassy recommended that people "stay indoors and wear masks if available" due to reports of toxic gases released from the blast.

Several port officials were put under house arrest during the investigation of negligence.

Hundreds of protestors took to the streets, seizing the Foreign Ministry, Energy Ministry, and Economy Ministry buildings and deeming Beirut a "disarmed" city. Many chanted "Terrorists, terrorists" in referring to Hizballah.

Some observers suggested that the fire was started by welders working nearby, according to the *New York Times*.

Hizballah leader Hasan Nasrallah warned in a televised address on *al-Manar* against blaming it for responsibility. Many Lebanese had blamed the group for problems that sparked the explosion, noting that it used the port for its smuggling operations and its parallel government had weakened official institutions that had become rife with negligence, corruption, and mismanagement.

Israel denied involvement, and Hizballah did not blame Israel in its condolence statement, despite conspiracy theories. The *Washington Post* and *Lebanese MTV* reported that Lebanese President Michel Aoun told journalists that "The case of the explosion has not yet been determined. There is a possibility of external interference via a missile, bomb or any other action."

Numerous senior Lebanese officials, including seven members of parliament and three cabinet ministers, resigned in the aftermath of massive protest demonstrations. Prime Minister Hassan Diab announced on August 10 that he and the rest of his administration had stepped down. On August 17, the *National News Agency* reported the arrest of Badri Daher, head of the customs authority.

Reuters reported on December 11, 2020 that Lebanese parties criticized the bringing of charges of negligence made by Judge Fadi Sawan against caretaker Prime Minister Hassan Diab and former ministers Ali Hassan Khalil, Ghazi Zeaiter and Youssef Finianos over the Beirut port explosion. Hizballah blamed political targeting. The United States earlier imposed sanctions on Finianos and Khalil, accusing them of enabling Hizballah.

September 5, 2020: *Naharnet* reported that the Lebanese Army Command-Orientation Directorate arrested members of a terrorist cell linked to ISIS that was plotting on conducting terrorist attacks inside Lebanon. The group was linked to the attack in Kaftoun in August. The cell's emir, Khaled Tellawi, remained at large. His vehicle was used in the Kaftoun attack that killed three municipal police guards. The arrests came on different dates in the North and Bekaa regions. The army said the terrorists had received military training, collected weapons and ammunition, and conducted thefts.

September 14, 2020: Four soldiers died while trying to arrest suspected terrorist Khaled al-Tallawi at his home in the north. He was shot dead.

September 22, 2020: The *Washington Post, AP, Reuters, al-Jadeed TV,* and the *National News Agency* reported that an explosion at a Hizballah arms depot in Ayn Qana injured several people.

September 26, 2020: *AFP* reported that police raided a house in Wadi Khaled and killed nine suspected ISIS members during a dragnet for "terrorists" linked to deadly attacks, including on soldiers. The attacks included an August 21, 2020 murder of two municipal policemen and the son of the mayor of Kaftoun. The safe house blew up during the operation, possibly burying other terrorists. The Internal Security Forces said the "terrorist cell" had more than 15 suspects, three of whom had been arrested earlier.

During the night, a terrorist on a motorcycle tried to enter an army post in Arman-Minyeh in the north. The terrorist and two soldiers were killed. Security forces confiscated grenades and an explosive belt, which they believed he intended to set off once inside the post. Other reports said the attack involved gunmen in a car and that one terrorist fled.

Libya

January 9, 2020: Two Eritrean asylum-seekers were shot to death in Tripoli ten days after the UNHCR forced them to leave its Gathering and Departure Facility because of overcrowding. 20010901

February 24, 2020: Turkish President Recep Tayyip Erdogan announced that two Turkish soldiers were killed in fighting in Libya.

May 2020: The UN migration agency reported that the family of a slain Libyan human trafficker attacked migrants in Mizdah, shooting and killing at least 30 migrants, mostly from Bangladesh. 20059901

May 16, 2020: Bombs exploded at a shelter for displaced people in Tripoli's Furnaj district during the night, killing seven people, including a 5-year-old Bangladeshi and wounding 17, including a Bengali migrant, 52, and his 5-year-old. The Bengali was also the father of the dead child. 20051601

October 6, 2020: Three Libyans broke into a factory in Tripoli's Tajoura neighborhood where African migrants work. They grabbed a Nigerian worker, poured gasoline on him, and set him on fire, burning him to death. Three other migrants were hospitalized with burns. Authorities arrested the trio, all in their 30s. No motive was announced. 20100601

Morocco

September 10, 2020: *AFP* reported that police arrested five members of an ISIS-affiliated cell, aged between 29 and 43, in raids in Tangiers and the Rabat region, seizing chemicals that were to be used in suicide bombings against public personalities, military figures, and the headquarters of the security services. Police found in homes and businesses explosive belts, three kilograms (6.6 pounds) of ammonium nitrate, electronic equipment and bladed weapons. They also confiscated pledges of allegiance to ISIS. Two suspects, in putting up "fierce resistance", seriously injured a policeman with knives. The suspected ringleader, 37, a fish salesman, was convicted of a common law crime in 2004 and was radicalized afterwards. Police found no evidence of direct contact with ISIS.

Red Sea

November 25, 2020: At 3 a.m., a mine damaged the *MT Agrari*, a Maltese-flagged, Greek-managed oil tanker docked at Shuqaiq, Saudi Arabia, near Yemen. No injuries were reported among the 25 crew members, including seven Greeks. Ambrey, a British security firm, said the *Agrari* had discharged cargo from Rotterdam, Netherlands, at the Shuqaiq Steam Power Plant. The Saudi state-run *al-Ekhbariya* television reported that the Saudi-led coalition blamed Yemeni Houthi rebels and said that it had intercepted and destroyed an explosives-laden boat, shrapnel from which hit the *Agrari*. 20112501

The Saudi-led coalition reported the previous day that it removed and destroyed five Iranian-made naval mines planted by the Houthis in the southern Red Sea.

Saudi Arabia

March 28, 2020: *Reuters, AP,* and *al-Arabiya* television reported that Saudi Arabia's Air Defense Forces used Patriot missiles to intercept two rockets above Riyadh and Jizan during the night. No injuries were reported. Houthi rebels in Yemen were suspected. 20032801

June 23, 2020: *Reuters* and *AP* reported that Yemeni Houthis claimed they fired a large missile and drone deep into Saudi Arabia that hit the Ministry of Defense, Ministry of Intelligence, the King Salman air base in Riyadh and military positions in Jizan and Najran. Saudi officials said the military intercepted one ballistic missile. A Houthi military spokesman warned that the Houthis planned to "carry out more, stronger and tougher military operations" in the future until Saudi Arabia stops the "aggression". 20062302

September 28, 2020: *Deutsche Welle* and the *Saudi Press Agency* reported that during the previous week, Saudi authorities arrested ten members of a terrorist cell that had received training from the Iranian Revolutionary Guards. Security forces seized more than five kilograms of gunpowder, 17 packages containing chemicals, military uniforms, listening devices, computers, knives, Kalashnikov machine guns, rifles, pistols, and ammunition from a house and a farm. Three had been trained in making explosives between October-December 2017; the other seven had ties to the Revolutionary Guards.

October 28, 2020: The *Washington Examiner* reported that the U.S. embassy had issued an alert for citizens in Riyadh, warning of a possible missile or drone attack. *Bloomberg* reported that the alert came an hour after Saudi Arabia announced it destroyed bomb-carrying drones Houthi rebels in Yemen had launched against targets in the south.

October 29, 2020: *Al-Jazeera* reported that a man attacked a Saudi security guard outside the French Consulate in Jeddah in Mecca Province. The guard was hospitalized. Authorities arrested the attacker. Police said he was a Saudi. 20102903

November 11, 2020: A bomb went off during an Armistice Day commemoration organized by the French Consulate at Jiddah's Non-Muslim Cemetery, injuring three, including a Briton, a Greek policeman serving in the Greek Consulate, and a Saudi security guard. People from 20 nations were in attendance. The next day, the Islamic State claimed credit on *Telegram* and *Amaq*, saying it was targeting French diplomats who were marking the end of WWI, saying it targeted the French Consul because of publication of caricatures of the Prophet Muhammad. 20111101

November 23, 2020: Yemeni Houthi rebels said they fired a Quds 2 missile that hit a Saudi Aramco oil storage facility in Jiddah in retaliation for the Saudi-led coalition's involvement in Yemen's war.

December 4, 2020: *Reuters* and Saudi state television reported that the Saudi-led coalition intercepted and destroyed a bomb-carrying drone launched by the Houthis in Yemen towards the kingdom.

December 14, 2020: The *Washington Post* and *UPI* reported that an explosion from an "external source" struck the Singapore-flagged *BW Rhine* oil tanker while it was in port in Jiddah at 12:40 a.m., damaging the hull but causing no injuries. The ship's owner, Hafnia, said it was investigating whether "some oil had escaped from the vessel". The firm said that a fire that broke out on board was extinguished and all 22 crew members were safe. The United Kingdom Maritime Trade Operations said Jiddah's port was closed following "unconfirmed reports of a second vessel being involved in an incident". The state-run Saudi Press Agency later quoted an unnamed official in the Energy Ministry as saying that the explosion was caused by a boat loaded with bombs. The Ministry noted a similar attack on a ship in Shuqaiq in northern Jiddah on November 25. Houthi rebels were among the suspects. 20121401

SYRIA

January 2020: The government claimed that divers had planted explosives on offshore pipelines in the Mediterranean Sea of the Banias refinery. The damage did not halt operations.

January 4, 2020: The bodies of 21 shepherds were found shot in the back of their heads. Their hands were tied behind their backs.

January 14, 2020: ISIS fighters stole 2,000 cattle from a village near Mayadeen. After one of four shepherds informed authorities, Syrian troops were fired on. ISIS gunmen killed 11 troops and pro-government militia and two shepherds. They also destroyed an armored vehicle.

Seven shepherds were found shot to death west of Deir el-Zour.

March 12, 2020: The *New York Daily News* and *Homeland Security Today* reported that ISIS issued a warning in its *al-Naba* newsletter for its members to avoid Europe during the coronavirus pandemic. Operatives should not go to Europe and those already there should remain "in the land of the epidemic". Terrorists were to wash their hands "before dipping them in the vessels" and cover their mouths when yawning and sneezing. *Military Times* and *The Observation Post* reported on March 14 that blogger Aymenn Jawad al-Tamimi had translated the newsletter's counsel on how to "deal with epidemics". ISIS followers have an "obligation of taking up the causes of protection from illnesses and avoiding them" and "flee from the one afflicted with leprosy as you flee from the lion". ISIS added, "When one of you wakes from his sleep, let him not dip his hand into the vessels until he washes it three times, for he does not know where his hand spent the night."

March 29-30, 2020: *CNN* and the *Washington Post* reported that overnight, several ISIS members broke out of the Ghweran prison in Hasakah by ripping off doors and using them to break down a wall during a riot. The Kurdish Syrian Democratic Forces run the detention facility.

April 9, 2020: ISIS attacked government positions in the Sukhna area. Two days of fighting led to the deaths of 32 troops and 26 ISIS gunmen.

April 15, 2020: Hizballah claimed that an Israeli drone fired two missiles at a four-wheel-drive vehicle carrying two members of the group traveling in rural Damascus near the Jdeidet Yabous border crossing with Lebanon. No one was hurt. One missile went off near the vehicle; the second hit after the driver exited the vehicle.

April 28, 2020: *Reuters* reported that a bomb exploded in central Afrin's market, killing 40 civilians, including 11 children. The Turkish Defense Ministry blamed the Syrian Kurdish YPG militia.

May 25, 2020: *Stars and Stripes* reported that a coalition airstrike killed one of ISIS's top three senior commanders, Mu'ataz Nu'man 'Abd Nayif Najm al-Jaburi, alias Hakim, alias Hajji Taysir, in Deir al-Zour Province. As of 2017, he was deputy emir for manufacturing, making him in charge of ISIS's chemical and biological weapons program in Syria. The U.S. Rewards for Justice program had issued a $5 million reward for his capture. The Syrian Democratic Forces said he was responsible for external terrorist attacks. He was also considered by ISIS as its governor for Iraq. The U.S. had listed him as a specially-designated terrorist. The U.S. Department of State said he was believed to have been born in Iraq in 1987 and had overseen bombmaking and insurgent activities.

A Rewards for Justice poster listed him with Sami Jasim Muhammad al-Jaburi and Amir Mohammed Abdul Rahman al-Mawli al-Salbi, Baghdadi's eventual successor, as three key ISIS members. Iraqi national Sami al-Jaburi, alias Hajji Hamid, was listed as an earlier member of al-Qaeda in Iraq and was instrumental in managing ISIS finances. Al-Salbi, variant Amir Muhammed Sa'id 'Abd al-Rahman al-Mawla, alias Hajji 'Abdallah, was a religious scholar in AQI. The Department of State offered a $5 million reward for the capture of each of them.

May 27, 2020: ISIS attacked a government post in the north, killing eight soldiers. Opposition activists claimed that Russian airstrikes killed 11 ISIS gunmen.

May 28, 2020: The bodies of three Kurdish-led Syrian Democratic Forces fighters were found with their throats slit in Deir el-Zour Province near the Iraqi border, a region where ISIS sleeper cells were reportedly active.

June 14, 2020: *Task and Purpose* reported on June 16, 2020 that a coalition drone fired a modified R9X variant of the non-explosive AGM-114 Hellfire missile full of swords at a vehicle, killing Jordanian citizen Qassam al-Urduni and Yemeni citizen Bilal al-Sanaani, two commanders of Horas al-Din, an al-Qaeda offshoot, in northern

Syria. Video showed that the vehicle was somewhat intact, with damage to the roof, windshield, and one side.

July 18, 2020: *AFP* and *SANA* reported that two bombs exploded next to a kiosk opposite the Anas bin Malik mosque in Damascus, killing one person and injuring two on the eve of Syria's third war-time parliamentary election. One gravely wounded person was hospitalized.

July 19, 2020: *Reuters* and *Anadolu* reported that a car bomb went off in Siccu in the Azaz region, across the border from Turkey's southern Kilis Province, killing five and wounding 85. Fifteen, some in critical condition, were hospitalized in a Turkish hospital. 20071901

August 24, 2020: *SANA* and *AFP* reported that after midnight, an explosion hit the Arab Gas Pipeline in the northeastern Damascus suburbs of Adra and Dumair that feeds three power stations, sparking a large fire and cutting off electricity throughout the country. Oil Minister Ali Ghanem condemned the "cowardly terrorist act", observing it was the sixth attack on the pipeline. U.S. Syria envoy James Jeffrey blamed ISIS.

October 15, 2020: Amina Omar, head of the Kurdish-led Syrian National Council, announced the release of 631 repentant ISIS prisoners who have "no blood on their hands"; the Syrian Democratic Forces halved the terms of another 253 as part of a general amnesty.

October 22, 2020: *AFP* and *SANA* reported that a bomb planted in his car in Qudsaya killed Damascus Province mufti Adnan al-Afiyuni, 66, who was considered close to President Bashar al-Assad, an Alawite Shi'ite.

October 22, 2020: The *Washington Examiner* reported on October 26 that U.S. Central Command spokeswoman Major Beth Riordan said that an October 22 air strike killed seven al-Qaeda leaders meeting near Idlib.

November 24, 2020: *Reuters* reported that two bombs killed seven people and wounded scores in northwest Syria near the Turkish border. A bomb went off at a road junction on the outskirts of al-Bab, killing five and wounding 20, some critically. Hours later, a car bomb went off in Afrin, killing two civilians and wounding 17. Turkey accused the YPG.

December 10, 2020: *ABC News* and *Anadolu* reported that a car bomb went off at a checkpoint in a Turkish-controlled area in Ras al-Ayn in northeastern Syria, killing two Turkish soldiers and two local security officers with the Syrian opposition. The UK-based Syrian Observatory for Human Rights said 16 were killed, including four Turks. The governor's office for the southern Turkish Sanliurfa Province said two Turkish soldiers and two Syrian security officers were killed and six, including two Syrian security forces, were wounded. No one claimed credit; ISIS was suspected. 20121001

TUNISIA

March 6, 2020: Two suicide bombers on a motorcycle set off an explosion at 11 a.m. less than 100 yards from the U.S. Embassy's main entrance, killing a policeman—52, a father of three—and injuring four other security personnel and a woman. No one claimed credit, but jihadis were suspected. Authorities blamed "terrorists". Local media said the two male bombers had served prison terms for terrorism-related crimes. The attorney of one of them said on *Wataniya* state television that his client was sentenced for a *Facebook* posting "with religious overtones". 20030601

July 20, 2020: The *North Africa Post* reported that the Tunisian Ministry of Interior claimed that authorities foiled a terrorist attack by arresting a would-be ISIS-affiliated terrorist planning to attack a military patrol with an IED in a southern governorate. The terrorist was not previously known to authorities. Authorities said he had been trained in making explosives and was plotting attacks against security personnel. The previous week, the Interior Ministry announced that an ISIS-linked terrorist was "rounded".

September 6, 2020: *AFP* reported that three terrorists rammed their vehicle into two officers of the national gendarmerie, then slashed to death

Tunisian National Guard officer Sami Mrabet, 38, father of two, and wounded another before the trio were shot to death in a firefight in Sousse. The terrorists had stolen the victims' guns and vehicle, and fled through the Akouda district of the city's tourist area of El-Kantaoui. Authorities recovered the car and two pistols. The next day, ISIS claimed credit. Tunisian authorities questioned 43 and arrested seven people, including the wife of an assailant, who called her husband a "martyr" during interrogation. The twins and a third man were from the Siliana region. Mrabet was buried in his home town of Moknine in a funeral attended by more than 1,000 people, including several government officials. Police said the attackers were twin brothers and a third man was from the Siliana region. The twins consulted *Facebook* pages regarding "explosive and armed attacks", but remained unknown to the authorities.

December 20, 2020: *Reuters* reported that IS-affiliated Ajned Kilafha jihadis were suspected when terrorists kidnapped and beheaded Okba Dhouibi, a young shepherd, in the Kasserine and Saloum mountains near the border with Algeria.

WEST BANK

April 22, 2020: *Reuters* reported that Israeli security forces shot to death a Palestinian man who drove his vehicle into a border policeman and then stabbed him with scissors at a checkpoint near Jerusalem in the West Bank. The policeman was moderately wounded. Police found a bomb at the scene near the Jewish settlement of Maale Adumim.

May 12, 2020: The *New York Times* and *Agence France-Presse* reported that a heavy rock struck in the head and killed Staff Sgt. Amit Ben Ygal, 21, of Ramat Gan, an Israeli soldier, while his unit was completing a nighttime arrest of four Palestinians in Yaabed, variant Yabad, a Palestinian village near Jenin, in the northern West Bank. Some of the detainees were suspected of throwing stones at passing Israeli motorists. The rock was thrown from a nearby house's rooftop. Ygal's helmet did not save him. Palestinian news agency *Wafa* reported that Israeli forces had arrested seven additional people by noon during the search for the killer. Kamel Abu Shamleh, a member of the village's municipal council, said two of his sons were arrested after his home was raided by about 10 soldiers at 4 a.m. Hamas praised the killing.

Reuters reported that police shot and wounded a Palestinian who tried to stab security staff at a checkpoint in the West Bank.

The *Washington Post* reported on August 19, 2020, that the previous week, a three-judge panel of the Israeli Supreme Court blocked the IDF from demolishing the home of a Palestinian man accused of killing Israeli Staff Sergeant Amit Ben Ygal, 49, on May 12. Nazmi Abu Bakr, 49, was accused in military court of dropping a block on an Israeli Army unit from the roof of his third-floor apartment in a 4:30 a.m. clash in Yabad in the West Bank. The panel ruled that it would be "disproportional" to displace his wife and eight children, who apparently were asleep during the attack. Prime Minister Netanyahu told the Knesset, "My policy as prime minister is to destroy the homes of terrorists, and I intend to continue with it." Abu Bakr had yet to be convicted. He confessed to attempting to cause injuries, not deaths.

May 13, 2020: *Reuters* reported that Israeli soldiers on an arrest raid shot dead a Palestinian, 15, in the Fawwar refugee camp after they were attacked with rocks and firebombs.

May 14, 2020: *Reuters* reported that an Israeli soldier shot dead a Palestinian who the military said drove at high speed towards troops at an army post outside Negohot settlement near Hebron, injuring one of them.

May 29, 2020: *Reuters* reported that Israeli soldiers shot and killed a Palestinian driver who tried to run them over with a car near Ramallah. No Israelis were hurt.

June 23, 2020: *Reuters* reported that at 4 p.m., Israeli police shot to death Ahmad Erekat, 27 or 28, a Palestinian man who tried to ram his car into a female police officer at the military Container Checkpoint near Abu Dis in the occupied West Bank. Israeli police spokesman Micky Rosenfeld said an officer was slightly injured.

Palestinian officials countered that Erekat was en route to Bethlehem to pick up family members from a hair salon on his sister's wedding day. *Al-Jazeera* reported that Palestine Liberation Organization Secretary General Saeb Erekat said Ahmad was his relative, and that his wedding was scheduled for the following week. The Palestinian news agency *Wafa* reported that the director of the Palestinian Red Crescent Society in Bethlehem said that a soldier prevented Palestinian medical personnel from approaching the man, who bled out. *CNN* reported that video showed the car turned sharply towards a police booth and hit female border police sergeant Shani Or Hama Kadosh. Relatives said he lost control of the vehicle, which accidentally jumped the curb. Erekat's cousin said he had worked in the ad industry. Kadosh was treated at a hospital and released. She told Israeli television, "A car pulled up and I pointed at it to stop. The car began slowing down. The moment I saw it starting to slow down, I moved in its direction. I took a step, [the driver] saw that I had made the step, he looked me in the eyes, turned the wheel, ran me over, and I was thrown in the opposite direction. In the beginning I never understood why he was looking at me. Only when I flew through the air did I understand it was an attempt at an attack."

November 25, 2020: *ABC News* reported that Israeli forces killed a Palestinian motorist who tried to crash his Fiat Punto into an Israeli soldier at a West bank checkpoint after presenting false documents. The soldier was lightly injured.

December 21, 2020: *Reuters* reported that Israeli police shot to death a Palestinian man from near Jenin who had fired shots at officers at a security post near one of the entrances to Jerusalem's walled Old City's Al-Aqsa mosque compound. The area is referred to by Muslims as the Noble Sanctuary and by Jews as the Temple Mount.

YEMEN

January 18, 2020: *AFP, al-Masdar Online,* and *BBC* reported that Houthi rebels fired missiles at a mosque in the al-Estiqbal army training camp in Marib Province during evening prayers, killing 116 troops and wounding dozens.

January 25, 2020: *AP* and *CNN* reported that tribal leaders said a suspected U.S. drone strike destroyed a building in the Wadi Ubaidah area in Marib Province that was believed to be an AQAP hideout, killing senior AQAP founder and current leader Qassim al-Rimi. President Trump retweeted several tweets and media reports suggesting that al-Rimi was killed. The local residents said there were three explosions.

February 6, 2020: The White House confirmed that an airstrike had killed AQAP leader Qassim al-Rimi in Yemen.

February 14, 2020: *AFP* reported that a Houthi rebels claimed credit for a shootdown when a Saudi Tornado fighter jet crashed in al-Jawf Province. The rebels' *al-Masirah* tv reported that "dozens" of people were dead or wounded.

February 19, 2020: A roadside bomb killed six guards of Yemeni Defense Minister Mohammed al-Maqdishi (who was unharmed) and wounded eight others when it exploded under a car in his convoy in Marib Province, where he was surveying his forces fighting against Shi'ite Houthi rebels from the area.

May 7, 2020: During a battle with government forces in Marib and Bayda Provinces, Shi'ite Houthi special forces commander Mohamed Abdel Karim al-Hamran, who was close to Houthi leader Abdul Malek al-Houthi, was killed. He was part of a Lebanese Hizballah-trained brigade. Dozens were killed and wounded on both sides, including 16 in Bayda, mostly Houthis.

A bomb hit a military checkpoint in Abyan Province during the night, killing three soldiers and wounding four others.

June 2, 2020: Gunmen shot to death Nabil al-Quaety, 34, a Yemeni video journalist and photographer who contributed to *AFP* during the previous five years, outside his home in the Dar Saad district of Aden. No group claimed credit. He left behind a pregnant wife and three children. In 2016, he was a finalist for the UK's Rory Peck Award for covering Yemen's war.

August 30, 2020: Saudi-led coalition spokesman Colonel Turki al-Malki announced it had foiled two attacks launched by Iran-backed

Houthi rebels, including a remotely-controlled explosives-laden boat dispatched into the Red Sea near international shipping lanes. Yemeni officials said an explosion killed three people and wounded five. He said the coalition also destroyed an explosives-carrying drone over Abha International Airport in southwestern Saudi Arabia. 20083001-02

October 14, 2020: *AP,* the *Wall Street Journal,* the *Washington Post,* and *CNN* reported that Houthi rebels released two Americans—humanitarian worker Sandra Loli and businessman Mikael Gidada—and the remains of a third—Bilal Fateen—in exchange for the return of 283 Houthi rebels from Oman. White House National Security Adviser Robert O'Brien offered "sincerest thanks to Sultan Haitham bin Tariq of Oman and King Salman of Saudi Arabia for their efforts to secure the release of our citizens". Loli had been held for three years; Gidada for about a year.

October 27, 2020: Gunmen shot to death Hassan Zaid, 66, who headed the Houthi rebel-run Youth and Sports Ministry, firing at his car in the Haddah neighborhood of Sana'a. His daughter, who was driving Zaid to his office, was wounded. No one claimed credit. The Iran-backed Houthis blamed the Saudi-led coalition. Zaid was wanted by Saudi Arabia for plotting attacks and in 2017 Riyadh offered a $10 million bounty for information leading to his arrest. In 2017, he called for school children and teachers in Houthi-held areas to go to the front lines to fight against forces of the internationally recognized government.

November 29-30, 2020: Eleven children, including a 1-month-old, died in two attacks attributed to Houthis. Shells hit Durayhimi, south of Hodeida, on November 29, followed by shelling in Usayfara in Taiz Province on November 30.

December 5, 2020: Drive-by gunmen on a motorcycle killed university professor Khalid al-Hameidi, a secular critic of jihadis, in Dhale, where he was dean of the university's education faculty. AQAP and IS were the leading suspects.

December 7, 2020: AQAP was suspected of using automatic rifles and rocket-propelled grenades in attacking a checkpoint in Lawdar district in Abyan Province during the night, killing six Yemeni troops and wounding four, two critically. The guards were trained by the United Arab Emirates.

December 24, 2020: During the night, Houthi rebels beat to death Ahlam al-Ashary, 25, in front of her two children in Ibb Province. They were looking for her husband for his alleged ties to rival forces loyal to the U.N.-recognized government. They instead kicked her and hit her with sticks and the backs of their pistols, killing her.

December 30, 2020: *Al-Arabiya, UPI, AP* and *Reuters* reported that three mortar rounds hit the airport hall in Aden shortly after members of a newly-announced unity government deplaned from a Yemenia flight from Saudi Arabia. Witnesses reported hearing gunfire. The blasts killed 22, including a journalist and three staffers of the International Committee of the Red Cross, and injured 58. Some 36 people required major surgery. No group claimed credit. The Houthis denied involvement. Saudi state media reported that the passengers included Prime Minister Maeen Abdulmalik Saeed, other cabinet members, and Saudi Arabia's ambassador to Yemen, Mohammed Said al-Jaber. None of the cabinet members were hurt.

The next day, the death toll had reached 25 or 26, with 110 injured. Prime Minister Saeed blamed Iran and the Houthi rebels for firing four rockets at the airport. 20123001

Hours later, a second explosion went off near Aden's Maasheq presidential palace where the cabinet members including Prime Minister Maeen Abdulmalik Saeed and the Saudi ambassador to Yemen had been brought to supposed safety. There were no immediate reports of casualties.

NORTH AMERICA

CANADA

April 18, 2020: *CNN* and *AP* reported that around 10:30 p.m., Gabriel Wortman, 51, dressed in a police uniform and driving a car disguised to look like an RCMP police cruiser, killed 17 people at 16 crime scenes in the rural, coastal Portapique area of Nova Scotia before he died. Among the dead was Nova Scotia RCMP Constable Heidi Stevenson, 23-year veteran of the RCMP, a mother of two. Wortman also injured a male RCMP officer. Wortman was not a member of the RCMP.

The following morning, just before noon, the RCMP arrested Wortman at a truck stop after a gun battle in the Shubenacadie and Enfield area of Nova Scotia, 57 miles from Portapique, northwest of Halifax. Police later announced he had died. Police did not provide a motive for the attack.

Many of the victims did not know the shooter. Police found several casualties inside and outside a home in Portapique. Some structures at crime scenes were on fire.

The RCMP said Wortman was a white man, bald, 6'2-6'3 with green eyes. About 100 people live in the Portapique area. Police said that his silver Chevrolet Tracker was not a police vehicle. The car had a number 28B11 on the C pillar behind the rear passenger window. He had worked as a denturist.

Reuters reported that Canadian Prime Minister Justin Trudeau said on April 20 that the death toll had reached 18. The murders occurred in Portapique on Cobequid Bay, Truro, Milford and Enfield.

AP and a GoFundMe site curated by Kori Hamilton and *Facebook* posts by family members indicated that the dead included:

- Lisa McCully, who taught grades 3 and 4 at the Debert Elementary School in Debert, Nova Scotia.

- Jaimie and Greg Blair

- Corrie Ellison; his brother, Clinton, stumbled across his body, saw the killer, and hid in the woods.

- Emily Tuck, 17 (making her the youngest victim), Aaron (Friar) Tuck and Jolene Oliver, who were killed in their home. Emily's aunt reported that she played fiddle, and enjoyed welding and fixing vehicles with her father. Aaron was a mechanic and leather worker. Jolene, youngest of three, loved poetry and books.

- Tom Bagley

- Heather O'Brien, a licensed practical nurse, according to Von Canada, a long-term health care company

- Gina Marie Goulet, 54

- Kristen Beaton, a home support worker and continuing care assistant who was caring for her elderly patients when she was gunned down, according to Von Canada. She was pregnant with her and husband Nick's second child.

- Officer Sean McLeod from Springhill Institute and correctional officer Alanna Jenkins from Nova Penitentiary.

- Constable Heidi Stevenson, Reg #45161, was a married mother of two children, aged 10 and 13. At one point, she was the media spokesperson for the province's RCMP force. Her husband, Dean, teaches at a Halifax-area high school. She was reporting to the "active shooter incident" when she was murdered.

- *AP* reported on April 20 that Justin Zahl, 22, was awaiting confirmation that his grandparents, Elizabeth Joanne Thomas, in her late 50s, and John Zahl, in his late 60s, were killed when their two-story log cabin burned down. The couple adopted and raised him and his brother, Riley, 19. They lived in Albuquerque, New Mexico, where they raised Justin and Riley before retiring to their dream home in Nova Scotia in 2017. John Zahl was originally from Minnesota and Elizabeth from Winnipeg, Manitoba. She worked for HCSC Blue

Cross Blue Shield in New Mexico and he worked for FedEx for 20 years and earlier worked for the Navy as a Russian translator. He had taught behaviorally challenged students at middle and elementary schools in Albuquerque.

CNN Ottawa reported on April 20 that Wortman had used two cars during his spree, pulling people over at random while driving his counterfeit police cruiser and executing them. Victims included a nurse and a teacher. Chris Leather, a Royal Canadian Mounted Police chief superintendent and criminal operations officer in Nova Scotia, said, "We're unable to fully examine the crime scenes because, for instance, we have had five structure fires, most of those being residences, and we believe there may be victims still within the remains of those homes which burnt to the ground." Police said Wortman apparently knew some, but not all, of his victims.

Wortman shot an old dog, which managed to survive; his owners did not.

Police said the spree began with a domestic violence incident at a home in Portapique, where Wortman was trying to track down his former significant other. He killed two people there, then fled. Police said the spree appeared to have been premeditated, pointing to the amount of time it must have taken to create the fake police cruiser and obtain a uniform. A neighbor told *CTV News* that Wortman had recently purchased two used police cars and parked them behind a clinic where he worked.

AP reported on April 21 that he lived part-time on Portapique Beach Road, location of a house inside and outside of which several bodies were found. Police believed they might find other bodies in the burned homes. Wortman owned a denture practice in Dartmouth, near Halifax. The Atlantic Denture Clinic had been closed because of the coronavirus pandemic.

Prime Minister Trudeau announced he would introduce gun control legislation prohibiting military-style assault weapons.

Reuters added on April 20 that a 19th person had died and by April 21, 22 were reported dead.

RCMP Commissioner Brenda Lucki told the *Canadian Broadcasting Corporation* that there was no indication that the killings were terror-ism-related. Police had not found any confessor note from the killer. The *National Post, AP* and *Global News* reported on April 23 that Wortman had argued with his girlfriend at a party before starting the spree. When they returned to his home, Wortman assaulted her and tied her up. He torched his home. She escaped and hid out in the woods, where police found her at 7 a.m. the next day. (A later *AP* report indicated that she emerged from the woods at 6 a.m. and called 911, telling the police he was driving a mock police car and wearing a police uniform.) He had returned to the party and killed several people. He killed two men and a woman—he knew at least two of them—and set their house on fire. He knocked on the door of people he knew, but they did not answer and told 911 he was armed and driving a police car. He shot a police officer in his replica cruiser, injuring him; the officer escaped. In Shubenacadie, Wortman apparently torched police vehicles after Constable Stevenson and her partner tried to run him off the road and crashed into his vehicle. Wortman shot Stevenson, grabbed Stevenson's gun, and torched the two vehicles. He killed a passerby and took an SUV. He drove to a home and killed a woman he knew. He dropped off his police uniform and stole her car. He was spotted in Central Onslow and in Brookfield. He stopped to get gas and was shot by a police officer who was refueling at 11:26 a.m.

AP added on April 21 that Nova Scotia court records showed that the killer had been ordered to receive counselling for anger management after pleading guilty to assaulting a man in the Halifax area on October 29, 2001. He pleaded guilty on October 7, 2002, as his trial was about to begin. Wortman was given nine months' probation, fined $50 and told to stay away from the man. He was barred from owning or possessing a weapon, ammunition or explosive substances.

AFP reported on April 23 that police were criticized for public communications snafus, using *Twitter* to alert the public to shelter in place rather than use systems that were more commonly used in the area.

Police said Wortman did not have a firearms license for the guns he used in the attacks. Wortman had acquired a pistol in Canada and several long guns in the U.S.

The *Broadcastify* website posted recordings of first responders and dispatchers.

AP reported on April 28 that Wortman had obtained the replica police cruiser at an auction, adding a light bar and decals. He owned four used police cars obtained at auction and collected police uniforms. *AP* and *Reuters* also noted that nine of the victims died in fires Wortman set, the others died by gunshots. Police believed Wortman spent the night in an industrial area, woke up before 6 a.m., and attacked other communities.

The *Washington Post* reported on May 1 that the Canadian government announced an immediate ban on some 1,500 makes and models of "military-grade" assault weapons. Prime Minister Justin Trudeau said, "These weapons were designed for one purpose and one purpose only: to kill the largest amount of people in the shortest amount of time... There is no use — and no place — for such weapons in Canada... you don't need an AR-15 to bring down a deer."

February 24, 2020: *AP* reported on May 19, 2020 that a 17-year-old stabbed a woman to death at a Toronto massage parlor. On May 19, he was charged with terrorism after police said they uncovered evidence he was inspired by an online incel community of sexually frustrated men. He initially was charged with first-degree murder and attempted murder after he stabbed Ashley Noelle Arzaga, 24, several times with the sword. She was found dead in the massage parlor.

June 19, 2020: *ABC News* reported that multiple gun shots were fired at St. Clair Avenue W and St. Clarens Avenue in Toronto, killing one person. Two men fled in a sedan.

July 2, 2020: *Reuters* reported that at 6:40 a.m., police arrested an armed man early on Thursday who had gained access to an exclusive part of Ottawa where Prime Minister Justin Trudeau, 48, lives. Trudeau was not at home at the time. Trudeau and his family live in a large house on the grounds of Rideau Hall, the residence of Governor General Julie Payette, the official representative of Queen Elizabeth. The next day, police said that an armed member of the Canadian military who drove a truck through the gates was

acting alone and faced numerous charges. *Fox News* reported on July 7 that Corey Hurren, 46, was charged with 21 weapons-related offenses, plus threatening to cause death or bodily harm to the prime minister. Prosecutors said Hurren brought a prohibited M-14 rifle, shotguns, a revolver, and a prohibited high-capacity magazine onto the Rideau Hall property. Hurren was an on-duty member of the Canadian military reserves who also ran a gourmet sausage business. He had driven from Manitoba. The *Guardian* reported that Hurren was seen carrying a rifle 13 minutes after he breached the gate before police surrounded him in a greenhouse on the grounds. Police arrested him two hours later.

September 25, 2020: *Al-Jazeera* and *CNN* reported that the Royal Canadian Mounted Police arrested Shehroze Chaudhry, alias Abu Huzayfah, 25, of Burlington, Ontario, for lying about his involvement with ISIS, including conducting executions. The RCMP cited media interviews in which he discussed traveling to Syria in 2016 to join ISIS and committing acts of "terrorism". He was charged with the criminal code offence of perpetrating a hoax related to terrorist activity and was scheduled to appear in court on November 16. He had told *CBC* in 2016 that he was an ISIS enforcer and often witnessed public lashings, beheadings and crucifixions. He appeared on the *New York Times* podcast *Caliphate*, describing shooting blindfolded, bound civilians in the back of the head. He was to appear in court in mid-November, facing charges that carry a five-year sentence.

UNITED STATES

January 11, 2020: *CNN* and the *Washington Post* reported that the federal authorities had decided that more than a dozen Saudi servicemen training at U.S. military installations were to be expelled from the United States after a review that followed the deadly shooting in December 2019 at a Naval Air Station in Pensacola, Florida. The Saudis were not accused of aiding the 21-year-old Saudi Air Force second lieutenant who killed three American sailors, but some were believed linked to extremist movements. Some were also accused of possessing child pornography. NPR reported on January 13 that more than 20 Saudis were to be expelled.

January 16, 2020: The *Washington Post*, *CNN* and *AP* reported that the FBI arrested three alleged white supremacist members of The Base (not the same as al-Qaeda—Arabic for The Base) at residences in Delaware and Maryland who planned to attend a pro-gun rally in Richmond, Virginia. The Department of Justice announced that two men were accused of possessing a machine gun, more than 1,000 rounds of ammunition and body armor parts. The trio were charged with multiple firearms and immigration-related offenses. Brian Mark Lemley, Jr., 33, was accused of transporting a machine gun and transporting a firearm and ammunition with intent to commit a felony. He and William Garfield Bilbrough, IV, 19, were accused of transporting and harboring an alien—Canadian citizen Patrik Jordan Mathews, 27, a former combat engineer in the Canadian Army Reserve. Mathews was charged with transporting a firearm and ammunition with intent to commit a felony, being an alien in possession of a firearm and ammunition, and illegally crossing into the U.S. from Canada in August 2019, days after a police raid on his house in rural Manitoba. The FBI said Lemley and Bilbrough drove from Maryland to Michigan to pick up Mathews after he entered the U.S. near the Manitoba-Minnesota border. They then drove to Maryland's Eastern Shore, where Bilbrough lives. Court documents indicated that Nemley ordered an upper receiver gun part online in November 2019. Court documents also said that in December 2019, Nemley and Mathews built a functioning assault rifle using the part. The two allegedly bought 1,650 rounds of 5.56 mm and 6.5 mm ammunition in January 2020 and practiced using the assault rifle at a Maryland gun range. The duo had been living in Newark, Delaware. Lemley earlier served as a cavalry scout in the Army. The Counter Extremism Project reported that the Base said it was an international network training its members to fight in a race war. Lemley and Mathews faced 10 years in prison. Bilbrough faced five years.

Virginia Governor Ralph Northam issued a temporary state of emergency around the rally, banning weapons on state Capitol grounds. A Richmond judge upheld the order.

NPR reported the next day that the Floyd County Police Department announced that three other white supremacists were in custody in Georgia. *CNN* and the *Washington Post* said Daculi resident Jacob Oliver Kaderli, alias Pestilence, 29; Michael John Helterbrand, 25; and Luke Austin Lane, 21, faced charges of conspiracy to commit murder and participation in a criminal gang known as The Base for planning to overthrow the government and kill a married Antifa couple in Bartow County. Police cited the FBI in saying, "The group was involved in recruiting new members online, meeting to discuss strategy and practicing in paramilitary training camps on a 100-acre tract in Silver Creek." They discussed "the creation of a white ethno-state" and "committing acts of violence against minority communities (including African-Americans and Jewish-Americans)" in encrypted online chat rooms.

Later that day, another alleged neo-Nazi Base member, Yousef O. Barasneh, 22, of Oak Creek, Wisconsin, was arrested for conspiring with other members of The Base in September 2019 to vandalize minority-owned property. The U.S. attorney's office for the Eastern District of Wisconsin charged him with conspiring to violate citizens' rights to use property free from threats and intimidation, saying he vandalized the Beth Israeli Sinai Congregation in Racine, Wisconsin, by spray-painting swastikas and anti-Semitic words on the outside of the synagogue. He faced up to 10 years in prison and up to $250,000 in fines.

The *Washington Post* added on January 18 that an FBI agent had infiltrated the Georgia group, participating in shooting drills run by Lane and Kaderli, apparently in preparation for the "Boogalo" — Base term for the "collapse of the United States and subsequent race war". The agent also learned of Helterbrand's admiration for white supremacist Dylann Roof, the killer of nine black parishioners at a historic church in Charleston, S.C. The agent, Lane, and Kaderli surveilled the target couple's home in Bartow County in December 2019, using code words to hide details of their "camping trip". Lane mused about killing other Base members over worry of the insecurity of the plot, saying they were "stupid" and "would likely talk about it".

February 2020: U.S. Army infantry Private First Class Jarrett William Smith, 24, pleaded guilty to two counts of providing information about explosives to an FBI undercover agent while stationed at Fort Riley, Kansas, in 2019. An FBI affidavit said he talked about targeting an unidentified news organization with a car bomb. *CNN* reported that it was the target. The Anti-Defamation League said Smith was associated with the international neo-Nazi group Feuerkrieg Division (FD) when arrested. FD expressed "consternation" with the arrest on its *Telegram* channel. *Army Times* reported on August 14, 2020 that he was linked to Satanism and hoped to overthrow the U.S. government. Federal public defender Rich Federico argued that Smith had suffered a lifetime of victimization, isolation and trauma and requested leniency, suggesting a 15 month sentence with three years of supervised release. A sentencing hearing was scheduled for August 2020. He faced 20 years in prison and a $250,000 fine. *Military Times* said he had distributed information via social media regarding bombmaking and manufacturing napalm. Smith was born with a cleft lip and palate and bullied in school for his consequent speech impediment. Federico claimed that as a freshman, Smith was on a classmate's "hit list" for a planned school shooting and related plot to bomb his high school. The classmate shot at and missed a high school resource officer and was detained with several pipe bombs in his bag. The shooter had written in a journal: "People would thank me for killing him" next to Smith's name. Federico said Smith's traumas made him "the perfect target for online extremist groups searching for new recruits". Smith joined the military in 2016, but did not fit in, continuing his depression and turning to alcohol.

February 9, 2020: *WJCT* and the *Florida Times-Union* reported that at 2:45 p.m., Gregory William Loel Timm, 27, crashed his GMC Safari minivan into a red tent in the Walmart Supercenter in the Kernan Village shopping complex in the 11900 Atlantic Boulevard area in the Sandalwood neighborhood of Jacksonville, Florida

where Republican volunteers were registering people to vote. He fled, but was captured 4½ hours later a mile away at his home in the 2000 block of Brighton Bay Trail by the Jacksonville Sheriff's Office, who held him on two counts of aggravated assault on a person older than 65 and one count each of criminal mischief and driving with a suspended license. No one was hurt. Circuit Judge Mark Borello ordered Timm held in lieu of $500,000 bail ($250,000 on the two aggravated assault charges; $5,003 on the criminal mischief count; and $2,503 on the suspended license count). Timm did not qualify for a public defender. Timm was not a registered voter. He told police he was a stage hand, and was a member of the local branch of the International Alliance of Theatrical Stage Employees. He had lived in Jacksonville for two years. He was born in Des Moines, Iowa.

The *Florida Times-Union* reported on February 12 that Timm said that someone "had to take a stand" against President Trump.

February 23, 2020: *CNN* reported that at 11:05 a.m., Albany, New York police were notified that a person affiliated with the local Jewish community center received an emailed bomb threat. New York State and local police and three K-9 units responded and found no device inside the center or the neighboring day care center. Rich Azzopardi, spokesman for New York Governor Andrew Cuomo, said that the threat was emailed to Jewish community centers across the state.

March 24, 2020: The *Washington Post 202* reported that Timothy Wilson, 36, who planned to bomb a Missouri hospital during the coronavirus crisis, was shot to death in Belton, Missouri after he went to pick up what he thought was a car bomb. The FBI did not announce whether the gunshot was self-inflicted or the result of a shootout. The FBI announced that he had been the "subject of a months-long domestic terrorism investigation, which revealed him to be a potentially violent extremist, motived by racial, religious, and anti-government animus". The *New York Times* reported that Wilson had also thought about attacking a school with a large population of black students, a mosque, and synagogue. *Vice News* reported that he believed in the neo-Nazi accelerationism view, in which society would collapse because of terrorist attacks.

March 31, 2020: *ABC News* reported that a California Highway Patrol officer arrested California train engineer Eduardo Moreno, 44, who at 1 p.m. allegedly tried to crash a train at full speed into the *USNS Mercy*, the hospital ship treating non-COVID-19 patients at the Port of Los Angeles. He was to be arraigned the next day on train wrecking charges. The train rammed through several concrete and chain barriers, before sliding through a parking lot nearly 250 yards from the *Mercy*, which was undamaged. No one was injured. The train leaked fuel. Moreno allegedly claimed to police and FBI agents that he was suspicious of the *Mercy's* intentions and thought it was part of a government takeover. The U.S. Attorney's Office in the Central District of California said, "Moreno stated that he acted alone and had not pre-planned the attempted attack… While admitting to intentionally derailing and crashing the train, he said he knew it would bring media attention and 'people could see for themselves,' referring to the *Mercy*." The affidavit said Moreno told the FBI that "he did it out of the desire to 'wake people up'".

April 30, 2020: *CNN* reported on May 13, 2020 that in the early morning of April 30, a gunman fired an assault rifle at the Cuban Embassy in Washington, D.C., causing no injuries. Cuban Foreign Minister Bruno Eduardo Rodriguez Parrilla complained of the Trump administration's "complacent silence", noting that "The attacker confessed that he aimed to kill. It's a very serious issue… Can you imagine that which would be the U.S. reaction in a similar case of a similar attack against an American embassy anywhere in the world?" Cuban embassy surveillance video showed the gunman arriving in a car at 2 a.m. and shooting through a fence with an automatic weapon, breaking a window and damaging a metal statue of Jose Martí. Police arrested Alexander Alazo, a Cuban citizen living in the US, and charged him with possessing an unregistered firearm and assault with intent to kill, plus charges related to attacking a foreign embassy. Police confiscated an AK-47 and 32 spent shells, and a gasoline-soaked Cuban flag with

hand-written messages including Trump 2020. Court documents quoted Alazo saying that he heard voices and attacked the Embassy "because he wanted to get them before they got him, referring to the Cuban government". He feared Cuban "criminal organizations" might be tracking him. He had lived out of his car for nine months before the Embassy attack. The court appointed a public defender. Rodriguez Parrilla said Alazo had completed his military service on Cuba and had no history of criminal conduct or mental illness before he moved to Mexico in 2003 and then to the U.S. He returned to Cuba eight times and had worked as a pastor in Cuba.

May 4, 2020: *KRDO* and *ABC News* reported that Bradley Bunn, 53, from Loveland, Colorado, was arrested after FBI and ATF agents found four pipe bombs and "potential pipe bomb components" in his house. Authorities believed he was planning an armed protest against the state's COVID-19 restrictions. Bunn had earlier encouraged people to bring assault rifles to a planned May 1 rally at the Colorado capitol in Denver. He faced 10 years in federal prison and a $250,000 fine.

May 21, 2020: *CNN* reported that a gunman tried to speed through the south Ocean Drive security gate, then opened fire, wounding the female Naval Security Forces base security guard at Naval Air Station Corpus Christi in Texas at 6:15 a.m. The injured guard rolled over and hit a switch that raised a barrier, preventing the gunman from getting onto the base. The gunman was soon "neutralized", according to the U.S. Navy. *AP* and *KWTX* clarified that security forces shot and killed the gunman. No explosives were found. The injured sailor was wearing Kevlar body armor and her protective vest stopped the round. *WOKV* and *AP* reported FBI Supervisory Senior Resident Agent Leah Greeves said that the FBI was investigating the shooting as "terrorism-related" and that authorities were searching for a second person of interest. *Navy Times* identified the suspected gunman as Syrian-born U.S. citizen Adam Salim Alsahli, 20, of Corpus Christi. *KRIS-TV* reported that federal agents seized electronic media from Alsahli's last known address. He had majored in business at Del Mar community college, attending classes in fall 2018, spring 2019 and fall 2019. The FBI said his social media posts on *Twitter*, *Facebook*, and *WhatsApp* showed support for the late AQAP spokesman Ibrahim al-Rabaysh and hardline clerics from Saudi Arabia. Some reports indicated that Alsahli had a pistol, assault rifle, and shotgun.

May 28, 2020: *WOKV* and *AP* reported that Muhammed Momtaz al-Azhari, 23, of Florida, was charged in a terror plot that targeted "busy beaches" by providing material support to ISIS after trying to acquire firearms. Prosecutors said he was arrested on May 24 after taking possession of weapons after negotiating with an undercover FBI employee to purchase guns and silencers, including an AK-47-style rifle allegedly to be used in an attack. He faced a 20-year sentence. The *Tampa Bay Times* reported that he had surveilled several Tampa-area locations. He also visited the site of the 2016 Pulse nightclub massacre of 49 people. Prosecutors said he was recorded as saying, "I don't want to take four or five, no. I want to take at least 50. You know like, brother Omar Mateen in Orlando did. He took 49 with him." Electronic surveillance on May 16 recorded him rehearsing his lines during a planned attack, including, "Know America. Today is your emergency. Today we kill from you guys like you killed from us. This is a revenge for Muslims." He purchased weapons parts via eBay from someone in Texas. USPS stopped the package's delivery and eBay flagged the purchase. The seller cooperated with the FBI, providing details. Public defender Sam Landes said, "The allegations misunderstand both the law and the evidence."

May 28, 2020: *CNN* reported on June 8, 2020 that the U.S. Attorney's Office for the District of Minnesota charged Branden M. Wolfe, 23, of St. Paul, Minnesota with aiding and abetting arson for his alleged role in the May 28 fire that heavily damaged the Third Precinct police station in Minneapolis during protests of George Floyd's murder. Authorities arrested Wolfe on June 3. Prosecutors said that he was wearing several items stolen from the Third Precinct, including body armor, a police-issue duty belt with hand-cuffs, an earphone piece, a baton and a knife. St. Paul police arrested him at a home improvement store while he was wearing the police equipment. Prosecutors noted that he had been fired from the store earlier that day after "referring to social media posts about him stealing items" from the police. Police found in his apartment a riot helmet, a pistol magazine and a police radio.

May 30, 2020: The *Florida Times-Union* reported on June 13, 2020 that the Jacksonville Sheriff's Office on June 11, 2020 arrested Jacksonville man Martin Bryan Silvera-Albor, 22, for the May 30 slashing of a police officer on the right side of his neck during a downtown protest in the Bay Street area. He was charged with aggravated battery of a police officer, battery, resisting an officer without violence and criminal mischief. In 2018 he pleaded guilty to a domestic battery charge.

May 30, 2020: Federal prosecutors in the U.S. District Court in Las Vegas announced the arrest on terrorism-related charges of three white Nevada men with ties to the Boogaloo movement of right-wing extremists advocating generating a civil war to overthrow the U.S. government. Prosecutors said they were conspiring to spark violence during recent protests in Las Vegas. Prosecutors said they conspired to carry out a plan that began in April in conjunction with protests to reopen businesses closed because of the coronavirus. The trio then decided to graft onto the massive protests over the police murder in Minneapolis of George Floyd, an African-American. The trio were en route to a protest in downtown Las Vegas after filling gas cans in a parking lot and making Molotov cocktails in glass bottles. The trio were identified as Stephen T. Parshall, 35, of Las Vegas; Andrew T. Lynam Jr., 23, of suburban Henderson; and William L. Loomis, 40, of Las Vegas. They were each held on $1 million bond in the Clark County jail. Lynam is from suburban Henderson and the others are from Las Vegas. The trio had U.S. military experience: Lynam is an Army reservist; Parshall formerly enlisted in the Navy; Loomis formerly enlisted in the Air Force. The trio faced federal charges of conspiracy to damage and destroy by fire and explosive, and possession of unregistered firearms. They also faced state charges of felony conspiracy, terrorism and explosives possession. Defense attorney Monti Levy represented Loomis on the state charges. A deputy public defender represented Parshall. An attorney was appointed to represent Lynam. A confidential informant met Lynam and Parshall at a Las Vegas rally in April when they were carrying firearms; Lyman said they were "not for joking around and that it was for people who wanted to violently overthrow the United States government". On May 27, according to the informant, Parshall and Loomis "discussed causing an incident to incite chaos and possibly a riot, in response to the death of a suspect". The criminal complaint said Loomis wanted to firebomb a power substation. On May 28, Lynam suggested hitting a fee station at Lake Mead on federal land north of the Hoover Dam, on May 30. The complaint said the group also discussed attacking a U.S. Forest Service ranger station. The informant said that Parshall and Loomis's "idea behind the explosion was to hopefully create civil unrest and rioting throughout Las Vegas".

May 31, 2020: *WOKV* and the *Florida Times Union* reported on June 8-9, 2020 that Ivan Jacob Zecher, 27, of Jacksonville, Florida, was charged with possessing a firearm as a convicted felon and unlawful possession of an unregistered firearm during a protest on May 31 in response to the murder of George Floyd in Minneapolis. The Department of Justice criminal complaint said he was part of a group blocking traffic and throwing things at police officers and cars at Market and Forsyth in Jacksonville. He was initially arrested for unlawful assembly. A search of his backpack revealed a liquor bottle that smelled like gasoline, with a lighter and a hatchet. He called the hatchet a "demolition hammer". Zecher admitted to holding the bottle for someone else and that he knew it had gas inside. The Bureau of Alcohol, Tobacco, Firearms and Explosives determined that the ingredients in the bottle including gasoline and polystyrene—a flammable gel—constituted a "Molotov cocktail" which can be a destructive device and is considered a firearm under federal law. He faced 10 years in prison on each count. He was released on bond. Zecher pleaded guilty on May 15, 2014 and was convict-

ed of aggravated assault with a deadly weapon in Clay County, Florida. He was sentenced to time served and 18 months probation.

June 5, 2020: Police arrested and charged Brooklyn attorneys Colinford Mattis, 32, and Urooj Rahman, 31, in connection with throwing a Molotov cocktail into a police patrol car during protests in Brooklyn following the Minneapolis police murder of George Floyd. A federal appeals court ruled they should not remain in home detention while prosecutors appealed their bail decision. They had been out on bail with electronic monitoring. Brooklyn federal prosecutors charged them with causing damage by fire and explosives to an NYPD car after they allegedly drove a tan minivan to the Fort Greene neighborhood and Rahman threw an explosive into the broken window of an empty patrol car. Mattis was driving. Soon after, police stopped the getaway vehicle and found "precursor items" to build explosives, including a lighter, a beer bottle stuffed with toilet paper and a gasoline tank. Court filings indicated that a witness claimed that Rahman "attempted to distribute" Molotov cocktails to others at the protest "so that those individuals could likewise use the incendiary devices in furtherance of more destruction and violence". Rahman, a Pakistani immigrant, graduated from Fordham Law School; she worked at Bronx Legal Services. Mattis, an African-American, completed New York University Law School after graduating from Princeton University. She was represented by attorney Paul Shechtman, who argued that "she had no intent to harm anyone. This was an empty police vehicle, badly vandalized, one-and-a-half blocks from the police station. There were only two other people around, both of them were taking photographs. There was no crowd nearby."

June 6, 2020: The FBI office in San Francisco announced it was working with the Santa Cruz County Sheriff's Department in investigating the ambush/murder of Santa Cruz Sheriff's Sergeant Damon Gutzwiller, 38, in which two other officers were wounded on the night of June 6 and the fatal drive-by shooting of Federal Protective Service officer David Patrick Underwood, 53, at 1:30 p.m. outside the Donald V. Dellums Federal

Building, which includes the U.S. courthouse in Oakland, California on May 29. Another FPS officer was critically wounded in the latter attack. Surveillance cameras captured a white Ford van. The FPS officers had been monitoring a protest over the police killing of George Floyd. Both attacks involved gunmen in a van. Gutzwiller was a 14-year veteran of the force. A 911 caller said there were guns and bomb-making devices in a suspicious van in Ben Lomond, an unincorporated area near Santa Cruz, on May 29. Deputies chased the van, which pulled into a residential driveway. Gunmen fired on the deputies when they exited their vehicle to investigate. The gunmen also used explosives. Gutzwiller died, a second deputy was hit by either gunfire or shrapnel and was hit by a vehicle. A third California Highway Patrol officer was shot in the hand. Gutzwiller left behind a young son and a pregnant wife. Suspect Steven Carrillo, 32, tried to hijack a car and was shot during his arrest. He was to be charged with first-degree murder. He had arrived at Travis Air Force Base, 50 miles from San Francisco, in June 2018, becoming a member of the 60th Security Forces Squadron. Monika Leigh Scott Carrillo, 30, his wife, who was also in the Air Force, was found dead in an off-base hotel in May 2018 while she was stationed in South Carolina. Sumter County Sheriff's Office and the Air Force Office of Special Investigations ruled her death a suicide.

CNN reported on June 17, 2020 that Steven Carrillo was a member of the right-wing Boogaloo movement. Carrillo was represented by attorney Jeffrey Stotter. CNN added that during the June 6 shootout with Santa Cruz sheriff's deputies, Carrillo wrote Boogaloo phrases "BOOG", "I became unreasonable" and "stop the duopoly" in his own blood on a vehicle he allegedly carjacked while trying to flee. Investigators suggested that he used a homemade AR-15-type "ghost gun" rifle in the shootings. It was recovered. DOD records listed him as serving in Kuwait, Texas, and Utah, and that he was a team leader for Phoenix Raven, a security team that guards Air Force aircraft in high-terrorist and high-crime areas overseas. He could face the death penalty.

Robert Alvin Justus, Jr., allegedly drove the van used in the Oakland shooting, and faced charges of aiding and abetting murder and attempted murder. He told the FBI on June 11 that he had driven the van, but "he did not want to participate in the murder, but that he felt that he had to participate because he was trapped in the van".

June 7, 2020: CNN and WTVR reported that the Henrico County Commonwealth's Attorney Shannon Taylor charged Harry H. Rogers, 36, of Hanover with attempted malicious wounding, felony vandalism, and assault and battery for driving his car through a group of Black Lives Matter protesters in Richmond, Virginia. Prosecutors said Rogers was an "admitted leader of the Ku Klux Klan and a propagandist for Confederate ideology". He was arraigned on June 8. His next hearing was scheduled for August 18. The Washington Post reported on June 25 that Henrico County Commonwealth's Attorney Shannon Taylor added hate crime charges, hit-and-run, and new felonious attempted malicious wounding charges.

June 10, 2020: CNN reported that around 3 a.m., a man opened fire at police cars outside a police station in Paso Robles, California, hitting a sheriff's deputy in the head. The deputy was hospitalized in serious but stable condition. San Luis Obispo County Sheriff Ian Parkinson said that "We feel that this was an ambush that he planned. He intended for officers to come out of the police department and to assault them." Police were searching for a man with dark hair in his 20s or 30s. Police suspected that another case was related after hours later, they found the body of a 58-year-old man near an Amtrak station in the city. He had been shot in the head "at close proximity".

June 10, 2020: CNN, NBC News, The Daily Beast, Reuters, Army Times, and The Guardian reported on June 22, 2020 that the Department of Justice and a federal grand jury indicted U.S. Army Private Ethan Phelan Melzer, 22, of Louisville, Kentucky, with conspiring and attempting to murder U.S. nationals, conspiring and attempting to murder military service members, providing and attempting to provide material support to terrorists and conspiring to murder and maim in a foreign country, in a plot to conduct a "mass casualty" attack against his own unit, spearheaded by members of the Order of the Nine Angles, a Europe-based "Satanist neo-Nazi group". The FBI arrested Melzer on June 10, 2020. The group was founded in the United Kingdom in the 1960s and early 1970s by former neo-Nazi David Myatt. The indictment noted that the Order "espoused violent, neo-Nazi, anti-Semitic, and Satanic beliefs, and have expressed admiration for both Nazis, such as Adolf Hitler, and Islamic jihadists, such as [Osama] Bin Laden, the now-deceased former leader of al-Qaida". Observing that he might die in the attack, Melzer said, "who gives a f-- … it would be another war." Assistant Attorney General for National Security John C. Demers said, "As the indictment lays out, Ethan Melzer plotted a deadly ambush on his fellow soldiers in the service of a diabolical cocktail of ideologies laced with hate and violence. Our women and men in uniform risk their lives for our country, but they should never face such peril at the hands of one of their own." Acting US Attorney Audrey Strauss called Melzer "the enemy within". Melzer was represented by attorney Jennifer Willis. U.S. District Judge Gregory Woods was to preside over the case. *Army Times* reported that Melzer confessed to the plot to the FBI on May 30. He faced a life sentence.

The indictment noted that when Melzer was informed of a redeployment of his unit from Italy to Turkey, where they would guard sensitive U.S. facilities, around April, he sent encrypted messages to the Order, the RapeWaffen Division, and a purported al-Qaeda member, including the unit's anticipated location and security details. He told the Order that although he could be killed, he "would've died successfully". He advocated a jihadi attack on his colleagues.

The *BBC* added that four British teens with ties to the Order had been jailed for terror offenses in the past year; one was convicted of planning a terrorist attack.

Army Times noted that Melzer enlisted as an infantryman through the Army's delayed entry program in December 2018. Army spokes-

man Lieutenant Colonel Emanuel Ortizcruz said Melzer began his active duty service in June 2019. Federal attorneys announced that the staff judge advocate from the 173rd Airborne Brigade, based in Vicenza, Italy, was involved in the investigation.

The Anti-Defamation League explained that the RapeWaffen Division uses *Telegram* to advocate rape and murder to spark a race war.

The FBI said his ideology developed from reading ISIS propaganda. His iCloud account included an ISIS document entitled "Harvest of the soldiers" which described attacks and murders of U.S. personnel.

The *Daily Beast* and *Reuters* reported that one of Melzer's interlocutors had been an FBI informant since May. The news services added that David Myatt wrote a guide for racist terrorists, "A Practical Guide to The Strategy and Tactics of Revolution", saying that they are engaged "in a real war for freedom and for the very future of our race" and listed anti-Nazi activists, "Zionists", judges, police officers, and government officials as appropriate targets for assassination. British police found a copy of the manual in the home of David Copeland in 1999, who was arrested for a bombing spree across London intended to spark a race war. The group of Holocaust deniers believes that "Adolf Hitler was sent by our gods to guide us to greatness". Myatt converted to Islam in 1988 and became an al-Qaeda supporter, although he later renounced extremism and Islam.

June 15, 2020: The *Washington Post, New York Times, Eastern New Mexico News,* and *KOB4* reported that a gunman fired four shots at protesters who wrapped a chain around the neck of a bronze statue in Albuquerque and tied to pull down a monument of Spanish conquistador Juan de Oñate. Militia men wearing military-like garb and carrying semiautomatic rifles formed a protective circle around the gunman, who had been surrounded by the protestors. One man was in critical but stable condition. New Mexico Governor Michelle Lujan Grisham (D) said, "The heavily armed individuals who flaunted themselves at the protest, calling themselves a 'civil guard,' were there for one reason: To menace protesters, to present an unsanctioned show of unregulated force. To menace the people of New Mexico with weaponry — with an implicit threat of violence — is on its face unacceptable; that violence did indeed occur is unspeakable." The militia calls itself the New Mexico Civil Guard. Police detained several militia members. Stephen Ray Baca, 31, was booked for aggravated battery.

June 17, 2020: *CNN* reported that at 1 a.m., Anthony Eaglehorse-Lassandro, 27, drove his car into a group of protesters calling for police reform near Southwest 3rd Avenue near Alder Street in downtown Portland, injuring three. Portland Police said he tried to escape by driving off at "a high rate of speed" and going the wrong way on streets. Police arrested him after he hit another car, a barrier, and tried to run away. He was held on charges of felony hit and run, reckless driving, and possession of a controlled substance.

June 20, 2020: *CNN* reported that at 12:27 a.m., in the 2900 block of Hennepin Avenue South in Minneapolis, a dozen people were shot, one fatally. No one was arrested and the motive was unclear. A witness said two groups were shooting at each other.

June 23, 2020: *BBC One's Panorama* reported that the Southern Poverty Law Center had shared with it secret recordings of efforts by the neo-Nazi The Base to recruit teens. The FBI said The Base tries to unite the world's white supremacists and incite a race war. *BBC* earlier reported that the group's American founder, Rinaldo Nazzaro, 47, was running the group from his apartment in St. Petersburg, Russia. The recordings indicated, according to *BBC*, that Nazzaro and a panel of senior The Base members hosted a conference call on an encrypted app to ask them about their personal history, ethnicity, radicalization journey and experience with weapons.

The *BBC* added that a prominent The Base member was Matthew Baccari, 25, an unemployed Southern Californian, who used the alias Mathias to run the Fascist Forge website, where terrorism and sexual violence were openly encouraged.

June 24, 2020: The *Washington Examiner* reported that the U.S. Department of State released its annual *Country Reports on Terrorism*. Highlights included the designation of Iran as the "world's foremost state sponsor of terrorism". "In the past, Tehran has spent as much as $700 million per year to support terrorist groups, including Hezbollah and Hamas, though its ability to provide financial support in 2019 was constrained by crippling U.S. sanctions." The report charged that Tehran's Islamic Revolutionary Guard Corps was involved in terrorist plots in North and South America, Europe, the Middle East, Asia, and Africa and that "Tehran also continued to permit an al-Qa'ida (AQ) facilitation network to operate in Iran, sending money and fighters to conflict zones in Afghanistan and Syria, and it still allowed AQ members to reside in the country."

Al-Jazeera added that the *Reports* noted that "Pakistan continued to serve as a safe haven for certain regionally focused terrorist groups. It allowed groups targeting Afghanistan, including the Afghan Taliban and affiliated HQN {Haqqani Network}, as well as groups targeting India, including LeT [Lashkar e-Taiba] and its affiliated front organisations, and JeM [Jaish e-Muhammad], to operate from its territory."

June 24, 2020: *Military Times* reported that an Army Criminal Investigative Command investigation of Fort Benning, Georgia-based Army infantry Major William Jeffrey Poole indicated that as Nebor, he had posted racist, far-right anti-government rants on *Reddit*, calling for armed insurrection involving mass murder and destruction. Moderators on an Army subreddit spotted his activity and compiled a 75-page report for CID. He appeared to have worked alone.

June 27, 2020: *WDRB* reported that Louisville Mayor Greg Fischer announced that a man opened fire from the edge of the protest area at a local park at around 9 p.m., killing Tyler Gerth, 27, a photographer capturing images of the protests. Police arrested the suspect, who was wounded and in custody at a hospital. The demonstrators were protesting police brutality and the death of Breonna Taylor. Fischer said "several people" fired weapons in Jefferson Square Park. Video showed a man in shorts and a tank top firing a gun in the direction of tents set up in the park. Interim police chief Robert Schroeder said the suspect had participated in the protests since they started. The man been arrested several times in recent weeks and protestors asked him to leave the park because of his "disruptive behavior". Jasmine Harris, 27, said she heard six shots.

July 4, 2020: *CNN* and *AP* reported that at 1:30 a.m., Dawit Kelete, 27, of Seattle, drove a white Jaguar into a group of Black Femme protestors on closed highway I-5 in Seattle, seriously injuring two women. A protestor hopped into a car and chased Kelete for a mile, eventually pulling in front of Kelete's car, stopping him. Captain Ron Mead of the Washington State Patrol said Kelete was held on two counts of vehicular assault. Bail was denied. Seattle veterinary worker Summer Taylor, 24, suffered life-threatening injuries. Diaz Love, 32, from Bellingham, Washington (according to *CNN*; *AP* said she was from Portland, Oregon), sustained serious injuries, including internal injuries and fractured arms and legs. Kelete attended Washington State University between 2011 and 2017, majoring in business and commerce. Summer Taylor died on July 7 at Seattle's Harborview Medical Center. The *Washington Post* reported on July 8 that the King County Prosecuting Attorney's Office charged Kelete with reckless driving, vehicular assault and vehicular homicide. A King County judge had earlier set bail at $1.2 million. Arraignment was scheduled for July 22. Kelete was represented by defense attorney John Henry Browne.

The *Washington Post* and *New York Times* reported that Ari E. Weil, an expert on terrorist tactics at the University of Chicago, found that since George Floyd's police killing in Minneapolis on May 25, drivers had attacked people more than 65 times. *USA Today* on July 10 put the number since May 27 at 66 vehicle-ramming attacks. Weil said at least 19 of the 59 civilian incidents were malicious.

July 6, 2020: *CNN* and *WRTV* reported that a red Toyota crashed into an electric scooter as a Black Lives Matter protest in Bloomington, Indiana was ending in the evening. A male passenger got out and threw the scooter aside. A woman, 29, stood in front of the car and put her hands on the hood. The female driver accelerated, throwing the 29-year-old onto the hood. A man, 35, grabbed the driver's side, holding on to the car as it sped off. The two people were injured, falling off when the car made a quick right turn. Geoff Stewart suffered abrasions to his arms; the woman was knocked unconscious and hospitalized with a laceration to her head.

July 15, 2020: *Business Insider* and *Reuters* reported that the Trump Administration in June released convicted Lebanese terrorist financier Kassim Tajideen, 65, who had pleaded guilty to laundering more than $1 billion for Hizballah, after he had served a year of a five-year prison sentence. A Lebanese security official and a senior Lebanese politician told *Insider* that he was freed from a federal prison in an ongoing series of prisoner swaps between the U.S. and Iran. The release was initially called a "purely judicial" humanitarian move over concerns he might contract COVID in prison. *Reuters* reported that General Abbas Ibrahim, the chief of Lebanon's General Security Directorate domestic intelligence service, brokered the arrangement.

July 29, 2020: The *Florida Times-Union, CNN, USA Today* and *Treasure Coast Newspapers* reported that all 50 U.S. states issued warnings about not opening mysterious, unsolicited packages of seeds that had arrived via mail throughout the U.S. in recent weeks. Florida logged 160 such packages. The U.S. Department of Agriculture said that it appeared that the packages included sender addresses from the official *China Post*, which the Chinese Foreign Ministry said were forged. Some of the labels indicated that the packages contained jewelry, although inside was a packet of seeds in clear, plastic packaging. The identity of the sender and his/her/their motivation was unclear. USDA said, "At this time, we don't have any evidence indicating this is something other than a 'brushing scam' where people receive unsolicited items from a seller who then posts false customer reviews to boost sales." Katherine Hutt, chief communications officer for the Better Business Bureau, said, "When people get a package that they didn't order, that's one of the first things that we suspect close up" and The Canadian Food Inspection Agency, the USDA's Animal and Plant Health Inspection

Service (APHIS), the Department of Homeland Security's Customs and Border Protection, other federal agencies, and state agriculture departments opened investigations. Authorities counseled recipients to not open the packages, not plant the seeds, and not throw them away to ensure that they did not sprout in landfills and pose an agricultural risk. Recipients should also keep the packaging and mailing label intact. Florida Agriculture Commissioner Nikki Fried warned "Plant seeds from unknown sources may introduce dangerous pathogens, diseases, or invasive species into Florida, putting agriculture and our state's plant, animal, and human health at risk."

August 13, 2020: *CNN* reported that the U.S. Department of Justice seized $2 million worth of cryptocurrency from ISIS, al-Qaeda, and the al-Qassam Brigades (the military wing of Hamas), saying that it likely would have been used by terrorist groups to purchase weapons and train likely attackers. It was the largest U.S. government seizure of terrorist online assets. John Demers, Assistant Attorney General in charge of DOJ's National Security Division, told reporters, "Two million dollars is a lot of equipment that they can buy, a lot of weapons, a lot of training that they can fund, a lot of tickets to fly people around the world... This is going to make a big difference in their operation." DOJ seized 300 cryptocurrency accounts, four websites, and four *Facebook* pages. One of the sites was allegedly created by ISIS in February 2020 to dupe purchasers into buying personal protective equipment to protect against the spread of the coronavirus. Teams from DOJ, Homeland Security and the IRS contributed to 87 pages of civil forfeiture complaints unsealed in federal court in Washington, D.C.

August 18, 2020: The *Washington Post* and *Defense One* reported that U.S. Attorney General William P. Barr sent a letter to British Home Secretary Priti Patel indicating that the U.S. would not pursue the death penalty for ISIS "Beatles" Alexanda Kotey and El Shafee Elsheikh if London by October 15 transferred evidence to aid their prosecution for suspected involvement in the executions of American, British and other foreign hostages in Syria. The

duo were otherwise to be handed over to Iraq for prosecution. The U.S. military was detaining them in Iraq. *Reuters* added on August 26 that the UK Supreme Court permitted the release of evidence to U.S. authorities, ending legal action by Elsheikh's mother, Maha el-Gizouli.

August 25, 2020: *CNN* reported that two demonstrators were shot to death and a third was seriously injured while protesting the police shooting of Jacob Blake, 29, a Black man, seven times in the back; Blake survived but was paralyzed from the waist down. Kenosha, Wisconsin Police Chief Daniel Miskinis announced the arrest of Kyle Rittenhouse, 17, of Antioch, Illinois, a former member of a youth police cadet program, on one count of first-degree intentional homicide. Rittenhouse was held in Lake County, Illinois; an extradition hearing was scheduled for August 28. He was also charged as a fugitive from justice. Under Wisconsin law, he would be tried as an adult. Miskinis added that the shooting might not have occurred if the demonstrators and accused gunman had obeyed the city's 8 p.m. curfew, observing, "Everybody involved was out after the curfew. I'm not gonna make a great deal of it but the point is the curfew's in place to protect. Had persons not been out involved in violation of that, perhaps the situation that unfolded would not have happened." A cell phone video of the incident recorded a young white man firing a semi-automatic rifle and saying, "I just killed somebody." Video showed him calmly walking past police while he carried the gun.

Police said Rittenhouse had an affinity for police, guns, and President Trump.

The victims were a 26-year-old from Silver Lake, Wisconsin and a 36-year-old from Kenosha. Rittenhouse faced felony charges of murdering Anthony M. Huber and Joseph Rosenbaum and felony attempted homicide for wounding Gaige Grosskreutz. He was also charged with misdemeanor possession of a dangerous weapon while under the age of 18.

CNN reported on November 20, 2020 the Rittenhouse was released after posting $2 million in bail. Attorney Lin Wood tweeted that Mike Lindell, CEO of My Pillow, Inc., and actor Ricky Schroder helped raise the money.

The *Washington Post* reported that Rittenhouse said he used federal stimulus money to purchase the gun he used.

August 29, 2020: *Business Insider* reported that the U.S. Department of Justice shut down an ISIS-affiliated website, FaceMaskCenter.com, that was selling fake N95 masks claimed to be FDA-approved and other fake personal protective equipment (PPE). The site accepted credit cards. A Syrian living in Turkey claimed that he could provide up to 100,000 N95 masks, which were manufactured in Turkey. The site said it was "the original online personal protective equipment supplier and was the first of its kind" since its inception in 1996, although it was created on February 26, 2020. The DOJ complaint named Turkey-based Murat Cakar an ISIS facilitator who was accused of managing the scheme and accepting $100,000 from Zoobia Shahnaz, an American who pleaded guilty in 2018 to financially supporting ISIS and attempting to travel to Syria to join the group. DOJ also said Cakar was involved in ISIS hacking operations.

September 2, 2020: *AFP* and *The Hill* reported that Texas-born Omer Kuzu, 23, who spent five years handling ISIS telecommunications operations before the Syrian Democratic Forces captured him in 2019, pleaded guilty to one count of conspiring to provide material support to a terrorist group. Omer and his brother, Yusuf, went to Turkey on October 16, 2014, then were smuggled by "ISIS taxi" into Syria and then to ISIS-held territory in Mosul, Iraq. Although trained as a fighter with 40 others in five days of physical and weapons courses, he helped to repair telecommunications equipment. Upon capture with 1,500 others in March 2019, he was sent to the United States. He appeared in federal court in Texas on August 1, 2019. He faced 20 years in prison. Sentencing was scheduled for January 22, 2021.

September 3, 2020: *CNN* and *Newsweek* reported that federal agents arrested Michael Robert Solomon, 30, of New Brighton, Minnesota, and Benjamin Ryan Teeter, 22, of Hampstead, North Carolina, members of the Boogaloo Bois, on charges of conspiring and attempting to become "assets" of a foreign terrorist organization (Hamas) that share their "anti-U.S. government views". A formal detention hearing was scheduled for September 9 in U.S. District Court in Minneapolis, Minnesota. The FBI noted that they had carried firearms at a George Floyd protest in late May and claimed to be members of the "Boojahideen" that planned to attack police officers and aimed at "overthrowing the government and replacing its police forces". The criminal complaint said they discussed stealing weapons and "bombs" from a National Guard Armory and would assassinate white supremacists while someone recorded it. In June, a confidential informant told the FBI that the duo told a purported Hamas member that they wanted to be "mercenaries" for the group. Solomon told an undercover FBI agent posing as a Hamas member that the duo "would be an asset to Hamas" because "we've got to be pretty valuable because two American-born white boys, right? We can move around like nothing. I can take anything anywhere." The duo told the FBI agent they wanted to destroy "government monuments, raiding the headquarters of a white supremacist organization in North Carolina, and targeting politicians and members of the media". Teeter allegedly added, "If I have to shoot someone I'm not going to call the cops and stick around." Solomon replied, "If you're carrying for self-defense you're going to call the cops and go through the process… If we are able to accomplish our goals, the US would be f***ing done." On tape, Solomon shied away from blowing up courthouses, preferring to "take down twenty senators while they're f***king playing baseball". The duo claimed they could make unmarked, untraceable and unregistered parts for guns and weapons with $700 of equipment.

Teeter told *CNN* in a June interview that he went to Minneapolis to protect protestors from police abuse and white supremacists. He claimed to be a non-voting "left anarchist" and a member of the LGBT community, observing, "people think I'm part of a Nazi group—I'm not… If people are going to initiate deadly force against us, we need to be willing and able to initiate deadly force in return… We are very careful to make sure that people realize that we are on their side. We are here to defend them… Once people realize that we are on their side and we are here to protect them, everybody has been—almost everybody—has been very happy to have us here."

September 18, 2020: *CNN, AFP, al-Jazeera, Reuters,* the *New York Times,* and the *Washington Post* reported that postal service officers at the White House mail handling facility intercepted a package containing ricin that was addressed to President Trump. The package apparently was mailed from St. Hubert, Quebec, Canada. *CNN* reported on September 20 that Quebec woman Pascale Cecile Veronique Ferrier, 53, who was carrying a knife and a loaded gun and suspected of sending the letter, was arrested while trying to enter the U.S. from Fort Erie, Ontario, Canada at the Peace Bridge border crossing into Buffalo, New York. She appeared before U.S. District Magistrate Judge H. Kenneth Schroeder, Jr., in federal court in Buffalo, New York on September 22 on charges of threatening the President of the United States. Canadian police searched a Montreal apartment linked to the French-Canadian dual national who was suspected of sending six letters. Five were sent to a sheriff's office and other law enforcement and detention facilities in south Texas. The police department in Mission, Texas, turned over one of the suspicious letters to the FBI. Investigators matched her fingerprints to four of the letters.

Hidalgo County District Attorney Ricardo Rodriguez Jr., said Mission police arrested her in early 2019 during a traffic stop. She was held on a weapons charge and record-tampering offense before being turned over to U.S. immigration officials and deported. He said she had been in Texas to protest construction of the U.S.-Mexico anti-immigrant border wall.

Ferrier appeared before U.S. District Judge H. Kenneth Schroeder, Jr., in federal court in Buffalo, New York on September 22 on charges of threatening the President of the United States. Via a French-English interpreter, she requested a court-appointed lawyer. Judge Schroeder entered a not-guilty plea on her behalf. A special hearing was scheduled for September 28. She was deemed a flight risk and was held without bail. The defense said it would exercise her right to contest her identity as the person named in the criminal complaint.

An FBI special agent bomb technician filed an affidavit indicating that she had enclosed a note in the letter which said, "I found a new name for you: 'The Ugly Tyrant Clown' I hope you like it… You ruin USA and lead them to disaster. Give up and remove your application for this election. So I made a "Special Gift" for you to make a decision. This gift is in this letter. If it doesn't work, I'll find better recipe for another poison, or I might use my gun when I'll be able to come. Enjoy! FREE REBEL SPIRIT." Investigators found six other letters sent to Texas in mid-September to people staffing detention centers where she was held in 2019 after her arrest for weapons possession.

Reuters reported on September 28 that Judge Schroeder declared Ferrier a flight risk and "a continuing danger" to Trump and to members of the community and ordered her detained and transferred via the U.S. Marshals Service to Washington, D.C., where she was indicted on charges of threatening to kill and injure the president. A grand jury had returned an indictment on September 24. He noted that she was carrying nearly 300 rounds of ammunition with her upon arrest. Traces of ricin were found at her Quebec home.

September 21, 2020: *CNN* reported that a group of people found 39 razor blades around playground equipment in Howe Park in Eaton Rapids, Michigan. City workers found two more in the grass at GAR Memorial Island. City police said that "Some of the blades appeared to have been placed intentionally to cause harm." Witnesses saw four teens on Howe playground equipment. The city offered a $2,500 reward for information leading to the arrest of the suspects.

September 28, 2020: *USA Today* cited a study by the University of Chicago's Project on Security and Threats that found that there were 104 incidents of people driving vehicles into protests from May 27 through September 5—96 by civilians and eight by police—causing two deaths. At least 43 were malicious; 39 drivers were charged.

September 30, 2020: *AFP* reported on October 1, 2020 that the previous day, the U.S. Department of Justice filed charges against a Trinidadian-American father and son who joined ISIS in 2015. DOJ claimed that it had repatriated 27 Americans who traveled to Syria and Iraq to join ISIS, and called on the rest of the world to follow its lead. It had filed terrorist support charges against some of the returnees, including

- Kazakhstan-born, naturalized U.S. citizen Ruslan Maratovich Asainov, 44, whom prosecutors identified as an ISIS sniper and weapons trainer.

- Texas-born Omer Kuzu, who at age 17 went to Syria with his brother in 2014 and worked as an ISIS communications specialist before his capture in 2019

- Samantha Marie Elhassani, who was charged in Chicago federal court with material support for a designated terrorist group in 2018. She argued that her husband forced her and her two children to go to Syria in 2015. Charges were reduced to providing financial support for a terrorist group after she admitted carrying money to Hong Kong for her husband. She faced a 10 year sentence.

October 6, 2020: U.S. District Judge Leonie Brinkema in Alexandria, Virginia denied the request for compassionate release of Ardit Ferizi, 24, a computer hacker who gave ISIS personal data of more than 1,300 U.S. government and military personnel, and ruled that the Kosovo native should remain in federal prison in Lewisburg, Pennsylvania, to serve his 20-year sentence. Ferizi was the first person convicted in the U.S. of both computer hacking and terrorism charges. He could be released in 2032 if he was to be credited for good behavior. He had asked for release because his asthma and obesity place him at greater risk of contracting COVID-19.

October 7, 2020: The *Washington Post* reported that the Department of Justice charged Alexanda Kotey and El Shafee Elsheikh, two of the British-accented ISIS "Beatles", in Alexandria, Virginia federal court for involvement in the torture and beheading of American journalists and aid workers. The duo had flown that day to the U.S. from Iraq to face charges of hostage-taking resulting in death, conspiracy to murder U.S.

citizens outside the United States, conspiracy to provide material support to a foreign terrorist organization and related conspiracy charges. They faced life in prison.

AFP reported on October 9 that the duo pleaded not guilty via videolink to the U.S. District Court in Alexandria, Virginia to charges of conspiracy to murder American journalists James Foley and Steven Sotloff and relief workers Peter Kassig and Kayla Mueller. Judge T.S. Ellis called the case "complex and unusual" and set the next hearing for January 15, 2021. The duo were also suspected of involvement in the killing of two Britons, Alan Henning and David Haines, and several other hostages, including two Japanese nationals. The eight-count U.S. grand jury indictment charged them with hostage-taking, conspiracy to commit murder and other offenses.

October 7, 2020: *NBC News, WXYZ, Washington Post, Reuters, Washington Post 202, USA Today* and *AP* reported that the FBI and Michigan State Police conducted a nighttime raid that extended into the morning on a home in Hartland Meadows near M-59 in Livingston County, arresting six militiamen—Adam Fox, Barry Croft, Ty Garbin, 24, Kaleb Franks, Daniel Harris, and Brandon Caserta—plotting to kidnap Michigan Governor Gretchen Whitmer (D) and try her at a "secure location" in Wisconsin for treason. Five of them were Michigan residents; Croft is from Delaware.

In July, informants attended and recorded a meeting in which the men "discussed attacking a Michigan State Police facility, and in a separate conversation after the meeting, Garbin suggested shooting up the Governor's vacation home". In a July 27 meeting, a defendant told an informant, "Snatch and grab, man. Grab the f---ing governor. Just grab the b----. Because at that point, we do that, dude — it's over." A member of a Michigan militia group who was involved in a Second Amendment rally at the Michigan statehouse in June, told the FBI that the group was considering killing police officers. Militia groups and others had opposed Whitmer's pandemic restrictions, including closing gyms. The six had apparently kept the larger militia out of their plans. Federal and state officials charged 13 people in planning to attack law enforcement, overthrow the government and ignite a civil war. The group had considered attacking police in their homes, had trained in firearms, and had experimented with explosives.

The *Detroit Free Press* reported that the group planned for 200 men to raid the state Capitol and throw Molotov cocktails at responding police cars, kidnapping Whitmer and others. They had purchased weapons and surveilled targets, but were infiltrated by the FBI, which became aware of them via social media in early 2020. The Bureau monitored a meeting in June 20 in Grand Rapids, Michigan. The FBI said that one member of the group, Adam Fox, contacted a local militia group already under FBI surveillance, saying he needed "200 men" for the attack on Whitmer, which could take place when she was entering or leaving her vacation home or the governor's official summer residence. The FBI said he used code words such as "cupcakes" for explosives and referred to a "baker", possibly a bombmaker.

Federal authorities charged six plotters with conspiracy to commit kidnapping. State officials charged another seven linked to the Wolverine Watchmen militia with providing material support to terrorists and other related offenses.

Whitmer, referring to President Trump's recent comments, observed, "When our leaders speak, their words matter. They carry weight… When our leaders meet with, encourage, or fraternize with domestic terrorists, they legitimize their actions, and they are complicit."

Caserta said on social media that he was an anarchist who opposes all forms of government and said in a *YouTube* video in 2020 that "every person who works for government is your enemy." He posted video of himself on *YouTube* on September 15 saying, "F--- the government" and aimed an assault-style rifle at a point off camera, showing how quickly he can load a magazine. His *LinkedIn* page said he was a mechanic at a bike shop. "I am inquiring about career opportunities in the manufacturing industry." He claimed he graduated from high school in 2006.

Croft last tweeted on June 8, 2019, complaining that *Facebook* had expelled him for violating its community standards. "Fascistbook hard at work protecting People who abuse chil-

dren." He tweeted on February 14, 2017 that he was "Standing with Trump!" He posted "Liberal: n. - 1. A spineless, jellyfish like creature, that goes wherever the current pushes them 2. A person with no moral compass."

Prosecutors said the Wolverine Watchmen met periodically for "field training" in preparation for "the boogaloo"—an expected civil war or violent uprising against the government. Joseph Morrison allegedly founded the Watchmen group and called himself "Boogaloo Bunyan" online. Morrison, 26, lives with Pete Musico, 42, in Munith, Michigan, hosting the training exercises.

Federal prosecutors said the Wolverine Watchmen trained and discussed possible attacks with Fox and five of his associates charged with federal crimes and that some of the Wolverine Watchmen group — Shawn Fix, 38; William Null, 38; Michael Null, 38; and Eric Molitor, 36 — helped surveill governor's private vacation home. Court documents alleged that another member of the Wolverine Watchmen, Paul Bellar, 21, was given the role of "sergeant" and helped train the group because of his expertise with firearms. The group had purchased an 800,000-volt Taser and night goggles. More than a dozen people from several states met in Dublin, Ohio on June 6, 2020 to discuss creating a society that followed the Bill of Rights.

Michigan Attorney General Dana Nessel said the plotters sought the home addresses of law enforcement officers to threaten them with violence. She announced that 19 state felony charges were filed against Paul Bellar, Shawn Fix, Eric Molitor, Michael Null, William Null, Pete Musico and Joseph Morrison, including allegations of providing support for terrorist acts. Six were arraigned by October 10. Bond for Eric Molitor, 36; Shawn Fix, 38; Michael Null, 38; and William Null, 38; was set at $250,000. The four were charged with providing material support for terrorist acts and carrying or possessing a firearm during commission of a felony. Joseph Morrison, 26, and his father-in-law, Pete Musico, 42, were given $10 million cash bond. They each faced the same charges as the others plus additional counts of a threat of terrorism and gang membership. Attorney Philip C. Curtis represented Musico. Attorney George D. Lyons represented Morrison. A seventh person, Paul Bellar, 21, was arrested in Columbia, South Carolina and awaiting extradition on charges of material support for terrorist acts, gang membership and carrying or possessing a gun during commission of a felony.

President Trump complained that Whitmer didn't thank him for his DOJ and FBI having stopped the plotters, noting she "has done a terrible job. She locked down her state for everyone, except her husband's boating activities. The Federal Government provided tremendous help to the Great People of Michigan... My Justice Department and Federal Law Enforcement announced they foiled a dangerous plot. Rather than say thank you, she calls me a White Supremacist."

Whitmer wrote in the *Washington Post* op-ed page on October 10:

"When I addressed the people of Michigan on Thursday to comment on the unprecedented terrorism, conspiracy and weapons charges against 13 men, some of whom were preparing to kidnap and possibly kill me, I said, "Hatred, bigotry and violence have no place in the great state of Michigan." I meant it. But just moments later, President Trump's campaign adviser, Jason Miller, appeared on national television accusing me of fostering hatred.

"I'm not going to waste my time arguing with the president. But I will always hold him accountable. Because when our leaders speak, their words carry weight.

"When our leaders encourage domestic terrorists, they legitimize their actions. When they stoke and contribute to hate speech, they are complicit. And when a sitting president stands on a national stage refusing to condemn white supremacists and hate groups, as President Trump did when he told the Proud Boys to "stand back and stand by" during the first presidential debate, he is complicit. Hate groups heard the president's words not as a rebuke, but as a rallying cry. As a call to action.

"2020 should be the year for national unity. In the midst of the worst public health crisis we have seen in our lifetimes, we should all come together as Americans to fight covid-19 and protect each other.

"But this country is more divided than ever. And instead of uniting the country, our president has spent the past seven months denying science, ignoring his own health experts, stoking distrust, and fomenting anger and giving comfort to those who spread fear and hatred and division. He has proved time and again that he is more focused on his chances in the upcoming election and picking fights with me and Democrats across the country than he is on protecting our families, front-line workers and small businesses from covid-19.

"As a result, at least 212,000 Americans are dead. More than 60 million have filed for unemployment. And still, the president has not developed a national strategy on testing, protective medical equipment or masks.

"This year has been hard for all of us. It's been hard for our doctors and nurses, for truck drivers and grocery store workers, for teachers and students and parents, and for those who have had to stay isolated to stay safe. And it is not over yet.

"I've said it many times—we are not one another's enemy. This virus is our enemy. And this enemy is relentless. It does not care if you are a Republican or a Democrat, young or old, rich or poor. It does not care if we are tired of it.

"It threatens us all—our lives, our families, our jobs, our businesses and our economy. It preys on our elderly and medically vulnerable residents, and it has exposed deep inequities in our society.

"For the past seven months, I have made the tough choices to keep our state safe. These have been gut-wrenching decisions no governor has ever had to make.

"When I get out of bed every morning, I think about the high school seniors, such as my daughter, who missed graduation ceremonies. I think about those who have missed weddings and funerals. I think about all the parents who are working from home, making breakfast every day, logging kids into their Zoom classes and doing laundry. I think about the small-business owners who spent a lifetime building something great, who are now hanging on by their fingernails just to keep the lights on.

"And I think about the 212,000 Americans

who have died as a result of this virus. Deaths that could have been avoided, had the president treated covid-19 like the crisis he has known it to be from the beginning.

"The disruption this virus has caused to our daily lives is immeasurable. But our hard work and sacrifices have saved thousands of lives. Michigan has one of the strongest economic recoveries in the nation.

"There will be more hard days ahead. But we must all show a little kindness and a lot more empathy. Give one another some grace. And let's take care of each other.

"Wear your mask. Stay six feet apart. Wash your hands frequently. And look out for your neighbors.

"We will get through this together."

Reuters reported that Musico, Michael Null, and William Null, all armed, had joined hundreds of protesters who entered the capitol building on April 30 as state lawmakers debated Whitmer's request to extend her emergency powers to battle the pandemic.

The *Washington Post* added that Fox was in tough financial straits and was living in a storage cellar, accessed through a trap door, beneath a friend's (Brian Titus) Vac Shack vacuum shop after his girlfriend kicked him out of her home. Fox held a planning meeting in the basement on June 20.

Attorney Parker Douglas represented Daniel Harris, 23, a former Marine who lived at home with his parents, did construction work, and attended a Black Lives Matter protest in June.

William Null had told Barry County Sheriff Dar Leaf that he wanted to start his own cause: My Life Matters, which he would eventually turn into the Michigan Liberty Militia.

Marine Corps Times reported that two of the accused were former Marines: Cpl. Daniel Harris and Lance Cpl. Joseph Morrison.

- Morrison, a reservist, joined the Corps in March 2015 and was discharged as a lance corporal the day he was charged. He was assigned to Engineer Support Company, 6th Engineer Support Battalion, 4th Marine Logistics Group, Battle Creek, Michigan. Awards included the National Defense Service Medal and the Selected Marine Corps Reserve Medal.

- Harris, an 0311, joined the Corps in June 2015 and was discharged in June 2019 after serving with 3rd Battalion, 2nd Marines, based out of Camp Lejeune, North Carolina. Awards included the Good Conduct Medal, the Humanitarian Service Medal, the National Defense Service Medal, the Global War on Terrorism Service Medal, the Korean Defense Service Medal and the Sea Service Deployment Ribbon.

The *Washington Post* reported on October 13 that FBI Special Agent Richard Trask testified at a court hearing in Grand Rapids, Michigan that the group had discussed also "taking" Virginia Governor Ralph Northam (D) during a meeting of suspects in Dublin, Ohio. They considered setting Whitmer adrift in Lake Michigan.

The *Detroit Free Press* reported on October 13 that Magistrate Judge Sally Berens ordered Kaleb Franks, Daniel Harris and Brandon Caserta to be held without bond, and would rule later on the bond status of Adam Fox and Ty Garbin.

CNN reported on October 26 that Mark Satawa, Ty Garbin's lawyer, said his client was just "playing army". Garbin was charged with conspiracy to commit kidnapping.

USA Today, the *Detroit Free Press*, and *Florida Times-Union* reported that the Michigan Attorney General's Office announced that Adam Fox's Plan A for the attack on the Michigan State Capitol would have entailed taking hostages and televising the execution of government employees, or locking the doors and setting the building on fire. The description was part of the brief filed by the Attorney General's Office in Jackson County's 12th District Court against Pete Musico, 42, of Munith, Michigan. Musico's bond was reduced from $10 million to $100,000 after his October 23 hearing. The Jackson County Sheriff's Office announced that Musico was freed on bond on October 30 with a GPS tether. The filing also said that Musico had claimed to have thrown a Molotov cocktail into a police officer's home and that he tried to get a Michigan State Police trooper to touch him at a rally at the Michigan State Capitol in 2020. Musico was represented by attorney Kareem Johnson. Fox was represented by federal public defender Kareem Johnson.

On December 16, 2020, federal prosecutors indicted Barry Croft, Daniel Harris, Ty Garbin, Kaleb Franks, Adam Fox and Brandon Caserta on a federal kidnapping conspiracy charge in the alleged plot. The latter five pleaded not guilty to the indictment in proceedings on December 17. The five defendants had been in custody since being arrested in October. Josh Blanchard, an attorney for Barry Croft, said his client had not yet been arraigned. The indictment said that between June 6 and October 7, the group conspired to "unlawfully seize, kidnap, abduct and carry away, and hold for ransom and reward" Whitmer, by planning to kidnap her from a vacation home and blow up a bridge to delay law enforcement. Michigan had charged another eight people; seven of them are associated with the Wolverine Watchmen group. A federal magistrate judge had ruled in mid-October that there was ample evidence of probable cause for Harris, Garbin, Franks, Fox and Caserta to stand trial.

October 13, 2020: The *Daily Beast* reported that the U.S. Attorney's office for the Eastern District of Virginia was seeking the extradition to the U.S. of five American citizens who had fled the country to Pakistan in 2009 to fight for the al-Qaeda-linked Lashkar-e-Taiba and Jaish-e-Mohammed terrorist groups. The five were identified as Waqar Hussain Khan, Ahmed Minni, Ramy Zamzam, Aman Yemer, and Umar Farooq. They were indicted in 2017; the indictment was unsealed in late 2019 without public notice. The FBI referred to them as the Five Guys, whom Pakistan arrested on terrorism charges and jailed in 2009. Federal prosecutors wanted to try them for conspiracy to provide material support to terrorists based on an indictment filed while they were in prison.

Ramy Zamzam, purported group leader, served as president of Howard University's Muslim Student Association and was a dental student.

In early December 2009, the five flew from Dulles Airport to Karachi. Pakistani authorities arrested them five days later at the house of a relative. They had been radicalized in part by jihadi online videos showing attacks on the U.S. Army.

Also potentially open to federal charges was Kary Kleman, a Florida man who converted to Islam in 2011 and moved to Syria in 2015. Turkey arrested him in 2017 and sentenced him to prison in 2018 on terrorism charges. His sentence ends in 2024.

October 22, 2020: The *Washington Post* and *WBTV* reported that federal court documents indicated that Alexander Hillel Treisman, alias Alexander S. Theiss, 19, had searched online for Democratic Party Presidential candidate and former Vice President Joe Biden's home address and for night-vision goggles and purchased an AR-15 in New Hampshire. He had posted in April 2020 "Should I kill Joe Biden?" on the meme-sharing site *iFunny*, popular with white nationalists and far-right propaganda. The *Daily Beast* reported that on May 3, Treisman went to a Wendy's within four miles of Biden's Delaware home. He was arrested on May 28 after tellers at the Fifth Third Bank in Kannapolis, North Carolina, reported a white Ford van abandoned in the parking lot. Police found in his van four rifles, a 9mm handgun, explosive materials, ammunition, books on bomb making, and $509,000 in cash, possibly his inheritance. Police initially arrested Treisman, who was carrying identification cards for Washington state, California and Florida, for carrying a concealed weapon; he had purchased weapons in at least four states. Federal officials then allegedly found 6,721 images and 1,248 videos of child pornography on eight digital devices. Treisman pleaded not guilty to three federal counts of child pornography in October. A federal magistrate judge filed an order in early October outlining why Treisman should remain in custody. Treisman's attorney said his client had been diagnosed with Asperger's syndrome. Judge Joe L. Webster, a federal magistrate in Durham, North Carolina, denied bail because "the record establishes by clear and convincing evidence that no combination of available release conditions would reasonably assure the safety of the community".

Federal authorities added that in October 2019, Treisman created a note on his phone that outlined "a plan to perform a mass shooting at a mall food court on Christmas or Black Friday". Posting on *Reddit* as AlextheBodacious, he talked about executing those he hated and stated that he was "going to do a columbine for a while,

[but] I think it would better to put it towards something more memorable". A video taken from Treisman's cellphone in April 2020 showed him driving by the Mandalay Bay Casino in Las Vegas and praising the 2017 massacre that killed 58 and injured more than 500. "That's the one, that's where they did it … nice," he said. In a cellphone video taken in April 2020 at O'Hare International Airport in Chicago, a male voice opined that it would be "awesome" to hijack a plane and crash it into a building.

October 28, 2020: *USA Today* and *WPVI* reported that Philadelphia police found propane tanks, torches, and possible dynamite sticks in a van following night of protests against the shooting death of Walter Wallace, Jr., a Black man with a history of mental health problems.

November 9, 2020: *Newsweek* reported that U.S. District Court Judge Philip P. Simon sentenced Samantha Elhassani, alias Samantha Sally, 35, formerly of Elkart, Indiana, to 78 months in prison for aiding ISIS terrorists by smuggling more than $30,000 in cash and gold in multiple trips from the U.S. to Hong Kong between November 2014 and April 2015 to help fund their actions in Syria. She pleaded guilty to financing terrorism and was to serve three years on supervised release after completing her sentence. In 2015, she traveled with her husband Moussa Elhassani, their two children and her brother-in-law to Syria, where the men fought with ISIS. He died in a 2017 drone strike in Syria. On her last trip, she bought rifle scopes, binoculars and other tactical gear for ISIS.

November 25, 2020: *Reuters* reported that federal prosecutors charged Maria Bell, 53, of Hopatcong, New Jersey, with concealing multiple efforts to transfer money to jihadis connected to the Nusra Front, a former al-Qaeda affiliate based in Syria's Idlib Province. She was charged with knowingly concealing her involvement in providing material support to a designated foreign terrorist organization, al-Nusra. U.S. Magistrate Judge Cathy Waldor in Newark declined to grant bail. Federal prosecutor Dean Sovolos said a search of Bell's residence yielded 136 pistols and rifles, 15 canisters of ammunition and an anti-tank rocket. FBI agent Matthew Hohmann

said that when offering al-Nusra assistance, she cited her professional experience, including specialized firearms training she underwent while serving on active duty in the U.S. Army and the Army National Guard. Bell was represented by public defender Rahul Sharma, who claimed that the guns were "antique weapons" that belonged to Bell's late husband. Bell faced up to 10 years in prison and a fine of $250,000. The U.S. Attorney's office in Newark alleged that starting around February 2017, Bell used mobile phone apps to advise, and to facilitate money transfers to, al-Nusra, also known as Hay'at Tahrir al-Sham (HTS). The FBI said she used encrypted apps to communicate with an al-Nusra member with whom she shared "thousands of encrypted communications". The Bureau indicated that Bell planned to meet him in Turkey and sent at least 18 payments totaling $3,150 to his associates via wire transfer.

December 16, 2020: *ABC News* reported that in July 2019, Philippines Criminal Investigation and Detection Group authorities arrested Kenyan national Cholo Abdi Abdullah, who, at the direction of the Somalia-based al-Shabaab, conspired to hijack aircraft in order to conduct a 9/11-style attack in the United States, in what acting U.S. Attorney Audrey Strauss called a "chilling callback" to September 11. Abdullah arrived in the U.S. on December 15, 2020, and appeared briefly for arraignment the next day via telephone from the Metropolitan Correction Center in Manhattan. He pleaded not guilty and was ordered held without bail. His next court date was set for January 6, 2021.

The indictment alleged that Abdullah obtained pilot training in the Philippines, and researched security on commercial airliners, how to breach a cockpit door, how to obtain a U.S. visa, and researched information about the tallest building in an unspecified "major U.S. city". He allegedly was directed by a senior al-Shabaab commander who planned the 2019 attack on a Nairobi hotel that killed 21 people, including a U.S. citizen who had survived the 9/11 attack.

December 25, 2020: The *Washington Post, CNN, WSMV* and *WTVF* reported that police suspected that a suicide bomber set off explosives in his recreational vehicle at 6:30 a.m. in Nashville, Tennessee, hospitalizing eight people with noncritical injuries, and severely damaging 41 buildings, including the AT&T building at 166 2nd Avenue N. where the vehicle had parked, near at the intersection of Second Avenue North and Commerce Street. One officer was knocked off his feet, another reported possibly temporary hearing loss. Numerous cars were burned. One building collapsed. The blast was heard 15 miles away. Second Avenue's Arts District is on the edge the hospitality and tourist district in an historic part of Nashville. A caller had indicated around 6 a.m. that they had heard shots fired in the area; when police arrived, they saw the suspicious vehicle. Six police officers went door-to-door to evacuate local residents when the vehicle's loudspeaker system started warning "This area must be evacuated now. If you can hear this message, evacuate now" and starting a 15-minute countdown and playing "Downtown" by Petula Clark. Police found bits of human tissue among the rubble. At least 500 tips came in to police switchboards. Police searched a residence in a Nashville suburb linked to the RV; neighbors said the vehicle had been parked at the house, but rarely saw the owner enter or leave the building. The *Washington Post* reported on December 27 that Don Aaron, a spokesman for the Metropolitan Nashville Police Department, confirmed that Anthony Quinn Warner, 63, was under investigation after a search of his home on Bakertown Road in Antioch, Tennessee, 10 miles southeast of the explosion. Nashville Mayor John Cooper said the location of the bombing, next to the AT&T building, indicated it was meant to be an attack on service. Police emergency systems in Tennessee, Kentucky and Alabama, Nashville's COVID-19 hotline, and several hospital systems were knocked out of service due to the A&T central office's being affected. Flight operations were affected at Nashville International Airport. By December 27, more than 75 percent of the cell sites affected by the explosion had been restored, including in the Birmingham and Huntsville, Alabama areas.

Later on December 27, authorities said that the remains of Anthony Quinn Warner were found in the rubble. Neighbors said he was an unmarried loner and that they had seen a similar RV in his backyard in the preceding months. The *Washington Post* noted that he once owned an alarm company, and installed numerous security cameras at his home. He had lived for years with his parents, and after his father died in 2011, he remained with his mother, Betty Christine Lane, before moving into a nearby house. Property records indicated that in November, a quitclaim showed that he transferred his property at 115 Bakertown Road to a Los Angeles woman for "$0". He had worked for 15 years as a computer consultant at the Nashville real estate firm Fridrich & Clark Realty, retiring in December. Warner's father had worked for AT&T.

CNN reported on December 28 that neighbor Rick Laude said Warner told him just before Christmas, "Yes, I'm going to be more famous. I'm going to be so famous Nashville will never forget me."

CNN reported on December 30 that Raymond Throckmorton, attorney for Pamela Perry, who claimed to be Warner's girlfriend, phoned the Metropolitan Nashville Police Department on August 21, 2019 to warn that Warner was making bombs in his RV. He said she had made "suicidal threats to him via telephone". Police visited her home, where they found two unloaded pistols near Perry, who claimed they belonged to Warner.

WTVF reported on January 2, 2021 that Warner sent packages containing odd messages to acquaintances. One package, postmarked December 23, which arrived on January 1, 2021, contained nine typed pages and two Samsung thumb drives containing Internet videos he made. The cover letter began, "Hey Dude… You will never believe what I found in the park… The knowledge I have gained is immeasurable. I now understand everything, and I mean everything from who/what we really are, to what the known universe really is." It was signed Julio, an alias he used in emails; it was also his dog's name. Warner wrote about 9-11 conspiracy theories, observing "The moon landing and 9-11 have so many anomalies they are hard to count… September 2011 was supposed to be the end game for the planet," when aliens and UFOs would attack earth. He said the media was covering up the alien plans. He also wrote of reptilians and lizard people that he believed control the earth and had tweaked human DNA, warning "They put a switch into the human brain so they could walk among us and appear human." He wrote about "perception", that "Everything is an illusion" and "there is no such thing as death." He did not mention AT&T or offer a motive for the bombing.

December 31, 2020: In an especially worrisome case of product tampering and a fitting close to 2020, *AP* reported that police in Grafton, Wisconsin arrested a pharmacist at Aurora Medical Center for deliberately spoiling more than 500 doses of Moderna coronavirus vaccine. Prosecutors recommended charges of first-degree recklessly endangering safety, adulterating a prescription drug and criminal damage to property. The limited supplies of vaccines are rationed for high-risk individuals. The estimated value of the doses was $11,000, but would have protected health-care workers on the front lines of the intensifying pandemic. Earlier in the week, Aurora Health Care dismissed the pharmacist, who admitted in writing that on December 26 he had removed 57 vaccine vials "knowing that if not properly stored the vaccine would be ineffective". Each vial has enough for ten vaccinations but can remain at room temperature for only 12 hours. The thawed vaccines cannot be refrozen. Hundreds of doses were discarded, but 60 believed to be useable were quickly administered on December 26; the recipients might not get full protection. Aurora Health leaders said the vials had been removed not once but twice. The pharmacist admitted to removing and returning the vaccine to refrigeration on Christmas Eve.

UPDATES OF PRE-2019 INCIDENTS

AFRICA

BURKINA FASO

December 15, 2018: Burkina Faso Security Minister Clement Sawadogo said Quebec, Canada resident Edith Blais, 34, and her Italian friend Luca Tacchetto, 30, were travelling by car in the southwest when all communication with their families abruptly ended on December 15. Family members said they planned to travel to Togo for a humanitarian aid mission. They were last heard from in Bobo-Dioulasso in southwestern Burkina Faso. Sawadogo and Canadian officials called the disappearance of the aid workers a kidnapping. Jihadis were suspected. 18121501

AP reported that the duo were free in good health on March 14, 2020. The *BBC* and *AFP* reported that the duo, wearing Tuareg clothing, apparently escaped, flagged down a passing car, and asked the driver to take them to the nearest U.N. post. The *New York Times* said that they were released in Mali. Mali's U.N. peacekeeping spokesman Olivier Salgado said the duo were brought to the MINUSMA base in Kidal in a civilian car. Mali said no ransom was paid. No jihadi groups in the area claimed credit.

CONGO

2017: On May 29, 2020, Congolese Kamwina Nsapu militia leader Trésor Mputu Kankonde was apprehended in Katole, nine miles north of Kanaga. He was accused of involvement in the murder of U.S. citizen Michael Sharp, Swedish national Zaida Catalan and local interpreter Betu Tshintela, who were working with the United Nations in 2017. They were reported missing while investigating human rights abuses in central Congo. Their bodies were found in March 2017. A mobile phone video of their murders was found later. Several dozen people were arrested. Some 36 defendants appeared at a court hearing in August 2019.

December 2018: *AP* reported on March 12, 2019 that the U.N. reported that intercommunal violence during three days in December 2018 had left 535 people dead in western Congo. Violence took place in Yumbi between the Banunu and Batende communities after a dispute over a burial for a Banunu customary chief. The UN report added that "The similarity in the way the attacks were carried out indicated prior consultation and organization. Certain chiefs of Batende-majority villages were cited by many sources as having taken part in the planning of the attacks."

KENYA

August 7, 1998: *AP* reported on February 24, 2020 that the Supreme Court heard the arguments of victims of the bombings of the U.S. embassies in Tanzania and Kenya that killed more than 200 and injured thousands. Among the survivors were Doreen Oport, 59, who had been a senior immigration assistant in Nairobi, and Tobias Otieno, 69, who assisted U.S. firms in selling to Kenyan clients. The Court was to decide what compensation they could receive from the government of Sudan for their injuries. At issue was the $4 billion in punitive damages that he been awarded initially, but quashed by an appeals court.

On May 18, 2020, *Bloomberg* reported that the U.S. Supreme Court in a 9-0 ruling upheld a 2012 federal court's $10.2 billion judgment against Sudan for the U.S. Embassy bombings in Nairobi and Dar es Salaam on August 7, 1998, saying that the Republic of Sudan could be held liable for both punitive and compensatory damages. The original ruling had been partially overturned on appeal in 2014, in which the appellate court held that a 2008 law that allowed compensatory damages to be applied retroactively to cases involving state sponsors of terrorism did not extend to punitive damages. The court thus cut $4.3 billion from the judgment. The Supreme Court ruled in Opati v. Republic of Sudan (17-1268) that Congress intended the 2008 law to compensate victims and punish wrongdoers. Doreen Oport, who worked in the U.S. Embassy in Nairobi and was badly injured in the attack, said, "The Supreme Court has reaffirmed Sudan's guilt and the basic American principle that the value of a life is not dependent on where a person is born."

The *New York Times* on July 26, 2020 ran an update on the status of the compensation due to some of the victims of the August 7, 1998 bombing of the U.S. Embassy in Nairobi. Doreen Oport, a Kenyan citizen when she was injured, was due to receive $400,000 from Sudan. Riz Khaliq was a U.S. citizen at the time of the attack, and was eligible for at least $3 million. Both were naturalized U.S. citizens. She had worked at the U.S. Embassy in Nairobi for 15 years before immigrating to the U.S. in 2002 and obtaining citizenship in 2010.

On November 13, 2020, the *New York Times, CNN, Business Insider,* and *Reuters* reported that during the night of August 7, 2020, Abu Mohammed al-Masri, believed to be the mastermind behind the al-Qaeda bombings of the U.S. Embassies in Tanzania and Kenya on August 7,

1998, was shot to death in his white Renault in a middle-class neighborhood in northern Tehran. A younger woman died with him. One of the four shots hit a passing car. Iranian news agencies said two gunmen escaped on a motorbike. Iranian news agencies initially reported that the dead were Lebanese academic Habib Dawood, variant Daoud, who had ties to Lebanese Hizballah, and his daughter, Maryam. No arrests were reported.

The media later identified the dead as Abdullah Ahmed Abdullah, alias Abu Mohammed al-Masri, 57, a former Egyptian-born professional soccer player and founding member of al-Qaeda, and his daughter, Miriam, 27, widow of Osama bin Laden's son Hamza. She married Hamza in 2005 or so. He had been held under house arrest in Iran since 2003, and was released from custody in 2015 to win the freedom of an Iranian diplomat whom al-Qaeda had kidnapped in Yemen. In 2018, the U.S. Rewards for Justice program offered a bounty on information on him and Saif al-'Adl of $10 million.

The *New York Times* and *Washington Post* reported that Israel was responsible for the attack; some believed they acted at the behest of the United States.

September 21, 2013: On January 14, 2019, *AP* reported that a magistrate's court ruled that three men must stand trial on charges they were involved in a deadly al-Shabaab attack on Nairobi's Westgate shopping mall on September 21, 2013 in which 67 people were killed. A fourth suspect was freed for lack of evidence. *AP, AFP* and *Deutsche Welle* reported on October 7, 2020 that Chief Justice/Magistrate Francis Andayi found guilty Mohamed Ahmed Abdi and Hassan Hussein Mustafa, variant Hussein Hassan Mustafah, for conspiring with and aiding the four al-Shabaab gunmen who attacked Nairobi's Westgate Mall. The four gunmen died of smoke inhalation during the four-day siege. Defendant Liban Abdullahi Omar, a brother of one of the attackers, was acquitted of all charges. The three defendants were ethnic Somalis; two were Kenyan citizens. Surviving victims included security guard David Odhiambo, who was shot in the head and fired from his job for his injuries. Omar's lawyer said his client was abducted by men believed to be security agents five minutes after his release. Abdi was represented by attorney Mbugua Mureithi. *Reuters* reported on October 30, 2020 that Chief Magistrate Francis Andayi of the Milimani Law Courts in Nairobi sentenced the duo to 18 years. Abdi received an additional 15 years for possession of materials promoting terrorism. The Magistrate announced that he would deduct the seven years they had spent on remand.

April 2, 2015: *AP* reported on June 19, 2019 that in a Nairobi court Chief Magistrate Francis Andayi found defendants Rashid Charles Mberesero, Hassan Aden Hassan, and Mohamed Abdi Abikar guilty of conspiracy to commit a terror attack after phone records and handwriting linked them to al-Shabaab's April 2, 2015 Garissa University College attack that killed 148 people. Sahal Diriye Hussein was acquitted. Sentencing was scheduled for July 3. Defense attorney Mbugua Mureithi planned to appeal.

On July 3, 2019, a Kenyan court sentenced three al-Shabaab members for the April 2, 2015 attack on Garissa University. Rashid Charles Mberesero was sentenced to life in jail. Hassan Aden Hassan and Mohamed Abdi Abikar were sentenced to 41 years each for being accomplices. Prosecutor Duncan Ondimu had asked the court for a 60-year sentence for each. "Sixty years will serve justice. Though it won't bring back the lives lost, it will go a long way to pass a message that such actions will not go unpunished." Attorney Mbugua Mureithi represented Hassan and Abikar, observing, "These men were not at Garissa University at the fateful day... never pulled the actual triggers of the actual guns."

November 26, 2018: On May 9, 2020, *AP* reported that Italian officials announced that Italian aid volunteer Silvia Costanza Romano, 25, who was kidnapped in Kenya's Chakama coastal trading center on November 26, 2018 had been freed. The Association of Former Intelligence Officers weekly newsletter reported that *Anadolu* and *Ahval* said that Turkey's National Intelligence Service (MİT) determined that she was alive and rescued her in coordination with Italian and Somali intelligence services. She was a volunteer with the Italian-based Africa Milele, variant Milelel Onlus, humanitarian group. She had been transferred to Somalia in the hands of an armed group linked to al-Shabaab. *Anadolu* reported that MİT delivered her to Italian authorities in Mogadishu. Italian media claimed that she converted to Islam while a hostage. Although Italian Prime Minister Giuseppe Conte and Foreign Minster Luigi Di Maio welcomed her to Rome's Ciampino Airport, others slammed her conversion. Alessandro Pagano, a lawmaker from the anti-migrant League Party, was reprimanded by the acting president of the Chamber of Deputies, Mara Carfagna, Democratic Party parliamentarian Emanuele Fiano, and colleagues in the lower house of parliament after he called her a "neo-terrorist" while complaining that the coalition government had a "strong anti-religious bent" in refusing to reopen churches during the COVID-19 lockdown. Social media criticized her conversion and for volunteering in a remote part of Kenya. The government was criticized for apparently paying a ransom. A glass bottle was thrown against her Milan home. Italian Premier Giuseppe Conte observed, "To whoever's speculating about her, first become a 23-year-old, kidnapped in Kenya, forced to walk nine hours a day, in a forest, by those with Kalashnikovs." Pagano apologized on *Facebook*, saying he intended to criticize the government, not Romano. 18112601

MALI

2012, 2016: On October 10, 2020, *TheLocal.ch*, *Keystone-ATS*, and *AP* reported that kidnappers killed hostage Beatrice Stoeckli, a missionary from Basel who was working in Timbuktu when she was abducted in 2016. Jihadis had also kidnapped her in 2012. Swiss authorities said they had been working for four years with Malian authorities and other partners for her release. French hostage Sophie Petronin, who had been released earlier in October 2020, told French authorities that Stoeckli had been killed by the al-Qaeda affiliate Jama'at Nusrat al-Islam Muslimeen (JNIM). *AP* noted that Stoeckli was freed from her first kidnapping on April 24, 2012, when she arrived by helicopter from Timbuktu, Mali at Ouagadougou, Burkina Faso, after being handed over by Ansar Dine. It remained unclear what happened to the four other foreign hostages—Australian doctor Ken Elliott, Colombian nun Gloria Cecilia Narváez Argoti, South African national Christo Bothma and Romanian citizen Julian Ghergut—being held by JNIM and its associates. 16999901, 12999901

March 2015: *AFP* reported on October 27, 2020 that the trial began against three jihadis accused of killing more than two dozen people in attacks targeting foreigners in 2015. In March 2015, gunmen fired at Bamako's La Terrasse nightclub and threw a grenade inside, killing a Frenchman, a Belgian, and three Malians. In November 2015, gunmen took guests and staff hostage at the 190-room Radisson Blu Hotel, killing 20 people, including 14 foreigners. The primary suspect was Mauritanian national Fawaz Ould Ahmed, believed to be a lieutenant of Algerian terrorist leader Mokhtar Belmokhtar. Ahmed was charged with masterminding the hotel attack and personally shooting the nightclub victims, using an assault rifle, as revenge for French satirical magazine *Charlie Hebdo* publishing cartoons of the Prophet Mohammed. *Daily News* reported on October 29, 2020 that two of the jihadi terrorists were sentenced to death. *AFP* reported that Fawaz Ould Ahmed and Sadou Chaka pleaded guilty and expressed no remorse for three attacks. *Reuters* reported that Ahmed said he was personally responsible for the March 2015 attack in which he shot the five people. Ould Ahmed and Chaka planned the November 2015 al-Mourabitoun attack and masterminded an attack on a Mali hotel in August 2015 that killed 17 people. Mali authorities captured Ould Ahmed in April 2016 while he was planning a new attack in Bamako. They confiscated grenades and a suitcase full of weapons.

December 24, 2016: *Reuters* and *AFP* reported on October 5, 2020 that the government released 180 alleged or convicted jihadis in the central Niono region and northern Tessalit region after arriving by plane on October 3-4, 2020 to obtain the release of two hostages.

- Former opposition Union for the Republic and Democracy leader and three-time presidential candidate Soumaïla Cissé, 70, was kidnapped on March 25, 2020 while campaigning in Niafounke/Timbuktu during legislative elections. Cissé served as Minister of Finance from 1993 to 2000.

- French charity worker Sophie Petronin, now 75, was kidnapped in Gao on December 24, 2016. She ran a charity for orphaned and malnourished children. She was the last French hostage in the world. Her last video appeared in June 2018. She appeared tired and emaciated while asking for French President Emmanuel Macron's aid. A follow-up video in November 2018, in which she did not appear, featured her kidnappers saying her health was going downhill.

Malian authorities believed an al-Qaeda-linked group in central Mali, led by cleric Amadou Koufa, was behind the kidnappings.

AFP reported that on late October 5 and early October 6, 2020, Mali released another 30 prisoners.

France 24 and *AP* reported on October 6, 2020 that the two hostages were freed, along with Italian hostages Nicola Chiacchio, variant Ciacio, and Reverend Pierluigi Maccalli. *Avvenire*, the newspaper of the Italian bishops' conference, reported that Rev. Maccalli is a Roman Catholic missionary priest from the Genoa-based African Missionary Society (SMA) who was kidnapped in September 2018 from his Bomoanga parish in Niamey, Niger. *AFP* and Menastream, an independent risk and research consultancy firm specializing in the Sahel and North Africa, said Chiacchio was kidnapped during a solo bike trip in February 2018 in central Mali. A video of the two Italians was released in April 2020.

Mali state broadcaster *ORTM, AP,* and *TV5 Monde* reported on October 10, 2020 that Cissé said he was constantly being moved in the desert, in "near permanent physical and moral isolation". The hostages were moved by motorcycle, boat, and camel to more than 20 locations during the six months Cissé was held. He said he was held apart from the European hostages. He was re-elected to his parliament seat during his captivity. He made a proof of life video on September 26, 2020.

It was not known whether a ransom was paid.

Petronin said she was treated well, and was now a Muslim named Mariam, not Sophie. "I was always highly respected during my captivity," and was permitted to listen to the radio. The guards shared messages and videos with her, including one from her son. "I hung on — I prayed a lot because I had a lot of time… I transformed detention … into a spiritual retreat, if one can say that… All of us, on while we are on this earth, we have or we will have ordeals to go through. If you accept what is happening, it will not go too badly. If you resist, you will hurt yourself." *Reuters* added that she said that at one point she felt like giving up hope, wandering into the desert, sat on the ground, and wept. A small voice in her head spoke to her, and she persevered. "It said you mustn't cry or be sad. I will stay with you. And until today it hasn't left." She lost some weight and four teeth.

Niger

October 4, 2017: The *New York Times* reported on March 15, 2020 that the Senate Armed Services Committee temporarily blocked the promotion to brigadier general of special forces Colonel Bradley D. Moses, who was involved in the incident that resulted in the deaths of four Americans in Niger. Colonel Moses was in charge of the Thrid Special Forces Group. His subordinates were punished earlier. He was scheduled for promotion after the end of his assignment in Afghanistan. The four Americans who were killed—Sgt. First Class Jeremiah W. Johnson, Staff Sgt. Bryan C. Black, Staff Sgt. Dustin Wright and Sgt. La David T. Johnson—received posthumous valor awards.

Somalia

October 2017: On July 10, 2019, *AP* reported that a military firing squad at a police academy executed three al-Shabaab men convicted of carrying out a deadly attack on the Nasa-Hablod hotel that killed 18 people and wounded 47 others in Mogadishu in October 2017.

June 8, 2018: Al-Shabaab forces in Jubaland killed by indirect fire U.S. Staff Sgt. Alexander

Conrad, 26, assigned to 1st Battalion, 3rd Special Forces Group. *Army Times* reported on May 2, 2019 that an April 19, 2019 airstrike killed two al-Shabaab terrorists, including the attack's orchestrator, Abdullahi Jibiyow, a mortar team leader responsible for multiple attacks in the Lower Juba River Valley.

Uganda

1999: *AP* and *Politico* reported on May 17, 2019 that Australian Prime Minister Scott Morrison said that former Hutu rebels Leonidas Bimenyimana and Gregoire Nyaminani who became Rwandan refugees resettled in Australia after 15 years in U.S. detention, were no longer suspects in the 1999 ax and machete slayings of four Britons, two Americans and two New Zealander tourists who were in a Ugandan wild park in 1999 to see mountain gorillas. *Politico* reported that the members of the Congo-based Liberation Army of Rwanda (now the Democratic Forces for the Liberation of Rwanda) were jailed in Virginia for more than a decade before they moved to Australia in 2018. A U.S. court held that their confessions were obtained under torture. The *Australian Broadcasting Corporation* reported that DeAnne Haubner Norton's older brother Rob Haubner, 48, and sister-in-law Susan Miller, 42, both senior executives of Intel Corporation from Oregon, were killed during their honeymoon. Scottish-born Australian David Roberts's son Steven Roberts, 23, a Briton who lived in Melbourne, was also killed. 99999901

ASIA

BANGLADESH

August 15, 1975: On April 7, 2020, Home Minister Asaduzzaman Khan said that police in Dhaka arrested former military Captain Abdul Majed, a fugitive killer of the country's independence leader Sheikh Mujibur Rahman, nearly 45 years after the assassination. Majed had publicly announced his involvement in the assassination and had reportedly been hiding in India for many years. He was one of 12 defendants whose death sentences were upheld by the country's Supreme Court in 2009. A trial court in 1998 had sentenced them to death for killing Rahman and most of his family members. Rahman was the father of current Prime Minister Sheikh Hasina. She and her younger sister Sheikh Rehana were the only survivors in the family, as they were visiting Germany during the attack. In 2010, five others who admitted to taking part in the assassination were hanged. One man died of natural causes in Zimbabwe. The other six convicts, including Majed, remained at large. Officials claimed that one was in Canada and another in the U.S. On April 11, 2020, authorities hanged Abul Majed at the central jail at Keranigani near Dhaka, at one minute past midnight. President M. Abdul Hamid had rejected a clemency request.

September 23, 1994: On July 3, 2019, a court sentenced nine Bangladesh Nationalist Party oppositionists to death and 25 others to life in prison for an attack on a train carrying political leader Sheikh Hasina on September 23, 1994. The BNP, led by former Prime Minister Khaleda Zia, called the verdict politically motivated. The current prime minister and then-opposition leader, Hasina was riding a passenger train at Pakshi Rail Station when attackers fired shots and threw bombs, injuring scores of people. Hasina was unhurt.

The Paban district trial court sentenced 13 other people to 10 years in jail in a case filed under the Explosives Substances Act of 1908.

October 31, 2015: On October 13, 2019, *AP* reported that Anti-Terrorism Special Tribunal Judge Majibur Rahman announced indictments of eight suspected jihadis tied to the banned domestic militant group Ansar al-Islam for the February 2015 killing of Faisal Abedin Deepan of the Jagriti Prokashoni publishing house, which published books on secularism and atheism. Six suspects pleaded not guilty. Another two, including a fired military official, were at large, and the judge issued arrest warrants for them.

On the same day, another publisher, Ahmed Rashid Tutul, survived an attack by suspected militants in Dhaka.

Both published the work of Bangladeshi-American writer and blogger Avijit Roy, who was hacked to death in February 2015.

July 1, 2016: In 2019, Judge Mojibur Rahman of an anti-terrorism tribunal sentenced seven members of the banned Jamatul Mujahedeen Bangladesh group to death for involvement in the attack on Dhaka's Holey Artisan Bakery that killed more than 20 people, mostly foreigners. Charges included planning the attack, making bombs, and murder. One person was acquitted.

INDIA

December 6, 1992: The *Washington Post* and *AP* reported on September 30, 2020 that India's Supreme Court acquitted 32 people who were accused of conspiring to destroy the 16th century Babri Mosque in Ayodhya which was leveled by a mob of Hindu extremists on December 6, 1992. The accused included four senior politicians from the ruling Hindu nationalist Bharatiya Janata Party and an incumbent member of Parliament. Ensuing rioting killed nearly 2,000 people. Judge Surendra Kumar Yadav, speaking from Lucknow, Uttar Pradesh State, held that the destruction was not a preplanned conspiracy and evidence was not sufficient for convictions. Four senior BJP defendants included

- Lal Krishna Advani, 92, former deputy prime minister
- Uma Bharti, a former government minister
- Murli Manohar Joshi

- Kalyan Singh, the senior elected BJP leader of Uttar Pradesh State when the attack occurred

Other defendants included Jai Bhagwan Goyal. Seventeen of the original 49 defendants died of natural causes during the trial. Four BJP leaders were accused of making inflammatory speeches that stoked the violent mob's actions.

Attorney Rishab Tripathi represented one of the defendants. Attorney I.B. Singh represented Joshi, a minister in a previous BJP government.

February 19, 2007: Bombs exploded on two coaches of the Samjauta Express (Friendship Express) train at Dewana, killing 68 people, mostly Pakistanis. On March 20, 2019, an Indian court in Mohali acquitted four Hindus charged with setting off the bombs on the train that was traveling from New Delhi to Atari. Defense attorney Mukesh Garg said the court ruled that investigators failed to conclusively prove that the accused were guilty. India's National Investigation Agency filed charges of criminal conspiracy to murder against the four in 2011.

November 26-29, 2008: On February 22, 2019, *AP* reported that Pakistan re-imposed a ban on two charities—Jamat-ut-Dawa and Falah-e-Insaniat Foundation—thought to be a front for Lashkar-e-Taiba, run by a U.S.-wanted suspect, Muslim cleric Hafiz Saeed, believed to be behind the 2008 Mumbai terror attacks. The groups were banned in February 2018, but the Pakistani Supreme Court in September 2018 allowed them to reopen.

On June 28, 2020, *Reuters* reported that India was seeking the extradition of senior Pakistani militant Sajir Mir, who was suspected to have been the "project manager" of the Mumbai attacks. The previous week, the U.S. said he was living free in Pakistan. India and the U.S. separately indicted Mir, of the Lashkar-e-Taiba group, for the attacks on hotels, a train station, and a Jewish center that killed 166 people, including six Americans. The FBI posted a $5 million reward for his capture. He was also wanted in a 2008-2009 plot against Denmark's *Jyllands-Posten* newspaper, which published cartoons of the Prophet Mohammad.

INDONESIA

October 12, 2002: *AP* reported on December 27, 2019 that Ni Luh Erniati, Balinese widow of one of the 202 people who were killed in the October 12, 2002 Bali nightclub bombing by Jemaah Islamiyah, had become friends with the brother of defendant Amrozi Nurhasyim. The brother, Ali Fauzi, had taught Amrozi how to make bombs. Their reconciliation efforts were part of the work of the Alliance for a Peaceful Indonesia (AIDA). The duo visited 8,000 students in 150 schools in parts of Indonesia known for extremist recruiting. Fauzi claimed he did not know of the plot, which was orchestrated by three of his brothers, Amrozi, Ali Imron and Ali Ghufron, alias Mukhlas.

April 2017: On December 26, 2019, Indonesian authorities in Depok on the outskirts of Jakarta arrested RM and RB, two members of an elite police mobile brigade, suspected in an acid attack on Novel Baswedan, a leading investigator at the Corruption Eradication Commission (KPK), in April 2017. Baswedan was nearly blinded by acid thrown at him near a mosque as he left dawn prayers. Police had questioned 73 witnesses.

JAPAN

March 20, 1995: *Newsweek* reported on September 23, 2020 that on July 26, 2020, Japan had executed the remaining six members of the doomsday cult Aum Shinrikyo which conducted the deadly nerve gas attack on the Tokyo subway system in 1995.

MALAYSIA

December 2018: *AP* reported on April 6, 2019 that Philippine Abu Sayyaf gunmen had kidnapped two Indonesians and a Malaysian off Malaysia's Sabah State on Borneo island and taken by speedboat to Sulu in the Philippines in December 2018. On April 4, 2019, one of the Indonesians, Heri Ardiansyah, escaped by swimming to a marine gunboat but another Indonesian, Hariadin, drowned. The kidnappers shot the Malaysian, Jari Bin Abudullah, in the back while trying to escape. The Malaysian was airlifted to Zamboanga city, where a hospital listed him as being in critical condition. The marines gunned down three Abu Sayyaf terrorists who were chasing the Indonesians. Philippine marines were attempting to rescue them on Simusa island in Sulu Province over the previous two days. The marines seized four assault rifles, a grenade launcher and various ammunition from the captors of the Indonesians. On April 5, 2019, Philippine Army troops clashed with 80 Abu Sayyaf gunmen in Sulu's mountainous Patikul town in a gun battle that killed three soldiers and four terrorists and wounded several people on both sides. The Islamic State group said it killed three and wounded 13 Philippine soldiers, but claimed "the mujahideen returned safely to base." The group was led by Hajan Sawadjaan. 18129901

MALDIVES

2014: *AP* reported on September 1, 2019 that Husnu Suood, president of the Maldives government-appointed commission, reported that their investigation determined that Ahmed Rilwan, a journalist for the *Maldives Independent* news website, in 2014 was kidnapped outside his Hulhumale island apartment, thrown into a car, taken to a boat and transferred to a bigger vessel at deeper seas and killed, possibly by those linked to fighters in Syria at the time. Suood said that Rilwan had been in touch with a group of Maldivians fighting in Syria and accused by its leader of being a non-believer in Islam. Conversations on *Facebook Messenger* indicated that Rilwan had received death threats. Suood said two groups active among the Maldivian radicals were recruiting for foreign terrorist organizations. He added that the same group was behind the stabbing death of blogger Yaamin Rasheed in 2017.

2015: On May 20, 2019, the High Court annulled the Criminal Court's conviction and 15-year prison term given vice president Ahmed Adeeb on allegations he conspired to assassinate former President Yameen Abdul Gayoom. The High Court ordered a new investigation. Adeeb was serving 33 years in prison after being convicted of corruption and causing an explosion on Yameen's speedboat in 2015. Adeeb was arrested after the explosion on the boat injured Yameen's wife. The U.S. FBI said it found no evidence of explosives on the boat. The High Court also annulled the ten-year jail terms given Adeeb's two bodyguards in the same case.

MYANMAR

January 29, 2017: A gunman assassinated Ko Ni, Supreme Court advocate for the National League for Democracy and a longtime adviser to Myanmar leader Aung San Suu Kyi, at the arrival gate at Yangon's airport from Indonesia as he held his 5-year-old grandchild. The assassin also shot taxi driver Nay Win, who tried to detain him. Police arrested the gunman, identified as Kyi Lin from Mandalay. On January 30, 2017, police arrested a second alleged conspirator, Myint Swe, in Karen State, saying he hired gunman Kyi Lin. On February 15, 2019, Yangon Northern District Court found Kyi Lin guilty of premeditated murder and illegal weapons possession and sentenced him to death. Kyi Lin received 20 years for killing the taxi driver who tried to chase him down. The court sentenced to death another man, Aung Win Zaw, for helping to plan the killing. Two men were given prison sentences for their involvement: alleged planner Zayar Phyo, who told the court he had been framed, received a five-year prison sentence, and Aung Win Tun, charged with harboring one of the suspects, was given three years. Alleged mastermind Aung Win Khine, alias Aung Win Khaing, remained at large, charged with premeditated murder. Police said the murder plot was hatched in April 2016; Kyi Lin was hired to be the gunman and was paid almost $60,000.

PAKISTAN

January 23, 2002: The *Washington Post, CNN,* and *AFP* reported on April 2, 2020 that two judges on the High Court of Sindh Province overturned the convictions of the men involved in the January 23, 2002 kidnapping and February 1, 2002 beheading of American journalist

Daniel Pearl, South Asia bureau chief of the *Wall Street Journal*. They included British-born Ahmed Omar Saeed Sheikh, who had been sentenced to death. The ruling can be appealed to Pakistan's Supreme Court. Defense attorney Khawaja Naveed said, "As per the court's judgment, Omar Saeed Sheikh has been found guilty of kidnapping and not of murder. The accused was in jail for 20 years." His kidnapping sentence was for only seven years. He had already served for 18 years, and could be released. The court also ordered the release of the trio convicted in 2002 of abetting Omar and sentenced to life sentences, including Fahad Naseem, a computer expert; Salman Saqib, a religious activist; and Sheikh Adil, a police officer. *AFP* reported on April 4, 2020 that the Interior Ministry announced that on August 3, authorities arrested the four defendants, who were to remain in jail "for a period of three months" while prosecutors appealed the ruling to the Supreme Court. Alleged al-Qaeda 9/11 mastermind Khalid Sheikh Mohammed, who was arrested in Pakistan in 2003 and has since been imprisoned at Guantanamo Bay, claimed to have killed Pearl.

AP reported on June 29, 2020 that the Pakistani Supreme Court rejected the government's request to suspend the April ruling by the Sindh High Court exonerating Ahmed Omar Saeed Sheikh of the January 23, 2002 kidnap/beheading of American journalist Daniel Pearl before a 90-day detention order was to expire on July 2, 2020. Saeed was likely to be freed. The Court refused to immediately hear the appeal, saying it would be heard on September 25. The Sindh court had upheld the kidnap charge. Saeed had been on death row for 18 years. He was represented by attorney Mahmood Ahmed Sheikh, no relation.

On July 2, 2020, *AP* reported that Superintendent of Karachi Central Prison Hasan Sehtoo said the foursome would remain in custody until September 30 under a law that allows authorities to detain any suspect for up to one year. He said the men's release would threaten public safety. Attorney Mahmood Sheikh said he was not aware of the 90-day extension.

AP reported on October 7, 2020 that the government ordered the continued detention for at least another three months of British-born Pakistani Ahmed Omar Saeed Sheikh, who had been on death row for the January 2002 beheading of U.S. journalist Daniel Pearl. A lower court acquitted Sheikh and three accomplices accused of murder charges in April 2020; the government and Pearl's family appealed the ruling to the Supreme Court. The four had been sentenced to life. The family was represented by attorney Faisal Siddiqi. The judges adjourned the hearing until October 21, 2020.

Reuters and *AFP* reported on December 24, 2020 that the Sindh High Court ordered the immediate release of four men accused of orchestrating the 2002 kidnapping and beheading. In April, the court had commuted the death sentence of the main suspect, British-born Ahmed Omar Saeed Sheikh, and acquitted three others citing a lack of evidence against them. The four were represented by attorneys Mahmood Sheikh and Nadeem Azar.

AP and *USA Today* added on December 30, 2020 that acting U.S. Attorney General Jeffrey Rosen said that the U.S. would not permit Sheikh to evade justice, observing "The separate judicial rulings reversing his conviction and ordering his release are an affront to terrorism victims everywhere." Rosen praised Pakistan for appealing the court's rulings. "If, however, those efforts do not succeed, the United States stands ready to take custody of Omar Sheikh to stand trial here." Pakistan's Supreme Court scheduled its next hearing for January 5, 2021.

August 13, 2011: On January 15, 2019, *AP* reported that Pakistani police officers raided a terrorist hideout in Faisalabad in Punjab Province before dawn, killing two members of the Islamic State group linked to the August 13, 2011 al-Qaeda kidnapping of American development worker Warren Weinstein in Lahore. He was accidentally killed in a U.S. drone strike in 2015 on the Afghanistan-Pakistan border. Rai Tahir of the Punjab counter-terrorism department said the two terrorists were Adeel Hafeez and Usman Haroon, who also were involved in the May 9, 2013 abduction of former Prime Minister Yusuf Raza Gilani's son, Ali Haider, who was rescued in Afghanistan by U.S. forces in 2016. Pakistani officers had foiled other attacks the pair had plotted. The duo were also behind the killing of two Pakistani intelligence officers in recent years and in some other high-profile crimes, according to Pakistani authorities.

November 23, 2018: On January 12, 2019, anti-terrorism court judge Abdul Malik gave police five days to investigate the five suspects accused of helping the Baluch Liberation Army separatist group attack the Chinese Consulate in Karachi on November 23, 2018, killing two civilians and two policemen. Senior officer Amir Sheikh said the men confessed to facilitating three terrorists who were killed.

PHILIPPINES

November 23, 2009: On December 19, 2019, the *Washington Post* and *Reuters* reported that the Philippine Supreme Court issued a 761-page decision that convicted more than 40 people, led by eight members of the Ampatuan political family dynasty as well as police officers and militiamen, of murder in the killings of 26 rivals and 32 journalists on November 23, 2009. Another 15 were guilty of accessory to the crime; 56 were acquitted. Reporters Without Borders said it was the deadliest attack on journalists ever recorded. There were only 57 murder counts because one victim's body was never found. Two brothers, Andal Jr. and Zaldy Ampatuan, were named as the masterminds that had backed Manila in battling Muslim separatists in the southern Philippines. They and other relatives faced life sentences, which means 40 years in the Philippines, without parole. The gunmen targeted the family of political rival Esmael Mangudadatu in the Maguindanao massacre. They planned to appeal.

Some 197 people had stood trial; 80, including 12 Ampatuans, remained at large. Eleven, including Sajid Ampatuan, the newly acquitted younger brother who is serving as a mayor in the province, were out on bail. Family patriarch and suspected architect of the massacre, Andal Ampatuan, Sr., died in prison of a heart attack in 2015.

Among the family members who cheered the decision was Jergin Dela Cruz Malabanan, 26, whose mother was killed, leaving her to raise her siblings and a newborn. Also killed were the sister and husband of Mary Grace Morales, 43, mother of three daughters. Esmael Mangudadatu, a congressman whose wife was shot more than a dozen times, said "this case has a long way to go."

In 2009, a motorcade of Mangudadatu's family and lawyers, accompanied by a media entourage, had been on the way to lodge his candidacy in a gubernatorial run when they were ambushed, shot to death, and buried in a mass grave surrounded by corn and grass fields.

Three witnesses were killed since the trial began. Victim families reported harassment and threats. The decade-long trial called 357 witnesses and generated 238 volumes of documents.

2012: *The Washington Post* reported on May 31, 2019 that Dutch bird watcher Ewold Horn, 59, was killed in crossfire during a raid in Sulu island by soldiers hoping to rescue him from 30 Abu Sayyaf Group kidnappers. Horn had been kidnapped in 2012 with Swiss birdwatcher Lorenzo Vinciguerra, who escaped in 2014. Brigadier General Divino Rey Pabayo Jr., commander of Joint Task Force Sulu, said, "Horn was shot by one of his guards when he tried to escape from the Abu Sayyaf." Soldiers recovered Horn's body and that of Abu Sayyaf leader Radullan Sahiron's second wife, Mingayan Sahiron. The military believed it had killed six ASG members and wounded a dozen. Eight soldiers were wounded by gunshots and shrapnel. 12999901.

2015: The *New York Times* reported on March 24, 2019 that Filipino couple Ellen Barriga and Mohammad Reza Kiram, alias Abdul Rahman, moved to Syria in 2015 to join ISIS and become key recruiters of other Southeast Asians. The duo surrendered in January 2019 to coalition forces. Barriga was a Catholic math whiz who earned an MBA. She converted to Islam after earning an accounting degree at Ateneo de Davao University, then worked as an accounting manager. Kiram beheaded a hostage in an ISIS propaganda video. In 2019, she was 38; he was 29. The couple had a daughter in the Philippines. Police said Kiram was involved in the 2012 bombing of a bus terminal in Zamboanga.

SRI LANKA

August 2005: On January 16, 2019, authorities in southwestern Germany arrested Navanithan G., 39, a suspected member of the Liberation Tigers of Tamil Eelam (LTTE, Tamil Tigers), alleged to have been involved in the August 2005 assassination of Sri Lankan Foreign Minister Lakshman Kathirkamar. G. was accused of membership in a foreign terrorist organization, murder and attempted murder. Prosecutors said G. was a member of LTTE's's secret police, participating in the killing of and the attempted killing of Eelam People's Democratic Party leader Douglas Devananda.

THAILAND

April 17, 2014: *AP* reported on September 3, 2019 that law enforcement officials in May found the remains of Porlajee ("Billy") Rakchongcharoen, an ethnic Karen community activist who disappeared on April 17, 2014 in suspicious circumstances. He was last seen in the custody of Kaeng Krachan National Park officials in western Thailand. He was leading the Karen community's lawsuit against park chief Chaiwat Limlikitaksorn over his efforts to evict them by burning their homes and possessions inside the park. Chaiwat said that Porlajee had been arrested for illegally collecting wild honey, then released with a warning. The Department of Special Investigation said it had discovered a 53-gallon oil drum sunk in a reservoir at the park with a bone fragment near it that matched the DNA of Porlajee's mother. The drum and the bone had been burnt. More bone fragments were later found nearby. Porlajee, then 30 years old, was survived by his wife, Phinnapha Phrueksaphan, and their five children.

VIETNAM

2018: *Reuters* reported on September 22, 2020 that a Ho Chi Minh City court sentenced 20 defendants of the Trieu Dai Viet group to prison terms of two to 24 years for terrorism regarding the 2018 detonation of two bombs at a police station that injured three people. The court found 17 guilty of terrorism and three of illegal use of explosives. Defense attorney Nguyen Van Mieng said all 20 had pleaded guilty and would be under house arrest after they leave prison. The Ministry of Public Security said the attack was funded by an exiled anti-regime group, the Canada-based Trieu Dai Viet (Viet Dynasty), for purchasing explosives and detonators for "terrorism activities to overthrow the state of Vietnam". Police said the group's motto was "fire all, kill all, destroy all, steal all". The Ministry said the group was founded by Ngo Van Hoang Hung, who broke out of prison in 1982 and went to Canada.

AUSTRALIA

2016: *AP* reported on May 2, 2019 that the New South Wales State Supreme Court in Sydney sentenced pharmacy student Ihsas Khan, 25, of carrying out a terrorist act by repeatedly stabbing passer-by Wayne Greenhalgh with a machete while shouting "I will kill you, you will die" in the Sydney suburb of Minto in 2016. During his sixth trial, a jury rejected Khan's mental illness defense. Four previous trials were aborted and the fifth jury could not reach a verdict. Justice Geoffrey Bellew scheduled sentencing submissions for May 23. Khan faced life in prison. Greenhalgh was injured in his right arm, left hand, face and lungs and had to take four months off work. Prosecutors said Khan was a "self-radicalized extremist Muslim" and ISIS supporter. Khan told a psychiatrist that a *jinn* directed him to kill someone.

December 11, 2016: *AP* reported on May 9, 2019 that a Victoria, Australia State Supreme Court jury convicted Sunni Muslim men Abdullah Chaarani, 28, Ahmed Mohamed, 26, and Hatim Moukhaiber, 31, of engaging in a terror act by burning down a Shi'ite Imam Ali Islamic Center in Melbourne on December 11, 2016. No one was injured. The words "Islamic State" were spray painted on the building's exterior. Mohamed and Moukhaiber denied involvement. Chaarani conceded that he was there, but argued he had been part of an act of protest, advocacy or dissent. Chaarani and Mohamed were found guilty of attempting to commit a terror act over a failed attempt to burn the mosque down on November 25, 2016. Sentencing was scheduled for mid-May 2019; they faced life in prison. Mohamed and Chaarani were earlier convicted of planning a terrorist attack on central Melbourne locations including the Federation Square restaurant and nightclub precinct, St. Paul's Anglican Cathedral and Flinders Street train station on December 25, 2016. They were among five men found guilty in November 2018 after the plot was foiled by police who listened to their plans and watched their reconnaissance at Federation Square. Sentencing had yet to be scheduled.

On July 24, 2019, *AP* reported that Justice Andrew Tinney sentenced the three Sunni Muslim men to prison terms of 16 and 22 years. Mohamed and Chaarani were imprisoned for 22 years. Mohamed and Chaarani will be eligible for parole in 17 years. Moukhaiber must serve 12 years of his 16-year sentence before parole could be considered.

AP reported on November 29, 2019 that Supreme Court of Victoria Justice Christopher Beale sentenced Ahmed Mohamed, 27, Abdullah Chaarani, 29, and Hamza Abbas, 24. Chaarani and Mohamed must serve at least 28 years and six months in prison. Hamza Abbas, who was involved in the conspiracy for a shorter time, was jailed for 22 years with a non-parole period of 16 years and six months. Ringleader Ibrahim Abbas was sentenced in 2018 to 24 years in prison. He had been a prosecution witness against his brother Hamza Abbas and Mohamed and Chaarani. Mohamed and Chaarani were serving 22-year prison terms for firebombing a Shi'ite mosque in Melbourne weeks before the planned Christmas attack.

January 2017: On February 22, 2019, *MSNBC* reported that Justice Mark Weinberg sentenced Australian man James Gargasoulas, 29, to life in jail for murdering six people and injuring 27 more in a vehicle attack on pedestrians in Melbourne's city center in January 2017. He had told the court that he acted on a premonition. Gargasoulas killed three-month-old Zachary Bryant, Thalia Hakin, 10, Jess Mudie, 22, Yosuke Kanno, 25, Bhavita Patel, 33, and Matthew Si, 33. He will be eligible for parole after 46 years. He

initially pleaded not guilty, but later admitted to the attack.

December 21, 2017: On March 28, 2019, Victoria State Supreme Court Justice Elizabeth Hollingworth sentenced ISIS sympathizer Saeed Noori, 37, who rammed his mother's SUV into pedestrians on a busy Melbourne sidewalk, killing one person and injuring 16 others on December 21, 2017, to life in prison. She ordered him to serve 30 years behind bars before he is eligible for parole. Noori had pleaded guilty in December 2018 to the murder of Antonios Crocaris, 83, who died in a hospital eight days after he was struck. Noori pleaded guilty to 11 counts of recklessly causing serious injury, which carries a maximum of 15 years in prison, and five counts of conduct endangering life, which carries up to 10 years in prison. He came to Australia from Afghanistan as a refugee in 2004 and became an Australian citizen. He has three children. His lawyers told the court he suffered from schizophrenia. Hollingworth mentioned Noori's mental health issues, years of heavy drug use and gambling addiction.

EUROPE

BELGIUM

May 24, 2014: *AP* reported on January 15, 2019 that French citizen Mehdi Nemmouche, 33, refused to testify at the Justice Palace in Brussels. He was accused of "terrorist murder" for shooting dead an Israeli couple and two museum workers at the Brussels Jewish Museum on May 24, 2014. Alleged accomplice Nacer Bendrer, 30, also appeared in court on charges of supplying to Nemmouche the revolver and assault rifle used in the killings. French authorities alleged Nemmouche was one of the jihadists who kept four French journalists hostage until they were freed in April 2014 in Syria. Defense lawyers claimed Israeli intelligence agents opened fire at the museum. Lawyer Virginie Taelman said, "The killing was not an attack by Islamic State, but a targeted execution by agents from Mossad."

Nemmouche was also represented by defense lawyer Henri Laquay. The trial was scheduled to run until March 1.

On January 30, 2019, prosecutors said that a baseball bat and false Kalashnikov assault rifle were left on a lawyer's desk after a theft at his office in an apparent attempt to intimidate him during the trial. Thieves stole a laptop computer containing the case file of Nemmouche. State broadcaster *RTBF* identified the lawyer as Vincent Lurquin, who was representing a woman at the museum when the attack happened. Nemmouche said he was not involved and that the intimidation attempt was a "catastrophe" for his case. "I ask that that all the magistrates and all the jurors be left alone… I have absolutely nothing to do with this theft, which I strongly condemn… I live in complete isolation, have been totally cut off from the outside world for years… I have no way to be in contact with anyone who might be in a position to make such threats… I am not the museum killer… I have nothing to do with, and I condemn, the attacks in Paris in 2015 and in Belgium in 2016."

On February 28, 2019, *AP* reported that defense attorney Sebastien Courtoy, who represented Mehdi Nemmouche, began his defense of his French jihadist client. He told Presiding Judge Laurence Massart that Israeli Mossad intelligence agents were the killers. A verdict was expected on March 7. Nemmouche faced 30 years in prison. He still faced French charges over a hostage taking in Syria.

On March 7, 2019, *AP* reported that the presiding judge at the Brussels criminal court, Laurence Massart, declared French ISIS member Mehdi Nemmouche guilty of four counts of "terrorist murder" for killing the four people at the Jewish museum. Nemmouche faced 30 years in prison. Accused accomplice Nacer Bendrer was found guilty of supplying the revolver and assault rifle used in the slayings. *AP* reported on March 12 that the court sentenced Nemmouche to life in prison. State broadcaster *RTBF* reported that Nacer Bendrer was sentenced to 15 years in prison.

On May 17, 2019, *AP* reported that Mehdi Nemmouche was transferred to a French prison to face charges of "abduction and illegal seques-

tration with links to a terrorist enterprise" in relation to the kidnapping of four French journalists held in Syria between June 2013 and May 2014. Nemmouche was sentenced in December 2018 to life in prison in Belgium on terror charges for shooting dead an Israeli couple and two people working at the museum.

March 22, 2016: *AP* reported on December 7, 2020 that pre-trial hearings began at the former NATO headquarters, now called Justitia, regarding the March 22, 2016 ISIS suicide bombings that killed 32 and injured hundreds at the Brussels subway and airport. The case involved 650 plaintiffs. Some 900 people suffered physical or mental trauma. Earlier in 2020, the federal prosecutor's office requested that eight of the 13 main suspects should be referred to the criminal court of assizes for charges of assassinations, attempted assassinations in a terrorist context, and belonging to a terrorist group. Among them was Salah Abdeslam, the lone known surviving suspect in the 2015 Paris attacks, and Mohamed Abrini, the Brussels native who left Brussels's Zaventem airport after his explosives failed to detonate. Abdeslam was captured in Brussels on March 18, 2016.

June 30, 2018: *AP* reported on November 25, 2020 that on November 27, 2020, the trial in Antwerp was to begin of four people, among them two Iranians including an Iranian diplomat believed to be the mastermind, accused of plotting to bomb a rally of 25,000 Iranian Mujahedeen-e-Khalq (MEK) opposition supporters in Villepinte, a Paris suburb, on June 30, 2018. The bomb destroyed an Army robot sent in to defuse the bomb that was found in the Mercedes car of Amir Saadouni and Nasimeh Naami, a couple arrested in a Brussels suburb. Luggage in the car contained 550 grams of triacetone triperoxide (TATP) and a detonator. The couple were of Iranian heritage but lived in Antwerp. Belgium's intelligence and security agency (VSSE) said diplomat Assadollah Assadi, 48, operated on orders of Iran's authorities and brought the explosives to Europe. VSSE believed Assadi was an officer of Iran's intelligence and security ministry Department 312 who operated under cover at Iran's Vienna embassy and recruited the couple years earlier. Assadi was represented by attorney Dimitri de Beco, who observed, "His defense will raise a number of procedural issues, including the question of his diplomatic immunity, since it is not disputed that he had diplomatic status, at least at the time of the facts." Defendant Mehrdad Arefani lived in Brussels and was suspected of traveling to Villepinte on the day of the planned attack. He had a phone with Assadi's number. Prosecutors claimed Assadi, code name Daniel, carried the explosives on the commercial flight to Austria, then transferred the bomb to Saadouni and Naami during a meeting in a Pizza Hut restaurant in Luxembourg just two days before their arrest. Naami said she believed the parcel contained fireworks. The defendants faced five and 20 years in prison on charges of "attempted terrorist murder and participation in the activities of a terrorist group".

BULGARIA

July 18, 2012: *AFP* and *al-Jazeera* reported on September 21, 2020 that Judge Adelina Ivanova of the Specialized Criminal Court in Sofia sentenced two Lebanese men in absentia to life in prison without parole for being accomplices in the July 18, 2012 bombing of a bus of Israeli tourists at Burgas Airport that killed five Israelis, including a pregnant woman, their Bulgarian bus driver, and the Franco-Lebanese bomber—Mohamad Hassan el-Husseini, 23—and wounded 38 people. Bulgaria's Interior Ministry blamed Hizballah for logistics and financing. The court found the duo guilty of complicity in an act of terrorism, manslaughter, attempted manslaughter, and using fake IDs. Lebanese-Australian Meliad Farah, 31 at the time of the attack, and Lebanese-Canadian Hassan El Hajj Hassan, 24, were charged in mid-2016 in absentia; they had long earlier fled Bulgaria. The court ruled that they must also pay damages to the families of those who died or were injured in the attack amounting to more than 100 million leva ($60 million). Prosecutor Evgenia Shtarkelova said that the duo was actively sought on an Interpol Red notice. The men had used faked U.S. driver's licenses, made by a printer at a Lebanese university. Public defender Zhanet Zhelyazkova represented Hassan.

CZECH REPUBLIC

2017: On January 14, 2019, *AP* reported that Prague's regional court convicted Czech national Jaromir Balda, 71, of carrying out two attacks on trains while blaming them on jihadis and sentenced him to four years in prison. Balda cut down two trees in 2017 that fell on train tracks near Mlada Boleslav, 30 miles north of Prague. Two passenger trains later hit the trees. No one was injured. He had placed pamphlets at the sites with threats of extremist attacks planned on Czech territory. He wanted to incite fear of Muslims and attacks. He pleaded guilty but claimed he did not want to harm anyone. The court ordered him to undergo psychiatric treatment. On April 16, 2019, *AP* reported that Prague's High Court upheld a four-year prison term issued by Prague's regional court for Balda.

FRANCE

August 1982: On September 9, 2020, *AFP* reported that Norwegian anti-terrorist police in Skien arrested Walid Abdulrahman Abu Zayed, who had lived in Norway since 1991. France had requested his extradition in 2015 for involvement in a 1982 attack in which two men threw grenades and fired into the Goldenberg restaurant in a Jewish neighborhood of the Marais quarter in Paris that killed six and injured 22. The attack had been attributed to the Abu Nidal Organization. Abu Zayed, now in his 60s, had earlier denied involvement. In 2015, he told the Norwegian daily *VG* he had never been to Paris. His wife told *AFP* in 2015 that he had never been in France. Abu Zayed was wanted for murder and attempted murder. France had issued four arrest warrants, including two against people in Jordan and another against a suspect believed hiding in the West Bank.

On November 27, 2020, *Reuters* reported that Norway announced that it would extradite Zayed to France. Zayed had moved to Norway in the 1990s. Norwegian authorities arrested him in September 2020. The Ministry of Justice cleared him for extradition to France on November 12; he appealed to the full Norwegian cabinet, which rejected his appeal.

1983: On January 29, 2019, *AP* reported the death from a heart attack of Varuzhan Karapetian, a Syrian of Armenian descent, who headed the French branch of the Armenian Secret Army for the Liberation of Armenia and carried out a 1983 bombing attack on Orly Airport in Paris that killed eight people. He confessed to paying a passenger to check a bomb-carrying bag for him onto a Turkish Airlines flight. He was sentenced to life imprisonment in France, but was released in 2001 on condition of his being deported to Armenia.

March 2012: On April 19, 2019, *AP* reported that a Paris appeals court convicted Abdelkader Merah of complicity to murder for his involvement in his brother's (Mohamed Merah) attack in March 2012 in the area that killed seven people. The court raised his sentence from 20 to 30 years after finding him guilty of an additional charge. He earlier was convicted in Toulouse and sentenced for ties to terrorism, but acquitted of conspiracy to murder, leading prosecutors to lodge an appeal. Mohamed Merah killed three soldiers, then fired on a Jewish school, killing a rabbi, his two young sons and a schoolgirl.

January 7 and 9, 2015: *AFP* reported on August 27, 2020 that on September 2, 2020, the trial would begin of 14 alleged accomplices, including a woman, of the January 7, 2015 jihadi attack against the *Charlie Hebdo* satirical weekly and the January 9, 2015 jihadi attack on a Jewish supermarket in Paris. Brothers Said and Cherif Kouachi killed 12 people at *Charlie Hebdo*'s office. Cherif's prison friend, Amedy Coulibaly, killed female police officer Clarissa Jean-Philippe, 27, during a routine traffic check on Montrouge on January 8, 2015. The next day, Coulibaly killed four Jewish men during a hostage-taking at the Hyper Cacher supermarket, claiming the attacks for ISIS. Three suspects were to be tried in absentia: Hayat Boumedienne, the wife of Coulibaly, and the Belhoucine brothers Mohamed and Mehdi. They were believed to have traveled to ISIS-held turf. Unconfirmed reports said they were dead. Mohamed Belhoucine, the elder of the two brothers, and Ali Riza Polat, 35, a French citizen of Turkish origin, were charged with complicity in terror, which carries a life sentence.

Prosecutors believed Polat was close to Coulibaly and helped build the terrorist trio's arsenal. He was also accused of helping "at all stages of the preparation". Polat tried to go to Syria but was in French detention since March 2015. Mohamed Belhoucine was accused of being the ideological mentor of Coulibaly, getting him in contact with ISIS, and writing the oath of allegiance that Coulibaly made to ISIS. Most of the other suspects were charged with association with a terror group and faced 20 year sentences. Attorneys for the *Charlie Hebdo* victims included Marie-Laure Barre and Nathalie Senyk. The Hyper Cacher victims' attorney was Patrick Klugman. Safya Akorri served as a defence attorney.

Among the cartoonists killed at *Charlie Hebdo* were director Stephane Charbonnier, known as "Charb", 47, Jean Cabut, known as "Cabu", 76, and Georges Wolinski, 80.

On September 1, 2020, *AP* reported that *Charlie Hebdo* reprinted the caricatures of the Prophet Mohammed (first run in 2006 by the Danish newspaper *Jyllands Posten*) cited by the killers, observing "history cannot be rewritten nor erased".

CNN, AFP, AP, and the *Washington Post* reported that on December 16, 2020, all 14 defendants were convicted in the trial of those linked the January 7-9, 2015 Paris attacks on *Charlie Hebdo* and a kosher supermarket. Defendant Ali Riza Polat, 35, lieutenant of the virulently anti-Semitic market attacker, Amédy Coulibaly, and two other defendants contracted COVID-19, forcing the suspension of the trial for a month. Polat was the only defendant present to face a life term. A handwriting expert testified Polat wrote a list of arms and munitions—plus their prices—which was linked to the attack. The minimum sentence requested by prosecutors was five years, for a suspect who shopped for weapons and a car, and watched as his friend removed the GPS tracker from a motorcycle. Judicial police said investigators examined 37 million bits of phone data. Coulibaly's wife, Hayat Boumeddiene, the only woman on trial, fled to Syria days before the attack with two other absent defendants, Mohamed and Mehdi Belhoucine; the brother were believed to now be dead. The French widow of an ISIS emir testified from prison that she met Boumeddiene in late 2019 at a camp in Syria. Boumeddiene was found guilty of financing terrorism and belonging to a criminal terrorist network. Five defendants were convicted only of involvement in a criminal conspiracy; the rest were charged with terrorist complicity. Polat was sentenced to 30 years in prison; 20 without parole.

April 19, 2015: *AP* reported on October 5, 2020 that the Paris trial began of Algerian man Sidi Ahmed Ghlam, 29, accused of killing female fitness instructor Aurelie Chatelain, 32, in her car and trying to blow up a church during Sunday Mass in Villejuif, a Paris Suburb, on April 19, 2015. He inadvertently shot himself in the leg and was arrested after calling emergency services. ISIS operatives in Syria allegedly orchestrated the attack. He was charged with murder and attempted terrorist murder, and faced life in prison. Nine other defendants joined him at trial; seven were charged with providing logistical assistance including weapons and protective vests. Police had killed Abdelhamid Abaaoud, a third sponsor, who had coordinated the attacks on November 13, 2015 on the Bataclan concert hall in Paris, France's national stadium and several cafes. Authorities in Algeria and France believed that in late 2014-early 2015 he went to Turkey, where he met Abaaoud and other operatives. He was represented by attorney Jean-Hubert Portejoie. Ghlam admitted to being directed by ISIS operatives Abdelhamid Abaaoud, Abdelnasser Benyoucef and Samir Nouad. Authorities believed Benyoucef was the sponsor of Amédy Coulibaly, who shot up a kosher supermarket in January 2015. Benyoucef and Nouad, a member of Algerian jihadi GIA in the 1990s, were believed to have died in suicide attacks in Syria; they were tried in absentia in the Villejuif case.

On November 5, 2020, a Paris criminal court sentenced Ghlam to life in prison. The sentence allows no chance for parole for at least 22 years. His attorney said he would appeal the verdict. Ghlam said an accomplice, who was never found, was the killer. Ghlam's DNA was found in Chatelain's car. Seven accomplices were sentenced to between three and 30 years in prison. The court convicted in absentia Abdelnasser Benyoucef

and Samir Nouad for orchestrating the attack, and sentenced them to life in prison.

August 21, 2015: The *New York Times* reported on May 24, 2020, that Alek Skarlatos, an American who helped stop a terrorist attack on the Thalys train en route from Amsterdam to Paris, was running as a Republican in Washington's 4th Congressional District.

AFP and *AP* reported on November 16, 2020, the trial began of Moroccan man Ayoub el-Khazzani, 31, for an attempted terrorist attack on August 21, 2015 on car No. 12 on the Thalys high-speed train. Three passengers—off-duty U.S. servicemen airman Spencer Stone and National Guardsman Alek Skarlatos, and Franco-American professor Mark Magoolian—foiled the attack. El-Khazzani shot and wounded the professor with a pistol. Student Anthony Sadler, 23, helped subdue the terrorist. Their actions were turned into a 2018 film, "The 15:17 to Paris", by Clint Eastwood. El-Khazzani had an AK-47, a box-cutter, and a bag of nearly 300 rounds of ammunition. Sadler had backpacked with the soldiers. El-Shazzani slashed Stone in the neck and eyebrow and almost cut Stone's thumb off. El-Khazzani joined ISIS in Syria in May 2015. He was charged with "attempted terrorist murder". He was tried with three alleged accomplices, including

- Bilal Chatra, who was 19 at the time of the attack. Chatra was represented by attorney Lea Dordilly. Chatra was an Algerian IS member. He was to be the second man on the train but bowed out a week before the attack.

- Mohamed Bakkali allegedly took in el-Khazzani and Chatra in Budapest, Hungary, which he denies. The two were arrested in Germany in 2016.

- Redouane el-Amrani Ezzerrifi, allegedly piloted a boat to help in their return to Europe.

Belgian Abdelhamid Abaaoud was believed to have been one of the masterminds behind the Thalys attack and have recruited Chatra in Turkey to be a scout for el-Khazzani getting into Europe.

El-Khazzani was represented by attorney Sarah Mauger-Poliak. The trial was scheduled to run until December 17. El-Khazzani faced life in prison.

The three heroes were represented by attorney Thibault de Montbrial.

As of the start of the trial, Eastwood, 90, had not responded to a summons.

On November 25, el-Khazzani told the court that he intended to kill only U.S. soldiers in retaliation for bombings of civilians in Syria, refusing Abdelhamid Abaaoud's directive to kill members of the European Commission he incorrectly believed were on the train's car 12.

Reuters reported on December 18, 2020 that a Paris court sentenced el-Khazzani to life in prison for attempted murder with intent to commit terrorism.

November 13, 2015: On March 15, 2019, *AP* reported that Dutch police detained two men, aged 29 and 31, in Amsterdam on suspicion of involvement in providing weapons used in the November 2015 terror attacks in Paris following an investigation by French, Belgian and Dutch detectives. Authorities seized computers, data carriers, documents and cell phones from their homes. An investigating judge ordered the 29-year-old detained for two weeks. The 31-year-old was released for health reasons.

AP and *DPA* reported on July 29, 2019 that prosecutors in Naumburg announced German authorities extradited a Bosnian man, 39, to Belgium, where he was sought in connection with the terrorist attacks in Paris that killed 130 people. He was arrested in June 2019.

MSN.com and *InsideEdition.com* reported on June 12, 2020 that a stolen painting by Banksy honoring the Bataclan concert hall victims was recovered in a home in Abruzzo, Italy.

2016: On February 12, 2019, *AP* reported that two individuals were placed in custody as part of the investigation of the 2016 slaying by Larossi Abballa of two police officers in their home in Magnanville, west of Paris, in the name of ISIS.

July 14, 2016: On June 23, 2020, *AP* reported that counter-terrorism prosecutors formally requested for nine suspects to be tried for the July 14, 2016 Bastille Day truck attack in Nice that left 86 people dead. The nine were not identified. Four suspects were earlier charged with terrorist conspiracy for alleged links to Mohamed Lahouaiej Bouhlel, who drove a 19-ton truck down Nice's Promenade des Anglais and into a crowd waiting for the fireworks display. Five other suspects were charged with other criminal counts, including for allegedly providing arms to the Tunisian attacker, who lived in France. The prosecutor's office said they likely did not have knowledge of his plans. One of the five was at large, avoiding a criminal arrest warrant. ISIS had claimed credit for the attack, although authorities said there was no evidence that ISIS orchestrated the attack.

September 3-4, 2016: On September 23, 2019, the *Guardian* reported that the trial began of five women who planned to conduct a car bomb attack against the Notre Dame Cathedral. They allegedly tried to set off firebombs in front of restaurants in central Paris near Notre Dame. A sixth young woman was tried for failing to denounce the planned attack. The trial was expected to run until October 11, 2019.

AP reported that during the night of September 3-4, 2016, Ines Madani, then 19, and Ornella Gilligmann parked Madani's father's grey Peugeot 607 loaded with six gas canisters but showing no license plates on a narrow street in front of busy restaurants near Notre Dame. They poured diesel fuel over the car and threw a lit cigarette at it. The diesel did not catch fire. No one was hurt. The women fled. Police found the duo's fingerprints and DNA on the gas canisters. Police arrested Gilligmann with her husband and three children in southern France two days later. She had attempted to reach Syria in 2014.

Madani, coached by her ISIS handler, went to Boussy-Saint-Antoine, joining other women, including a cleaner, 23, in a psychiatric clinic, who had become radicalized. The women fled the apartment, fearing police surveillance. One left a note written in lipstick on a mirror saying: "Mummy loves you." One woman attempted to stab a plainclothes officer. Madani was injured in the legs by police officers firing as she attempted to escape.

Ines Madani was reportedly in touch with ISIS in Syria and recruited other women in France, using aliases of male ISIS fighters on *Telegram* and in phone calls. She was represented by attorney Laurent Pasquet-Marinacce, who said she was manipulated by ISIS string-pullers in Syria. Court documents identified Syria-based ISIS fighter Rachid Kassim as coordinating the plot along with other attacks in France, such as the attack on a French priest inside his Normandy church and the murder of a French police couple at their home, in front of their child. He was tried in absentia, although observers suspected he died in a 2017 drone strike in Mosul, Iraq. On social media, he had suggested group stabbing or "filling a vehicle with gas cylinders and spraying them with fuel". Madani and Gilligmann sent Kassim videos pledging allegiance to ISIS, according to court documents.

The suspects faced from 30 years to life in prison if convicted.

AP reported on October 10, 2019 that prosecutor Jean-Michel Bourles sought prison sentences of 25 and 30 years for the duo, saying only Inès Madani's youth prevented the prosecution from seeking a life term instead of 30 years. He requested 25 years for Gilligmann. Both women acknowledged roles in the plot but fingered each other as the instigator. On October 14, 2019, the two women were convicted of terrorism charges and sentenced to 30 (Madani) and 25 (Gilligmann) years in prison after apologizing for their actions. Two other women, Amel Sakaou and Sarah Hervouet, were sentenced to 20 years each. The group plotted a new attack in Sakaou's suburban apartment, which was under police surveillance. Sakaou refused to appear during the trial. Hervouet, who was once betrothed to Kassim without ever meeting him, said she accepted her conviction. Kassim was convicted in absentia and given a life sentence.

June 6, 2017: *CBS News* reported that Farid Ikken, 43, an ISIS follower, charged a police officer outside the Notre Dame cathedral in Paris with a hammer, yelling "This is for Syria!" In early October 2020, a court sentenced him to 28 years in jail.

December 11, 2018: On January 29, 2019, *AP* reported that a French judicial official said five people were arrested and detained as part of the investigation into the Christmas market attack that left five dead in Strasbourg on December 11, 2018. They were suspected of helping gunman Cherif Chekatt obtain his weapon. On February 2, three people detained in the investigation were handed preliminary terrorism charges. The other two suspects were freed without being charged on January 30.

GERMANY

September 26, 1980: *AP* reported on September 23, 2020 that the German government established a 1.2 million-euro ($1.4 million) fund to help survivors of the September 26, 1980 far-right attack on Munich's Oktoberfest that killed 13 people, including three children, and wounded more than 200. Among the dead was the bomber, student Gundolf Koehler, a supporter of a banned far-right group. The federal and Bavarian state governments and the city of Munich will contribute to the fund. The initial investigation indicated that Koehler acted alone and was closed in 1982. In 2014, a new witness resurfaced and federal prosecutors reopened the case. In July 2020, prosecutors said there might have been co-conspirators but the report could not be corroborated, so the second probe was closed.

June 11, 2000: *Deutsche Welle* and *DPA* reported on June 11, 2020 that residents of Dessau commemorated the memory of Mozambican Alberto Adriano, 39. The father of three had lived in East Germany and then reunified Germany for 12 years before he was beaten to death by three drunken neo-Nazis outside his home near the Stadtpark, Dessau's historic city park, on June 11, 2000. He died on June 14 of massive head injuries, never recovering from a coma. The trio confessed, showed no remorse, and were convicted. The eldest got life in prison. The other two, were who both 16 years old, received nine-year sentences. Adriano had worked in a meat-processing plant and came to Dessau from Mozambique in 1988, one of the last East German

Vertragsarbeiter (contract workers), named after the bilateral migrant worker contracts the GDR signed with other socialist countries.

July 23, 2016: On October 25, 2019, Bavaria's state criminal police office had decided to classify the July 23, 2016 shooting in front of a Munich fast food restaurant in which German-Iranian David Ali Somboly, 18, killed nine people and then himself as a "politically motivated crime", noting that "the radical right-wing and racist views of the perpetrator should not be ignored". The dead were of Hungarian, Turkish, Greek, and Kosovo Albanian extraction. The court noted that Somboly had researched online the murder of 77 people by Norwegian right-wing extremist Anders Behring Breivik five years earlier. The court also cited revenge for bullying by schoolmates, some of immigrant origin, mental illness, a lack of social contacts and excessive playing of combat video games. In 2018, a man was sentenced to seven years in prison for selling a pistol and ammunition to Somboly. In a separate trial, a man who ran the web forum where illegal goods, including the weapon, were traded was sentenced to six years.

December 19, 2016: *AP* reported on February 22, 2019 that the German government rejected *Focus* media reports claiming authorities sought to cover up the involvement of Bilal Ben Ammar, a second man in the December 19, 2016 truck attack on a Berlin Christmas market, by deporting him. *Focus* claimed Ammar was arrested days after the attack and deported to Tunisia a month later, despite having frequent contacts with the attacker, Tunisian asylum-seeker Anis Amri, including having dinner with him on the eve of the attack. German media reported that Ben Ammar had ties to Moroccan intelligence. German Interior Minister Seehofer said authorities had acted lawfully in the deportation to Tunisia on February 1, 2017.

On April 19, 2019, *AP* and *Der Spiegel* reported that Anis Amri was part of a Europe-wide jihadi network. Amri died in a shootout with Italian police days after the attack. His contacts with ISIS supporters included extremists tied to the 2015 attacks in Paris. The German Federal Prosecutors Office and federal police cited recordings made of prison conversations involving Frenchman Clement Baur, who was arrested in 2017 for planning an attack during the country's presidential election. Police said Baur claimed Amri was part of a plan to stage simultaneous attacks in Europe and that he was fascinated by the 2016 Nice truck attack.

June 15, 2018: Police arrested Tunisian Sief Allah H., in his apartment at Osloerstrasse 3 in the Chorweiler neighborhood of Cologne, on suspicion of producing biological weapons to use in an attack in Germany. A month later, authorities arrested his German wife, Yasmin H. *AP* reported on March 7, 2019 that federal prosecutors charged Sief, 30, and his wife, 43, with preparing a severe act of violence over a plot to use the toxin ricin. Prosecutors said they followed ISIS ideology. They bought thousands of castor beans and developed ricin and turned fireworks into explosives. He had tried unsuccessfully to travel to Syria twice in 2017 to join ISIS as a fighter. Prosecutors said she helped him by buying plane tickets, booking accommodation and sending him money. Investigators found about 3,150 castor bean seeds and 84.3 milligrams of ricin along with bomb-making components. He was charged with two additional counts of preparing severe acts of violence; she was accused of having supported him in both cases. He was also charged with trying to join a foreign terrorist group.

August 26, 2018: *AP* and *DPA* reported on March 18, 2019 that Syrian male asylum seeker Alaa Sheiki went on trial in Dresden state court for manslaughter in the August 26, 2018 stabbing in Chemnitz that killed Daniel Hillig, 35, a German carpenter. Iraqi co-defendant Yousif Ibrahim Abdullah remained at large and was sought on an international arrest warrant. On August 22, 2019, *AP* reported that the state court in Dresden convicted Syrian asylum-seeker Alaa S., 24, of manslaughter and dangerous bodily harm. The court sentenced the defendant to nine years and six months in prison; prosecutors had requested 10 years. An Iraqi suspect was sought on an international arrest warrant.

October 2018: *AP* reported on April 17, 2019 that prosecutors indicted Mine K., 47, a German woman who was arrested in October 2018 as she attempted to return to Germany after allegedly marrying an ISIS fighter in a January 2015 video-call ceremony from Germany, joining him with her son in Turkey in February 2015, and living in a Tal Afar, Iraq, home seized by the group. Her husband was killed on guard duty later in 2015. She decided in 2016 to leave ISIS. She and her son left ISIS-controlled territory for Turkey, then returned to Germany in 2018. She was charged in a Duesseldorf court with membership in a foreign terrorist organization and having appropriated opponents' property in violation of international law.

October 2018: On March 25, 2019 Austrian authorities in Vienna arrested an Iraqi man, 42, suspected of carrying out unsuccessful attacks on trains in Germany in October and December 2018 and sympathizing with ISIS. The suspected terrorist lived in Vienna. In October 2018, a high-speed train hit a steel cable stretched over the tracks between electrification masts on the Nuremberg-Munich line, damaging a window in the driver's cab but causing no injuries. An Arabic-language threatening note was found nearby as well as other documents suggesting a link to ISIS. On December 25, 2018, police found damage to overhead wires on a railway line in Berlin's eastern suburbs, a note in Arabic, and an ISIS flag. Prosecutors and police in Berlin and Bavaria said that the Iraqi man was suspected of attempted murder, causing serious damage to property, membership in a terrorist organization and dangerous interference in railway traffic.

GREECE

June 14, 1985: *AP* reported on September 21, 2019 that Greek police had arrested a Lebanese suspect, 65, on the island of Mykonos on September 19 in response to a warrant from Germany in the June 14, 1985 hijacking of Trans World Airlines flight 847 from Athens, diverting it to Beirut International Airport, Lebanon. The terrorists shot to death U.S. Navy diver Robert Stethem, 23, after beating him unconscious. The

flight originated in Cairo and was destined for San Diego, with stops in Athens, Rome, Boston, and Los Angeles. They released the other 146 passengers and crew members after stops in Beirut and Algiers. The last hostage was freed after 17 days. The suspect was held on the Greek island of Syros, and was to be transferred to the Korydallos high security prison in Athens for extradition proceedings. The Lebanese Foreign Ministry said the suspect was Lebanese journalist Mohammed Saleh. Several Greek media outlets identified the detainee as Mohammed Ali Hammadi, who was arrested in Frankfurt in 1987 and convicted in Germany for the skyjacking and Stethem's murder. Hammadi, an alleged Hizballah member, was sentenced to life in prison but was paroled in 2005 and returned to Lebanon. The U.S. had demanded his extradition from Germany, but Germany demurred after Hizballah kidnapped two Germans in Beirut. Hammadi, fellow hijacker Hasan Izz-al-Din, and accomplice Ali Atwa were on the FBI's list of most wanted terrorists. The FBI offered a reward of up to $5 million for information leading to each man's capture. On September 23, Greek authorities said the arrest was a case of mistaken identity, and released the suspect, who had been held without charges for four days. He had been detained on Mykonos during a cruise stop. He was put up in a hotel on Syros island. He had been a journalist for the Lebanese daily *as-Safir* until it closed in 2016.

December 17, 2018: *AP* reported on January 8, 2019 that the Popular Fighters Group claimed credit for setting off a bomb at the Athens offices of *Skai TV* and radio station and daily newspaper *Kathimerini* on December 17, 2018 to protest the media organization's "support" for austerity policies during Greece's eight-year financial crisis. No one was injured.

ITALY

1981: In 1981, Cesare Battisti escaped from an Italian prison while awaiting trial on four counts of murder allegedly committed when he was a member of the Armed Proletarians for Communism. In 1990, he was convicted in absentia and faced a life term for killing two police officers, a jeweler, and a butcher. He fled to France, joining dozens of Italian left wingers protected by the French Socialist government. He ran off to Mexico, then escaped extradition from there by fleeing to Brazil. He was arrested in Rio de Janeiro in 2007, but then-Brazilian President Luiz Inacio Lula da Silva denied Italy's extradition request and granted him asylum in 2010. He was released from jail and wrote a book about his Rio prison experience, attending an April 12, 2012 book presentation. He was arrested in 2017 while trying to cross the Brazil-Bolivia border with the equivalent of $7,500 in undeclared cash, but was freed within days. Bolivia's public defender, David Tezanos, said Battisti formally requested asylum in Bolivia on December 21, 2018. Brazilian Supreme Federal Tribunal Justice Luiz Fux announced in December 2018 that Interpol had issued an arrest request on tax evasion and money laundering charges, leading him to issue a Brazilian warrant. Outgoing Brazilian President Michel Temer signed the decree ordering extradition. Battisti fled to Bolivia. Bolivian police, working with Italian agents, arrested Battisti, now 64, in Santa Cruz de La Sierra, Bolivia on January 12, 2019, after intelligence agents spotted him using a mobile device. Italy sent a military aircraft to pick him up on January 13, 2019; he arrived at Rome's Ciampino militiary airport shortly after 11:30 a.m. on January 14, 2019. Brazilian President Jair Bolsonaro applauded the capture. Italian Premier Giuseppe Conte said Battisti would begin serving his life sentences upon returning to Italy. Italian Interior Minister Matteo Salvini called Battisti a "delinquent who doesn't deserve to live comfortably on the beach but rather to finish his days in prison". Under Brazilian law people extradited to serve life sentences must have their sentences capped at 30 years, a concession rejected by Italian officials who instead took him into custody in Bolivia. Battisti was scheduled to serve his sentence at Rome's Rebibbia prison. He was transferred to the maximum-security Oristano prison in remote western Sardinia. Justice Minister Alfonso Bonafede said security concerns prompted the change.

Malta

October 16, 2017: On November 20, 2019, the *Guardian, AFP,* and *Reuters* reported that armed forces personnel boarded a yacht at about 5:30 a.m. and arrested prominent Maltese hotelier and power company director Yorgen Fenech, 53, as his yacht, *Gio,* was heading out to sea from Portomaso, in an operation linked to the murder by car bomb of the Maltese anti-corruption journalist Daphne Caruana Galizia on October 16, 2017. Some 24 hours earlier, Maltese Prime Minister Joseph Muscat offered immunity from prosecution to an alleged middleman in exchange for information about those who ordered the murder. One of the last investigations that Caruana Galizia was working on was a massive leak of data from Fenech's business. On November 30, 2019, prosecutors charged Fenech with being an accomplice to the murder. He pleaded innocent, and was remanded into custody.

On November 26, 2019, Tourism Minister Konrad Mizzi, Economy Minister Chris Cardona and Muscat's chief of staff, Keith Schembri, resigned, denying wrongdoing. On December 1, Prime Minister Joseph Muscat said he would resign in January 2020.

CNN reported on July 22, 2020 that Melvin Theuma, a taxi driver alleged to have been a middleman in the murder of Daphne Caruana Galizia, was in critical condition following a nighttime knifing on July 21. He sustained injuries on the right side of his torso and his neck. Police suggested that the knife wounds were self-inflicted. Theuma was granted a presidential pardon in exchange for testifying in the case. He was due to attend a court hearing on July 22. The *Times of Malta* reported that the murder case against Yorgen Fenech continued.

On August 16, 2020, *CBS News 60 Minutes* reported that fellow journalists were continuing the investigation of bribery, cronyism, organized crime, and money laundering that Galizia wrote about until she was killed by a car bomb. The Daphne Project, a consortium of major international news organizations, including *Reuters* and *The Guardian,* followed her leads.

NETHERLANDS

December 15, 2015: *AP* reported on July 18, 2019 that Amsterdam District Court convicted Naoufal F., 38, a career criminal, of organizing the murder of Iranian-born Ali Motamed, who lived in the Netherlands. Two hit men who shot him outside his home on December 15, 2015 were convicted earlier in 2019. The court sentenced F. to life for arranging the murder, but said the motive was unclear. In January 2019, the Dutch government said it was "probable that Iran had a hand" in the killing of Motamed and another individual in The Hague in 2017.

August 11, 2018: On January 31, 2019, Dutch prosecutors demanded a 20-month prison sentence for a man, 35, who threw home-made fire-bombs at the Turkish consulate in Amsterdam on August 11, 2018, saying he wanted to draw attention to the "Kurdish question". He was waving a knife when police arrested him near the consulate on Amsterdam's Museum Square. One of the devices caused a small blaze on the grounds of the consulate. The verdict was expected on February 14, 2019.

August 31, 2018: On September 3, 2019, prosecutors requested a 25-year sentence at the trial of Afghan asylum-seeker Jawed S., 20, for stabbing two 38-year-old American male tourists in the back at Amsterdam's Central railway station on August 31, 2018. Prosecutors said it was a terrorist attack to force authorities to take action against anti-Islam lawmaker Geert Wilders. Jawed S. was tried for attempted murder. Police shot him after the men were stabbed. Prosecutors said S. did not know his victims were Americans.

On November 16, 2020, an Amsterdam appeals court upheld the conviction for attempted murder with a terrorist motive of Jawed S., 21. The court reduced the sentence of the attacker from nearly 27 years to 25 years based on sentences in similar cases and on his young age. The court said he took a train from Germany to Amsterdam to avenge what he perceived as insults to Islam. The attacker was ordered to pay the victims $3.55 million in damages.

September 2018: *AP* reported on October 8, 2020 that the Rotterdam District Court convicted six jihadi men of plotting to fire AK-47 assault rifles at a festival and set off a car bomb and sentenced them to 10-17 years. They planned to set off their explosive vests when police arrived. Acting on intelligence agencies' tips, an undercover policeman infiltrated the gang and thwarted the attack. Police arrested them in September 2018. The group's ringleader, a man of Iraqi descent, was sentenced to 17 years.

NORTHERN IRELAND

November 21, 1974: *AFP* reported on November 18, 2020 that West Midlands Police and counterterrorism officers from the Police Service of Northern Ireland detained a 65-year-old man at his Belfast home under the Terrorism Act for the November 21, 1974 bombings of the Mulberry Bush and Tavern in the Town pubs in Birmingham that killed 21 and injured 182. In 1975, the "Birmingham Six" were wrongly jailed. The Court of Appeal in 1991 ruled that their conviction was "unsafe" and freed them. The bombings were blamed on the Provisional Irish Republican Army (PIRA), which never claimed responsibility. Among those who died were John Rowlands and Maxine Hambleton, 18. *AP* reported on November 20, 2020 that West Midlands Police released the suspect after searching his Belfast home.

1975: *AFP* reported on May 13, 2020 that the UK Supreme Court ruled for former Sinn Fein leader Gerry Adams's appeal against his 1970s jailbreak convictions. Adams, now 71, had been sentenced twice in 1975 for trying to escape from prison. He successfully argued that his 1973 detention under the government's internment program of holding terrorism suspects without trial was invalid. A unanimous court agreed, holding that the original interim custody order (ICO) issued on July 21, 1973, should have been made personally by the Minister for Northern Ireland at the time, not a junior minister. Thus, "The making of the ICO in respect of the appellant (Adams) was invalid. It follows that he was not detained lawfully... It further follows that he was wrongfully convicted of the offences of attempting to escape from lawful custody and his convictions for those offences must be quashed." Adams tried to escape in December 1973 and July 1974 from the Maze prison near Belfast with IRA assistance. He was jailed in 1975 for 4½ years for the attempts. Adams ran Sinn Fein, the IRA's political wing, from 1983 until February 2018. He was charged with IRA membership in 1978; the case was dropped for insufficient evidence. He claimed he was not part of the paramilitary leadership.

NORWAY

July 2011: On September 16, 2020, *Reuters, Verdens Gang* and *AFP* reported that Oeystein Storrvik, the attorney for Anders Behring Breivik, said he planned to seek parole when he becomes eligible in July 2021.

RUSSIA

April 3, 2017: On December 10, 2019, *AP* and *AFP* reported that a military court in St. Petersburg convicted 11 people for the suicide bombing of a St. Petersburg subway train on April 3, 2017, killing 16 people, including Kyrgyz suicide bomber Akbarjon Djalilov, 22, and wounding more than 50. The court sentenced Abror Azimov, 29, a man from Kyrgyzstan, to life in prison and sentenced nine men and one woman to 19 to 28 years. The woman, Shokhista Karimova, 48, was sentenced to 20 years. Police had arrested 20 people, declaring 11 of them accomplices of the perpetrator and charging them with terrorism. Their lawyers said they would appeal the ruling. Ten of the defendants were accused of acting as accomplices, such as providing Djalilov with explosives and false documents. Charges included organizing a terrorist group, perpetrating an "act of terror", weapons trafficking, and making explosive devices. Prosecutors said the defendants formed two "terrorist cells" in Moscow and Saint Petersburg, then wired money and gave explosives to Djalilov. The Imam Shamil Battalion, which experts said is linked to al-Qaeda, claimed credit.

SLOVAKIA

February 21, 2018: *AP* reported on March 14, 2019 that police charged a suspect with ordering the slaying of investigative reporter Jan Kuciak and his fiancee Martina Kusnirova on February 21, 2018, in their home in a case that brought down the Slovak government. Slovak authorities believed it was a contract killing linked to Kuciak's investigating possible government corruption and ties between politicians and Italian mobsters. Four suspects were charged. The mastermind was believed to be at large.

SPAIN

August 17-18, 2017: *AFP* and *Reuters* reported on November 10, 2020 that the trial began in Spain's National Court in San Fernando de Henares near Madrid of three men accused of helping members of an ISIS cell that conducted two attacks in Barcelona and the nearby seaside town of Cambrils that killed 16 people and wounded 140 on August 17-18, 2017. Two defendants, a Spaniard and a Moroccan, were accused of membership in the cell; another Moroccan of collaborating with the group. A driver had crashed a van into pedestrians on Barcelona's Las Ramblas boulevard, killing 14, including two children aged 3 and 7. While at large, the terrorist killed another person but was shot dead by police several days later. Five accomplices of the driver rammed into pedestrians in Cambrils and stabbed to death a woman. Police shot to death the five terrorists. Observers expected the trial to end on December 16.

Prosecutors requested

- 41 years in prison for Mohamed Houli Chemlal, 23, for belonging to a jihadist group, manufacture and possession of explosives, and conspiracy to wreak havoc. He admitted that they had been planning attacks "on an even greater scale", with Barcelona's Sagrada Familia basilica, the Camp Nou football stadium in Barcelona and the Eiffel Tower among the suspected targets. An accidental explosion in Alcanar changed their plans. Chemlal lived, but imam Abdelbaki Es Satty, 44, who allegedly radicalized the group, died.

- 36 years for Driss Oukabir, 31, whose brother was one of the attackers. Driss allegedly rented the van used in the Barcelona attack and faced the same charges as Chemlal.

- Eight years for Said Ben Iazza, 27, for collaborating with a terror group and lending them his van and ID.

SWEDEN

February 28, 1986: *AP*, *AFP* and *CNN* reported on June 10, 2020 that Swedish investigators named disgruntled Swedish graphic designer Stig Engström, then-52, who worked at the Skandia insurance company near the scene of the crime, as the assassin of Prime Minister Olof Palme on February 28, 1986. As the suspect died at age 66 in 2000 from an apparent suicide, Sweden decided to close the case. Chief prosecutor Krister Petersson said that investigators did not conclusively link a weapon to the assassination. Engström, the "Skandia Man", had been active in a military shooting club. Investigations had questioned more than 10,000 people; 134 people confessed. Police noted that the suspect had changed his story several times. The similarly-named Christer Pettersson, a petty criminal and drug addict, was convicted of the crime in July 1989 after Palme's widow Lisbet identified him in a line-up. He was freed on appeal months later. He died in 2004; Lisbet died in 2018. Police never found the weapon, despite testing 788 revolvers.

April 7, 2017: *AP* reported on July 18, 2019 that Justice Minister Morgan Johansson said Iryna Zamanova, a Ukrainian woman who lost her leg in a Stockholm terror attack, could not be granted a permanent residence permit out of compassion because "clemency only applies to criminal cases, not residence permits". The tourist received a temporary permit after the April 7, 2017 attack to give evidence in the trial of Rakhmat Akilov, who drove a stolen truck into a crowd in Stockholm. Akilov was sentenced to life in June 2018.

TURKEY

2013: On May 13, 2019, *AP* and *Anadolu* reported that an Ankara court sentenced Yusuf Nazik, who was accused of planning a deadly 2013 bombing, to life in prison for murder, disrupting the unity of the state and membership in a terrorist group, among other charges. Turkish intelligence agents captured him in Syria in September 2018 and brought him to Turkey. He was accused of planning and organizing two car bombings that killed 52 people in Reyhanli, near the border with Syria. Turkey said a Turkish Marxist group with alleged links to Syria's intelligence agency carried out the attack. Two other suspects were sentenced for aiding a terrorist group.

2016: *AP* and *Anadolu* reported on May 17, 2019 that a court in Istanbul sentenced 14 people to life imprisonment without parole for two Kurdistan Freedom Falcons (TAK) car-and-suicide bombings near Istanbul's Besiktas soccer stadium in 2016 that killed 47 people. Four defendants were convicted of attempting to disrupt the unity and integrity of the state and of premeditated murder through bombing. Ten other defendants were convicted of disrupting Turkey's unity and of assisting the bombings.

January 1, 2017: On February 18, 2019, *Anadolu* reported that Uzbek national Abdulkadir Masharipov denied all charges against him, including membership in a terror group and murder. He was the main suspect in the January 1, 2017 attack that killed 39 people in Istanbul's Reina nightclub. He was arrested 15 days later. He said that although he had admitted the attack to police, he was not the man with the AK-47 rifle. Some 58 suspects, mostly foreigners, were on trial. Only 39 were in custody.

UKRAINE

July 17, 2014: Malaysia Airlines Flight 17, a B-777, was shot down over Grabovo, Ukraine. On November 3, 2020, the trial in a Dutch courtroom began of Oleg Putalov, who was one of four people charged in the case. Putalov denied involvement. Prosecutors said that a Russian-made Buk missile launched from territory controlled by pro-Russian rebels hit the jet, killing all 298 passengers and crew on board en route from Amsterdam to Kuala Lumpur. Also accused were two other Russians—Igor Girkin and Sergey Dubinskiy—and Ukrainian Leonid Kharchenko.

July 20, 2016: *AP* reported on December 12, 2019 that Ukrainian police arrested several suspects in the car-bomb killing of prominent Belarus-born journalist Pavel Sheremet in Kyiv on July 20, 2016, but had not determined who ordered the killing. One of the suspects, Andrii Antonenko, a rock musician who earlier served as a special forces sergeant, announced his arrest on *Facebook* and said that his apartment was being searched. Other detainees included Iuliia Kuzmenko, a doctor who helped troops in the east as a volunteer, and Yana Dugar, a soldier who fought in the conflict. Deputy national police chief Yevhen Koval said that Antonenko and Kuzmenko were accused of planting an explosive device under Sheremet's car, citing footage from surveillance cameras and other evidence. Two other suspects were in custody on charges related to a different criminal case.

UNITED KINGDOM

1974: On January 31, 2019, *AP* reported that Surrey Coroner Richard Travers ruled that the inquest into the 1974 Guildford pub bombings, carried out by the Irish Republican Army, at the heart of the film "In The Name of the Father", were to be resumed. Proceedings were suspended after four people were convicted in 1975. The convictions were later overturned.

July 20, 1982: *AP* reported on December 18, 2019 that British Judge Amanda Yip ruled in a civil case that John Downey, 67, an Irishman, was an "active participant" in the July 20, 1982 IRA nail bombing of London's Hyde Park that killed four soldiers and horses from a detachment of the Queen's Household Cavalry and injured 31 other people. Relatives of the dead brought the suit five years earlier, after the criminal case against Downey failed. The ruling made it possi-

ble for the families, including Sarahjane Young, daughter of a victim, to sue Downey for damages. Downey remained in prison in Northern Ireland, awaiting trial for another attack during the Troubles.

December 21, 1988: *AFP* reported on August 21, 2020 that after winning permission to appeal, the family of convicted Lockerbie Pan Am 103 bomber Abdelbaset Mohmet al-Megrahi began a formal legal challenge to overturn his conviction. Al-Megrahi died of cancer in Libya in 2012, the only person convicted in the bombing which killed 243 passenegers and 16 crew as it flew from London to New York on December 21, 1988 over Lockerbie, Scotland. Another 11 people in Lockerbie also died. Three Scottish judges serving in a special court in the Netherlands jailed him for life in 2001; he was released on health grounds in 2009. The family was represented by attorney Aamer Anwar.

AFP reported on November 24, 2020 that al-Megrahi's posthumous appeal began in a Scotland court. Scotland's most senior judge, Lord Justice General Colin Sutherland, and four other judges in Scotland's highest criminal court were to hear the case via video link. The legal team for Megrahi's family took part remotely from Glasgow. The Scottish Criminal Cases Review Commission (SCCRC) referred al-Megrahi's family's appeal to the High Court of Justiciary in Edinburgh in March 2020.

The *Washington Post*, *Wall Street Journal*, *USA Today*, and the *New York Times* reported on December 16, 2020 that the Department of Justice planned to unseal charges the next week against Libyan intelligence officer Abu Agila Mohammad Mas'ud, variant Abu Agela Mas'ud Kheir al-Marimi, another Pan Am 103 bombing suspect, who allegedly helped build the bomb that brought down the plane. Mas'ud's last known location was a Libyan prison where he was serving time for unrelated offenses.

CBS News, UPI, AFP, the *Washington Post,* and *Bloomberg* reported on December 21, 2020 that one of Attorney General Bill Barr's last acts as AG was to file the charges that included destruction of an aircraft resulting in death and destruction of a vehicle of interstate commerce by means of an explosive resulting in death.

The U.S. requested extradition to the U.S. from Libya, where he was serving a separate 10-year sentence for bomb making. The complaint was mostly based on a confession Mas'ud had made to Libyan authorities in 2012, plus his travel records indicating the he traveled from Tripoli to Malta, where he allegedly made the bomb. Scottish authorities received the information in 2017. In 1991, then-AG Barr announced charges against Libyan officials Abdel Basset Ali al-Megrahi and Lamen Khalifa Fhimah regarding the bombing. Barr said that the Scottish government had not ruled out charging Mas'ud. Mas'ud also admitted to making the bomb used in the 1986 attack on the LaBelle Discotheque in Berlin, West Germany that killed two American service members and a Turkish woman and injured hundreds. Barr said the operation was ordered by the leadership of Libyan intelligence, and that then-Libyan leader Muammar Qadhafi thanked Mas'ud.

September 16, 2010: *BBC* and *AP* reported on June 18, 2020 that an anti-terrorism court in Islamabad, Pakistan sentenced three men to life in prison for the September 16, 2010 murder of Pakistani exile politician Dr. Imran Farooq, 50, a senior leader in the Muttahida Qaumi Movement, who was stabbed to death outside his home in London's Edgware neighborhood. He had lived in the UK since 1999. The court ruled that MQM founder Altaf Hussain ordered the murder and issued an arrest warrant. The Pakistani court assured British police that the accused would not be sentenced to death. The court sentenced MQM members Khalid Shamim, Mohsin Ali and Moazzam Ali to life in prison and fined them Rs1m ($6,000; £4,800) each, to be paid to Dr. Farooq's family. The court ordered property confiscated from four other absent suspects and issued arrest warrants for four men living in the UK, identified as Altaf Hussain, Iftikhar Hussain, Mohammad Anwar and Kashif Kamran.

2015: On June 9, 2019, the *Telegraph* reported that Iran- and Hizballah-linked terrorists were caught stockpiling tons of explosives in a northwest suburb of London. MI-5 and the Metropolitan Police found thousands of disposable ice packs containing three tons of ammonium nitrate, which is often used in homemade bombs. Authorities uncovered the cache in autumn 2015. Police raided four properties. The *Sun* added that a man in his forties was arrested on suspicion of plotting terrorism before being released without charge.

2015: *AP, ABC News, CNN, AFP, Bloomberg* and *Time* reported on July 16, 2020 that the Court of Appeal in London ruled that Shamima Begum, now 20, a UK-born woman who left the country as a teenager in 2015 to join ISIS, is entitled to return to Britain to appeal her citizenship status. The UK government had taken away her citizenship in 2019. Her infant son died in a refugee camp in Syria.

May 22, 2017: *AP* reported on July 17, 2019 that Ahmed Bin Salem, a spokesman for the Tripoli-based Special Deterrence Force in Libya, said it had extradited Hashem Abedi, brother of the Manchester Arena suicide bomber, to face charges in the United Kingdom. Hashem's brother, Salman Abedi, set off a bomb at the end of an Ariana Grande concert on May 22, 2017, killing 22 people and wounding more than 260. British authorities said Hashem, then 18 years old, was involved in the attack. Hashem and the boys' father, Ramadan Abedi, were detained by Libyan forces shortly after the attack. Hashem had told investigators that he and Salman belonged to ISIS and that he knew about the attack. The father was not charged and was later released. A Westminster Magistrates' Court judge issued the arrest warrant for Hashem Abedi. Abedi was represented by attorney Zafar Ali, who told Westminster Magistrates' Court his client denied the 22 charges of murder, one count of attempted murder relating to the more than 260 people who were injured, and one count of conspiring to cause explosions.

On February 4, 2020, the murder trial began in London's Central Criminal Court of Hashem Abedi. The prosecution argued that Hashem was just as guilty as the attacker for conspiring with Salman during "months of planning", assembling metal containers, nails and screws for shrapnel and chemicals to make explosives. Hashem Abedi had traveled to Libya, his parents' homeland, before the attack. He was detained in Tripoli by a militia allied with a U.N.-recognized government and returned to the UK in 2019. He said he was not guilty of 22 counts of murder for the attack's victims, one count of attempted murder for those injured and one count of conspiring with his brother to cause explosions.

NBC News and the *British Press Association* reported on March 17, 2020 that Hashem Abedi was found guilty of 22 counts of murder, one count of attempted murder encompassing the remaining injured, and one count of conspiring with Salman to cause explosions. The judge said sentencing would be announced after collection of victim impact statements from the families. *Reuters* reported that Hashem was in Libya when the bomb went off. He was extradited to the UK in July 2019. The family arrived in the UK in the 1990s during Qadhafi's rule and moved from London to the Fallowfield area of south Manchester. Hashem was born in Manchester. Their father returned to Libya after Qadhafi was ousted in 2011.

Billboard, AFP, Reuters, New York Daily News, and the *Hollywood Reporter* reported on August 20, 2020 that Judge Jeremy Baker sentenced Hashem Abedi, 23, to at least 55 years in prison for helping to plan the attack. Hashem was found guilty of murder, attempted murder, and conspiring to cause explosions. Sentencing had been postponed due to travel restrictions during the pandemic. Judge Baker said the brothers were "equally culpable for the deaths and injuries caused by the explosion… Although Salman Abedi was directly responsible, it was clear the defendant took an integral part in the planning." If Hashem had been 21 at the time of the bombing, he would have given him a "whole-life term". The brothers were born in Manchester to Libyan parents and visited Libya with them a month before the attack. Salman returned to the U.K. on May 18, 2017; Hashem stayed in Libya until his extradition to the UK and was arrested at a London airport in July 2019. Prosecutors said Hashem ordered the chemicals for the bomb and arranged their transport. Among the dead were a 51-year-old woman, and ten people under the age of 20, including Liam Curry, 19, and an 8-year-old.

June 12, 2018: Jack Renshaw, 23, an alleged member of the banned British neo-Nazi group National Action and White Jihad, pleaded guilty to planning to murder Labour Party legislator Rosie Cooper and a police officer who had previously interviewed him about alleged race-hate offenses. Renshaw was accused of buying a machete for the attack in 2017. He pleaded guilty to preparing acts of terrorism as he went on trial alongside five other alleged members of the outlawed group. All six denied belonging to the group. Prosecutors said the plot was foiled when a disenchanted member of the group reported it to an anti-racism organization. On May 17, 2019, High Court Judge Maura McGowan sentenced Renshaw to life in prison.

August 14, 2018: On July 17, 2019, *AP* reported that London's Central Criminal Court convicted Salih Khater, 30, a British citizen originally from Sudan, of attempted murder. On August 14, 2018, he drove a car into several pedestrians and cyclists outside Parliament before colliding with a security barrier guarded by police. Three people were injured. He claimed he was looking for the Sudanese embassy to get a visa, got lost and panicked. Sentencing was scheduled for October 2019.

On October 14, 2019, *AP* reported that Judge Maura McGowan of London's Central Criminal Court sentenced Khater to life in prison for attempted murder in a bid "to kill as many people as possible". Khater must serve a minimum of 15 years. McGowan said, "Even acting alone, you acted for a terrorist purpose… All the evidence is consistent with that conclusion." Khater was represented by attorney Peter Carter.

December 31, 2018: On November 27, 2019, Judge Jeremy Stuart-Smith sentenced Mahdi Mohamud, 26, a Dutch extremist from a Somali family, who lived in the UK since age 9, who stabbed commuters at random with a steak knife in Manchester's Victoria Train station on New Year's Eve, to at least 11 years in prison. The judge ordered that his sentence begin in a high-security psychiatric hospital. Mohamud was diagnosed as suffering paranoid schizophrenia. Mohamud pleaded guilty. He had screamed "Allahu Akbar!" and stabbed James Knox, 54, repeatedly. He then stabbed Knox's companion, Anna Charlton, 57, across her face. Sgt. Lee Valentine, 31, was stabbed in the shoulder while confronting Mohamud.

LATIN AMERICA

ARGENTINA

July 18, 1994: On February 28, 2019, an Argentine court ruled that former President Carlos Menem, 88, was not guilty of charges of interference with the investigation into the July 18, 1994 bombing of the Argentine Israelite Mutual Association Jewish cultural center that killed 85 people. He and other officials had been accused for years of trying to divert attention away from a Syrian businessman who was a family friend. Menem was president from 1989 to 1999. He was now serving as a senator.

The *Washington Post* reported on December 23, 2020 that a federal court cleared former auto dealer Carlos Telleldín in the bombing in Buenos Aires. He denied knowing that the truck he sold would be used as a bomb in the attack.

BRAZIL

2005: On April 18, 2019, *AP* reported that police rearrested Regivaldo Pereira Galvão, a farmer convicted of ordering the 2005 assassination of American missionary Dorothy Stang in 2005. Brazil's supreme court overruled a May 2018 injunction that had blocked him from serving his 2010 sentence for hiring two ranch hands to kill Stang, an environmental activist.

March 14, 2018: *AP* reported on March 12, 2019 that police arrested two suspects, Ronnie Lessa and Elcio Vieira de Queiroz, both former police officers, in the March 14, 2018 killing of Rio de Janeiro councilwoman Marielle Franco and her driver, Anderson Gomes. Lessa allegedly shot Franco and De Queiroz allegedly drove the getaway car.

EL SALVADOR

1981: *AP* reported on February 17, 2019 that police arrested a man convicted of participating in the 1981 killing of two American labor advisers and the head of the country's land reform agency. Jose Dimas Valle Acevedo had been a corporal in the since-disbanded National Guard. He was one of two men who confessed to gunning down land reform chief Jose Rodolfo Viera, as well as Michael Peter Hammer and Mark David Pearlman, U.S. citizens working with the AFL-CIO. The gunmen were freed under a 1987 amnesty law that was overturned in 2016. A U.N. truth commission said the murders apparently were ordered by prominent businessmen; charges were dropped.

November 16, 1989: *AP* reported on June 8, 2020 that Spain's National Court began the trial of two former Salvadoran military officers for killing five Spanish priests at the Central American University in San Salvador in El Salvador on November 16, 1989. They were identified as

- Former Colonel Inocente Orlando Montano, who served as El Salvador's vice minister for public security during the country's 1979-1992 civil war. He faced up to 150 years in prison. The U.S. extradited him to Spain in 2017 to face charges of terrorist murder and crimes against humanity. He was in his 70s and in ill health.

- René Yusshy Mendoza, an army lieutenant and member of the Atlacatl battalion that allegedly killed the priests. Prosecutors requested a 5 year sentence. He had confessed. His lawyer claimed that his client should be excluded from the case per the statute of limitations.

El Salvador refused to extradite 16 other suspects who had been charged in the case.

Among the victims was Father Ignacio Ellacuría, dean of the Central American University and a prominent mind behind Liberation Theology. He and other Jesuit priests were helping organize peace talks to end the war. Also killed in the attack were another priest from El Salvador, their housekeeper and her daughter. The Spanish court was not trying the defendants for those killings.

The trial was expected to run until July 16.

HONDURAS

March 3, 2016: *AP* reported on February 5, 2019 that Honduran prosecutors said they planned to bring charges against former executive Roberto David Castillo Mejia whom they alleged was a mastermind behind the 2016 murder of indigenous and environmental activist Berta Caceres. Castillo was president of Empresa Desarollos Energeticos in 2016. Caceres led the fight against the company's construction of a dam, and was honored with a Goldman Environmental Prize. Castillo, who was arrested in 2018, was represented by attorney Juan Carlos Sanchez. Prosecutors said that Castillo was in charge of providing logistics and other resources to one of the convicted killers. On December 2, 2019, a Honduran court sentenced seven people convicted of participating in the 2016 murder of Berta Caceres to prison terms of up to 50 years. The seven men were convicted in November 2018. Elvin Rápalo, Henry Hernández, Edilson Duarte and Oscar Torres Velásquez were sentenced to 34 years for the murder and 16 years for attempted murder. Three others were sentenced to 30 years.

VENEZUELA

May 2017: On July 10, 2019, *AP* reported that Venezuelan senior prosecutor Tarek William Saab tweeted that Spanish authorities had arrested Enzo Franchini Oliveros, who was sought by Venezuela for public disorder, intentional homicide and terrorism charges related to the burning of Orlando Figuera, 22, during anti-government protests in May 2017. A Spanish National Court spokesman said he was jailed in Madrid after his July 9 arrest in a town near Madrid. Franchini told Judge Santiago Pedraz that he did not want to be extradited.

MIDDLE EAST

AFGHANISTAN

November 2008: *The Hill, USA Today, Reuters,* and *al-Jazeera* reported that on October 28, 2020, federal authorities charged Haji Najibullah, 42 (or 44), an Afghan man, for the November 2008 kidnapping of former *New York Times* journalist David Rohde, Afghan journalist Tahir Ludin, and their Afghan driver Asadullah Mangal. He was arrested and transferred to the U.S. from Ukraine, and was arraigned before a federal judge in New York. The indictment said that Najibullah, Akhund Zada, and Timor Shah kidnapped their victims at gunpoint in Afghanistan in November 2008. Five days later, Najibullah and six armed guards forced the hostages to hike to Pakistan from Afghanistan, where the hostages were held for seven months. The Taliban trio forced the hostages to make videos and calls seeking help, and made them create at least three videos showing them begging for help surrounded by masked guards armed with machine guns. The kidnappers demanded money from Rohde's family and the release by the U.S. of Taliban prisoners. The *New York Times* reported that Rohde and Ludin escaped in June 2009 by dropping down a wall with a rope and escaping to a Pakistan militia post. Mangal escaped a few weeks later. Najibullah was charged with one count of hostage taking, conspiracy to commit hostage taking and kidnapping, and two counts of using and possessing a machine gun in furtherance of crimes of violence. He faced life in prison on each charge. Rohde now writes for the *New Yorker.* Manhattan-based federal public defender Mark Gombiner represented Najibullah.

Rohde was also held hostage by Bosnian Serbs for nearly two weeks in 1995, when he was working for the *Christian Science Monitor.*

June 30, 2009: *Military.com* reported on June 28, 2019 that Bowe Bergdahl's attorneys argued in front of the Army's Court of Criminal Appeals that the case should be reconsidered or Bergdahl given clemency because of prejudicial comments and tweets by the Commander in Chief. President Trump tweeted on November 3, 2017 that

Bergdahl getting no jail time was "a complete and total disgrace to our Country and to our Military". Bergdahl's attorney, former Coast Guard judge advocate and Yale University Law School lecturer Eugene Fidell, argued that Trump's comments constituted "apparent" unlawful command influence that influenced the case's decisions or outcomes. As a candidate, Trump said Bergdahl should be executed by firing squad, pushed out of an airplane without a parachute or dropped back into Afghanistan. "Let them have him. That's cheaper than a bullet."

Army Times reported on July 18, 2019 that an Army Court of Criminal Appeals panel ruled 2-1 to reaffirm Bowe Bergdahl's guilty plea and previous sentence of reduction in rank to private, a $10,000 fine and a dishonorable discharge, setting aside President Donald Trump's comments about a conviction and prison time, which the defense deemed undue command influence and interference with his right to a fair trial. Bergdahl's attorney told *Army Times* that the defense would appeal to the U.S. Court of Appeals of the Armed Forces, a civilian court with jurisdiction over the U.S. armed forces in Washington, D.C.

Military.com reported on August 27, 2020 that the Court of Appeals for the Armed Forces upheld the 2017 conviction and sentence of former Army Sereant Robert "Bowe" Bergdahl on charges of desertion and misbehavior before the enemy, holding the public comments by President Donald Trump and the late Senator John McCain condemning him did not invalidate his prosecution via unlawful command influence. Two of the five judges filed partial dissents. Defense attorney Eugene Fidell planned to continue to seek dismissal of charges.

February 25, 2012: *Stars and Stripes* reported that on May 29, 2020, the Afghan government released from a Parwan Province prison Abdul Saboor, who killed two US service members in an insider attack on February 25, 2012. The dead were Army Major Robert J. Marchanti, II, 48, of Baltimore, a member of the Maryland National Guard and Lt. Col. John Darin Loftis. Saboor had been sentenced to 20 years in prison in 2016. Saboor had served in the Afghan military and was an Afghan Tajik who had snuck off to study in a Pakistani madrassa. He told the *BBC*

in 2016 that he had heard that the U.S. military desecrated Qurans. He had been at large for four years before being arrested in his Parwan home in 2016. He freely admitted to the murders and was unrepentant. The Taliban had claimed credit, but on June 1, 2020, Hezb-e-Islami said Saboor had conducted the attack for them. Saboor was freed as part of a 2016 reconciliation agreement between Kabul and Hezb-e-Islami. Fazal Ghani Haqmal, spokesman for HeI, said the 164 prisoners were freed due to Covid concerns.

October 2012: Canadian Joshua Boyle and his American wife, Caitlan Coleman of Stewartstown, Pennsylvania, were kidnapped by a Taliban-linked group while backpacking. The couple had three children while in captivity. Pakistani forces rescued them in 2017. Boyle was arrested in December 2017. *AP* reported on March 25, 2019 that Joshua Boyle went on trial in Canada on charges that he repeatedly assaulted his wife. He faced 19 charges, including sexual assault, all but one of which related to his wife. *AP* reported on December 19, 2019 that Canadian Judge Peter Dooby acquitted Boyle of 19 charges including assault, harassment, sexual assault and forcible confinement. The couple had been held by the Haqqani Network between October 2012 and October 2017. The couple had three children while held captive, mostly in Pakistan. Coleman alleged that Boyle had abused her during and after their captivity. Coleman lives in the United States with their four children. The duo met through an online Star Wars forum in 2002 and married in 2011.

ABC News reported on May 12, 2020 that the U.S. government offered $1 million for information leading to the capture of the Taliban terrorists who kidnapped and held the family. Coleman said that her Taliban guards once sexually assaulted her and that Boyle abused her physically and psychologically during their captivity. Some observers suggested that he was an Islamist who wanted to meet the Taliban, but the deal went awry. He was acquitted of assault in a Canadian court in December 2019. They had often lived in separate Taliban compounds while hostages.

August 28, 2013: *Army Times* reported on June 12, 2019 that the Pentagon upgraded the Silver Star of Staff Sergeant Michael H. Ollis, 24, an infantryman with the 10th Mountain Division out of Fort Drum, New York who was killed while shielding Polish Army Lieutenant Karol Cierpica from a suicide bomber on August 28, 2013 in Ghazni Province. Cierpica had been wounded in both legs and was unable to walk. The Pentagon upgraded the medal to the Distinguished Service Cross, the second highest military honor that can be awarded to a U.S. soldier. Cierpica named his newborn son Michael. The VFW named a post after Ollis. Ollis also received the Army Gold Medal from Poland, the highest honor a foreign soldier can receive from Poland.

August 7, 2016: *AP* reported on November 1, 2019 that U.S. Special Representative for Afghanistan Reconciliation Zalmay Khalilzad was in Kabul to negotiate a prisoner exchange that would include two Western professors, American Kevin King, 63, and Australian Timothy Weeks, 50, who worked at the American University of Afghanistan and were kidnapped by the Taliban on August 7, 2016. The duo would be freed for the release of 11 Taliban prisoners, including Anas Haqqani, the younger brother of Sirajuddin, deputy head of the Taliban and leader of the Haqqani Network, and an uncle of the Haqqanis. Anas Haqqani was arrested in Bahrain in 2014 and handed over to the Afghan government. He was sentenced to death. Overall, the Taliban was demanding the release of 80 prisoners. The government demanded that the Taliban agree to a cease-fire before any prisoner exchange.

AP reported on November 12, 2019 that Afghan President Ashraf Ghani announced that his government had granted "conditional release" to three prominent Haqqani Network prisoners at Bagram Air Base—Anas Haqqani, Haji Mali Khan and Hafiz Rashid—in an effort to get the Taliban to free the professors. The American University in Kabul said it was not part of any negotiations with the Taliban. On November 15, 2019, Taliban spokesman Zabihullah Mujahid complained that the trio had yet to be released

from Bagram Prison. On November 19, 2019, *NPR* reported that the Taliban prisoners were flown to Qatar, and the Western hostages were freed in Zabul's Naw Bahar district, a region largely under Taliban control.

On December 1, 2019, Weeks told a news conference that he believed that U.S. Navy SEAL teams tried and failed six times to free the duo, sometimes missing them by hours. He and King were moved to various remote locations in Afghanistan and Pakistan, often held in tiny, windowless cells. Some Taliban guards were "lovely people… I don't hate them at all… And some of them, I have great respect for, and great love for, almost. Some of them were so compassionate and such lovely, lovely people. And it really led me to think about … how did they end up like this? … I know a lot of people don't admit this, but for me, they were soldiers. And soldiers obey the commands of their commanders. (They) don't get a choice."

The *Washington Post* reported on February 27, 2020 that the Taliban invited Timothy Weeks to Doha, Qatar ahead of the signing of the peace agreement.

2018: *AP* reported on May 28, 2019 that UNICEF determined that attacks on Afghan schools tripled in 2018—from 68 in 2017 to 192 in 2018—in part because militants targeted schools that were used as polling stations in the October parliamentary elections.

EGYPT

November 21, 2013: *AP* and *al-Ahram* reported that on July 27, 2020 Egypt executed in a Cairo prison seven people convicted of killing a police officer in Ismailia in November 2013. They were accused of killing the officer who was attempting to break up a fight and attempted murder of a civilian after seizing the officer's weapon before escaping. A criminal court sentenced them to death. Egypt's highest criminal appeals court upheld the verdict in 2018. Three had confessed on television on November 26, 2013, with bruises on their faces. Amnesty International noted that there were numerous allegations of torture and due process violations.

2014: On February 8, 2019, *AP* reported that Human Rights Watch said that Egypt executed on February 7 three Muslim Brotherhood members sentenced to death following torture and beatings to extract confessions. The trio were convicted in 2018 for the 2014 killing of a judge's son in the Nile Delta town of Mansoura.

June 29, 2015: On February 20, 2019, *AP* reported that Egypt executed nine suspected Muslim Brotherhood members convicted of involvement in the 2015 bombing that killed Hisham Barakat, the country's top prosecutor. Egypt's highest appeals court upheld the death sentences in November 2018 and commuted six other death sentences to life in prison.

March 2016: On September 24, 2019, *AP* reported that the Alexandria (Egypt) Criminal Court sentenced Seif Eddin Mustafa to life in prison after he was convicted of hijacking a domestic EgyptAir flight to Cyprus in March 2016. He used a fake suicide belt. After six hours of negotiations at Cyprus's Larnaca airport, he released all 72 passengers and crew and was arrested. He claimed he was protesting Egypt's government. Cypriot prosecutors said he told authorities that he wanted to be reunited with his estranged Cypriot family. He was extradited to Egypt in 2018.

October 2017: On June 27, 2020, *AP* reported that Egypt hanged Abdel-Rahim al-Mosmari, a Libyan terrorist from Derna, Libya, convicted of plotting an ambush with rocket-propelled grenades that killed 16 police officers and wounded 13 security forces as they were conducting a raid southwest of Cairo in October 2017. He was arrested a month after the attack. A military court sentenced him to death in November 2019. A military appeals court upheld his death sentence in mid-June, and he was hanged in a Cairo prison.

The court had sentenced 15 other defendants for the attack, including 10 in absentia, to life in prison. Another 17 got 5- to 15-year sentences.

Authorities said police likely ran out of ammunition in the hours-long gun battle in the al-Wahat al-Bahriya area, gateway into the Western Desert. The terrorists captured and later killed several police officers. The military rescued one kidnapped officer. Some reports indicated that more than 50 police were killed.

IRAN

November 4, 1979: In an interview with *AP* on October 29, 2019, Ebrahim Asgharzadeh, 63, one of the Iranian student leaders of the 1979 U.S. Embassy takeover, expressed regret for the seizure of the diplomatic compound and the 444-day hostage crisis. He said that despite efforts by the Revolutionary Guard to claim it directed the attack, the students were in control. "Like Jesus Christ, I bear all the sins on my shoulders", Asgharzadeh said.

March 9, 2007: On March 9, 2019, *Newsweek* reported former Air Force intelligence officer Bob Kent on December 10, 2018 was about to board a plane in New York with $250,000 earmarked to pay for the ransom of ex-FBI agent Robert Alan Levinson, who had disappeared on March 9, 2007 from a hotel on Iran's Kish Island. The Trump Administration refused to issue a waiver allowing payment to Iran. The FBI posted a $5 million reward for "information that could lead to Bob Levinson's safe return".

On November 4, 2019, the Trump administration offered $20 million for information about Levinson. As of November 4, he had been missing for 4,624 days. On November 9, 2019, *AP* reported that Iran's Justice Department acknowledged for the first time to the U.N.'s Working Group on Enforced or Involuntary Disappearances that it had an open case before its Public Prosecution and Revolutionary Court of Tehran regarding Levinson. The next day, Foreign Ministry spokesman Abbas Mousavi said the case "was a missing person" filing, not an indication that Levinson was being prosecuted. Mousavi said Levinson "has no judicial or criminal case in any Islamic Republic of Iran court whatsoever... It is normal that a case is opened like it's done for any missing people anywhere in Iran."

On March 9, 2020, U.S. District Judge Timothy Kelly held Iran responsible for the kidnapping of former FBI agent Robert Levinson, entering a 25-page default judgement against the regime. Levinson's family sought more than $1.5 billion in damages.

The *Washington Post* reported on March 25, 2020 that Levinson's family and National Security Advisor Robert O'Brien announced that he had died in Iranian custody. The family noted, "We don't know when or how he died, only that it was prior to the COVID-19 pandemic… How those responsible in Iran could do this to a human being, while repeatedly lying to the world all this time, is incomprehensible to us… They kidnapped a foreign citizen and denied him any basic human rights, and his blood is on their hands." O'Brien said that the U.S. believed Levinson "may have passed away some time ago".

BBC reported on March 26, 2020 that Iran denied that Levinson died in custody there, saying he left the country years earlier. A Foreign Ministry spokesman cited "credible evidence" that he left Iran for an "unspecified destination".

AP reported on October 6, 2020 that Judge Timothy J. Kelly in the District Court in Washington, D.C. ordered Iran to pay $1.45 billion ($107 million in compensatory damages and $1.35 billion in punitive damages) to the family of former FBI agent Robert Levinson.

On December 14, 2020, the Trump administration formally blamed Iran for the presumed death of Levinson. The administration announced sanctions, including blocking their assets in the U.S., against Mohammad Baseri and Ahmad Khazai, two Iranian intelligence officers believed responsible for his abduction.

2008: The *Washington Post* reported on August 1, 2020 that the Intelligence Ministry claimed it had detained Jamshid Sharmahd, 65, alleged Iranian-German leader of the Tondar ("thunder" in Farsi) militant wing of the little-known Glendora, California-based Anjoman-e Padeshahi-e Iran (Kingdom Assembly of Iran) monarchist opposition group for allegedly planning the 2008 attack on the Hosseynieh Seyed al-Shohada Mosque in Shiraz that killed 14 people and wounded more than 200. The Ministry claimed he planned other attacks throughout Iran, including an attack on a dam and using cyanide bombs at Tehran's annual book fair, and that the group was behind the 2010 bombing of Ayatollah Ruhollah Khomeini's mausoleum in Tehran

that wounded several people. Iranian Intelligence Minister Mahmoud Alavi said on state TV that Sharmahd was arrested in Iran. The U.S. Department of State had earlier issued the "Outlaw Regime: A Chronicle of Iran's Destructive Activities" report that mentioned how he had been targeted for assassination. His family said that Iranians abducted him in Dubai, then took him to Iran via Oman. The family had last heard from him on July 28. The Iranian Intelligence Ministry denied that he was arrested in Tajikistan. The family said he suffers from Parkinson's disease, diabetes and heart trouble that require medication and careful monitoring.

IRAQ

January 20, 2007: *Military Times* reported that on December 5, 2019, the U.S. Department of State offered $15 million for information on financial activities, networks and associates of Yemen-based Islamic Revolutionary Guard Commander-Qods Force commander Abdul Reza Shahlai, who planned one of the most sophisticated attacks against coalition troops in Iraq, killing five soldiers and wounding three on January 20, 2007 in an attack on the Karbala provincial headquarters. The bounty was not for his death or capture. The U.S. added that he "provided weapons and explosives to violent Shia extremist groups", funded and directed a plot to kill Saudi ambassador to the United States Adel al-Jubeir, and plotted follow-on attacks in the U.S. that could have killed nearly 200 Americans. In the Karbala attack, terrorists drove Suburbans and black Chevy Tahoes with distinct IED jammers operated by coalition forces and carried proper vehicle placards known to be on U.S. coalition vehicles in Iraq. They used American uniforms and weapons, and spoke some English. He was also suspected of being behind some of the sophisticated weaponry going from Iran to Houthi rebels. The U.S. Department of the Treasury sanctioned him in 2011 for his role in the attempted assassination of the Saudi ambassador to the U.S.

April 2009: *AP* and *Army Times* reported on June 19, 2019 that on June 17, U.S. District Judge

Roslynn Mauskopf in Brooklyn federal court sentenced Canadian citizen and Iraqi national Faruq Khalil Muhammad 'Isa to 26 years in a U.S. prison for his role in supporting a group of jihadists who conducted a 2009 suicide attack outside the gate of the U.S. base in Mosul, Iraq that killed five U.S. soldiers. Several family members of the soldiers demanded 'Isa get a life sentence. Among those killed were Jason Pautsch and Gary Lee Woods, Jr. Judge Mauskopf said that 'Isa played a "comparatively limited role" in the conspiracy from Canada and did not plan the attack. 'Isa was to be deported to Canada following his release and placed on federal probation for the rest of his life. 'Isa was arrested in 2011 on a U.S. warrant after an investigation by authorities in New York, Canada and Tunisia. A Tunisian terrorist network used a suicide bomber to set off an explosives-laden truck outside the U.S. base in Mosul. Court filing reported that 'Isa admitted corresponding by email with two jihadis while they were in Syria and "facilitators" who were trying to get the attackers into Iraq, wiring one of them $700 and providing "words of encouragement and religious guidance" to his co-conspirators. Defense attorney Samuel Jacobson was a former Marine who served in Iraq.

ISRAEL

1970: *CNN* reported in April 2019 that Chicago-area resident Rasmieh Odeh pleaded guilty in 2017 to illegally obtaining American citizenship by not disclosing her 1970 conviction in Israel for her role in a pair of bombings, one of which killed two people. She became an American in 2004. The U.S. pulled her citizenship and expelled her.

June 27, 1976: On March 26, 2019, Michel Bacos, 95, the chief pilot of the 12-member crew of the Air France Airbus jetliner that was hijacked on a flight from Israel and landed at Entebbe Airport in Uganda, died. Israeli commandos freed the 100 hostages. Bacos was awarded the French Legion of Honor for refusing to leave the plane's passengers.

July 31, 2015: On May 18, 2020, *AP, Haaretz,* and *Reuters* reported that the Central Lod District Court found Israeli extremist Amiram Ben-Uliel, 25, guilty of three counts of murder and two counts of attempted murder by killing the sleeping Dawabshe Palestinian family when he threw a Molotov cocktail through a window of their home in Duma in the West Bank during the morning of July 31, 2015. The court did not find him guilty of membership in a terrorist organization. The dead included Saad and Reham Dawabshe and their 18-month-old son, Ali. Another son, Ahmad, 4, suffered severe injuries. Authorities called the attack a "price tag" incident after finding Hebrew graffiti calling for "Revenge", with an image of the Jewish Star of David on a building. The defendant was the son of a prominent West Bank rabbi. Upon arrest, he was formally charged six months later, along with a minor. He confessed, saying the attack was "revenge" for the drive-by murder of Malachi Rosenfeld, an Israeli killed a month earlier by a Palestinian near Duma. Police said that although he planned the attack, with the minor, the latter did not show up during the attack. Ben Uliel threw two Molotov cocktails into the home and another residence. The attacker hailed from the northern West Bank settlement of Shilo. He was also convicted on two counts each of attempted murder and arson, plus with one count of conspiracy to commit a hate crime. He faced a life sentence. His attorney said he would appeal the verdict to the Supreme Court.

April 2017: *AP* reported on January 10, 2019 that as part of a plea bargain, the Jerusalem District Court sentenced Palestinian Jamil Tamimi, 60, to 18 years for stabbing to death British exchange student Hannah Bladon, 20, on the Jerusalem light rail before an off-duty policeman pulled the emergency brake and subdued him in April 2017. Tamimi's defense team claimed he suffered from a mental illness. Bladon was an exchange student at Hebrew University from the University of Birmingham.

LEBANON

October 23, 1983: The *Florida Times-Union* reported on May 13, 2019 that the Semper Fidelis Society proposed building a memorial to those

220 Marines, 18 Navy sailors, and three Army soldiers who were killed by a Hizballah suicide bomber who attacked the four-storey Marine barracks in Beirut on October 23, 1983. The memorial would be similar to the "They Came in Peace" memorial outside Camp Gilbert H. Johnson, part of Marine Corps Base Camp Lejeune in Jacksonville, North Carolina. Among those killed was Lance Corporal John Blocker of Yulee, Florida; Staff Sergeant Patrick Prindeville of Gainesville, Florida; and Lance Corporal Nathaniel Jenkins of Daytona Beach, Florida. Some 22 Marines came from Florida.

February 14, 2005: On September 16, 2019, the Special Tribunal for Lebanon in the Netherlands announced five new counts, including terrorism and intentional homicide, against Hizballah fighter Salim Jamil Ayyash, a Lebanese who was accused of assassinating former Lebanese Prime Minister Rafiq Hariri on February 14, 2005 and being involved in three bombings targeting Lebanese politicians in 2004 and 2005. The court also issued an international arrest warrant for Ayyash. The indictment had been issued under seal in June 2019, accusing him of bombings on October 1, 2004, June 21 and July 12, 2005, targeting politicians Marwan Hamadeh, Georges Hawi and Elias el-Murr. Hawi and two other people died; the other two politicians and nearly 20 other people were wounded.

AP and *CNN* reported on August 18, 2020 that the UN Special Tribunal for Lebanon found Hizballah member Salim Jamil Ayyash, alias Abu Salim, 56, guilty as a co-conspirator of five charges for his involvement in the suicide truck bombing that killed 22 people, including former Lebanese Prime Minister Rafik Hariri, and wounded 226 others outside a seaside hotel in Beirut on February 14, 2005. The court acquitted three other Hizballah members: Assad Sabra; Hassan Oneissi, alias Hassan Issa; and Hassan Habib Merhi, variant Merei. Presiding Judge David Re said that there was no evidence that the leadership of Hizballah and Syria were involved, although they "may have had motives to eliminate Hariri and some of his political allies". The written judgment was more than 2,600 pages long and had 13,000 footnotes. Judge Janet Nosworthy said that four different networks of

mobile phones "were interconnected and coordinated with each other, and operated as covert networks at the relevant times". The trial, held in Leidschendam, near The Hague, Netherlands, began in 2014 and included 415 days of hearings and evidence from 297 witnesses. Charges against a fifth Hizballah member, Mustafa Badreddine, one of its senior military commanders, were dropped after he was killed in Syria in 2016. *CNN* reported that the four suspects had been charged with conspiracy to commit a terrorist act, intentional homicide, attempted intentional homicide, and related charges. The verdicts were issued in absentia.

The *Washington Post* reported on August 25, 2020 that Lebanese citizen Ayyash was part of Hizballah's still-active Unit 121 hit team that had conducted four other assassinations, including deadly car bombings targeting Lebanese military and political leaders and journalists over at least a decade. Victims who were killed by car bombs between 2007 and 2013 included Wissam Eid, a Lebanese investigator of the Hariri killing; Wissam al-Hassan, a Lebanese army brigadier general and Hariri security chief; François al-Hajj, a Lebanese major general; and Mohamad Chatah, an economist and diplomat.

AP reported on December 11, 2020 that presiding Australian judge David Re announced that the special tribunal set up to prosecute those responsible for the assassination of al-Hariri sentenced Hizballah member Salim Jamil Ayyash to five life sentences for conspiring to commit an act of terrorism; criminal association; committing acts of terrorism; intentional homicide with premeditation; and attempted intentional homicide with premeditation. He was tried in absentia. A new international arrest warrant was issued for him.

2013: Lebanon's state-run *National News Agency* reported that on November 1, 2019 that the Judicial Council sentenced to death Youssef Diab for two car bombings in 2013 that targeted two Sunni mosques in Tripoli, killing 47 people and wounding 300 others. Diab detonated one of the bombs remotely.

Libya

September 11, 2012: The *Washington Post* reported on June 13, 2019 that a jury found Mustafa al-Imam, 47, guilty on one count each of conspiracy to provide material support to terrorists and maliciously destroying government property in the September 11, 2012 Benghazi attacks. U.S. District Judge Christopher R. "Casey" Cooper directed jurors to continue deliberating on 15 counts, including murder and attempted murder, on which they were deadlocked.

2018: *AP* reported on May 17, 2019 that a South Korean and three Filipino hostages were freed after months of captivity by unnamed groups. The release of the four civilian engineers who were working at a desalination plant was mediated by the United Arab Emirates, which worked with the Libyan National Army militia led by commander Khalifa Hifter. Joo, the South Korean, 62, was held for 315 days. 18999901

Morocco

December 17, 2018: *AP* and Moroccan state news reported on April 12, 2019 that on April 11 a Moroccan terrorism court sentenced to ten years in prison a Swiss man, 33, on charges including "deliberately helping perpetrators of terrorist acts" and training terrorists. He was linked to jihadis who allegedly killed two female tourists, one from Denmark and one from Norway, in their tent in the Atlas Mountains on December 17, 2018. The online advertising technician was arrested in December 2018. He was married to a Moroccan woman, according to a lawyer representing another Swiss suspect in the case. Moroccan prosecutors earlier filed terrorism charges against 25 individuals suspected of links to the killers. Authorities blamed followers of the Islamic State.

AP reported that Danish student Louisa Vesterager Jespersen, 24, and her Norwegian friend Maren Ueland, 28, were found dead in their tent near the base of Mount Toubkal with stab wounds to their necks. One of them was beheaded. On May 3, 2019, the *Washington Post* reported that the previous day, two dozen suspects went to trial in Salé, Morocco, including three men Moroccan officials said participated in the women's killings. Some of them could face the death penalty. One of the suspects was a dual Spanish-Swiss citizen. Some pledged allegiance to ISIS. *Reuters* quoted Moroccan police spokesman Boubaker Sabik saying that they acted as "lone wolves". In April 2019, Moroccan state news reported that a Swiss man tied to the attack was sentenced to 10 years in prison for "deliberately helping perpetrators of terrorist attacks". In early 2019, Danish police sought legal action against 14 people who allegedly shared video footage of the killing of one of the women on social media. The trial of 24 people began on May 16, 2019, with the Moroccan government included as a civil party. Hafida Makssaoui served as the government-appointed lawyer representing the four chief suspects, aged 25-30, who pleaded guilty.

On July 11, 2019, *AP* reported that the trial of nearly two dozen suspects for the stabbing was nearing completion. The three main suspects claimed allegiance to ISIS, recording the murders, and posting the video online. The trio, aged 25 to 30, pleaded guilty and said they regretted their actions. They were represented by state-appointed attorney Havida Maksaoui, who claimed mitigating circumstances and ask the court to order psychological tests. Attorney Khalid Fataoui represented Jespersen's family. The prosecutor said that he would seek death sentences, calling them "human beasts". The suspected accomplices included several imams and ex-convicts. Only one accused accomplice, a Swiss-Spanish convert to Islam, Kevin Zoller, pleaded innocent. Investigators said he had direct contact with members of ISIS in Syria via the encrypted messaging service *Telegram*. He was represented by attorney Saad Sahli. Another Swiss male accomplice was sentenced in April 2019 to 10 years in prison, on charges including "deliberately helping perpetrators of terrorist acts" and training terrorists. On July 18, 2019, the court convicted carpenters Jounes Ouzayed and Rashid Afatti and street merchant Abdessamad al-Joud and sentenced them to death. A fourth suspect, Khaiali Abderahman, who fled the scene, was sentenced to life in prison. The court sentenced 19 accomplices to jail terms ranging from five to 30 years. Kevin Zoller was sentenced to 20 years.

SYRIA

2013: The *New York Times* and *Washington Post 202* reported on April 15, 2019 that the Red Cross said that in late 2013, ISIS kidnapped Luisa Akavi, 62, a New Zealand nurse and midwife in Idlib. By April 15, 2019, the ICRC believed that she was alive. The ICRC and New Zealand government had kept her existence quiet, but the ICRC now asked the public for tips to help find her and her two Red Cross drivers, both Syrians, who were kidnapped with her. Akavi was of Cook Islands descent and lived in Otaki, north of Wellington. The ICRC said that two people at a clinic in Sousa, Syria, saw her in December 2018. There were also sightings in 2016 and 2017. In 2014, ISIS moved her and other hostages hours before a raid by U.S. special forces designed to rescue them. *AP* reported that she might have been offered for ransom and was used as a human shield. New Zealand Foreign Minister Winston Peters said the government did not approve the release of her name. 13999901

2015: *NBC News* reported on July 23, 2020 that Alexanda Kotey and El Shafee Elsheikh, two of the British ISIS terrorists called the "Beatles" who were in U.S. military custody in Iraq, said in an interview that they had mistreated Western hostages in Syria, including American Kayla Mueller, an aid worker who was held captive and tortured and sexually abused before her death in 2015. Kotey recalled, "She was in a room by herself that no one would go in." Elsheikh added, "I took an email from her myself," i.e., he obtained an email address for ISIS to demand ransom from the family. "She was in a large room, it was dark, and she was alone, and… she was very scared." ISIS had demanded 5 million euros from her family, or they would send the family "a picture of Kayla's dead body". U.S. and UK authorities said the ISIS "Beatles" were behind 27 killings, including the beheadings of Americans James Foley, Steven Sotloff and Peter Kassig, and British aid workers David Haines and Alan Henning. Kotey and Elsheikh had denied

in a 2018 interview ever having heard of Mueller. In the latest interview, Kotey said, "I never denied that they was ever hit," admitting that he hit a Dutch captive in the chest to make a mark that would be visible in a photo that would be sent to his family. The State Department had reported that "Elsheikh was said to have earned a reputation for waterboarding, mock executions, and crucifixions while serving as an ISIS jailer." State said Kotey, as a jail guard, "likely engaged in the group's executions and exceptionally cruel torture methods, including electronic shock and waterboarding". The other two "Beatles" were Mohammed Emwazi, alias Jihadi John, who was killed by a Hellfire missile strike in 2015, and Aine Lesley Davis, was sentenced to seven and a half years in prison in Turkey in 2017.

2015: The *New York Times* reported on May 5, 2019 that Sri Lanka citizen and ISIS fighter Mohamad Muhsin Sharhaz Nilam was killed in a coalition airstrike in Syria in 2015. He had been a school principal and karate instructor from central Sri Lanka.

April 2016: *AP* reported on April 5, 2019 that Italian businessman Sergio Zanotti, who was kidnapped in Syria in April 2016 by al-Qaeda-linked terrorists, was released. He was from Brescia, Italy. Zanotti appeared in a video in November 2016 asking the Italian government to intervene to ensure he was not killed. The Prime Minister's office announced, "at the end of a complex and delicate activity of intelligence, investigation and diplomacy… today we succeeded in obtaining the release of Sergio Zanotti."

October 2016: Italian Defense Minister Elisabetta Trenta announced on May 22, 2019 that Alessandro Sandrini, who went missing in October 2016 and was presumed to be a hostage, was released and returned to Italy. Sandrini, in his early 30s, disappeared after traveling to Turkey. In July 2018, a video showed him wearing an orange jumpsuit flanked by masked men brandishing automatic weapons, asking Italy to help free him as quickly as possible. A group in Syria affiliated with the al-Qaeda-linked Hayat Tahir-al-Sham claimed a criminal gang had kidnapped him. 16109901

TUNISIA

March 18, 2015: On January 29, 2019, the trial reopened in Tunis regarding the Islamic State attack on the Imperial Hotel in the Sousse beach resort that killed 38 people, most of them British tourists. More than 40 people were summoned to face trial. Fourteen were not in custody. Six others were security agents accused of failing to prevent or stop the attack.

On February 9, 2019, *AP* reported that Tunisian authorities sentenced seven suspects to life in prison and handed out other sentences in a trial for the two 2015 attacks that killed 60 people, mainly tourists. Samir Ben Amor, who served as defense attorney for one of the 44 defendants, said some defendants received jail terms ranging from 16 years to six months, while charges against 27 suspects were dismissed. Charges included premeditated murder, threatening national security and belonging to an extremist-linked group. The prosecution said it would appeal the verdicts. The suspected mastermind of the attacks, Chamseddine Sandi, was believed to be hiding in Libya. Several defendants acknowledged having provided logistical assistance to Sandi. On March 18, 2015, terrorists killed 22 people at the Bardo Museum in Tunis. On June 26, 2015, Aymen Rezgui walked onto the beach of the Imperial Hotel in the coastal city of Sousse and used an assault rifle to shoot at tourists, killing 38 people. The Islamic State group claimed responsibility.

WEST BANK

September 2018: On January 18, 2019, *AP* reported that Israeli forces used explosives to demolish the apartment of Khalil Jabarin, 17, in Yatta, West Bank. The Palestinian was charged with fatally stabbing U.S.-born settler activist Ari Fuld at a mall near a West Bank settlement in September 2018.

December 9, 2018: In a drive-by shooting from a vehicle driven by Palestinian Salah Barghouti, 29, an assailant wounded seven people who were standing at a bus stop at the entrance to Ofra, a Jewish settlement in the West Bank. A pregnant woman, Shira Ish-ran, 21, was hit in the stomach and was in critical condition. Her baby boy, Amiad, died on December 12. Barghouti was killed on December 12 while attempting to harm Israeli forces in an arrest raid. *AP* reported on April 17, 2019 that the Israeli military demolished Barghouti's family home in Khobar, West Bank. Israel arrested more than 100 Palestinians during the manhunt for Barghouti. He and his brother, Aasem, were accused of the drive-by. Aasem was arrested and his home was also demolished.

YEMEN

October 12, 2000: *Fox News* reported on January 6, 2019 that President Trump tweeted that an airstrike in Yemen killed Jamel Ahmed Mohammed Ali al-Badawi, variant Jamal, an al-Qaeda operative tied to the 2000 attack on the guided-missile destroyer *U.S.S. Cole.* "Our GREAT MILITARY has delivered justice for the heroes lost and wounded in the cowardly attack on the USS Cole. We have just killed the leader of that attack, Jamal al-Badawi. Our work against al Qaeda continues. We will never stop in our fight against Radical Islamic Terrorism!" Navy Capt. William Urban, a spokesman for U.S. Central Command, said that the airstrike occurred on January 1, 2019. *Navy Times* reported that al-Badawi was on the FBI's list of Most Wanted Terrorists. He was driving alone in a vehicle in Yemen's Ma'rib Governorate at the time of the strike, according to a U.S. administration spokesman. Yemeni authorities arrested al-Badawi in December 2000 for his part in the attack, but he escaped from prison in April 2003. He was sentenced to death in 2004; the sentence was reduced to 15 years in prison on February 26, 2005. He escaped in 2006 when he and other inmates tunneled out of the prison and into an adjacent mosque. The *Washington Post* reported that he surrendered in 2007. Yemen permitted him to remain free in exchange for aiding in the search and capture of other al-Qaeda operatives. The U.S. Department of State's Rewards for Justice Program had offered up to $5 million for information leading to his capture.

The FBI's "Most Wanted Terrorist" listing said that he was wanted for murder and conspiracy to murder U.S. nationals and U.S. military personnel; conspiracy to use and using a weapon of mass destruction; damaging and destroying government properties and defense facilities; and providing material support to a terrorist organization. His aliases included Jamal Muhsin al-Tali; Abu Abdul Rahman al-Badawi; Abu Abdul Rahman al-Adani; Jamal Mohammad Ahmad Ali al-Badawi; and Jamal Mohammad Ahmad, with dates of birth as July 22, 1960; October 23, 1960; and 1963. He was born in al-Shargian, Makiris, Yemen. He was 5'5" and weighed 175 pounds.

CNN reported on March 26, 2019 that the U.S. Supreme Court by an 8-1 (Thomas) vote ruled against victims and families of the October 2000 attack on the *U.S.S. Cole* in their lawsuit against Sudan, holding that the victims did not properly serve notice of their lawsuit to the government of Sudan. The decision put in jeopardy the more than $314 million default judgment that was awarded to the families.

AP reported on April 16, 2019 that a three-judge panel from the U.S. Court of Appeals for the District of Columbia Circuit unanimously ruled that former military judge since-retired Air Force Colonel Vance Spath "created a disqualifying appearance of partiality" by pursuing a position as an immigration judge while also overseeing the case. The decision threw out more than three years of proceedings in the case against Abd al-Rahim al-Nashiri, alleged mastermind of the 2000 bombing of the *U.S.S. Cole* that killed 17 Americans and wounded 39 others. The panel voided Spath's 2018 order that required two defense attorneys to return to the case involuntarily. Navy Lt. Alaric Piette was a member of Nashiri's defense team. Michael Paradis represented Nashiri in the D.C. Circuit case.

On February 13, 2020, *AP* and *Fox News* reported that Sudan's transitional government's Ministry of Justice announced that on February 7 it had reached a $70 million settlement with families of the victims of the al-Qaeda attack on the *U.S.S. Cole*. Khartoum was aiming to be removed from the U.S. list of state sponsors of terrorism. Khartoum was also negotiating with families of victims of the 1998 bombings of U.S. embassies in Kenya and Tanzania that killed more than 200 and wounded more than 1,000 people.

NORTH AMERICA

CANADA

January 29, 2017: On February 8, 2019, Quebec Superior Court Justice Francois Huot sentenced French-Canadian Alexandre Bissonnette, 29, who shot dead six Muslim men in a Quebec City mosque on January 29, 2017, to serve 40 years in prison before becoming eligible for parole. Bissonnette had pleaded guilty in March 2018 to six charges of first-degree murder and six of attempted murder. Huot rejected the prosecution's request for six consecutive life sentences, which would have prevented Bissonnette from seeking parole for 150 years. Huot declared that the section of the Criminal Code allowing consecutive life sentences violates Canada's bill of rights. Among those injured was Aymen Derbali, who was shot seven times and left paralyzed from the waist down. Bissonnette killed Mamadou Tanou Barry, 42; Abdelkrim Hassane, 41; Khaled Belkacemi, 60; Aboubaker Thabti, 44; Azzeddine Soufiane, 57; and Ibrahima Barry, 39.

June 2017: *Fox News* reported on July 28, 2020 that Syrian-born Rehab Dughmosh, who charged employees at a tire shop in Toronto in June 2017 in an ISIS-inspired attack was denied parole on July 27, 2020 after prosecutors quoted her as saying that she would "do another attack" if she was not sent back to Syria. In the attack, she grabbed golf clubs, a bow and arrow, and a hammer from Canadian Tire at Cedarbrae Mall in Scarborough, threatening people in the store and yelling "Allahu Akhbar" and "This is for ISIS." She told police she was disappointed that there were no injuries. In 2019, she was sentenced to seven years in prison for trying to join ISIS and conduct the attack. Her parole date had been scheduled for August 7, 2020. *Global News* reported that in February 2020, she wrote a threatening note to parole officers in which she said, "If you release me from jail, I will do another terrorist attack, so tell your government to send me back to my country." The court noted that she kept an ISIS flag in her jail cell, sought out radical literature, and fought with another Muslim inmate who was not wearing a hijab. The court wrote, "You have threatened to kill or maim inmates you deem to be in conflict with your ideologies, and have threatened to burn down your living unit with no regard to human life." Justice Maureen Forestell indicated Dughmosh's mental illness, which was likely related to schizophrenia, had "rendered her vulnerable" to extremist beliefs. The parole board noted that Dughmosh has "no pro-social associates, lack employment prospects and financial resources, your motivation for further intervention is low, and you continue to believe it is acceptable to use violence as a method of achieving your goals."

April 23, 2018: Alek Minassian, 25, was accused of driving a rental van into crowds of pedestrians on Yonge Street in the north Toronto neighborhood of North York, killing eight women and two men aged 22 to 94. On September 27, 2019, a video showed him telling police hours after the attack that he belonged to an online incel (involuntarily celibate) group of men who plotted attacks against people who were sexually active. He was charged with ten counts of first-degree murder and 16 counts of attempted murder. Minassian's trial was scheduled to start in February 2020. He told police, "I feel like I accomplished my mission... I know of several other guys over the internet who feel the same way... too cowardly to act on their anger... I felt it was time to take action and not just sit on the sidelines and just fester in my own sadness." He claimed he was in contact with Elliot Rodger, a community college student who killed six people and wounded 13 in shooting and stabbing attacks in 2014 near the University of California, Santa Barbara, before apparently shooting himself to death. Minassian said he was laughed at by women at a 2013 Halloween party, observing, "I was angry that they would give their love and affection to obnoxious brutes." After planning the attack for a month, he determined that "The van was the perfect medium size to use as my weapon... I'm thinking that this is it, this is the day of retribution... I was driving down Yonge because

I knew it would be a busy area and then as soon as I saw the pedestrians, I just decided to go for it... The only reason I stop my attack was because someone's drink got splashed on my windshield and I was worried that I would crash... I wanted to do more but I've kind of been foiled by a lack of visibility."

On November 10, 2020, Minassian pleaded not guilty to ten counts of first-degree murder and 16 counts of attempted murder. His attorney, Boris Bytensky, claimed Minassian was not criminally responsible because he has autism spectrum disorder and did not understand that what he was doing was wrong.

Reuters reported on December 18, 2020 that the trial presided over by Justice Anne Molloy, of Alek Minassian was due to end on December 18. Minassian pleaded "not criminally responsible".

UNITED STATES

September 15, 1963: *CNN* reported that on June 26, 2020, former Ku Klux Klan member Thomas Edwin Blanton, Jr., the last of the September 15, 1963 Birmingham, Alabama 16th Street Baptist Church bombers that killed four African-American girls, died in prison. Sarah Jean Collins, then 12, lost an eye in the blast which killed her sister, Addie Mae Collins, 14. The dead included Carole Robertson, 14; 8,000 people attended her funeral at which Dr. Martin Luther King, Jr., gave a eulogy. Also killed were Denise McNair, 11, and Cynthia Wesley, 14. Fourteen other people were injured. The bomb collapsed a basement wall; the girls were in a lounge they used for changing into their choir robes. Three KKK members were convicted of murder; Blanton was convicted in 2001 and sentenced to life in prison. Blanton, 82, went into cardiac arrest at the William Donaldson Correctional Facility, according to Chief Deputy Coroner Bill Yates of the Jefferson County Coroner's Office, which found no evidence of trauma or foul play.

The church was declared a national historic landmark in 2006. It had served as a staging area for the civil rights marches that were opposed by Birmingham Public Safety Commissioner Bull Connor. The church bombing marked a turning point in the civil rights movement and contributed to the passage of the Civil Rights Act of 1964. Fifty years after the attack, President Barack Obama awarded the four girls posthumous Congressional Gold Medals.

The FBI initially suspected Blanton and fellow Klansmen Robert Edward Chambliss, Bobby Frank Cherry and Herman Frank Cash. Alabama Attorney General Bill Baxley convicted Chambliss, then-73, in 1977. Chambliss died in prison in 1985.

Cherry was convicted in 2002 and died in prison in 2004. Cash died in 1994 and was never charged in the case.

The Alabama Board of Pardons and Paroles rejected Blanton's parole request in 2016, ruling he would be eligible in 2021.

June 5, 1968: *BBC* and *TMZ* reported that on August 30, 2019, Sirhan Sirhan, 75, the man convicted of assassinating Presidential primary candidate Robert F. Kennedy on June 5, 1968, was stabbed at the Richard J. Donovan Correctional Facility near San Diego, California in the afternoon. Sirhan, a Palestinian with Jordanian citizenship, was serving a life sentence. The attacker, a fellow inmate, was placed in isolation.

1981: On April 17, 2019, *CNN* reported that Michael Cardozo, attorney for former radical activist Judith (Judy) Clark, 69, who had been jailed for 38 years for her role in the 1981 robbery of a Brink's armored truck in suburban Nyack, New York, was granted parole. Clark was convicted of murder in the robbery that left a security guard and two police officers dead. New York State Department of Corrections records indicated that she described herself as "a blinded revolutionary" and "single-minded fanatic ... at war with America". Prosecutors called her a "cold-blooded cop killer" who chose to participate in "bank robbery, anarchy and murder". Kevin Gilleece, the acting Rockland County district attorney, said, "Because of her complete disregard for human life and the sheer brutality of the crime, parole should never have been granted for this convicted murderer." She was initially sentenced to 75 years to life in prison. New York Governor Andrew Cuomo commuted her sentence in 2016, opening the possibility of parole. She trained service dogs used by law enforcement, taught prenatal care, created an AIDS counseling program and became a chaplain at Bedford Hills Correctional Facility in Bedford Hills, New York.

January 1996: Daniel Lewis Lee, a member of a white supremacist group, was found guilty of murdering an Arkansas family of three, including an 8-year-old girl, in January 1996 in Arkansas. He was convicted of murder in aid of racketeering three years later and was sentenced to death. He hailed from Yukon, Oklahoma. His group had plotting to build a whites-only nation in the Pacific Northwest. On July 14, 2020, *CNN* reported that he was executed at age 47 by lethal injection at 8:07 a.m. in Terre Haute, Indiana in the first federal execution in 17 years after the U.S. Supreme Court by a 5-4 vote quashed a lower court order that had temporarily blocked his execution. His last words were "I didn't do it. I've made a lot of mistakes in my life but I'm not a murderer. You're killing an innocent man." He was represented by attorney Ruth Friedman, who said, "It is shameful that the government saw fit to carry out this execution during a pandemic... It is shameful that the government saw fit to carry out this execution when counsel for Danny Lee could not be present with him, and when the judges in his case and even the family of his victims urged against it. And it is beyond shameful that the government, in the end, carried out this execution in haste, in the middle of the night, while the country was sleeping. We hope that upon awakening, the country will be as outraged as we are." Earlene Peterson, whose daughter, granddaughter and son-in-law were tortured, killed and dumped in a lake by Lee and an accomplice, had opposed the execution.

September 11, 2001: *AP* reported on February 28, 2019 that German prosecutors were investigating how Moroccan Mounir el-Motassadeq, who was convicted of helping the Hamburg-based 9/11 suicide pilots—Mohammed Atta, Marwan al-Shehhi and Ziad Jarrah—was apparently paid 7,000 euros ($7,960) before he was deported to Morocco in October 2018. He had nearly finished his 15-year sentence for membership in a terrorist organization and being an accessory to murder. *Der Spiegel* reported that el-Motassadeq was on a list of terror suspects whose assets are frozen and are not allowed to receive any funds from his prison account. El-Motassadeq was arrested in Hamburg in November 2001.

CNN reported on June 29, 2019 that Luis Alvarez, 53, a retired NYPD bomb squad detective who described for Congress his 9/11-related medical issues during an impassioned appeal with comedian Jon Stewart for an extension of the September 11th Victim Compensation Fund, died in a hospice in New York.

CNN reported on July 18, 2019 that FDNY announced that 200 firefighters had lost their lives from illnesses stemming from working at the World Trade Center after 9/11. Richard Driscoll was the 200th firefighter to succumb to an illness. He served in FDNY for 32 years, and was cited for bravery five times during his career. He retired from Engine 91 in East Harlem in 2002. Kevin Nolan, the 199th firefighter to die from 9/11-related conditions, served from 1989 to 2007, retiring with Engine Company 79 in the Bronx. Another 343 FDNY members died on 9/11.

On September 12, 2019, *NBC News* reported that the FBI and U.S. Department of Justice declassified the name of an individual who allegedly directed two men in California who assisted the 9/11 hijackers. The 9/11 families and their lawyers believe the person may be a Saudi official, but the name was redacted when a 2012 summary of the FBI's inquiry into the matter was earlier released. The administration declined to release the name publicly, instead disclosing it to the plaintiff's lawyers under a protective order.

October 2002: The *Washington Post* reported on March 18, 2019 that the Supreme Court announced that it would consider whether Lee Boyd Malvo, 34, the then-17-year-old half of the Beltway snipers who terrorized the Washington region in 2002, may challenge his sentence in Virginia of life in prison without parole. Between September 5 and October 22, 2002, John Allen Muhammad and Malvo killed 10 people and wounded others in sniper attacks in Virginia, Maryland and the District of Columbia. Muhammad was executed in 2009. Malvo received sentences of life without parole in Virginia and Maryland. The Supreme Court case is *Mathena*

v. Malvo. On March 10, 2020, the *Washington Post* reported that imprisoned sniper Lee Boyd Malvo, 35, was married on March 6, 2020 in a ceremony at Red Onion State Prison in Virginia. Malvo was serving life sentences without parole for two murders in Virginia and six murders in Maryland.

September 14, 2009: Authorities in Queens arrested suspected al-Qaeda associate Najibullah Zazi, 25, of Aurora, Colorado. He pleaded guilty on February 22, 2010 in the U.S. District Court in Brooklyn to conspiracy to use weapons of mass destruction, to commit murder in a foreign country, and to provide material support for a terrorist organization. Department of Justice officials said Zazi's team had planned to attack the New York City subway on September 14, 15, or 16. He told the judge, "In spring 2008, I conspired with others to join the Taliban, to fight along with the Taliban against the United States. We were recruited to al-Qaeda instead." On September 28, 2019, *CNN* reported that U.S. District Court Judge Raymond Dearie in Brooklyn, who had sentenced Zazi to 10 years after the trial, said Zazi would effectively serve no additional prison time after prosecutors cited Zazi's "extraordinary cooperation" with US investigators. Prosecutors said he had met with the government more than 100 times, testified in multiple trials and "provided critical intelligence and unique insight regarding al-Qaeda and its members". Zazi remained under lifetime supervision. While in prison, he received his GED. He was represented by attorney William Stampur, who said his client "has unequivocally disavowed radical Islam in no uncertain terms". Zazi came to the U.S. from Pakistan at age 15.

2011: *CNN* reported on November 17, 2019 that federal court documents filed on November 13, 2019 in connection with a pending appeal by Dzhokhar Tsarnaev, Tamerlan Tsarnaev's younger brother and April 15, 2013 Boston bombing co-conspirator, of his conviction and death sentence, provided new details about a triple homicide at a Massachusetts residence in 2011 that a friend of Tamerlan said they took part in. Oral arguments were scheduled to begin on December 12. Ibragim Todashev described the killings while being questioned on May 21, 2013, saying he and Tsarnaev bound, beat and slit the throats of three young men in Waltham, Massachusetts.

April 15, 2013: *CNN* reported on December 12, 2019 that lawyers representing Dzhokhar Tsarnaev, 26, the surviving Boston Marathon bomber who was earlier convicted and sentenced to death for his role in the bombing that killed four and injured hundreds and left the city under siege during a five-day manhunt in April 2013, began their appeal of the 2015 death sentence to the 1st US Circuit Court of Appeals, arguing that the Boston jury pool was tainted and biased.

The *Washington Post* reported on July 31, 2020 that the 1st U.S. District Court of Appeals for the First Circuit set aside the death penalty for Dzhokhar Tsarnaev, who had been found guilty of planting the two bombs that killed three people and injured dozens at the 2013 Boston Marathon. The Court held for additional hearings. The Court added, "Just to be crystal clear, Dzhokhar will remain confined to prison for the rest of his life, holding that the lower court judge did not adequately consider the impact of extensive pretrial publicity on the jurors who recommended the death sentence. The case was to return to the lower court, "with the only question remaining being whether the government will end his life by executing him."

AP reported on October 6, 2020, that the U.S. Department of Justice petitioned the U.S. Supreme Court to review the case of Dzhokhar Tsarnaev. Tsarnaev, now 27, was convicted of all 30 charges against him, including conspiracy and use of a weapon of mass destruction and the killing of a Massachusetts Institute of Technology police officer. Tsarnaev was represented by attorney David Patton.

2015: The *Boston Herald*, *CBS Boston* and *al-Jazeera* reported on September 28, 2020 that federal Magistrate Judge Donald Cabell in Boston extended the sentence of David Daoud Wright of Everett, Massachusetts, to 30 years for planning to behead anti-Muslim public figure/blogger Pamela Geller on behalf of ISIS in 2015. He was sentenced to 28 years in 2017. In 2019, the 1st U.S. Circuit Court of Appeals overturned his conviction on conspiracy to provide material

support to a designated foreign terrorist organization. He remained convicted of conspiracy to commit acts of "terrorism transcending national boundaries" and other crimes. He had a hearing in June 19, 2015, represented by attorney Jessica Hedges. In 2015, Geller organized a Prophet Muhammad cartoon contest in Garland, Texas, where police shot to death two Muslim gunmen. A few days later, Ussamah Rahim, Wright's uncle, told him in a phone call that he could not wait to attack Geller and would instead attack "those boys in blue". Hours later, he pulled a knife on officers in a Boston parking lot; they fatally shot him. Prosecutors sought a life sentence, calling him "extremely dangerous" and "a serious threat to the United States". Defense attorneys countered with a call for 14 years, saying the Covid-19 pandemic put his life at risk behind bars. They claimed he "continues to renounce ISIS and radicalism" and "seeks to educate others about the destructiveness of radicalism".

In August 2020, a judge reduced the sentence to time served due to the pandemic of Nicholas Rovinski, 29, of Warwick, Rhode Island. He had testified against Wright at his trial. Rovinski was to be released in 2028, but his attorneys argued that he was especially susceptible to Covid-19 symptoms due to his cerebral palsy and hypertension. Rovinski was to spend the next decade in home confinement with electronic monitoring; the first six months were to constitute "strict home confinement".

December 2, 2015: *CNN* reported on October 23, 2020 that Enrique Marquez, 28, who purchased guns for Syed Rizwan Farook in 2011 and 2012 before Farook and his wife, Tashfeen Malik, conducted a terrorist attack on December 2, 2015 on the Inland Regional Center in San Bernardino, California that killed 14 people and wounded 22, was sentenced to 20 years in prison. Marquez pleaded guilty to conspiracy to provide material support and resources to terrorists, and making false statements in connection with the acquisition of the semiautomatic rifles by serving as the "straw buyer". Federal prosecutors said that the rifles were purchased, prosecutors said, in preparation for attacks that never happened— one against Riverside City College, a community college that Marquez and Syed Rizwan Farook had once attended, the other on a busy freeway. Assistant U.S. Attorney Tracy Wilkison said, "By his own admissions, this defendant collaborated with and purchased weapons for a man he definitively knew held radical and anti-American beliefs—and who wanted to kill innocent people." On December 3, 2015, Marquez told a 911 operator that Farook was responsible for the San Bernardino attack, observing, "The f***** a***** used my gun in the shooting…They can trace all the guns back to me." The prosecution's sentencing memorandum noted that that Marquez "was a full, willing, and motivated participant of the conspiracy who not only provided the agreement necessary for the conspiracy to attack (Riverside City College) and (motorists on State Route 91), but also co-designed the attacks with Farook, purchased the two firearms and ammunition to facilitate the attacks, researched bomb making and obtained explosive powder and other bomb-making materials, and visited RCC and SR-91 to sketch out how he and Farook would attack the two locations to maximize casualties." U.S. District Judge Jesus Bernal denied Marquez's request for a five-year sentence. After completing his sentence, Marquez will be on supervised release for 15 years.

Prosecutors said that Farook's mother, Rafia Sultana Shareef, will be sentenced November 16, 2020 after she pleaded guilty in March 2020 to a federal charge of intending to impede the investigation by shredding a map her son made. Prosecutors said they would ask for a sentence of no more than 18 months.

June 12, 2016: On April 1, 2020, a three-judge panel of the 4th District Court of Appeal in Florida rejected negligence lawsuits filed against G4S Secure Solutions (USA), Inc., the employer of Omar Mateen, who shot to death 49 people and wounded dozens at the Pulse gay nightclub in Orlando on June 12, 2016. The court upheld the ruling of the Palm Beach County circuit judge.

2017: On February 13, 2019, *WPIX11* reported that a New York court sentenced James Jackson, 30, a white supremacist who traveled from Baltimore to Manhattan to kill Timothy Caughman, 66, a black man, with a sword in 2017. He had pleaded guilty. He was sentenced to life in pris-

on without the possibility of parole, according to Manhattan District Attorney Cyrus Vance. Jackson had stalked other black men in New York City and said the attack was practice for further assaults on black people. Jackson had served in Afghanistan.

February 2017: Robert Lorenzo Hester, Jr., of Missouri, was arrested after reaching out to undercover FBI agents posing as ISIS members saying he was willing to assist with an attack on "buses, trains and a train station in Kansas City" on Presidents Day. *Fox News* reported on September 24, 2019 that the Department of Justice announced that he pleaded guilty to attempting to provide material support to ISIS from October 2016 to February 2017. The government recommended a 20-year sentence in a federal prison under terms of a plea agreement; he would receive at least 15 years.

The Department of Justice said he suggested targets such as "oil production" locations, "military bases", "federal places", "government officials" and "Wall Street". "Any government building in D.C. would get attention of everyone." Hester also claimed proficiency with "assault weapons", preferring the AK-47, citing his enlistment in the Army for less than a year. He received a general discharge in 2013 for violating Army regulations, according to the *Kansas City Star*.

He was arrested in 2016 in Columbia, Missouri in an unrelated case.

June 21, 2017: Quebec, Canada resident Amor M. Ftouhi, 49, knifed airport police Lieutenant Jeff Neville in the neck at 10 a.m. in Flint, Michigan's Bishop International Airport before he was apprehended. Ftouhi was charged with committing an act of violence at an airport. A witness said the attacker yelled "Allahu Akbar" and "you have killed people in Syria, Iraq and Afghanistan and we are all going to die" before striking. *FBI.gov* reported on July 8, 2019 that Ftouhi had viewed anti-Western videos online and had looked into how to purchase a gun in the United States; he thought Michigan would be the best place to buy one. He often tried to purchase an assault rifle in Michigan, but was refused because he was not a U.S. citizen. He was convicted of terrorism charges in November 2018 and sentenced to life in prison in April 2019.

August 12, 2017: On March 27, 2019, avowed neo-Nazi James Alex Fields, Jr., 25, of Ohio, who killed one woman and injured 35 others when he plowed his gray Dodge Charger into a group of counterprotesters at a white supremacist rally in Charlottesville, pleaded guilty to hate crimes in federal court. He was convicted on 29 of 30 counts as part of a deal with prosecutors, who agreed they would not seek the death penalty. He was convicted in state court and sentenced to life in prison in December for first-degree murder and other counts for killing Heather D. Heyer, 32, and injuring dozens at the Unite the Right rally on August 12, 2017. One woman testified that she had five surgeries and was expecting a sixth. Another sustained a broken pelvis. Another person pushed his fiancee out of the way before he was struck by Fields's car.

The *Washington Post* reported on June 28, 2019 that Judge Michael Urbanski in U.S. District Court in Charlottesville, Virginia sentenced Fields to life in prison. Fields told the courtroom, "Every day I think about how things could have gone differently, and how I regret my actions… I am sorry." A Virginia jury voted for a life term plus 419 years in state prison on state charges; sentencing was scheduled for July 15, 2019. Prosecutor Christopher R. Kavanaugh deemed the attack "domestic terrorism".

AP reported on July 14, 2019 that Charlottesville Circuit Court Judge Richard Moore sentenced white supremacist James Alex Fields, Jr., 22, to life plus 419 years on Virginia state charges for killing Heather Heyer, 32, and injuring dozens during the Unite the Right rally in Charlottesville on August 12, 2017. The previous month, he received a life sentence on 29 federal hate crime charges.

October 1, 2017: *AP* and the *Washington Post* reported on January 29, 2019 that the FBI's Behavioral Analysis Unit concluded that gunman Stephen Paddock, who killed 58 people and injured 869 at a country music festival from the Mandalay Bay Resort and Casino in Las Vegas on October 1, 2017, did not appear to have a "single or clear motivating factor" for his actions.

On October 3, 2019, MGM Resorts International reached a settlement that could pay $800 million to families of the 58 people who died and hundreds who were wounded.

CNN reported on November 19, 2019 that Kimberly Gervais, 57, a Mira Loma, California woman who was paralyzed from the neck down after she was shot in the October 1, 2017 Las Vegas massacre, died. She became the 59th fatality, suffering spinal injuries.

February 14, 2018: *AP* and the *Florida Times-Union* reported that Broward Circuit Judge Elizabeth Scherer on June 22, 2020 indefinitely postponed the capital murder trial of Nikolas Cruz, 21, because of the Broward County courthouse's closure due to the coronavirus. Cruz was on trial for killing 17 people and wounding 17 others with an AR-15 rifle at the Marjory Stoneman Douglas High School in Parkland, Florida on February 14, 2018. The Courthouse had been closed since March 16, 2020. Defense attorneys said he would plead guilty in exchange for a life sentence. Among his court-appointed attorneys was Gabriel Ermine. Scherer set the next status hearing for August 25, 2020. The Florida Department of Health listed more than 11,300 coronavirus cases and 373 deaths in Broward County.

October 26, 2018: Authorities arrested Cesar Altieri Sayoc, 56, at an AutoZone parking lot in Plantation, Florida in connection with a series of mail bombs to prominent critics of the Trump administration. On March 21, 2019, Sayoc pleaded guilty in federal court in the Southern District of New York to 65 counts, including charges of using a weapon of mass destruction and illegally mailing explosives with the intent to kill or injure people. "I knew these actions were wrong. I'm extremely sorry." He claimed that he did not intend for the devices to detonate, but "I was aware of the risk that they would explode." He faced life in prison. Sentencing was scheduled for September 12, 2019. The *Washington Post* reported on August 5, 2019 that U.S. District Judge Jed Rakoff sentenced Sayoc to 20 years in prison.

October 27, 2018: On January 29, 2019, *AP* reported that the Justice Department filed a superseding 66-count indictment against Pittsburgh Tree of Life synagogue shooting suspect Robert Bowers, 46, of Baldwin, Pennsylvania detailing a list of stridently anti-Semitic statements on social media. The indictment included 13 violations of the Matthew Shepard and James Byrd, Jr. Hate Crimes Prevention Act, plus other charges. He faced a possible death sentence.

On February 11, 2019, Robert Bowers pleaded not guilty to hate crimes and dozens of other counts in federal court. He was represented by prominent death penalty litigator Judy Clarke.

On August 26, 2019, the U.S. attorney's office in Pittsburg filed a notice of intent to seek the death penalty against Bowers, citing allegations of substantial planning and premeditation, the vulnerability and number of victims, motivation of religious hostility, injury, harm and loss caused to the victims and the choice of the Tree of Life synagogue.

December 17, 2018: *WSVN* reported that the FBI arrested Pakistan-born U.S. citizen Tayyab Tahir Ismail, 33, in a raid on his parents' Pembroke Pines, Florida home along Southwest 64th Street and 191st Avenue. He was suspected of distributing information on how to build a bomb and sympathizing with ISIS. Ismail lived at the home with his wife and two children. Investigators said Ismail in 2010 made terrorist threats against a homeless shelter. Ismail befriended James Medina who in 2016 was arrested for targeting an Aventura synagogue; Medina later was sentenced to 25 years. At that time, Ismail told an FBI informant that jihad was an Islamic duty, and wanted to go to the Caliphate. He traveled in Pakistan in December 2017, reportedly returning with several copies of ISIS propaganda. Authorities said he cited lectures given by Anwar al-Aulaqi and allegedly knew about Medina's plot but did not notify law enforcement.

Authorities said that his uploads included "You are surrounded by methods to hit them … kill them devil's soldiers without hesitation. Make them bleed even in their own homes." He also posted, "There are plenty of methods to attack my brother – take poison in injections and enter malls and inject products with poison – at night come out and cause the fire of houses." His site included a step-by-step video on how to build a suicide vest. The FBI said, "On at least five occasions in or around July, August and September 2018, Ismail posted bomb making instructions on a mobile messaging platform." He was also arrested in 2015 in a domestic violence case. *NPR* and *WPTV* reported on July 19, 2019 that U.S. District Judge K. Michael Moore sentenced the Broward County man to 20 years in prison, the maximum possible sentence. Ismail was represented by defense attorney David Nunez.

BIBLIOGRAPHY

GENERAL

Max Abrahms, Matthew Ward and Ryan Kennedy "Explaining Civilian Attacks: Terrorist Networks, Principal-Agent Problems and Target Selection" 12, 1 *Perspectives on Terrorism*, February 2018, pp. 23-45.

R. A. Bates "Dancing with Wolves: Today's Lone Wolf Terrorists" 4, 1 *Journal of Public and Professional Psychology*, 2012.

Sarah L. Desmarais, et al., "The State of Scientific Knowledge Regarding Factors Associated with Terrorism" 4, 4 *Journal of Threat Assessment and Management*, 2017, pp. 180-209.

Daniel Dory "L'analyse Geopolitique du Terrorisme: Conditions Theoriques et Conceptuelles" 33 *L'Espace Politique*, 2017.

Daniel Dory "Compte-rendu de l'Atlas du Terrorisme Islamiste de M. Guidere" *L'Espace Politique*, 2017.

Daniel Dory "Le Sentier Lumineux: un Laboratoire pour l'Etude du Terrorism" 16 *Securite Globale* Hiver 2018, pp. 93-112.

Daniel Dory "Le Terrorisme Comme Objet Geographique: un Etat des Lieuz" ("Terrorism as a Geographical Object: An Inventory") 728, *Ann. Geo.*, 2019, pp. 5-36.

C. Ellis, et al. "Analysing the Processes of Lone-Actor Terrorism: Research Findings" 10, 2 *Perspectives on Terrorism*, 2016, pp. 33-41.

Walter Enders, Todd Sandler, and Khusrav Gaibulloev "Domestic Versus Transnational Terrorism: Data, Decomposition and Dynamics" 48, 3 *Journal of Peace Research*, 2011, pp. 319-337. A comparison of ITERATE and GTD.

Abigail R. Esman *Rage: Narcissism, Patriarchy, and the Culture of Terrorism* Lincoln: University of Nebraska Press/Potomac Books, 2020, 232 pp.

H. Eudeline "Le Terrorisme Maritime, une Menace Reelle Pour la Stabilite Mondiale" 163 *Herodote*, pp. 9 31.

R. Ezcurra and D. Palacios "Terrorism and Spatial Disparities: Does Interregional Inequality Matter?" 42 *European Journal of Political Economy*, 2016, pp. 60-74.

Michael Freeman with Katherine Ellena and Amina Kator-Mubarez *The Global Spread of Islamism and the Consequences for Terrorism* Lincoln: University of Nebraska Press/Potomac Books, 2020, 248 pp.

J.-F. Gayraud *Theorie des Hybrides: Terrorisme et Crime Organise* Paris: CNRS Editions, 2017, 253 pp.

Paul Gill and Emily Comer "There and Back Again: The Study of Mental Disorder and Terrorist Involvement" 72, 3 *American Psychologist*, 2017, pp. 231-241.

Nicholas Grossman *Drones and Terrorism: Asymmetric Warfare and the Threat to Global Security* I.B. Tauris, 2018, 240 pp.

Global Terrorism Index 2017 Sydney, Australia: Institute for Economics and Peace, 2018, 117 pp.

John Horgan "Psychology of Terrorism: Introduction to the Special Issue" 72, 3 *American Psychologist*, 2017, pp. 199-204.

Darren Hudson, Arie Perliger, Rile Post and Zachary Hohman *The Irrational Terrorist and Persistent Terrorist Myths* Rienner, 2020.

R. Jackson and D. Pisoiu *Contemporary Debates on Terrorism*, 2nd edition London/New York: Routledge, 2018, 292 pp.

Charlotte Klonk *Terror: When Images Become Weapons* Manchester University Press, 2020.

O. Koren "Why Insurgents Kill Civilians in Capital Cities: A Disaggregated Analysis of Mechanisms and Trends" 61 *Political Geography*, 2017, pp. 237-252.

Gary LaFree "Terrorism and the Internet" 16, 1 *Criminology and Public Policy*, 2017, pp. 93-98.

Gary LaFree, et al., "The Contagious Diffusion of World-Wide Terrorism: Is It Less Common Than We Might Think?" 41, 4 *Studies in Conflict and Terrorism*, 2018, pp. 261-280.

S. Pinero Kluch and A. Vaux "The Non-Random Nature of Terrorism: An Exploration of Where and How Global Trends of Terrorism Have Developed Over 40 Years" 39, 12 *Studies in Conflict and Terrorism*, 2016, pp. 1031-1046.

Charles W. Mahoney "More Data, New Problems: Audiences, Ahistoricity and Selection Bias in Terrorism and Insurgency Research" *International Studies Review*, 2017.

Aaron Mead-Long "Mass Attacks in Public Spaces: An Analysis of Key Indicators, Including Operational and Strategic Recommendations" 25, 3 *The Intelligencer: Journal of U.S. Intelligence Studies* Winter-Spring 2020, pp. 19-32.

Aki Peritz *Disruption: The 2006 Liquid Bomb Plot and Terrorists' Half-Century Love Affair with the Air Industry* Potomac Books, 2020.

Bart Schuurman "Research on Terrorism, 2007-2016: A Review of Data, Methods and Authorship" *Terrorism and Political Violence*, 2018.

Anja Shortland *Kidnap: Inside the Ransom Business* London: Oxford University Press, 2019, 248 pp.

Andrew Silke and Jenifer Schmidt-Petersen "The Golden Age? What the 100 Most Cited Articles in Terrorism Studies Tell Us" 29, 4 *Terrorism and Political Violence*, 2017.

Joshua Sinai *Bibliography of Terrorism and Counter-Terrorism* Routledge, 2020.

Y. Tominaga "There's No Place Like Home! Examining the Diffusion of Suicide Attacks Through Terrorist Group Locations" 25 *Applied Spatial Analysis and Policy*, 2017.

Bernard Touboul "The Role of Money Laundering in International Organized Crime and Terrorism" 24, 3 *The Intelligencer: Journal of U.S. Intelligence Studies* Winter 2018-2019, pp. 41-55.

U.S. Department of State *Country Reports on Terrorism 2019* Washington, D.C., June 2020.

AFRICA

Prudence Bushnell *Terrorism, Betrayal and Resilience: My Story of the 1998 U.S. Embassy Bombings* Washington, D.C.: Potomac Books, 2018, 246 pp.

J. Guido *Terrorist Sanctuary in the Sahara: A Case Study* Carlisle Barracks: U.S. Army War College, 2017, 72 pp.

Andrew Milburn *When the Tempest Gathers: From Mogadishu to the Fight Against ISIS, a Marine Special Operations Commander at War* Pen and Sword Military, 2020.

Isha Sesay *Beneath the Tamarind Tree: A Story of Courage, Family and the Lost Schoolgirls of Boko Haram* Dey St/William Morrow, 2019, 382 pp.

ASIA

Navin A. Bapat *Monsters to Destroy: Understanding the War on Terror* London: Oxford University Press, 2019.

Musa Khan Jalalzai *Spy War in South Asia: Intelligence Failure, Reforms and the Fight Against Cross Border Terrorism in Pakistan, Bangladesh, India and Afghanistan* Vij Books India, 2019.

Rommel Ranlaoi *Terrorism in the Philippines: From al-Qaeda to ISIS* 2019

EUROPE

Anthony M. Amore *The Woman Who Stole Vermeer: The True Story of Rose Dugdale and the Russborough House Art Heist* NY: Pegasus, 2020, 262 pp.

San Charles Haddad *The File: Origins of the Munich Massacre* Post Hill Press, 2020.

Patrick Radden Keefe *Say Nothing: A True Story of Murder and Memory in Northern Ireland* Doubleday, 2019, 448 pp.

Michael Kenney *The Islamic State in Britain: Radicalization and Resilience in an Activist Network* Cambridge University Press, 2018, 298 pp.

Thomas Leahy *The Intelligence War Against the IRA* London: Cambridge University Press, 2020.

Christophe Naudin *Diary of a Survivor of the Bataclan* France, n.d.

Maria Papageorgiou "Dismantling 17 November" 26, 1 *The Intelligencer: Journal of U.S. Intelligence Studies* Fall 2020, pp. 41-43.

Michael Pullara *The Spy Who Was Left Behind: Russia, the United States, and the True Story of the Betrayal and Assassination of a CIA Agent* New York: Scribner, 2018, 352 pp.

F. Reinares and C. Garcia-Calvo *Actividad Yihadista en Espana, 2013-2017: de la Operacion Cesto a Los Atentados en Cataluna* Madrid: Real Instituto Elcano, Documento de trabajo 13/2017, 34 pp.

Bart Schuurman *Becoming a European Homegrown Jihadist: A Multilevel Analysis of Involvement in the Dutch Hofstadgroup*, PhD dissertation, Leiden University, 2017.

Bart Schuurman "Conducting Qualtitative Research on Terrorism: Finding and Using Primary Sources" *Research Methods* London: Sage, 2019.

LATIN AMERICA

L. Taylor "Sendero Luminoso in the New Millennium: Comrades, Cocaine and Coutnerinsurgency on the Peruvian Frontier" 17, 1 *Journal of Agrarian Change*, 2017, pp. 106-121.

Z. Toll "Terrorism in Colombia: The Revoluitonary Armed Forces of Colombia and National Liberation Army" 4, 1 *Journal of Masson Graduate Research*, 2017, pp. 16-30.

MIDDLE EAST

Esther Ahmad *Defying Jihad: The Dramatic True Story of a Woman Who Volunteered to Kill Infidels—and Then Faced Death for Becoming One* Tyndale Momentum, 2019.

Fred Burton and Samuel M. Katz *Beirut Rules: The Murder of a CIA Station Chief and Hezbollah's War Against America* Berkley, 2018, 390 pp.

Sarah M. Carlson *In the Dark of War: A CIA Officer's Inside Account of the U.S. Evacuation from Libya* Fidelis Books, 2020.

Christopher Catherwood *ISIS: The Killing Caliphate: The Ideology of Terror* Frontline Books, 2019.

Patrick Cockburn *War in the Age of Trump: The Defeat of ISIS, the Fall of the Kurds, the Conflict with Iran* Verso, 2020.

Margaret Coker *The Falcons: The Untold Story of the Elite Iraqi Spy Unit that Helped Bring Down the Islamic State* Dey Street, 2020.

Ed Darack *The Warriors of Anbar: The Mariens Who Crushed Al Qaeda: The Greatest Untold Story of the Iraq War* Da Capo Press, 2019.

Aimen Dean with Tim Lister and Paul Cruick-shank *Nine Lives: My Time as the West's Top Spy Inside al-Qaeda* Oneworld Publications, 2018, 467 pp.

Sam Faddis *The CIA War in Kurdistan: The Untold Story of the Northern Front in the Iraq War* Casemate, 2020.

Thomas Hegghammer *The Caravan: Abdallah Azzam and the Rise of Global Jihad* New York: Cambridge University Press, 2020.

Shaker Jeffrey and Katharine Holstein *Shadow on the Mountain: A Yazidi Memoir of Terror, Resistance and Hope* Da Capo Press, 2020.

Samuel M. Katz *No Shadows in the Desert: Murder, Vengeance, and Espionage in the War Against ISIS* Hanover Square Press, 2020.

Barry Meier *Missing Man: The American Spy Who Vanished in Iran* New York: Farrar, Straus and Giroux, 2016, 273 pp.

Azadeh Moaveni *Guest House for Young Widows: Among the Women of ISIS* New York: Random House, 2019, 338 pp.

Andrew Mumford *The West's War Against Islamic State: Operation Inherent Resolve in Syria and Iraq* I.B. Tauris, 2020.

Colonel Keith Nightingale *Eagle Claw to Osama Bin Laden: A Personal Account of the Difficult Birth of Modern U.S. Special Operations* Casemate, 2020

Dana J. H. Pittard and Wes J. Bryant *Hunting the Caliphate: America's War on ISIS and the Dawn of the Strike Cell* Post Hill Press, 2019.

Pat Proctor *Lessons Unlearned: The U.S. Army's Role in Creating the Forever Wars in Afghanistan and Iraq* University of Missouri Press, 2020.

Julie Salamon *An Innocent Bystander: The Killing of Leon Klinghoffer* New York: Little, Brown, 2019, 349 pp.

Richard H. Shultz, Jr. *Transforming US Intelligence for Irregular War: Task Force 714 in Iraq* Washington, D.C.: Georgetown University Press, 2020.

Patrick J. Sloyan *When Reagan Sent in the Marines: The Invasion of Lebanon* Thomas Dunne Books, 2019.

Brian Steed *ISIS: The Essential Reference Guide* ABC-Clio, 2020.

Susan M. Stein *On Distant Service: The Life of the First U.S. Foreign Service Officer To Be Assassinated* Potomac Books, 2020.

Christopher Strom, Jerome Preisler and Michael Benson *Brooklyn to Baghdad: An NYPD Intelligence Cop Fights Terror in Iraq* Chicago Review Press, 2019.

Richard Vaux with Brad Kuhn *Dirty Work: The Untold Story of My Secret Mission to Steal Back TWA Flight 847 from Hezbollah* s.p., 2019, 110 pp.

Beau Wise and Tom Sileo *Three Wise Men: A Navy SEAL, a Green Beret, and How Their Marine Brother Became a War's Sole Survivor* New York: St. Martin's, 2021.

Graeme Wood *The Way of the Strangers: Encounters with the Islamic State* New York: Penguin Random House, 2019, 368 pp.

I. Zhen "Confrontation on the Issue of Terrorism Between Iran and the U.S. After 1979" 29, 2 *Terrorism and Political Violence*, 2017, pp. 236-253.

NORTH AMERICA

Cynthia Beebe *Boots in the Ashes: Busting Bombers, Arsonists and Outlaws as a Trailblazing Female ATF Agent* Center Street, 2020.

Seyward Darby *Sisters in Hate: American Women on the Front Lines of White Nationalism* New York: Little, Brown, 2020, excerpted as "One Woman's Descent Into Hate" *New York Times*, July 19, 2020.

E. E. Fridel "A Multivariate Comparison of Family, Felony, and Public Mass Murders in the United States" 1, 27 *Journal of Interpersonal Violence*, 2017.

Garrett M. Graff *The Only Plane in the Sky: An Oral History of 9/11* Avid Reader Press/Simon & Schuster, 2019.

Daryl Johnson *Hateland: A Long, Hard Look at America's Extremist Heart* Prometheus Books, 2019.

Seth Jones, Catrina Doxsee, and Nicholas Harrington "The Escalating Terrorism Problem in the United States" *Center for Strategic and International Studies Briefs*, June 17, 2020.

A. Lankford and S. Tomek "Mass Killings in the United States from 2006 to 2013: Social Contagion or Random Clusters?" *Suicide and Life-Threatening Behavior* doi:10.1111/sltb.12366 2017.

Talia Lavin *Culture Warlords: My Journey into the Dark Web of White Supremacy* Hachette, 2020, 273 pp.

Alexander Meleagrou-Hitchens, Seamus Hughes, and Bennett Clifford *Homegrown: ISIS Inside America* I.B. Tauris, 2020.

J.R. Meloy and M. Amman "Public Figure Attacks in the United States, 1995-2015" *Behavioral Sciences and the Law* 2016.

Arie Perliger *American Zealots: Inside Right-Wing Domestic Terrorism* Columbia University Press, 2020.

William Rosenau *Tonight We Bombed the U.S. Capitol: The Explosive Story of M19, America's First Female Terrorist Group* Atria Books, 2019.

Jeffrey D. Simon *The Alphabet Bomber: A Lone Wolf Terrorist Ahead of His Time* Lincoln: University of Nebraska Press/Potomac Books, 2019, 272 pp.

U.S. Secret Service National Threat Assessment Center "Mass Attacks in Public Spaces 2017", No. 35, 2018.

U.S. Secret Service National Threat Assessment Center "Mass Attacks in Public Spaces 2018", 2019.

The Violence Project "Mass Shooters" https://wwwtheviolenceproject.org/mass-shooters 2019.

Mitchell Zuckoff *Fall and Rise: The Story of 9/11* HarperCollins, 2019, 589 pp.

Responses

Alec Bierbauer and Colonel Mark Cooter with Michael Marks *Predator Rising: How a Team of Renegades Broke Rules, Shatered Barriers, and Launched a Drone Warfare Revolution* Skyhorse, 2020.

Patrick T. Brandt, Justin George, and Todd Sandler "Why Concessions Should Not be Made to Terrorist Kidnappers" 44 *European Journal of Political Economy,* May 2016, pp. 41-52.

John O. Brennan *Undaunted: My Fight Against America's Enemies, At Home and Abroad* Macmillan, 2020, 464 pp.

Willard Chesney with Joe Layden *No Ordinary Dog: My Partner from the SEAL Teams to the Bin Laden Raid* New York: St. Martin's, 2020.

Edward W. Dunbar, ed. *Indoctrination to Hate: Recruitment Techniques of Hate Groups and How to Stop Them* Praeger Pub Text, 2021.

Federal Bureau of Investigation "Making Prevention a Reality: Identifying, Assessing and Managing the Threat of Targeted Attacks" www.fbi.gov/file-repository/making_prevention_a_reality_identifying_assessing_managing_threats_of_ta.pdf 2015.

Michael R. Gordon *Degrade and Destroy: The Inside Story of the War Against the Islamic State* Farrar, Straus and Giroux, 2019.

C. Heath-Kelly "Survivor Trees and Memorial Groves; Vegetal Commemoration of Victims of Terrorism in Europe and the United States" 64 *Political Geography*, 2018, pp. 63-72.

Stefanie von Hlatky, ed. *Countering Violent Extremism and Terrorism: Assessing Domestic and International Strategies* McGill-Queen's University Press, 2020.

Bruce Hoffman and Jacob Ware "The Challenges of Effective Counterterrorism Intelligence in 2020" lawfareblog.com June 21, 2020.

Homegrown Violent Extremist Mobilization Indicators, 2019 Edition, produced by the FBI, the National Counterterrorism Center, and the Department of Homeland Security Washington, D.C.: Office of the Director of National Intelligence, 2019.

L. Jarvis and T. Legrand "The Proscription or Listing of Terrorist Organizations: Understanding, Assessment, and International Comparisons" 30, 2 *Terrorism and Political Violence*, 2018, pp. 199-215.

Jenna Jordan *Leadership Decapitation of Terrorist Organizations* Stanford University Press, 2019.

Chappell Lawson, Alan Bersin, and Juliette N. Kayyem, eds. *Beyond 9/11: Homeland Security for the Twenty-First Century* Cambridge: MIT Press, 2020.

T. Legrand "More Symbolic—More Political—Than Substantive: An Interview with James R. Clapper on the U.S. Designated Foreign Terrorist Organizations" 30, 2 *Terrorism and Political Violence*, 2018, pp 356-372.

Philip Mudd *Black Site: The CIA in the Post-9/11 World* Liveright, 2019, 272 pp.

Thomas Pecora *Guardian: Life in the Crosshairs of the CIA's War on Terror* Post Hill Press, 2019

Christian Picciolini *Breaking Hate: Confronting the New Culture of Extremism* Hachette, 2020.

Dennis Pluchinski *Anti-American Terrorism: From Eisenhower to Trump—A Chronicle of the Threat and Response: Volume I: The Eisenhower Through Carter Administrations* World Scientific Publishing Europe Ltd., 2020.

Dennis Pluchinski *Anti-American Terrorism: From Eisenhower to Trump—A Chronicle of the Threat and Response: Volume II: The Reagan and George H.W. Bush Administrations* World Scientific Publishing Europe Ltd., 2020.

Justin K. Sheffield *The Gospel of War: A SEAL Team Six Operator's Battles in the Fight for Good Over Evil* Center Street, 2019.

Tracy Walder with Jessica Anya Blau *The Unexpected Spy: From the CIA to the FBI, My Secret Life Taking Down Some of the World's Most Notorious Terrorists* New York: St. Martin's, 2020.

Cliff Watts *Messing with the Enemy: Surviving in a Social Media World of Hackers, Terrorists, Russians and Fake News* Harper, 2018.

FICTION

Andrew Altschul *The Gringa* New York: Melville House, 2020, 421 pp.

Fernando Aramburu *Homeland,* translated by Alred MacAdam New York: Pantheon, 2019, 608 pp.

Johannes Anyuru *They Will Drown in Their Mothers' Tears,* translated by Saskia Vogel Two Lines Press, 2019, 278 pp.

Randy Boyagoda *Original Prin* John Metcalf/Biblioasis, 2019, 223 pp.

Jack Carr *True Believer* Atria/Emily Bestler Books, 2019, 496 pp.

John Elliott *After the Eleventh Hour* Amazon/CreateSpace, 2019, 190 pp.

Lars Kepler *Rabbit Hunter* NY: Knopf, 2020, 512 pp.

Megha Majumdar *A Burning* New York: Alfred A. Knopf, 2020, 293 pp.

Edna O'Brien *Girl* New York: Farrar, Straus and Giroux, 2019, 230 pp.

Chris Pavone *The Paris Diversion* New York: Random House, 2019, 384 pp.

John Woods *Lady Chevy* Pegasus Crime, 2020, 296 pp.

Juli Zeh *Empty Hearts,* translated by John Cullen Nan A. Talese/Doubleday, 2019, 288 pp.

ABOUT THE AUTHOR
EDWARD MICKOLUS, PHD

Edward Mickolus, after graduating from Georgetown University, wrote the first doctoral dissertation on international terrorism while earning an M.A., M.Phil, and Ph.D. from Yale University.

He then served in analytical, operational, management, and staff positions in the Central Intelligence Agency for 33 years, where he was CIA's first full-time analyst on international terrorism; analyzed African political, economic, social, military, and leadership issues; wrote political-psychological assessments of world leaders; and managed collection, counterintelligence, and covert action programs against terrorists, drug traffickers, weapons proliferators, and hostile espionage services.

He founded Vinyard Software, Inc., whose products include ITERATE (International Terrorism: Attributes of Terrorist Events) text and numeric datasets and DOTS (Data on Terrorist Suspects). Clients include 200 universities in two dozen countries.

His 45 books include a series of multi-volume chronologies and biographies on international terrorism; more than two dozen book chapters; 100 articles and reviews in refereed scholarly journals and newspapers and presentations to professional societies; and 14 humorous publications.

For the following ten years, he was a senior instructor for SAIC and its spinoff, Leidos, Inc. He served as the Deborah M. Hixon Professor of Intelligence Tradecraft and Board of Advisors member at the Daniel Morgan Graduate School in Washington, D.C.

He is married to Susan Schjelderup.

In addition to his terrorism and intelligence books shown at the front of this book, he is also the author of:

More Funny Covid Memes

America's Funniest Memes: Coronavirus Edition

The Secret Book of CIA Humor

The Secret Book of Intelligence Community Humor

Two Spies Walk Into a Bar

His Words: Inspirational Quotations from Jesus Christ

Food with Thought: The Wit and Wisdom of Chinese Fortune Cookies

with Tracy Tripp White Noise Whispers (forthcoming)

with Joseph Rendon Take My Weight… Please!

with Harlan Rector I Matter: Finding Meaning in Your Life at Any Age, Volume 1

with Harlan Rector I Matter Too: Finding Meaning in Your Life at Any Age, Volume 2

with Harlan Rector I Still Matter: Finding Meaning in Your Life at Any Age, Volume 3 (forthcoming)

with Joseph T. Brannan Coaching Winning Model United Nations Teams

www.ingramcontent.com/pod-product-compliance
Lightning Source LLC
Chambersburg PA
CBHW080415030426
42335CB00020B/2462